BEFORE THE HOLOCAUST

HERMANN BECK

BEFORE THE HOLOCAUST

antisemitic violence and the reaction of
German elites and institutions during
the Nazi takeover

OXFORD
UNIVERSITY PRESS

OXFORD
UNIVERSITY PRESS

Great Clarendon Street, Oxford, OX2 6DP,
United Kingdom

Oxford University Press is a department of the University of Oxford.
It furthers the University's objective of excellence in research, scholarship,
and education by publishing worldwide. Oxford is a registered trade mark of
Oxford University Press in the UK and in certain other countries

First Edition published in 2022

Impression: 1

Published in the United States of America by Oxford University Press
198 Madison Avenue, New York, NY 10016, United States of America

British Library Cataloguing in Publication Data
Data available

Library of Congress Control Number: 2021953511

ISBN 978–0–19–286507–6

DOI: 10.1093/oso/9780192865076.001.0001

Printed and bound in the UK by
Clays Ltd, Elcograf S.p.A.

PREFACE

The focal point of this book is the wave of antisemitic violence that engulfed Germany in the early spring of 1933 and the reactions of German institutions and elites to the antisemitic attacks and discrimination. When I first discovered the existence and magnitude of local, grassroots anti-Jewish violence perpetrated mostly by SA units and uncoordinated from above, setting in a mere five weeks after Hitler was appointed Chancellor, my first reaction was incredulity, for neither the fact that it happened nor its enormous extent are adequately recognized in the historical literature. "Why was it not stopped?" was my first question after discovering evidence of this antisemitic violence in the archives, since by early March 1933 the Nazi dictatorship was not yet fully ensconced in power and some opportunities to oppose certain actions and policies still seemed to exist. My attention therefore naturally turned to those institutions in the German State and society, and the elites who led them, that might have intervened in the early spring of 1933. If German institutions and elites could not put a halt to antisemitic violence at this early stage of the Nazi takeover, how could anyone reasonably expect that this might happen at a later point, in 1938 or during the war, when the repressive apparatus of the dictatorship was fully established? Was it not the case that forfeiting the chance to put a stop to antisemitic violence and legislation in March and April 1933 meant that the opportunity would be lost for good?

These thoughts crossed my mind over a decade ago while I was researching the relationship between the Nazi Party and Hitler's conservative coalition partner, the German National People's Party (DNVP, or

German Nationals).[1] As I went through conservative party files, I came across an unexpectedly large number of complaints about antisemitic attacks and pleas for help from German Jews who were close to the DNVP. This struck me as paradoxical and difficult to comprehend, since these attacks began immediately after the elections of 5 March 1933, only five weeks after Hitler's accession to the chancellorship. The spirit that informed the institutions of the Weimar Republic, during which the rule of law was largely intact and antisemitic attacks and other transgressions were punished (though not as severely as they might have been),[2] should still have been very much alive, since even after the March elections the NSDAP (with 43.9 percent of the popular vote) did not have a majority. This instinctively raised further questions: Why was there no immediate outcry against such pervasive violence? Where were Germany's conservative elites in the administrative and judicial bureaucracy, the DNVP, the army, and the Christian Churches? They surely must have been horrified at what they could not have failed to notice and should have voiced their strongest exception to antisemitic attacks and violence—be it only for reasons of patriotism, since random violence that went unpunished did not accord with their image of Germany, and because they staunchly opposed any kind of popular lawlessness, social and political unrest, and disruptive "disorder."

When I encountered a large number of protests from foreign consulates in Berlin in the holdings of the Reich Chancellery (hundreds of complaints from the Polish Consulate alone) remonstrating about violent attacks perpetrated against their Jewish citizens that dated from mid-March 1933, my interest was piqued. How was it possible that such enormous numbers of attacks occurred a little over a month after 30 January? What also gave me pause was that previous research had rarely

---

1. See *The Fateful Alliance. German Conservatives and Nazis in 1933: The Machtergreifung in a New Light* (Oxford and New York: Berghahn Books, 2008); "Konflikte zwischen Deutschnationalen und Nationalsozialisten während der Machtergreifungszeit," *Historische Zeitschrift*, 292 (2011), 645–681; "The Antibourgeois Character of National Socialism," *Journal of Modern History*, 88 (2016), 572–609.
2. Cyril Levitt, "The Prosecution of Antisemites by the Courts in the Weimar Republic: Was Justice Served?" *Leo Baeck Yearbook*, 36 (1991), 151–167.

emphasized the prevalence of anti-Jewish attacks in the spring of 1933, let alone made them the focus of their investigation. Yet the numbers of attacks I encountered in DNVP party files and the numerous protests from foreign consulates to the Reich Chancellery and Interior Ministry indicated that anti-Jewish attacks were far more prevalent than previously assumed. What I had seen so far might, after all, be just the tip of an iceberg. As I began to dig deeper, I found my suspicions confirmed. The present book is the outcome of my quest in the archives.

The origins of my interest in the topic of this book can indirectly be traced back to Henri Lefebvre's seminar on twentieth-century Marxism in the *Centre Historique* in the Marais in Paris in the spring of 1982. It was then that I first became intrigued by the notion of the "paradox." Lefebvre, the grand old man of the French Left, had a peculiar way of looking at politics and society that could not fail to impress his students, leaving an indelible mark, even if they did not agree with his political views. Lefebvre never tired of arguing that modern history is replete with paradoxes, with which we have learned to live, quite possibly without even being fully aware of them. Ever since, I have been captivated by such inherent paradoxes whenever I stumbled upon them in my own scholarly endeavors and, perhaps without realizing it, even selected the themes of my research topics accordingly.

My first longer research project on the social thought of Prussian conservatives and Prussian officials, in what some historians have termed the age of bureaucratic absolutism between 1815 and 1848, had its origin in what I then considered the strongly felt and seemingly paradoxical animosity Prussian conservatives harbored for Prussian officials, an extreme aversion and loathing that went beyond a mere struggle for power. Conservatives accused high-ranking officials of having applied a kind of utopian social engineering during the Reform Era (1807–11), thereby destroying the old Prussian state. In their own approach to social and political reality, conservatives had always stressed the importance of taking vested rights and privileges, as well as local and regional particularities, into account, emphasizing the importance of safeguarding institutions that had evolved historically, and accusing bureaucrats of violating what they considered the rules of gradual historical development. These charges were unfounded, as I subsequently demonstrated, for internal memoranda within the Prussian civil service showed that high-echelon bureaucrats were pervaded by a similar mindset and the same approach to social reality, urging their subordinate officials to be mindful of regional particularities and vested rights when conceiving legislation. Another intriguing paradox concerns the strong social concerns evinced by Prussian conservatives, such as Joseph Maria von Radowitz and Hermann Wagener, their closeness to the extreme Left of their day, and the numerous commonalities in the social and political thought of contemporary Prussian conservatives and socialists in the 1840s through 1860s. In fact, several scholarly works in the 1930s pointed to those Prussian conservatives as forerunners of National Socialism and praised their concept of an authoritarian social kingdom.[3]

My second longer project, focusing on a topic in which I had long been interested, embodied another vexing paradox: the fascination of Germany's educated bourgeois elite, the *Bildungsbürgertum*, with National Socialism during the beginning stage of the regime's consolidation of power in 1933. This cultured elite included the established professional classes, the professoriate, administrators with a university education, and the Protestant clergy. It had been instrumental in earning Germany's reputation for learning and technical expertise.[4] Before the German defeat in the First World War and the economic turmoil and inflation following it, this educated elite had enjoyed significant material security

3. *The Origins of the Authoritarian Welfare State in Prussia: Conservatives, Bureaucracy, and the Social Question, 1815–1870* (Ann Arbor: Michigan Press, 1995); "The Social Policies of Prussian Officials: The Bureaucracy in a New Light," *Journal of Modern History*, 64 (1992), 263–298; "Die Rolle des Sozialkonservatismus in der preußisch-deutschen Geschichte als Forschungsproblem," *Jahrbuch für die Geschichte Mittel- und Ostdeutschlands*, 43 (1995), 59–92; "Konservative Politik und Modernisierung in Preußen, 1815–1918," in Thomas Stamm-Kuhlmann, ed., *Pommern im 19. Jahrhundert. Staatliche und gesellschaftliche Entwicklung in vergleichender Perspektive* (Cologne: Böhlau, 2007), 13–30.
4. The constituent element of the *Bildungsbürgertum* was the common *Bildung* of its members. The notion was shaped by a belief in human perfectibility, specifically that an individual's potential could be realized through personal improvement and education. This was the central notion of German Idealism and a cornerstone of Wilhelm von Humboldt's reform of the Prussian university system, from where the concept spread throughout Germany.

and comfort, as well as greater social prestige than its counterparts in most other European countries. To them, defeat in the war was more than a military disaster; it signified a personal humiliation and the loss of a distinct cultural identity. During the Weimar Republic the majority of the then predominantly conservative and intensely nationalistic educated bourgeoisie (before the 1880s its political orientation was mostly liberal) initially viewed the rising Nazi movement with thinly veiled contempt and favored the conservative DNVP at the ballot box. Even though some common ground did exist in extreme nationalism and hatred of what was considered the flagrant injustice of Versailles and dismay over Germany's treatment by the former Entente powers, the political message advanced by National Socialism was too simplistic to be readily accepted by the educated upper middle classes, whose cultural elitism ran counter to the essential anti-intellectualism of the NSDAP. Yet, beginning in 1932, large sections of the established members of the educated upper middle class voted in disproportionate numbers for the NSDAP, and after Hitler became Chancellor the academically trained flocked into the Nazi party. In the same way that the respected bookstore owner and member of the educated bourgeoisie Wilhelm Spannaus made the Nazi party socially acceptable in the northern German town of Northeim, as William S. Allen so vividly portrays in his The Nazi Seizure of Power, the cultivated bourgeoisie's initial enthusiasm for the regime helped to legitimate and consolidate Hitler's dictatorship. The major motivational shift in the educated elite's political orientation toward National Socialism seemed to me well worth investigating, especially since opportunism alone clearly could not explain the apparently genuine enthusiasm with which the "national revolution" was welcomed. To what exactly could National Socialism appeal in this segment of the population which, by virtue of education, breeding, and often social background, would be unlikely prey for the "temptations" of Nazism, whose public image was initially dominated by vulgarity, social animosity, and street violence?

The actual search for specific reasons to explain the educated elite's preference for Nazism proved difficult. Perusals of civil service organization files yielded no concrete results, and what little I found in literary bequests, autobiographies, letter collections, and other sources of a more personal nature were often too dependent on the individual case to permit generalization. It quickly became clear that the prominent members of the educated bourgeoisie who had left their personal papers to archives or had their correspondence published left out any compromising material that might provide evidence of their former partiality for Nazism. Searches in local archives revealed that even the protocols of city council meetings in the winter and spring of 1933 had been cleansed to obfuscate evidence of complicity. Yet, in researching the elusive reasons why so many members of the educated elite enthusiastically embraced the new regime, I happened upon what seemed to be another paradox. During the last phase of the Weimar Republic, the remaining established members of the educated elite had voted mostly for the German National People's Party (DNVP), which had entered a coalition with the Nazi party on 30 January 1933, thus facilitating Hitler's accession to the chancellorship. In DNVP party files I discovered documents that contradicted basic assumptions regarding the supposedly close relationship between Nazis and their conservative coalition partner during the first phase of the Nazi seizure of power between 30 January and 14 July 1933.

Conservative party files told a tale of Nazi hostility and loathing toward their conservative allies that was often expressed in physical terms, that is, extensive and hitherto little-known Nazi violence against DNVP members and organizations, and pitched battles fought between the SA and members of German National organizations. I also encountered widespread denigration of conservative symbols and *Honoratioren*, Nazi efforts to undermine existing hierarchies (in the judicial branch of the civil service, for example), and campaigns against the conservative bourgeoisie that revealed the pronounced anti-bourgeois thrust of Nazism. Given the impact of these unexpected findings and the dearth of relevant archival materials on the educated bourgeoisie, the focal point of my analysis turned to the relationship between conservative German

Nationals and the Nazis after Hitler became Chancellor on 30 January 1933. It was in conservative party files that I first discovered evidence of widespread antisemitic violence setting in more than three weeks before the 1 April boycott. While researching the dealings between the DNVP and their more powerful coalition partner, the attitude of German conservatives toward anti-Jewish violence also inexorably came into focus. As it became clear that the DNVP party leadership rebuffed calls for help from conservative and national-minded Jews, who had fought for Germany in World War I and whose families had lived in the country for generations, I wondered about the responses of other entrenched institutions, such as the Protestant and Catholic Churches and the administrative and judicial bureaucracies.

The answers I found constitute the paradox that lies at the heart of this book: How could institutions, and the elites who ran them, that claimed to be the standard-bearers of national morality, patriotism, and *Rechtsstaat* values abandon Jewish Germans during the first onslaught of antisemitic violence and discrimination? I quickly sensed that the prevalent anti-Jewish mood in the winter and spring of 1933 made antisemitism *salonfähig* in a way it had never been before, so that now ingrained antisemitic prejudices could be freely vented in public. In view of the fact that antisemitism was now a publicly sanctioned ideology fueled by formerly mostly private prejudices, it would also be less difficult to find excuses for the innumerable violent acts committed against Jews in Germany.

CONTENTS

List of Abbreviations   xvii

List of Archives   xix

Introduction   1

The Search for Archival Evidence   1

The Wider Implications: Which Institutions Were in a
    Position to Help?   7

Overview of Contents   18

Previous Literature on Antisemitic Violence in 1933   33

PART I. VIOLENCE AGAINST FOREIGN JEWS

1. Violence against *"Ostjuden"* in the Winter and Spring of 1933   47

   A Few Statistics   49

   A Litany of Violent Attacks in Early 1933   53

   Economic Damage and Ruin   57

   Rituals of Humiliation   62

   Abduction and Forced Deportation   65

   Grievous Bodily Harm and Murder   70

2. "Ostjuden" as Predetermined Targets: a History of
       Marginalization   73

   Roots of Prejudice   73

   Stigmatization and Violence during the Weimar Republic   78

   The Difficult Path to Citizenship   86

   The Policies of the NSDAP–DNVP Coalition Government   91

   German Jews and *"Ostjuden"*   98

3. Attacks against American and West European Jews,
   among Others   103
   Attacks on American Nationals   104
   Attacks on West European, Czech, and Rumanian Jews   112

PART II. VIOLENCE AGAINST GERMAN JEWS

4. Violent Attacks   123
   Antisemitic Violence in the Weimar Republic   124
   Documentary Evidence for Crimes against Jews   130
   Forcible Expulsion through Violence and Threats   138
   Attacks in Jail and on Jewish Livestock Dealers   148

5. Pillory Marches and the Perfidy Decree   151
   Pillory Marches   151
   The Perfidy Decree   166

6. Murder   175
   Categories of Anti-Jewish Murder   175
   The "Spontaneous" Murder   181
   Murder while in Custody   194
   The Planned Murder   201

7. Boycott   211
   Boycott Movements before 1 April 1933   211
   Global Protests and Boycotts against Germany   214
   The Boycott of 1 April 1933   219
   Psychological Implications of the Boycott   228
   Continuation of the Boycott Movement   231

8. Legal and Economic Discrimination   237
   The Antisemitic Legislation of April 1933   237
     The Law on the Restoration of a Professional Civil Service   239
     The Law on Admission to Legal Practice   244
     The Decree on the Admission of Physicians to the Statutory Health
       Insurance System   249
     The Law against the Overcrowding of German Schools and
       Universities   253

Impact of the April Legislation   256

Economic Discrimination   260

Other Discriminatory Measures   265

PART III. REACTIONS TO ANTISEMITIC VIOLENCE

9. The Protestant Church and the "Jewish Question:" the
   Church as Conscience of the Nation   275

   Fragmentation and Efforts to Form a Unified Organizational
   Structure   278

   The Church as a Moral Authority   280

   The Church in Politics: Interconnections with the DNVP   284

   The Church and Politics at the End of the Weimar Republic   286

   Political Groupings within the Church   291

   After 30 January 1933: a "Church-friendly National Socialism"   297

10. Protestant Church Leaders and the "Jewish Question:"
    Conscience Betrayed   311

    Foreign Reactions   311

    Church Reactions to Foreign Protests   314

    The Church and the Boycott of 1 April 1933   319

    Church Reactions to Pleas for Help and Reports
    of Discrimination   326

    Letter Exchanges between Wilhelm Menn and Ernst Stoltenhoff   331

    Growing Consensus with the Regime   335

    Otto Dibelius's Position on Antisemitism and his
    Relationship to the New State   338

11. The Protestant Church between Action and Silence   346

    The World Alliance for International Friendship Through the
    Churches and the Situation in Germany   346

    The Protestant Churches under Pressure: Prelude to the
    26 April Meeting   352

    Church Leaders on the "Judenfrage:" Opinions and Comments   356

    The Memorandum on the "Judenfrage"   371

CONTENTS

12. The German Catholic Church between Doctrine and
      Self-Preservation   377
      Before 30 January 1933   378
      After 30 January 1933   384
      The Church, the April Boycott, and Intervention on
        Behalf of Jews   389

13. Reactions of the German Administrative and Judicial
      Bureaucracy   400
      Officials Minimize Attacks   403
      Fabricated Charges against Victims   405
      Antisemitic Attacks and the Reaction of the Judicial Bureaucracy   412

14. Reactions of Hitler's Conservative Coalition Partner   420
      The DNVP and the "Jewish Question" during the Weimar Republic   421
      The DNVP and National-minded German Jews in March 1933   434
      Protests by Members of the DNVP and Active Help   438
      The Boycott and *Völkisch* Antisemitism   444
      Lacking Determination and Fearing to Decide   450

Epilogue: How Could it Happen?   457

Bibliography   475
Acknowledgements   521
Index   523

LIST OF ABBREVIATIONS

ADGB	Allgemeiner Deutscher Gewerkschaftsbund, General German Trade Union Federation
AdR	Akten der Reichskanzlei, Files of the Reich Chancellery
BNSDJ	Bund Nationalsozialistischer Deutscher Juristen, National Socialist Association of German Jurists
DDP	Deutsche Demokratische Partei, German Democratic Party
DEKA	Deutscher Evangelischer Kirchenausschuss, German Evangelical Church Committee
DNVP	Deutschnationale Volkspartei, German National People's Party
DVP	Deutsche Volkspartei, German People's Party
KPD	Kommunistische Partei Deutschlands, German Communist Party
NS	Nationalsozialismus/nationalsozialistisch, National Socialism/National Socialist
NSBO	Nationalsozialistische Betriebszellenorganisation, National Socialist Factory Cell Organization
NSDAP	Nationalsozialistische Deutsche Arbeiterpartei, National Socialist German Workers' Party
NYT	*New York Times*
SA	Sturmabteilung, "Stormtroopers" (Nazi paramilitary force)
SOPADE	Sozialdemokratische Partei Deutschlands im Exil, Social Democratic Party of Germany in Exile
SPD	Sozialdemokratische Partei Deutschlands, Social Democratic Party of Germany
SS	Schutzstaffel, "Protection Squad" (Nazi special elite formation)
USPD	Unabhängige Sozialdemokratische Partei Deutschlands, Independent Social Democratic Party of Germany
VJHZ	*Vierteljahrshefte für Zeitgeschichte*

LIST OF ARCHIVES

Bayerisches Hauptstaatsarchiv München, BayHStaA
Bundesarchiv Berlin-Lichterfelde, BA Berlin
Bundesarchiv Koblenz, BA Koblenz
Bundesarchiv-Militärarchiv Freiburg, BA Freiburg
Evangelisches Zentralarchiv Berlin, EZA Berlin
Geheimes Staatsarchiv Preußischer Kulturbesitz, Berlin-Dahlem GStAPK Dahlem
Hauptstaatsarchiv Düsseldorf, HStA Düsseldorf, now Landesarchiv Nordrhein-Westfalen
Hauptstaatsarchiv Stuttgart, HStA Stuttgart
Hessisches Hauptstaatsarchiv Wiesbaden, HHStA Wiesbaden
Institut für Zeitgeschichte, Munich IfZ
Landesarchiv Baden-Württemberg, formerly Generallandesarchiv Karlsruhe, LABW Karlsruhe
Landesarchiv Berlin, LA Berlin
Landesarchiv Schleswig-Holstein, LASH
Landeshauptarchiv Schwerin, LHA Schwerin
Landeskirchenarchiv der Evangelisch-Lutherischen Landeskirche Sachsens, Dresden LAKA Dresden
Niedersächsisches Hauptstaatsarchiv Hannover, NHStA Hannover
Nordelbisches Kirchenarchiv Kiel, NEKA Kiel
Nordrhein-Westfälisches Hauptstaatsarchiv, Düsseldorf HStA Düsseldorf
Sächsisches Hauptstaatsarchiv Dresden, SHStA Dresden
Staatsarchiv Hamburg, StA Hamburg
Staatsarchiv München, StA München

The passivity, the silence of the respectable people . . . [was] just as important for the success of National Socialism as the bellowing of the enthusiasts.

—Fritz Stern, *Das feine Schweigen*

INTRODUCTION

The Search for Archival Evidence

In the Preface I outlined how I happened upon the problems and events discussed in this book while researching the conflict-ridden relationship between the Nazi Party and the conservative German National People's Party, whose coalition brought Hitler to power at the end of January 1933. As I went through what is left of the conservative party files,[1] I was surprised by the large number of complaints about antisemitic attacks from members of the conservative party, by the violent attacks on Jewish businesses, and pleas for help from conservative Jewish Germans. Had Weimar's legal system, which was still largely functional in February, stopped working so abruptly within the space of less than a month? Once I fully realized the extent of antisemitic violence in March and April 1933, one question immediately sprang to mind: if anti-Jewish violence was so widespread during this time, why has previous research on the period of the Nazi takeover rarely stressed the prevalence of violent antisemitism? Studies dealing with the period from the perspective of the fate of German Jews focus primarily on the economic aspects of violence and exclusion, such as the boycott of shops and lawyers' and doctors' offices on 1 April 1933, as well as on the discriminatory legislation of April 1933, but antisemitic violence as such, though mentioned, is rarely thoroughly examined, let alone in the

---

1. Until the early 1990s, these were housed in the Zentrales Staatsarchiv I of the German Democratic Republic in Potsdam and then relocated to the Bundesarchiv Berlin in Berlin-Lichterfelde.

Before the Holocaust: Antisemitic Violence and the Reaction of German Elites and Institutions during the Nazi Takeover.
Hermann Beck, Oxford University Press. © Hermann Beck 2022. DOI: 10.1093/oso/9780192865076.003.0001

context of relevant social and political forces that may have impacted or mitigated it.[2] The answer gradually became clear: the surviving documentation, as far as it still exists, is deeply hidden in different archival holdings, since antisemitic attacks went, for the most part, unreported and therefore cannot be found in police files. This section thus deals with the search for archival evidence to gain as complete a picture as possible of the extent of antisemitic violence, though it should be kept in mind that since many crimes against Germany's Jews went unrecorded, even a systematic exploration of German archives can yield only fragmentary results.

As the vast number of complaints in conservative party files left no doubt that there must have been countless attacks, I began to dig deeper and searched for further information in other archival holdings. In the files of the Reich Chancellery I found hundreds of complaints from foreign delegations in Berlin that protested against violent attacks perpetrated against their Jewish citizens, including reports from the Polish, French, Swiss, and United States consulates about acts of provocation and violence directed against Jewish citizens of those countries.[3] In the holdings of the Prussian Ministry of Justice in the Geheimes Staatsarchiv Preußischer Kulturbesitz in Berlin-Dahlem I discovered documents relating to several antisemitic murders committed in the spring of 1933.[4] And among the files of the British military government after 1945 I found trial documents on anti-Jewish attacks, murders, and so-called *Prangermärsche* ("pillory marches") that occurred in 1933 but were prosecuted only after the Second World War and collected under the heading "Crimes Committed during the National Socialist Revolution."[5]

2. For previous research on antisemitic violence in 1933, see the fourth section of this Introduction.
3. BA Berlin, R43 II, no. 1195, "NSDAP," 29–53; 67–97; 91–112; 113–120; 150–161; 164–204.
4. GStAPK Dahlem, Rep. 84a, no. 54815, "Wegen Ermordung des jüdischen Milchhändlers Max Kassel, März–Mai 1933;" Rep. 84a, no. 54897, "Wegen Ermordung des jüdischen Rechtsanwalts Schumm aus Neidenburg;" Rep. 84a, no. 53389, "Ermittlungsverfahren gegen Unbekannt wegen Ermordung des jüdischen Zahnarztes Dr. Alfred Meyer, Kommunist in Wuppertal-Barmen am 16. Mai 1933."
5. See, for example, BA Koblenz, Oberster Gerichtshof für die Britische Zone, Z38, no. 216, "Strafsache gegen Karl Saucke wegen Freiheitsberaubung und Misshandlung von Angehörigen linksgerichteter Parteien und Juden in Seesen;" no. 239, "Tötung eines jüdischen

On the other hand, it quickly became apparent that the direct approach yielded few results when it came to the specifics of the actual crimes. The usual place to look for evidence of antisemitic attacks would be the police records of larger German cities. Yet, there was barely any evidence of antisemitic attacks in these records. After spending a considerable amount of time going through police files for March and April 1933 in the Munich Staatsarchiv and in Hannover's Niedersächsisches Landesarchiv, for example, it became clear that research in police files would yield no appreciable results.[6] I soon discovered the reason for this: already in March, police officers had been instructed not to record antisemitic crimes and not to offer help to the victims. In Prussia, Hermann Göring's admonitions (as head of the Prussian police) not to deploy police officers as protection squads for Jewish homes set the tone. In one case in Dresden, five uniformed SA men forced their way into the home of a Polish rabbi and beat him with rubber truncheons. The policemen summoned to the scene refused to get involved, with the standard excuse, "It is not the obligation of the police to protect Jews."[7] In fact this particular phrase—"Die Polizei ist nicht dazu da, um Juden zu schützen"—seems to have been a standard formulation repeatedly encountered in the reports. Indeed, if victims called in the police in March 1933, they could be in for a nasty shock, for already in mid-February about 50,000 members of the SA, SS, and the veterans' organization *Stahlhelm* were amalgamated with the Prussian police, so that assault victims might open the door to a Nazi stormtrooper now vested with official police authority. Other German states then rapidly followed the Prussian example. The fact that no assistance could be expected from

Hauptschriftleiters des sozialdemokratischen 'Volksblattes' in Detmold auf dem Transport nach Dachau;" no. 391, "Anprangerung eines jüdischen Geschäftsmanns, Pinneberg 1933."

6. Staatsarchiv München, Polizeidirektion München, nos. 6758; 6761–6764; 6766–6771; Niedersächsisches Landesarchiv, Hauptstaatsarchiv Hannover, Hann. 180 Hannover, Hann. 180 Hildesheim.
7. BA Berlin, R43 II, no. 1195, "NSDAP," fol. 201.

the police quickly became known to attackers, victims, and potential victims alike, thus emboldening perpetrators.

After carefully perusing the federal German and central Prussian archives in Koblenz and Berlin and the central archives of German Protestantism in Berlin in search of further evidence, I turned to the regional archives of the different German states, from Bavaria to Saxony, Baden, Hessen, some of the other lesser German states, and former Prussian provinces such as Schleswig-Holstein.[8] In several regional archives I found further revealing evidence of antisemitic violence as, for example, in the so-called *Wiedergutmachungsakten* (compensation files) at the main Hessian archives in Wiesbaden.[9] In the Landesarchiv Schleswig-Holstein in Schleswig and Nordrhein-Westfälisches Hauptstaatsarchiv in Düsseldorf I discovered files on post-war trials that dealt with antisemitic murder cases from the period of the Nazi takeover. Already in 1933, public prosecutors' offices were compelled to launch an investigation into murder cases, and German authorities had accordingly initiated legal proceedings and gathered evidence against potential suspects in the spring of that year. In several instances murder suspects had been clearly identified and overwhelming evidence against them had been collected. Yet, even in cases where the killers were known, no sentences were passed in 1933. All offenders were released under the amnesty of 25 July 1933 for "Crimes Committed during the National Socialist Revolution."[10]

But the files of the original investigation occasionally survived the war, and in several instances murder cases were revived after 1945, especially

---

8. Bayerisches Hauptstaatsarchiv München; Sächsisches Hauptstaatsarchiv Dresden; Landesarchiv Baden-Württemberg, formerly Generallandesarchiv Karlsruhe; Niedersächsisches Landesarchiv in Hannover, Hessisches Hauptstaatsarchiv Wiesbaden; Landesarchiv Nordrhein-Westfalen, formerly Hauptstaatsarchiv Düsseldorf; Landesarchiv Berlin; Landeshauptarchiv Schwerin; Staatsarchiv Hamburg; Landesarchiv Schleswig-Holstein in Schleswig; Landesarchiv Thüringen in Weimar.
9. Hauptstaatsarchiv Wiesbaden, Abt. 518.11, *"Entschädigungsakten."* Of the 110, 000 files documenting claims of Nazi victims (*Entschädigungsakten*), about 6,000 were digitalized in the 1990s. Among these there were eleven cases that referred to crimes committed in 1933.
10. GStAPK Dahlem, Rep. 84a, no. 54771, "Gnadenerweise aus Anlass der Beendigung der nationalsozialistischen Revolution, aufgrund des Erlasses vom 22. Juni 1933 in Verbindung mit der allgemeinen Verfügung des Justizministers vom 25. Juli 1933."

when the killers were suspected or known.[11] Resumption of legal proceedings after the war was often prompted when friends or relatives of the victims urged the German authorities, or, before 1949, the occupation authorities, to reopen proceedings and bring the murderers to justice. Some of these post-war murder trials extended into the late 1950s and early 1960s. But even after the war convictions were rare and sentences, when passed, exceedingly clement by the standards of the time. This was due mostly to lack of hard evidence and because the politically restorative political climate of the 1950s worked in favor of the defendants. In some instances the trail had gone cold, former murder suspects had been killed during the war, or witnesses had disappeared. In other cases murder suspects, mostly former SA or SS men, gave each other alibis, or put the blame on comrades whom they believed to have been killed in the war and were thus beyond the reach of the law. Those convicted were often criminal types with a long charge sheet, since even former Nazi judges had no qualms about sentencing such people to long terms of imprisonment.[12]

Taken together, the files tell the appalling and largely unknown story of massive antisemitic attacks in the spring of 1933. The attacks began immediately after 5 March and then gradually abated during the summer. Since the crimes were mostly not directly recorded, they have to be pieced together from complaints in conservative party files, files from prosecutors' offices from the spring of 1933, post-1945 British occupation authority files, trial records on *Prangermärsche*, regional incidents that might be recorded in the archives of German states or former Prussian provinces, such as Schleswig-Holstein, and information gleaned from post-war trials. We also have no clear notion of the actual number of attacks. The *New York Times*, *Chicago Daily Tribune*, London

---

11. This happened, for example, in the murder cases of Max Kassel, Peter Stieldorf, Friedrich Schumm, Felix Fechenbach, Fritz Solmitz, Wilhelm Spiegel, and Alfred Meyer, all of which are discussed in Chapter 6 below.
12. This occurred, for example, in the post-war murder trials of Max Kassel and Felix Fechenbach. In the latter case the chauffeur, who was only marginally involved, was sentenced to five years' imprisonment.

Times, Manchester Guardian, and countless other newspapers and magazines in the Western democracies carried accounts of antisemitic attacks, but the reporting was too unspecific, since precise details, such as names of victims and informants, were usually not revealed, in order to shield them. And much of the information was based on reports from Germans who wanted to remain anonymous. The same is true for the numerous diplomatic reports and commentaries from the time of the Nazi takeover. They mentioned the attacks in some detail, but were based mostly on hearsay and oral accounts from unnamed informants and cannot be used as a basis for a statistical assessment.[13] We have one concrete figure. An American journalist, Michael Williams, who visited Germany from early April until mid-June, mentions the figure of about 300 antisemitic murders and 3,000 other violent crimes against Germany's Jews in a *New York Times* article from mid-June 1933.[14] This figure was not based on statistics or other concrete evidence. If we accept this as a possible yardstick, however, the magnitude of antisemitic crimes becomes starkly clear: since, during the depth of the Depression in 1931, there were 1,336 cases of murder and manslaughter in the entire population in Germany, the number of attacks that Williams mentions for the late spring of 1933 would account for more than one fifth of all murders committed in Germany in 1931 within a span of only three months. Projected to twelve months, it would amount to 1,200 murders, that is, very close to the 1931 figure of all cases of murder and manslaughter for the entire population.[15] This onslaught of anti-Jewish violence set in exactly five weeks after Hitler became Chancellor. One critical question we have to answer now is: in the conditions of the late winter and spring

---

13. *Documents on British Foreign Policy 1919–1939*, 2nd series, IV (London: HMSO, 1950), 395–481; vol. V (London: HMSO, 1956), 1–55; *Foreign Relations of the United States. Diplomatic Papers 1933*, vol. II (Washington: Government Printing Office, 1949), 183–255.
14. Michael Williams, "Nazi Deeds Worst in History," *NYT*, 16 June 1933.
15. The figure for murders and manslaughters compares with 13,134 male and 5,491 female suicides (1931); *Statistisches Jahrbuch für das Deutsche Reich*, 52 (Berlin: Statistisches Reichsamt, 1933), 44–45.

of 1933, which parties and other institutions of the German State and society were in a position to intervene on behalf of the victims?

The Wider Implications: Which Institutions Were in a Position to Help?

In order to assess which institutions of the German State and society might have been able to protest, help, or actively intervene on behalf of Jews in Germany, the specific political conditions of the winter and spring of 1933 have to be taken into account. The first effective measure of the new regime to stifle potential opposition was the presidential decree of 4 February 1933, authorizing the prohibition of newspapers and public meetings that attacked institutions or leading officials of State. This so-called *Schubladenverordnung* thus gave the new government the power to (temporarily) ban the opposition press.[16] But the system of law courts still functioned in February and many newspaper prohibitions could be successfully contested. Still, in these economically precarious times even a temporary loss of advertisement revenue might mean economic ruin, and so the opposition press moderated its critical tone toward the new government from early on.

Especially in the largest federal state, Prussia, whose domestic politics were conducted with implacable ruthlessness by Hermann Göring as acting Interior Minister (after 30 January) and Minister President (after 11 April), and which accounted for 62.45 percent of Germany's population and 61.16 percent of its size, the Nazi takeover made rapid progress.[17] The higher administrative bureaucracy, such as provincial and district governors and police commissioners, was ruthlessly purged. This amounted to

16. Ironically, it was drafted by Hitler's predecessors in office with an eye toward controlling the activities of the Nazi Party.
17. In 1933, Prussia had 292,771.65 sq. km (Germany without the Saar 468,779.58 sq. km), with a population of 39,958,073 (total German population: 65,335,879 million); *Statistisches Jahrbuch* (1933), 5–6.

a removal of pro-Republican forces that followed closely on the heels of the previous purge after the *Preußenschlag*—the overthrow of the Prussian government by the Reich under Papen's government on 20 July 1932. On 22 February 1933 large contingents of SA, SS, and *Stahlhelm* units (about 50,000) were employed as auxiliary police and merged with the Prussian police force, so that if anyone was attacked by Nazi stormtroopers in the street and appealed to the police for help, SA men in auxiliary police uniform might well come to their assistance. This meant that the 5 March election campaign was no longer free, with the scales heavily tipped against the SPD (Social Democratic Party), Center, and other pro-Republican parties, since meetings of the democratic opposition were now ruthlessly broken up. At the beginning of February, Kurt Schumacher and other SPD deputies still believed that Nazi leaders were mere pawns in the hands of the capitalists around the DNVP (German National People's Party) leader Alfred Hugenberg (a view also shared by many in the Center Party); already by the end of that month Nazi violence showed considerable effect in that many SPD politicians, such as Berlin's former police chief Albert Grzesinski, had resignedly stopped campaigning or fled Germany, even before the electoral showdown of 5 March, as in the case of the former Prussian Prime Minister Otto Braun.[18]

The decisive event that smoothed the road to dictatorship was the Reichstag fire—the burning of the houses of parliament—on the night of 27 February. At the time a majority of Germans believed the version propagated by the government that communists had set fire to the Reichstag and that a communist coup attempt was imminent. Due to fear of a communist uprising, President Hindenburg signed "The Decree for the Protection of the People and the State," the so-called Reichstag fire decree that suspended the basic rights of citizens, such as freedom of expression and the right of assembly, and outlawed the Communist

---

18. Heinrich August Winkler, *Der Weg in die Katastrophe. Arbeiter und Arbeiterbewegung in der Weimarer Republik 1930 bis 1933*, 2nd ed. (Bonn: Dietz, 1990), 878; Erich Matthias, "Die Sozialdemokratische Partei Deutschlands," in Erich Matthias and Rudolf Morsey, eds., *Das Ende der Parteien 1933* (Düsseldorf: Droste, 1960), 234–235.

Party. Now letters could be opened, houses searched, and suspects held without a warrant. Those interned had no right of appeal and redress for false arrest. Since the Reichstag fire decree was not accompanied by provisions about how to implement the law, as was customary, its execution was left to the ministers of interior of the different German states. It also authorized the Reich government to take over full powers in any of the German states whose governments were unable to restore public order, which was significant in the case of those states where the NSDAP was not yet part of government. These states— Hamburg, Bremen, Lübeck, Schaumburg-Lippe, Hesse-Darmstadt, Baden, Württemberg, Saxony, and Bavaria—were taken over in the weeks following the 5 March elections.

Perhaps most significant of all was the fact that the Reichstag fire and the seemingly decisive actions of the new Nazi government against the perceived communist threat (by early March the NSDAP was clearly considered the dominant force in the coalition) changed the public mood in favor of Hitler and the NSDAP, widely seen as the only leader and party ready to save Germany from communism. As the Nazi opponent Theodor Eschenburg wrote in his memoirs, the Reichstag fire was "the first event that sent chilling fright through our bones...A premonition went through Germany: Now things are getting dangerous."[19] During the last week of the election campaign the NSDAP therefore enjoyed a decided advantage that was reflected in the voter turnout (88.8 percent) and, to a certain extent, in election results: the NSDAP gained 5.5 million votes (from 11.7 to 17.2 million) and rose from 33.1 to 43.9 percent of the national electorate, while conservative support remained stagnant at 8 percent. Together the NSDAP/DNVP coalition enjoyed an absolute majority after 5 March 1933. Nazi tactics of outlawing the KPD while letting voters cast their ballot for the communists now bore fruit. The 81 Communist deputies who had been elected (the KPD

---

19. Theodor Eschenburg, *Letzten Endes meine ich doch. Erinnerungen, 1933–1999* (Berlin: Siedler, 2000), 13.

had received 12.3 percent of the vote) went into hiding or were arrested, and without them the 288 Nazi deputies alone had an absolute majority in parliament.

All of this had been accomplished without flagrantly violating constitutional provisions, which is the reason why some historians emphasize that this was a "legal" or "semi-legal" takeover, though political violence increased throughout March and reached a first high point in the course of the Nazi takeover of the German *Länder* between 5 and 10 March.[20] As a result of National Socialist successes and the lack of resistance to the takeover, there was growing defeatism in the ranks of those political forces that had opposed Nazism. With the Communist Party already outlawed, resignation now spread within the ranks of the SPD and Center Party. In February and March, long-standing members of the Social Democratic Party returned their membership cards,[21] and after 5 March countless members of the Republican *Reichsbanner* applied to the veterans' organization *Stahlhelm* for membership to protect themselves from Nazi retribution, while the leadership of the General German Trade Union Federation (ADGB) declared its willingness to sever its long-standing ties with the SPD.[22] All were stunned by the energy and dynamism of the movement and the ruthlessness with which any opposition was swept aside. The leaders of the *Reichsbanner* and other organizations, whose rank and file would have been willing to oppose the new regime more openly, were also paralyzed by the seeming legality of the Nazi conquest of power, since open rebellion against the new government would have

20. Karl Dietrich Bracher stresses the "pseudo-legal" character of the Nazi takeover in *Die nationalsozialistische Machtergreifung*, while Klaus Hildebrand speaks of a "semblance of legality." See Karl Dietrich Bracher, Wolfgang Sauer, and Gerhard Schulz, *Die Nationalsozialistische Machtergreifung*, 2nd ed. (Cologne and Opladen: Westdeutscher Verlag, 1962); Karl Dietrich Bracher, *Die deutsche Diktatur. Entstehung, Struktur, Folgen des Nationalsozialismus*, 7th ed. (Berlin: Ullstein, 1997); Klaus Hildebrand, *Das dritte Reich*, 3rd ed. (Munich: Oldenbourg, 1987), 2.
21. NHStA Hannover, Hann 310 II A, no. 41, 1932–1933.
22. Hermann Beck, *The Fateful Alliance. German Conservatives and Nazis in 1933: The Machtergreifung in a New Light* (New York and Oxford: Berghahn, 2010), 253–270.

automatically summoned up the forces of law and order and the institutions of the State against them.[23]

The Center and liberal parties' support for the 23 March Enabling Act, in which Hitler asked for absolute rule for four years and which required a parliamentary two-thirds majority, was another ominous sign of the momentous change in the political climate. While there were threats and intimidation outside and inside the Kroll Opera House in which the voting took place, its ready acceptance cannot be explained solely as a combination of opportunism and fear of Nazi reprisals if the decree were rejected. As one of the liberal deputies, Hermann Dietrich, wrote after the war, never before in his life had he received such an enormous acclaim of approval as on the occasion of this vote. The outcome (442 to 94 in favor of approval, with only SPD deputies voting against) was thus greatly favored by the public mood, which demanded acceptance.[24] In the spring of 1933, the overbearing propaganda and domineering publicity for the Hitler government went to such extremes that even the newly appointed Propaganda Minister Joseph Goebbels (13 March 1933) spoke out against "nationalist kitsch," which a contemporary (anti-Nazi) diarist commented upon: "All the lowest instincts of taste seem to have been unleashed by the National Socialist movement and its victory. Busts of the Führer made out of lard are the least of it. Toilet paper: 'we crack down' is not bad either. And the postcard industry!"[25] In petitions to the Reich Chancellery, owners of coffeehouses asked permission to name their shops after Hitler, rose growers their roses, and the mayor of the East Prussian village Sutzken requested a name change to "Hitlershöhe," while a registrar official in Düsseldorf reported to local Nazi Party authorities that a party member requested to name his child "Hitlerine" but had to

23. On the willingness of the rank and file of the *Reichsbanner* to resist at the local level, see William S. Allen, *The Nazi Seizure of Power*, rev. ed. (New York: Watts, 1984), 169–233.

24. Rudolf Morsey, *Das Ermächtigungsgesetz* (Düsseldorf: Droste, 1992), 129–183; Eric Kurlander, *Living with Hitler. Liberal Democrats in the Third Reich* (New Haven: Yale University Press, 2009), 13–19.

25. Erich Ebermayer, *Denn heute gehört uns Deutschland* (Hamburg and Vienna: Zsolnay, 1959), 65 (entry from 18 April 1933).

settle for "Adolfine" instead.[26] And this was just the tip of an adulation iceberg. As administrative reports suggested, a generally favorable mood toward the new government seemed to catch on even among former opponents. In the second half of April, for example, the *Regierungspräsident* (district governor) of middle and upper Franconia summarized reports from his counties to the effect that "the takeover is viewed more sympathetically, even among those not previously well disposed toward the NSDAP, and there are indications, namely in workers' circles, that point to a certain leaning toward the new government."[27]

This powerful wave of hopeful enthusiasm, which was often boosted by opportunism but sometimes also genuine, buoyed and sustained the "semi-legal" conquest of State and society. It was one characteristic of the period; violence was another. This violence manifested itself not only in rabble-rousing grassroots initiatives by local Nazi organizations against perceived opponents and, after 5 March, antisemitic attacks throughout Germany, but also in countless acts of revenge and intimidation against political opponents, neighbors, business rivals, or anyone who had ever crossed prominent Nazis or Nazi organizations. Ubiquitous terror was the essential lubricant in eliminating opponents and in rendering innocuous potential enemies, convincing them that accommodation with the new regime was the only option they had. It would be wrong to assume that social and political prominence was a protective shield against Nazi attacks even at the beginning of Hitler's rule. Every German, regardless of social standing, who had ever fallen foul of the Nazis was now in danger. There were house searches in the homes of prominent parliamentarians, such as Siegfried von Kardorff, the former Vice-President of parliament, the house of former President Ebert's widow was searched for Republican flags, and in Einstein's (empty) house Nazi stormtroopers looked for explosives. Any pretext would do to intimidate those seen as enemies.

26. Beatrice Heiber and Helmut Heiber, eds., *Die Rückseite des Hakenkreuzes. Absonderliches aus den Akten des Dritten Reiches*, 2nd ed. (Munich: DTV, 1994), 119–122.
27. Martin Broszat et al., eds., *Bayern in der NS Zeit*. Vol. 1, *Soziale Lage und politisches Verhalten der Bevölkerung im Spiegel vertraulicher Berichte* (Munich and Vienna: Oldenbourg, 1977), 210.

In the same vein, members and even leaders of the German National People's Party, the NSDAP's coalition partner, were not spared either. Many German National mayors were forcibly replaced by SA leaders, and numerous pitched battles were fought between the SA and members of the conservative German National *Kampfring*. Since conservatives were usually outnumbered, they mostly came out on the losing side. Attacks against members and leaders of the conservative party were carried out with astonishing brutality. The files meticulously list the injuries, such as knocked-out teeth, head wounds, and the occasional bullet wound. Even prominent conservative politicians, such as Paul Rüffer, leader of the German National workers' movement, were subjected to such attacks.[28] It goes without saying that the political Left suffered incomparably more. Terror against KPD, SPD, the trade unions, and the Republican *Reichsbanner* was more systematic and on a much larger scale. Hermann Göring's so-called *Schießerlaß* of 17 February, demanding co-operation with "national associations" and the ruthless use of firearms against the political Left, created a legal double standard and amounted to an invitation to attack leftist parties and organizations. The vast majority of the 27,000 inmates kept as "protective detainees" in camps, the more than 100,000 prisoners temporarily kept in the "wild" concentration camps of the SA, and the 500–600 murdered political opponents were members of the Left.[29] The opening of the first large concentration camp in Dachau had been announced in the newspapers, and the existence of a large number of SA "wild" camps and torture cellars was widely known. So was the fact that neither the law courts nor the police could offer protection, and rumors as to what was happening inside these "extra-legal

28. Hermann Beck, "Konflikte zwischen Deutschnationalen und Nationalsozialisten während der Machtergreifungszeit," *Historische Zeitschrift*, 292 (2011), 645–681; BA Berlin, R43 II, no. 1195, fols. 323–324v.
29. Winkler, *Katastrophe*, 889; Michael Schneider, *Unterm Hakenkreuz. Arbeiter und Arbeiterbewegung 1933 bis 1939* (Berlin: Aufbau, 1999), 455; Martin Broszat, "Nationalsozialistische Konzentrationslager 1933–1945," in Hans Buchheim, Martin Broszat, and Hans-Adolf Jacobsen, eds., *Anatomie des SS-Staates*, 6th ed. (Munich: DTV, 1994), 323–449, esp. 336; Nikolaus Wachsmann, *KL. A History of the Nazi Concentration Camps* (New York: Farrar, Straus & Giroux: 2015), 27–70.

spaces" abounded. Fear nipped potential resistance in the bud. It was this atmosphere of nationalist ecstasy and lawlessness, of seeming euphoria and wanton arbitrariness, of fear, brutal repression, and the beginning of tight surveillance coupled with hopes for a better tomorrow that characterized the political climate of the late winter and spring of 1933 and that forms the backdrop of assessing the problem of who remained in a position to protest against antisemitic violence and come to the aid of the victims.

Given the speed of the Nazi takeover and the political and psychological implications arising from the largely unopposed conquest of State and society, few German State or societal institutions remained in a position to intervene and lend active support on behalf of the victims by the end of March 1933. Those democratic parties of the Weimar Republic that had traditionally opposed antisemitism, in particular the left liberal German Democratic Party (DDP) and the Social Democratic Party (SPD), had been severely weakened. The DDP, once the third strongest party in the early Republic with 18.5 percent of the vote and seventy-five deputies in Weimar's first elections on 19 January 1919, whose predecessor in the Empire had already stood up for the rights of German Jews, had merged with the antisemitic *Jungdeutscher Orden* (Young German Order) in 1930, even though this supposed accretion of its strength had failed to arrest its decline. By 1932 it had been reduced to a splinter party with a mere 1 percent of the vote. In the second half of March 1933, it was fighting for its very survival and its five deputies elected in March 1933 all voted in favor of the Enabling Act.[30]

The SPD, which had emerged as far and away the strongest party after the first elections in January 1919, had managed to salvage parts of its support base and remained (a distant) second to the NSDAP in the elections of 1932, with about one fifth of the electorate behind it. The party had once been a vigorous defender of the position of German Jews,

30. On their position on the "Jewish Question," see Philip Bernard Wiener, "Die Parteien der Mitte," in Werner E. Mosse, ed., *Entscheidungsjahr 1932. Zur Judenfrage in der Endphase der Weimarer Republik*, 2nd ed. (Tübingen: Mohr Siebeck, 1966), esp. 289–306.

but this particular concern had gradually receded into the background during the Republic's last phase.[31] Given their own precarious position in the spring of 1933, leading Social Democrats were first and foremost concerned about the survival of their party and saving their own remaining members and leaders. The issue of antisemitic attacks does not seem to have been a major issue of discussion among party leaders.[32] My suspicions in this respect were confirmed during a visit to the Friedrich Ebert Stiftung in Bonn-Bad Godesberg, where I found little information on this issue,[33] but was surprised to see that the prevailing preoccupation of the SPD leadership at the very end of the Republic, much more so than in the 1920s, was to present the party as national-minded. Exertions to emphasize one's loyalty to the nation left even less space for the defense of German Jews, who, in popular consciousness and despite all evidence to the contrary, were frequently regarded as unpatriotic. At the end of the day, of course, by the second half of March 1933 all political parties other than the NSDAP were most concerned about fighting for their very survival. They were then banned or dissolved between 22 June and 5 July. In fact, among the political parties, only Hitler's alliance partner, the conservative German National People's Party, retained vestiges of political influence. This small but still very influential party, representing large parts of the Protestant elites, was a doubtful last resort, since its own past was tinged with antisemitism. The party's position, as well as the divergent views of some of its members and leaders on how to respond to anti-Jewish discrimination and often-violent attacks, still deserve to be

---

31. See Donald Niewyk, *Socialist, Anti-Semite, and Jew. German Social Democracy Confronts the Problem of Anti-Semitism, 1918–1933* (Baton Rouge: LSU Press, 1971); Hans-Helmuth Knütter, "Die Linksparteien," in Mosse, ed., *Entscheidungsjahr*, 323–348, esp. 323–334: On the historical background, see Lars Fischer, *The Socialist Response to Antisemitism in Imperial Germany* (Cambridge: Cambridge University Press, 2007).

32. See also David Bankier, "German Social Democrats and the Jewish Question," in David Bankier, ed., *Probing the Depths of German Anti-Semitism. German Society and the Persecution of the Jews, 1933–1941* (New York: Berghahn, 2000), 511–532. The meticulously researched accounts of the SPD's history from 1930 to 1933 by Winkler, *Katastrophe*, and from 1933 to 1939 by Michael Schneider, *Unterm Hakenkreuz*, also have little to say about the SPD's reaction to antisemitism.

33. In the holdings of the "SOPADE," and in the available literary bequests and press organs.

examined here in some detail, not least in order to show that in 1933 Jews in Germany had very few influential champions left.[34]

Apart from the DNVP, there were only three institutions in German society that remained in a position to protest effectively, insofar as they had preserved at least a semblance of independence: first, the Christian Churches, in particular the Protestant Church, to which almost two-thirds of all Germans belonged as tax-paying members.[35] As will be discussed comprehensively in Chapters 9, 10, and 11 below, leaders of the Protestant Church considered themselves as moral authorities, responsible for upholding ethical standards throughout the country, and frequently got involved in the political issues of the day; in 1932, several Protestant leaders outspokenly opposed the Nazi party on a variety of issues. Secondly, the administrative bureaucracy, which tackled complaints from foreign consulates, and the judicial branch of the civil service, which was charged with prosecuting and sentencing the perpetrators of antisemitic crimes. The reasons for their failure to do so constitute an important part of the story presented in this book. Thirdly, the Reichswehr, Germany's small but highly professional army, which still seemed autonomous and nominally free of Nazi influence in the first half of 1933. Yet it quickly became apparent that army leaders were, for the most part, not interested in the issue, and not prepared to lend succor in any form. At the German military archives in Freiburg, for example, only two slender folders deal with antisemitism in 1933. They focus on the prehistory of the introduction of the "Aryan clause" in the Reichswehr in February 1934 and also contain appeals by national-minded German Jews to have their war service recognized as frontline duty.[36] In the early 1950s, the Institute for Contemporary History in Munich prepared

---

34. See Chapter 14 below.
35. According to article 137, section 6, of the Weimar Constitution, as institutions under public law religious communities were entitled to levy taxes based on the legal provisions of the individual German states.
36. BA Freiburg, Allgemeines Wehrmachtsamt, RW 6, nos. 73a, 73b. During the Weimar Republic and the early years of the Third Reich (until the introduction of general conscription on 16 March 1935), the official name of the German armed forces was "Reichswehr;" thereafter the term "Wehrmacht" was used.

questionnaires dealing with the "Reichswehr and National Socialism before 1933," which German generals were asked to fill out. One central question was: "What did you not like about National Socialism?" I found only one case among the more than three dozen *Fragebögen* I perused, in which a General emphasized that he was offended, as he put it euphemistically, by the "Überspitzung des Rassegedankens," the undue weight accorded to "racial issues" in National Socialism.[37] One main reason for the overall lack of any concern was undoubtedly entrenched antisemitic convictions within the officer corps, and the widespread belief, as *Reichswehr* Chief Hans von Seeckt once put it, that "...the Jewish talent is purely critical, hence negative, and can never help in the construction of a State," or in the words of Werner von Fritsch, later Commander-in-Chief of the Wehrmacht (1935–8), "...Ebert, pacifists, Jews, democrats, Black, Red, and Gold, and the French are all the same, namely the people who want to destroy Germany."[38] A second reason was the increasing closeness of the officer corps to the new regime. As the leading magazine for *Reichswehr* officers, the *Militär-Wochenblatt*, wrote during the summer: "It has to be clear to the German officer that if his own [political] views are in contradiction to those of National Socialism, he will have to revise them."[39] It would thus be illusory to expect help from an allegedly

37. At the military archives in Freiburg, I was given a list of possible research assistants who, for a fee, would scour the files for visiting historians. Some of these researchers had worked there for decades and knew the files probably better than some of the archivists. After having spent a week in Freiburg with little to show for my efforts, I decided to discuss my topic with some of the most experienced of these paid researchers. Without exception they told me that they did not want to squander their time and my money. In their opinion, senior German officers were simply not interested in this particular issue. In 1933 the *Reichswehr* thus abdicated any responsibility for protecting Jewish Germans from Nazi attacks, even those who had been decorated during the First World War, and it is therefore not a topic of discussion in this book.
38. The first quotation is from a March 1919 letter Seeckt wrote to his wife; the second from a letter Fritsch wrote to his friend Joachim von Stülpnagel in November 1924, quoted in Francis L. Carsten, *The Reichswehr and Politics* (Oxford: Clarendon Press, 1966), 31, 203. For a later period see Omer Bartov, *The Eastern Front, 1941–1945. German Troops and the Barbarization of Warfare* (London: Macmillan, 1985); Omer Bartov, *Hitler's Army. Soldiers, Nazis, and War in the Third Reich* (Oxford: Oxford University Press, 1991).
39. "Der Soldat und die nationale Revolution," *Militär-Wochenblatt*, 118 (18 August 1933), 209–211, esp. 211.

apolitical army that proved only too eager to jump on the Nazi bandwagon.[40]

Overview of Contents

Part I: This book is subdivided into three parts: Part I focuses on violence against foreign Jews (mostly from Eastern Europe) who lived in Germany without citizenship; Part II on different forms of violence, from assaults to pillory marches, murder, and boycotts against German Jews; and Part III on the reaction of those institutions that were still in a position to protest in the spring of 1933—the Christian Churches, the bureaucracy, and Hitler's coalition partner, the DNVP. Foreign Jews were the most vulnerable and thus became the initial targets of attacks by SA and SS bands, who felt free to vent their hatred on them in the most brutal fashion, unencumbered by fear of legal accountability. Chapter 1 deals with violence against "*Ostjuden*" (mostly from Poland), since they constituted the largest group and attacks against them are best documented. Violence against them fell into five categories: (i) physical violence and robbery; (ii) financial damages such as the forced cancellation of debts, vandalism of property, and destruction of goods; (iii) rituals of humiliation, such as "pillory marches," in which victims were paraded through streets; (iv) kidnapping, often in combination with pressure on victims to relinquish their businesses and emigrate; and (v) aggravated bodily assault and murder. While German authorities were initially reluctant to introduce specific discriminatory legal measures against Polish Jews, as these might trigger administrative retaliation against the German minority in Poland, SA and SS members felt themselves under no such constraints as they threatened, humiliated, and intimidated "*Ostjuden*."

40. There were exceptions to this rule. For example, former Chancellor Kurt von Schleicher intervened with Hindenburg in the spring of 1933 with regard to the treatment of German Jews; BA Koblenz, N42/94, fol. 17 (my thanks to Professor Thomas Weber for this reference).

Physical violence was abundant, as was the wanton destruction of property and countless other forms of personal degradation that served the attackers' twisted sense of visceral satisfaction to pressure the reviled "*Ostjuden*" into leaving Germany quickly. In addition to pillory marches, the demolition of religious artifacts and the shearing of beards were means to demoralize and humiliate victims.

Chapter 2 investigates the roots of prejudice against "*Ostjuden*," the stigmatization and violence against them during the Weimar Republic, their thorny path to citizenship, the policies of the NSDAP–DNVP coalition government, and the often-ambivalent relationship between German Jews and "*Ostjuden*," who, by some, were perceived as dangerous brothers from the East whose distinctly foreign identity might trigger antisemitic resentments at home, while others saw them as a pure unspoiled force capable of rejuvenating Judaism in the West. Already in 1921 the Prussian government resorted to a policy of committing "undesirable *Ostjuden*" to internment camps.[41] This chapter also highlights the difficulties of obtaining German citizenship, even if born in Germany. When obtained after seemingly unending bureaucratic complications, it was then quickly rescinded with a stroke of the pen in 1933. Since Germany knew no national citizenship before February 1934, applicants had to apply for the citizenship of a specific German state, which further complicated the process.

Chapter 3 concentrates on attacks against American and Western European Jews, as well as on Czech and Rumanian Jews who had property in Germany and cannot easily be subsumed under the "*Ostjuden*" category. As this chapter makes clear, not even an American passport guaranteed safety from attacks, and women (in what might still be considered a more chivalrous age) were also not spared mistreatment by the SA. Monetary gain was a frequent motive for violent assaults,

---

41. In Germany, discrimination against "*Ostjuden*" goes back to the Empire. In the United States, immigrants from Eastern Europe were also identified as an undesirable group of newcomers. Leonard Dinnerstein, *Anti-Semitism in America* (Oxford: Oxford University Press, 1994), 58–104.

many of which are reminiscent of organized crime, and politics was often used as a pretext for enrichment and for venting pent-up frustration on defenseless victims. One *cause célèbre*, the July 1933 attack on the American businessman Philip Zuckerman in Leipzig, shows that even when attacks were an embarrassment for Germany's reputation, so that it would have been in the government's interest to apprehend the attackers, arrests proved difficult as the perpetrators were shielded by their SA superiors. As a result of the publicity the attacks received worldwide, Germany's image abroad, which had just begun to recover from the country's stigmatization following World War I thanks to Gustav Stresemann's foreign policy, rapidly deteriorated.

Part II: The second part of this book concentrates on violence against German Jews. Since boycott actions were often causally connected to physical violence, they are discussed here as well. Chapter 4, "Violent Attacks," begins with a brief examination of antisemitic violence in the Weimar Republic. While there was a significant amount of anti-Jewish crime during the Weimar Republic, including assaults and cemetery and synagogue desecrations, political opponents of the Nazi Party, in particular the SPD and DDP, usually made them public, if only to show up their political adversary. Offenders, when apprehended, were sentenced by the courts, though punishments were often lenient. In early March 1933, by contrast, violence was widespread, and the perpetrators mostly went unpunished even when they were apprehended, as the documentary evidence for crimes against Jews for the two-day period between 13 and 15 March 1933 in this chapter illustrates. Following these case studies is an investigation into the frequent instances of expulsions from Germany instigated by violent attacks and threats, which tore many families apart. The chapter concludes with attacks in prisons and in the workplace, such as against Jewish livestock dealers and butchers in stockyards.

Chapter 5 focuses on pillory marches and the so-called "Perfidy Decree," which was designed to repress rumors, criticism, and news unwelcome to the regime. A widespread form of violence directed against Jews and those who remained on a friendly footing with them was public branding in its various forms. In "pillory marches" victims were paraded through town by foot or on an oxcart accompanied by a posse of SA men. Like other antisemitic crimes, pillory marches were registered only indirectly through allusions in diplomatic reports, judicial documents, intra-bureaucratic complaints, or newspaper articles. While it is impossible to gauge their exact number, frequent references to pillory marches in newspapers make it likely that most adults in Germany would at least have heard of this very conspicuous form of public humiliation in the spring of 1933. Photographs of such events have even been reprinted in history schoolbooks, though historical scholarship has rarely focused on them. Another widespread form of pillorying was the publication on city hall billboards or in newspapers of the names of those who continued buying in Jewish shops. In 1933 (and on various occasions throughout the Third Reich) Nazis considered public stigmatization an effective means of socially destroying potential opponents, while enforcing conformity on others. In fact, the elimination of the private sphere and the remorseless dragging into the public realm of matters that were previously private were hallmarks of the dictatorship. This chapter also traces the origins of pillory marches as a form of medieval and early modern punishment, which Nazis took up instinctively as an effective means of destroying potential enemies, forcing doubters into line and compelling them to profess allegiance to the new regime. Those who stood apart were met with hostility as potential opponents of the regime, lukewarm toward the "national revolution," and traitors to the German people.

The *Heimtücke-Verordnung* (Perfidy Decree), signed by President Hindenburg on 21 March 1933, punished the circulation of rumors "designed to seriously harm the welfare of the Reich or a *Land* or the reputation of the Reich or a *Land* government or the parties or associations that support these governments."[42] It granted authorities wide-ranging discretionary

---

42. Paragraph 3 of the ordinance read: "Whoever intentionally puts forward or circulates an untrue or grossly misrepresented claim of a factual nature that is designed to seriously harm the welfare of the Reich or a *Land* or the reputation of the Reich or a *Land*

powers and gave them great latitude as to which elements of a criminal offense to prosecute. The decree was meant as a deterrent against whispering campaigns and furtive rumors, since criticism behind closed doors was punished as severely as that spoken in public. As shown in this chapter, penalties for criticism were especially harsh if uttered by members of an ostracized minority. Examples from the files, contrasting the sentences for Jews and non-Jews for very similar offenses, show that Jewish Germans suffered more than others when denounced under the Perfidy Decree. The Perfidy Decree also created a field day for informers, since the mere mention of truths unwelcome to the regime could be penalized. It brought out the worst in people and fostered denunciations, sowed distrust, and imposed on many an unnatural discretion to the point of secrecy. Its psychological effect on social intercourse outlasted the regime.

The third chapter in Part II centers on the murder of German Jews in the late winter and spring of 1933. Based on the available documentary evidence, it is possible to classify antisemitic murder cases during this period into three approximate categories, though occasional overlap cannot always be avoided. The more spontaneous murder without prior planning accounted for the majority of cases, especially since for SA units, shorn of scruples and restraint, the line between grievous bodily harm and murder had become blurred. It is impossible to say how many victims succumbed to their wounds in the days or weeks after the attacks, and the number of unknown cases is high. In the rapturous exultation of victory, attackers committed their crimes with horrifying brutality and the insouciance of knowing that they were not accountable to the law. The second category of murder comprised those already in prisons or

government or the parties or associations that support these governments will...be sentenced with imprisonment for up to two years and, if the assertion is publicly put forward or circulated, with imprisonment of no fewer than three months." Herbert Michaelis and Ernst Schraepler, eds., *Ursachen und Folgen. Vom deutschen Zusammenbruch 1918 und 1945 bis zur staatlichen Neuordnung Deutschlands in der Gegenwart*, vol. IX: *Das Dritte Reich. Die Zertrümmerung des Parteienstaates und die Grundlegung der Diktatur.* (Berlin: Wendler, 1964), 281–282; Bernward Dörner, *"Heimtücke:"Das Gesetz als Waffe Kontrolle, Abschreckung und Verfolgung in Deutschland 1933–1945* (Paderborn: Schöningh, 1998), 320–321.

camps, so that killings were occasionally camouflaged as "shot while trying to escape." As will be seen, non-Jews who had been arrested at the same time and for similar political "offenses" as the Jewish victims who were murdered mostly survived their time in detention or were released. The third category consists of planned "revenge" murders. Many of these attracted some attention already in 1933 and were then reopened after 1945 once political circumstances permitted. This chapter examines a few cases from each of the three categories, illustrating patterns, and examining them in as much detail as the sources permit.

The reaction of judicial authorities to the murder cases, demonstrating the corruption of the legal system, is intertwined with the narrative. Files from different archival holdings on the same cases—from 1933, when the murder occurred, and the post-war period, when it was prosecuted—add nuance and detail. In 1933, Jewish victims were often labelled communists by SA perpetrators, who knew that if prosecutors could be convinced that victims had supported communists or made derogatory remarks about Hitler or the Nazi movement, they would be cut some slack. While public prosecutors understood that such charges were mostly absurd, they bought into this method of framing victims, thereby justifying SA violence and murder and providing an alibi for their leniency and acquittals of SA perpetrators. Prosecutors knew full well that the SA murderers would not be sentenced, making it easier for them to succumb to the vicissitudes and pressures of the zeitgeist. This chapter thus illustrates that in 1933 the law was not employed to aid Jewish victims, but rather to falsely characterize victims in such a way that SA violence and murder against them could be legitimated. It looks at the type of killers, brawlers and thugs who were die-hard racists and misfits in civilian life and to whom their stormtrooper role offered a release for translating their brutal fantasies into reality—not unlike the SA men depicted in Anna Seghers's 1942 novel *The Seventh Cross*. Legal proceedings were initiated against some of them in 1933, quite often with conclusive proof, but due to two amnesties for "Crimes Committed during the National Socialist Revolution" in March and July 1933, they got off scot-free, though in some cases the law caught up with them after 1945. Several of the anti-Jewish murder cases were resurrected by friends or relatives of the victims after 1945 and then dragged on during the 1950s, occasionally even into the early 1960s.

Chapter 7, on the April boycott, begins by briefly highlighting boycott movements before 1 April 1933 and then examines global protests against Germany as a reaction to Nazi antisemitic violence, before dealing with the April boycott, the regionally ongoing boycott activities, and the resulting psychological reverberations. The alleged official reason for the boycott of Jewish shops and lawyers' and doctors' offices was anti-German protests and the boycott of German goods in the United States and some Western European countries. After the boycott was officially declared ended, massive social pressure extending to physical threats was exerted on some groups of the population, especially civil servants, not to buy in Jewish-owned shops. Those who continued patronizing them were publicly stigmatized. In contrast to the traditional view of the April boycott, this chapter demonstrates that the actual day of the boycott—Saturday, 1 April—saw countless assaults on German Jews all over the Reich, and that boycott actions were often used as a pretext for violent attacks, especially in the more rural regions of Germany, so that in some places the events of the day resembled a Reich-wide pogrom.

The fifth and final chapter of Part II deals with the violent attacks on Jewish professionals and discriminatory local actions that helped blaze the trail for the antisemitic legislation of April 1933. It examines in some detail the discriminatory measures contained in the laws that (barring certain exemptions) excluded Jews from the upper echelons of the civil service, banned large numbers of Jewish judges, public prosecutors, and attorneys from practicing law, debarred Jewish doctors from the national health insurance system, and introduced rigid quotas for Jewish *Gymnasium* and university students. The implementation decrees of the laws gave ample scope for translating broad mandates into practice. In some states Nazi government officials blatantly violated the letter of the laws to impose even more draconian measures against Jewish professionals.

As a result, the laws were applied differently in various states and localities, so that local and regional interpretations often went far beyond the laws' original discriminatory intent to the point that, already by the end of 1933, life for most Jewish professionals in Germany had become unbearable.

The second part of the chapter shows that the application of the "Aryan clause" spilled over into the private sector of the economy. While the legislation was initially meant to remain confined to the public realm, the "Aryan clause" soon came to play a role in the private sector as well, since the public sector dovetailed in many ways with the private economy in that state ministries or municipal governments awarded orders or contracted out to private firms. Orders and contracts to private firms thus often depended on whether they were deemed to be "free of Jewish influence." This part discusses in detail economic discrimination and other discriminatory measures, such as proscribing trade with "non-Aryans," barring Jews from entering towns for any reason, and discouraging them, often with threats, from visiting resort towns as tourists—all of which went far beyond the discriminatory measures stipulated in the April legislation. While antisemitic violence and the April boycott mostly met with public disapprobation, in particular among the middle classes, existing sources seem to indicate that the restrictions on entry into the professions by Jewish Germans, as well as the removal from office of high-ranking Jewish officials, judges, public prosecutors, and lawyers, aroused less displeasure, possibly because these restrictions and expulsions created increased opportunities for non-Jewish Germans' own advancement.

(For the locations and intensity of antisemitic violence, attacks, pillory marches, and murder in Germany in 1933, please see the map on page 44).

Part III: The third part focuses on the reaction of those German institutions that were still in a position to protest against antisemitic violence in the conditions of the late winter and spring of 1933. The potentially most influential of these (apart from the *Reichswehr*) was the Protestant Church and, to a lesser extent, its Catholic counterpart. Given the importance of the Protestant Church in German society at the time, three chapters are devoted to investigating the reaction of Protestants to assaults on Jews in Germany. The first of these looks at the identity, structure, and political orientation of the Protestant Church, whose leaders considered it to be a moral authority and the conscience of the nation. On account of the Church's traditional connectedness with the State and in the face of foreign adversaries, Protestant Church leaders considered it their duty to continue their unconditional support of German interests from World War I into the Weimar Republic, to get involved in politics, and, if necessary, to issue proclamations on the pressing political concerns of the day. In 1918–19 they condemned the Allied blockade and the continued confinement of German POWs after the armistice, voiced their disapproval of the injustices of the Versailles Peace Treaty (as they perceived them), and denounced the Allied injunction on Austria joining the Reich as a violation of Wilson's principle of self-determination. The feeling that Germany was treated unfairly by the Allies also influenced the attitude of the Church toward the rise of National Socialism. Before 1933 a majority of Protestant Church dignitaries considered the rise of the Nazi movement to be a reaction to the ongoing humiliation of their country by foreign powers, a view that tended to generate a certain elective affinity with the nationalist aims of National Socialism. Once Hitler had come to power, this was reflected in a disinclination to criticize a political party with whose essential foreign policy goals most Church leaders agreed. At the end of the Republic, Church dignitaries became increasingly involved in politics and were asked by the German Interior Minister to support the State in the prevention of public violence; in 1932 several Protestant Church leaders even criticized the lawless behavior of the Nazi Party in public, despite an overall agreement with the Party's nationalist orientation.

On 30 January 1933, the advent of the new regime was initially welcomed, partly because Protestant Church dignitaries overrated the position of conservatives in the NSDAP/DNVP coalition. During the first two months of the new regime, Hitler presented himself as Church-friendly.

Most heads of the Protestant *Land* Churches responded favorably, stressing the theme of having been rescued from the danger of communism owing to the decisive actions of the new government. Initially common ground prevailed, such as the view that the former Entente powers had been responsible for the war, dismay over the oppressive shackles of Versailles, and a joint belief in the "corroding influence" of Weimar culture. Despite some misgivings, a majority of Church leaders initially believed that National Socialism would continue to exert a positive effect on Germany's future. Hitler's promises to honor the rights of the Church and his assurance that the Christian confessions would continue to be "the most important factors in the safeguarding of our people" during his speech supporting the Enabling Act on 23 March 1933 left an especially positive impression. Still, there was a certain underlying fear mixed in with the hopeful enthusiasm, as some Protestant leaders warned of the danger that the Church might be ceding its independence to an increasingly powerful State.

Chapter 10 begins by examining the Church's response to the vigorous foreign protests remonstrating against anti-Jewish violence in Germany and the boycott of 1 April 1933. Throughout March and April, a great many pleas for help from German Jews who had converted to Protestantism reached the Church leadership, so that it is impossible to argue that Church officials were not aware of the hopeless situation in which Protestants of Jewish descent found themselves. Particularly revealing for the mindset of the Church hierarchy and political divisions within the Church is the letter exchange between a progressive Rhenish Church leader, who found the Nazi takeover anathema, and a conservative Rhenish *Generalsuperintendent*, who, like most of his peers, was so critical of public life under the Weimar Republic that he essentially welcomed the new government. Their exchange also highlights the predicament in which the Church found itself. While there were still some voices among Church leaders warning of the rapidly growing dictatorial powers of the new regime in the second half of March and early April, the eagerness to conform to the prevailing zeitgeist was palpably on the rise.

When the first news of massive anti-Jewish attacks became known in the weeks after the elections of 5 March 1933, the Western press covered the incidents in long articles. When some foreign Church leaders demanded of their German counterparts that they speak out against this violence, it quickly became clear that the German Protestant Church hierarchy would not live up to its self-proclaimed ethical mission. Anti-semitic violence was not openly disavowed; instead, Church leaders defended the government and minimized the attacks; some even disputed that there had been attacks at all. A frequent reason given for this behavior was the charge that the Allied press campaign, just as the alleged "atrocity propaganda" against Germany in World War I, had been vastly exaggerated. An analysis of the reactions of Church dignitaries shows them to be convinced that they had moral right on their side. In late March, numerous Church leaders demanded that the head of the *Kirchenausschuß* (Church executive committee), Hermann Kapler, speak out against the injustices. Yet, between the end of March, when many seemed prepared to protest, and 26 April, when the decisive meeting on the "Jewish Question" took place, there was a noticeable swing in the political mood in favor of the regime. The politics of Otto Dibelius, one of the most colorful figures of German and world Protestantism in the twentieth century, illustrates the conflicted mentality as well as the underlying antisemitism that produced this temporary allegiance. Even though openly critical of National Socialism in 1932, he welcomed the advent of the new government in March 1933 and defended the boycott in a radio speech to an American audience, but then turned irrevocably against the Nazi regime. Though an avowed anti-Nazi after 1933, Dibelius also made no bones about his antisemitism and, as described in this chapter, openly acknowledged it in 1933 and also long after 1945.

Throughout the early spring of 1933, leaders of the Western European and American Protestant Churches, as well as some Protestants inside Germany, had been urging German Church leaders to finally speak out against Nazi crimes. Chapter 11 analyzes the tension between the small minority that was prepared to protest and the overwhelming majority who advocated silence and inactivity. On 26 April 1933 about forty Protestant Church leaders met to decide this issue definitively. This chapter examines the mindset of Church leaders regarding antisemitic attacks, the (few) arguments advanced in favor of protest, and the (multitude) of reasons moved forward in support of silence and inactivity. The true attitudes and beliefs of German Protestant leaders were misunderstood abroad, since it was not merely out of fear that Church dignitaries failed to speak out against Nazi violence and antisemitic legislation. Their reticence was also due to the fact that they often agreed with the legal measures and other aims of National Socialist discriminatory policies put forward in March and April 1933. Due to misreading their German counterparts, foreign Church leaders occasionally exhibited restraint and failed to press German Protestants with the necessary urgency, assuming that German Churches were in mortal danger and that leaders remained silent solely out of fear.

Henri-Louis Henriod, General Secretary of the World Alliance for International Friendship Through the Churches, who visited Berlin in mid-April, adopted the argumentation patterns of German Church leaders with regard to anti-Jewish Reich legislation and recounted the rationalizations of conservative Protestants when reviewing the situation in Germany. These included blaming attacks on the large number of Eastern European immigrants, who had "quickly gained great influence within communist and socialist parties," and the "predominant Jewish influence" in public service positions, law courts, hospitals, institutions of higher learning, social services, and the press. During the critical meeting of 26 April, in which the issue of whether or not the Church should raise its voice in public and protest against the antisemitic violence and legislation, only one of the Executive Committee members passionately argued in favor of protest. In dealing with the arguments advanced in favor and against public protest, this chapter investigates in detail the mode of reasoning and mindset of the Church leadership with regard to their politics and the "Jewish Question."

Chapter 12 on the reaction of the Catholic Church opens with an analysis of the Church's relationship to National Socialism. In contrast to the Protestant Church leadership, Catholic bishops issued a series of warnings against the ideological teachings of National Socialism beginning in the fall of 1930 that remained in effect until after the passing of the Enabling Act. It was mainly out of concern for the safety of Catholic civil servants, the integrity and continued functioning of the vast networks of Catholic organizations, and fear that Catholics might again find themselves banished from the national community, at a time when many Catholics were clearly eager to be part of it, that the Catholic episcopate revoked its earlier warnings on 28 March 1933.[43] The fate of German Jews came into focus only shortly before the 1 April boycott, when it could no longer be avoided. Led by Cardinal Archbishop Adolf Bertram of Breslau, *primus inter pares* among German archbishops, the episcopate chose to remain silent.

The reasons for the absence of protest were clearly spelled out by Bertram: remote aloofness to the Jewish minority whose "economic struggle" was of no concern to the Catholic Church and fear that interference with the regime's policies might do harm to the Church itself. In his correspondence with American Church leaders, another key figure, Cardinal Archbishop Michael von Faulhaber of Munich and Freising, downplayed and even negated reports of antisemitic attacks. He, too, advocated that silence was the better part of valor and that protests against Nazi antisemitism would imperil Catholics, while arguing that Jews could well help themselves, using the rapid end to the boycott to justify his position. In his correspondence with those German Catholics who claimed that the Church must speak out, he staunchly defended the inactivity of the episcopate, maintaining that at a time when the Catholic Church was under severe attack other more pressing matters existed than extending help to Jews. Yet, when the fate of Catholic officials was at stake with the passing of the 7 April legislation because of its political discrimination, Catholic bishops were capable of quickly relinquishing their attitude of appeasement toward the regime; the anti-Jewish

43. As once before in the nineteenth century (1871–87) during the so-called *Kulturkampf*.

discrimination of the legislation did not compel them to criticism or action in the same way. Thus, this chapter illustrates that while there were a few individual Catholic voices in the spring of 1933 that favored strong protests, the Catholic episcopate as a whole remained silent in the face of antisemitic outrages.

Chapter 13 focuses on the reaction of the administrative and judicial branch of the bureaucracy to the multitude of attacks against Germany's Jews. Foreign embassies and consulates directed complaints about attacks against their Jewish nationals mostly to the interior ministries of the different German states, whose high-ranking officials then dealt with them in internal memoranda, where they discussed recommendations of how to respond. The reactions of those German administrative officials who decided the outcome of the grievances brought forward by foreign diplomatic missions were thus revealing with regard to the bureaucracy's overall position on the treatment of Jews and its orientation toward the new Nazi regime. While high-ranking members of the bureaucracy were fully informed of what was happening, in their reports they minimized the crimes and shielded the perpetrators, thereby becoming their willing accomplices. The intra-bureaucratic correspondence gives the impression that the victims themselves had been responsible for the attacks, simply because of their presence in Germany. Since SA members who perpetrated these attacks got off scot-free, they quickly realized that the judicial bureaucracy was willing to cover up their crimes—another sign of encouragement to the attackers.

Antisemitic murders in the late winter and spring of 1933 were brought before the judicial branch of the civil service, which initiated legal proceedings. In the case of the judicial bureaucracy, prosecutors often adopted a defense counsel's version of events by disparaging the victims and maligning their character. Their tendentious reports, in which they frequently labelled the mostly Eastern European Jewish victims as "people's parasites," swindlers, and opponents of the national government, and in which prejudice often assumed the force of legal fact, always made sure to create extenuating circumstances for the perpetrators' actions, however lawless. Already months after Hitler's accession to the chancellorship, the administration of justice was thus unable to act with any degree of objectivity. Political pressure based on the anticipated expectations of those in power, which judicial officials anxiously strove to fulfill, clearly played a decisive role. In the first revolutionary phase of the National Socialist takeover, much remained undecided and was held in abeyance, so that judicial officials felt under a weight of anxiety to live up to what the zeitgeist seemed to demand of them. Their reports were thus ideologically colored, endowing anti-Jewish crimes with certain "moral," or at least "legitimate," justification. And perpetrators knew quite well that they could count on this leniency. As a consequence, they not only felt free to behave in a brazen and impertinent fashion but often saw themselves as agents of restoring "moral justice." In Nazi eyes, after 5 March 1933 the time had come to seek revenge and demand punishment for all the alleged wrongs suffered, many of them attributed to the very presence of Jews in Germany.

Chapter 14 assesses the reaction of Hitler's conservative coalition part- ner, the DNVP, to anti-Jewish attacks in the winter and spring of 1933. It starts out with a brief analysis of the DNVP's position on the "Jewish Question" during the Weimar Republic and then examines in detail the response of party leaders to cries for help from national-minded German Jews in March 1933. Fully assimilated Jews who had fought for Germany in the war and lost their savings in the 1923 inflation, and who were now victimized and unjustly blamed for Germany's misfortunes, found them- selves in an inescapable predicament as they realized that all their exer- tions and privations had been in vain. Some individual conservatives were appalled by what was happening and willing to protest and help, sending strongly worded (if vain) appeals to DNVP leaders who, like the Protestant Church hierarchy and the Catholic episcopate, were unwilling to become involved. During the period of the Nazi takeover, DNVP leaders also evinced a lack of determination, in part based on the fear of deciding certain issues—if, for example, an applicant who was "half- Jewish" could be accepted into the party, a determination that was often based on anxiety that the party might incur the stigma of being *juden-freundlich*, that is, friendly towards Jews, which would be tantamount to political suicide in the atmosphere that prevailed in the spring of 1933.

Fear of laying themselves open to criticism by their more radical coalition partner was all-pervasive and well founded, given that SA attacks on German National organizations that resulted in skirmishes and pitched battles were not infrequent in April and May 1933. Yet, to a much greater extent than was the case with the Protestant and Catholic Church leadership, German Nationals were very active in their complicity: there were die-hard *völkisch* antisemites in the party, who freely spoke of annihilating "alien race elements" as early as 1933 and liberally shared their effusions with others. The sole political difference between them and even the most extreme Nazis paradoxically lay in rejecting any form of public health care and welfare policies. In addition, many regional DNVP associations willingly (even eagerly) participated in the 1 April boycott. Even though the DNVP never introduced an "Aryan clause" at the national level (though some *Land* associations had adopted it for their region), party leaders frequently refused membership even to those Jews who had converted to Christianity, despite an often-outstanding patriotic pedigree, while (barring some notable exceptions) the party as a whole shunned those German Jews who turned to it as their last resort. The only political party that still had a modicum of influence left in March and April 1933 refused to take a stand on behalf of those persecuted, no matter how valuable their services had been to the Fatherland in the past.

Previous Literature on Antisemitic Violence in 1933

There is no systematic study of antisemitic violence during the period of the Nazi seizure of power, though numerous historians have dealt with this topic in the context of other larger themes, mentioning antisemitic violence in more or less detail. The following offers a short overview of where antisemitic violence in 1933 is discussed. In particular, Richard Bessel's article on "The Nazi Capture of Power" examines antisemitic violence within the framework of the Nazi takeover, interpreting it in the context of "a deep desire to visit revenge on those deemed responsible for the dire state of affairs in Weimar Germany."[44] Bessel makes the interesting point that, in contrast to attacks on the Left, violence against Jews was essential to the campaign to capture power and that the violent antisemitism of Nazi activists should not be regarded as politically instrumental, but as an end in itself. Bessel stresses the "sadistic nature of the attacks on Jews," which "appears to have satisfied emotional urges," and, alluding to the underlying component of social envy, aptly observes that the violence resembled "an almost festive sadistic outburst by young toughs who wanted to enjoy themselves at Jews' expense and demonstrate to their one-time social betters that they were the masters now."[45] Bessel is familiar with anti-Jewish assaults from his earlier study on SA violence in East Elbian Prussia before and during the period of the seizure of power, in which he provided a succinct account of the plethora of attacks in Silesia, Pomerania, and East Prussia in March 1933, pointing out that Hermann Göring's infamous Essen speech of 10 March, in which he declared that the police were no "protection squad for Jewish shops," undoubtedly contributed to the reluctance of the police to interfere on behalf of the victims.[46] Other historians who focus of the history of the SA during this period also mention antisemitic violence in the late winter and spring of 1933.[47]

Violence against Jews in pre-war Nazi Germany is discussed in Michael Wildt's article on "Violence against Jews in Germany, 1933–1939," in

---

44. Richard Bessel, "The Nazi Capture of Power," *Journal of Contemporary History*, 39 (2004), 169–188, esp. 175–179; quotation on 174.
45. Ibid., 176, 178.
46. Richard Bessel, *Political Violence and the Rise of Nazism. The Storm Troopers in Eastern Germany 1925–1934* (New Haven and London: Yale University Press, 1984), 105–109.
47. Eric Reiche, *The Development of the SA in Nürnberg, 1922–1934* (Cambridge: Cambridge University Press, 1986), 187–188; Peter Longerich, *Die braunen Bataillone. Geschichte der SA* (Munich: Beck, 1989), 169–173; and Daniel Siemens, *Stormtroopers. A New History of Hitler's Brownshirts* (New Haven: Yale, 2017), 124–125; 128–131.

which he emphasizes that "NSDAP organizations gave free rein to their antisemitic hatred" immediately "after the Reichstag elections on 5 March 1933," though his analysis concentrates mostly on the period after 1935 in the small Franconian town of Treuchtlingen. Wildt's article was part of a larger project that was then brought to full fruition in his perceptive study on violence against Jews in the rural parts and small towns of Germany between 1919 and 1939, *Volksgemeinschaft als Selbstermächtigung*, now also available in translation.[48] In his piece on "The Nazi Party and its Violence against the Jews, 1933–1939," Armin Nolzen writes that "as far as the persecution of the Jews between 1933 and 1939 is concerned, little is known about the anti-Jewish violence of the Nazi party." For the year 1933, he barely mentions violent attacks and focuses instead on boycott actions and the consequences of *Gleichschaltung*, which often had the effect of socially isolating "non Aryans."[49] Two contemporary reports, the *Braunbuch* on the Reichstag fire and subsequent "Hitlerterror" and the *Schwarzbuch* on the situation of Jews in Germany, also list a plethora of violent transgressions (though mostly without mentioning names, places, or precise dates, in order to protect victims who still remained in Germany), while Timothy Ryback's account of a brave public prosecutor's struggle for justice (a rare phenomenon indeed in the spring of 1933) deals with Jewish murder victims in Germany's first official concentration camp, Dachau.[50]

More recently, physical violence against Jews, the April boycott, and the indignant reaction abroad have been discussed in Peter Fritzsche's *Hitler's First Hundred Days* on the basis of diaries and autobiographies

48. Michael Wildt, "Violence against Jews in Germany, 1933–1939," in Bankier, ed., *Probing the Depths*, 181–212, quotation 181; Michael Wildt, *Volksgemeinschaft als Selbstermächtigung. Gewalt gegen Juden in der Deutschen Provinz 1919 bis 1939* (Hamburg: Hamburger Edition, 2007), esp. 101–132; Wildt's fine book has been translated into English as *Hitler's Volksgemeinschaft and the Dynamics of Racial Exclusion* (New York: Berghahn, 2012).
49. Arnim Nolzen, "The Nazi Party and its Violence against the Jews, 1933–1939: Violence as a Historiographical Concept," *Yad Vashem Studies*, 31 (2003), 245–285, esp. 247; 249–256.
50. *Braunbuch über Reichstagsbrand und Hitler-Terror* (Basel: Universum Bücherei, 1933, repr. 1973), 222–269; Comité des Dlegations Juives, ed., *Das Schwarzbuch. Tatsachen und Dokumente. Die Lage der Juden in Deutschland 1933* (Paris: Edition du Rond-Point, 1934); Timothy Ryback, *Hitler's First Victims. The Quest for Justice* (New York: Knopf, 2014).

which viscerally capture the horrors of exclusion,[51] and Kim Wünschmann, in her carefully researched study of Jewish prisoners incarcerated in pre-war Nazi concentration camps, also devotes some attention to the period of the Nazi takeover. While, before 1938, Jews were held in camps not solely on account of being Jewish but because they had fallen foul of the regime in one way or another, once in the hands of SA guards they were singled out for exceptionally brutal treatment. The proportion of Jews among the total camp population lay at around 5 percent until 1918.[52] In his thought-provoking *A World Without Jews*, Alon Confino highlights the ability of the Nazi regime to bring forth the endorsement, acquiescence, and passive collusion of large parts of the German population for their anti-Jewish policies, arguing that anti-Jewish measures and attacks presumed a set of beliefs, preconceptions, and assumptions about Jews that were prevalent in German culture. Though not based on archival documents and focusing on a later period, Confino's work also highlights physical brutality in the spring of 1933 and points out that there were no organized groups in the German State or society that actively opposed anti-Jewish measures.[53]

General surveys of the history of Nazi Germany also make reference to antisemitic violence in the spring of 1933, though a general rule seems to apply: the earlier a book was published, the less attention was paid to antisemitic transgressions other than the April boycott and the April legislation. This is to be expected, since historians' interest in the fate of German Jews during the Nazi period has increased dramatically since the 1960s, when the first surveys by Karl Dietrich Bracher and Martin Broszat appeared. The massive, and in its detail still unsurpassed, analysis of the Nazi takeover by Karl Dietrich Bracher, Wolfgang Sauer, and Gerhard Schulz, *Die nationalsozialistische Machtergreifung* (first published in 1960),

51. Peter Fritzsche, *Hitler's First Hundred Days. When Germans Embraced the Third Reich* (New York: Basic Books, 2020), 229–262.
52. Kim Wünschmann, *Before Auschwitz: Jewish Prisoners in the Prewar Concentration Camps* (Cambridge: Harvard University Press, 2015), esp. 17–57; 58–67; see also Chapter 6 below.
53. Alon Confino, *A World Without Jews: The Nazi Imagination from Persecution to Genocide* (New Haven: Yale University Press), esp. 27–55.

devotes some attention to the April boycott and antisemitic legislation in the first part of the thousand-page study written by Bracher, but the reader gets no sense of the ubiquitous random violence, acts of revenge, SA units out of control, and innumerable instances of anti-Jewish bestiality, though Gerhard Schulz briefly deals with SA violence in his section and mentions several murders of Germany's Jews.[54] In his *Die deutsche Diktatur*, first published in 1969, Bracher again devotes much attention to the Nazi takeover, stressing the "semblance of legality" that characterized the process, but does not mention the mobilization of grassroots violence against Jews.[55]

The same is true for the other well-known overviews of the history of Nazi Germany by Martin Broszat, Klaus Hildebrand, and Hans-Ulrich Thamer published between the late 1960s and mid-1980s, all of which mention the April boycott but fail to discuss the widespread antisemitic violence in 1933.[56] This changes somewhat with the surveys published between the late 1980s and late 1990s by Norbert Frei and Jost Dülffer (which briefly mention violence against Jews) and especially Ludolf Herbst, who speaks of "pogrom-like disturbances against Jews" after the 5 March elections.[57] The more recent studies by Michael Burleigh and Richard Evans, as well as by Ian Kershaw in the first volume of his biography of Hitler, also mention antisemitic violence in 1933, Evans and Kershaw in some detail.[58] Quite possibly, British authors, such as

54. Bracher, Sauer, and Schulz, *Die nationalsozialistische Machtergreifung*, 276–282, 872–874.
55. Karl Dietrich Bracher, *The German Dictatorship. The Origins, Structure, and Effects of National Socialism* (New York: Holt, Rinehart & Winston, 1970).
56. Martin Broszat, *Der Staat Hitlers*, 7th ed. (Munich: DTV, 1978); English trans.: *The Hitler State. The Foundation and Development of the Internal Structure of the Third Reich* (London: Longman, 1981); Hildebrand, *Dritte Reich*; Hans-Ulrich Thamer, *Verführung und Gewalt. Deutschland 1933–1945* (Berlin: Siedler, 1986).
57. Norbert Frei, *National Socialist Rule in Germany. The Führer State 1933–1945* (Oxford: Blackwell, 1993), 46–47, 1st German ed. pub. 1987; Jost Dülffer, *Nazi Germany 1933–1945. Faith and Annihilation* (London: Arnold, 1996), 140–141, 1st German ed. pub. 1992; Ludolf Herbst, *Das nationalsozialistische Deutschland, 1933–1945. Die Entfesselung der Gewalt: Rassismus und Krieg* (Frankfurt: Suhrkamp, 1996), 73–75, esp. 73.
58. Michael Burleigh, *The Third Reich. A New History* (New York: Hill & Wang, 2000), 281–283; Richard Evans, *The Coming of the Third Reich* (New York: Penguin, 2004), 434–437; Ian Kershaw, *Hitler. 1889–1936: Hubris* (New York: Norton, 1999), 471–473.

Burleigh, Kershaw, and Evans, tend to be more aware of violent anti-Jewish attacks at the very beginning of the Nazi regime because these had been part of contemporary knowledge in Britain, where newspapers reported on them in detail, while their existence was denied in Germany. Several overarching studies on other subjects that cover the transition from the end of Weimar to the Third Reich, even if their focus is not explicitly on German Jewish history, also mention antisemitic violence. Noteworthy in this context are the brief but well-informed synopsis in the third volume of Heinrich August Winkler's history of the Social Democratic Party during the Weimar Republic and the incisive assessment in Klaus Scholder's two-volume history of the Christian Churches between the end of World War I and 1934.[59]

There are several studies that provide new and detailed information on antisemitic violence during the Weimar Republic. First and foremost among them is Dirk Walter's monograph on antisemitic crime, with a host of information on antisemitic violence in Munich and Bavaria in the immediate post-World War I period that culminated in the fall of 1923, desecrations of cemeteries and synagogues throughout Germany in the 1920s, violence against politically active Jews, and violent attacks by the SA, including the so-called *Kurfürstendammkrawall* in September 1931.[60] Also valuable is Cornelia Hecht's study on German Jews and antisemitism in the Weimar Republic, which offers details on a variety of acts of violence, including verbal insults, economic boycotts, the "cold pogrom" of social boycotts, the desecrations of synagogues and cemeteries, personal threats, and murder (of Walter Rathenau, for example); Dirk Schumann's *Political Violence in the Weimar Republic* mentions a few instances of antisemitic crime within its main theme of political violence, though Schumann makes the point that during the Republic "physical violence of the SA before the seizure of power primarily concentrated on

59. Winkler, *Katastrophe*, 898–900; Klaus Scholder, *Die Kirchen und das Dritte Reich. Vorgeschichte und Zeit der Illusionen* (Frankfurt: Propyläen, 1977), 322–326.
60. Dirk Walter, *Antisemitische Kriminalität und Gewalt. Judenfeindschaft in der Weimarer Republik* (Bonn: Dietz, 1999), esp. 97–110; 115–139; 200–243.

the political opponent of the left," not on Jews.[61] Violence against Eastern
Jews is highlighted in Trude Maurer's *Ostjuden in Deutschland 1918–1933*, the
indispensable monograph on the subject—with close to one thousand
pages it highlights every aspect of the history of Eastern Jews during the
Weimar Republic, with detailed chapters on expulsions, deportations,
consignment to camps, and violent attacks.[62]

Widespread antisemitic violence is also commented upon in works that
deal with the exclusion of Jews from the German economy, since boycotts
and other methods of preventing Jews from participating in economic life
were often causally linked with violence. Here, too, the general rule seems
to apply that older publications tend to de-emphasize anti-Jewish violence
in March and April 1933, while the more recent ones pay it some heed. The
first significant study by Heinrich Uhlig on department stores in the Third
Reich from the mid-1950s does not mention antisemitic violence in a
separate section in the text, but Uhlig provides a detailed listing of
instances of violence at the end of his book, whereas Helmut Genschel's
1966 study focuses exclusively on boycott actions with little mention of
violence in the spring of 1933, though Genschel does refer to foreign
protests about the mistreatment and arrests of foreign citizens.[63] Books
published on boycotts, economic exclusion, and the expropriation of
property since the late 1980s usually devote a short section containing
graphic examples of antisemitic violence in March and April 1933. These

61. Cornelia Hecht, *Deutsche Juden und Antisemitismus in der Weimarer Republik* (Bonn: Dietz,
2003); Dirk Schumann, *Politische Gewalt in der Weimarer Republik 1918–1933. Kampf um die
Straße und Furcht vor dem Bürgerkrieg* (Essen: Klartext, 2001), quotation on p. 334, n. 197; Dirk
Schumann, "Gewalt als Methode der nationalsozialistischen Machteroberung," in Andreas
Wirsching, ed., *Das Jahr 1933. Die nationalsozialistische Machteroberung und die deutsche
Gesellschaft* (Göttingen: Wallstein, 2009), 135–155.
62. Trude Maurer, *Ostjuden in Deutschland 1918–1933* (Hamburg: Christians, 1986), esp. 324–435,
and Walter, *Antisemitische Kriminalität*, 52–79; for the years 1933–1939, Trude Maurer,
"Ausländische Juden in Deutschland, 1933–1939," in Arnold Pauker, ed., *Die Juden im
nationalsozialistischen Deutschland* (Tübingen: Mohr, 1986), 189–210, and Yfaat Weiss,
"'Ostjuden' in Deutschland als Freiwild. Die nationalsozialistische Außenpolitik zwischen
Ideologie und Wirklichkeit," *Tel Aviver Jahrbuch für deutsche Geschichte*, 23 (1994), 215–232.
63. Heinrich Uhlig, *Die Warenhäuser im Dritten Reich* (Cologne: Westdeutscher Verlag, 1956),
77–92; 209–212. Helmut Genschel, *Die Verdrängung der Juden aus der Wirtschaft im Dritten Reich*
(Göttingen: Musterschmidt, 1966), 43–59, esp. 44.

include Avraham Barkai's *From Boycott to Annihilation: The Economic Struggle of German Jews, 1933–1943*, Frank Bajohr's "Aryanisation" in Hamburg, with an excellent short chapter on antisemitism "from below," in which antisemitic attacks are discussed, and Hannah Ahlheim's *"Deutsche, kauft nicht bei Juden!" Antisemitismus und politischer Boycott in Deutschland 1924 bis 1935*, which mentions violence in the spring of 1933, though not to the same extent as the less widespread but better-known violent attacks of the summer of 1935.[64] Also useful is Christoph Kreutzmüller's *Foreign Sale in Berlin. The Destruction of Jewish Commercial Activity 1930–1945*, which offers some detail on violence in the economic boycott actions of March and April 1933.[65]

Studies on the fate of Jews in Nazi Germany between 1933 and 1939 and on the prehistory of the Holocaust also occasionally take account of antisemitic violence in the late winter and spring of 1933. These include Helmut Krausnick's long article "Judenverfolgung," in which he briefly discusses violence in law courts and against businesses preceding the April 1933 boycott, and Karl Schleunes's *The Twisted Road to Auschwitz*, which makes the interesting points that "no directives, not even mild ones, were forthcoming from the offices of Hitler's chancellery or party headquarters to indicate the imminence of an anti-Jewish campaign" and that local SA units that initiated the violence were "unaware that such uncoordinated actions served to undermine rather than strengthen Hitler's position."[66] Schleunes also correctly emphasizes that Hitler's

---

64. Avraham Barkai, *Vom Boykott zur "Entjudung." Der wirtschaftliche Existenzkampf der Juden im Dritten Reich 1933–1943* (Frankfurt: Fischer, 1988), 23–26, English trans. pub. 1989 by University Press of New England; Frank Bajohr, *"Arisierung" in Hamburg. Die Verdrängung der jüdischen Unternehmer 1933–1945*. Hamburger Beiträge zur Sozial- und Zeitgeschichte, 35, 2nd ed. (Hamburg: Christians, 1998), 27–33, English trans. pub. 2002 by Berghahn; Hannah Ahlheim, *"Deutsche, kauft nicht bei Juden!" Antisemitismus und politischer Boycott in Deutschland 1924 bis 1935*, 2nd ed. (Göttingen: Wallstein, 2012).

65. Christoph Kreutzmüller, *Ausverkauf. Die Vernichtung der jüdischen Gewerbetätigkeit in Berlin 1930–1933*, 2nd ed. (Berlin: Metropol, 2013), English trans., *Foreign Sale in Berlin. The Destruction of Jewish Commercial Activity 1930–1945* (New York: Berghahn, 2015), 99–117.

66. Helmut Krausnick, "Judenverfolgung," in Hans Buchheim, Martin Broszat, Hans-Adolf Jacobsen, and Helmut Krausnick, eds., *Anatomie des SS-Staates*, 5th ed., vol. 2. (Munich: DTV, 1989), 257–260; Karl Schleunes, *The Twisted Road to Auschwitz. Nazi Policy toward German Jews 1933–1939* (Urbana: University of Illinois Press, 1970), 71–74, esp. 71. Schleunes also mentions that the SA "failed to appreciate Hitler's need for masking all of his actions behind a facade of legality" (*Twisted Road*, 71).

"continued appeals" to stop the rampant violence "were to little avail."[67] Uwe Dietrich Adam's *Judenpolitik im Dritten Reich* offers details on violence against Jewish lawyers and judges that led to the antisemitic legislation of April 1933; Kurt Pätzold, in his *Faschismus, Rassenwahn, Judenverfolgung*, provides interesting information on attacks on Jewish businesses, Robert Gellately's insightful *Hitler's True Believers* contributes valuable details on pillory marches, while Helmut Berding's otherwise useful and succinct *Moderner Antisemitismus in Deutschland*, which covers the period from 1780 to 1945, has little to say on the subject of antisemitic violence in 1933.[68] In the first volume of his stellar *Nazi Germany and the Jews*, covering the years from 1933 to 1939 and written with an informed heart, Saul Friedländer mentions that the violence following the March elections began with attacks on Eastern Jews, "traditionally the first targets of German-Jew hatred," noting that the foreign press gave wide coverage to the attacks, so that foreign protests then became the pretext for the "retaliatory" April boycott.[69] Peter Longerich's *Politik der Vernichtung* mentions antisemitic violence in some detail, while Longerich's *"Davon haben wir nichts gewusst!" Die Deutschen und die Judenverfolgung 1933–1945* focuses almost exclusively on the public reaction to the boycott in April 1933.[70] Collections of primary sources on the persecution of Jews in Nazi Germany also provide examples of antisemitic attacks in the spring of 1933 and are a valuable source of information.[71]

---

67. Schleunes, *Twisted Road*, 74.
68. Uwe Dietrich Adam, *Judenpolitik im Dritten Reich* (Düsseldorf: Droste, 1972), esp. 46–51; Kurt Pätzold, *Faschismus, Rassenwahn, Judenverfolgung. Eine Studie zur politischen Strategie und Taktik des faschistischen deutschen Imperialismus* (Berlin/GDR: Verlag der Wissenschaften, 1975), 41–52; Robert Gellately, *Hitler's True Believers. How Ordinary People Became Nazis* (Oxford: Oxford University Press, 2020), 239–252; Helmut Berding, *Moderner Antisemitismus in Deutschland* (Frankfurt: Suhrkamp, 1988).
69. Saul Friedländer, *Nazi Germany and the Jews*. Vol. I: *The Years of Persecution* (New York: HarperCollins, 1997), 18–20; Peter Longerich, *Politik der Vernichtung. Eine Gesamtdarstellung der nationalsozialistischen Judenverfolgung* (Munich: Piper, 1998), 26–30.
70. Longerich, *Politik der Vernichtung*; Peter Longerich, *"Davon haben wir nichts gewusst!" Die Deutschen und die Judenverfolgung 1933–1945* (Munich: Pantheon, 2007), 55–73.
71. In particular, Paul Sauer, ed., *Dokumente über die Verfolgung der jüdischen Bürger in Baden-Württemberg durch das nationalsozialistische Regime 1933–1945*, 2 vols. (Stuttgart: Kohlhammer, 1966); Otto Dov Kulka and Eberhard Jäckel, eds., *Die Juden in den geheimen NS-Stimmungsberichten 1933–1945* (Düsseldorf: Droste, 2004), esp. 45–57 (document nos. 1–20),

Finally, there are several essay collections in which some individual contributions provide essential background information and insight into the history of Jews in Germany. Proceeding in chronological order, the first of these is *Juden im Wilhelminischen Deutschland*, edited by Werner E. Mosse, with penetrating articles on the history of the "Jewish Question" in nineteenth-century Germany by Reinhard Rürup, Jewish involvement in the German economy and society by Werner E. Mosse, and Jewish participation in German politics by Peter Pulzer, as well as the incisive *tour de force* on the structure and function of German antisemitism between 1871 and 1914 by Werner Jochmann.[72] Equally invaluable is Werner E. Mosse's *Deutsches Judentum in Krieg und Revolution 1916–1923*, with discerning articles by Saul Friedländer on how the political changes wrought by the First World War shaped public perception of the "Jewish Question" during the war and in the immediate post-war period, and Werner Angress's monograph-length study on the role Jewish leaders played during the revolutionary period. Also important are Wilhelm Treue's essay on economic motivations in fueling German antisemitism, Werner Jochmann's study on the spread of antisemitism in the decade between 1914 and 1924, and Eva Reichmann's astute article on changes in consciousness among German Jews during this period.[73] With a focus on

and nos. 1–47, CD-ROM; Wolf Gruner, ed., *Die Verfolgung und Ermordung der europäischen Juden durch das nationalsozialistische Deutschland 1933–1945*, vol. 1, *Deutsches Reich 1933–1937* (Munich: Oldenbourg, 2008), 74–169.

72. Werner E. Mosse, ed., *Juden im Wilhelminischen Deutschland* (Tübingen: Mohr Siebeck, 1998), first pub. 1976; Reinhard Rürup, "Emanzipation und Krise – Zur Geschichte der 'Judenfrage' in Deutschland vor 1890," in Mosse, ed., *Juden*, 1–56; Werner E. Mosse, "Die Juden in Wirtschaft und Gesellschaft," in Mosse, ed., *Juden*, 57–113; Peter Pulzer, "Die jüdische Beteiligung an der Politik," in Mosse, ed., *Juden*, 143–239; Werner Jochmann, "Struktur und Funktion des deutschen Antisemitismus," in Mosse, ed., *Juden*, 389–477. This last essay, together with other pieces on antisemitism in the Weimar Republic and the Protestant Church, is reprinted in Werner Jochmann, *Gesellschaftskrise und Judenfeindschaft in Deutschland 1870–1945*, 2nd ed. (Hamburg: Christians, 1991), 30–99.

73. Werner E. Mosse, ed., *Deutsches Judentum in Krieg und Revolution 1916–1923* (Tübingen: Mohr Siebeck, 1971); Saul Friedländer, "Die politischen Veränderungen der Kriegszeit und ihre Auswirkungen auf die Judenfrage," in Mosse, ed., *Deutsches Judentum*, 27–65; Werner T. Angress, "Juden im politischen Leben der Revolutionszeit," in Mosse, ed., *Deutsches Judentum*, 127–315; Wilhelm Treue, "Zur Frage der wirtschaftlichen Motive im deutschen Antisemitismus," in Mosse, ed., *Deutsches Judentum*, 387–408; Werner Jochmann, "Die

the end of Weimar, several of the articles in Werner E. Mosse's edited volume *Entscheidungsjahr 1932* make essential reading for anyone interested in the years preceding 1933, including George L. Mosse's piece on "The German Right and the Jews," Werner E. Mosse's article on the increasingly imperiled position of German Jews during Weimar's last years, and the shorter essays on the Churches and political parties.[74] Finally, Arnold Paucker's edited collection on Jews in Nazi Germany, which contains mostly shorter articles in German and English, offers only a few essays on the very beginning of the dictatorship. Among these, Reinhard Rürup's brief summary of Nazi anti-Jewish policies before World War II and Avraham Barkai's examination of the economic plight of German Jews are especially valuable.[75] The entire literature to date does not include a systematic study on antisemitic violence during the period of the Nazi seizure of power—a time when protest and remonstrations against policies and actions of the nascent dictatorship would still have been possible. Parts I and II of the present study examine antisemitic violence during this period as comprehensively as the documentary evidence permits, as both important in itself and as a prelude to the horrors that would come later. Part III then investigates in detail the reasons why none of the institutions and elites who led them, which were still in a position to protest or oppose Nazi antisemitic discrimination and violence in March and April 1933, availed themselves of the opportunities to do so before it was too late.

Ausbreitung des Antisemitismus, "in Mosse, ed., *Deutsches Judentum*, 409–510; and Eva G. Reichmann, "Der Bewußtseinswandel der deutschen Juden," in Mosse, ed., *Deutsches Judentum*, 511–612.

74. Mosse, ed., *Entscheidungsjahr*; Werner E. Mosse, "Der Niedergang der Weimarer Republik und die Juden," in Mosse, ed., *Entscheidungsjahr* 3–49; George L. Mosse, "Die deutsche Rechte und die Juden," in Mosse, ed., *Entscheidungsjahr*, 183–246; Hans-Joachim Kraus, "Die evangelische Kirche," in Mosse, ed., *Entscheidungsjahr*, 249–270; Karl Thieme, "Deutsche Katholiken," in Mosse, ed., *Entscheidungsjahr*, 271–289," and Wiener, "Parteien, 289–321.
75. Pauker, ed., *Die Juden* (Tübingen: Mohr Siebeck, 1986); Reinhard Rürup, "Das Ende der Emanzipation: Die antijüdische Politik in Deutschland von der 'Machtergreifung' bis zum Zweiten Weltkrieg," in Pauker, ed., *Die Juden*, 97–114; Avraham Barkai, "Der wirtschaftliche Existenzkampf der Juden im Dritten Reich, 1933–1938," in Pauker, ed., *Die Juden*, 153–166.

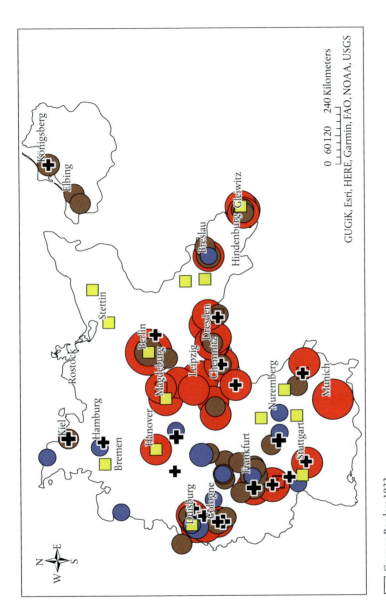

Königsberg
Elbing

Breslau

Hindenburg Gleiwitz

Stettin

Berlin
Dresden
Magdeburg
Leipzig
Chemnitz

Rostock

Kiel
Hamburg
Bremen

Hanover

Nuremberg

Munich

Duisburg
Cologne

Frankfurt

Stuttgart

N
W — E
S

0 60 120   240 Kilometers

GUGiK, Esri, HERE, Garmin, FAO, NOAA, USGS

German Borders 1933

✚ Murder and Attempted Murder

◻ Forceable Shop Closures and Boycotts before and after April 1, 1933

● Attacks and other Actions against Foreign Jews - Ostjuden, Americans, Dutch, Czech

● Violence against German Jews including Forced Expulsions

● Pillory Marches

PART I

VIOLENCE AGAINST FOREIGN JEWS

1

VIOLENCE AGAINST "*OSTJUDEN*" IN THE WINTER AND SPRING OF 1933

Eight months after Hitler had become chancellor, the spiritual leader of German Jews, Leo Baeck, was forced to recognize that "the thousand-year-old history of German Jewry has come to an end."[1] His statement was prompted in part by the nationwide boycott of shops and lawyers' and doctors' offices, as well as the April 1933 antisemitic laws that excluded German Jews from the civil service; banned judges, attorneys, and public prosecutors from practicing law; and excluded doctors from the statutory health insurance system. Accompanying these well-known antisemitic measures, however, were even more pernicious actions, not well documented in historical records, which underscore the veracity of Baeck's assertion. Countless violent attacks, armed robbery, assaults by SA gangs that wounded and incapacitated victims, as well as blackmail, extortion, abduction into SA torture cellars and "wild" concentration camps, and outright murder meant that German and foreign Jews were threatened already at the very beginning of Hitler's reign by economic and physical destruction.[2] Contemporaries were often aware of the attacks; historians, for the most part, are not. In February 1946, for

---

1. At the founding of the *Reichsvertretung der Juden in Deutschland* (hereafter *Reichsvertretung*) in September 1933. See Moshe Zimmermann, *Die Deutschen Juden 1914–1945* (Munich: Oldenbourg, 1997), 57.
2. See, for example, Bessel, "Nazi Capture," 169–188, esp. 176–179, and Wildt, *Volksgemeinschaft*, 101–138; the general focus of the literature is more on the economic aspects of violence and exclusion than on physical violence.

Before the Holocaust: Antisemitic Violence and the Reaction of German Elites and Institutions during the Nazi Takeover. Hermann Beck, Oxford University Press. © Hermann Beck 2022. DOI: 10.1093/oso/9780192865076.003.0002

example, prompted by the soul-searching caused by the still raw wounds of the catastrophic events that accompanied total defeat, Konrad Adenauer (the first chancellor of post-war Germany) wrote to a Catholic clergyman: "The Jewish pogroms of 1933 and 1938 occurred in full public view."[3] As Adenauer pointed out, many acts of violence against foreign Jews did indeed take place in the plain light of day, as did the countless "pillory marches" during which victims were led by foot or on an oxcart through town, a humiliating experience that left those who suffered through it demoralized and broken. These attacks set in immediately after the March 1933 Reichstag elections and only gradually abated during the summer.

This wave of violence first engulfed those Jews who lived in Germany without German citizenship. These were the most vulnerable and thus became the initial targets of personal acts of revenge carried out by members of the SA and SS. Among them, those most significantly affected were Jews from Eastern Europe or their descendants—those who had fled from the pogroms initiated after the murder of Tsar Alexander II that devastated the Jewish settlement rayons in the Russian Empire (the "Pale of Settlement"), as well as Jews from Austrian Galicia, Hungary, and Rumania.[4] Some of these refugees remained in Central Europe on their way to the New World.[5] German Jews and Christians

---

3. Konrad Adenauer, *Briefe 1945–1947*, ed. Hans-Peter Mensing (Berlin: Siedler, 1983), 172.
4. In 1897 about 5.2 million Jews lived in the Russian Empire, of whom 94% were concentrated in former "Congress Poland" and the settlement rayons of western Russia and western Ukraine. The so-called "May Laws" of 1882 forbade Jews from purchasing land and moving from towns to the countryside. Jews in the Russian Empire were declared to be "non-natives" (*inorodtsy*). In 1887 a *numerus clausus* was introduced for Jews attending schools and universities; in 1891–2 violent expulsions of Jewish artisans from Moscow and St. Petersburg followed. See Werner Bergmann, *Geschichte des Antisemitismus*, 2nd ed. (Munich: Beck, 2004), 58–65, esp. 58–59; John D. Klier, *Imperial Russia's Jewish Question, 1855–1881* (Cambridge, 1995); Hugh Seton-Watson, "Two Contending Policies Toward Jews: Russia and Hungary," in Herbert A. Strauss, ed., *Hostages of Modernization. Studies on Modern Anti-Semitism 1870–1933/1939*. Vol. 3/2: *Austria-Hungary-Poland-Russia* (Berlin and New York: De Gruyter, 1993), 948–960, esp. 953; Heinz-Dietrich Löwe, "Anti-Semitism at the Close of the Tsarist Era," in Strauss, ed., *Hostages*, 1188–1207, esp. 1196–1197; Hans Rogger, "Reforming Jews – Reforming Russians," in Strauss, ed., *Hostages*, 1208–1229, esp. 1214, 1220–1222.
5. According to Shalom Adel-Rudel, of the 2.725 million Jews who left Europe between 1880 and 1914, the greater number left from German ports. From Hamburg alone, 62,000 departed in 1887; 136,000 in 1892; about 70, 000 annually between 1892 and 1904; and

referred to these Eastern European Jews who got stuck in Germany on their way to the United States as "*Ostjuden*," a term that was always tinged with "something of the scornful German attitude toward eastern Europe."[6]

A Few Statistics

According to the census of June 1933, 98,747 Jewish foreigners lived in the German Reich, comprising 19.8 percent of Germany's Jewish population. Of this number, 57.2 percent (about 56,000) were Polish, roughly 20 percent were stateless, mostly Russian, followed by Austrian, Czech, Hungarian, and Rumanian Jews, respectively.[7] Thus, about 80 percent of foreign Jews in the German Reich can be classified as "*Ostjuden*." Close to 40,000 of the foreign Jews had been born in Germany and a further 2,400 in the territories Germany had lost after the First World War. Citizenship in the German states was governed by the descent principle (*jus sanguinis*). If Germany had adhered to the territorial principle (*jus soli*), as in the United States, this group would have possessed German citizenship.[8] Of the foreign Jews, 73,025 (74 percent) lived in Prussia (41,122 in Berlin and 12,000–15,000 in the Ruhr area), 12,804 in Saxony, 4,640 in Bavaria, und 2,000 in Baden.[9] Of those Jews who lived in Germany in 1933 but were born abroad, only about 16,000 had acquired German

109,000 annually between 1904 and 1914; Adler-Rudel, *Ostjuden in Deutschland 1880–1940* (Tübingen: Mohr, 1959), 5.

6. Esra Bennathan, "Die demographische und wirtschaftliche Struktur der Juden," in Mosse, ed., *Entscheidungsjahr*, 87–131.
7. Bennathan, "Struktur," 98; Maurer, "Ausländische Juden," 189–210, esp. 189. In 1925, the national distribution had been slightly different: Polish: 50,993 (47.3%); Austrian: 13,509 (12.5%); "stateless:" 9,908 (9.2%); Czechoslovakian: 5,620 (5.2%); Rumanian: 3,240 (3.0%); Hungarian: 3,179 (3.0%); Soviet: 9,505 (8.8%); Lithuanian: 1,710 (1.6%); Latvian: 1,353 (1.3%); other countries: 7,706 (7.2%). Maurer, *Ostjuden*, 74.
8. Maurer, "Ausländische Juden," 189.
9. Maurer, "Ausländische Juden," 189; Zimmermann, *Die deutschen Juden*, 22–23.

citizenship.[10] As a result of emigration and delayed transit of Eastern Jews through Germany, the percentage of foreigners among the German Jewish population rose from 7 percent in 1900 to 19.1 percent in 1925 and finally to 19.8 percent in 1933. In 1933, 13 percent of all foreigners living in Germany were Jewish.[11] The number of foreign Jews was highest in Berlin, Munich, Leipzig, and Dresden. In 1933 they comprised about 30 percent of the Jewish population in Berlin, 26.7 percent in Munich, 60.7 percent in Dresden, and even 73.9 percent in Leipzig.[12] Foreign Jews comprised an especially high percentage in tanning and leather processing (63 percent) and in the fur trade (54 percent), making them an important part of the fur trade in Leipzig, the center of the German leather and fur industry.[13]

Numbers had also risen as a result of the First World War. Before 1914, about 90,000 foreign Jews had lived in Germany, including 10,000–11,000 from West European countries.[14] As Saul Friedländer mentions, during World War I a total of 35,000 Polish Jewish workers were "transferred voluntarily or forcibly to the Reich."[15] In the chaos of the immediate post-war years, tens of thousands of Eastern Jews entered the country, so that at the beginning of the 1920s about 160,000 foreign Jews lived in Germany.[16] Since the governments of the Weimar Republic did not adopt a welcoming attitude toward "*Ostjuden*," their number was reduced by emigration and deportation (and to a lesser extent by naturalization) to about 108,000 by the mid-1920s. Already in 1920 about

10. Werner E. Mosse, "German Jews: Citizens of the Republic," in Paucker, *Die Juden*, 45–55, esp. 47.
11. Bennathan, "Struktur," 98.
12. In 1925 the percentages had been as follows: Berlin: 25.4%; Munich: 27%; Dresden: 60%; Leipzig: 80.7%. See Bennathan, "Struktur," 98; Wilhelm Treue, "Zur Frage der wirtschaftlichen Motive im deutschen Antisemitismus," in Mosse, ed., *Deutsches Judentum*, 387–409, esp. 399.
13. Bennathan, "Struktur," 92–93; 121–122.
14. Werner Jochmann, "Die Ausbreitung des Antisemitismus," in Mosse, ed., *Deutsches Judentum*, 409–510, esp. 414.
15. Friedländer, "Die politischen Veränderungen," in Mosse, *Deutsches Judentum*, 27–65, esp. 35; Jochmann, "Die Ausbreitung," 411; Adler-Rudel, *Ostjuden*, 34–47; Egmont Zechlin, *Die deutsche Politik und die Juden im ersten Weltkrieg* (Göttingen: Vandenhoeck, 1969), 260–262.
16. Treue, "Zur Frage," 397.

1,500 East European Jews left Germany per month to migrate westward, mainly to the United States, and 12,000 returned to Eastern Europe, while a series of political crises resulted in more reimmigration during the early years of the Republic.[17] During the 1923 Ruhr crisis about 9,000 East European Jews left Germany, and a further 12,000 left during the first years of the rise of National Socialism.[18] In Saxony, for example, numbers of "Eastern foreigners" fell from about 10,000 at the beginning of the 1920s to 6,000 by 1925. After 1925, numbers rose again until 1933. For the year 1929, Saxony's Interior Ministry gave the following figures for the state's larger cities: 3,000 in Dresden; 2,802 in Leipzig; and 1,400 in Chemnitz.[19]

The fate of these Eastern Jews has attracted some scholarly attention, notably with regard to the German Empire and the Weimar Republic; little, however, is known about the violence directed against them in 1933.[20] The majority of attacks on foreign Jews, especially on "Ostjuden," are not registered in police files, since the police almost always refused to record violent attacks against non-German Jews and because victims feared reporting attacks. Reasons for refusing or failing to report offenses varied: victims of attacks feared retribution from SA members working as so-called Hilfspolizisten (auxiliary police) for the police force,[21] or police squads contacted by telephone failed to appear to help the victims,[22] or

17. Maurer, Ostjuden, 74, 355–415.
18. Zimmermann, Die deutschen Juden, 22–23.
19. Sächsisches Hauptstaatsarchiv Dresden (hereafter cited as SHStA Dresden), Innenministerium, Bestand 10736, Nr. 11708, "Einwanderung und Ausweisung von Ostjuden," fols. 125–126. Saxony's parliament debated the "Ostjuden Question" on 28 June 1927.
20. See, for example, Steven Aschheim, Brothers and Strangers. The East European Jew in German and German Jewish Consciousness (Madison: University of Wisconsin Press, 1982); Jack Wertheimer, Unwelcome Strangers. East European Jews in Imperial Germany (New York: Oxford University Press, 1987); Maurer, Ostjuden; Zechlin, Die deutsche Politik; Weiss, "'Ostjuden'," 215–232; and Jerzy Tomaszewski, "Położenie Żydów w Niemczech na Wiosnę 1933 r. w Reportach Poselstwa RP oraz Konsulatu Generalnego RP w Berlinie," Biuletyn Żydowskiego Instytutu Historycznego, nos. 3–4 (1986), 131–142 (English title: "The Situation of the Jews in Germany in Spring 1933 as Reflected in Reports of the Polish Republic Legation and Consulate General in Berlin.")
21. 15 March 1933 at, Bundesarchiv, Berlin-Lichterfelde (hereafter BA Berlin), R43 II, no. 1195, "Auswärtiges Amt an Preußisches Ministerium des Innern," Akten der Reichskanzlei, NSDAP, fol. 107.
22. BA Berlin, R43 II, no. 1195, fol. 108.

the police simply declined to officially record statements from anyone with foreign citizenship.[23] In Wanne-Eickel in the Ruhr area, for example, the police went so far as to say to a Polish Jew that "foreigners [had] no right to police protection."[24] Yet in 1933 police reactions were still not uniform and varied considerably by region. In Duisburg, for example, police even prevented a degrading "pillory march," many of which had occurred in other locations. Regardless of the reaction of local police, foreign Jews had the opportunity of complaining to their embassies and consulates on German territory. It is ironic in view of their disadvantaged status as non-citizens that attacks on non-German Jews are therefore often better documented than attacks on German Jews.

Immediately after the Reichstag election of 5 March 1933, as the long pent-up anti-Jewish hatred on the part of the SA, SS, and ordinary members of the NSDAP could be vented freely, a wave of pogrom-like actions took place throughout the Reich. Before the election, the attention of National Socialist organizations and SA members in auxiliary police uniforms had been focused mainly on the struggle against political opponents, especially the KPD and SPD, so that before 5 March anti-Jewish attacks remained isolated. In addition to occasional acts of violence, shop windows of Jewish stores were often smashed, as in Essen and Duisburg-Hamborn between 15 and 25 February.[25] A more concerted wave of violence set in during the night of 5/6 March 1933. It first engulfed those Jews who lived in Germany without a German passport, making them the most vulnerable targets of personal acts of revenge carried out by SA and SS members. (For attacks against foreign Jews, see the map on page 44).

23. 23 March 1933 at BA Berlin, R43 II, no. 1195, "Auswärtiges Amt an Reichsministerium des Innern," fol. 173.

24. 27 March 1933 at BA Berlin, R43 II, no. 1195, "Polnische Gesandtschaft an Auswärtiges Amt," fol. 204.

25. BA Berlin, R43 II, no. 1195, fols. 116–117. In February, several attacks occurred in Silesia, such as in Beuthen and Laband on 20 February (R43 II, no. 1195, fols. 171–172); Bessel, *Political Violence*.

The following account deals mainly, though not exclusively, with Polish Jews, since they constituted the largest group and attacks against them are best documented.[26] These attacks are divided into five categories: (i) physical violence and aggravated robbery; (ii) economic/financial damages such as boycotts and the forced cancellation of debts, vandalism of property, and destruction of goods; (iii) rituals of humiliation such as "pillory marches," in which victims were paraded through the streets in degrading conditions; (iv) violent kidnappings, often in combination with pressure on victims to give up their businesses and emigrate; and finally (v) aggravated bodily assault and murder.

A Litany of Violent Attacks in Early 1933

More than two-thirds of violent attacks against non-German Jews were carried out against Polish nationals. On 5 April 1933 the Polish Embassy sent its fifth formal letter of complaint to the Foreign Ministry in Berlin, in which numerous violent attacks against Polish Jews who lived in the German Reich were recorded.[27] Since this account documents events that have remained largely unknown in the literature, numerous examples of violence against Polish Jews are enumerated in what follows to show how widespread antisemitic attacks were in the winter and spring of 1933. A large number of them took place in Berlin's so-called *Scheunenviertel*, the area around Dragonerstraße, Schönhäuser Tor, Landsbergerstraße, Alte Schönhauserstraße, and Grenadierstraße, where many Polish and other East European Jews resided. On 6 March two uniformed men forced their way into Wolf Leibowitz's shop

26. See also Jerzy Tomaszewski, "Polish Diplomats and the Fate of Polish Jews in Nazi Germany" *Acta Poloniae Historica*, 61 (1990), 183–204, esp. 187–90.
27. 5 April 1933 at BA Berlin, R43 II, no. 603, "Polnische Gesandtschaft an Auswärtiges Amt," Akten der Reichskanzlei, Judentum: Stellung und Behandlung der Juden im nationalsozialistischen Deutschland, fols. 16–29. German Foreign Minister Neurath forwarded these complaints to Interior Minister Frick, demanding that an end be put to the attacks as they might "seriously endanger the reputation of the German government and the German nation abroad." See 6 April 1933 at BA Berlin, R43 II, no. 603; Neurath an Frick," fols. 8–10.

in Gellnowstraße 15, beat him up, and stole twelve suits and a coat. On 24 March Israel Gernstein was attacked by two men in front of the synagogue at Grenadierstraße 37 and beaten up; Isaak Moses Kalb suffered the same fate on the same date and in the same street—five people assaulted him and forcibly cut off his beard. Gustav Ganz, of Metzerstraße 14, was attacked and beaten up by two uniformed men on Linienstraße 8 and suffered a concussion as a result.[28] In Chemnitz on 25 March six Polish Jews were forced to wash communist slogans off the sides of buildings and were beaten up as they did so. In Gelsenkirchen five men pushed their way into the apartment of Hersz Weissmann on 27 March and demanded that he "pay back" 600 Reichsmarks that one of the five had paid him for furniture. On the following night, three men again forced their way into Weissmann's apartment and demanded money. Since none was at hand, the men punched Weissmann's 15-year-old son and stole two gold watches.[29] Also in Gelsenkirchen on 28 March around 4:30 p.m. two uniformed men forced their way into Josef Issler's shop, at Hochstraße 73, and demanded that he immediately close it down. Half an hour later fifteen men raided Issler's private abode and beat both him and his son until they were unconscious. Neighbors took them to a hospital. A similar fate befell Abraham Tanne and Jakob Neimann, as well as Mojzes Erlich and his sister Cyla Erlich, who were beaten up and had their valuables stolen.[30] In Leipzig several men in uniform grabbed Uszer Haim Schenker, of Blücherstraße 33, on 26 March and beat him until he was bleeding heavily; Moszek Aron Syne was called into a pub frequented by National Socialists on 22 March, searched, and beaten up. Chaim Baruch Durst suffered the same fate: on 12 March he was attacked by three men in his Munich apartment, at Agnesstraße 46, and beaten with rubber truncheons, after which his attackers stole 200 marks in cash, four prayer books, and several official identification documents

---

28. 5 April 1933, ibid., fol. 17; see also Jerzy Tomaszewski, "Położenie Żydów," 132–138, for reports by the Polish ambassador Alfred Wysocki of specific attacks on Polish Jews. In early July 1933 Wysocki was posted to Rome and replaced by Józef Lipski.
29. 5 April 1933 at BA Berlin, R43, no. 603, fols. 21, 23.
30. Ibid., fol. 24.

from him.[31] In Wiesbaden I. Schleider was attacked in his shop, at Nerostraße 3, by half a dozen men in uniform on 23 March and so brutally beaten up that he suffered a double-fractured skull and had to be taken to hospital.[32]

This inventory of violent acts can be extended based on the reports of the Polish Embassy. Already on 11 March 1933 the Polish Embassy recorded about twenty violent attacks on Polish Jews in Berlin alone, including raids on several Jewish-owned restaurants that served a predominantly Jewish clientele. During attacks on Jewish restaurants on 5 and 9 March in the Alte Schönhauserstraße that were carried out by groups of SA men, guests were wounded with rubber truncheons, all the furnishings destroyed, food thrown on the floor, and a "fee" imposed upon the owner for the subsequent search of the premises.[33] Criminal SA bands obviously felt quite free to vent their hatred and frustration in this fashion, unencumbered by any fear of the law. On 8 March a Jewish-owned hotel was attacked by uniformed men, the guests beaten and wounded with knives, the windows smashed, and the furniture demolished.[34] During attacks by bands of SA men on the Café Engländer in Schönhäuser Allee on 9 March, guests were beaten so badly that they had to be taken to hospital. When the SA descended upon the café again on 15 March, guests were forced to accompany the attackers to an SA meeting point, where they were searched, robbed, and "beaten unconscious with rubber truncheons."[35] One of the victims was taken to a nearby hospital. The Café New York in Schönhauserstraße 59 was likewise raided several times. On 2 March 1933 a group of uniformed men went into the restaurant and took food from the buffet without paying; on 5 March a different group of SA men threatened to throw a bomb into the café if it was not shut down, and during another attack on 15 March guests were

---

31. Ibid., fols. 25–26.   32. Ibid., fol. 27.
33. 11 March 1933 at BA Berlin, R43 II, no. 1195, "Polnische Gesandtschaft an Auswärtiges Amt," Akten der Reichskanzlei, NSDAP, fols. 114–15.
34. Ibid., fol. 117.
35. 23 March 1933 at BA Berlin, R43 II, no. 1195, "Auswärtiges Amt an Ministerien," Akten der Reichskanzlei, NSDAP, fols. 166–168.

yet again beaten until they fell unconscious.[36] The Polish Embassy informed the official in charge of such matters in the German Foreign Ministry, *Legationsrat* Alexander von Bülow-Schwante,[37] that the perpetrators of the attacks were "exclusively SA and SS men in *Hilfspolizei* uniforms."[38]

Most of the attacks took place in Berlin, in 1933 the fourth largest city in the world after London, New York, and Tokyo, with more than 4.2 million inhabitants. As memoranda from the Polish Embassy to the German Foreign Ministry on 11, 18, and 27 March clearly indicate, however, violent attacks were intensifying in other German cities as well. Regional focal points of attacks on Polish Jews included Düsseldorf and Duisburg-Hamborn, each with a dozen reported attacks, as well as Essen, Cologne, Gelsenkirchen, and Wanne-Eickel in the Prussian Rhine province. A multitude of further attacks took place in Saxony's large cities—Leipzig, Dresden, Chemnitz, and Plauen—as well as in Worms in Rhine-Hessen, in Wiesbaden, the capital of the Prussian province of Hessen-Nassau, in the Upper Silesian cities of Beuthen, Gleiwitz, and Hindenburg, as well as in the Silesian provincial capital, Breslau. The Upper Silesian industrial center, to which Beuthen, Gleiwitz, and Hindenburg belonged, was part of the so-called *Optionsgebiet*, in which a plebiscite had been held in 1921 to decide whether the territory would be incorporated into Poland or remain part of the German Reich. Nazi attacks on Polish Jews in Upper Silesia undermined the 1922 Convention on the protection of minorities.[39]

36. Ibid., fols. 165–166, 168.
37. Vicco von Bülow-Schwante (1891–1970) was one of the experts on Jewish affairs in the Foreign Ministry. See Eckart Conze, Norbert Frei, Peter Hayes, and Moshe Zimmermann, *Das Amt und die Vergangenheit. Deutsche Diplomaten im Dritten Reich und in der Bundesrepublik* (Munich: Pantheon, 2012), 42–51.
38. 23 March 1933 at BA Berlin, R43 II, no. 1195, "Auswärtiges Amt an Ministerien," Akten der Reichskanzlei, fol. 164.
39. In the Versailles Treaty, Upper Silesia was designated a German–Polish mixed-language area, the legal status of which would be decided by plebiscite. In 1921, 59.6% of the area's population opted for remaining in Germany and 40.3% for being part of Poland. At the behest of France, 3,200 square kilometers with about 950,000 inhabitants were awarded to Poland, including cities with a German majority such as Kattowitz (Katowice) and Königshütte (Chorzów) with 57% and 75% Germans respectively, which were surrounded by a

Economic Damage and Ruin

Direct physical attacks were the most frequent but certainly not the only form of assault on "*Ostjuden*." Another type of aggression was aimed at inflicting economic damage or causing ruin, often initiated by envious competitors. In addition, victims were often prevented from offering their merchandise at markets, such as at a commercial fair in Deggendorf in Bavaria, where Polish Jews had rented stalls in full compliance with official regulations but were then informed by the local town council that they ought not to participate in the fair since their personal security could not be guaranteed.[40] Rejections of applications to sell goods at markets and removal of market stalls were also issued at the behest of competing non-Jewish traders. In a letter to the Breslau police chief of 17 June 1933, for example, the street trader Luise Rupprecht requested that her Jewish competitors be expelled from their places in the Breslau market. Adroitly using the jargon of the day, Rupprecht complained that "of all people, a Jewish trader of foreign race and doubtlessly also a communist has limited the few remaining opportunities we Germans have to earn money in this part of town."[41] Breslau's police chief in March 1933 was the infamous Silesian SA leader and convicted murderer Edmund Heines, who had made Breslau notorious nationwide for its anti-Jewish orientation. He was a man with an open ear for such requests. The petition was successful.

The removal from market stalls also became a formidable method of discrimination in Saxony. When the Austrian Consulate General in Dresden complained to Saxon authorities that the Jewish Austrian citizen

predominantly Polish population. On 15 May 1922 Germany and Poland negotiated a bilateral Convention on the protection of minorities. See R. Blunke, "The German Minority in Interwar Poland and German Foreign Policy–Some Reconsiderations," *Journal of Contemporary History*, 25 (1990): 87–102.

---

40. 2 May 1933 at SHStA Dresden, Bestand 10717, no. 1723, Judentum 1933–1935, "Polnische Gesandschaft an Auswärtiges Amt," fol. 22.
41. Gruner, ed., *Die Verfolgung*, 193–194.

Berta Rosenbaum had been denied access to markets in the Saxon cities of Bautzen, Pirna, and Reichenbach, even though she had the required permissions, the Saxon Economics Ministry responded that there existed no police regulations concerning the removal of Jewish traders; the order denying access was a "spontaneous" measure concerning public order and security.[42] The Austrian Consulate thereupon asserted that Frau Rosenbaum's rejection was based solely on the fact that she was Jewish, and that it should be taken into consideration that she had lived in Saxony for over thirty years and now her entire livelihood was at stake.[43]

A Polish complaint from early May 1933 makes it clear that Rosenbaum's case was no isolated incident, but that hundreds were affected by similar actions. In more than twelve cities "Polish merchants of the Mosaic religion" had been removed from city markets—forty in Halle, thirty in Dessau, and fifty-five in Erfurt.[44] Elsewhere, Christian merchants demanded in the presence of city officials that their Jewish counterparts be removed; in some cases the local police had prevented their participation in the markets.[45] Others received letters from state authorities, "according to which their presence in markets was denied because of their heritage," or they were "assigned to special, so-called Jewish rows" in the marketplace.[46] Comparable actions occurred not only in Saxon cities such as Leipzig, Apolda, and Bautzen but also in southern German cities such as Landshut, Nuremberg, Karlsruhe, Freiburg, and Konstanz.[47] To justify the rejection of both foreign and German Jews from markets in Saxony, the Saxon Interior Ministry claimed that in some places "disturbances to public peace and order had already occurred" and that the "national population" was negatively predisposed toward "Jewish market traders, whether of German or foreign citizenship."[48] For this reason, the

---

42. 21 April 1933 at SHStA Dresden, Bestand 10717, no. 1723, "Österreichisches Generalkonsulat an sächsisches Ministerium der auswärtigen Angelegenheiten," fols. 1–3, esp. 3.
43. Ibid., fol. 3.
44. 2 May 1933 at SHStA Dresden, Bestand 10717, no. 1723, "Polnische Gesandtschaft an Auswärtiges Amt," fols. 20–22.
45. Ibid., fols. 20–21.   46. Ibid., fol. 21.
47. Ibid., fol. 21.   48. Ibid., fol. 22.

Interior Ministry asserted, it was unable to counteract police regulations against the Jewish traders, even if the papers of the persons concerned were in order.[49] Ministry officials emphasized that there were no special regulations for foreign Jews, but that the measures pertained to all Jewish traders.[50]

Thus, already in the spring of 1933 "spontaneous" local ordinances and decrees annulled existing rights and legislation, even if these had been in place for decades. These "spontaneous" ordinances and decrees that were initiated on the spur of the moment replaced existing laws and affected Jewish daily life in Germany already in the months after 30 January 1933. In Ernst Fraenkel's terminology, the *"Maßnahmenstaat"* based on ad hoc local ordinances and decrees had partly superseded the statutes and legislation of the State based on legal norms, the *"Normenstaat,"* insofar as it applied to Jewish daily life, as early as the spring of 1933.[51] To preserve the veneer of legality, Saxony's Interior Ministry repeatedly ordered subordinate authorities to make it clear in their directives that Jewish traders were not to be excluded from markets "merely because they were Jews."[52] At the end of May 1933 the Foreign Office in Berlin entered the fray and, for reasons of expediency, insisted on a more legalistic position: all previous measures, such as the boycott of 1 April, had been directed solely against German Jews and excluded foreign business owners. It would be advisable to refrain from introducing measures against foreign Jews in future, since these "could give the Polish government cause for reprisals against German citizens or administrative harassment of the German minority in Poland."[53]

49. 27 May 1933 at SHStA Dresden, Bestand 10717, no. 1723, "Ministerium der auswärtigen Angelegenheiten an Reichsministerium des Innern," fol. 25.
50. Ibid., fol. 23.
51. Ernst Fraenkel, *Der Doppelstaat* (Hamburg: Europäische Verlagsanstalt, 1974). See also Wildt, *Volksgemeinschaft*, 133–137.
52. 15 June 1933 at SHStA Dresden, Bestand 10717, no. 1723, "Sächsisches Ministerium des Innern an Kreishauptmannschaften und Polizeidirektionen," fol. 31. See also Weiss, "Ostjuden," 221.
53. 31 May 1933 at SHStA Dresden, Bestand 10717, no. 1723, "Auswärtiges Amt an Oberbürgermeister der Stadt Berlin," fols. 28–29.

In July 1933 the Saxon Interior Ministry's directive regarding the "admittance of Jewish traders to public markets" was also modified to read: "[The] admission of foreign, Jewish traders may be denied only in those cases in which business practices or the character of the claimant justify rejection."[54] Even though these new directives leave room for interpretation, foreign Jews still enjoyed certain advantages for fear of "countermeasures on the part of foreign governments against German citizens or members of German minorities."[55] Or, as the County Office in Zwickau wrote to the Interior Ministry in Dresden, rejection of foreign traders "provides unwelcome material to the charge of *Greuelpropaganda* [atrocity propaganda] abroad regarding agitation of Jews in the German Reich."[56] Here foreign Jews were clearly in a more advantageous position, since *raison d'état* forced German authorities to be more lenient toward Polish Jews. How things actually looked at the local level, where the SA ruled and made decisions, was another question altogether.

The theme of "atrocity propaganda" played an important role in the political discourse in the spring of 1933. Beginning in mid-March, soon after the onset of violent antisemitic attacks throughout Germany, the Western press, especially in England and the United States, reported in detail about events in Germany.[57] Under government auspices, but with the willing cooperation of large parts of German society, a domestic front against foreign reports formed throughout the whole country. The German press initiated a countercampaign, arguing that foreign press

---

54. 15 July 1933 at SHStA Dresden, Bestand 10717, no. 1723, "Sächsisches Ministerium des Innern an Kreishauptmannschaften und Polizeidirektionen," fol. 35.
55. Ibid., fol. 35. See also Weiss, "Ostjuden," 220–225.
56. 18 September 1933 at SHStA Dresden, Bestand 10717, no. 1723, "Kreishauptmannschaft Zwickau an das Ministerium des Innern," fols. 42–45, esp. 45.
57. See, for example, the articles in *The New York Times* in March 1933: 21 March, "Terror in Germany;" 26 March, "Herr Hitler's Nazis Hear an Echo of World Opinion;" 27 March, "German Jailings Spread Terror;" and many others. For the British press reaction, see "The Persecution of Jews in Germany," Bayerisches Hauptstaatsarchiv Munich, (hereafter BayHStaA), Abt. V, Sammlung Varia 231.

reports were either fabrications or else vastly exaggerated, and comparing them to the Allied "atrocity propaganda" during World War I, that is, to French and British propaganda in 1914/15 regarding German atrocities in Belgium and northern France.[58] Not only the (censored) German press but also the Churches, notably the Protestant Church, were in complete agreement that these "vastly exaggerated" reports about antisemitic attacks constituted just another anti-German plot. Who, German press reports asked, had cared about the manifold injustices committed against the German minorities in Poland and Czechoslovakia?

Another type of violent transgression mentioned in Polish diplomatic reports involved extensive material damages: destruction of goods and merchandise and the annihilation of property. In March and April 1933 countless Jewish shop windows were smashed throughout the Reich.[59] Jahnka Rand's window, for example, in Alleestraße 126 in Duisburg-Hamborn, worth 700 marks, was smashed on 27 March; on 22 March in Groß-Strelitz fruit and vegetable stands had been thrown over by uniformed men, while other Jewish traders were forbidden to sell their merchandise.[60] In Hindenburg in Upper Silesia, a group of fifty uniformed men forced a heavy-goods truck from the Jewish firm Ginsberg & Rosenberg off the street and turned it over, wrecking the truck and damaging the goods inside.[61] Another terse report of an incident, typical for this time, fails to adequately convey the potential tragedy behind it: in

---

58. While the essence of Allied charges regarding the shooting of Belgian civilians was true, beginning in the late 1920s German wartime atrocities came to be largely interpreted as Allied propaganda. In 1928, a book by the British Labour MP Arthur Ponsonby, *Falsehood in Wartime*, showed some of the atrocities to be deliberate fabrications. The book was quickly translated, went through several German editions, and shaped German public perception of Allied war propaganda, especially since German authorities had consistently maintained that the Allied charges were invented. See John Horne and Alan Kramer, *German Atrocities 1914. A History of Denial* (New Haven and London: Yale University Press, 2001), esp. 3, 369, 374, and 417.

59. Geheimes Staatsarchiv Preußischer Kulturbesitz Dahlem (hereafter GStAPK Dahlem), I. HA, Innenministerium, Rep. 77/127, "Politische Ausschreitungen und Zusammenstöße," Monatsberichte, Beiheft 1b, 1932–1933.

60. 5 April 1933 at BA Berlin, R43 II, no. 603, "Polnische Gesandtschaft an Auswärtiges Amt," fols. 25, 26.

61. Ibid., fol. 27.

Hamborn, "in the marketplace an unknown person attacked Simon Leib Herszberg, Hagedornstraße 25, and knocked over his basket with 500 eggs, while spewing out abuse."[62]

Rituals of Humiliation

The wanton destruction of property or carefully stacked-up goods in market stalls already contained elements of humiliation: perpetrators wanted to show the hated and reviled "*Ostjuden*" that they were now completely at the mercy of the arbitrary violence of attackers and that they should leave Germany and leave it fast. Over and above this, another category of anti-Jewish crime involved forms of personal degradation and served exclusively the attackers' goal of twisted amusement and visceral satisfaction. Even though official Polish reports only succinctly summarized the nature of the attacks and refrained from detailed descriptions, several assaults can be classified in this category. The demolition of religious instruments and the shearing of beards are included in this category as specific ways of demoralizing and humiliating victims.

Toward this end Isaak Moses Kalb was assaulted by five people, two of them in uniform, on 24 March around 7:00 p.m. in Grenadierstraße in Berlin. He was not only "badly beaten up" but also had to undergo the indignity of having his "beard cut off."[63] Similar incidents took place throughout March and April. On 9 March at around 5:00 p.m. in Dragonerstraße in Berlin, four uniformed men not only cut off the beard of the victim, Aron Schegel, and ripped his wallet from his hands, but also beat him badly;[64] the following day in Düsseldorf, Salomon Laas had parts of his beard singed off.[65] A synagogue in

---

62. 27 March 1933 at BA Berlin, R43 II, no. 1195, "Polnische Gesandtschaft an Auswärtiges Amt," fol. 203.

63. 5 April 1933 at BA Berlin, R43 II, no. 603, "Polnische Gesandtschaft an Auswärtiges Amt," fol. 17.

64. 23 March 1933 at BA Berlin, R43 II, no. 1195, "Auswärtiges Amt an Ministerien," fol. 165.

65. Ibid.

Blankenfelderstraße in Berlin was stormed on 1 April by uniformed men who wore armbands of the auxiliary police. The attackers sheared off the beard of one victim, searched everyone present in the synagogue, beat them with rubber truncheons, threatened them with revolvers, and then smashed the synagogue's entire inventory, including sacred religious instruments. At the end of all the tumult, the victims were forced to sing "nationalist" songs—"those who refused to do so were beaten up." It was practically de rigueur in this and similar attacks that the perpetrators went one step further and demanded a declaration from the victims that all present had been treated well.[66]

An even more infamous means of public humiliation, which recalled the pillories of the Middle Ages, was the so-called "pillory march" (*Prangermarsch*), whereby chosen victims were led through the streets of their hometowns either on foot or in a cart. Victims of pillory marches were mostly well-established Jewish Germans who owned businesses and were well known in the community; they thus must have felt the public humiliation especially deeply. In the Germany of the 1930s geographical mobility was limited due to the absence of economic opportunities and other factors, so that most inhabitants of German cities and towns rarely ventured beyond the confines of their hometown or province. For this reason, people knew each other all the better inside their respective familiar surroundings. The public running of the gauntlet of a pillory march therefore also caused victims indelible personal trauma and economic damage. In the case of foreign Jews, most of whom were not well known in their places of residence, pillory marches were a less frequent, but not unknown, type of assault.

A report of the Polish Mission of 5 April 1933 recounts how Fischel Häusler was prepared for such a *Prangermarsch* on 25 March in Duisburg. At a Nazi Party meeting place red paper flowers were stuck on his suit and both communist and black-red-gold flags pressed into his hands,

---

66. 5 April 1933 at BA Berlin, R43 II, no. 603, "Polnische Gesandschaft an Auswärtiges Amt," fol. 19.

after which he was to be forcibly marched through the streets of the city. The police were able to prevent this act at the last moment. David Schimmel and David Miller, however, could not be spared the humiliation: both were forced to "carry a black-red-gold flag that had been tied around their necks through the streets of Duisburg."[67] A still worse fate befell the Duisburg rabbi Jakob Bereisch, who was attacked by five uniformed men on 18 March in his apartment and beaten with rubber truncheons. The riot squad that had been called in declared that "it is not part of police duties to protect Jews."[68] Five days later, uniformed men forced their way into his synagogue, wrapped Bereisch up in the republican black-red-gold flag, and chased him through several well-populated streets in Duisburg, all the way to the city theatre.[69]

Another form of humiliation was devised by the SA in Worms, where on 9 March Chaim and Milan Ormianer, as well as Hermann Grünebaum, were dragged to an SA meeting place and forced to "punch each other," as it was described in the report of the Polish Diplomatic Mission of 11 March.[70] Documents from another archival collection, which deal with political disturbances during the seizure of power in general, make it clear that this form of humiliation enjoyed special popularity with the SA in Worms:

> In Worms SA men brought the Jewish leather merchants G. (father and son) and the Jewish gentlemen R. and Gl. to the "Brown House", [where they] were forced to beat each other up under threat of being shot dead. Then they all had to sign a declaration in which they promised to keep quiet about the events that had occurred. Otherwise, they would be shot. The mistreated victims now lie in the Jewish hospital in Frankfurt am Main.[71]

67. Ibid., fols. 22–23.
68. 27 March 1933 at BA Berlin, R43 II, no. 1195, "Polnische Gesandtschaft an Auswärtiges Amt," fol. 201.
69. Ibid., fol. 202.
70. 11 March 1933 at BA Berlin, R43 II, no. 1195, "Polnische Gesandtschaft an Auswärtiges Amt," fol. 118.
71. GStAPK Dahlem I. H.A. Rep. 90p, no. 71, Heft 2, "Ausschreitungen: März 1933," fol. 47. The beginning of the document (dated 25 April 1935) reads: "The collated documents in the supplement... have been given to me today by Herr ORR Flothow, to whom they were

The same dossier records another, similar incident: "In Worms the Jewish merchants, the brothers K. were forced to punch each other under threat of being shot [if they refused]. They are [now] hospitalized in Mannheim suffering from serious injuries."[72] Not all of the attacks in this dossier are recorded in the Polish Diplomatic Mission records, since not all of the countless attacks were officially reported to foreign missions, given that victims correctly feared that an official complaint might result in making them the renewed targets of attacks.

Abduction and Forced Deportation

A further type of crime was the forced closing of shops and businesses in conjunction with the abduction and maltreatment of shop owners. Dozens of such cases appear in the March aide-memoires of the Polish Diplomatic Mission. A typical example of this type of attack reads as follows: "On the 13th of the month six uniformed men [in Hindenburg, Upper Silesia] forced their way into the shop of Herszlik Saper and threatened him with the destruction of all his wares if he did not close his shop. Upon their departure one of them ripped out the telephone line."[73] Demands to close shops were frequently connected with the threat to demolish the entire inventories if the victims refused to comply. Another case, typical for its brutality, occurred in Berlin:

> On the 20th of the month at around 4:00 pm two people ... in uniform and *Hilfspolizei* armbands went into the shop of the butcher Gedalli Scheck, Kielstraße 34. They demanded from the son of the aforementioned, Isaak Leib Scheck, that he immediately close the shop. ... [Then] he was brought

given by Herr Staatssekretär Landfried during his time in office, with the instruction not to record them and also not to include them in the files. Signed: Schröder, Amtsrat." Surprisingly, the documents survived, despite the order not to include them in the official records.

---

72. GStAPK Dahlem, I. H.A. Rep. 90p, no. 71, Heft 2, "Ausschreitungen: März 1933," fol. 50.
73. 18 March 1933 at BA Berlin, R43 II, no. 1195 "Auswärtiges Amt an Ministerien," fol. 172.

to the police station, Steinstraße 5. There he was made to kneel with his face against the wall in a special room and, at gunpoint, beaten with a rubber truncheon over his head and on his face. At around 7:00 p.m. he was let go, although under threat of death if he were again to open his shop.[74]

These and similar attacks were often initiated by business owners who had close ties to the SA or NSDAP, considered victims disagreeable competitors, and now seized the opportunity offered by the political situation and their party connections to get rid of them. Thus, victims of attacks who were physically menaced unless they immediately closed down their shops were usually known to the perpetrators; many of these attacks were in effect "commissioned." A frequently used pretext to lend weight to the threatened shop closure was that a victim had not settled an alleged debt and could avoid further demands for repayment only if the shop was immediately shut down.[75] In a case in Duisburg in March 1933, in which a certain Joseph Mond had requested help from the police after receiving repeated threats, police officers claimed that they were "not in a position to take remedial action," so that Mond had no alternative but to close his shop.[76]

In the course of March, abductions, which were always accompanied by brutal mistreatment and theft, became ever more prevalent. Erwin Wellner, of Immanuel Kirchstraße 31 in Berlin, for example, was seized on 26 March by six people in uniform and taken to an empty apartment in Prenzlauer Straße, where he was "beaten up and manhandled in an especially drastic way for two hours."[77] Chaim Juda Safier was carried

---

74. 27 March 1933 at BA Berlin, R43 II, no. 1195, "Polnische Gesandtschaft an Auswärtiges Amt," fols. 200–201.
75. 23 March 1933 at BA Berlin, R43 II, no. 1195, "Auswärtiges Amt an Ministerien," fol. 170. The violent antisemitic wave of 1933 was supported only by the SA and Nazi party organizations, not by popular attitudes: neighborhood disputes played a role only when Nazi officials or Party members were involved.
76. 27 March 1933 at BA Berlin, R43 II, no. 1195, "Polnische Gesandtschaft an Auswärtiges Amt," fol. 202.
77. 5 April 1933 at BA Berlin, R43 II, no. 603, "Polnische Gesandtschaft an Auswärtiges Amt," fol. 18.

off to the Nazi Party meeting place in General Pape Straße in Berlin on 30 March after he had refused to yield to extortion and pay 850 Reichsmarks "protection money." He was held there for two days and "beaten up and mistreated." The report emphasized that the police presidium refused "to instruct the official medical district officer to examine the injured person."[78] Often victims were kidnapped directly out of their own apartments. A group of eleven uniformed men, for example, broke into Abraham Pinkus Seile's residence at Fürstenstraße 8 in Leipzig, threatened him at gunpoint, and took him away.[79] In a majority of cases victims were let go on the same day or after a few days. It also happened, however, that relatives of kidnapping victims went for weeks without hearing any news. Lajbus Fauszlegier, as a case in point, was arrested on 23 March at around 11:30 p.m. at the Café Dobberstein in Berlin and brought to the 12th police district. On 1 April the police presidium reported in response to an inquiry that no trace of Fauszlegier was to be found anywhere; by 5 April his wife still had received no information as to his whereabouts or fate.[80]

The assault on Juda Tager on 20 March in Dresden is revealing regarding the mindset of the attackers; in his case a Dresden police station took down details of the incident. Tager was snatched from his apartment at around midnight by three SA men and taken to an SA meeting place. He told the police afterwards that he was placed with his face against the wall and asked which German woman he had already raped. Then he was told that he would be shot "on the count of three" if he did not reveal the name. When repeated attempts at this "procedure" failed to illicit the desired response from him, Tager was shown a Social Democratic Party flag and told that he had donated money to the party. Throughout, he was repeatedly manhandled with bare fists and rifle butts. Finally, he was told that he had to leave Germany forthwith or else the SA would come for him again. Tager, born in 1898, informed the police that he had been a resident of Germany since 1913 and, beginning

---

78. Ibid., fol. 18.   79. Ibid., fols. 25–26.   80. Ibid., fol. 15.

in 1916, had fought for Austria in the First World War, for which service he had received several official commendations.[81] The police protocol indicated that Tager had blood-suffused eyes, a bloody nose, and suffered acute pain all over his body. His case illustrates the standard prejudices that lay behind the attacks and that had been disseminated in Nazi newspapers and magazines such as *Der Stürmer*. There, Jews were frequently viewed as "seducers" or even as "rapists" of German women and girls.[82] Responding to the complaint of the Polish Consulate in Leipzig about Tager's abduction, the Saxon Foreign Ministry asserted that investigations of this case had been initiated, but that Tager had been arrested again on 19 April on suspicion of "having spread atrocity propaganda,"[83] an accusation often employed to excuse SA attacks. A letter of the Saxon Interior Ministry of 9 May made clear that Tager's complaint would not be further investigated, "since the alleged actions of the members of the SA, in so far as they can be classified as criminal acts, fall under the amnesty."[84]

The obsession with "atrocity propaganda" and the fear that film clips and documentary proof of attacks would come to light were indeed widespread. In this context, the American tourist Michael van Buren, a 32-year-old architect from New York, was arrested on 1 April at 2:00 p.m. in Dresden's main train station. Van Buren was traveling from Berlin to Prague, when the train stopped in Dresden and was searched in the early morning of Saturday, 1 April. As van Buren later stated in the official report at the American Consulate in Prague, "Every person, German or foreigner, who had a Jewish name or was Jewish looking was taken aside

81. 21 March 1933 at SHStA Dresden, Bestand 10717, no. 4846, "Beschwerden ausländischer Vertreterbehörden wegen Übergriffen an ihren jüdischen Staatsbürgern," "Polizeipräsidium Dresden," fols. 83–85.

82. Daniel Roos, *Julius Streicher und "Der Stürmer"* (Paderborn: Schöningh, 2014).

83. 13 May 1933 at SHStA Dresden, Bestand 10717, no. 4846, "Ministerium der auswärtigen Angelegenheiten an Polnisches Konsulat," fol. 86.

84. 9 May 1933 at SHStA Dresden, Bestand 10717, no. 4846, "Sächsisches Ministerium des Innern an Ministerium der auswärtigen Angelegenheiten," fol. 82. On the amnesty, "Betrifft Gnadenerweise aus Anlass der Beendigung der nationalsozialistischen Revolution vom 22.7.1933 in Verbindung mit der allgemeinen Verfügung des Justizministers vom 25. Juli 1933" at GStAPK Dahlem, Rep. 84a, no. 54771.

and commanded to leave the train with their luggage and wait outside the platform."[85] Van Buren, who "saw the sad faces of the Jews" and took several snapshots, was taken off the train by National Socialist "auxiliary policemen," beaten, and taken into custody for being a "spy" who, as Saxony's Interior Ministry later put it, "took snapshots for anti-German foreign propaganda."[86] Van Buren was accused of having attempted to "procure phony evidence and lies in order to promote anti-German attacks by the foreign press."[87] He then was transferred to a police prison, searched, and put in a cell; his camera was taken away from him. His request to contact the American Consulate was ignored. In the afternoon van Buren was released; he continued his journey to Prague, where he lodged a complaint with the U.S. General Consulate. His camera with the film, which had meanwhile been developed, was returned to him, though the shots taken at the Dresden train station had been confiscated.[88]

The searches at Dresden's main train station during the night of 31 March to 1 April 1933 had been planned, as documented in a written statement of the Dresden Interior Ministry of 2 May: at the end of March it had been observed that "in connection with the boycott of Jewish shops, designed to counter foreign atrocity propaganda," many "Jewish families attempted to leave Germany."[89] Since it was suspected that "foreign atrocity propaganda is supported in these circles," the Dresden police undertook checks on foreign travelers during the early-morning hours of 1 April. As the train had been used by many "Jewish travelers," not all of them could be examined during the short waiting period, so that only "suspicious persons" were intercepted.[90] Such kinds of "special actions" by the SA and the police throughout the Reich accounted for innumerable encroachments and violent attacks that took place

85. 20 April 1933 at SHStA Dresden, Bestand 10717, no. 4858, "Sächsisches Ministerium des Innern an Ministerium der auswärtigen Angelegenheiten," (contains the 7 April 1933 report of the U.S. Consulate in Prague), fol. 57.
86. 20 April 1933 at SHStA Dresden, Bestand 10717, no. 4858, fol. 49.
87. 7 April 1933, ibid., fol. 58.   88. 7 April 1933, ibid., fol. 47–60.
89. 2 May 1933 at SHStA Dresden, Bestand 10717, no. 4858, fol. 93.
90. Ibid., fols. 93–94.

alongside the boycott of 1 April. In Leipzig, for example, the son of the Greek tobacco merchant Charilaos Perpessa, who had been a local resident for forty years, was beaten up by SA men because he allegedly had spoken out against the boycott and incited the public.[91]

Grievous Bodily Harm and Murder

From the records of foreign diplomatic missions, it would appear that fewer foreign than German Jews were victims of murder and attempted murder. It is difficult to judge if this really was the case, since the number of attacks that went unreported, whether out of fear or because victims had no next of kin to report the crimes, was high. Written records are incomplete and, given that many crimes went unreported, faulty in the extreme in terms of providing reliable figures as to the total number of assaults against specific groups. A case in Cologne on 20 March, the attack on Martes Abraham, can be classified as attempted murder. According to the Polish Diplomatic Mission, "two young people, one of them in uniform," armed with revolvers, pushed their way into his apartment and threatened him. To escape his attackers, Abraham sprang out the window and lay—after a 9-meter fall—badly injured in the inner courtyard, where the attackers caught up with him and continued to beat him.[92] In Wiesbaden eight SA men attacked the silk-wares trader Salomon Rosenstrauch on 23 March in his store, beat him up, destroyed his furnishings, and ordered him to close his shop immediately—otherwise he would be killed. When Rosenstrauch, who suffered several broken ribs as a result of the attack, reopened his shop weeks later in spite of the threats, it became clear that the SA men had been in earnest. On 22 April several men appeared at Rosenstrauch's apartment and shot him dead. Apparently, the murder was committed by his former attackers, who had

91. 21 April 1933 at SHStA Dresden, Bestand 10717, no. 4858, fols. 174–177.
92. 27 March 1933 at BA Berlin, R43 II, no. 1195, "Polnische Gesandschaft an Auswärtiges Amt," fol. 203.

now carried out their threat.[93] On the very day of her husband's murder, Rosenstrauch's widow was ordered to the hospital to identify the body and asked to sign a declaration that her husband had died of a sudden heart attack. According to the statement in her compensation claim, she refused to do this since she had seen that her husband's dead body showed distinct signs of violence.[94] Even though no charges were brought against Rosenstrauch's murderers (which would have aided his widow's claims for compensation after the war), the case was mentioned in short notices in the *Frankfurter Zeitung*, the *Deutsche Allgemeine Zeitung*, and the *London Evening Standard* on 24 April 1933.[95]

As testified by a further Polish Diplomatic Mission aide-memoire of 22 May 1933, violent attacks and abductions of Polish Jews continued, if in reduced intensity, throughout April and May.[96] Forced shop closings also continued, and cases from Württemberg—in Esslingen on the Neckar und Cannstatt near Stuttgart—were mentioned, as well as another case of the murder of Mendel Zelig Haber.[97] He had disappeared from Dortmund on 25 April and was consigned to an SA guardhouse; subsequently he was pulled lifeless out of a tributary of the Dortmund–Ems Canal. Haber's body showed signs of gunshot wounds in his head, neck, and back, as well as numerous indications of severe maltreatment.[98]

As indicated by their enormous volume, antisemitic attacks against "Ostjuden" in 1933 were markedly different from those in the Weimar Republic: attacks were carried out with greater brutality since the police turned a blind eye and attackers could now be certain that they would get away with their crimes. During the Republic, antisemitic crimes were reported to the police and legal proceedings instituted.[99] In addition,

93. Entschädigungsakten, Hauptstaatsarchiv Wiesbaden Abt. 518, no. 48634, Salomon Rosenstrauch.
94. Ibid.
95. See copies of these notices in Rosenstrauch's compensation claim file, ibid.
96. Gruner, ed., *Die Verfolgung*, 160–162.
97. Ibid., fol. 161.   98. Ibid., fol. 161.
99. Walter, *Antisemitische Kriminalität*, 97–151; 166–171; 200–244; Hecht, *Deutsche Juden*, 101–345; Wildt, *Volksgemeinschaft*, 69–101; and Schumann, *Politische Gewalt*, 199, 221, 238, 262, 333–334, 367.

violent antisemitic attacks did not go unnoticed since they drew the attention of the Social Democratic, Communist, and at times even the (Left) liberal party press.[100] From the attackers' point of view, the *"Ostjuden"* were especially fair game. After 5 March 1933 members of the SA and other Nazi organizations also used antisemitic attacks to "excel" within their peer group by demonstrating their "ferocity" and their allegiance to the Nazi cause. Sebastian Haffner, writing in 1939 after leaving his native Germany in 1938, emphasized that for the Nazis anti-Jewish violence functioned as a test of courage, a means of selection, and a bonding of the Nazi "in-group," "through the iron trammels of jointly committed crimes."[101] At around the same time, the head of the Frankfurt School in exile, Max Horkheimer, emphasized that antisemitic violence was used "as a means of intimidating the population at large by showing that the system is ruthless and will stop at nothing. Politically speaking, pogroms are aimed at the onlookers."[102] More recently, Michael Wildt has argued that antisemitic attacks contributed to the creation of the *Volksgemeinschaft*, whereby those who belonged strengthened their internal coherence by persecuting and attacking those who did not.[103] The antisemitic policies of the regime, which found their most brutal expression in violence against Jews, also served to undermine traditional civil society and public order and, by implication, helped blaze the trail for the construction of the Nazi State.

100. Schumann, *Politische Gewalt*, 334.
101. Sebastian Haffner, *Germany: Jekyll & Hyde* (Berlin: Verlag 1900, 1996), 69–70.
102. Max Horkheimer, "The Iron Heel," in Roger Griffin, ed., *Fascism* (Oxford: Oxford University Press, 1995), 272. Original quotation from Max Horkheimer, "Die Juden und Europa," *Zeitschrift für Sozialforschung*, 8 (1939), 132–133; 135–136.
103. Wildt, *Volksgemeinschaft*, 26–68, 352–374.

2

"OSTJUDEN" AS PREDETERMINED TARGETS

a History of Marginalization

In antisemitic propaganda, from the NSDAP to parts of the DNVP, *"Ostjuden"* were the preferred object of hatred. The bulk of the national-oriented conservative and moderate liberal bourgeoisie viewed the Jews from the East, some of whom stood out through their dress and speech, with mistrust. The list of prejudices directed against them was endless. In the winter and spring of 1933 Nazi stormtroopers therefore knew quite well that their attacks were directed against a group that was exposed to general contempt and whose members would find no defenders.[1] This chapter examines the main causes of prejudice, the stigmatization of *"Ostjuden"* and violence against them during the Weimar Republic, and discriminatory practices when they wanted to acquire citizenship; it concludes with a brief analysis of the difficult relationship between Jews from Eastern Europe and German Jews, and the policies of the Hitler Cabinet after 30 January 1933.

Roots of Prejudice

Popular prejudices were all-encompassing. *"Ostjuden"* were a target of vicious animosity already during the German Empire. In the wake of the

---

1. Weiss, "Ostjuden," 215–232.

Before the Holocaust: Antisemitic Violence and the Reaction of German Elites and Institutions during the Nazi Takeover. Hermann Beck, Oxford University Press. © Hermann Beck 2022. DOI: 10.1093/oso/9780192865076.003.0003

First World War, quite often an automatic link was made in the popular consciousness between "*Ostjuden*" and revolutionaries. Kurt Eisner, who had proclaimed the Socialist Republic in Bavaria on 7 November 1918, quickly became a symbol of such a "Jewish revolutionary." German and foreign newspapers emphasized his Jewish background and, though born in Berlin, to many Germans he came to epitomize a "Galician Jew." The Bavarian correspondent of the Paris *Le Temps* characterized him as a "Shylock in a glittering frock coat," who "covered his head with a greasy little cap."[2] Because Eisner had instigated the publication of excerpts of Bavarian documents about the onset of war in August 1914 that stressed German responsibility for its outbreak, he also appeared as a traitor to the nation, another causal nexus that quickly took root in the minds of national-oriented Germans.[3] After Eisner's assassination in February 1919, other Jewish revolutionaries stepped into the limelight in connection with the short-lived Bavarian Soviet Republic, such as Eugen Leviné-Nissen, who was born in St. Petersburg in 1883 and received German citizenship in 1913, and Towia Axelrod, who was also Russian-born. Both had experience as revolutionaries in the 1905 Russian Revolution.[4] Their notoriety as importers of revolution was surpassed only by the Polish-born Rosa Luxemburg, who was murdered in January 1919. She had acquired German citizenship through marriage.[5] These specific examples were sweepingly generalized and elevated to the level of a causal relationship between Eastern Jews on the one hand and revolution

2. Friedländer, "Die politischen Veränderungen," 27–66, esp. 51; Allan Mitchell, *Revolution in Bavaria 1918–1919. The Eisner Regime and the Soviet Republic* (Princeton: Princeton University Press, 1965).
3. Heinrich August Winkler, *Weimar 1918–1933*, 4th ed. (Munich: Beck, 2005), 77. Since, as Winkler writes, important passages were omitted from Eisner's document collection, Eisner also laid himself open to charges of manipulation.
4. Angress, "Juden," 137–317, esp. 226–234, 286–298. Of the twenty-seven government members of the Bavarian Soviet Republic, many of the more influential had Jewish roots—besides Leviné-Nissen and Axelrod, Frieda Rabiner (alias Friedjung), Ernst Toller, Erich Mühsam, Gustav Landauer, and Arnold Wadler. The blame for shooting captives in the cellar of the Luitpold Gymnasium in Munich was later laid at their doorstep. Friedländer, *Nazi Germany and the Jews*, vol. I, 92, 355.
5. Maurer, *Ostjuden*, 310.

and treason on the other. This soon became the most destructive prejudice held against foreign (and often also German) Jews.[6]

After the Russian Revolution, fear of a worldwide Jewish conspiracy from the East was so widespread that even Thomas Mann subscribed to it. In May 1918 Mann made notes about a conversation with Ernst Bertram: "We also spoke about the type of Russian Jew, the leader of the worldwide revolutionary movement, this volatile mixture of Jewish intellectual radicalism and effusive Slavic passion about Christ. A world that still possesses a survival instinct must gather all energy to proceed against this scum with the finality of an execution squad."[7] In this context, often absurd theories were propounded. In March 1919, for example, Reinhold Wulle, editor-in-chief of the *Deutsche Zeitung* and a well-known figure in *völkisch* circles, who played an important role in the antisemitic wing of the DNVP until 1922, claimed that international Jewry had prepared the revolution in Germany and carried it through. According to Wulle, Polish and Russian Jews had been brought to Germany during the war, where they recruited German allies with Russian-Jewish money to prepare the revolution. Since the Reich government (led by the SPD politician Gustav Bauer in the spring of 1919) supposedly owed its existence to the Jews, it would not take action against them.[8]

It was this unsubstantiated connection between the alleged Jewish-instigated 1918 revolution and the resulting defeat of the German army (which, it was claimed, had remained undefeated until then and was brought down only because of the "stab in its back") that endowed National Socialist hatred of Jews with its unconditional and limitless

---

6. In this context, Saul Friedländer quotes the Vichy-friendly historian Jacques Benoist-Méchin: "In Magdeburg it is Brandes; in Dresden Lipinsky, Geyer, and Fleissner; in the Ruhr Markus and Levinsohn; in Bremerhaven and Kiel Grünewald and Kohn; in the Pfalz Lilienthal and Heine." See Friedländer, *Nazi Germany and the Jews*, vol. I, 92.
7. Thomas Mann, *Tagebücher, 1918–1921*, ed. Peter D. Mendelsohn (Frankfurt: Fischer, 1979), 223; entry of 2 May 1918.
8. Reinhold Wulle, "Der Stern Judas," *Deutsche Zeitung*, 24, no. 3 (13 March 1919), quoted in Jochmann, "Ausbreitung," 451.

brutality.[9] In Nazi eyes it also turned them into formidable opponents who had to be eliminated.[10] What the *Ostdeutsche Rundschau* wrote on 25 June 1919, days before the German ratification of the Versailles Treaty, expressed the feelings of many German nationalists, antisemites, and parts of the national-minded bourgeoisie:

> The Jews have obstructed our military winning run and defrauded us of the fruits of our victories. The Jews have laid an axe to the thrones and smashed the monarchical constitution to pieces. The Jews have destroyed our middle classes, spread profiteering like the plague, stirred up the cities against the countryside, and the workers against the State and Fatherland. The Jews have brought us the revolution, and if now after the lost war we also lose the peace, then the Jew [Juda] has amassed his fair share of guilt.[11]

Here all social and political ills were projected onto a single culprit. The *"Ostjuden"* were the most obvious and visible target. These charges, based on a selective distortion of the facts, which purposely negated the substantial Jewish-German contribution to the war effort and the large

9. Boris Barth, *Dolchstosslegenden und politische Desintegration. Das Trauma der deutschen Niederlage im ersten Weltkrieg 1914–1933* (Düsseldorf: Droste, 2003). Since German territory was free of enemy troops by the time of the armistice, Friedrich Ebert greeted the returning troops in Berlin as undefeated by the enemy. Hindenburg's statement to the Reichstag Committee on the Investigation of the German Collapse to the effect that an English general had told him that the German army had been stabbed from behind, further contributed to putting the blame for Germany's defeat on "revolutionaries" in the hinterland and their wire-pullers—the Jews. In the minds of most Germans, the "shameful dictate" of Versailles and the chaotic economic and political developments between 1919 and 1923 were a corollary of defeat. Erich Eyck, *Geschichte der Weimarer Republik*, vol. I (Zurich: Rentsch, 1956), 189.
10. Comparable to Saul Friedländer's concept of redemptive antisemitism, which he apprehends as an extreme form of racial antisemitism, a "synthesis of a murderous rage and an 'idealistic' goal," a brand of antisemitism, "born from the fear of racial degeneration and the religious belief in redemption," where the struggle against Jews becomes "the dominant aspect of a worldview." In Friedländer's understanding, "redemption would come as liberation from the Jews – as their expulsion, possibly their annihilation." Quotations in Friedländer, *Nazi Germany and the Jews*, vol. I, 3 and 87.
11. O. Stauf von der March, ed., *Die Juden im Urteil der Zeiten. Eine Sammlung jüdischer und nichtjüdischer Urteile* (Munich: Boepple: 1921), 179, quoted in Friedländer, "Die politischen Veränderungen," 53. In his *Der politische Charakter der Deutschen* (Leipzig: Hammer, 1919), 5, Georg Heydner wrote in 1919: "Every Jew was a voluntary agent of the Entente." Quoted in Friedländer, "Die politischen Veränderungen," 53.

number of Jewish war dead, would later be taken up by National Socialist propaganda, widely circulated, and, most damning of all, believed.[12]

The alleged higher-than-average crime rate among "Ostjuden" was used, as Wilhelm Treue wrote, as "one of the most striking and effective arguments against them – though no one had furnished proof of this."[13] Through frequent house searches and raids in places where Eastern Jews lived, such as Berlin's Scheunenviertel, the police were on the lookout not only for people illegally residing in Germany but also for receivers of stolen goods, since suspicion that "Ostjuden" were implicated in racketeering and shady business practices was widespread.[14] This image of the crafty rogue who cheated upstanding people was already common in nineteenth-century novels, such as Gustav Freytag's bestselling Soll und Haben (1854) or Wilhelm Raabe's Der Hungerpastor (1864). There were few members of German bourgeois households before World War I who were not familiar with the malicious characters of Freytag's Veitel Itzig (a more vicious version of Dickens's Uriah Heep) or Raabe's rancorous Moses Freudenstein.[15] The widespread image of crime and dishonest business dealings was heightened by the fact that "Ostjuden" often worked as peddlers and street hawkers, trades in which foreign Jews were overrepresented.[16] In the real estate trade foreign Jews similarly occupied an important position; their share substantially exceeded their percentage of the total employed Jewish population in Germany.[17] In 1927, 3 percent of all developed properties in Prussian cities of more than 100,000 were owned by resident foreigners (9 percent in Berlin);

12. On the approximately 12,000 Jewish Germans who died in the First World War, see BA Freiburg RW 6, "Allgemeines Wehrmachtsamt," no. 73 a. The number of Jewish war losses was constantly called into question by the political Right. See also Tim Grady, The German-Jewish Soldiers of the First World War in History and Memory (Liverpool: Liverpool University Press, 2011), and Tim Grady, A Deadly Legacy. German Jews and the Great War (New Haven: Yale University Press, 2017).
13. Treue, "Wirtschaflichen Motive," 403.   14. Jochmann, "Ausbreitung," 505.
15. George L. Mosse, "Die deutsche Rechte," in Mosse, ed., Entscheidungsjahr, 183–246, esp. 230. See also Chapter 14 below.
16. Bennathan, "Struktur," in Mosse, ed., Entscheidungsjahr, 114–115. On accusations of prostitution, see Donald L. Niewyk, The Jews in Weimar Germany (Baton Rouge: Louisiana State Press, 1980), 118.
17. Treue, "Wirtschaftliche Motive," 400–402.

87 percent of these properties had been acquired since July 1918.[18] Wilhelm Treue emphasized that the often conjured-up problem of "foreign infiltration of city properties" was connected "with the problem of foreign Jews, especially the Ostjuden," whereby the phenomenon of "foreign infiltration" was linked with inflation, since almost 90 percent of the foreign-owned properties in larger cities was acquired by foreign owners only after 1 July 1918.[19] According to Treue, there were frequent complaints until 1924–5 about the expanding "proportion of foreigners and property owners living abroad" who owned German city properties.[20] The political and psychological implications of this were significant, since facts were often blown out of proportion and politically exploited. Contrary to contemporary assumptions, foreign property ownership was not identical with "*Ostjuden*" ownership, since almost 20 percent of foreign owners were Dutch.[21]

Stigmatization and Violence during the Weimar Republic

Already during the Weimar Republic prejudices based on biased and cherry-picked facts were reflected in repressions against "*Ostjuden*"—mostly

---

18. See Bennathan, "Struktur," 115, n. 37; Treue, "Wirtschaftliche Motive," 400.
19. Bennathan characterizes the circumstances as follows: "On a scale, which cannot be ascertained quantitatively, this goes back to the time of the German inflation after the First World War. Property and houses, which later produced substantial profits, were bought up by foreign buyers, including immigrants from Poland, Austria, Czechoslovakia, Russia, and the Baltic states. This phenomenon, which has often been criticized as a foreign take-over of real estate and property in German cities in political debates, can be traced back to citizens of neighboring countries with stronger currencies (in Prussia, the citizens of Holland represented the largest group of buyers). Jews comprised a significant percentage of these immigrants from neighboring countries.... Inhabitants of these countries possessed ... experience in avoiding inflationary losses ; the currencies of some neighboring countries had also stabilized before the German Reichsmark." See Bennathan, "Struktur," 116–117; Treue, "Wirtschaftliche Motive," 402.
20. *Preußische Statistik*, 299 (Berlin: Statistisches Amt, 1930), in Treue, "Wirtschaftliche Motive," 400.
21. According to Treue's estimate, about 68.5% of foreign owners might have been Jewish. While the fewer than 14,000 Eastern Jewish property buyers in Prussia (after 1 July 1918) had little influence on the overall economy, the unintended psychological impact of their property acquisitions was significant. See Treue, "Wirtschaftliche Motive," 402.

in the form of deportations, internment in camps, and violent attacks. After the overthrow of the Bavarian Soviet Republic and suppression of the revolution in Munich, the situation in Bavaria was especially tense. The Munich revolution was generally considered the work of foreign Jews, given the leading role played by the Russian-born revolutionaries Towia Axelrod, Eugen Leviné-Nissen and Max Levien, even though the latter was not Jewish.[22] In a November 1919 Munich police memorandum it was argued that the April 1919 revolution in Munich had been a "deed of individuals...who were alien to the Bavarian national character and nature of its people," and that the majority of its leading figures were of Jewish, predominantly "Eastern Jewish descent."[23] When Gustav von Kahr became Bavarian Minister-President in the course of the Kapp Putsch in March 1920, he enacted a new decree regarding resident foreigners, which could lead to deportations or internment in the Ingolstadt internment camp.[24] Since no separate Reich citizenship existed, deportations as well as naturalizations and annulments lay within the jurisdiction of the *Länder*.[25] Internments and deportations continued to be encouraged during the early years of the Republic, since the Berlin press (and not just right-wing papers) discovered the *"Ostjuden"* theme after 1919 and called for the closing of borders as well as for confinements and expulsions to put a stop to further immigration. German National and antisemitic publications were even more discriminatory in tone and openly warned of the *"Ostjuden"* danger.[26]

22. Thomas Weber, *Becoming Hitler. The Making of a Nazi* (Oxford: Oxford University Press), 58.
23. Werner Angress, "Juden," 137–315; Walter, *Antisemitische Kriminalität*, 52–79, esp. 54.
24. Walter, *Antisemitische Kriminalität*, 64. The decree had been created to "free the country of at least those foreigners who had immigrated first during and after the war...especially of those fundamentally foreign elements, who...frequently were carriers and distributors of eastern Bolshevik ideas" (ibid., 272). During the First World War, Russian Jews were often placed under arrest in camps as hostile elements, while Austro-Hungarian Jews were drafted into the German or Austro-Hungarian army. See Zimmermann, *Die deutschen Juden*, 7.
25. Walter, *Antisemitische Kriminalität*, 52.
26. Ibid., 59–64; Maurer, *Ostjuden*, 326–425; Jochmann, "Ausbreitung," 409–510. According to Walter, moderate German Nationals viewed focusing on the *"Ostjuden"* question as an alternative to radical "pogrom-antisemitism." This meant that they could place more consensual antisemitic themes on the agenda, since large sections of the population shared prejudices against *"Ostjuden"* and fear of further *"Ostjuden"* immigration. See Walter, *Antisemitische Kriminalität*, 60.

The Bavarian deportation policy of the early 1920s was seen as more rigorous than that in Prussia, though Prussia deported higher numbers of Eastern Jews, largely because of the concentration of foreign Jews in Prussia's eastern provinces and Berlin.[27] Trude Maurer estimated that between 1922 and the end of September 1932 more than 4,000 Jews were deported from Prussia.[28] The most spectacular action during the entire Weimar period was the so-called Bavarian "*Ostjuden* Deportation" of October 1923, initiated by Gustav von Kahr, who had become *General-staatskommissar* (State Commissioner General) of Bavaria in September 1923.[29] Theoretically every foreigner was liable for deportation without cause provided his or her continued presence was not in the national interest of Bavaria. In reality, deportation orders often affected Eastern Jews who owned businesses or who had other economic interests and properties that could not be liquidated in a matter of days. Victims of this policy were told that they had arrived in Germany destitute but had now prospered after having enriched themselves at a time when the German nation suffered from dire poverty. Philipp Löwenfeld, a Social Democratic attorney from Munich, whose professional work included deportation cases, quoted one such deportation order: "You have immigrated to Bavaria in 1887 as a poor tobacco worker. As has been established, you currently own a profitable factory and three houses in Munich. In a house search two gold watches were found to be in your possession. By virtue of this you are a thorn in the flesh of the Bavarian people and will be deported. You have to hand over your business enterprise within a week to a trustee to be named by the *Generalstaatskommissar*; failing that, it will be confiscated without compensation for the benefit of the

27. Maurer, Ostjuden, 415; Dieter Gosewinkel, Einbürgern und Ausschließen: Die Nationalisierung der Staatsangehörigkeit vom deutschen Bund bis zur Bundesrepublik Deutschland (Göttingen: Vandenhoeck & Ruprecht, 2001), 356–363, 370–376. In 1923 and during the great depression deportation activity was intense. See Zimmerman, Die deutschen Juden, 23.

28. Maurer, Ostjuden, 398–399. The Prussian statistics during the Weimar period do not offer precise figures of "Ostjuden" deported from Prussia.

29. Kahr was named Generalstaatskommisar by the Bavarian government on 26 September 1923. See Maurer, Ostjuden, 405–416; Walter, Antisemitische Kriminalität, 75–79.

Bavarian people."[30] The implied de facto expropriation in the deportation process (during the inflation of 1923 material assets could be disposed of only at a great loss) and its wanton capriciousness led to national (especially from the Prussian government) and international protests, so that the bulk of the deportations were not carried out, especially since Kahr resigned from office on 18 February 1924. Those who had already been deported were ruined.[31]

After the signing of the Versailles Treaty, when there was no longer any need to be mindful of foreign public opinion, the Prussian government (SPD, DDP, and Center) established a policy of sending certain categories of "Ostjuden" to camps, if their country of origin, mostly Poland, refused to take back those slated for deportation. In 1921 "undesirable Ostjuden" were committed to internment camps in Cottbus and Stargard.[32] Conditions in Stargard, the larger of the camps, quickly came under public criticism over insufficient rations, poor accommodations, maltreatment at the hands of guards, and censoring of the internees' letters.[33] Under the title "Stargard Hell," The Jewish Worker's Voice wrote on 1 June 1921:

> In the Stargard camp the old Prussian militarism runs riot...here reigns basest insult, abuse and the rifle bud. We have before us letters in which shocking scenes are written down. Insults such as "bastard," "Jewish pig," and similar unmentionable examples are part of the daily fare. The muck

30. Maurer, Ostjuden, 407; Reiner Pommerin, "Die Ausweisung von 'Ostjuden' aus Bayern 1923. Ein Beitrag zum Krisenjahr der Weimarer Republik, " VJHZ 34 (1986), 311–340.
31. Pommerin, "Ausweisung;" Maurer, Ostjuden, 405–416; Walter, Antisemitische Kriminalität, 75–79.
32. Jochmann, "Ausbreitung des Antisemitismus," 504–506; Maurer, Ostjuden, 416–435; Adler-Rudel, Ostjuden, 114–119. The internment decree of 17 November 1920 was preceded by conflicts between the DDP and the SPD. Interior Minister Severing (SPD) consented reluctantly to the establishment of camps. See Maurer, Ostjuden, 420–422.
33. Maurer, Ostjuden, 427–431. In the early months of 1921, the situation of the "Ostjuden" had deteriorated, since the SPD had left the Prussian government and Carl Severing was replaced by Alexander Dominicus (DDP), who was responsible for the internments. According to Scholem Adler-Rudel, who was a member of the Jewish Welfare Office for Workers, which assisted Eastern Jews living in Prussia, this meant that "instead of convicted and dishonest elements...innocent people, who were without residency documents, were indiscriminately arrested off the street and taken off to camps." See Adler-Rudel, Ostjuden, 116.

that passes for food is inedible, the barracks are overcrowded. After 8:00 p.m. no one is allowed out of the barracks. Given the heat and the large number of cooped up inmates the air is extremely unhealthy. The interned are constantly sick. Mistreatment by guards is par for the course. Currently several people who were cruelly beaten up with rifle butts lie in the camp sick bay. Censorship has been established for incoming and outgoing letters.[34]

This report was reprinted by several daily papers and caused great uproar. Eventually Social Democratic deputies investigated the issue and made the outrage public. When the Social Democrats returned to the Prussian government and Carl Severing to the Interior Ministry, internments were limited explicitly to those with criminal records and people considered hostile to the State in August 1923; in the fall internments were revoked and done away with altogether.[35]

As in cases of deportation and internment, violent attacks against "Ostjuden" also reached a peak in the crisis year of 1923. In 1920, there already occurred occasional lootings in Berlin during the Kapp Putsch, but no systematic assaults against Jews in particular.[36] In the early 1920s there had been violent attacks by both Germans and Poles in the contested Upper Silesian plebiscite area, especially during the summer of 1922 in Kattowitz after the city was handed over to Polish administration.[37] After the division of East Upper Silesia on 15 May 1922, many Jews left the part that would become Polish. They had overwhelmingly voted for Germany in the plebiscite. Fear of Polish antisemitism was pervasive, especially since

---

34. Adler-Rudel, Ostjuden, 117.
35. See Mauer, Ostjuden, 433–435; Adler-Rudel, Ostjuden, 118–119. Internment camps also existed in Bavaria, though the camp in Ingolstadt was much smaller than that in Stargard. Severing was Interior Minister from 29 March 1920 until 21 April 1921 and then again from 7 November 1921. Dominicus held the post from 21 April until 7 November 1921. Wolfgang Neugebauer, ed., Handbuch der preußischen Geschichte, vol. 3 (Berlin and New York: DeGruyter, 2001), 314–315.
36. Maurer, Ostjuden, 326. David Clay Large mentions "some attacks against Ostjuden in the Scheunenviertel" during the Kapp Putsch, in his "'Out with the Ostjuden:' The Scheunenviertel Riots in Berlin, November 1923," in Christhard Hoffmann, Werner Bergmann, and Helmut W. Smith, eds., Exclusionary Violence: Antisemitic Riots in Modern German History (Ann Arbor: University of Michigan Press, 2002), 123–140, esp. 127.
37. Maurer, Ostjuden, 328.

violent antisemitic attacks in Poland and Ukraine between 1919 and 1921 were widely known.[38] In 1923 there was also antisemitic violence in the part of Upper Silesia that remained German, in particular in Beuthen, and then again in Berlin during the "*Scheunenviertel* pogrom" on 5 November 1923 (which took place four days before the Beer Hall Putsch in Munich).

What lent political explosiveness to the pogrom-like violence in Berlin's *Scheunenviertel*, the residential area of Eastern Jews, was the fact that blame for attacks cannot be put solely at the feet of the political Right. As the Social Democratic *Vorwärts* indicated, the bulk of perpetrators originated from the "lumpen proletariat." In this case social protest had been steered into antisemitic channels.[39] At noon on 5 November 1923 thousands of unemployed workers streamed through the streets of the *Scheunenviertel*, especially Dragoner-, Grenadier-, and Münz-streets, ransacked shops, beat up shopkeepers, and even broke into homes. Anyone who looked Jewish was a preferred target. The police took action only in the later afternoon and at first arrested mostly Jews, purportedly for their own protection. Even groups of the Reich Association of Jewish Frontline Soldiers, who had rushed into the *Scheunenviertel* to protect Jewish residents, were detained. When darkness set in, attacks began anew; they could be completely quelled only in the course of the coming days. Altogether, the violent assaults on 5 and 6 November resulted in several dozen injured, including members of the Reich Association of Jewish Frontline Soldiers, as well as one death. Unrest also erupted in other sections of Berlin. Between 3 and 7 November 1923 more than 200 shops were looted in Berlin—146 with Christian and 61 with Jewish owners. In the *Scheunenviertel*, antisemitic motivations clearly

---

38. Hecht, *Deutsche Juden*, 164. For voting behavior and the results of the vote, see Peter Maser and Adelheid Weiser, *Juden in Oberschlesien. Historischer Überblick: Jüdische Gemeinden*. Part I: *Historischer Überblick, Jüdische Gemeinden* (Berlin: Mann, 1992), 46. Yisrael Gutman, "Poles and Jews Between the Wars: Historic Overview," in Herbert A. Strauss, ed., *Hostages of Modernization. Studies on Modern Antisemitism 1870–1933/1939*. Vol. 3/2: *Austria-Hungary-Poland-Russia* (Berlin and New York: De Gruyter), 1038–1061; Dietrich Beyrau, "Antisemitismus und Judentum in Polen, 1918–1939," *Geschichte und Gesellschaft*, 8 (1982), 205–233.

39. Walter, *Antisemitische Kriminalität*, 151–154, esp. 152.

predominated, and shopkeepers tried to protect themselves with signs such as "Christian shop."[40]

Violent disturbances in the *Scheunenviertel* had begun in the late morning of 5 November, when thousands of unemployed workers, who had gathered in front of the labor exchange near Alexanderplatz, learned that there was no more money to pay out to them. A rumor that spread like wildfire had it that Galician Jews from the neighboring *Scheunenviertel* had somehow gotten hold of the *Notgeld* (which at this time of galloping inflation maintained its value for a short time) that was expected to be distributed that day. Here versions of events diverge: the *Berliner Tageblatt*, the Social Democratic press, and the Director of the Jewish Worker Welfare Bureau, Alfred Berger, emphasized the role of well-dressed agitators who incited unemployed workers against the Jews and directed the fury of the crowd to the nearby *Scheunenviertel*. This version, stressing the role of the nationalist agitators, is favored by Trude Maurer and Cornelia Hecht. According to Hecht, "Professional antisemitic agitators intermingled with the crowd and launched rumors that 'Galicians' were buying up the paper money in the *Scheunenviertel*. Their rabble-rousing propaganda fell on fertile ground."[41] This version is also supported by Rainer Zilkenat and Bernd Kruppa, who both assume that nationalist agitators were mixed in with the crowd.[42]

Robert Scholz, in contrast, interprets the unrest as food riots, caused by the rising food prices, especially bread, since the price of this staple had risen sharply. Ever since 1916 such food riots with antisemitic overtones were not unusual in Berlin.[43] Dirk Walter argues that manipulation

40. See Walter, *Antisemitische Kriminalität*, 152–153; Hecht, *Deutsche Juden*, 177–186; Large, "Out with the Ostjuden"; Maurer, *Ostjuden*, 329–344.
41. Maurer, *Ostjuden*, 329–330; Hecht, *Deutsche Juden*, 177–178.
42. Rainer Zilkenat, "Der Pogrom am 5. und 6. November 1923," in Thomas Raschke and Verein Stiftung Scheunenviertel, eds., *Spuren eines verlorenen Berlin. Das Scheunenviertel* (Berlin: Haude & Spener, 1994), 95–101; Bernd Kruppa, *Rechtsradikalismus in Berlin, 1918–1928* (Berlin: Overall, 1988), 242.
43. Robert Scholz, "Ein unruhiges Jahrzehnt: Lebensmittelunruhen, Massenstreiks und Arbeitslosenkrawalle in Berlin 1914–1923," in Manfred Gailus, ed., *Pöbelexzesse und Volkstumulte in Berlin: Zur Sozialgeschichte der Straße 1830–1980* (Berlin: Europäische Perspektiven, 1984), 79–123; Gerald Feldman, *The Great Disorder* (Oxford: Oxford University

and assertions that professional agitators were involved "cannot be verified from the sources." It was more likely that right-wing extremists "rushed to the site" when unrest in the *Scheunenviertel* became known. As Walter emphasizes, even the liberal press acknowledged that the pogrom was not carried out by members of nationalist groups, but that the perpetrators "more likely originated from supporters of leftist parties."[44] David Clay Large equally stresses the lack of evidence indicating that antisemitic agitators had been involved or that detailed planning and coordination played a role: "On the contrary, precisely because the rioting was essentially spontaneous, and because the majority of participants belonged to the traditional constituency of the Left, rather than that of the radical Right, this case was particularly ominous."[45] Large explicitly emphasizes that the attacks constituted a pogrom. When the raging mob pushed its way through the *Scheunenviertel* with cries of "out with the Ostjuden," every one taking part could be certain that their acts were somehow in accord with official policies. From the closing of the eastern border in April 1918 to the frequent raids in the *Scheunenviertel*, deportation orders, and internment camps, State organizations had made it clear that Eastern Jews enjoyed no protection. According to Large, it was this aspect of the events in the *Scheunenviertel* that corresponded to the classic model of a pogrom, in which attackers believe themselves to be in tacit agreement with State power.[46] Fewer than ten years later the "*Ostjuden*" would again be among the first to feel the wanton brutality of National Socialist violence.

Press, 1993), 754–780; Wolfgang Ribbe, ed., *Geschichte Berlins*, vol. 2: *Von der Märzrevolution bis zur Gegenwart* (Munich: Beck, 1987), 838–845; Belinda Davis, *Home Fires Burning: Food, Politics, and Everyday Life in World War I Berlin* (Chapel Hill: University of North Carolina Press, 2000).

---

44. Walter, *Antisemitische Kriminalität*, 152. Walter holds that the presence of agitators from the *völkisch* milieu was an argument of expediency: if the extreme Right could be blamed, "the authorities and the democratic spectrum did not have to take responsibility. It distracted from the fact that the members of the general public had been involved in a major antisemitic incident" (152).

45. Large, "Out with the *Ostjuden*," 125.   46. Ibid., 126.

The Difficult Path to Citizenship

The low number of naturalizations indicates how difficult it was for immigrant Jews from Eastern Europe to obtain German citizenship.[47] This was partly due to German citizenship legislation. In Germany the "descent principle" (*jus sanguinis*)—citizenship determined by "blood"—had been in effect since the introduction of the first citizenship laws in Bavaria in 1818, Württemberg in 1819, and Prussia in 1842. This descent principle had also governed French citizenship since the introduction of the *Code Civil* in 1803. In the North German Confederation (1867–71) and in the German Empire after 1871 no national citizenship existed, so that inhabitants continued to hold the citizenship of the member states in which they resided. Germans were thus citizens of Prussia, Bavaria, Saxony, Württemberg, Baden, or of any other German Empire member state. The Reich and State Citizenship Law of 22 July 1913 did ensure that citizenship in all states of the Empire was based on the same foundation, and its rules remained in effect throughout the Weimar Republic. It was not until the 30 January 1934 "Law on the Reconstruction of the Reich" and the 5 February 1934 decree of Interior Minister Wilhelm Frick on German citizenship that a uniform and standardized German citizenship was created. In the course of the National Socialist centralization policies, the sovereignty of the *Länder* was abolished and a Reich citizenship put in place. The creation of a centralized structure was popular with many Germans, including liberals, and established Hitler as the one politician who could achieve the long-coveted internal unification of the Reich.[48]

Before February 1934 Germans had to apply for citizenship from a specific *Land* (German state). Thus, a German who lived in Nuremberg

---

47. Of Jews not born in Germany, only about 16,000 had acquired German citizenship by 1933. See Mosse, "German Jews," 47.
48. Ingo von Münch, ed., *Gesetze des NS-Staates*, 3rd. ed. (Paderborn: UTB, 1994), 43–44; Gosewinkel, *Einbürgern und Ausschließen*; Ingo von Münch, *Die deutsche Staatsangehörigkeit. Vergangenheit—Gegenwart—Zukunft* (Berlin: De Gruyter, 2007).

was a citizen of Bavaria, one who lived in Leipzig of Saxony, a Berliner was a Prussian, and a resident of the city of Schwerin a citizen of Mecklenburg-Schwerin. Applications for citizenship in the *Länder* were discussed in the *Reichsrat*, the State Council of the representatives of the German *Länder*. *Reichsrat* members of every state could raise objections to the naturalization applicants of other German states. During the naturalization procedure, petitions of all applicants from all member states of the Reich had to be submitted to the representatives of the German *Länder* in the *Reichsrat*, so that each German state had the opportunity to object to an application put forward by another state. It was, however, possible to overturn rejections of one or more states against specific applicants by a majority vote in the *Reichsrat*.[49] This happened, for example, in the *Reichsrat* session on 21 August 1924, in which the opposition of the Bavarian delegation to a Romanian's citizenship application in Prussia was rejected by a majority vote.[50] If the applicant was a *"fremdstämmiger Ostjude"* (foreign *"Ostjude"*), in the bureaucratic jargon of the day, the naturalization process promised to be protracted due to objections raised by other *Länder*. Initial citizenship applications of Eastern Jews would be denied almost as a matter of principle: as the Prussian Interior Minister Wolfgang Heine explained in 1919, the tenet that "first generation Jewish Poles are to be excluded from naturalization" had been strictly upheld.[51]

An interesting case in point for the difficulty of obtaining citizenship is that of Hermann Frisch, born on 24 October 1878 in Galicia. His first application to the Mecklenburg authorities in 1919 was denied because he had not yet resided in Germany for twenty years.[52] Frisch's second

---

49. In *The Twisted Road to Auschwitz*, 110–112, Schleunes seems to assume that this possibility did not exist. Trude Maurer also discusses overturns of rejections, *Ostjuden*, 308–323.
50. 18 September 1924 at Landeshauptarchiv Schwerin (hereafter LHA Schwerin) , Bestand 5.12–3/1, no. 11148a, fol. 390.
51. Maurer, *Ostjuden*, 309.
52. LHA Schwerin, no. 11148b, fols. 619–621. This was not a fixed rule. According to the Citizenship Law of 1913, there was no minimum residency requirement at the Reich level, but relevant administrative regulations were in place for individual *Länder*. In Prussia a residency requirement of ten years was applied to all those who had adapted to the German language, customs, and culture. According to a 23 May 1925 memo of the Prussian

petition in 1927 was opposed by several German states: Württemberg doubted that the applicant, "who is a foreign *Ostjude*, feels himself in sync with the German character and constitutes a desired addition to the resident population, despite his long stay in the country." Hamburg voiced its opposition because Frisch had been fined by the Wismar tax authorities for evading payment of capital gains tax; Saxony because "the basic question of the naturalization of Polish nationals" had not yet been regulated; and Bavarian representatives followed suit due to "fundamental reservations about the naturalization of foreign Polish nationals given the hostile attitude of Polish authorities toward Germany."[53]

Mecklenburg-Schwerin, which had approved naturalization in the Frisch case, thereupon turned to the interior ministries in Stuttgart, Dresden, and Munich, as well as to the Reich and Foreign Affairs Office in Hamburg, and backed up its position with the arguments that Frisch had resided in Germany since 1903, had earlier held Austrian citizenship, and, for the most part, had a clean record.[54] Frisch's life up to this point was then scrutinized in response to further unease: Saxony demanded that the German Consulate in Krakow be contacted, and Bavaria would let its objections drop only "if the applicant demonstrably maintains no further relationships with Polish circles."[55] Hamburg withdrew its objections; Württemberg deputies maintained theirs. At this point Wismar local tax authorities and the Mecklenburg state tax authorities in Schwerin voiced misgivings due to Frisch's attempted capital gains tax evasion.

Interior Ministry, "foreigners from the East" should be naturalized only after twenty years of residency. See Maurer, *Ostjuden*, 314.

---

53. 1 April, 6 April, 8 April, 11 April 1933 at LHA Schwerin, Bestand 5.12–3/1, no. 11148b, fols. 591–601. In general, arguments for the rejection of Jewish applicants from Eastern Europe were fairly standard: the applicant was said to have "fought against German troops or [those of its allies]" (fol. 589); was a "foreign Jew from the East" (fol. 589 v.), or could not be regarded as "a desired contribution to the [German] population" (fol. 590). In bureaucratic communications, Frisch's former Galician name "Hersch Frisch recte Blüher" was used ("recte," meaning *gerade gerückt*—the last name of the mother is included with that of the father when children were classified as illegitimate).

54. 1 July 1927 at LHA Schwerin no. 11148b.

55. 9 July 1927, 18 July 1927 at LHA Schwerin, no. 11148b, fols. 604–607.

The German Consulate in Krakow reported that while nothing unfavorable was known about the applicant, he evidently came from "that circle of eastern elements who according to their whole mentality are hardly disposed to integrate themselves into other national traditions [*Volkstum*]."[56] Württemberg now doubled down on its rejection, adopting the concerns of the German Consulate in Krakow and observing that Frisch was applying for naturalization purely for "reasons of self-interest."[57] Following further inquiries, the president of the Mecklenburg state tax office finally withdrew his reservations in October 1928 and the case was again placed before the *Reichsrat*.[58] Even though Bavaria, Saxony, and Württemberg continued to vote against Frisch's naturalization, the *Reichsrat* rejected all objections in its 18 October 1928 session, thus finally clearing Frisch's path for Mecklenburg-Schwerin citizenship.[59] Protracted delays and denials of naturalization of this kind were often used by state governments to preserve their main weapon against unwanted foreigners: deportation.[60] In 1921, the Reich Interior Minister issued guidelines clarifying how state governments should treat naturalization applications: "The cultural interests of the Reich demand restraint with regard to citizenship applications from States whose inhabitants are, on the whole, not on a cultural level commensurate...with that of Germany." Applications from "members of Eastern States" thus required special attention in order "to prevent a gradual penetration of German culture with elements that are alien in nature and detrimental to the upholding of the German character and temperament."[61] Naturalization applications of "*Ostjuden*" were therefore deliberately delayed, even in states where the percentage of the Jewish population was very low, as in

56. 2 January 1928, 14 October 1927 at LHA Schwerin, no. 11148b, fols. 611–615.
57. 20 January 1928 at LHA Schwerin, no. 11148b.
58. 15 September 1928, 11 October 1928 at LHA Schwerin, no. 11148b, fols. 632–633.
59. 18 October,26 October 1928 at LHA Schwerin, no. 11148b, fols. 636–638.
60. Maurer, *Ostjuden*, 309.
61. Maurer, *Ostjuden*, 312. Between 1919 and 1932 a total of 11,254 "eastern foreigners of non-German descent" were naturalized in Prussia (Maurer, *Ostjuden*, 857).

Mecklenburg-Schwerin, where fewer than 0.2 percent of the population was Jewish in 1925.[62]

The naturalization request of the merchant Markus Fischl, who had resided in Mecklenburg-Schwerin since 1 January 1909, first in Wismar and then in Güstrow, illustrate this strategy. In contrast to Hermann Frisch, Markus Fischl's own state, Mecklenburg-Schwerin, made things difficult for him. During his first naturalization attempt in December 1921 he was notified that "for naturalization a minimum of fifteen years of residency within the country is required."[63] According to a 1925 memorandum of the Prussian Interior Minister, "Eastern foreigners" could be naturalized only after twenty years of residency, while Saxony had a thirty-year residency requirement.[64] In the course of a renewed attempt in March 1924 (Fischl having now met the fifteen-year requirement), Fischl's attorney was informed by the Schwerin Interior Ministry that his client's application had no chance of success, since the period of residency required for the naturalization had meanwhile been increased and because "the government has an interest in not giving foreigners a permanent lawful residence here in order to be able to get rid of these people, that is, deport them."[65] The official rejection of Fischl's application for naturalization followed on 28 April 1925.[66]

Fischl's attorney now attempted to have Markus Fischl's son, Dr. Hermann Fischl, who in 1925 had been awarded a Ph.D. from Mecklenburg's state university in Rostock, naturalized.[67] In this case no major objections were raised, though meticulous inquiries were conducted about his past life, among others to the town council of Güstrow, where it was confirmed that he was "known as an especially industrious, respectable, and hard-working young man," who "feels and thinks of

62. *Statistisches Jahrbuch* (1933), 18. In 1925, 632,156 Protestants, 36,724 Catholics, and only 1,225 Jews resided in Mecklenburg-Schwerin.
63. 4 February 1924 at LHA Schwerin, Bestand 5.12–3/1, no. 11148a, fol. 383.
64. See Maurer, *Ostjuden*, 314.
65. 7 March 1924 at LHA Schwerin, no. 11148a, fols. 385–386.
66. 28 April 1925 at LHA Schwerin, no. 11148a, fol. 393.
67. 14 January 1927at LHA Schwerin, no. 11148a, fol. 395. Dr. Hermann Fischl was born in 1901 in the part of Poland that belonged to the Russian Empire; he moved to Wismar in 1908.

himself as completely German."[68] Inquiries were also made to authorities in places where he had studied, including Rostock, the district administration office in Heidelberg, and Baden's Interior Ministry in Karlsruhe, in whose administrative purview the University of Heidelberg was situated. Since nothing negative was reported against him, there were no further objections to his citizenship, and on 19 November 1927 Hermann Fischl's Certificate of Naturalization was presented to him.[69] Six and a half years later, on 12 April 1934, in the wake of the 14 July 1933 law on revoking naturalizations, Dr. Fischl's citizenship, acquired in a protracted tug of war with the authorities, was declared null and void with the stroke of a pen.[70] The Mayor of Fürstenwalde on the Spree, a town in Brandenburg with about 25,000 inhabitants where Fischl resided, thereupon withdrew his Certificate of Naturalization from the state of Mecklenburg-Schwerin.[71]

The Policies of the NSDAP–DNVP Coalition Government

After 30 January 1933 the political climate quickly changed, to the detriment of the "*Ostjuden*." Already on 9 March, Hans Heinrich Lammers, Hitler's Undersecretary of State at the Reich Chancellery, submitted a proposal for a new *völkisch* law to National Socialist Interior Minister Wilhelm Frick.[72] In it, Lammers called for legal measures to be taken against the immigration of "*Ostjuden*" and the annulment of all personal name changes ("the revocation of changes to inherited names") that had

---

68. 21 February 1927 at LHA Schwerin, no. 11148a, fol. 401.
69. 19 November 1927 at LHA Schwerin, no. 11148a, fol. 420.
70. 13 April 1934 at LHA Schwerin, no. 11148a, fol. 430. Joseph Walk, ed., *Das Sonderrecht für die Juden im NS-Staat: eine Sammlung der gesetzlichen Maßnahmen und Richtlinien—Inhalt und Bedeutung*, 2nd ed. (Heidelberg: Müller, 1996), 36. Article 1 of the law stipulated that "Naturalizations that occurred during the period from 9 November 1918 to 30 January 1933 can be rescinded as undesirable."
71. 16 May 1934 at LHA Schwerin, Nr. 11148a, fol. 432.
72. *Akten der Reichskanzlei. Die Regierung Hitler*, part I, vol. I: *1933–1934*, ed. Karl-Heinz Minuth (Boppard: Boldt, 1983), 182–183. Hans Heinrich Lammers (1879–1962): from 30 January 1933 *Staatssekretär* and Head of the Reich Chancellery.

been made since November 1918, as well as the "expulsion of at least a certain percentage of immigrated but not yet naturalized *Ostjuden*."[73] The purpose of name changes was to prevent German and foreign Jews from assimilating by eliminating their own Jewish-sounding names. This annulment of official name changes subsequently became a law in the Third Reich, so that, for example, the famous Bismarck biographer Emil Ludwig became "Emil Ludwig Cohn." The authorities in the Weimar Republic had already laid the groundwork for this insofar as they often refused to recognize or simply ignored the Germanization of Jewish names.[74]

With regard to the draft legislation to invalidate the naturalization of East European Jews, Frick responded to Lammers on 15 March 1933: he had requested that German state governments require police authorities responsible for foreigners to take tough measures against "*Ostjuden*" immigrants and deport those East European Jews who had no authorization to reside in the Reich.[75] It may be taken for granted that Frick and Lammers agreed on measures against "*Ostjuden*" and that the members of the NSDAP–DNVP coalition government supported these policies, just as they could be certain that they would be popular with the public at large. Lammers's original plan was then followed up in an Interior Ministry meeting in mid-March 1933 that focused on a draft law mandating the revocation of naturalizations granted between 11 November 1918 and 30 January 1933, if the new citizens "did not constitute a desired increase in [Germany's] population." It was directed mainly against "*Ostjuden*."[76] On the occasion of the passing of the law, On the Revocation of Naturalizations and the Rescinding of German Citizenship, on 14 July 1933, Hitler emphasized in the Cabinet that he constantly heard that "while there was

---

73. *Akten der Reichskanzlei*, vol. 1, 182–183.
74. This was the case with the aforementioned Hermann Frisch. In bureaucratic communications, he was consistently referred to as "Hersch Frisch recte Blüher." See n. 53 above.
75. *Akten der Reichskanzlei*, part I, vol. I, 183 (also at BA Berlin, R43 II, no. 134, fols. 13–14).
76. *Akten der Reichskanzlei*, part I, vol. I, 457–458 (also at BA Berlin, R43 II, no. 134, fols. 16–19).

no sympathy for actions against Jews *per se*, actions against *Ostjuden* generally met with understanding."[77]

This law made possible the rescinding of all naturalizations that had been carried out during the Weimar Republic; after 14 July 1933 naturalizations were screened for the possibility of revocation. The review of whether naturalizations were to be viewed as undesirable proceeded "according to *völkisch* national (and racial) principles."[78] In August 1933 it was further specified that "non-Aryans could no longer be granted German citizenship."[79] Revocation also extended to naturalized relatives and those whose German citizenship was based on a relationship with the naturalized person through birth or marriage. Persons whose citizenship was revoked became stateless unless they could reacquire their old citizenship; they now needed a residency permit to remain in Germany. As a result, the number of foreign Jews who became stateless rose from 19.9 to 41.5 percent between 1933 and 1939. Since opportunities to emigrate were significantly reduced for stateless persons, the Third Reich ultimately undermined the goal of its own policy, namely to have the highest possible number of Jews leave the country.[80]

The law regarding German residency was also tightened in 1933. East European Jews, who had hitherto held unlimited residency permits, were now summoned by the police and issued permits that limited their stay in the country from three to six months.[81] In some German states, such as Württemberg, interior ministries issued instructions in the years after 1933 designed to "deny residency permits in principle...to Jewish foreigners...in order to avoid this undesired accretion to the population."[82] Thüringen systematically expelled its "*Ostjuden.*" Amendments to the

77. *Akten der Reichskanzlei*, part I, vol. I, 659–660.
78. Walk, *Sonderrecht*, 36, 42 (laid out in the implementation ordinance of the law on 26 July 1933).
79. Walk, *Sonderrecht*, 49; Maurer, "Ausländische Juden," 193.
80. Maurer, "Ausländische Juden," 189–195.   81. Ibid., 192.
82. "Erlass des württembergischen Innenministeriums vom 13 Dez. 1935," in Paul Sauer, ed., *Dokumente über die Verfolgung der jüdischen Bürger in Baden-Württemberg durch das nationalsozialistische Regime 1933–1935*, part 2 (Stuttgart: Kohlhammer, 1966), 101.

Criminal Code in the summer of 1933 made it possible to expel foreigners from Germany if convicted of a three-month prison sentence, whereas formerly the persons in question were merely expelled from their respective *Land*. This new practice resulted in numerous deportations of Polish citizens in the summer of 1933. In 1935 and 1936 numerous stateless persons were expelled on the basis of mere misdemeanors. Since no other country would take them in, they were packed off to detention camps. This also happened to Soviet Jews in January 1938, when their deportation was ordered, since the Soviet Union refused to take in their expelled countrymen.[83]

Initially, German authorities were still careful not to direct measures exclusively against foreign Jews. During the April boycott, businesses owned by foreign Jews were exempted from boycott measures. When attacks on foreign businesses did occur, those affected could at least lodge official complaints with their embassies or consulates.[84] In a similar vein, the Law against the Overcrowding of German Schools and Universities of 25 April 1933 applied only to citizens of the Reich, so that foreign Jews could stay in their educational institutions. The later prominent literary critic Marcel Reich-Ranicki, for example, could continue to attend his Berlin *Gymnasium*.[85] In a decree of the Reich Interior Ministry of 3 May this exemption was partly modified: "In order to avoid diplomatic complications," schools were advised to apply the law also to "foreign non-Aryans," albeit without "revealing the actual reason for non-acceptance."[86]

Even Reich President Paul von Hindenburg, at whose insistence Hitler had to concede to significant and, on the whole, beneficial modifications for Jewish Germans in the 8 April 1933 civil service legislation, showed no

---

83. Maurer, "Ausländische Juden," 195–196.
84. As recorded in the files, this happened occasionally.
85. See von Münch, ed., *Gesetze des NS-Staates*, 175–176; Marcel Reich-Ranicki, *Mein Leben* (Stuttgart: DVA, 1999), 68–131; Marcel Reich-Ranicki, ed., *Meine Schulzeit im Dritten Reich. Erinnerungen deutscher Schriftsteller* (Munich: DTV, 1998), 7th ed., 50–67.
86. "Zulassung von Ausländern bzw. ausländischen Nichtariern...," Walk, *Sonderrecht*, 19.

sympathy for Eastern Jews.[87] In a respectfully worded reply to Prince Carl of Sweden, who had appealed to Hindenburg in his role as president of the Swedish Red Cross on behalf of Jews living in Germany, Hindenburg blamed antisemitic attacks on the influx of "Ostjuden" into Germany.[88] Hindenburg maintained that, where attacks had occurred, the authorities had stepped in. If anything else was claimed abroad, it was due solely to exaggeration, and "in some countries systematic atrocity propaganda [occurred]." Overall, the German people had maintained "exemplary discipline."[89] In the original draft of Hindenburg's letter, he mentioned that "things had occurred that I condemn and regret just as much as the Reich government,"[90] a modification omitted from the final version. To appreciate the measures taken by the Reich government, the specific conditions that existed in Germany had to be kept in mind: "The geographical position of Germany has exposed our country to the immigration of undesirable elements from Eastern Europe," while "in the wake of the [1918] revolution elements have come to the fore, from whom established German Jewry strongly disassociates itself."[91]

Whereas Hindenburg clearly distinguished between Jewish immigrants from Eastern Europe and "home-grown established Jewry" (alteingesessenes Judentum), a distinction consciously made by many Jewish Germans and Austrians,[92] no such distinction was made in an official declaration

---

87. For Hitler's answer to Hindenburg's intervention, see *Akten zur Deutschen Auswärtigen Politik, 1918–1945*, Series C, 1933–1937, vol. I, part 1: *30 January–15 May 1933* (Göttingen: Vandenhoeck & Ruprecht, 1971), 253–255. Chapter 8 below.

88. Prince Carl of Sweden had written to Hindenburg on 4 April 1933 that the Jewish population in Germany, which was obviously subjugated to serious oppression, was entitled to "kind and just treatment." He doubted that those "who currently hold power in Germany" provided the necessary consideration and requested that Hindenburg do his utmost "to spare the world this oppressive spectacle of racial persecution among the German people, who are rightly admired on account of their high cultural standards." *Akten der Reichskanzlei*, part I, vol. I, 391, n. 2.

89. Ibid., 391.   90. Ibid., 391, n. 3.   91. Ibid., 392.

92. In his memoirs the Jewish refugee Stefan Zweig wrote: "The family of my father came from Moravia. In the small rural villages, the Jewish communities lived in complete harmony with the local farmers and petty bourgeoisie; they did not exhibit at all the oppressed spirits and, on the other hand, the slick, pushy impatience of the Galicians – the eastern Jews" (*Die Welt von gestern. Erinnerungen eines Europäers* (Frankfurt: Fischer, 2010), 20); Shulamit Volkov, "Die Dynamik der Dissimilation: Deutsche Juden und die ostjüdischen

issued by the Foreign Office concerning the "spread of Jewish influence in Germany." On 30 April 1933 Vicco von Bülow-Schwante, head of the German section in the Foreign Office since March 1933,[93] dispatched a memorandum to German diplomatic and consular representatives abroad that was meant to "help foreign countries understand the nature of the Jewish question in Germany."[94] This dispatch, largely free of National Socialist jargon, was to be disseminated to foreign countries to provide the Foreign Office's official position on German antisemitic measures. It is revealing as it makes clear the orientation and prejudices of this institution. Bülow-Schwante argued that since 1918 the attitude toward Jews inside Germany had fundamentally changed, both politically and economically. For many decades, Germany had been a "transition point for millions of Jews from the east who, without being assimilated, moved on in the next generation after a more or less extended stay." Since 1918, Social Democrats had used their political influence to encourage "the influx of Eastern Jews and their naturalization in Germany" and "to grant them disproportionate influence in public life, government, the judiciary and the administration."[95] Bülow-Schwante then focused on the alleged political radicalism of Eastern Jewish immigrants, referring to "Jewish districts" that furnished "the most fertile breeding grounds for communism," such as Grenadierstraße [in the *Scheunenviertel*] in Berlin. These Jewish neighborhoods entertained close connections to upper-class Jewish circles in the western part of Berlin: "The many-layered connections between Marxism and Communism on the one hand, and world Jewry, on the other, are…of particular significance." Here the

Einwanderer," in Shulamit Volkov, ed., *Jüdisches Leben und Antisemitismus im 19. und 20. Jahrhundert* (Munich: Beck, 1990), 166–180.

93. Vicco von Bülow-Schwante (1891–1970) was appointed head of the "Sonderreferat Germany" in the Foreign Office on 20 March 1933. A DNVP member since 1928, later Nazi party member, and SA *Standartenführer* (Colonel), Bülow-Schwante was one of the leading experts in the Foreign Office responsible for the "Jewish Question." See Conze et al., *Das Amt und die Vergangenheit*, 42–46; Magnus Brechtken, *Madagaskar für die Juden: Antisemitische Idee und politische Praxis, 1885–1945* (Munich: Oldenbourg, 1997), 173.

94. *Akten der Reichskanzlei*, part I, vol. I, 419–422 (also at BA Berlin, R43 II, no. 600, fols. 163–164).

95. *Akten der Reichskanzlei*, part I, vol. I, 420.

communist-plutocratic world conspiracy that would play a central role in National Socialist propaganda during World War II is already hinted at.[96] The reality was different: many affluent and well-established German Jews regarded the newcomers from Eastern Europe with wary distrust, and the more conservative among them feared, not without reason, that the "*Ostjuden*" might incite German antisemitism.

Two examples serve to illuminate Hitler's view of "*Ostjuden*." At a meeting in the Reich Chancellery in the early fall of 1933, in which discussion centered on the approximately 50,000 refugees who had left Germany since the beginning of the Hitler government, a Foreign Office official proposed issuing a statement that refugees could return to Germany at any time.[97] Hitler took issue with this, arguing that it was a great advantage for Germany that the political refugees had left the country, "since this group of people consists predominantly of Ostjuden...."[98] Factually, this was not accurate and is merely an example of how reality was distorted by ideological bias and prejudice. In a conference of Reich Governors on 28 September several hundred complaints from different countries were discussed. The common theme was the "alleged illegal treatment of foreign Jews," including 139 complaints by the Soviet Embassy "about personal attacks, especially on the part of the SA against Russian citizens, most of whom were Jewish."[99] Hitler remarked that, where the Jewish question was concerned, he could not give way and compromise, commenting that he would have preferred to first pass a

96. *Akten der Reichskanzlei*, part I, vol. 1, 421; Jeffrey Herf, *The Jewish Enemy. Nazi Propaganda during World War II and the Holocaust* (Cambridge: Harvard University Press, 2006), 92–138; Jeffrey Herf, "'Der Krieg und die Juden.' Nationalsozialistische Propaganda im Zweiten Weltkrieg," in Jörg Echternkamp, ed., *Das Deutsche Reich und der zweite Weltkrieg*, vol. 9, part II (Munich: DVA, 2005), 159–202.

97. *Akten der Reichskanzlei*, part I, vol. 2, 834–836. This statement that refugees who had not lost their citizenship would remain under German protection and could return at any time was conceived to forestall a Dutch application to the League of Nations about German political refugees that aimed to resolve the refugee problem through international cooperation (ibid., 834).

98. *Akten der Reichskanzlei*. part I, vol. 2, 835. According to Hitler, Germany had taken in hundreds of thousands of people who had emigrated from the East despite its defeat in the First World War.

99. *Akten der Reichskanzlei*, part I, vol. 2, 864–871, esp. 866.

new citizenship law that would have led to harsher treatment of Jews in Germany.[100] Foreign opinion on the Jewish question was bound to change because "Jewish emigres would become a burden to foreign countries and interfere in offensive ways in the political life of their host countries."[101] This was another prediction that was based solely on prejudice. It was completely unfounded and would not turn out to be the case.

German Jews and *"Ostjuden"*

The attitude of established German Jews vis-à-vis *"Ostjuden"* was characterized by ambiguity.[102] As Egmont Zechlin observed, most German Jews viewed Eastern Jewry "primarily from the vantage point of their own position as German Jews" in German society.[103] That may be too sweeping a characterization, but it hits the mark for those German Jews who felt themselves completely at home in German culture and were convinced of the existence of a German–Jewish symbiosis. Leo Baeck, the leading voice of Judaism in Germany, spoke in this context of that rare "living, creative bond between Jews and Gentiles that in modern times existed only in German-speaking lands."[104] Many feared that the advances made since 1871 would be undermined if the German population painted German Jews with the brush of negative stereotypes

---

100. Ibid., 865. This new citizenship law was passed in September 1935.
101. Ibid., 867.
102. This had already been the case long before the First World War. While Gerson Bleichröder and other Jewish philanthropists donated vast sums on behalf of Eastern Jews, as early as 1881 spokesmen for Berlin Jews threatened to suspend all collaboration with the *Alliance Israelite* in Paris if the latter continued to encourage Russian Jews to pass through the German capital. Fritz Stern, *Gold and Iron. Bismarck, Bleichröder, and the Building of the German Empire* (New York: Vintage, 1979), 346, 481, 526; Aschheim, *Brothers and Strangers*, 3–58.
103. Zechlin, *Die deutsche Politik*, 165.
104. Niewyk, *Jews in Weimar*, 100; Leo Baeck, "Kulturzusammenhänge," in *Der Morgen*, I (1925), 72–83.

associated with East European Jews.[105] Inside the *Centralverein* and among German Jews as a whole, controversial discussions were held as to whether to support or oppose the closing of the eastern border on 23 April 1918 to prevent the influx of more Jewish workers from the East.[106] And there was concern that special legislation directed against Polish Jews might soon apply to long-established German Jews as well. As the liberal *Centralverein* official and Rabbi Felix Goldmann discerned in December 1915, "A special law directed against Polish Jews is really oriented against the members of a certain religious community.... Those clever people who believe that one should silence antisemitism by sacrificing the *"Ostjuden"* to it are sorely mistaken.... Today the tide goes against Polish Jews, tomorrow against naturalized Jews, the day after against established German citizens."[107]

Those who argued against a further influx of Eastern Jews or even for their repatriation or expulsion were convinced that the reason for the growing antisemitism after the First World War was connected with the immigration of *"Ostjuden"* and the encouragement of this immigration by Jewish organizations in Germany. At the beginning of the 1920s, this attitude was prevalent even in the left-liberal German Democratic Party (DDP), which was disparaged by its opponents as a *"Judenpartei."* Otto Fischbeck, DDP member and Prussian Minister of Trade and Industry, accused party comrades who helped Eastern Jewish refugees of further stirring up antisemitism.[108] And representatives of the Jewish community in Munich declared in the city's leading newspapers at the beginning of the 1920s that established Jewish fellow citizens should not be

---

105. The negative stereotype of the *"Ostjude"* is discussed in detail in Maurer, *Ostjuden*, 104–128. As Moshe Zimmermann noted, antisemites did in fact make use of stereotypes of East Europeans—lazy, corrupt, criminal, revolutionary, "Asian,"—in order to denigrate not only *"Ostjuden"* but also German Jews. See Zimmermann, *Die deutschen Juden*, 94.

106. Zechlin, *Die deutsche Politik*, 260–278; Avraham Barkai, *"Wehr Dich!" Der Centralverein deutscher Staatsbürger jüdischen Glaubens 1893–1938* (Munich: Beck, 2002), 73–86.

107. Felix Goldmann, "Deutschland und die Ostjudenfrage," *Zeitschrift des Centralvereins deutscher Staatsbürger jüdischen Glaubens*, 21 (November/December 1915), 195–213, esp. 200–201; Barkai, "Wehr Dich!," 79.

108. Jochmann, "Ausbreitung," 409–510, esp. 496–497; Zimmermann, *Die deutschen Juden*, 94; Maurer, *Ostjuden*, 283 (on Otto Fischbeck).

confused with those immigrants from the East who threatened law and order. Munich was, of course, a special case in that many *"Ostjuden"* were automatically associated with the short-lived Bavarian "Soviet Republic" of 1919.[109] The position of the *Centralverein* was divided. Apart from Rabbi Felix Goldmann, there were other voices, such as that of the attorney Jakob Marx from Karlsruhe, who argued that a significant minority of *"Ostjuden"* were black marketeers, con men, stock market fraudsters, thieves, or criminals.[110] In Saxony's large cities—Leipzig, Dresden, and Chemnitz—*"Ostjuden"* were disadvantaged within their local Jewish communities: until 1923 they did not have the right to vote and after that they could propose only a limited number of representatives to the Jewish Community Council. In Dresden, they were not allowed to hold an office within the Jewish religious community, and in some Prussian cities the payment of taxes to the Jewish congregation was a prerequisite for being eligible to vote in community elections.[111] The most disapproving attitude toward *"Ostjuden"* was displayed by Max Naumann's Association of National German Jews (1921–35). Naumann (1875–1939) had become a reserve officer in the Bavarian army in 1902 and distinguished himself as a highly decorated infantry officer in the First World War. He was convinced that emphasizing a distinct Jewish identity triggered antisemitic resentments and therefore insisted on distinguishing between assimilated and established German Jews, on the one hand, and *"Ostjuden"* on the other.[112] "To the national German Jew," Naumann wrote in 1920, "the

109. Treue, "Wirtschaftliche Motive," 398; Angress, "Juden im politischen Leben," 137–316, esp. 286–299; Mitchell, *Revolution in Bavaria, 1918–1919.*
110. Jakob Marx, *Das deutsche Judentum und seine jüdischen Gegner* (Berlin: Philo, 1925), 25; quoted in Niewyk, *Jews in Weimar*, 115. "It cannot be denied that in the hour of our greatest need many of these people engaged in dealings that were highly dangerous for the national economy" (ibid.).
111. Niewyk, *Jews in Weimar*, 119–121; "In 1930 Zionists charged that fully 29 liberal-dominated communities denied the vote to Eastern Jews by one measure or another; among them were Leipzig, Mainz, Stuttgart, Würzburg, Augsburg, Aachen, und Hannover" (120); Maurer, *Ostjuden*, 610–644.
112. Robert S. Wistrich, *Who's Who in Nazi Germany* (London: Routledge, 1995), 177; Matthias Hambrock, *Die Etablierung der Außenseiter. Der Verband nationaldeutscher Juden 1921–1935* (Cologne: Böhlau, 2003); Carl J. Rheins, "The Verband nationaldeutscher Juden 1921–1922," *Leo-Baeck-Institute Yearbook*, 25, 1: 243–268; Niewyk, *Jews in Weimar*, 165–177;

Ostjude is a stranger – a stranger emotionally, spiritually, physically.... Germany is too sick to provide asylum to the dangerous guests from the East, may they be of Jewish or Slavic origin.... For us, the Ostjuden problem is not a Jewish, but rather a German problem."[113]

While for Max Naumann uniquely Jewish traits had no innate positive value, as he saw in them "only the culpable superannuated spirit of the ghetto that must be relinquished as soon as possible,"[114] for Zionists and national-oriented Jewish or Orthodox circles the encounter with the wider sphere of Judaism offered the opportunity of a renewal of faith and a revival of their own unique identity. In a special issue of the *Süddeutsche Monatshefte* of February 1916 that focused on "*Ostjuden*," a more positive note was struck: "Whoever approaches the study of the Ostjuden with an open mind a whole world opens up—so rare and unique as no other in Europe and few in other parts of the world."[115] For many German Zionists the discovery of Eastern Judaism was the great Jewish experience of wartime: "a strong unbroken Judaism..., rooted in its own ethnic traditions and full of passionate hope for the future," compared to which their own way of life seemed to be "completely abstract and devoid of substance."[116] The encounter with Jewish

Barkai, *"Wehr Dich!"*, 138–42; 234–38; Zimmermann, *Die deutschen Juden*, 32. The historian Hans-Joachim Schoeps, who knew Naumann personally, characterized him in his memoirs as "a figure of absolute integrity, but stifled in the style of Hugenberg" ["eine absolut integre Erscheinung, aber hugenbergisch beschränkt"]; Schoeps, *Die letzten dreißig Jahre. Rückblicke* (Stuttgart: Klett, 1956), 99.

113. Max Naumann, *Vom nationaldeutschen Juden* (Berlin: Goldschmidt, 1920), 21–22; Eva Reichmann, "Der Bewußtseinswandel der deutschen Juden," in Mosse, ed., *Deutsches Judentum*, 511–612, esp. 541. Friedrich von Oppeln-Bronikowski, who had close ties to the DNVP, was equally critical of "*Ostjuden*" in his *Gerechtigkeit! Zur Lösung der Judenfrage* (Berlin: Huch, 1932), published by the *Centralverein*. See Arnold Paucker, "Der jüdische Abwehrkampf," in Mosse, ed., *Entscheidungsjahr*, 405–499, esp. 425–26.

114. Eva Reichmann, "Diskussionen über die Judenfrage 1930–1932," in Mosse, ed., *Entscheidungsjahr*, 503–531, esp. 518.

115. LHA Schwerin, Bestand 5.12–7/1, no. 9014, "Staatsrechtliche Stellung der Juden, 1847–1934" (Ostjuden, *Süddeutsche Monatshefte*, 13, Febr. 1916, Heft 5, fols. 673–856, esp. 673); Reichmann, "Bewußtseinswandel," 511–612, esp. 537–545.

116. Gerhard Holdheim, *Der jüdische Wille*, I (1918/1919), 222–224 (quoted in Reichmann, "Bewußtseinswandel," 538). The student Fritz Loebenstein reported, for example, via army mail from Russia in 1918: "For three weeks I was lucky enough to live here among many thousands of Jews.... Such strength emanates from within these people

life in its East European setting became an essential part of the revival of Judaism in Central Europe in the 1920s. As Donald L. Niewyk argues, this revitalization grew out of Jewish reactions to World War I, the upsurge of antisemitism that came in the wake of war, and the vulgarity of Weimar popular culture.[117] Niewyk maintains that, during the war in the East, German Jews had encountered a natural, pure, and unspoiled "Judaism" that was "unsullied by intercourse with Western civilization."[118] Hermann Cohen (1842–1918), one of the intellectual leaders of German Judaism, praised the "*Ostjuden*" in an essay during the First World War, in particular their "compelling force of spirit and warm-heartedness, their serenity and composure in the face of suffering, their simplicity and unspoiled nature, which everyone whose sense for noble unaffected naturalness has not been dulled must value and love."[119] And Steven Aschheim's assessment, despite his realization of the problematic aspects in the relationship between German Jews and "*Ostjuden*," is also emphatically positive: "By and large the encounter left most Jews with a deepened Jewish consciousness."[120]

that we, who have come here as strangers, ourselves become strengthened by them" (Reichmann, "Bewußtseinswandel," 538).

117. Niewyk, *Jews in Weimar*, 101.
118. Ibid.: "Their example inspired a few young Orthodox rabbinical students to take part of their training at east European yeshivas. This new interest in the Talmudic tradition and the influx of eastern Jews helped temporarily to stay the decline of Orthodox Judaism in Weimar Germany."
119. Hermann Cohen, "Der polnische Jude," in *Der Jude*, 1 (1916/17), 149–156, esp. 153. In addition to the "social creativeness and resourcefulness" of the "*Ostjuden*," Cohen believed that "they are still imbued with much genuine Judaism [Judentum] .... With their sheer superhuman ability to suffer in silence...they will give new momentum to our ideal sense of morality, and our willingness to make sacrifices in the name of extraordinary goals (154). See also Barkai, 'Wehr Dich!', 85–86. On Hermann Cohen, see Hermann Lübbe, *Politische Philosophie in Deutschland* (Munich: DTV, 1974), 83–123; Julius Ebbinghaus, "Hermann Cohen," in *Encyclopedia of Philosophy*, vol. 2 (New York: Macmillan, 1972), 125–128.
120. Aschheim, *Brothers and Strangers*, 151. For a succinct characterization of East European Judaism in Germany, see Zimmermann, *Deutsche Juden*, 22–25.

3

ATTACKS AGAINST AMERICAN AND WEST EUROPEAN JEWS, AMONG OTHERS

On the basis of the available archival records, it can safely be assumed that attacks against Polish Jews made up well over half of all attacks on foreign Jews. In addition, there were numerous attacks on American, Swiss, Italian, Dutch, Czech, Rumanian, and Austrian Jews. Documentary evidence of some of these attacks exists because victims occasionally lodged complaints at their respective embassies or consulates which, in turn, forwarded these to the German Foreign Office or other German authorities with demands for explanation or clarification. In March and early April 1933, for example, Foreign Minister Freiherr Konstantin von Neurath forwarded the bundles of complaints from the Polish Embassy to the acting Prussian Interior Minister Hermann Göring, Hitler's State Secretary in the Reich Chancellery Heinrich Lammers, and Reich Interior Minister Wilhelm Frick, as well as occasionally to the Berlin chief of police, with the urgent request that an immediate stop be put to the attacks.[1] Neurath called for an end to the attacks to prevent damage to the rapidly deteriorating international reputation of the Reich and to keep foreign criticism of its new government within bounds. The myriad of attacks against foreign and German Jews had already led to

---

1. Konstantin von Neurath (1873–1956), German Foreign Minister, 2 June 1932 to 4 February 1938; Hermann Göring (1893–1946), acting Interior Minister of Prussia from 30 January 1933 and Prussian Minister-President from 11 April 1933; Hans Heinrich Lammers (see Chapter 2 above); Wilhelm Frick (1877–1946), Reich Minister of the Interior from 30 January 1933 to 18 July 1943.

Before the Holocaust: Antisemitic Violence and the Reaction of German Elites and Institutions during the Nazi Takeover. Hermann Beck, Oxford University Press. © Hermann Beck 2022. DOI: 10.1093/oso/9780192865076.003.0004

loud protests from Western countries in March, often in the form of disparaging articles in *The New York Times*, London *Times*, *Manchester Guardian*, *Observer*, and other British newspapers, remonstrations from the Anglican Church, questions in the British House of Lords, and a dangerous worsening of relations with Poland that threatened to have adverse repercussions for its German-speaking minority. In the spring of 1933 even the threat of impending war could no longer be discounted.[2] To make matters worse, an international movement to boycott German goods had begun to form in March. In early May 1933 the Hamburg Chamber of Commerce assembled reports from Hamburg firms in a memorandum to the city government that described in detail how German products were being boycotted in North Africa, the Near and Middle East, the United States, England, and other European countries such as France, Belgium, Poland, Czechoslovakia, and Rumania.[3]

Attacks on American Nationals

Especially embarrassing in this context were attacks on American Jews, which might have caused serious diplomatic complications and unwelcome publicity. They also were documented in greater detail than the collective complaints from the Polish Embassy, where dozens of cases were dealt with in one aide-memoire. Violent attacks on American Jews make it evident that not even a U.S. passport could offer protection from the SA, despite the fact that Prussian and Reich authorities treated these cases more seriously than attacks on "*Ostjuden.*" A few examples may illustrate the nature of these attacks and their repercussions: on 11 March

2. BayHSta, V. Hauptabteilung, Sammlung Varia, no. 231, "The Persecution of Jews in Germany;" Stephanie Seul, "Herr Hitler's Nazis Hear an Echo of World Opinion: British and American Press Responses to Nazi Anti-Semitism, September 1930–April 1933," *Politics, Religion, and Ideology*, 14 (September 2013), 412–430; see also BA Berlin, R43, II, nos. 602, 1399, and 1480.
3. 4 May 1933 at Staatsarchiv Hamburg (hereafter StA Hamburg), Bestand 132–1, no. 828, "Boykottbewegung im Ausland als Gegenbewegung zu antisemitischen Bewegungen in Deutschland."

the naturalized American citizen Julian Fuchs was threatened by a gang of SA stormtroopers in his wife's pub on Nürnberger Straße in Berlin, then beaten and reviled as a "dirty Jew," before his attackers extorted money from him that he allegedly owed them. The police, who took his attackers to the nearest police station, finally rescued him.[4] During the night of 10 March the American citizen Jean Klauber and her husband were attacked and mistreated by a group of SA men in their own home in Munich. Envy and hatred appear to have been the driving motivation behind the attack, as one of the group revealed when his eyes fell on Klauber's new suits: "Hey look here, four suits, and we have been starving for fourteen years."[5] When Mrs. Klauber asked about the reason for the action, she received only the reply: "Jews! We hate you! Fourteen whole years we have waited for this, and tonight we are going to hang many of you."[6] The couple was repeatedly subjected to brutal assaults, whereby Mr. Klauber's arm was broken and his wife beaten with a rubber truncheon.

The SA man's threat of violence was meant very seriously. Walter Gyssling, journalist and member of the *Centralverein*'s Office for Defense against Antisemitism, confided to his diary that there had been several excessively vicious antisemitic attacks on 9 and 10 March in Munich. A completely apolitical businessman, for example, was attacked by the SA at night and, as Gyssling wrote, "With the words, 'We've gone hungry for fourteen years and you pig Jew have blown all the money,' the inhuman beasts literally ripped his arm out of its socket."[7] The wife of a Jewish attorney was barbarically attacked by "SA men who forced their way into her home," because her husband had fled. A Jewish furniture dealer was hospitalized in the surgical ward with a cracked skull "following a night-time house search by the SA," and numerous Jewish

---

4. 14 March 1933 at BA Berlin, R43 II, no. 1195, fols. 96–98.
5. 11 March 1933 at BA Berlin, R43 II, no. 1195, fols. 99–101, esp. 100.
6. Ibid.
7. Walter Gyssling's diary entry from 10 March 1933 is reprinted in Gruner, ed., *Verfolgung und Ermordung*, vol. I, *Deutsches Reich*, 76–78.

merchants had been arrested "simply because of some proscription list."[8] Rabbi Leo Baerwald, head of the Israelite Religious Community in Munich, was dragged to the SA headquarters, the "Brown House," later tied to a tree, and tortured with a series of mock executions.[9] A married Jewish couple well known to Gyssling was attacked in their home together with their son, stripped, and beaten with wire whips until they fell unconscious.[10] The most notorious incident was the pillory march of the well-known Munich attorney Dr. Michael Siegel, who intervened on behalf of a friend at the police presidium and, as a result, was mistreated by the SA and led through the streets of Munich with slashed clothing and a sign that read, "I, the Jew Siegel, will never again complain about National Socialists." Gyssling ended his diary entry with the telling sentence: "Starting today, I know what a pogrom is."[11]

In early March 1933 the U.S. Embassy recorded accounts of attacks on Nathaniel S. Wolff and Max Schussler.[12] The 38-year-old Wolff from New York, a painter by profession who had arrived in Berlin only in early February 1933, was attacked in the early morning of 6 March by a group of SA men, vilified as "dirty Russian Jew," tied hand and foot, and hauled to an SA quarters. His request to telegraph the U.S. Consulate in Hamburg was rejected with the brusque comment, "As a foreigner you have no rights, and especially not as a Jew."[13] Later the SA offered to release him provided he would sign the following document: "1. I am a Jew. 2. I will leave this evening for Paris. 3. I promise never to set foot on German soil again. 4. I certify that I have not been subjected to physical violence and that none of my property has been stolen."[14] This, too, was a lie, since a Kodak camera worth 200 Reichsmarks had been stolen from Wolff's room—a typical action, as attacks were often accompanied by

8. Ibid., 77.
9. Ibid., 77. Dr. Leo Baerwald (1883–1970). In 1933 Munich had a population of 735,388, of which about 1.2% (8,825) were Jewish; Thamer, *Verführung und Gewalt*, 258.
10. Gyssling quoted in Gruner, ed., *Verfolgung und Ermordung*, vol. I, *Deutsches Reich*, 77–78.
11. Ibid., 78.
12. 6 March 1933 at BA Berlin, R43 II. no. 1195, fols. 42–47; 7 March 1933, ibid., 48–50. The report, prepared by the U.S. Embassy, was then forwarded to the German Foreign Office.
13. Ibid., fol. 44.   14. Ibid., fol. 42.

theft. In the end the SA set Wolff free, with the threat that they would "clear him out of the way" unless he "left on the evening train to Paris."[15] The demand to leave Germany immediately in conjunction with the customary threats and phony declarations that no harm had been done, which Wolff had to sign, was very common in these kinds of attacks, since SA members wanted to be sure that they remained safe from criminal prosecution.

The attack on Max Schussler belongs to a different category. Schussler, originally from Poland, was an American citizen and owned several rental properties in Berlin. In March 1933 he gave notice to a dilatory tenant who had been in arrears for an entire year, whereupon the tenant brought his connections to the SA into play. According to his own testimony, Schussler was assaulted by several National Socialists in his home on 7 March at 2:00 a.m. and forced at gunpoint to retract the notice to his defaulting tenant.[16] When Schussler asked the intruders about their authority to carry out this action, they "pointed to the swastika on their lapels." Once Schussler had signed the retraction, his assailants left him with the words, "If you revoke this tomorrow, you are a dead man."[17] Rent and property disputes were frequently a driving motivation in antisemitic assaults, though the same perpetrators would hardly have dared to utter death threats against a non-Jewish U.S. citizen, given that the notice to the defaulting tenant was justified. It may also have played a role that Schussler, who had lived in Berlin since October 1930, was known to be from Poland.

The most spectacular physical attack on a Jewish American citizen was that on the businessman Philip Zuckerman, who was knocked down and badly injured by SA men in Leipzig on Sunday, 16 July 1933.[18] Compared to other incidents, this attack caused a big stir: "American Ambassador

15. Ibid., fol. 47.   16. 7 March 1933 at BA Berlin, R43 II, no. 1195, fols. 48–50.
17. Ibid., fol. 50.
18. SHStA Dresden, Außenministerium, Bestand 10717, no. 4858, "Beschwerden ausländischer Vertreterbehörden an sächsische Stellen," fols. 238–280; 28 July 1933, Bestand 10717, no. 4846.

evinces utmost displeasure at the incident, especially since he is not aware of police intervention against perpetrators," the *Staatssekretär* in the Reich Interior Ministry anxiously noted.[19] In the subsequent investigation the following facts emerged: the New Yorker Philip Zuckerman was visiting his brother-in-law Israel Stein in mid-July 1933 in the Saxon city of Leipzig, the center of the German fur trade, in order to purchase furs. As he was walking with his family in the city center on 16 July, a Sunday afternoon, he was "attacked and beaten without cause by a passing troop of…SA men" at the corner of Brühl- and Nikolai Straße.[20] On that particular day, tens of thousands of SA men had gathered in Leipzig for the NSDAP *Gau-Parteitag* (district Party Day) and to parade in front of Hitler.[21] The attack on the busy Brühl thoroughfare commenced when two uniformed SA men suddenly bounded from a marching SA group and attacked Zuckerman with the exclamation "dirty Jew." Even though Zuckerman tried to explain that he was an American citizen, another throng of twenty stormtroopers came running toward him, ignoring his protests, and beating and bashing him on the head, as the 22 July edition of *The Times* of London reported. According to *The Times*, Zuckerman had to be hospitalized for about fourteen days. American authorities already had registered more than twenty similar cases "since the beginning of the revolution."[22]

This attack on a Sunday afternoon on one of the busiest commercial boulevards in Germany's fifth-largest city, at a time when Hitler had declared the "revolution" ended, resulted in a more vigorous reaction from the authorities.[23] On 28 July, Hans Pfundtner, *Staatssekretär* in the Reich Interior Ministry, dispatched a circular memorandum to all

---

19. SHStA Dresden, Bestand 10717, no. 4858, fol. 238.
20. 22 July 1933 at SHStA Dresden, Bestand 10717, no. 4858, fol. 240.
21. Hitler spoke in front of 25,000 Party functionaries and 140,000 SA and SS men at the *Sachsentreffen* in Leipzig. In his speech he called for the elimination of class barriers. Ernst Christian Schütt, *Chronik 1933. Tag für Tag in Wort und Bild*, 2nd ed. (Dortmund: Chronik, 1993), 128; Max Domarus, ed., *Hitler. Reden und Proklamationen*, vol. 1, *Triumph*, part 1 (Wiesbaden: Löwit, 1973), 290.
22. *The Times*, 22 July 1933, 12, at SHStA Dresden, Bestand 10717, no. 4858, fol. 243.
23. In 1933, Leipzig had a population of 713,470, of which 1.6% (about 11,400) were Jewish.

German state governments: the incident, he warned, had "led to sharp complaints from the American Embassy" and "obviously greatly affected the new American Ambassador, who had only just arrived in Germany, and adversely influenced his judgment of conditions in Germany, which is far from favorable."[24] Therefore, state governments should "try to ensure by every means available that such incidents, which are highly injurious of Germany's standing in the world, are not repeated."[25] In future, Pfundtner continued, the police should make every effort to punish the perpetrators; it was intolerable that a foreigner could be knocked down and badly injured in a busy street in broad daylight without the police intervening. Here, Pfundtner finally broaches a problem in his official capacity that had been rampant throughout the Reich since early March, when terror reigned the streets and increasingly began to encroach on other facets of daily life throughout the spring. The regular police forces, largely powerless in any case, had refused to intervene and counter the SA to prevent attacks. Pfundtner's demand that immediate action be taken "against police officials, who are unwilling to carry out their duty, prevent crime and energetically prosecute offenses" fell on deaf ears.[26] Quite to the contrary, soon after the Leipzig attack in the second half of July 1933 a general amnesty for crimes committed in connection with the "national revolution" was passed, which, in turn, frustrated any attempt to prosecute members of the SA and other National Socialist organizations who had committed crimes.[27] Still, with regard to the attack on Zuckerman, the Saxon Minister-President

---

24. 28 July 1933 at SHStA Dresden, Bestand 10717, no. 4858.
25. Ibid. Pfundtner remarked that he "need waste no breath" about the disastrous consequences "from this for our foreign policy." Hans Pfundtner (1881–1945) studied economics and law. From 1925 to 1933 he worked as a lawyer and notary. In 1935 he took a leading role in the formulation of the Nuremberg Laws. A former confidant of Hugenberg, Pfundtner was one of those officials in Hitler's coalition government who came from the DNVP. He was an expert in administrative issues and, as Hans Mommsen wrote, had "significant influence as a Staatssekretär in the Reich Interior Ministry on the administrative-political decisions of the Third Reich." See Hans Mommsen, *Beamtentum im Dritten Reich* (Stuttgart: DVA, 1966), 29–31.
26. Ibid., and 28 July 1933 at SHStA Dresden, Bestand 10717, nos. 4858 and 4846.
27. "Betrifft Gnadenerweise...," at GStAPK, Dahlem, Rep. 84a, no. 54771.

Manfred von Killinger followed up Pfundtner's warning with a further urgent directive:[28] In his communication to *Obergruppe IV* of the Saxon SA, Killinger stated the obvious: in Saxony, cases in which foreigners were subjected to physical attacks had increased, though it was not the behavior of the foreigners, "but more than anything else the fact that they were members of the Jewish race that instigated the attacks."[29] These not only forced the German Foreign Office into "unsatisfactory negotiations with the foreign representatives of the countries concerned" but also stood in the way of a revival of the Saxon economy, since "the maltreated Jewish foreigners would hardly furnish commissions and contracts for Saxony's economy after the ill-treatment that had befallen them."[30]

Killinger's statement makes it obvious that attempts to stop anti-Jewish attacks that ran counter to the national interest were made purely for reasons of *raison d'état* and not out of any humanitarian considerations. On 11 August Pfundtner forewarned officials in the Saxon capital, Dresden, that "the government of the United States insists on a complete clearing up of the incident, punishment of the perpetrators, and an indemnity for the victims." He thus also emphasized the need to apprehend the culprits; since more than a hundred men had taken part in the assault, it should not have been too difficult to detain at least a few of them.[31] Yet all inquiries turned out to be fruitless. At the end of September, the Saxon Interior Ministry reported that even the highest Saxon SA leader failed to apprehend any of the perpetrators, since "more than a hundred thousand men" had marched through Leipzig during the district Party Day and "several hundred thousand participants and spectators were present."[32] Clearly, the SA took care of its own. Given the circumstances, the Interior Ministry's suggestion that Zuckerman or his relatives

28. 15 August 1933, SHStA Dresden, Bestand 10717/4846, 11. Manfred von Killinger (1886–1944), served as an officer in World War I and was then leader of a Freikorps, in which capacity he participated in the plot to murder Matthias Erzberger. In 1933 he became Reich Commissioner and Minister-President of Saxony.
29. Ibid.   30. Ibid.
31. 11 August 1933 at SHStA Dresden, Bestand 10717, no. 4858. If perpetrators could not be identified through the police investigation, the Saxon SA leadership was to be contacted.
32. 27 September 1933 at SHStA Dresden, Bestand 10717, no. 4858.

should provide descriptions of the attackers or their uniforms sounded like mockery.[33] The continued pursuit of the Leipzig attackers by German authorities merely served to signal to the American Embassy that German officials took these incidents seriously; in reality, it was more of a smokescreen to prevent adverse foreign-policy consequences.

This particular incident had repercussions well beyond the diplomatic sphere, since the assault on Philip Zuckerman coincided with the visit of a high-level delegation of American clerics and intellectuals to Berlin. On 21 July, Army District Chaplain Ludwig Müller, then head of the German Protestant *Kirchenbund* (Church Association) gave a talk to this group, "the first and foremost goal of which was to convince the Americans of the untruth and exaggeration of Jewish atrocity propaganda."[34] According to a report by Admiral Ernst Meusel, a member of the Protestant Church leadership, "the Germans at the delegation meeting had great difficulty convincing the Americans that the situation in Germany was under control and in no way reflected the atrocity rumors spread abroad."[35] When, during the evening following the speech, the American guests heard about the assault on Zuckerman, they "declared indignantly that what they had been told earlier in the day was apparently not true," and "departed obviously convinced that they have been lied to in Berlin."[36]

Since members of this delegation had influential connections in American Protestant churches and society, it can be assumed that they helped to impart a more realistic picture of German conditions to an American audience. As Peter Novick argued, already before World War II the image of the Nazi regime in American public opinion was so negative due to detailed press reports of antisemitic attacks that there was nothing Hitler was not deemed capable of doing.[37] Articles and analyses about the

---

33. The Saxon Foreign Ministry also advised the police to contact the American Consulate to get a description of Zuckerman's attackers (see 4 October 1933, SHStA Dresden, Bestand 10717, no. 4858).
34. 27 July 1933 at SHStA Dresden, Bestand 10717, no. 4858. Müller was the military district (*Wehrkreis*) pastor of East Prussia.
35. 24 July 1933, ibid.   36. 24 July 1933, ibid.
37. Peter Novick, *The Holocaust in American Life* (Boston and New York: Houghton Mifflin, 1999).

Nazi regime's antisemitic policies in literary magazines for the educated reader, such as *The Nation, Contemporary Review, Current History, Foreign Affairs, The Literary Digest, The Living Age, Harper's Monthly,* and *The Nineteenth Century and After* also helped to convey a more realistic picture of conditions in the Third Reich.[38] Yet more and accurate information did not lead to a loosening of restrictions on the quota for refugees from Nazi Germany,[39] even though within months of Hitler's accession to the chancellorship the Western world had understood the character of the regime that had come to power in Germany. One sure indicator of this comprehension was that already during the 1933 summer season German tourist statistics recorded a decline in foreign tourists of almost 50 percent compared to 1931. And after 1933, foreign students from Western countries, including those of the United States, who had traditionally been well represented at German universities, stayed away. Foreign students now increasingly came from Turkey, Bulgaria, and China.[40]

Attacks on West European, Czech, and Rumanian Jews

While assaults on Polish Jews and other *"Ostjuden"* were most frequent and attacks on American Jews received the most attention internationally, Jewish citizens of many nationalities were affected by violent

38. See the following articles in *The Nation*: "Back to Barbarism" and "The Folly of Adolf," 12 April 1933; "The Nazi Revolution at Work," 19 April 1933; "Germany's Lowest Depths," 3 May 1933; *Contemporary Review*: "Impressions of Hitler's Germany," June 1933, 669–676; *Current History*: "Germany's Anti-Jewish Campaign," May 1933, 142–145; "Nazi Treatment of the Jews," June 1933, 295–300; *Foreign Affairs*: "Hitler's Reich: The First Phase," July 1933, 589–608; *The Literary Digest*: "American Outcry at German Jew Baiting," 1 April 1933, 3–5; "The Two-Edged Sword of Nazi Boycotts," 8 April 1933, 3–4; *The Living Age*: "The Terror in Germany," May 1933, 198–202; *Harper's Monthly*: "The German Revolt Against Civilization," August 1933, 295–283; *The Nineteenth Century and After*: "Reflections on the German Revolution," May 1933, 513–526.
39. Dinnerstein, *Antisemitism in America*; Hertha Nathorff, *Das Tagebuch der Herta Nathorff: Berlin-New York. Aufzeichnungen 1933–1945* (Frankfurt: Fischer, 1988). Nathorff often complained about the difficulties involved in emigrating to the U.S. and the demoralizing treatment and hour-long lines at the American Consulate in Berlin.
40. Schütt, *Chronik 1933*, 135; Michael Grüttner, *Studenten im Dritten Reich* (Paderborn: Schöningh, 1995), 108–109.

assaults. On 8 March 1933, for example, the Swiss citizen Willy Guggenheim was badly mauled by SA men in a Jewish-owned restaurant in Magdeburg, even though he had identified himself as a Swiss citizen.[41] A group of Italians was abused and injured in the same SA attack.[42] In his official complaint the head of the Swiss legation pointed out that 140,000 Germans currently lived in Switzerland and that "public opinion in the Swiss Confederation would demand reprisals against these Germans if Swiss citizens came to harm in Germany."[43] One would have thought that arguments like these were another reason for German authorities to pursue investigations into attacks on foreign Jews more aggressively and to do everything possible to stop them.

The Diplomatic Mission of the Netherlands also issued formal complaints because of attacks on several Dutch Jews who lived in Berlin and who had been threatened or forced to close their shops, as happened on 9 March in the case of Max Franken, a fur dealer in Berlin-Charlottenburg. The riot squad that had been called in declared that nothing could be done to protect him. In the case of the Dutch citizen Siegfried Cohen, who notified the police after having been attacked, uniformed men surrounded his shop and prevented customers from purchasing his products.[44] Further complaints by Dutch diplomats with regard to assaults in Hanover and Stuttgart followed in the second half of March.[45]

Officials' complaints addressed to Foreign Minister Konstantin von Neurath make it clear that not only foreign Jews but occasionally people who simply "looked foreign" became targets of SA attacks. This explains the attack on two Indians, Messrs. Naidu and Nambiar (both British citizens), who were taken to an SA barracks at the end of February and, according to the British Embassy, "savagely thrashed." Both were then

---

41. 10 March 1933 at BA Berlin, R43 II, no. 1195, fol. 69.
42. 11 March 1933 ibid., fols. 76–77. On 9 June 1933 the Foreign Office wrote to the Italian Embassy that the public prosecutor's office had called off the criminal prosecution because the perpetrators could not be identified (11 March 1933, ibid., fol. 79).
43. 10 March 1933 at BA Berlin, R43 II, no. 1195, fol. 70.
44. 10 March 1933 at BA Berlin, R43 II, no. 1195, fols. 74–75.
45. 25 March 1933 at BA Berlin, R43 II, no. 1195, fols. 179–182.

conveyed to the police and released in early March. The British Ambassador, Sir Horace Rumbold, was especially indignant that the police "referred to such an arrest and such treatment merely as a misunderstanding and left it at that without an apology."[46] In an attempt to vindicate the behavior of the SA men, Neurath explained to the Ambassador that at least one of the attacked (Nambiar) was a communist, whose actions were also directed against the British government.[47] In the course of the enormous wave of anti-Jewish violence in March 1933, politically motivated crimes, such as attacks against communists, were thus occasionally mixed in with xenophobic assaults against foreigners or those who "looked foreign," as with the two Indians Naidu and Nambiar. Some attacks were exclusively based on hostility toward foreigners, such as the assault on five Greek students by a group of SA men on 8 March in Fasanenstraße in Berlin-Charlottenburg. The report of the Greek diplomatic mission rendered it abundantly clear that this had not been the only attack on Greek citizens in March 1933.[48]

One prominent example of an attack based on both political and antisemitic motives was the arrest of the well-known journalist Egon Erwin Kisch, generally considered one of the preeminent German-speaking journalists of the twentieth century, who was politically close to the communists. A Czechoslovak citizen from Prague, Kisch had worked in Vienna and Berlin since 1913.[49] On the day after the Reichstag fire, Kisch was arrested and in March deported to Czechoslovakia.[50]

46. 10 March 1933 at BA Berlin, R43 II, no. 1195, fols. 71–72.
47. Ibid., 72. Narayanan Nambiar (1896–1986) was an Indian Nationalist. After the war he served as the Indian diplomatic envoy to West Germany from 1955 to 1958. See Margarete Buber-Neumann, *Von Potsdam bis Moskau* (Stuttgart: DVA, 1958), 107.
48. 15 March 1933 at BA Berlin, R43 II, no. 1195, fols. 111–112.
49. Egon Erwin Kisch (1885–1948) made a name for himself during the Weimar Republic by virtue of his lively reporting and his books *Der rasende Reporter* (1924), *Write that Down, Kisch* (1922 and 1929), and *Tsars, Popes, and Bolsheviks* (1927). The West German magazine *Stern* established the Egon Erwin Kisch Prize in the 1970s for the best German-language reportage. See the collection of Kisch's best stories, *Nichts ist erregender als die Wahrheit*, 2 vols. (Frankfurt: Büchergilde Gutenberg, 1981).
50. 15 March 1933 at BA Berlin, R43 II, no. 1195, fol. 104.

On the day of his arrest, he had the opportunity to observe his jailers in the corridor of the Berlin police presidium at Alexanderplatz:

> The swastika-bedecked new officials...are without exception men with the blunt faces of professional thugs, "*Schläger*" as they are called in their world. To these men, for whom the police count as the epitome of the enemy, their role as policemen is new. How do rogues behave when they are disguised as representatives of State authority?...They make sneering remarks about us, and when they yell at you, they call you "dirty swine," "red pig," and address you with the condescending "Du."[51]

The list of assaults on Czechoslovak citizens is long; most of the victims were Jewish. On 9 March 1933, for example, Albert Deutsch, a Jewish furniture dealer who had lived in Berlin for seven years, was threatened by the SA. The motive was an act of revenge on the part of a less successful competitor—in this case, a non-Jewish furniture dealer who owed money to Deutsch and was then sued by him, whereupon the debtor threatened Deutsch with reprisals by his Nazi friends.[52] The case is reminiscent of Lion Feuchtwanger's novel *Die Geschwister Oppermann*, written in the spring and summer of 1933 and published in the fall of that same year. In it Feuchtwanger describes how the furniture business of Martin Oppermann, owner of the long-established eponymous chain of furniture stores in Berlin, was taken over by his smaller and less successful National Socialist competitor Heinrich Wels with the help of Wels's connections to the NSDAP.[53]

As with the attacks on Polish Jews, assaults on Czechoslovak Jews frequently took place in cafés, as happened to the Czechoslovak national Anatole Friedmann, who was beaten with steel rods by twenty SA men in a cafe in Berlin's Schönhauser Allee and so badly wounded that he had to be conveyed to a hospital. The police station responsible for the

---

51. As opposed to the habitual and more polite form of "you" (*Sie*);" the more informal *Du* used to be reserved for close friends and relatives. Egon Erwin Kisch, "Der Erste Schub," in Kisch, *Nichts erregender*, vol. II, 67–70, esp. 69.
52. 15 March 1933 at BA Berlin, R43 II, no. 1195, fols. 106–107.
53. Leon Feuchtwanger, *The Oppermanns* (New York: Carroll & Graf, 2001).

Friedmann case refused to accept the report of the attack and file charges. Friedmann did not dare go to police headquarters, "since my acquaintances have had the experience that instead of receiving their rights, they received only more beatings by the SA men employed at the police headquarters [as auxiliary police]."[54] Other attacks, such as that on Abraham Spira on Hamburger Straße in the eastern part of Berlin, had the forced closure of shops as their main motive, or, as with the married couple Hermann und Selma Leitner, were followed by abduction to instill fear into victims and their families.[55] Hermann Leitner, for example, was thrashed and abducted to an SA barracks on 11 March. His wife suspected that an act of revenge on the part of their neighbor, the baker Schiff, was behind the attack. Schiff had lost a court case against Leitner, after which he sent a threatening letter to Leitner, which Leitner forwarded to the police on 9 March. The attack and abduction took place two days later.[56]

Acts of personal revenge, some involving an intensely private background, also provide a recurring theme in the official complaints of the Rumanian Diplomatic Mission. In addition to the forced closure of textile and fashion stores, as well as boycott actions, motives for attacks centered on disputes over rental payments and acts of vengeance arising from them.[57] A typical case in point is that of Robert Rubin Oling, who was arrested on 18 March 1933 and dragged to an SA barracks, where castor oil was forced down his throat as he was "invited" to "donate money."[58] The reason for the abduction was that Oling, owner of a tenement house and landlord, had been at loggerheads for some time with two of his tenants, Messrs. Glootz and Uhlig, over issues not uncommon between landlords and tenants.[59] In a lawsuit that had already been settled before 30 January 1933, Glootz had been ordered to

---

54. 15 March 1933 at BA Berlin, R43 II, no. 1195, fol. 107.   55. Ibid., fol. 108.
56. 15 March 1933 at BA Berlin, R43 II, no. 1195, fols. 108–109.
57. 4 April 1933 at SHStA Dresden, Bestand 10717, no. 4858.   58. Ibid.
59. These were mostly petty in nature: Oling accused his tenants of throwing cigar butts out of the window and wasting water; the Glootz family accused the Olings of importing bugs from Galicia.

vacate his apartment. Looking back on this verdict in the autumn of 1933, Saxon Interior Ministry officials conceded that "the court attached greater veracity to the accusations of Oling."[60] Yet, after Hitler had come to power the balance of rights and attitudes, especially the criteria used to determine whose arguments to believe, had dramatically shifted by March 1933. Now Oling, whose critical attitude toward the new regime was well known, was accused of insulting Glootz's son, a member of the NSDAP, as a "Nazi pig," and was taken into "protective custody" from 18 March until 14 April.[61]

Here it becomes clear how much the purely private realm was affected by politics. As was all too common in Nazi Germany, the personal became the political and vice versa, especially if one of the parties concerned was Jewish. According to a statement by Uhlig, a member of the veterans' organization *Stahlhelm* and the second hostile tenant in the above lawsuit, Oling was said to have vilified the national government: "Those pigs will not be at the top for much longer."[62] Even though Oling vehemently (and believably, given the political environment in July 1933) denied having made this comment, he was this time taken into regular police custody from the end of July until 10 August for slander against the regime. Since the Rumanian Consulate had already lodged an official complaint with the German Foreign Ministry in March protesting Oling's first arrest, the Foreign Ministry now turned to the Saxon authorities, demanding an investigation into the specific facts of the case.[63] The five-page report on Oling's case, composed by the Saxon Interior Ministry, which then served as the basis for the report to the German Foreign Ministry, is characterized by blatant one-sidedness and reads like a justification of the attackers.[64] The Saxon authorities also documented that Oling had been questioned, pleaded that the matter be put to rest, and explained that the complaint of the Rumanian Consulate had been

60. 19 October 1933, SHStA Dresden, Bestand 10717, no. 4858.
61. Ibid.   62. Ibid.
63. 23 March 1933 at SHStA Dresden, Bestand 10717, no. 4858.
64. 19 October 1933, ibid.

issued against his will.[65] Apparently intimidated, Oling maintained that "during his time in protective custody he had had no cause for complaint about any mistreatment."[66] But this "co-operative" attitude did not help him. It was the version of events put forward by his tormentors that served as the basis for the Interior Ministry's report, which vindicated their actions against Oling. In his case, the official account of Saxon administrators is representative of the way in which the German authorities dealt with anti-Jewish attacks.

Between the beginning of Hitler's chancellorship on 30 January and the Reichstag Fire Decree on 28 February, SA and SS assaults were directed mainly against political opponents. After that, dams of pent-up hatred against Jews broke, especially since it was now apparent that Jews were no longer in a position to have recourse to the law. In these attacks, which were frequently based on private quarrels—such as disputes over debt, property, or rental payments—the perpetrators could conveniently use National Socialist propaganda as a pretext to make their Jewish victims out to be communists—that is, gravediggers of the established order—child molesters,[67] or seducers and rapists of "German women."[68] These accusations were used as an ideology of self-justification and as pretexts on which crimes were committed. They then served an alibi function and moral justification for the attackers, who sought to protect themselves from the criminal prosecution in case charges were brought against them.[69] The perpetrators could thus present themselves as righteous avengers who simply demanded atonement for "crimes" already committed by those who had allegedly enriched themselves for "fourteen

---

65. 26 May 1933, ibid.   66. 26 May 1933, ibid.
67. On the Bremer case, see also Chapter 6.
68. Such stereotypical accusations were repeated ad nauseam to the readership of *Der Stürmer*. See Roos, *Julius Streicher*. Commenting on the *Stürmer-Kästen*, the showcases in which the paper was displayed, Roos argues that "the mixture of sex and crime, combined with the corresponding drawings and photographs, incited the attention of passers-by, whose interest was stirred by the sensationalist style and presentation and the prurient curiosity in sexually explicit scandal stories" (442–443).
69. On 23 July 1933, a general amnesty for crimes committed during the period of the seizure of power was enacted. See n. 27 above.

whole years" during the Weimar Republic, "on the backs of the German people." In actual reality, those members of Nazi organizations who initiated the attacks were often driven by the wish to rid themselves of irksome competitors by forcibly closing their shops, or to avoid having to repay a debt, or to prevent a threatened eviction or seizure of possessions for failure to pay rent. This could be managed if the owners, creditors, or landlords in question were Jewish, since their private rights had already been eroded both officially and in the public consciousness by March 1933.[70]

70. Bernd Rüthers, *Die unbegrenzte Auslegung. Zum Wandel der Privatrechtsordnung im Nationalsozialismus,* 7th ed. (Tübingen: Mohr Siebeck, 2012).

PART II

VIOLENCE AGAINST GERMAN JEWS

4

VIOLENT ATTACKS

In the winter and spring of 1933, most measures taken against German Jews were motivated by violence. Violence could assume a host of different shapes: in boycotts it played an ancillary role, but it was central in pillory marches, assaults, extortions coupled with robbery, intimidation, abduction into SA torture cellars, and grievous bodily harm and murder. Mistreatment was often followed by pressure to leave one's home town and Germany (underlined by the threat of murder in the case of non-compliance). There had already been some isolated antisemitic attacks in Prussia's eastern provinces and Hesse in February 1933,[1] but it was mostly after the elections of 5 March 1933, once the focus could be shifted away from political opponents, that they became rampant throughout the entire Reich. With few exceptions, the German press remained silent, though the conservative *Deutsche Allgemeine Zeitung* is cited by *The Times* of London as "setting an example of courage and plain speaking" for admitting what was actually going on in Germany and warning that brutal personal acts of revenge must no longer be tolerated:

> Between the lines of this cautious admonition, in which the references to arrest and concealment by private individuals and to blood revenge deserve particular notice, may be read most of that which has been lately whispered in Berlin – a tale of raids, beatings, brutal torment, and killing. Most of this violence has not been the street brawling of former times but

---

1. Longerich, *Bataillone*, 165–179; Bessel, *Political Violence*, 105–109.

Before the Holocaust: Antisemitic Violence and the Reaction of German Elites and Institutions during the Nazi Takeover.
Hermann Beck, Oxford University Press. © Hermann Beck 2022. DOI: 10.1093/oso/9780192865076.003.0005

the killing or injuring of unarmed people by armed people. The whole tale may never be told..."[2]

English newspapers could freely report the actual conditions. On 15 March *The Times* wrote of "unauthorized arrests, unlawful detentions, the maltreatment and sometimes the murder of persons detained." And on 25 March *The Manchester Guardian* summarized the events of the past nine days as follows:

> The anti-Semitic outrages of the last few weeks are far more horrible than could reasonably have been imagined at first.... hundreds of Jews have been beaten, but no one dare say so publicly or dare complain without the risk of another beating.... There is not a word in the press – any newspaper that dare give even a hint of the truth would share the fate of the hundreds of newspapers that have been totally ruined by the terrorist dictatorship.... Jewish shops have been closed and raided, Jewish homes have been searched and thrown into disorder and hundreds of Jews have been beaten and robbed.... The police have either not interfered at all or with deliberate ineffectiveness when these outrages have been committed.[3]

In the United States, every major paper, including *The New York Times, The Wall Street Journal, The Chicago Daily Tribune*, and many others, reported in depth on the antisemitic attacks in Germany.

Antisemitic Violence in the Weimar Republic

There had been violent infringements and attacks against Jews during the Weimar Republic, but the extent of this new type of violence all across the vast geographic expanse of Germany had not been experienced since the Middle Ages. In addition to the more spectacular, almost pogrom-like,

---

2. *The Times*, 13 and 14 March 1933, BayHStA, Hauptabteilung V, Sammlung Varia 231, "Zur Judenfrage:" "The Persecution of the Jews in Germany," fols. 16, 17.
3. Ibid., fols. 18–21. *The Manchester Guardian*'s special correspondent reported on several concrete incidents, albeit without specific dates and locations and, of course, without naming names, since victims might suffer if an account of the events were to be published.

attacks in Berlin's *Scheunenviertel* in November 1923 and the assaults on Berlin's Kurfürstendamm—the *Kurfürstendammkravalle* of 12 September 1931—the Weimar Republic had seen attacks on functionaries of Jewish organizations and prominent Jews in its early phase,[4] as well as desecrations of cemeteries and synagogues, social ostracizing (such as the resort and spa antisemitism that already existed during the Empire), insults, and occasional physical assaults.[5] The main difference between the antisemitic attacks during the Republic and the violence of March 1933 was that the former were prosecuted by the police and the courts and occasionally stiff sentences were handed down, even though there is controversy regarding the effectiveness of prosecution and severity of punishments.[6] The *Centralverein* in particular directed the attention of the authorities to the existence of antisemitic crime and wrote up detailed reports on the development of related incidents and assaults. In October 1928, for example, the *Centralverein* sent a detailed compilation of thirteen cemetery and five synagogue desecrations to the Prussian Interior Minister, emphasizing that all these cases had occurred since its last survey of 30 May 1927. Annotations of the Interior Ministry show that all cases reported in May 1927 were individually prosecuted by the authorities.[7]

Still, one would be wrong to assume that antisemitic hooliganism was a peripheral phenomenon during the Weimar Republic and confined to the years of turmoil and inflation before 1924 and those of the Great

4. On attacks in Berlin's *Scheunenviertel*, see Chapter 1 above. On the *Kurfürstendammkravalle*, see Hecht, *Deutsche Juden*, 236–268; Walter, *Antisemitische Kriminalität*, 211–221, and Andreas Wirsching, *Vom Weltkrieg zum Bürgerkrieg. Politischer Extremismus in Deutschland und Frankreich 1918–1933/39* (Munich: Oldenbourg, 1999), 462–463.
5. Frank Bajohr, *Unser Hotel ist judenfrei, Bäder-Antisemitismus im 19. und 20. Jahrhundert* (Frankfurt: Fischer, 2003); Hecht, *Deutsche Juden*, 119–130, 225–235, 269–331; Walter, *Antisemitische Kriminalität*, 157–176, 186–199.
6. Donald Niewyk, "Jews and the Courts in Weimar Germany," *Jewish Social Studies*, 37 (1975), 99–113; Niewyk, *Jews in Weimar*, 74–78. A more critical attitude is taken by Cyril Levitt, "The Prosecution of Antisemites by the Courts in the Weimar Republic: Was Justice Served?," *Leo Baeck Yearbook*, 36 (1991), 151–167. See also Walter, *Antisemitische Kriminalität*, 139–142; Hecht, *Deutsche Juden*, 368–376.
7. 4 and 31 October 1928 at GStAPK Dahlem, Rep. 77, no. 259, "Antisemitische Ausschreitungen," fols. 24–29. On the activity of the *Centralverein*, see Walter, *Antisemitische Kriminalität*, 192–199; Barkai, "*Wehr Dich!*," 171–190; Paucker, "Abwehrkampf," in Mosse, ed., *Entscheidungsjahr*.

Depression after 1930. It existed as a potential threat even throughout what are often called the "golden years" of Weimar. One example from the small central German state of Thuringia with a population of only 1.489 million (3,603 of whom were Jewish, a miniscule percentage) may suffice to illustrate this.[8] During the first Nazi Party congress after Hitler's release from jail, held in Thuringia's capital, Weimar, in early July 1926, hooliganism and violent denunciations of Jews were rampant, with choruses of marching Nazi gangs shouting, "Throw out the Jew band from our German Fatherland."[9] And in Thuringia's largest city, Erfurt, tombstones in the Jewish cemetery were defiled in March 1926, Jews attending synagogues insulted and attacked in the street, and display windows of Jewish shops and company business plaques of Jewish firms defaced with tar paint.[10]

During the Republic the law exacted justice through court proceedings, even if punishments seemed light by the standards of the time. One example might suffice to illustrate this: during the night of 27/28 December 1931, two well-established Jewish citizens were accosted "in the meanest possible way" by National Socialists in the Rhine-Café in Beuel, a town near Bonn on the right bank of the Rhine. Their protests were met by blows to the face. A plainclothes police officer who happened to be present and wanted to mediate was knocked down as well. The publican was powerless. Only an alerted police patrol succeeded in restoring order, so that the names of the perpetrators could be taken down and charges brought against them. To make matters worse, during that same night the two main offenders, both members of the SA, smashed several windows of Jewish residents in Beuel. The whole incident attracted a great deal of attention well beyond the area of Bonn. A detailed report of the events went from local police authorities to the county government

8. The figures are from 1925; *Statistisches Jahrbuch* (1933), 18.
9. Volker Mauersberger, *Hitler in Weimar* (Berlin: Rowohlt, 1999), 222–234, esp. 227. The original went as follows: "Haut sie heraus, die Judenbande, aus unserem deutschen Vaterlande."
10. Christoph Kreutzmüller and Eckart Schörle, *Stadtluft macht frei? Jüdische Gewerbetreibende in Erfurt 1919–1939* (Berlin: Hentrich, 2013), 17.

in Bonn, from there to the district government in Cologne, then to the provincial government in Düsseldorf, and finally to the Interior Ministry in Berlin.[11] On 30 April 1932, the provincial government reported to Berlin that the two accused SA men had been sentenced to two and a half months in jail for bodily harm, coupled with personal insults.[12] Though in view of what had happened this was a laughably lenient sentence, the police followed procedure to charge the perpetrators, various levels of government followed up on the incident, the SA men were jailed, and the wider public was made aware of the case. What would be legal routine during the Republic would quickly fall by the wayside after 30 January 1933.

During the Republic there also existed parliamentary *Interpellationen*— inquiries in which parliamentary factions of the Nazi party in state parliaments were formally called upon to account for anti-Jewish offenses. These were occasionally instrumentalized by political opponents to discredit the NSDAP and make themselves or their party look good by taking the moral high ground. Yet, even if the motivation of the accusers was self-serving, these interpolations focused the attention of the public on antisemitic attacks.[13] On 29 March 1932, for example, the Prussian *Landtag* deputy Adam Barteld from Hanover, a member of the liberal *Staatspartei* (successor of the DDP) castigated the "desecration of synagogues and cemeteries by members of radical organizations," referring to Nazi actions over the last two years. He emphasized that "through such desecrations against places that decent people would never dare to profane, the reputation of the German State and people also [suffers] severe damage. Such actions by elements imbued with hate disparage Germany as a civilized nation throughout the world."[14] Desecrations of cemeteries and synagogues were not uncommon: between 1923 and 1932

11. 28 December 1931 and 16 January 1932 at GStAPK Dahlem, Rep. 77, no. 259, fols. 179–181.
12. 30 April 1932 at GStAPK Dahlem, Rep. 77, no. 259, fols. 181–181v.
13. On efforts to disclose the danger emanating from National Socialism before 1933, see Klaus Schönhoven and Hans-Jochen Vogel, eds., *Frühe Warnungen vor dem Nationalsozialismus* (Bonn: Dietz, 1998); Wiener, "Die Parteien der Mitte," in Mosse, ed., *Entscheidungsjahr*, 289–321 (here emphasis is placed on how antisemitism was instrumentalized).
14. 29 March 1932 at GStAPK Dahlem, Rep. 77, no. 259, fols. 182–186. Johann Adam Heinrich Barteld, postal employee (*Postamtmann*), member of the Prussian *Landtag* from 1921 to 1932.

there were 127 cases of cemetery and 54 cases of synagogue desecration. In those cases where information was provided on whether or not culprits had been apprehended, the *Aufklärungsquote* (percentage of cases solved) stood at 30 percent.[15] In the more spectacular cases, such as the attempt to blow up the synagogue in Frankfurt's West End in 1924, or the vandalism of the old Israelite cemetery in Erfurt in March 1926, when 95 of 135 tombstones and monuments were overturned or damaged, sentences were stiffer, and the main culprits were sentenced to longer custodial sentences—six years' detention in a state penitentiary in the Frankfurt case.[16] In an age when great respect was accorded to those who had given their lives for their country, when every year new World War I memorials were erected as wreaths were laid at existing ones, and every family mourned relatives and friends who had died in the Great War, Jewish places of commemoration, as all others, commanded respect, and even extreme nationalist and *völkisch* papers did not dare to defend perpetrators.[17]

In this environment, the case of Trebnitz in Lower Silesia attracted the attention of the general public and the authorities alike. As Barteld reported to the Prussian *Landtag*,

In November 1930 thirty-four tombstones in the Jewish cemetery were smeared with swastikas, and the windows of the mortuary were completely smashed. The inner wall of the mortuary was defaced with three

---

15. Walter, *Antisemitische Kriminalität*, 155–165, esp. 164. In 1928, opposition against cemetery and synagogue desecrations emerged across a wide spectrum of society. The national-minded novelist and president of the Prussian Writers Academy (*Dichterakademie*) Walter von Molo called them "the most un-German, un-Christian, crudest, most contemptible and cowardly" phenomenon of the present day. Prominent politicians, such as the Reich Minister of Justice Erich Koch-Weser, and scholars, such as the Protestant theologian Adolf von Harnack, joined the protest movement; the number of cemetery defilements fell to six cases in 1929. Hecht, *Deutsche Juden*, 225–235.

16. Walter, *Antisemitische Kriminalität*, 158–160; Marion Neiss, "Diffamierung mit Tradition – Friedhofsschändungen," in Wolfgang Benz, ed., *Antisemitismus in Deutschland. Zur Aktualität eines Vorurteils* (Munich: DTV, 1995), 140–155.

17. In 1928, as disapprobation of cemetery defilements reached a high point, Goebbels's *Der Angriff* published a ditty: "We're the last ones to defend, opponents in graves to still offend" ["Wir sind die letzten, die es verteidigen, Gegner im Grabe noch zu beleidigen"]. As witness in a court case in December 1929, Hitler also tried to distance himself from "crimes of brutality such as cemetery desecrations." See Walter, *Antisemitische Kriminalität*, 162, 300; Hecht, *Deutsche Juden*, 232.

red swastikas that carried the inscription: "Heil Hitler, Juda Verrecke!" In the center a gallows was drawn from which hung a Jewish figure.[18]

Suspicion immediately fell on members of the NSDAP. Yet the party not only vehemently denied having been involved but even published a notice in the local *Trebnitzer Anzeiger*: "The National Socialist Workers Party does not tolerate defilers of monuments in its midst. Therefore, the party will pay a reward of 50 RM to anyone who will name the scrawlers who misused the swastika for their nefarious actions in a Jewish cemetery so that they can be properly punished."[19] Shortly after the publication of this notice, two members of the NSDAP were arrested; they soon confessed. Trebnitz quickly attracted the attention of the Berlin papers, and the *Reichsbanner* held a public protest meeting against the cemetery defilements in the Trebnitz concert hall, in which a resolution was passed that was reprinted in the local Republican press and in the prominent democratic papers of the capital, such as the *Vossische Zeitung* and the *Berliner Tageblatt*.[20] In the notice, the NSDAP was accused of "a great number of similar crimes," and it was affirmed, "No other country knows similar deeds. Germany's name and its reputation throughout the world are disgraced by them." At the meeting demands were raised that "the governments of Reich and *Länder* intervene with all lawful means against the political agitation and calculated indoctrination that gives rise to such deeds."[21] After 5 March 1933 the time for declarations of solidarity with the victims had passed. Members of the Republican *Reichsbanner* who had initiated the protest meeting in Trebnitz had now themselves become the persecuted.[22] And the attention of the perpetrators now shifted from the dead to the living.

18. 29 March 1932 at GStAPK Dahlem, Rep. 77, no. 259, fol. 183. Trebnitz, town in Silesia with 9,000 inhabitants (1933); *Der Neue Brockhaus*, vol. IV (Leipzig: Brockhaus, 1938), 462.
19. *Berliner Volks-Zeitung*, 18 November 1930, at GStAPK Dahlem, Rep. 77, no. 259, fols. 194, 191.
20. 28 November 1930 at GStAPK Dahlem, Rep. 77, no. 259, fol. 197.
21. GStAPK Dahlem, Rep. 77, no. 259, fol. 199.
22. Founded in 1924 by members of the SPD, DDP, and Center Party, the *Reichsbanner Black-Red-Gold* was an association for the defense of the Republic with about 3.5 million members in 1932. Its paramilitary formations had about 400,000 members. The *Reichsbanner* dissolved itself in March 1933. See Karl Rohe, *Das Reichsbanner Schwarz-Rot-Gold* (Düsseldorf: Droste,

Documentary Evidence for Crimes against Jews

The *Times* correspondent who commented upon the anti-Jewish violence with the words, "The whole story may never be told," had good reason to be skeptical. The documentation of crimes against Jews in the winter and spring of 1933 is indeed unsatisfactory, since offenses went unrecorded for the most part in the heated atmosphere of the national revolution, especially since the position of the NSDAP in the coalition had become all-domineering after 5 March (with the increasing eclipse of the NSDAP's conservative coalition partner an accomplished fact by mid-May, Nazi leaders then used the term "German revolution" or "National Socialist revolution").[23] Attacks against foreign Jews are better documented than those against German citizens, since the former were recorded by foreign consulates and embassies and then passed on to German authorities, the Reich Interior Ministry, or the interior ministries of the different German states. In the case of attacks against foreign Jews, *raison d'état* alone mandated a greater effort to solve the case and stop further encroachments, in order to avoid unwelcome foreign-policy interventions.

When it comes to attacks on German Jews, accident and chance determine the extent of specific documentation and what the researcher is likely to find. Some victims close to the Reich Association of Jewish Frontline Soldiers or the DNVP turned to the latter in the (mostly vain) hope that help might be forthcoming from the NSDAP's coalition partner.[24] Descriptions of another group of violent attacks, albeit watered down by bureaucratic formalities and the decades that had

---

1966); Roger Chickering, "The Reichsbanner and the Weimar Republic, 1924–1926," *Journal of Modern History*, 40:4 (December 1968), 524–534.

23. BA Berlin, R43 II, no. 1195, Akten der Reichskanzlei, NSDAP, "Dr. Goebbels über den Stand der deutschen Revolution," fols. 327–333.
24. BA Berlin, R 8005, nos. 19, 44, and 48. Hermann Beck, "Between the Dictates of Conscience and Political Expediency: Hitler's Conservative Alliance Partner and Antisemitism during the Nazi Seizure of Power," *Journal of Contemporary History*, 41 (2006), 611–640; Beck, *Fateful Alliance*, 174–218.

passed between 1933 and the 1950s, can be found in the "compensation" files of survivors, who submitted claims for injustices suffered after the passing of the Federal Compensation Law (*Bundesentschädigungsgesetz*) in 1953. Here victims recounted the crimes that had been perpetrated against them.[25] Files documenting further anti-Jewish crimes are to be found in some of the court documents of the immediate post-war period—in the holdings of the Supreme Court for the British Zone (1945–9), for example, or in the court documents of West German legal proceedings after 1949.[26] Also revealing are some of the cases dealt with by the so-called *Sondergerichte* (special courts) that were in charge of sentences pertaining to the *Heimtückeverordnung* (Perfidy Ordinance).[27] Records and testimonies relating to violent crimes and murder can also be found in various state archives and in the holdings of the Reich Chancellery in the federal archives, now housed in Berlin-Lichterfelde.[28] In addition, the files of the Prussian Ministry of Justice in Berlin-Dahlem offer some case materials on legal proceedings dealing with attacks against Jews that had been initiated in 1933.[29]

25. See the compensation claims documents in the Hessisches Hauptstaatsarchiv Wiesbaden (HHStA Wiesbaden), Abt. 518. On compensation claims, see Hans-Ulrich Wehler, *Deutsche Gesellschaftsgeschichte*, vol. V (Munich: Beck, 2008), 253–257; Hans Günter Hockerts, "Wiedergutmachung in Deutschland. Eine historische Bilanz 1945–2000," *VJHZ* 49 (2001): 167–214; and Hans Günter Hockerts and Christiane Kuller, eds., *Nach der Verfolgung. Wiedergutmachung nationalsozialistischen Unrechts in Deutschland* (Göttingen: Wallstein, 2003).

26. BA Koblenz, Z 38, "Oberster Gerichtshof für die Britische Zone." For other court documents, see the files of the State Prosecutors' offices at the Landesarchiv Nordrhein-Westfalen (formerly Hauptstaatsarchiv Düsseldorf), Staatsanwaltschaft Düsseldorf, Rep. 372; Kleve, Rep. 224; Cologne, Rep. 231; Krefeld, Rep. 08, as well as the files of the Landesarchiv Schleswig-Holstein in Schleswig for the Staatsanwaltschaft Kiel, Abt. 352.3 and Staatsanwaltschaft Lübeck, Abt. 352.4.

27. See, for example, Landesarchiv Baden-Württemberg (formerly Generallandesarchiv) in Karlsruhe, Bestand 507, Sondergericht Mannheim; and Hessisches Hauptstaatsarchiv Wiesbaden, Abt. 462, Sondergericht Frankfurt.

28. In the Hessisches Hauptstaatsarchiv in Wiesbaden, the Landesarchiv Schleswig-Holstein in Schleswig, the Landesarchiv Baden-Württemberg in Karlsruhe, the Sächsisches Hauptstaatsarchiv in Dresden, and the Bundesarchiv in Berlin-Lichterfelde.

29. GStAPK Dahlem, Preußisches Justizministerium, Rep. 84a. Due to the amnesty for crimes committed during the "National Socialist revolution," none of the accused were convicted, even though in several cases there was overwhelming evidence that the accused were guilty. Numerous investigative records survived the Third Reich.

One set of documents in the Prussian state archives in Dahlem provides a clear impression of the extent of anti-Jewish violence and its geographic diffusion. (For locations and intensity of forcible expulsions and attacks against German Jews, see map on page 44). This *Aktenbestand* logs the registration of antisemitic incidents unedited, in telegram style and without mentioning full names. Quite obviously this set of files was meant for destruction and survived only because of the disobedience of an archival administrator.[30] Yet these files, too, offer only a part of the whole story, since many other attacks that occurred on the dates mentioned were not reported in them; the incidents below focus on East and West Prussia, Silesia, Brandenburg, Berlin, and parts of Hesse. Still, this partial record provides an instructive and not entirely random sample of what actually occurred with respect to the density of antisemitic attacks in the 48-hour period between the nights of 12/13 March and 14/15 March 1933, that is, after Hitler's forceful pleas to his followers to immediately put a stop to individual actions.[31] The detached and matter-of-fact language of the documentation softens a more brutal reality:

"During the night of 12–13 March, the Jewish Doctor L. in Elbing was taken away from his apartment by uniformed SA men. Barefoot and in his shirt, he had to follow the SA men to a car waiting outside his door. While boarding the car and during the ride he was mistreated. Through the intervention of a National Socialist doctor, who was asked for help by Doctor L.'s wife, it was possible to free Doctor L. from the office of the National Socialist Party in Elbing, to where he had been carried off."[32]

30. GStAPK Dahlem, I.H.A. Rep. 90P, no. 71, Heft 2, "Ausschreitungen März 1933." In the introduction to the file it is recorded that "the...collated documents were given to me today by Herr ORR [*Oberregierungsrat*] Flothow, to whom they had been handed by Undersecretary of State Landfried with instructions not to enter them into the official record and also not to include them in the documents. Berlin, 25 April 1935, signed: Schröder, Amtsrat. These documents were thus not meant to be preserved.
31. BA Berlin, R43 II, no. 1195, "Reichskanzlei, NSDAP," "Ermahnungen des Reichskanzlers," fols. 61–62 (Hitler's appeal to the SA and SS of 11 March 1933).
32. GStAPK Dahlem, I.H.A. Rep. 90P, no. 71, Heft 2, "Ausschreitungen März 1933," fol. 34. (Following notes 33–42 are from the same source.)

"During the night of 12–13 March, the Jewish Mr. K. was assaulted near the Gesundbrunnen Station [in Berlin] by four to six men who pounced on him with shouts of 'Heil Hitler' and maltreated him severely. According to the hospital doctor, K. has suffered a severe concussion. K.'s statement, which confirms the diagnosis, is as follows: 'I dragged myself along this unknown street until I saw the light of a first aid station. Then I heard that I was in a hospital."[33]

"During the night of 12–13 March, the Jewish brothers S. in Langen (Hesse) were seized by SA men from their second-floor apartment. The SA men had used a ladder for the purpose. The brothers S. were forced at gunpoint to accompany them to the city hall. There they were received by a uniformed SA-patrol, ten strong, who fell upon them without a word. They were so badly beaten that they were unable to move.... Both are now in the local hospital with severe injuries."[34]

"On 13 March 1933 the Jewish Mr. L. was beaten by an auxiliary policeman with a rubber truncheon in a café in Hindenburg without any reason."[35]

"On 13 March 1933 the Jewish merchants B. in Marienburg/West Prussia were carted off to the camp in the supply barracks. There they were held for two days and one night and were released only after the payment of a ransom."[36]

"Also, on 13 March 1933 in Marienburg/West Prussia the Jewish livestock dealer N. was abducted by the SA into the cellar of the bookstore vendor G., where he was so badly tortured that the doctor determined that he had third-degree burns."[37]

"On 13 March 1933, the Jewish merchant Y. in Königsberg/Prussia was forcibly hauled out of bed and brought to the SA post with his two sons. Y. and his two sons were badly mauled and roughed up, forced

33. Ibid., fol. 35. Elbing, town in East Prussia, pop. 68,206 (1925); *Statistisches Jahrbuch* (1933), 11.
34. Ibid., fol. 36. Langen, town in Hesse, pop. 8,900 (1933); *Neuer Brockhaus*, vol. III, 30.
35. Ibid., fol. 27. Hindenburg in Silesia, pop. 122,671 (1925); *Statistisches Jahrbuch* (1933), 12.
36. Ibid., fol. 38. Marienburg, in West Prussia, pop. 21,039 (1925); *Statistisches Jahrbuch* (1933), 12.
37. Ibid., fol. 37.

through a cargo door into a separate room, and there again beaten with rubber truncheons. As Y. fainted due to the abuse, he was forced to drink castor oil. The trousers of one of his sons, who had also been forced to drink castor oil, were tied up. All three had to march and practice military drills together with the other kidnapped members of the bourgeoisie. Intermittently the captives were beaten with rubber truncheons and badly battered. When Y. asked for the reason of his arrest, he received the answer that this was because of an order from the *Gauleitung*. Y. has died in hospital in the meantime."[38]

"The son G. of Mr. Y. who was also kidnapped in Königsberg, confirms his father's statements and added that all captives had their hair cut, that they were later beaten with truncheons, blackjacks, and rifle butts, and that SA men forced them to sing a song with the text, 'In the synagogue there hangs a big black pig.'"[39]

"On 13 March 1933 the two Jewish brothers G., Berlin, one of whom served on the front [in World War I] were assaulted in their apartment by five men in SA uniform, one of whom wore the insignia of an SA leader, beaten, and kicked. They were then forced to carry their three typewriters to the apartment of a former client (the two gentlemen have a legal office), where they had to declare in writing that they owed this client 500 RM and that they would leave the typewriters as security until the debt was liquidated. In a second declaration, which they also had to sign, it was stated that the typewriters and the signature under the promissory note had been given voluntarily."[40]

"On 13 March 1933 in Königsberg/Prussia, the Jewish baker and master craftsman X. (frontline soldier and holder of the Iron Cross) on whose shop an incendiary bomb attack had already been made on 9 March, was carried off by eight SA men to the SA station, ... and badly abused and brutalized. While being continually beaten, he had to completely undress and then run the gauntlet through rows of SA

---

38. Ibid., fol. 40. Königsberg, city in East Prussia, pop. 287,312 (1925); *Statistisches Jahrbuch* (1933), 12.
39. Ibid., fol. 39.   40. Ibid., fol. 42.

men; following this he was forced through a narrow door into a windowless dungeon and there incessantly maltreated. He received stab wounds on his legs and shoulder, severe wounds on the head with a pointed object, his hair was plucked out, he had to wipe his shoes with his own blood, and he was then put up against the wall and threatened with execution. He was also forced to sing the song, 'When Jew blood spurts from the knife.' On the morning after his release, two SA men appeared at Mr. X.'s door and threatened to kill him if he notified the police."[41]

"On 13 March 1933 about thirty SA men forced their way into the houses of fourteen Jewish families in Gedern, including that of an 80-year-old gentleman, mistreated the male family members, stole from them a gold watch and a wallet with money in it, and extorted a receipt for two unpaid bills from others. Apart from wounds from blows, two of the victims had stab wounds."[42]

"On 14 March 1933 the apartment of the Jewish couple H. in Hindenburg was searched, during the course of which the search party made off with a gold and silver watch, an alarm clock, and a sum of money."[43]

"On 14 March 1933 the Jewish merchant E., Luckenwalde, on his way home from concluding a business deal, was attacked in the hall of his home and badly wounded by stabbings with a knife. This had been preceded by significant unrest on the occasion of the closing of Jewish shops in Luckenwalde."[44]

"On 14 March 1933, the Jewish businessman M., Berlin, Neue Friedrich Straße, was taken from his business together with his Jewish partner and a Jewish employee by several persons in SA uniform, brought to the SA barracks... and there mistreated. He was forced to

41. Ibid., fol. 41.
42. Ibid., fol. 43. Gedern, a small town in Upper Hesse, pop. 1,700 (1900); *Meyers Großes Konversations-Lexikon*, 6th ed., vol. 7 (Leipzig: Bibliographisches Institut, 1904), 427.
43. GStAPK, I.H.A. Rep. 90P, no. 71, Heft 2, "Ausschreitungen März 1933," fol. 28. (Following notes 44–48 are from the same source.)
44. Ibid., fol. 25. Luckenwalde in Brandenburg, pop. 24,796 (1925); *Statistisches Jahrbuch* (1933), 12.

partially undress, then he was beaten with a rubber truncheon and forced to sing the Horst Wessel song."[45]

"On 14 March 1933 the Jewish Mr. S., Berlin, Andreasstraße, was arrested by SA men. His brother, who inquired at an SA station for his whereabouts, was also detained. Both brothers were so badly mauled and mistreated that they had to be taken to the Berlin-Friedrichshain hospital. The one arrested first suffered a severe concussion. He has to be fed artificially."[46]

"During the night of 14–15 March, the shoemaker S. in Alsfeld (Hesse) was taken from his apartment and badly beaten up."[47]

"During the night from the 14th to the 15th of March, also in Alsfeld, the Jewish Mr. S. was attacked in the street and beaten raw."[48]

These incidents constitute merely a segment—we will never exactly know how large or small—of the entire sum of antisemitic attacks during this forty-eight-hour period. They not only prove the utter ineffectiveness of Hitler's exhortations to maintain order and discontinue "individual actions" but also show that Jews had become fair game by mid-March 1933.[49] There were no sanctuaries left; no place was "off limits." Groups of SA men freely broke into homes to carry off victims, and subsequent savage beatings could and occasionally did lead to death. It was also clearly an objective of the perpetrators to inflict humiliations beyond physical suffering, and in the case of small towns, such as Gedern in Hesse, the entire resident Jewish population might as well have been afflicted by a modern form of the plague, which devastated everything in its path. Still, reality was more multifarious, nuanced, and in the end

45. Ibid., fol. 24.   46. Ibid., fol. 19.
47. Ibid., fol. 44. Alsfeld, town in Hesse, pop. 6000 (1933); *Neuer Brockhaus*, vol. I, 67.
48. Ibid., fol. 45.
49. David Bankier overestimates the effect of Hitler's appeal. Richard Evans argues that "Hitler's intervention only caused a temporary let-up in the sequence of violent incidents, and altogether failed to halt them completely," while Bankier assumes that after Hitler's appeal they diminished in intensity for good. Evans, *Coming of the Third Reich*, 433; David Bankier, *The Germans and the Final Solution. Public Opinion Under Nazism* (Oxford: Blackwell, 1992), 67.

more cruel than this listing can convey, based on information that a few Prussian officials could get their hands on in March 1933. Some of the more specific archival dossiers permit further and more detailed glimpses into the perplexity and forlornness of the Jewish population, the specific causes of the attacks, the reactions of the judicial bureaucracy to the violent assaults, and, perhaps most disturbing of all, the motivation of the perpetrators—for whom material enrichment, personal revenge, and a perverted desire to inflict suffering were often wellsprings of their actions.[50]

In addition to beatings, grievous bodily harm, and murder, the hatred and destructive frenzy of perpetrators were occasionally reflected in vandalism and veritable orgies of destruction. Both the sheer pleasure of destroying and distinct social envy appear to be dominant motivating factors. A case in point is the wanton act in May 1933 of four SS men who forced their way into the empty Kiel villa of the Jewish physician Dr. Steilberger at night and, in a whipped-up rage of destruction, smashed the glassed-in porch, ripped window panes complete with their frames out of their moorings, tore off part of the roof, knocked over the chimney, and destroyed the doors. According to the police report, "Everything that had not been nailed down was demolished."[51] The offenders had been so absorbed by their demolition of the villa that they took scant notice of having hurt themselves when breaking the windows and the fence, so that they could easily be identified by the trail of blood left in their wake. When charges were filed against them in 1933, they had to clear away most of the damage themselves; sentencing, however, had to wait until after the war in 1949.[52] Of the four perpetrators, three received prison sentences of five, four, and three months

---

50. Bruce B. Campbell, "The SA in the *Gleichschaltung*: The Context of Pressure and Violence," in Hermann Beck and Larry E. Jones, eds., *From Weimar to Hitler. Studies in the Dissolution of the Weimar Republic and the Establishment of the Third Reich, 1932–1934* (New York: Berghahn, 2019), 194–221. For information on the reaction of the judicial bureaucracy to violent assaults and the motivation of the perpetrators, see Chapter 13 below.

51. LASH, Staatsanwaltschaft Kiel, Abt. 352.3, no. 2689, "Zerstörung des Hauses des jüdischen Arztes Dr. Steilberger im Mai 1933," esp. fols. 3, 8.

52. LASH, Staatsanwaltschaft Kiel, Abt. 352.3, no. 2689. The case was reopened after the war.

respectively; the fourth suspect was released. The prison time of all three SS men was considered to have been served due to their internment in Allied camps.

Forcible Expulsion through Violence and Threats

Attacks on German Jews with the express purpose of expelling them from Germany were widespread in the spring of 1933. In some cases, purely personal motives, such as revenge, played the main role. Victims were assaulted, often in their homes, and then abducted to SA torture cellars, where they were mauled and brutalized. They were beaten half-dead and let go again with the proviso that they leave Germany immediately or else be killed. After what they had suffered already, murder was a believable threat, especially since rumors abounded that there had been numerous killings of German Jews in the spring and summer of 1933.[53] Detailed reports with concrete facts about the course of these attacks are rare, since victims often had to leave Germany from one day to the next, and were naturally reluctant to notify authorities or turn to them for help. After all, in most cases they had been threatened by quasi-State organs—members of the SA or SS in the uniform of auxiliary policemen—and warned not to turn to the regular police. Adding to the absence of any recourse for relief, the state apparatus in the different German *Länder* and municipalities was becoming increasingly infiltrated by members of the NSDAP and its organizations. Between February and the summer of 1933, the posts of mayors, police presidents, leaders of interest groups, artisan guilds, and professional organizations, as well as leading positions in the bureaucracy, such as county counselors, district presidents, and provincial governors, were taken over by Nazi Party members, so that there were no public authorities left to which one

---

53. See Chapter 6, below, on "Murder."

could turn for help.[54] With hostile officials acting more in accordance with what they perceived as the demands of the new regime than Weimar legal norms, most of the victims disappeared so quickly that they left hardly any trace, as has been amply documented in post-war compensation files.[55]

An appalling and yet typical case is that of the neurologist Dr. Fritz Fränkel, born in 1892 in Berlin, who was arrested in his practice on 21 March by a gang of SA men, abducted, and badly maltreated. On 23 March he was released "through the personal intervention of National Socialists known to him and upon the recommendation of the political police," after having to sign a statement that he would leave Germany immediately and for good. With his wife and 2-year-old child, he fled to Switzerland after hurriedly dismissing his secretary and a servant girl. From there he conveyed a report to the German Diplomatic Mission in Bern that recounted his fate.[56] Fränkel, who was awarded the Iron Cross First Class after serving two years as an army physician at the front in World War I, established a neurology practice in Berlin in 1925. He was arrested because he had been denounced. The charges against him were that he had worked for free for the International Workers Aid Society and that he had applied "psychoanalytic methods" in his work. After his

---

54. With the *Gleichschaltung* (coordination) of the *Länder*—that is, the capture of power by the NSDAP in those German states that had hitherto not been governed by the NSDAP (Hamburg, Bremen, Lübeck, Hesse-Darmstadt, Saxony, Württemberg, Baden, and Bavaria)—formerly democratic administrators were dismissed and replaced by Nazi Party members or by known nationalists. In Prussia, the removal of administrators faithful to the Republic had begun after the *Preußenschlag* of 20 July 1932. See Bracher, Sauer, Schulz, *Nationalsozialistische Machtergreifung*, 2nd ed., 413–509; Broszat, *Staat Hitlers*, 82–173.

55. HHStA Wiesbaden, Abt. 518. The cases discussed below are from the spring of 1933. The behavior of officials is well captured in Ian Kershaw's concept of "Working Towards the Führer;" see his *Hitler 1889–1936. Hubris* (London and New York: Norton, 1999), 527–591.

56. 28 March 1933 at BA Berlin R43 II, no. 603, fols. 214–219. The letter of the German Consulate in Bern to the Foreign Office in Berlin, to which Fränkel's report was attached, emphasizes that the Consulate obtained Fränkel's report through the foreign editor of the conservative (and German-friendly) *Berner Tageblatt*. Everything had been done to keep Fränkel's report secret, but the Consulate wanted the Foreign Office to verify the details. Because the torture he had endured had physically handicapped him, and given that foreign exchange rules allowed him to take only 200 Reichsmarks per person across the border, Fränkel's search for work ran into serious difficulties, making his financial situation in Switzerland especially precarious.

practice was searched, he was carried off to one of the SA headquarters in Berlin—the barracks in General-Pape-Straße in Schöneberg. What he experienced there was not untypical for the fate of many. In Fränkel's own words,

> Here the mistreatment was repeated in the cruelest fashion. I was strapped on a wooden bench and my naked back was so badly beaten that the shirt later stuck to it. Then, as with other prisoners, my suit and coat were taken away. I had to put on a dirty jacket and torn pair of pants (statement of an SA guard: "we have cleaned the john with it") and was quartered in a cellar with about twenty-five other prisoners. We all suffered from the cold. Since the two beds were reserved for the gravely injured, I had to lie on the stone floor. Mistreatment and abuse went on the whole night. While I had to examine another doctor who had almost been beaten to death (Dr. Philippsohn from Biersdorf near Berlin), someone poured a bucket of water over my head. Then the seriously injured doctor got another bucket. I was incessantly exposed to invective and indignities, for example, I constantly had to declare: "I am a stinking Jew." Apart from my personal suffering, it was hard for me that I had to witness the continued maltreatment of other people [who were] unknown to me. One prisoner had the skin under his soles burned off by fire, first with a cigarette, then with matches, then with a paper torch (sole and between the toes). Then he was pressed into a kind of closet, in which he almost suffocated. The doctor I mentioned earlier had to chew on sweaty socks. During the shrieks of the tortured, people sang and played the accordion on the first floor.[57]

It was hardly surprising that Dr. Fränkel left Germany as soon as possible after being subjected to and having to witness such treatment. This kind of expulsion from the country in which Fränkel and others had lived for generations was a mass phenomenon, as is shown by the Hessian compensation files.[58] To be eligible for compensation payments, each applicant's case was minutely examined, and documents had to be furnished to prove persecution in every individual instance. The fate of

---

57. 28 March 1933 at BA Berlin, R43 II, no. 603, fol. 217.
58. Of the approximately 110,000 compensation claim files in the HHStA Wiesbaden, about 6,000 were intensively evaluated (1989–96) in the course of a research project on "Widerstand und Verfolgung unter dem Nationalsozialismus in Hessen," making possible a thorough, full-text search for specific details. Several of these cases that focus on crimes in the spring of 1933 are referred to here.

the respective applicants and the motives that induced them to flee the country are frequently revealed in the biographical narratives included in the applications. The following cases focus on physical attacks, comparable to those on Fränkel: threats of murder and the well-grounded fear of being earmarked for assassination that prompted victims to flee Germany. Some of the victims were known and hated by the local SA, or they were members of the Republican *Reichsbanner Schwarz-Rot-Gold*, or the SPD, which also marked them for attack.

A few brief examples will suffice to illustrate the extent of expulsions of Jewish Germans. The merchant's apprentice Joseph Aron, member of the *Reichsbanner*, received a series of threatening letters after 23 March, demanding that he leave Germany. Several attacks by members of the SA followed in April, so that Aron saw no alternative but to leave his country in May 1933.[59] Norbert Weil, SPD member from northern Hesse, was assaulted by a gang of SS men, threatened with execution, imprisoned in a cellar and physically abused, finally driven into a forest, and there again threatened with hanging. He had barely recovered from his wounds when he was again arrested and committed to the Breitenau concentration camp near Kassel. Upon his release he immediately fled Germany.[60] Karl Bender left Germany in May 1933, since his father had been sentenced by a special court in Darmstadt to a three-month prison term, while he himself was threatened to be packed off to a concentration camp.[61] The 52-year-old Baruch Steinlauf operated a shop in Wiesbaden that specialized in gold and silver wares. According to his own testimony, he was forced to leave Germany in April 1933:

> In April 1933 my son Sidney knocked down an SA man who wanted to force his way into our shop with two other blokes. Connected to this

59. HHStA Wiesbaden, Apt. 518, no. 33295; Joseph Aron was born on 13 May 1914 in Frankfurt.
60. HHStA Wiesbaden, Apt. 518, no. 3542; Norbert Weil was born on 25 January 1904 in Schenklengsfeld-Hesse.
61. HHStA Wiesbaden, Apt. 518, no. 3112; Karl Bender was born on 30 December 1908 in Seligenstadt in Hesse. Bender declared that his parents, August and Amalie Bender, had been missing without trace since the Nazi period.

event, I was told that I should disappear from Germany right away, unless I wanted to risk life and limb. I thereupon fled Germany and had to leave my thriving business behind."[62]

Ludwig Wolfgang Schwarzschild was attacked and badly beaten up on 10 March 1933 by a group of fifteen SS members, led by SS man Moeller, whom Schwarzschild knew well. After the attack, he had repeated bouts of head and back pain, dizziness, sleeplessness, and anxiety attacks. According to this testimony, the SS gang had beaten him almost to death:

> The SS men beat me with their truncheons for about five minutes, mostly on the head, and were intent on clubbing me to death. Even after I stopped whimpering and felt at the end of my strength, they continued beating me, then ran off and left me to my fate. When I came to after some time and was brought home, the perpetrators stood about in the street laughing and gesticulating.[63]

Due to a well-grounded fear of further persecution, Schwarzschild escaped with his family to Austria that same month.

Jakob Stein, the owner of a furrier's shop, was already besieged in his house by the SA on the eve of the 5 March elections. He called out to his persecutors through a closed door that he was armed, but knew quite well that they would return the next day and that his life was in danger. On the morning of 6 March, he therefore fled Germany and went to France.[64]

In the spring of 1933, Dutch, Belgian, French, Czechoslovak, and Swiss authorities reported a stream of thousands of Jewish refugees. We shall never know how many hundreds or thousands were forced out of Germany for these or similar reasons. That the number must have been

---

62. HHStA Wiesbaden, Apt. 518, no. 896; Baruch Steinlauf was born on 11 August 1880. The facts of this case were confirmed by other witness statements in the files.
63. HHStA Wiesbaden, Apt. 518, no. 5165; Ludwig Wolfgang Schwarzschild, born on 23 December 1900 in Hamburg, stated that he was in a physician's care since this attack and unable to hold down a regular job.
64. HHStA Wiesbaden, Section 518, no. 5578; Jakob Stein was born on 6 July 1896 in Kirchheim (Palatinate) in Bavaria.

high is documented by the fact that contemporary diaries mention similar incidents and motivations for precipitous and hasty departures from Germany. A case in point is that of the son of the Breslau *Gymnasium* teacher Willy Cohn, who had to flee to Paris in April 1933. He felt he had no choice, since he had received credible threats of murder after a National Socialist student had to leave the *Gymnasium* because of him.[65] Of the thousands of refugees who fled to neighboring countries, many had to leave because their lives were in immediate danger. They had no chance to remain, or even to emigrate in a regular fashion.

Apart from direct violent attacks, a lawsuit coupled with good relations between the victim's opponent and the SA could also ruin a middle-class existence and turn people into homeless refugees overnight. This was the fate suffered by Ignaz Merker. What befell Merker has been passed down to posterity in detail, since he was still a Polish citizen even though he had lived in Germany since 1915, so that his case was also taken up by the Polish Consulate in Essen. To avoid foreign-policy complications, German authorities pretended to take part in bringing the culprits to justice, though with a pointed lack of success. Merker, born in Warsaw in 1894, owner of a lingerie shop in Cologne, was attacked by a gang of ten SA men in his shop on 1 July 1933, then forcibly abducted, first to an SA barracks in Cologne, then to the SA hostel Schloss Jägerhof in Düsseldorf, and there most brutally maltreated. He was beaten with leather whips and rubber truncheons until he fainted. During his three days of torture, ether was forced down his throat, so that he was unable to swallow for days afterwards.[66] Grievously wounded, Merker was consigned to a Cologne hospital. The attending physician at the St. Vincenz Hospital wrote the following report about Merker's condition on 7 July:

---

65. Willy Cohn, *Kein Recht-Nirgends. Breslauer Tagebücher* (Cologne: Böhlau, 2008), 11–13.
66. 6 July 1933, 7 July 1933 at GStAPK Dahlem, Rep. 84a/54847, 2–5; 6, "Wegen Verschleppung und Mißhandlung des jüdischen Kaufmanns Ignaz Merker in Köln 1933."

Big broad-shouldered man, now completely exhausted and broken. The slightest touch causes him enormous pain. The parts around the eyes, especially the right side of his forehead...are discolored blue.... The whole back, especially the shoulders, is much swollen with deep blue discolorations.... Both arms are suffused with blood and swollen from the shoulder joints to the tips of the fingers, so that he can barely move them. In almost its entire extension, the chest is discolored blue and yellow.[67]

According to the report of the Cologne state police of 6 July 1933, Merker should have "[remained] in hospital two to three months to recover his health as directed by the physician," but he felt it safer to leave Germany in the second half of July, long before his full recovery.[68] At the behest of the Polish Consulate in Essen, the German authorities began to search for the perpetrators. Yet the only person they managed to lay their hands on was one of the drivers of an SA vehicle, who purported to have loaned his car and did not know those who used it. Neither the secret state police office in Cologne, nor the police headquarters in Düsseldorf, nor the district governor in Trier managed to unearth the culprits.[69] Even though Merker was interrogated by the German authorities as to the precise course of events, he confided the true reason for the attack only to the Polish Consul. On 30 June a certain Hans Becker and his attorney Keil, who had lost a civil suit against Merker, had threatened retaliation against him during the legal proceedings to the point that they had to be called to order by the presiding judge. Their vengeance struck Merker the following day, when he was abducted by the SA. On 2 July Merker's opponents appeared in his cell, accompanied by the SA *Sturmführer* Hermann Pfeiffer (who had organized the action against Merker), and "all gloated over the sight of Merker, who had been tortured almost to death in the most cynical fashion."[70] After Merker had left Germany, his wife was continually

---

67. 7 July 1933 at GStAPK Dahlem, Rep. 84a, no. 54847, fols. 2–5; 6.
68. 25 July 1933 at GStAPK Dahlem, Rep. 84a, no. 54847, fol. 8. According to the report of the Cologne *Regierungspräsident* of 25 July 1933, Merker had by then been abroad for some time.
69. 13 July, 14 July, 25 July 1933, 26 August 1933 at GStAPK Dahlem, Rep. 84a, no. 54847, fols. 6–12.
70. 21 September 1933, ibid., fols. 13–16.

threatened with reprisals and was thus forced to also flee abroad, "leaving behind the shop and all the furnishings."[71]

Merker's case, along with the incidents previously mentioned, reveals the utter lawlessness prevailing in Germany just months after Hitler had become Chancellor. Jews, whether of German or foreign nationality, were without any rights. In fact, they had become fair game for their personal opponents, who could use quasi-State functionaries, such as the SA, to enrich themselves at their expense, beat and humiliate them at will without fear of legal consequences, and chase them out of the country. It goes without saying that the Polish Consul in Essen overrated the actual reach and capabilities of the German authorities (and probably also their sense of right and wrong) when he wrote, "The cruel deeds done to Merker testify to such gross brutality that I must assume as a matter of course that, with the help of the names and places I provided, you will do everything in your official capacity to track down the culprits so that they receive their just punishments."[72]

Following the amnesties in the second half of July 1933, the case files of virtually all crimes committed against Jews in Germany during the spring and early summer of 1933 were shelved. In assault cases committed during the late summer, regular police authorities seem to have made an effort to arrest the main culprits, though usually no sentences were handed down. On 28 August, for example, a gang of five to six SS men from Aschaffenburg attacked three Jews from nearby Hörstein near the town of Alzenau in northern Bavaria and mistreated them "in a bestial fashion." The report from the civilian authorities in Alzenau makes it clear that there had been no cause for the attack: "The Jews in Hörstein were so scared by this incident that they hid in large numbers in the forest...and returned to their homes only after midnight."[73] In tacit understanding with the National Socialist *Kreisleiter* (county leader), the

---

71. Ibid., fol. 16.   72. Ibid., fol. 16.
73. Kulka and Jäckel, eds., *Juden in NS-Stimmungsberichten*, no. 42, CD-ROM. Alzenau, in the lower Franconia region of Bavaria, pop. 1,718 (1900); Aschaffenburg, pop. 34,056 (1925); Meyers *Großes Konversations-Lexikon*, vol. I, 402; *Statistisches Jahrbuch* (1933), 11.

SS leader who had been responsible for the attack was taken into custody, but had to be released already at the end of August on orders from the Bavarian political police.[74]

Forced expulsions also destroyed families, as happened in the case of the Wiesbaden lawyer Dr. Emil Höchster. On 24 March Höchster was attacked in his office by three men, one of whom was in NSDAP party uniform. They pounced upon him with the words, "You are an enemy of our Party," and wounded him severely. Höchster's assistant, who witnessed the attack, was prevented by force from calling the police.[75] In his report to the Wiesbaden police presidium, Höchster emphasized that he had never belonged to a political party and that he was "not interested in the prosecution of the attackers," a remark that says much about the climate of fear in the spring of 1933.[76] On 28 March Johanna Höchster brought her severely injured husband to Saarbrücken in the Saar region (administered by the League of Nations until January 1935) and then to Paris, where he remained for fear of further attacks. Yet Johanna Höchster had to return to Wiesbaden in the spring of 1933 to care for her ailing father, who had suffered a stroke. According to her own testimony, her husband suggested divorce in 1935, so that she could return to the Protestant faith and finally be safe from harassment by the SA and other NS organizations.[77] In 1936, the Höchsters were divorced by mutual consent. The reason given—in the jargon of the age—was straightforward: "Due to the long separation, the difference in race, and the discrepancy that was thereby caused in the interpretation of matters involving general philosophical (*weltanschauliche*) issues..."[78]

74. Kulka and Jäckel, *Juden in NS-Stimmungsberichten*, nos. 41 and 43, CD-ROM.
75. HHStA Wiesbaden, Abt. 469–33, no. 4345, "Überfall auf den Wiesbadener Rechtsanwalt und Notar, Dr. Emil Höchster, am 24. März in dessen Kanzlei," fol. 7.
76. Ibid., fol. 9.   77. Ibid., fol. 19.
78. Ibid., fol. 12. Emil Höchster remained in Paris. In the early 1950s Johanna Höchster filed a compensation claim. Her former husband was missing and presumed dead. In order for her claim to be successful, she had to find out something about his whereabouts or have him officially declared dead by the authorities. As it was succinctly put in the files, the investigation revealed that "...the missing person was transferred to the concentration camp in Auschwitz on 17 December 1943. There can thereby be no doubt about his fate after that." Ibid., fol. 19.

The wave of violence aimed at expelling selected Jewish victims from Germany continued, albeit with diminished intensity, into the summer of 1933. The same was true for the pillory marches (*Prangermärsche*), designed to humiliate the victims, which went on well into the summer.[79] Already in mid-March, the notorious Breslau SA leader Edmund Heines had argued that violent attacks had to continue in order "to propel forward the national wave."[80] This not only countermanded Hitler's orders to stop "individual actions" but misleadingly suggested that anti-Jewish assaults were part of a long-term plan. In fact, the attacks that took place at the local level were mostly uncoordinated, directed against individuals or (sometimes random) groups of people, and were often prompted by a desire for revenge, monetary gain, or the sheer lust to vent one's anger and frustration upon others. Such "actions" continued throughout the spring and summer and finally abated only during the fall.

The following cases illustrate these ongoing persecutions: Max Goldschmidt, a self-employed traveling salesman from Limburg/Lahn in Hesse, reported in his compensation application:

> On the occasion of the then-current attacks against Jewish inhabitants, I was physically abused in Homberg (Hesse) in April 1933 and then imprisoned for eight days in Wabern. After my release I was arrested again after two days by SA men who were then active as so-called auxiliary police and who consigned me to the prison in Kassel for eight days.[81]

To avoid further persecution, he actively pursued his emigration and fled to Palestine in October. A man by the same name, Max Goldschmidt, a cattle dealer from the Melsungen area in Hesse, reported an event from the summer of 1933: "In August 1933, as I came with five other Jewish men

---

79. On *Prangermärsche*, see Chapter 5 below.
80. Kulka and Jäckel, eds., *Die Juden in NS-Stimmungsberichtung*, 45–46 (book). Edmund Heines (1897–1934), SA-*Obergruppenführer*, participant in the Hitler Putsch of 1923, and since May 1931 one of Röhm's deputies.
81. HHStA Wiesbaden, Abt. 518, no. 4634; Max Goldschmidt was born on 18 March 1906 in Homberg, a town in Hesse, pop. 4,000; Limburg/Lahn, a town in Hesse, pop. 11,501 (1925); *Neuer Brockhaus*, vol. II, 436; *Statistisches Jahrbuch* (1933), 12.

out of the synagogue, we were forced at gunpoint by the Frankfurt SA to erase communist graffiti from a house wall...." The group was then forced to gather on a square: "Rumor had it that a public flogging of Jews was on their agenda. County Counselor von Gagern prevented this humiliation."[82] Goldschmidt emigrated in 1936. Small towns and villages were often the scene of attacks on whole groups of Jews. In Gladenbach, a small town in Hesse, for example, during the night of 25/26 June, "the Jews Max Schiff, Moritz Stern, Julius Michael, Ernst Michael, Max Jonas, Löwenstein, August Schiff, Adolf Adler, Felix Adler, Albert Strauss, Berthold Leder, and others" were arrested, "kicked and beaten during the course of arrest," and "held in prison in Biedenkopf for about ten days."[83]

Attacks in Jail and on Jewish Livestock Dealers

It would also be wrong to assume that Jewish Germans were protected from mistreatment in 1933 while in custody in regular prisons. The files of the Kleve public prosecutor's office provide evidence that Jewish Germans were often subjected to cruel physical maltreatment while incarcerated. Victor Klemperer's experiences in detention in Dresden, where he was treated relatively well (by the standards of a Nazi prison at the beginning of the war) and not abused, were not representative and should not be generalized.[84] To give but one example: in 1949, the unskilled laborer Max Froebel from Lemgo was sentenced to one year

82. HHStA Wiesbaden, Abt. 518, no. 4636; Max Goldschmidt, born on 11 March 1894 in Felsberg, Kreis Melsungen; Felsberg, a village in the district of Kassel, pop. 897 (1900), Meyers *Großes Konversations-Lexikon*, vol. 6, 409.
83. 14 December 1945 at HHStA Wiesbaden, Abt. 483, no. 4156a, "Antijüdische Ausschreitungen in Gladenbach, Hessen, März bis August 1933." In the summer of 1935 incidents took place in which the public prosecutor's office intervened and several NSDAP members were arrested. Biedenkopf, a town in the district of Wiesbaden, pop. 2,853 (1900); Gladenbach, pop. 1,476 (1900); Meyers *Großes Konversations-Lexikon*, vol. 2, 831; vol. 7, 876.
84. Viktor Klemperer, *Ich will Zeugnis ablegen bis zum letzten*, vol. I: *1933–1941* (Berlin: Aufbau, 1995), 602–644. Klemperer was sentenced to a one-week imprisonment because he had accidentally disregarded the blackout orders. His main hardships were "the complete inactivity, the infuriating emptiness, and inability to move" (615). Kleve, town in the Prussian Rhineland, pop. 20,241 (1925); *Statistisches Jahrbuch* (1933), 11.

and six months of imprisonment for "[beating] the Jew Goldschmidt in the most nauseating fashion with a cane or rubber truncheon in the hall of the Kleve prison in the spring of 1933, to the point that Goldschmidt suffered serious wounds and lost several teeth."[85] Froebel's co-defendant, the bank employee Josef Rameil from Krefeld, was accused of having "twisted the already mentioned Jew Goldschmidt's ear until it turned blue. In doing so, Rameil forced Goldschmidt to eat bacon against his will."[86] In the opinion of the court, "the treatment of prisoners was simply barbaric."[87] Already months after 30 January, regular prisons had thus become places of lawlessness for German Jews. Neither the police nor law courts could be appealed to for protection.

For Jewish cattle dealers and butchers, stockyards had become dangerous places, in particular in the context of the ongoing manhunt in connection with the boycott of 1 April. Attacks and violent incidents are well documented for the Cologne stockyards, where on 3 April a Nazi "Action Committee" organized the expulsion of Jewish butchers, livestock dealers, and commission agents.[88] At 9:00 a.m. that day a mob of SS men appeared and drove all Jews who could not escape in the nick of time from their stalls and offices, an action accompanied by violence and beatings. While this was going on, butchers close to the Nazi Party pointed out their fellow Jewish workers and colleagues with expressions such as "This one is another dirty Jew" or "Over there stands another stinking Jew," whereupon the SS attacked the persons in question and

---

85. 3 February 1949 at HStA Düsseldorf (now Landesarchiv NRW), Gerichte Rep. 224, no. 147, "Staatsanwaltschaft Kleve nach 1945," fol. 5.
86. 3 February 1949 at HStA Düsseldorf, Gerichte Rep. 224, no. 147, fol. 6. After the war, Josef Rameil was fined 400 Deutschmarks for grievous bodily harm while holding office ("gefährliche Körperverletzung im Amt").
87. Ibid., fol. 9.
88. Files in several archival holdings speak to this: BA Koblenz, Z 38, Oberster Gerichtshof für die Britische Zone, no. 401, "Vertreibung jüdischer Metzger aus Köln;" HStA Düsseldorf, Gerichte Rep. 231, no. 120, "Hubert König wegen Misshandlung jüdischer Händler;" HStA Düsseldorf, Rep. 231, nos. 1429 and 1430, "Peter Stieldorf wegen Körperverletzung mit Todesfolge an dem jüdischen Viehhändler Max Moses bei der Vertreibung der Juden vom Gelände des Schlachthofs in Köln am 3. April 1933;" Institut für Zeitgeschichte München, GK 08.11, vol. I, "Körperverletzung mit Todesfolge an dem jüdischen Viehkaufmann Max Moses am 3. April 1933."

drove them from the stockyard.[89] This expulsion turned into a veritable manhunt. Those apprehended by the SS were battered with truncheons. The chase extended well beyond the stockyards into Cologne's green belt surrounding the inner city. One of those who had participated in the identification of Jewish butchers and doled out invective and punches, Hubert König, was sentenced to a three-month prison term after the war for his participation in the manhunt.[90] Given that witnesses testified that König had taken part in beatings and had also been a Nazi Party member long before 1933, this was an exceedingly mild punishment, especially since the court had established that the expulsion from the stockyards had been carried out in "a degrading, inhumane fashion."[91] König nevertheless appealed the sentence in 1948 to avoid prison. At first, the appeal was dismissed and the original sentence confirmed in October 1948. A second appeal was equally rejected, whereupon König filed a petition to commute the prison sentence into a fine, which was finally accepted. In 1949, König paid 1,500 Deutschmarks to the "Synagogen-Gemeinde" of Cologne, thereby carrying out his sentence.[92] This payment of 1,500 DM was all it took to settle the penalty and avoid prison.

89. BA Koblenz, Z 38, Oberster Gerichtshof für die Britische Zone, no. 401, "Vertreibung jüdischer Metzger aus Köln."
90. HStA Düsseldorf, Gerichte Rep. 231, no. 120. "Hubert König, wegen Misshandlung jüdischer Händler im Schlachthof Köln." In the course of these attacks two murders were committed; see Chapter 8 below.
91. HStA Düsseldorf, Gerichte Rep 231, no. 120, fols. 6–8, 38, und 41.
92. 23 May 1949 at HStA Düsseldorf, Gerichte Rep 231, no. 120. In a letter to the public prosecutor the synagogue community of Cologne had requested earlier not to accede to the defense's clemency plea in waiving the prison sentence, since König was considered a convinced antisemite who had welcomed the Judenaktion in order to eliminate unwelcome competition. The already far-too-mild punishment should at least be adhered to. The synagogue community eventually relinquished its opposition, since the fine of 1,500 DM would be used to help the poor in the Jewish community. In 1949, this was a not insignificant sum given that, with the introduction of the Deutschmark on 20 June 1948, each inhabitant of the western zones received only 40 DM, and old Reichsmarks were exchanged at a ratio of 10 RM:1 DM.

5

PILLORY MARCHES AND THE PERFIDY DECREE

Pillory Marches

A widespread form of violence directed against Jews, as well as those non-Jews who continued friendly relations with their Jewish friends or neighbors and complained about SA attacks, was "pillorying" and public branding in its various forms. Photographs or the names of those who continued buying in Jewish shops were posted on billboards at city halls, another form of psychological harassment by the regime to keep the population in line. A more active form of public shaming were the so-called "pillory marches." During these parade-like processions, victims were marched through town on an oxcart or on foot, accompanied by a posse of SA or SS men, and wearing a sign around their necks that referred to their alleged misdemeanor or crime. Photographs of such events have been passed down; some even found their way into history schoolbooks, but historical scholarship has rarely focused on them.[1] Between March and the summer of 1933, such pillory marches were not infrequent. Judging from countless allusions in the files and in contemporary newspapers, there must have been many hundreds of them, though only a small number of examples that include accompanying details have been preserved in the form of archival documentation or short newspaper articles.[2] A typical example of the latter is a brief note

---

1. An exception is Wildt, *Volksgemeinschaft als Selbstermächtigung.*
2. See, for example, BA Berlin, R 8005, no. 19; GStAPK, Rep. 77, Titel 4043, no. 123; Rep. 90P, no. 71, Heft 2; BA Koblenz Z 38, nos. 213 and 391.

Before the Holocaust: Antisemitic Violence and the Reaction of German Elites and Institutions during the Nazi Takeover. Hermann Beck, Oxford University Press. © Hermann Beck 2022. DOI: 10.1093/oso/9780192865076.003.0006

that appeared in Berlin newspapers on 8 April 1933 recounting an incident in Breslau under the headline "Women in the Pillory:"

> Yesterday, spontaneous demonstrations occurred here directed against Aryan women who, in opposition to the *völkisch* principles of the new State, live in close relationships with Jews. In a procession of seasoned SA men, posters with the names of these women were carried through town, preceded by a bugler. Many peoples' comrades joined the parade. In front of the houses of the pilloried women, the SA men got in line, and bugle calls and the old battle cry "Germany awake!" drew the attention of the neighbors of those pilloried. Names of the respective women were written in white paint on the pavement. Under the heading "Brand Them" the names of Aryan women who have entertained relationships with Jews have systematically been published in the *Schlesische Tageszeitung*, the leading NS paper in Silesia.[3]

The nature of this advertised event resembles a public festival. The pillory march also acted as a type of alliance amongst all those who wanted to demonstrate their allegiance to the new regime and gather together behind the national flag. Allegiance among the "upright thinking" was all the more firmly welded together by the manifest expulsion of those who did not acknowledge the standards and beliefs of the new State. Additional evidence of similar pillory marches can be found in situational reports of local authorities, such as the official statement of the Oberhausen police presidium on 28 March: "Five Jews, among them the rabbi, were led through the streets while carrying placards."[4] At the end of August, the state police in the *Regierungsbezirk* Kassel reported:

> During the last few days, Jews who have had intimate relations with German girls have been consigned to the central police station with the help of the SS. Before their committal, they were led in a public procession

---

3. BA Berlin, R 72, no. 1476, "Antisemitismus, Diskriminierung der Juden, März 1925 bis April 1935," fol. 1.
4. Kulka and Jäckel, *Juden in NS-Stimmungsberichten*, no. 3, CD-ROM; 47–48, book.

through the streets, during which time there were spontaneous antisemitic demonstrations of the excited populace. The Jews here were taken into protective custody and then released after several days.[5]

These parade-like ceremonies evince all the characteristics of medieval and early modern *Schand- und Ehrenstrafen* (punishment of ignominy and dishonor), which were designed to dishonor victims by the very publicity of the punishment. In the medieval and early modern world between the thirteenth and eighteenth centuries, when these punishments were applied, individual honor was of central importance to individuals' legal position and capacity. Guilds, for example, would accept in their midst only those artisans who had a blameless reputation; those who had committed a crime and thus lost their honor could not pursue an "honorable" trade or profession, nor could they credibly bear witness.[6] Public punishments entailed a dramatic lessening of one's social standing and respectability. *Schand- und Ehrenstrafen* were thus designed to undermine individuals' reputations by virtue of public exposure, mockery, and abuse.[7]

In the later Middle Ages and early modern times, individuals were wholly dependent on their social position and reputation, for they were

---

5. Kulka and Jäckel, *Juden in NS-Stimmungsberichten*, no. 39, CD-ROM; 54, book. *"Rassenschande"* (racial ignominy) became a criminal offence only with the Nuremberg Laws in September 1935 (Article 2 of the *Blutschutzgesetz*, which prohibited "mixed marriages" and out-of-wedlock sexual relations between "Jews and nationals of German or related bloodlines." See Lothar Gruchmann, "'Blutschutzgesetz' und Justiz. Entstehung und Anwendung des Nürnberger Gesetzes vom 15. September 1935," *VJHZ*, 31 (1983), 418–442.

6. Paul Münch, *Lebensformen in der Frühen Neuzeit* (Frankfurt and Berlin: Ullstein, 1996), 273–314; Wolfgang Schild, *Folter, Pranger, Scheiterhaufen. Rechtssprechung im Mittelalter* (Munich: Bassermann, 2010); Johann Heuzinga, *Herbst des Mittelalters. Studien über Lebens- und Geistesformen des 14. und 15 Jahrhunderts in Frankreich und in den Niederlanden*, 11th ed. (Stuttgart: Kröner, 1975); Richard van Dülmen, *Kultur und Alltag in der Frühen Neuzeit. Dorf und Stadt*, 2nd ed. (Munich: Beck, 1999), 194–274. Included as "dishonorable" were minstrels, traveling entertainers, those born out of wedlock, vagabonds, actors, fortune tellers, traveling salesmen, hawkers, knife sharpeners, medical quacks, disposers of dead animals, and executioners. They were unable to obtain full citizen status in towns, function as godparents, or give testimony in legal proceedings.

7. A mild form of public humiliation was the so-called *Stiegenstrafe* (public steps punishment), whereby the offender had to stand on the town hall steps and listen to a public proclamation of his sentencing, together with his own admission of guilt, which were read out to him. Schild, *Folter*, 180.

not yet abstract legal subjects who acted out different social roles.[8] Degrading punishments thus altered the identity of those concerned; the respected housewife who kept house and was in charge of the household could quickly turn into a harlot, whose adulterous behavior was held up to public ridicule.[9] This could have grievous consequences in an age when geographic mobility and thus also the opportunity to escape a personal stigma were virtually non-existent. The real punishment consisted of the public derision exhibited by the town community. Aside from being a source of considerable entertainment, public branding contributed to the internal cohesion of the onlooking urban population, whose members could feel superior to the branded delinquent.

Of all the degrading punishments, standing in the pillory was the most widespread. According to the *Constitutio Criminalis Carolina*, the legal codex and court rules introduced by Charles V at the Imperial Diet in Regensburg in 1532 and valid until the reforms of the eighteenth century, branding was applied as punishment for a whole series of infractions, reaching from theft and insult to sexual offenses.[10] For the purpose of punishment, the offender was chained to the pillory or exhibited in an iron cage. This was done in places where one could count on attracting a large public audience, either in front of the town hall or on market days in the center of the market square.[11] Persons of noble birth were allowed to escape this degrading form of punishment by paying a fine. The ultimate purpose of the punishment was to make the delinquent

---

8. Ralf Dahrendorf: *"Homo Sociologicus." Ein Versuch zur Geschichte, Bedeutung und Kritik der Kategorie der sozialen Rolle*, 14th ed. (Wiesbaden: Westdeutscher Verlag, 1974).
9. Schild, *Folter*, 182.
10. The *Constitutio Criminalis Carolina* was the first general German criminal code. It established a Reich law on criminal proceedings as well as the classification of criminal offenses and their legal consequences. Regional classifications were in part adapted to the Code's framework. The center of the criminal proceeding was the admission of guilt on the part of the accused, which was required to pass judgment, and which could be extorted through torture. The *Carolina* indicated a turning point from the Middle Ages to the modern era, away from the concept of "trial by ordeal" (*Gottesurteil*). It remained in place until the great legal codifications of the Enlightenment.
11. The pillory itself was mostly a column, to which the victim was tied, often standing on a platform with a stage. Its name came from the verb "prangen" (in the meaning of "to press") and was an instrument of criminal justice punishment (*Hochgerichtsbarkeit*).

known, so that the general public was alerted and could recognize the branded individual. In practice, public pillorying and stigmatization (a kind of physical branding of the type used on cattle, a form of degradation we know from Alexandre Dumas's *The Three Musketeers*) were often combined with banishment from towns or provinces.[12]

In the course of the pillory march and during public exhibitions and mocking accusations, onlookers could bombard the delinquent with filth and feces as they pleased. On the *Schandtafel*, the "placard of infamy" that hung around the offender's neck, the particular offense committed was rendered as either a picture or in writing—harlots had to wear a wreath of straw, blasphemers were forced to hold a candle and a rod as a symbol of penitence, and thieves bore a depiction of the object that they had purloined around their neck. In cases of prostitution or adultery, female malefactors had to push a cart filled with dung through the streets or wear straw wreaths or *Schandmasken* ("masks of shame") while they were led through the busiest streets of town accompanied by catchy music so that the largest number of onlookers could cheer, revel in the victims' misery, gloat over their misfortune, freely abuse them, and pelt them with rotten vegetables and other refuse.[13] In such cases the *Prangerstrafe* turned into a *schimpflicher Aufzug* ("griping parade"). In this way, not only public infractions but also misdeeds of a private and personal character

12. Dülmen, *Kultur und Alltag*, 269; Münch, *Lebensformen*, 290. The pillory punishment was often issued together with a branding and expulsion from one's hometown. As Dülmen indicates in an example from Danzig, between 1558 and 1731 the pillory punishment was levied for theft, break-ins, fraud, adultery, sexual offenses, and *Kuppelei* (illicit matchmaking), 250.
13. Dülmen, *Kultur und Alltag*, 207–212; Grete Bader-Weiß and Karl-Siegfried Bader, *Der Pranger. Ein Strafwerkzeug und Rechtswahrzeichen des Mittelalters* (Freiburg: Waibel, 1935). "Masks of shame" were often fitted with huge ears, devil's horns, or long tongues hanging out of the mask's mouth as a way to project the perceived qualities of the alleged perpetrator and as a symbol of his or her offense in an exaggerated, mocking way. A specific punishment for men was a ban on wearing a sword or, as it remained until the late nineteenth century, the public smashing of the sword, as, for example, in the case of Alfred Dreyfus (see the vivid representation of this event in Barbara Tuchman's *The Proud Tower* (New York: Bantham, 1969)). *Ehrenstrafen* (public humiliations) were pronounced mostly by town councils rather than town courts.

were publicly exposed and offenders laid bare to everyone's contempt.[14] It was in keeping with the nature of the National Socialist regime, with its emphasis on a hermetically sealed "*völkisch* community," that it resuscitated forms of punishment from the closed societies of the medieval and early modern worlds.[15] This was one of the feudal elements of National Socialism that was diametrically opposed to modernization.[16] With the National Socialist brandings and pillory marches, the very concept of "honor" was rendered absurd. While in medieval and early modern times a tangible offense was indeed committed by the standards of the time, the degrading punishments of 1933 were based solely on deliberate exclusion and the pleasure of jeering and inflicting humiliation on the victims. With non-Jewish victims, the "offense" could at best be interpreted as "treason" against an imaginary *völkisch* community.

During the spring and summer of 1933, municipal councils used the nationwide antisemitic wave to outlaw business dealings with Jewish shops, often branding those who continued patronizing them as "traitors of the people." On 17 July 1933, for example, the municipal council of Burgbernheim, in the governmental district of Central Franconia, passed the following resolution:

> In the year of the National Socialist revolution, which has seen the success of the triumph of our people's Chancellor Adolf Hitler, at a time in which "*Alljuda*" ("the Jew"), the mortal enemy of our people, has been ejected from its dominating position and reduced to his initial starting point, while the National Socialist movement staunchly

14. In addition to theft and fraud, these offenses included mostly blasphemy and perjury, as well as all types of moral and sexual transgressions.
15. In his *The Open Society and its Enemies*, Vol. II: *Hegel and Marx* (London and Henley: Routledge & Kegan Paul, 1966), Karl Popper, writing in 1943–5, considered the Third Reich to be one example of a closed society. His comparison between the "ideal types" of an "open" and a "closed" society and the affiliated mentalities is interesting psychologically. Nazi supporters viewed the *Volksgemeinschaft* as an "organic community" as opposed to the "mechanical," and thereby alienating, societies of the West. See Michael Stolleis, "Gemeinschaft und Volksgemeinschaft. Zur juristischen Terminologie im Nationalsozialismus," *VJHZ*, 20 (1972): 16–38.
16. Robert Koehl, "Feudal Aspects of National Socialism," in Henry Turner, ed., *Nazism and the Third Reich*, 151–174; Jens Albers, "Nationalsozialismus und Modernisierung," *Kölner Zeitschrift für Soziologie und Sozialpsychologie*, 41 (1989): 345–365.

continues its struggle against Jewry in the attempt to solve the Jewish question once and for all, the following citizens of our municipality have performed *Knechtsdienste* (slave labor) for the Jew and supported him by shopping from him and doing business with him. These hirelings in the service of the Jew shall be made known and reported to the public, our contemporaries, and descendants, because we consider them traitors to our beloved German Fatherland.[17]

In August 1933, other municipalities in Central Franconia followed this example by publishing lists of persons who "buy from the Jew or sell to them" in order "to brand them as traitors to the Fatherland."[18] In Altenstadt (Hesse) a billboard at the city hall read: "This people's comrade... has made his purchases with the Jew. He is to be considered a traitor to the people."[19] At a rally of artisans and tradesmen in Konstanz in the state of Baden, the names of all those who had recently bought goods in Jewish-owned shops and department stores were publicly read out: "During this procedure, many broke out into a cold sweat and quit the room humiliated."[20] On 2 October, under the heading "*An den Pranger*" ("Into the Pillory"), the *Kurhessische Landeszeitung* published the names of all those who had conducted business with Jews in the Marburg region in Hesse.[21] In other places, such as Freienwalde in Brandenburg, Waldenburg in Silesia, Stargard in Pomerania, and Schleusingen in Thuringia, anyone who made purchases in Jewish shops was photographed. The resulting snapshots were then published in newspapers or otherwise disseminated. The *Suhler Beobachter* in Thuringia justified such measures with the following argument: "All those who continue entertaining tacit

---

17. BA Berlin, R43 II, no. 594, fol. 97. Burgbernheim, a small town in Central Franconia, Bavaria, pop. 1,740 (1900); *Meyers Großes-Konversationslexikon*, vol. 3, 619.
18. BA Berlin, R43 II, no. 594, fol. 98.
19. Ibid., 97. Altenstadt, pop. 1,400 (1933); *Neuer Brockhaus*, vol. V, 70.
20. *Bodensee Rundschau*, no. 221, 22 September 1933 at BA Berlin, R43 II, no. 594, fol. 99; Konstanz, pop. 31,250 (1925), *Statistisches Jahrbuch* (1933), 12.
21. BA Berlin, R43 II, no. 594, fol. 99. In Wenings, a small town with about 4,000 inhabitants (1933) in Hesse, the Nazi *Kreisleiter* made it known in September 1933 that the names of "those who buy from Jews will be put on a public notice board and [they] will be taken to the concentration camp in Osthofen" (fol. 100). This referred to the Osthofen concentration camp near Worms, made notorious by Anna Seghers, *Das Siebte Kreuz* (Berlin: Aufbau, 1996), first published in 1942.

business relationships with Jews are among the unteachable, who either cannot or do not want to understand that such behavior enables the Jew to stay here with us, even though he is our mortal enemy."[22]

This remorseless dragging into the public realm of things that used to be considered private—in fact, the virtual elimination of the private sphere—marked one of the decisive ruptures between the nascent dictatorship and the Weimar Republic. It was probably more intuitive than consciously calculated that National Socialists borrowed from medieval and early modern punishments. To put someone in the pillory and lead them in processions through town was instinctively seen as an effective means of socially destroying stigmatized persons, while also enforcing conformity in others. The mutual solidarity among the "in-group" of those who joined and participated was automatically enhanced, while they also shared a modicum of guilt by association, since they supported the manhunts of the new regime and helped to translate these inhumane punishments into practice.[23] The relentless publicity of marches, processions, and parades, of which the pillory marches were certainly the most macabre, also served the function of forcing doubters into line and compelling them to profess allegiance to the new regime. Whoever stood apart was met with hostility as an opponent of the government, as lukewarm, and as a traitor to the German people. Hitler's famous dictum, "Whoever is not for me is against me," was ubiquitous in daily life. The pressure to conform had remained high since March 1933. The compulsion to make everything public was an expression of the anti-bourgeois and anti-elitist orientation of National Socialism that was directed toward enforcing social egalitarianism.[24] This may seem paradoxical,

---

22. *Suhler Beobachter*, 13 December 1933, at BA Berlin, R43 II, no. 594, fols. 100–101. Freienwalde in Brandenburg, pop. 12,000 (1933); Schleusingen, in Thuringia, pop. 4,700 (1933); *Neuer Brockhaus*, vol. II, 112; vol. IV, 95; Waldenburg in Silesia, pop. 44,120 (1925); Stargard in Pomerania, pop. 32,545 (1925); Suhl, pop. 15,582 (1925), *Statistisches Jahrbuch* (1933), 13. From Waldenburg, where SS men photographed customers in Jewish shops, it was reported that "[t]he measures were successful in that Jewish shops are avoided" (BA Berlin, R43 II, no. 594, fol. 101).
23. This argument is also made in Michael Wildt, *Volksgemeinschaft als Selbstermächtigung*.
24. Hermann Beck, "The Antibourgeois Character of National Socialism," *Journal of Modern History*, 88:3 (September 2016), 572–609.

since National Socialists were extremely exclusive, intolerant, and elitist in the fields of race and biology. Yet within the still-to-be-created racially homogeneous *völkisch* community there was to be no social hierarchy, and, unlike medieval and early modern penal practices, this time no one who belonged to the upper classes could buy his or her way out of being put in the pillory. Anyone who crossed the newly created lines of acceptable behavior was exposed to relentless public scrutiny.

Given surviving documentation, we have to assume that the majority of pillory marches took place in March and April 1933.[25] Since the estimated number of unknown cases was high, and since pillory marches, like other antisemitic crimes, were registered only indirectly— occasionally through allusions in diplomatic reports, judicial documents, or intra-bureaucratic complaints—definitive statements as to when the bulk of them took place are not possible. But it is beyond doubt that contemporaries were familiar with pillory marches and that they caused a stir among them—in particular, since victims were not only individuals but often entire groups of people. Newspaper articles about such events make it reasonable to assume that in 1933 most adults in Germany would at least have heard of this very conspicuous form of public humiliation. (For instances of pillory marches in 1933, see the map on page 44).

One such event that attracted a great deal of attention took place on the morning of Thursday, 30 March 1933, in Frankfurt am Main, when the Vice-President of the Chamber of Commerce was arrested, alongside thirty-eight of Frankfurt's leading Jewish businessmen. They had met that morning to confer on how to deal with the impending boycott, and the SS had been told by an anonymous informer of the meeting.[26] As a contemporary witness wrote, after the arrest "a large number of the most respected members of the Jewish business community were marched in single file with their hands raised high through the busiest

25. See, for example, 25 March at BA Berlin, R43 II, no. 603, fols. 22–23; 23 March at BA Berlin, R43 II, no. 1195, fol. 202; 10 March, 16 March, 18 March at GStAPK, Rep. 90 P, no. 71, Heft 2; on pillory marches in 1933, see also Gellately, *Hitler's True Believers*, 239–250.
26. 30 March 1933, 3 May 1933 at GStAPK Dahlem, Rep. 77, Titel 4043, no. 123, fols. 169, 171–172.

streets of town."[27] Other incidents from March were reported from the Prussian Rhine province.[28] There, on 16 March, "the Jewish merchant S. in Hamborn (near Duisburg) was forced by men in SA uniform to fasten a black-red-gold flag to his back and take part in an SA parade in this get-up." When the parade broke up, "S., who had fought on the front during the entire World War, was forced to set the flag ablaze."[29] In another case, in Ruhrort (also near Duisburg) "an almost 60-year-old Jewish citizen had paint poured all over him" and "a swastika was smeared on his back. In this state, he was dragged through the streets."[30] According to a report from Öhringhausen (near Olpe), thirteen Jewish citizens were arrested there: "Eight were maltreated; three of the arrested were forced to march at the head of a torchlight parade of the SA in a thoroughly degrading condition that same evening. They were also forced to sing in unison: 'We have lied, we have cheated, and we have to disappear'."[31]

Non-Jewish Germans could become victims of pillory marches if they were suspected of being "Jew-friendly" (*judenfreundlich*). In 1933, "Jew-friendliness" was not yet a punishable offense (as opposed to during the war years), but after the threatening propaganda that accompanied the nationwide manhunt before and during the boycott of 1 April, it was clear that anyone could get into trouble by publicly supporting Jewish friends or neighbors, or even by taking legal or any kind of professional action on behalf of a Jewish client or customer.[32] Help of this kind had unfortunate consequences for the Flensburg lawyer Dr. Hans Hansen, who executed a perfectly legal *Zwangsvollstreckung* (foreclosure) against a farmer in Schleswig-Holstein on behalf of a Jewish client. Hansen was

27. 30 March 1933, ibid., fol. 169; and the report of the Vice-President of the Frankfurt Appellate Court to the DNVP headquarters in Berlin: 3 April 1933 at BA Berlin R 8005, no. 19, fol. 64.
28. GStAPK Dahlem, I. H.A., Rep. 90 P, no. 71, Heft 2.
29. 16 March at GStAPK Dahlem, Rep. 90 P, no. 71, Heft 2, fol. 16. Duisburg-Hamborn, pop. 421,217 (1925); *Statistisches Jahrbuch* (1933), 11.
30. 16 March at GStAPK Dahlem, Rep. 90 P, no. 71, Heft 2, fol. 21.
31. Ibid., fol. 18. Olpe, town in Westphalia, pop. 7,600 (1933); *Neuer Brockhaus*, vol. III, 431.
32. Viktor Klemperer's diaries, *Ich will Zeugnis ablegen. Tagebücher*, vol. I: *1933–1941*, contain comments such as: "The whole world is afraid of facing the slightest suspicion of friendliness toward Jews; the fear appears to be constantly growing" (546, 578).

thereupon paraded by the SA through the streets of Flensburg at the head of a procession. A placard was hung around his neck stating, "As a lawyer I have supported a Jew and I have chased a farmer from house and home." The police finally broke up the procession. Hansen brought charges against the organizers, but the matter was followed up only after World War II and, even then, with no action taken.[33] Politically motivated pillory marches were directed mostly against members of the leftist parties. On 10 May 1933, for example, the entire political leadership of the SPD in the Berlin working class district of Kreuzberg—Mayor Hertz, his deputy Schweikart, and the director of the party's district office—were led through the streets by a jeering crowd. Hertz was forced to wear a sign that read, "I am the biggest scoundrel in Berlin." In Kreuzberg's market hall, Hertz and his fellow sufferers were pelted "with the entrails of dead animals, rotten fruit, and other items by market stand personnel who were Nazi-minded...."[34]

There were further instances of pillory marches in August 1933, even though Hitler had proclaimed the end of the revolution in his speech to the Reich governors of 6 July, exhorting his audience to transfer "the free torrent of revolution into the safe bed of evolution."[35] The Law Against the Establishment of Political Parties of 14 July 1933, which anchored the monopoly of power in the NSDAP and turned Germany into a one-party State, marks an end to the first phase of the seizure of power.[36] At the same time, the *Hitlergruß* (Hitler salute) became obligatory for all civil servants. Interior Minister Frick pointedly instructed them in a memo: "Whoever does not want to be suspected of being intentionally opposed [to the regime] will perform the Hitler salute."[37] Despite the official end

---

33. Landesarchiv Schleswig-Holstein in Schleswig, Abt. 354, Staatsanwaltschaft Flensburg, nos. 2940 and 801. The legal proceedings against the alleged perpetrator were called off in 1949.
34. GStAPK Dahlem, Rep. 90 P, no. 71, Heft 2, fol. 62. The entry ends with the succinct observation: "Mayor Hertz has been hit hard by this. He looks back on a spotless record."
35. Axel Friedrichs, ed., *Die nationalsozialistische Revolution 1933* (Berlin: Junker & Dünnhaupt, 1935), 58.
36. Michaelis and Schraepler, eds., *Ursachen und Folgen*, vol. IX, 235.
37. Josef Becker and Ruth Becker, eds., *Hitlers Machtergreifung. Dokumente vom Machtantritt Hitlers 30. Januar bis zur Besiegelung des Einparteienstaates 14 Juli 1933*, 2nd ed. (Munich: DTV), 378.

of the revolution, numerous SA and other party formations refused to discontinue the humiliating rituals. At the end of August, for example, the secret state police office in Berlin complained in a letter to Göring about conditions in Nuremberg, fearing potentially damaging propaganda abroad. According to the report, the Nuremberg *Gauleiter* Julius Streicher had removed the president of the Nuremberg police, an SS leader, because the latter would not tolerate "that the SA mistreats Jews and shaves women who had relationships with Jews, [leading them] in a triumphal parade through the streets of Nuremberg, as has happened repeatedly."[38] During these incidents in Nuremberg, the report continued, the son of the new American Ambassador William Dodd had witnessed "how a girl, who was said to have sexual relations with a Jew, was led through town with her hair cut off and wearing a placard that referred to this relationship."[39] Streicher had also given orders that "a number of Jewish inhabitants of Nuremberg be led by an SA posse...to a meadow, compelled to kneel down and, with threats to life and limb, forced to gobble up grass." On this last occasion, there had also been unwelcome visitors, since "a tour bus filled with numerous foreign visitors...had passed the scene of these events," so that "the passengers could fully observe what was going on."[40] Small wonder, then, that foreign tourists eschewed Germany after Hitler came to power.[41]

Other German regions also reported pillory marches in the summer of 1933. A press report of 19 August, for example, stated: "A Jewish baker in Weenen in East Friesland, who had mistreated his apprentice, was forced to wear a sign around his neck that read: 'I have seriously mistreated my

38. 30 August 1933 at GStAPK, Rep. 90 P, no. 5813, fols. 5–16, esp. 5.
39. Ibid., fols. 7–8. See also Erik Larson, *In the Garden of Beasts: Love, Terror, and an American Family in Hitler's Berlin* (New York: Broadway Books, 2012).
40. 30 August 1933 at GStAPK, Rep. 90 P, no. 5813, fol. 8. In addition, "on the occasion of the suicide of a Jewish industrialist," Streicher "was said to have taken a position on this incident in the press to the effect that if a Jew disappears, it is only to be welcomed as an example for the others" (ibid.).
41. Based on a sample of Germany's 175 most important holiday places, the German tourism statistics reported a decline of foreign visitors by almost 50% as compared to 1931 (22.9% compared to 1932). See Schütt, *Chronik 1933*, 135.

apprentice, a German peoples' comrade.'" With the sign around his neck, the baker was led through town by the SA.[42] Though hard to imagine by the standards of our own day, it was at that time not unusual for craftsmen to slap their 14- or 15-year-old apprentices as punishment for making mistakes. From March 1933 on, that could have fateful consequences for Jewish master craftsmen.

Long before the Nuremberg Laws of September 1935, the SA criminalized amorous relationships between Jews and non-Jews and made them public. On 30 August 1933 the *Hessische Volkswacht* reported such an incident from Kassel:

> The Jew Walter Lieberg, Lessingstr. 18, son of one of the co-owners of the Lieberg & Company metal works in Bettenhausen, has a relationship with the Christian girl Jandy from the Uhlandstraße. The mother of the girl doesn't do anything against the relationship but tolerates it. The "Christian" girl is of the opinion that the government cannot forbid them the relationship. To present these fine people to the population and make them realize the reprehensibleness of their characters, SS pioneers led the Jew, his mistress, and the mother through the streets of Kassel.[43]

The addresses of those concerned were listed conspicuously and with great precision, undoubtedly to rub in the stigma, so that everyone could freely abuse them in person. An article in the Mannheim *Hakenkreuzbanner* of 27 August 1933, entitled "You are Looking at Jews' Little Mistresses," exposes people in a similar way. First the article condemns the "false doctrine" that all men are equal, which is vilified as the fateful dogma of a passé liberal age that had been willingly adopted by "the good philistines" and would have resulted "in our race being adulterated and watered down and the morals of our people destroyed."[44] Then the names, addresses, and

---

42. BA Berlin, NS 5-VI, no. 17196, "Deutsche Arbeitsfront: Presseberichte zur Judenfrage," fol. 98; from *Der Deutsche*, no. 185, 10 August 1933.

43. BA Berlin, NS 5-VI, no. 17209, fol. 101. On the same page of the *Hessische Volkswacht* the following appeared further below: "A similar case took place on Saturday, 28 August, as the *Oberhessische Zeitung* reported from Marburg/Lahn." Pillory marches clearly were not rare events in 1933.

44. BA Berlin, R43 II, no. 594, fol. 134.

occupations of about twenty Mannheim citizens were listed and showered with invective: "...the wife of a municipal official...maintains an affectionate close friendship with a Jew, tolerated by her husband. The designation 'German woman' no longer applies to this lady, especially since the Hebrew comes and goes in and out of her house as he pleases." The article flaunts an unusually direct language and, at least theoretically, anticipates the practice of future years: "For a few years now, Alma Krieger has been on friendly terms with the Jew Stern...for her too it'll be good if she leaves for Palestine before she is sterilized."[45] With articles such as this one, the Nuremberg Laws had become reality more than two years before they were passed.[46]

Since information on pillory marches has been passed down to us only in the form of short newspaper articles, diplomatic protests, and excerpts from internal bureaucratic correspondence, details about the victims and the specific motivations of perpetrators are mostly missing. One set of files from the Supreme Court for the British Zone provides a little more background information on two specific cases. These records deal with the prosecution of offenders who were accused of having committed crimes specifically directed against their fellow German citizens in 1933. The first case deals with the businessman Wilhelm Söffge, a long-time member of the SPD in Goslar and, from 1921 to 1933, also a member of Goslar's town council responsible for agricultural matters. Söffge owned a great deal of property; he was obviously a wealthy man, and some of his fellow citizens in Goslar may have been envious of his achievements.[47] In the spring of 1933, he was charged with having used his political office to obtain building commissions from the municipality. Under this pretext, Söffge and the Jewish merchant Hochburg were forced by the SA on 5 May 1933 to mount an oxcart borrowed from a butcher's shop in front of the Goslar inn "Kaisersaal." From there the two

45. Ibid., fol. 136.   46. Walk, ed., *Sonderrecht*, 127.
47. BA Koblenz, Z 38, Oberster Gerichtshof..., no. 389, "Öffentliche Anprangerung zweier Juden." Goslar, in the *Regierungsbezirk* Hildesheim, pop. 21,229 (1925); *Statistisches Jahrbuch* (1933), 11.

were led in a procession of fifty to sixty uniformed SA men through Goslar. The procession was preceded by the SA members playing drums and fifes. Other SA men were armed with rifles, no doubt to mete out justice in case the victims tried to escape; the remainder of the SA gang that followed the cart was unarmed. Söffge and Hochburg both wore placards around their necks with degrading texts. Söffge's sign, to which he was forced to point with his finger during the duration of the procession, read: "I am the racketeer Söffge." Once back at the Kaisersaal, the procession broke up and Söffge and Hochburg were let go. Söffge survived the Third Reich and was able to bring action against the instigators of the pillory march after 1945. The main offenders received a six-month prison sentence. Their appeal was rejected and they had to serve the full term.[48]

The second case was similar insofar as economic motives again played a central role. On 26 June 1933 the tobacco wholesaler Adolf Siekmann from Pinneberg near Hamburg was led through the streets of the town by SS men in a procession with a sign around his neck reading, "I am the biggest cutthroat and usurer in Pinneberg."[49] The pillory march had been instigated by the tobacco dealer Pump, who was indebted to Siekmann. As Pump had no intention of repaying his debts, Siekmann filed a claim against him to get his money. Pump thereupon threatened Siekmann that he should either withdraw the claim or he would be paraded through town as a usurer. Since Siekmann was not to be intimidated, Pump carried out his threat. During Siekmann's pillory march, which was accompanied by about thirty to fifty people and lasted for about an hour, he was badgered by invectives such as *Schweinehund*" from the surrounding populace. The humiliating parade was followed by disparaging newspaper articles about him, his formerly thriving business was brought to a standstill, and in the end the once affluent and respected

---

48. BA Koblenz, Z 38, Oberster Gerichtshof..., no. 389. Hochburg is characterized as "the later-deceased Jewish merchant." For the trial against the instigators, see Z38, no 213, "Strafsache gegen Willi Lotzing wegen Verbrechen gegen die Menschlichkeit."
49. BA Koblenz, Z 38, no. 391, "Anprangerung eines jüdischen Geschäftsmannes, Pinneberg 1933." Pinneberg, in Schleswig-Holstein, pop. 12,700 (1933); *Neuer Brockhaus*, vol. III, 554.

tobacco wholesaler suffered a nervous breakdown.[50] Not long after, the town auditor, on orders of the mayor, examined the business dealings between Siekmann and Pump. He came to the conclusion that Siekmann had acted honorably, since the interest he had charged Pump was the same he would have had to pay the bank, so that Siekmann did not practice usury and could not be accused of profiteering. Yet all attempts at public rehabilitation failed. Newspapers refused to correct their earlier statements, and Pump went on boasting that he had been the guiding force behind the pillory march and that Siekmann was a profiteer. In 1939, Siekmann sued Pump for slander, which surprisingly led to a conviction. Pump was sentenced to pay 50 Reichsmarks, and the court's summary plainly stated: "The behavior of Mr. and Mrs. Pump in their business dealings with Siekmann was borderline criminal."[51] Even during the Third Reich, the legal standards that were applied could depend on the political orientation or capriciousness of local officials After the war, four people who had taken part in Siekmann's pillory march, including Heinrich Pump, were sentenced to prison terms of six to eight months.[52]

Since most pillory marches were never actually recorded, we must assume that the cases briefly outlined here form but the tip of the iceberg. Their number and the very public forum in which they played out leads to the assumption that many tens, possibly hundreds, of thousands of Germans, must have actually borne witness and watched these degrading spectacles, while millions, in fact a majority of adult Germans at the time, must have been aware of their existence, if only through rumors and newspaper reports.

The Perfidy Decree

A more hidden form of discrimination and indirect violence were the stiff punishments meted out to German Jews under the so-called *Heimtücke-*

---

50. BA Koblenz, Z 38, no. 391, fol. 11.   51. Ibid.
52. The appeal submitted by the defendant was unanimously denied by the Supreme Court for the British Zone of occupation.

Verordnung (Perfidy Decree). This decree had been signed by Hindenburg on 21 March 1933 as the Decree of the Reich President to Avert Perfidious Attacks against the National Government two days before the Enabling Act. The Perfidy Decree left the decision about which elements of a criminal offence would be prosecuted to the discretion of the authorities, thus giving them great latitude in addition to providing a field day for informers.[53] In connection with the press campaign against foreign "atrocity propaganda," the Perfidy Decree was designed to curb any negative "propaganda" on the domestic front—rumors, criticism, and in general the spreading of news unwelcome to the regime. The foreign and domestic campaigns were thus causally connected. The Perfidy Decree imposed severe penalties on the spreading of "untrue assertions of a factual kind" (*unwahre Behauptungen tatsächlicher Art*), as it was put in the tortuous bureaucratic jargon of the day.

Since private criticism against the regime was punished just as harshly as critical comments made in public, the decree was meant as a deterrent against whispering campaigns, furtive rumors made through the grapevine, and criticism uttered behind closed doors. It gave authorities the opportunity to punish even the slightest criticisms or (and this happened often) to prosecute as a serious crime the mere mentioning of grievances or abuses of power as denigrations of the government and the blackening of Germany's reputation.[54] This crossed the threshold into the absurd when Jews were punished for speaking to others in private about crimes they had heard of perpetrated against other Jews. Examples from the files

53. The most detailed study is Dörner, "*Heimtücke.*" It granted the authorities wide-ranging discretionary powers. Paragraph 3 of the ordinance read: "Whoever intentionally puts forward or circulates an untrue or grossly misrepresented claim of a factual nature that is designed to harm seriously the welfare of the Reich or a *Land* or the reputation of the Reich or a *Land* government or the parties or associations that support these governments will, as long as regulations do not threaten a severe punishment, be sentenced with imprisonment for up to two years." Michaelis and Schraepler, eds., *Ursachen und Folgen*, vol. IX, 281–282; Dörner, "*Heimtücke,*" 320–321.

54. On 20 December 1934 the *Heimtückegesetz* superseded the *Heimtückeverordnung*. Klaus-Michael Mallmann and Gerhard Paul, "Allwissend, allmächtig, allgegenwärtig? Gestapo, Gesellschaft und Widerstand," *Zeitschrift für Geschichtswissenschaft*, 41 (1993): 984–999; Robert Gellately, *The Gestapo and German Society. Enforcing Racial Policy 1933–1945* (Oxford: Clarendon Press, 1990), Dörner, "*Heimtücke,*" 20–25.

follow below. The mere mentioning of truths unwelcome and unpleasant to the regime could thus be penalized, and criticism was punished especially ruthlessly if uttered by members of an ostracized minority. As will be shown below by contrasting the sentencing of Jews and non-Jews for similar offenses, Jewish Germans thus suffered more than others when denounced under the Perfidy Decree.

Assertions and utterances made in the private sphere could be punished with a prison term if the accusations of the denouncers sounded believable. In conjunction with this decree, *Sondergerichte*—that is, special courts in the jurisdiction of all higher court districts (*Oberlandesgerichtsbezirke*)—were established that ruled on violations against the Perfidy Decree and punished the offenders. The rights of the accused were severely curtailed, since decisions of the *Sondergerichte* could not be appealed. In 1933 alone, 3,744 violations of the Perfidy Decree met with punishments.[55] The decree proved to be an effective instrument of terror. A seemingly harmless conversation about the contemporary political situation could have fateful consequences. Informers were taken at their word in accordance with their political position and the likelihood of the circumstances; facts in a specific case were interpreted in light of Nazi Party predilections, so that the Perfidy Decree nipped in the bud conversations about politics, especially if people were not sure that they could fully trust their conversation partners. Interlocutors or even mere listeners might deem it necessary to notify authorities of any "subversive," "seditious," or even merely critical remarks for reasons of self-protection, since concealment or withholding of information might signal complicity. The case of Dr. Kuno Ruhmann from Northeim, mentioned in William S. Allen's *The Nazi Seizure of Power*, is typical here: Ruhmann had imitated Hitler at an evening get-together in order to entertain the other guests. The next day, his hostess denounced him to the police in order to protect herself. Allen's point: "Given the atmosphere of terror,

---

55. Wolfgang Benz, Hermann Graml, and Hermann Weiß, eds., *Enzyklopädie des Nationalsozialismus* (Munich: DTV, 1997), 501. In 1937, 17,168 persons were denounced to the Gestapo under the *Heimtückeverordnung*; Dörner, "Heimtücke," 9.

even people who were friends felt that they must betray each other in order to survive..." The result of this behavior: "Social life was cut down enormously – you couldn't trust anyone anymore."[56] Over time, citizens of the dictatorship were bound to develop a pair of scissors in their heads, automatically censoring spontaneous speech, since careless talk could easily get them in jail or ruin their careers.

The case of Heinz Stern, a student at the University of Heidelberg whose father was Jewish and mother Protestant, is instructive in this regard. Since his school days, Stern had been a frequent customer at the Wolff bookstore in Heidelberg.[57] He knew the owners well and felt quite at ease in their shop. When he entered the bookstore on Saturday, 24 June 1933, he had a chat, as often before, with the owner, Frau Wilhelmine Wolff. On the previous evening, the Conti News Agency in Berlin had spread an intentionally false report concerning "foreign planes over Berlin," and this was front page news on 24 June in all the major German dailies. This particular report had the rather obvious purpose of impressing on the population at large that German air defenses were insufficient and of psychologically preparing the ground for rearmament.[58] The indictment mentions that Stern discussed this headline news with Frau Wolff, predicting that "this story about flyers over Berlin will fizzle out," for it was "just a ruse by Germany, a public relations stunt by the government like the other case about which no one talks anymore." Stern continued: "Foreign countries will expose this whole thing; they have the greatest interest in doing so, since Germany is making the claim

56. Allen, *Nazi Seizure of Power*, 189–190; see also Robert Gellately, "Crime, Identity and Power: Stories of Police Imposters in Nazi Germany," *Crime, Histoire & Sociétés*, 4 (2000), 5–18.
57. Ibid., 5, 7. Heidelberg, city in Baden, pop. 78,196 (1925); *Statistisches Jahrbuch* (1933), 12.
58. The report read as follows: "Above the Reich capital foreign airplanes of a type that is not produced in Germany appeared and dropped flyers over the eastern parts, as well as over the government quarter, that contain excessive abuse of the Reich government. The perpetrators could get away without being identified." In conclusion it was mentioned: "This time it was flyers. Germany is just as defenseless against deadly gas and fireballs that are hurled from the air onto its territory as it is against propaganda from the air." Evidence of the purported dropping of flyers was never produced. The false report was meant to speed up preparation for military rearmament and public air defense measures. See Schütt, *Chronik 1933*, 123.

for air defenses."[59] The remark about "the other case" was an allusion to the Reichstag fire, for which Stern implicitly seemed to hold the government responsible. According to the official version of events, a communist conspiracy had been behind the Reichstag fire as a beacon for the allegedly planned coup d'état against the national government. Émigré circles and foreign newspapers had hinted that the Nazis themselves had set the fire to create a pretext for cracking down on the leftist opposition. The issue was therefore extremely sensitive, and Stern would hardly have spoken so freely to Wilhelmine Wolff, whose husband and daughter also overheard the gist of the conversation, if he had not completely trusted the family based on their long acquaintance. In this case, confidence in their discretion proved sadly unfounded.

Further police investigations brought to light that Stern had joined the SPD in 1932. Since three people—the Wolff father, mother, and daughter—testified against him, Stern could hardly plead that what he had said was based on a misunderstanding, all the more so as it was emphasized in the indictment that Stern was a highly educated person who would not "mindlessly babble," so that one had to take "his utterances as the manifestation of a mean and malignant attitude against the State in its present-day form." The special court in neighboring Mannheim sentenced Stern to a one-year prison term. The summing up of the court draws attention to Stern's further derogatory remarks about a new consignment of national literature that, in his opinion, would turn out to be dead stock, and about the decline of tourism in Heidelberg that was due to foreign guests "staying away from Germany because of all the National Socialist processions"—remarks he allegedly uttered in a "mocking superior tone" and "in the impudent taunting way in which he comports himself."[60] Quite obviously, the bookstore owners had resented the ways of their long-time customer for quite some time, yet had given him the impression that they were to be trusted and that they shared his political

59. 10 July 1933 at Generallandesarchiv Karlsruhe, now Landesarchiv Baden-Württemberg, Bestand 507, no. 11669a, "Badische Staatsanwaltschaft Mannheim," fol. 3.
60. 22 July 1933 at Generallandesarchiv Karlsruhe, Bestand 507, no. 11669a, fols. 29–30.

views to a certain extent. Otherwise, Stern would have been more cautious and not vented his sentiments so freely. The Perfidy Decree now gave them the means to have him incarcerated because of a mere trifle. According to the court's summing up, the deed warranted "severe retribution" since it "counts among the vilest atrocity rumors leveled against the national government."[61] Stern had to serve two-thirds of this prison term; the remainder was suspended.[62] In May 1934, Stern continued his studies in the Swiss capital, Bern. After the war, in 1954, after having emigrated to the United States, Stern succeeded in having the 1933 sentence annulled.[63]

It is clear that Jewish Germans sentenced for violations under the perfidy measures were punished more severely than non-Jews.[64] For example, an elderly small business owner, Minna Bloch, who was from Rheinbischofsheim near Kehl in Baden and who suffered from a weak heart and high blood pressure, was sentenced to a six-month term for an injudicious remark.[65] In a conversation with her cleaning lady in May 1933, Bloch said that she could not understand why Jews were treated so badly, since Hitler himself was descended from Jews.[66] When the cleaning lady responded that this was out of the question as she had seen photographs of Hitler's relatives, Bloch retorted that it was after all possible that Hitler's mother might have borne him out of wedlock. Incensed, the cleaning lady reported these remarks to the authorities. The sole mitigating circumstances the court accepted in Minna Bloch's favor were that "as a Jewish small business owner she did not have an easy time...with the population," and that "her husband was killed in action during the war."[67] Even though it came to light during the

---

61. Ibid., fol. 33. Mannheim, city in Baden, pop. 260,871 (1925); *Statistisches Jahrbuch* (1933), 12.
62. 19 March 1934 at Generallandesarchiv Karlsruhe, Bestand 507, no. 11669a, fol. 49.
63. 12 August 1954 at Generallandesarchiv Karlsruhe, Bestand 507, no. 11669a (not paginated).
64. After the 9 November 1938 pogrom, discussions about anti-Jewish crimes that were committed during its course were eschewed during trials; Dörner, "Heimtücke," 231.
65. Kehl, opposite Strasbourg, pop. 11,600 (1933); *Neuer Brockhaus*, vol. 2, 617.
66. 29 August and 23 September at Generallandesarchiv Karlsruhe, Bestand 507, no. 11752, fols. 1–2; 9–11.
   23 September 1933 at Generallandesarchiv Karlsruhe, Bestand 507, no. 11752, fol. 11.
67. Ibid.

proceedings that Bloch's brother, a brother-in-law, and a cousin had also been killed in action fighting for Germany, Bloch was sentenced to half a year in jail. The public prosecutor's office also remained adamant and rejected the plea by her defense counsel that she was not physically fit to undergo detention because of her poor health.[68] In October 1933, Minna Bloch was consigned to the women's penitentiary in Bruchsal in northern Baden.

Another case in point is that of the livestock dealer Meier Buchheim, from Frankenberg in Hesse, who was sentenced to an eight-month prison term in April 1933. In a conversation with his shoemaker, he had maintained that times were bad for Jews in the Rheinpfalz (Bavarian Palatinate on the left bank of the Rhine), since "already...several Jews have been strung up there."[69] The shoemaker immediately denounced Buchheim to the authorities for these remarks. Since, by any standards, times were indeed "bad" for Jews and there had also been several murders in the Rheinpfalz, Buchheim's remarks were fully warranted. The court justified the prison term with the opinion that Buchheim's "untrue assertion" had the potential to "severely damage the welfare of the Reich and the Bavarian state," since from what he had said it followed that "currently lawless conditions prevail and the respective governments fail to do anything about it."[70] Whether the judges recognized the irony of their summing-up remains open to question. Meier Buchheim had fought and been wounded in the service of Germany during World War I. While this was considered a mitigating circumstance, the court considered it an aggravating factor that Buchheim had "violated German hospitality that he enjoys as a Jew in Germany."[71] The obvious paradox that, had he been a mere "guest" in Germany he would not have fought for his host country in a world war, was not appreciated.

68. 9 January 1934 at Generallandesarchiv Karlsruhe, Bestand 507, no. 11752, fol. 53.
69. 21 April 1933 at HHStA Wiesbaden, Abt. 40914, no. 789, "Gefangenenakte des Strafgefängnisses Frankfurt-Preungesheim," fols. 10–11."
70. 21 April 1933 at HHStA Wiesbaden, Abt. 40914, no. 789, fol. 11.
71. Ibid.

The Heidelberg student Rudolf Ernst Feith, scion of an old-established mercantile family from the nearby industrial city of Mannheim who had been expelled from Heidelberg University during the summer of 1933 because of his membership in the Communist Party, had become friends with the SA candidate Valentin Wittemann during a short stay in hospital, where the two shared a room. Wittemann even offered Feith the familiar "Du," in those days still a meaningful gesture of comradery. In a confidential conversation about an article in the (formerly liberal) *Frankfurter Zeitung* that dealt with the Reichstag fire, Feith expressed the opinion that "Göring and Goebbels had set the Reichstag ablaze," and that Hitler's book *Mein Kampf* contained several lies.[72] Wittemann did not report Feith, but he mentioned Feith's assertions to a medical orderly, who reported them to the Heidelberg NSDAP headquarters. For this expression of his views, Feith was punished with a one-year prison term; his KPD membership was an aggravating factor in the sentence.

Non-Jewish defendants got off more lightly. When the unemployed Protestant stucco mason, Wilhelm Dietz, was indicted for telling good acquaintances stories about attacks and other incidents concerning Jews in Gießen (Hesse) that involved pillory marches and other humiliations, all of which sounded quite believable, he was acquitted in the end.[73] This occurred despite the fact that his wife had been forced to confirm the main counts of the indictment.[74] In another case, on 26 June 1933, the Frankfurt dressmaker Katharina Wolff said in front of several witnesses in the hairdressing salon she frequented that "in Munich a Jew was shot dead and another severely wounded," "the Reichstag was set ablaze by the NSDAP," and "it was German planes that had dropped flyers over Berlin."[75] With regard to the weight of the offense, this was a more severe delinquency than that of Heinz Stern. Yet Katharina Wolff was sentenced to only four months' imprisonment, not one year as Stern had been. The fact that her husband was Jewish counted as a

---

72. 8 November 1933 at Generallandesarchiv Karlsruhe, Bestand 507, no. 11773a.
73. 6 October 1933 at HHStA Wiesbaden, Abt. 461, no. 7331, "Strafsache gegen Wilhelm Dietz."
74. 14 August and 24 November 1933 at HHStA Wiesbaden, Abt. 461, no. 7331.
75. 6 December 1933 at HHStA Wiesbaden, Abt. 461, no. 7356.

mitigating circumstance in this case, since "through her marriage she was unable to get along without social contacts in circles in which rejection of the government of the national uprising was prevalent."[76]

The Perfidy Decree had an immediate effect on interpersonal relations and social intercourse. It was bound to bring out the worst in people and fostered denunciations by informers, sowed distrust, and imposed on people an unnatural discretion to the point of secrecy. It also created barriers to the formation of common behavioral standards and expectations among individuals, thus introducing elements of hostility and suspicion into society that remained in force for years, even after the fall of the dictatorship, and would only gradually dissipate. Totalitarian regimes tend to eliminate trust in society by destroying social bonds and any "horizontal links" in the form of independent associations or networks. These are replaced by ties to Party organizations to guarantee both organizational control and individual loyalty.[77] To have too much trust in one's neighbors or "friends" might well have disastrous consequences. During the Third Reich, the lack of trust promoted an atmosphere of all-pervasive fear and the constant feeling of always having said one word too many, a kind of inner panic that has been aptly depicted in Bertolt Brecht's *Fear and Misery in the Third Reich*.[78]

76. Ibid.
77. See also Klaus-Dietmar Henke, ed., *Totalitarismus. Sechs Vorträge über Gehalt und Reichweite eines klassischen Konzepts der Diktaturforschung* (Dresden: Hannah-Arendt-Institut für Totalitarismus Forschung 1999); Gisela Diewald-Kerkmann, *Politische Denunziation im NS-Regime oder die kleine Macht der Volksgenossen* (Bonn: Dietz, 1995); Robert Gellately, "Denunciations in Twentieth-Century Germany: Aspects of Self-Policing in the Third Reich and the German Democratic Republic," in Sheila Fitzpatrick and Robert Gellately, eds., *Denunciatory Practices. Denunciation in Modern European History, 1789–1989* (Chicago: University of Chicago Press, 1997), 185–221.
78. See, for example, scene 10, "Der Spitzel," in Bertolt Brecht, *Furcht und Elend des Dritten Reiches* (Frankfurt: Suhrkamp, 1970), 66–76.

6

MURDER

Categories of Anti-Jewish Murder

Between the beginning of March and the summer of 1933 murders motivated by antisemitism were by no means rare. On the whole, written sources on this issue are sparse, since police files on antisemitic murder investigations barely exist. Still, a number of murder cases can be reconstructed in some detail, especially when contemporary judicial files can be supplemented with post-war trial documents. In several instances murder cases from the period of the Nazi takeover were reopened in the immediate post-war period, especially when the murder case in question had attracted attention in 1933 but was then dismissed by the authorities on the basis of the 22 July Amnesty for Offenses Committed in Connection with the National Socialist Revolution.[1] Reliable numerical data about anti-Jewish murder cases in 1933 does not exist. Estimates are vague, as they are based solely on subjective impressions. No agency or individual—including foreign correspondents and diplomats—had an overview of the situation in the Reich as a whole. As indicated above, German authorities did their best to play down attacks and murders, while foreign reports of antisemitic outrages were characterized as "atrocity propaganda" and equated with alleged calumnies of British propaganda during the First World War.[2] Even non-Nazis and potential opponents of the regime were thus loath

---

1. An emergency decree of the Reich President had already granted a first amnesty on 21 March 1933 for criminal acts "carried out in the struggle for the national uprising, its dissemination, or in the struggle for German territory;" Becker and Becker, eds., *Hitlers Machtergreifung*, 424.
2. On this, see also Seul, "'Hitler's Nazis," 412–431.

Before the Holocaust: Antisemitic Violence and the Reaction of German Elites and Institutions during the Nazi Takeover.
Hermann Beck, Oxford University Press. © Hermann Beck 2022. DOI: 10.1093/oso/9780192865076.003.0007

to acknowledge the justification of foreign criticism, since France, Great Britain, and even the United States continued to be viewed with suspicion, not only as former wartime enemies but also as the countries that kept Germany to one degree or another under the yoke of Versailles.[3]

German authorities also lacked a holistic perspective by which to gauge the Reich-wide number of antisemitic murders. Since these were generally not recorded by the police, the German authorities were not in a position to assess the number of murder victims even in a single governmental district, in particular since they were unwilling to concede the facts even when they were put before them. In cases where foreign consulates and diplomatic missions directly confronted the Reich Interior Ministry or the interior ministries of the German states with anti-semitic attacks (as happened with "*Ostjuden*" who complained to their consulates), the authorities minimized these deeds, put forward flimsy reasons in defense of the perpetrators (such as the omnipresent excuse that the victims had been communists), and generally adopted the viewpoint of the offenders. In intra-departmental correspondence they called for a united front against foreign accusations.[4] In those few cases in which a seemingly genuine effort was made to bring criminals to book for fear of diplomatic entanglements (as, for example, in the attack on the American businessman Philip Zuckerman and his wife in Leipzig), the German authorities remained powerless and ineffective when confronted with the obstructionism, delaying tactics, and collusion of the SA groups that protected and, if necessary, covered for each other.[5]

Several Prussian Ministry of Justice files from 1933 and documents from public prosecutors' offices relating to trials during the immediate post-war period provide more detailed information about some murder

3. R. W. Whalen, *Bitter Wounds: German Victims of the Great War, 1914–1939* (Ithaca: Cornell University Press, 1984), 155–179; Ulrich Heinemann, *Die verdrängte Niederlage. Politische Öffentlichkeit und Kriegsschuldfrage in der Weimarer Republik* (Göttingen: Vandenhoeck & Ruprecht, 1983).
4. For details, see Chapter 13 below.
5. See Chapter 3 above. See also, "Hitler Troopers Beat New Yorker," *NYT*, July 22, 1933, 4; Frederick T. Birchaul, "Dodd to see Hitler Today on Assaults," *NYT*, October 13, 1933, 15.

cases, so that they can be partially reconstructed with regard to the motivation of the perpetrators, the actual course of events, and the reaction of the authorities. A number of cases that had attracted attention in 1933 but could not be prosecuted were then reopened after the war by friends or relatives of the victims. In some instances suspects had been arrested in the spring of 1933, but due to the amnesty judicial authorities were under pressure to construct explanations and bend the truth so that these suspects (most of whom were guilty beyond a shadow of a doubt) could be set free under flimsy pretexts. These explanations are most revealing when it comes to exposing the collective mentality of judicial officials.[6] They also show that the German justice system betrayed its legal principles already during the first months of Nazi rule and that its officials were all too willing to make any concessions demanded of them.

The American journalist Michael Williams, publisher of *The Common-weal* and president of the Calvert Association, spent about eight weeks in Germany from the beginning of April to mid-June 1933 to investigate antisemitic violence. His estimate was quoted in *The New York Times*: "Recorded cases of physical molestation, serious enough to be note-worthy, at least 3,000. Deaths ranging from outright killings to deaths resulting from injuries or shock produced by physical violence, at least 300." He then continued:

> I am positive that those in the best position to know the facts, the foreign newspaper correspondents in Berlin and the American consular officials, would agree that in spite of the exaggerated first reports of wholesale deliberate slaughter, which were quickly proved false, there was and there continues to be a persecution of Jews which in its extent probably surpasses any recorded instance of persecution in Jewish history. For it goes deeper and is more inclusive in its intent to absolutely eliminate the Jewish portion of the German nation than any other outbreak of its kind.[7]

6. For more details, see Chapter 12 below.
7. "Nazi Deeds Called Worst in History," *NYT*, 14 June 1933, 4. In the spring of 1933 there were many other articles on this topic in *The New York Times*. The next surge of antisemitic violence then followed between July and December 1935; BA Koblenz, ZSg 117, "Presseausschnitts-Sammlung: Hauptarchiv der NSDAP," no. 372, vol.4, "Amerikanische Stellungnahmen zu Maßnahmen gegen Juden, Mai 1933 bis März 1944."

Even though Williams had met Protestant and Catholic Church leaders during his extended stay and traveled throughout the country, these figures are a conjectural assessment, not based on any statistical data, and quite possibly influenced by the shock of immediate experience. Yet in view of the surviving evidence, they are certainly well within the realm of probability. Given the fact that in the crisis-ridden year 1931 there were 1,336 murder and manslaughter cases in the entire country (806 that involved men and 530 that involved women), the number of 300 murders in this short period of time was immense.[8] Murders, like other antisemitic crimes, fell under the Amnesty for Offenses Committed in Connection with the National Socialist Revolution.[9] In some murder cases, legal proceedings against the perpetrators had been instituted but never got to the sentencing stage before the cases were terminated.[10] In the event that preliminary proceedings had been initiated, the general pattern of argumentation of the judicial authorities can be discerned: authorities did everything to minimize the crimes and shield the perpetrators, while public prosecutors often acted like defense counsels.[11]

Some murder cases were documented by the administrative authorities, such as the murder of the "Israelite trader of goods Otto Selz in Straubing," who, as is mentioned in the neutrally worded report of the district commissioner of Lower Bavaria on 30 March 1933, had been abducted by several men "in dark uniform...who carried him off from his apartment in nightclothes." Later Selz was found shot to death in a forest. The hijackers' car with its Munich license plate was occupied by six uniformed men, on whom eyewitnesses had noticed "the red armband

8. There were also 13,134 male and 5,491 female suicides recorded in Germany in 1931; *Statistisches Jahrbuch* (1933), 44–45. See also Christian Goeschel, *Suicide in Nazi Germany* (Oxford: Oxford University Press, 2009), 11–55.
9. "Betrifft Gnadenerweise...," at GStAPK, Rep. 84a, no. 54771; on the March amnesty, see Lothar Gruchmann, *Justiz im Dritten Reich 1933–1940. Anpassung und Unterwerfung in der Ära Gürtner*, 3rd ed. (Munich: Oldenbourg, 2001), 324–328.
10. A few prominent murder cases were reopened in post-war Germany and several sentences passed.
11. See Chapter 13 below on the reaction of the judicial and administrative bureaucracy.

with the swastika."[12] More murder cases are briefly referred to in the above-mentioned dossier at Berlin-Dahlem, which had been destined for destruction. One case from the region near Worms is especially reveal-ing, as it may deal with a case in which another person (Meier Buchheim) was convicted under the "Perfidy Decree" for spreading false rumors:[13] "The Jewish merchant F. was carried off from Worms to Dolgesheim by SA men at night. There he was found after a few hours hanged in the fire station with terrible injuries covering his whole body."[14] Other murder cases described in this particular dossier of files similarly deal with instances of grievous bodily harm; victims then died as a result of their injuries within hours or days. One of the most infamous murder cases, already notorious among contemporaries in 1933, occurred in the small Württemberg town of Creglingen, where, on Saturday, 25 March 1933, sixteen Jews were taken from the local synagogue to the town hall and savagely beaten by SA troopers with rubber truncheons and steel rods. One of them, Hermann Stern, a 67-year-old local, well-respected real estate agent who had unsuccessfully tried to escape, died of his wounds the same day, while another victim, Arnold Rosenfeld, passed away in hospital two days later.[15] The case made such waves that Lion Feucht-wanger devoted several pages to this and other pogrom-like attacks during the spring 1933 in his novel *The Oppermanns*, written between April and October 1933 in French exile. The main culprit, the SA leader Fritz Klein from Heilbronn, is mentioned by name in the novel, though

---

12. Broszat, Fröhlich, and Wiesemann, eds., *Bayern*, 432; Kulka and Jäckel, eds., *Juden in NS-Stimmungsberichten*, 48 (book).
13. See Chapter 5 above, and HHStA Wiesbaden, Abt. 40914, no. 789.
14. GStAPK Dahlem, Rep. 90 P, no. 71, Heft 2, fol. 51. The way the incidents were recorded suggests that the individual cases were separately typed up, with the family name shortened.
15. See Gellately, *Hitler's True Believers*, who emphasizes that the SA "outdid themselves in their cruelties" (242). See also Evans, *Coming of the Third Reich*, 434, and Stefan Schurr, "Die 'Judenaktion' in Creglingen am 25. März 1933. Eine Quellendokumentation," in Gerhard Naser, ed., *Lebenswege Creglinger Juden. Das Pogrom von 1933. Der schwierige Umgang mit der Vergangenheit*, 3rd ed. (Bergatreute: Eppe, 2002), 59–82.

Creglingen is turned into "Künzlingen" and Hermann Stern into "a seventy-year-old man by the name of Berg."[16]

Based on available written evidence, it is possible to classify antisemitic murder cases during the period of the Nazi seizure of power into three approximate categories, whereby occasional overlap cannot always be avoided.

i) The more or less spontaneous murder without prior planning. In their triumphant certainty that they would never be brought to account, and propelled by the hatred bred by incessant antisemitic propaganda, SA units were devoid of scruples and restraint to the point that the transition between grievous bodily harm and murder had become fluid. In these actions, extreme antisemitism, the desire for personal revenge, and frequently also the simple lust to torture and kill were the driving forces. It is impossible to say how many victims succumbed to their wounds in the days, weeks, or even months after the attacks.[17] But it is certain that most murders fell into this category, in which the estimated number of unknown cases is highest. In the rapturous exultation of wielding power, attackers proceeded not only with unspeakable brutality but also with carefree insouciance and the certainty of being beyond the reach of the law.[18]

ii) Murders of people already under arrest or in the custody of the SA and SS, so that killings could occasionally also be camouflaged as "shot while trying to escape." This category deals with specifically anti-Jewish murders, since non-Jews who had been arrested at the

---

16. Feuchtwanger, *The Oppermanns*, 282–286, esp. 283. "...[T]he historical novel won rave reviews when it was published around the world in 1933 and 1934" (Introduction, viii); the book was first published in the United States by Viking in 1934.
17. Cases in which victims died of their wounds months after the abuse are addressed below.
18. A witness in the Kassel murder case (see below) observed: "What especially attracted my attention was that the people left the courtyard in a leisurely way [after committing murder],... and what stood out to me was their unnatural calm." 25 April 1933, HHStA Wiesbaden, Abt. 468, no. 424, fol. 24.

same time as the Jewish victims who were later murdered either survived their time in detention or were released earlier.[19]

iii) Planned and "revenge" murders. Documented cases that have been passed down to us already attracted a great deal of attention in 1933, so that they could be reopened after 1945 as soon as political circumstances permitted.

Below follow a few examples in each of the three categories, described in as much detail as the documentary sources permit and possibly also illustrating the pattern and typical recurring traits of these murders. (For the locations and relative frequency of murders of Jews in 1933, see the map on page 44).

The "Spontaneous" Murder

During the night of Saturday, 22 April, to Sunday, 23 April 1933, several SA men forced their way into the apartment of the Jewish dairy merchant Max Kassel in Wiesbaden. Kassel's door was kicked in and, following a violent scuffle, Kassel himself was shot and killed by more than a dozen bullets.[20] Due to the brazenness and brutality of the murder, several high-ranking police officers inspected the scene of the crime on Sunday morning. There can be no doubt that initially the Wiesbaden police took the case seriously. The investigation quickly revealed that the almost 60-year-old Kassel was completely apolitical and belonged to no political party (contradicting later allegations that he had supported the Communists). Kassel, born in 1874 in Friedberg (Hesse), was known as a thoughtful, reserved, and guarded person who had a housekeeper to look after him. She also helped out in his shop and lived in the same

19. An example is the case of the Baden *Landtag* deputy Ludwig Marum (SPD), who was murdered in the Kislau concentration camp near Bruchsal. Other prisoners who had been arrested together with Marum were released earlier. Generallandesarchiv Karlsruhe, Bestand 309, nos. 4806–4820; Bestand 480, no. 7700; Monika Pohl, *Ludwig Marum. Gegner des Nationalsozialismus* (Karlsruhe: Info, 2013).
20. 23 April 1933 at HHStA Wiesbaden, Abt. 468, no. 424 "Ermittlungsakte im Mordfall Kassel."

block of apartments. During World War I, Kassel had been held captive for four years in French internment camps. According to his loyal housekeeper, Kassel "was met with hostility from various persons in words and phrases because he was a Jew." Especially malevolent and antagonistic was the son of the owner of the house, Rösch, who was a member of the NSDAP and regularly offered free meals to unemployed National Socialists.[21] Kassel's maid, whom he had recently dismissed without references, was engaged to an SS man, and Kassel's daughter believed that the revengeful fiancé of the maid was involved in the attack. Since the fiancé had made threats against Kassel, the dairy merchant began to feel increasingly uneasy in Webergasse 46 and sold his dairy shop effective 1 May 1933.[22]

While the initial police investigation from the days following the murder strictly adhered to the facts, the reports of the Wiesbaden public prosecutor to the Prussian Ministry of Justice sang a very different tune. The public prosecutor surmised that the murder "evidently concerns an act of revenge and political motivations possibly played a role;" he averred that "the suspicion of being party to the crime has focused on two members of the Communist Party."[23] That this was extremely unlikely was clear to anyone familiar with the case. At the beginning of May, several SA men—Johannes Lerch, Johann Haas, and Ernst Franzreb—came under suspicion. All three were detained in nearby Frankfurt but then escaped to Munich with the help of their SA superiors. The responsible SA officer in Frankfurt had at first refused to hand over the perpetrators to the police, "since carrying out the criminal proceedings might possibly endanger State interests."[24] Initially, the Wiesbaden public prosecutor seemed intent on upholding the law by pursuing the

---

21. 25 April 1933, ibid., fol. 23.   22. 23 April 1933, ibid., fols. 9–10 v.
23. 30 April 1933 at GStAPK Dahlem, Rep. 84a, no. 54815, "Wegen Ermordung des jüdischen Milchhändlers Max Kassel," fols. 2–2 v. The emphasis on the victim's religion in the court file is meant to indicate that the case would be handled separately, as it fell under the category of the "amnesty."
24. 12 May 1933 at GStAPK Dahlem, Rep. 84a, no. 54815, fol. 3; 9 June at ibid., fol. 10; and 24 July 1947 at HHStA Wiesbaden, Abt. 520-BW, no. 2085, Spruchkammerakte zu Ernst Franzreb, fols. 36–48.

(obviously guilty) SA men. According to the prosecutor, this might mean jeopardizing the national interest, but "nonetheless another course except that of strict legality...is not possible."[25] Yet his attitude was to soon change.

The post-war investigation revealed that the two main offenders, Johannes Lerch and Ernst Franzreb, had been in hiding in an SA training facility in Munich in 1933. Members of the Wiesbaden criminal police and the examining magistrate ferreted them out and brought them back to the Wiesbaden Remand Prison. The SA regiment to which Lerch and Franzreb belonged thereupon appealed for help to Ernst Röhm, the SA chief of staff, and succeeded in having the proceedings quashed and the two murder suspects set free. This happened in early July, before the promulgation of the 22 July amnesty.[26] The Wiesbaden public prosecutor, who could anticipate these developments as soon as Röhm involved himself in the proceedings, now found his hand forced to rationalize the cancellation of the arrest warrant and the release of the two main murder suspects, whom the investigation had clearly shown to be guilty. In an astonishing volte-face, he now produced a plethora of mitigating circumstances: there had, after all, been no real witnesses to what happened, except Lerch and Franzreb; the shots had probably not been fired with the intention to kill; possibly there was another unknown perpetrator from whose pistol the deadly bullets came. In addition, the accused were tired out and they had been drinking. Finally, the accused "had been fighting against organizations" that wanted to harm the National Socialist movement, and no one had been able to refute their assertions that "Kassel had supported the German Communist Party with monetary funds to bloodily suppress the SA and had also called the Reich

25. 12 May 1933 at GStAPK Dahlem, Rep. 84a, no. 54815, fol. 3v.
26. 25 March 1950 at HHStA Wiesbaden, Abt. 520-BW, no. 2085, "Spruchkammerakte zu Ernst Franzreb," fols. 5–6. After the war Franzreb received a prison sentence of ten years for the Kassel murder. In Franzreb's first trial, in a German denazification court (*Spruchkammer*) in 1947, a witness who had been locked up with him said, "it was a sensation that National Socialists were put in prison." On Lerch's and Franzreb's speedy release in 1933 the witness commented, "They were released for committing murder, and we were put in jail for distributing leaflets." 24 July 1947, ibid., fols. 43–44.

Chancellor a scoundrel [*Lump*]."[27] The public prosecutor, who had read the character assessments of Kassel, knew quite well that the retiring, cautious, and completely apolitical dairy merchant had done none of these things, but he had to think of his own political survival. He must have known that these were mere trumped-up allegations, frequently used by the SA both as an excuse and to vilify victims. SA perpetrators were well aware that if they could promulgate the accusation that the victim had supported communists, had been a communist himself, or made derogatory remarks about Hitler or the National Socialist movement, prosecuting counsel was bound to cut the perpetrators some slack and make their offense appear in a different light. The Wiesbaden prosecutor thus must have been aware that his arguments were preposterous and absurd. But they enabled him to do what he felt he had to do in any case—quell the proceedings and release the prisoners while at the same time try to save face.[28] He, too, was subject to the pressures of the zeitgeist, and the zeitgeist demanded the elimination of Jews from public life to end violence rather than using the law to put a stop to it. The law was not used to help victims; victims were characterized in such a way that SA violence could be justified.

But the case was not yet at an end. It lived on in two ways, the first indicating how the simple utterance of a fact could lead to arrest if it countered Nazi interests. In March 1934, the barber Adam Daum from Mainz (situated across the Rhine from Wiesbaden) was arrested for offenses under the "Perfidy Decree," because he had maintained that "three SA men killed a Jew in Wiesbaden." Since the prosecutor of this case actually requested the files of the Kassel murder, one may assume that Daum got off lightly.[29] The second was the reopening of the Kassel murder in a series of trials against Ernst Franzreb after 1945. The other principal offender, Lerch, had been killed during the war in Russia.[30]

27. 16 August at GStAPK Dahlem, Rep. 84a, no. 54815, fols. 16 v.–17.
28. 24 August 1933 at GStAPK Dahlem, Rep. 84a, no. 54815, fol. 19.
29. 28 March 1934 at GStAPK Dahlem, Rep. 84a, no. 54815, fol. 20.
30. 8 February and 24 July 1947 at HHStA Wiesbaden, Abt. 520-BW, no. 2085, fols. 9, 35–48.

Franzreb, though a very different type of offender from the high-ranking SS officers, was a typical Nazi criminal of the rough and ready sort:[31] born in 1900, he completed elementary school and two years of secondary school (*Realschule*) before being apprenticed as a gardener. In 1924 he joined the KPD and thereafter repeatedly fell afoul of the law: "His list of previous convictions leaves not the slightest doubt that he is [a] criminal by nature," as the Wiesbaden prosecutor's office summed it up in 1950.[32] In 1930, Franzreb joined the NSDAP and the SA. When his criminal record was discovered, he was expelled from the Party, but not the SA presumably—according to the post-war assessment—because "one did not want to do without such unscrupulous and brutal characters as the person concerned."[33]

Once the Nazis were in power, Franzreb outdid himself in house searches, knife attacks on communists, and brutal abuse of other political opponents. In the case of Max Kassel, Franzreb happened to run into a group of four SA men on the night of the murder, who told him that they had been ordered to arrest Kassel. Since Franzreb was the only one familiar with the building in which Kassel lived (he had been a frequent guest at Rösch's free dinner table for unemployed National Socialists), he led the group to Kassel's apartment and then took a leading role in his murder. Shortly thereafter, in the summer of 1933, Franzreb was named as the principal offender in the murder of a Wiesbaden communist.[34] In November 1938, he again "attracted attention by the havoc he wreaked on Jewish shops and in setting the Wiesbaden synagogue ablaze."[35] In another wanton attack, he broke into the apartment of the Jewish lawyer Guthmann in November 1939 (he had no orders to do so) and seriously

---

31. On high-ranking SS officers, see Ronald Smelser and Enrico Syring, eds., *Die SS. Elite unter dem Totenkopf. 30 Lebensläufe* (Paderborn: Schöningh, 2000); Michael Wildt, *Generation des Unbedingten. Das Führungskorps des Reichssicherheitshauptamtes* (Hamburg: Hamburger Edition, 2003); Campbell, "SA in the *Gleichschaltung*," 194–221.
32. 25 March 1950 at HHStA Wiesbaden, Abt. 520-BW, no. 2085, fol. 2.
33. 25 March 1950, ibid., fol. 3.
34. 24 July 1947 at HHStA Wiesbaden, Abt. 520-BW, no. 2085, fols. 35–48; 25 March 1950, ibid., fols. 1–10.
35. 25 March 1950, ibid., fol. 7.

injured Guthmann and his son with a knife. This last action, according to the court in 1950, "was too much even for those in power then."[36] In 1940, Franzreb was sentenced by a special court in Frankfurt to ten years *Zuchthaus* (prison for capital offenders). He remained in custody, except for a brief spell in a penal battalion at the very end of the war. Already on the occasion of Franzreb's first denazification trial in 1947, his victims turned out in force to make their complaints—former KPD members, Max Kassel's housekeeper, the widow of the lawyer Guthmann, as well as an assortment of senior members of Wiesbaden's criminal police department.[37] In a series of trials up to 1950 he was sentenced to another five years' imprisonment for his active participation in the demolition of the Wiesbaden synagogue, to ten years for the murder of Max Kassel, and to an additional ten years of heavy labor for his role as a Nazi criminal. He was also classified in the first group of those incriminated by post-war German denazification courts as a major Nazi criminal, the most severe of the five categories of incrimination.[38] In 1950, the court regretted in its summing up that "in view of the cruel and inhuman behavior" of the accused, the law does not "permit a punishment greater than ten years of heavy labor."[39]

36. 25 March 1950, ibid., fol. 8.
37. 8 February, 24 July 1947 at HHStA Wiesbaden, Abt. 520-BW, no. 2085, fols. 9, 35–48.
38. Franzreb's lawyer objected that Franzreb, through "placement in Group I would be equated with political criminals who are responsible for the death of millions of people." The court dismissed the objection (25 March 1950, ibid., fol. 9). In the American zone every German who had occupied a function in public life or who wanted to obtain such a position had to fill out a 131-question questionnaire. By March 1946, 1.39 million question-naires had been completed. Starting in March 1946 German civilian denazification courts (*Spruchkammern*) became involved. Beginning in February 1947, *Spruchkammer* proceedings were also taken up in the French and British Zones. There were five categories of incrimination: i) Major Offenders (*Hauptschuldige*); ii) Offenders (*Belastete*); iii) Lesser Offenders (*Minderbelastete*); iv) Fellow Travelers (*Mitläufer*); v) Exonerated (*Entlastete*). By 1950 more than 3,660,000 proceedings had been carried out, wherein 1,667 people were categorized as major main offenders, 20,060 as offenders, 150,425 as lesser offenders, and more than a million as fellow travelers. See Lutz Niethammer, *Die Mitläuferfabrik. Die Entnazifizierung am Beispiel Bayerns* (Berlin: Dietz, 1982); Jörg Echternkamp, *Nach dem Krieg. Alltagsnot, Neuorientierung und die Last der Vergangenheit 1945–1949* (Zurich: Pendo, 2003), 160–175; Angela Borgstedt, *Entnazifizierung in Karlsruhe 1946–1951* (Konstanz: UVK, 2001); Martin Broszat, "Siegerjustiz oder strafrechtliche 'Selbstreinigung.' Aspekte der Vergangenheitsbewältigung der deutschen Justiz während der Besatzungszeit," VJHZ, 29 (1981), 477–544.
39. 25 March 1950 at HHStA Wiesbaden, Abt. 520-BW, no. 2085, fol. 9.

When public prosecutors' offices did not automatically reopen a case after the war, close relatives or friends occasionally filled the breach. This happened in the case of the livestock dealer Max Moses from Wesseling near Cologne. Moses's daughter and son-in-law, Liselotte and Alfred Heilberg, who returned to Germany after 1945, brought the killing of Max Moses in early April 1933 to the attention of the authorities (in Moses's case, the precise designation of the crime was "grievous bodily harm resulting in death"). According to the Heilbergs, the following had taken place: the ardent Nazi Peter Stieldorf, who had been in charge of expelling Jewish livestock dealers and butchers from the Cologne stockyard in April 1933, had Moses arrested, then kicked and mistreated him, and subsequently ordered a gang of Nazi thugs to kill him in the green belt near Cologne's stockyards. Moses was beaten up so severely by the gang of hired ruffians (presumably SS men in civilian clothing) that he never recovered and, despite long stays in hospital and rehabilitation centers, eventually succumbed to his internal injuries.[40] Direct eyewitnesses to the crime could not be named and the doctor treating Moses at the time was no longer alive, but the Heilbergs found several reliable witnesses who had known Moses well, knew what had happened to him, were familiar with the facts, and also agreed to give testimony. Cologne's criminal investigation department then began an inquiry and summoned witnesses.[41]

The testimonies of these witnesses and the former director of the stockyard seriously incriminated Stieldorf, confirmed the charges against him, and generally depicted him as a widely feared and violent Nazi. After

40. 19 October 1959 at HStA Düsseldorf (Landesarchiv NRW), Abt. Rheinland, Gerichte Rep. 231, Staatsanwaltschaft Köln, no. 1429, fols. 1–1 v. Alfred Heilberg had reported Stieldorf's crime already in 1946, only to receive the reply that Stieldorf was no longer registered as a resident there.

41. 2 November, 10 November, 28 November, 7 December, 13 December, 29 December 1959 at HStA Düsseldorf, Abt. Rheinland, Gerichte Rep. 231, no. 1429, fols. 5–15. The original indictment "against unknown to the detriment of the cattle dealer Moses" of 27 June 1933 on account of battery was abandoned on 1 July 1933. The records of the original investigation were presumed to have gone missing due to the impact of war; 30 October 1959, ibid., fol. 4.

some to and fro, a warrant was issued against Stieldorf, who had moved back to Cologne in 1959, and since there he was at risk of escape and suppression of evidence, he was taken into custody.[42] In the arrest warrant of 14 March 1961, Stieldorf was "urgently suspected... as head of the Action Committee of expelling Jews from the stockyard Köln-Ehrenfeld [and] of having instigated other unknown persons to mistreat the Jewish livestock dealer Max Moses, whereupon they injured him so severely that he died on 19 January 1934."[43] To obtain further information about a now almost thirty-year-old case, the Cologne prosecutor's office turned to the local population in a newspaper ad, which also drew attention to another unsolved murder of which Stieldorf was suspected:

> Who witnessed the instances of assault and battery in the stockyard? During a raid by the NSDAP Cologne North in the spring of 1933 Jewish cattle dealers were expelled from the stockyard. In the course of this action, brutal attacks took place as a result of which the livestock dealer Max Moses (from Wesseling) died. The Jewish livestock agent Kahn (Wesseling) is also reported to have lost his life through comparable abuse. The population is asked for its participation in the solution of these crimes by furnishing information to the head prosecutor at the *Landgericht* (district court) in Cologne.[44]

In the unambiguously worded bill of indictment, Stieldorf was charged with "grievous bodily harm resulting in death."[45] The indictment also illuminated his career as a National Socialist: Stieldorf joined the Party in 1930, became a "block warden" shortly thereafter, and advanced to become *Personalamtsleiter* (head of personnel) of the NSDAP in Cologne and surroundings in August 1933, that is, a few months after the events at the stockyard.[46] Beginning in late March 1933, Stieldorf headed a committee whose task it was to expel Jewish livestock dealers and butchers

---

42. 14 March 1961 at HStA Düsseldorf, Staatsanwaltschaft Köln, no. 1430, fols. 140–143.
43. Ibid., fol. 141.
44. Ibid., fol. 215. The wording of the notice in the *Kölnische Rundschau* of 19 April 1961.
45. 8 November 1961 at Institut für Zeitgeschichte (IfZ), Munich, GK 08.11, vol. I, fols. 1–15.
46. This was a responsible position, given that Cologne, with its 756,000 inhabitants (1933), was the third largest city in the Reich after Berlin and Hamburg.

from the premises of the stockyard. There he was known as "a fanatical champion of Nazi ideology and a Jew-baiter," who "carried through the expulsion of Jews in the most ruthless fashion."[47] It also became clear that during the course of the investigation "the accused had demonstrably and repeatedly told lies." In 1933, he had obviously used his position in the stockyard to boost his own standing. On 1 May 1933, for example, during the new National Day of Labor, the entire workforce of the stockyard had to march past his apartment in review. The prosecution thus came to the conclusion that "despite the absence of direct witnesses to the action, there can no longer be doubts as to the accused's participation in the murder."[48]

In light of the evidence, corresponding testimonies of witnesses (who, for the most part, did not know each other), and Stieldorf's repeated lies, there could hardly be any doubt as to his guilt, the more so since he was also described as a brutal Nazi criminal in a related case.[49] All the more surprising, therefore, was the actual sentence, which acquitted Stieldorf of all charges in the absence of proof (*mangels Beweises*) and referred court costs to the public purse. In the opinion of the court, Stieldorf's assertion that he had nothing to do with the offense could "not be refuted with the necessary certainty."[50] The sentence must have appeared farcical to members of Moses's family, especially when reading the initial pages of the court's opinion, which emphasized Stieldorf's evasions and contradictions and his extreme antisemitism, which he obviously used for his advancement in the NSDAP. Grounds given for the acquittal were the absence of immediate witnesses and lack of persons who could testify from their own actual experience, as well as doubts as to whether it really had been Stieldorf who gave the order for the crime. Here aspersions are cast on the memory of the murdered Moses, on whose reports witnesses

47. 8 November 1961 at IfZ Munich, GK 08.11, vol. I, fol. 8.
48. Ibid., fol. 13.
49. HStA Düsseldorf, Gerichte Rep. 231, no. 120, "Hubert König wegen Misshandlung jüdischer Händler."
50. 15 June 1962 at IfZ, Munich, GK 08.1, "Strafverfahren gegen Peter Stieldorf. Misshandlung eines jüdischen Viehhändlers mit Todesfolge," fols. 1–12, esp. 7.

and the prosecution had relied and referred to. His recall, the court opined, might have suffered from "severe injuries to the head" and "in these circumstances, his account significantly loses its probative force [Beweiskraft]."[51] One can only assume that personal prejudice and the preferences of the three presiding judges, as well as the restorative political and social climate of the 1950s and early 1960s, promoted this far-fetched construct. In West Germany no significant renewal and exchange of the judicial elites had taken place, so that large parts of the judiciary were still dominated by former NSDAP members and sympathizers, as well as judges, whose sentencing practices were imbued with the values of the Third Reich.[52]

The most widely known anti-Jewish crime in the spring of 1933 was the murder of the lawyer Friedrich Schumm from Neidenburg (East Prussia) in Kiel on 1 April. Otto Dibelius, one of Germany's most prominent Protestant theologians, even mentioned this case in his radio address about the anti-Jewish boycott to an American audience on 4 April 1933. In this speech, Dibelius justified the legality and essential peacefulness of the present "revolution." According to Dibelius, the day of the boycott, too, had passed peacefully: "There had been only one bloody incident. This was in Kiel on the Baltic. There a Jew shot down a young National Socialist and was then himself shot by the crowd before the police could get him to safety."[53] But here Dibelius erred; the actual circumstances of the case were quite different: on 30 March the lawyer Friedrich Schumm from East Prussia visited his father, the furniture merchant Georg Schumm, in Kiel. As he tried to enter his father's shop at around 11:00 a.m. on 1 April, the day of the boycott, two SS guards barred his entrance.

---

51. Ibid., fols. 9–10.
52. Wilfried Loth and Bernd-A. Rusineck, eds., *Verwandlungspolitik—NS-Eliten in der westdeutschen Nachkriegsgesellschaft* (Frankfurt and New York: Campus, 1998); Norbert Frei, *Vergangenheitspolitik. Die Anfänge der Bundesrepublik und die NS-Vergangenheit* (Munich: DTV, 1996); Norbert Frei, ed., *Hitlers Eliten nach 1945*. 2nd ed. (Munich: DTV, 2004); Manfred Görtemaker and Christoph Safferling, *Die Akte Rosenburg. Das Bundesministerium der Justiz und die NS-Zeit* (Munich: Beck, 2016).
53. EZA Berlin, Bestand 51, E2e8,1, "Die nach Amerika gerichtete Rundfunkrede des Herrn General-superintendenten Dibelius vom 4. April 1933," fol. 3. See also Chapter 10 below.

It was only when his father came out of the shop that Schumm was finally let in. When the SS men told Schumm that he should have said right away that he was the son of the owner, Schumm responded, "You can't force us to do anything," a remark the SS men obviously "interpreted as an insult."[54] Therefore, as Schumm left the shop a little while later, the SS men were not willing to let pass what they considered a provocation; they got into an argument with him that quickly turned into a scuffle with one of them. The other SS man thereupon set upon Schumm, the lawyer drew his pistol, and injured his first antagonist, the SS man Wilhelm Asthalter, with a shot in the stomach. Schumm escaped back through the shop, but then quickly turned himself into a police station, from where he was immediately taken to police headquarters.[55] Witness statements taken down on the very day of the incident differ greatly. According to statements from SA and SS men, the argument, as well as the physical attack, had been begun by Schumm, whereas Schumm's sister, Anni Schumm, and the shop's managing clerk, Alma Bracker, held the SS guard who had been shot responsible, since he had jostled against Schumm and threatened him with a beating. The reader of all witness statements gains the impression that the SS guards precipitated the physical attack, but also that Schumm would not put up with any insults.[56]

The report of Kiel's police chief, Count von Rantzau, naturally gives preference to the version of the SA and SS men. But then Rantzau felt that he had some explaining to do, given that what occurred subsequent to the incident outside the furniture store was all too reminiscent of "revolutionary excesses," something Prussian authorities were not meant to tolerate in their districts. According to Rantzau's report, after the SS

---

54. 1 April 1933 at GStAPK Dahlem, Rep. 84a, no. 54897, "Wegen Ermordung des jüdischen Rechtsanwalts Schumm aus Neidenburg," fols. 16–25, esp. 18.
55. 2 April 1933, ibid., fol. 25.
56. Schumm had apparently decided to defend himself against possible attacks. Shortly before this incident, he had purchased a weapon, the license of which was dated 22 February 1933. Asthalter, the SS man who was shot, did not die, as initially reported in many newspapers and also repeated by Dibelius. He recovered after an operation.

man Asthalter was shot, "the indignation of the national population" vented itself on "the furniture, furnishings, and fixtures on the premises of the merchant Schumm's establishment, which were totally wrecked."[57] Yet, as the post-war investigation brought to light, popular anger played no role in this: Kiel's Nazi *Kreisleiter* and subsequent Lord Mayor, Walter Behrens, supported by the SS *Sturmbahnführer* (Major) Jahnke, ordered the throngs of SA and SS men, whom the goings-on had brought to the scene, to destroy Schumm's furniture shop.[58] The news that Friedrich Schumm had been conveyed to the prison in the police headquarters spread like wildfire, and all entrances to it were soon blocked by the SA and SS, so that it was impossible to transfer Schumm to the nearby prison in Rendsburg in the early afternoon, as initially planned.[59]

There are again different versions as to what happened next. According to police chief Count von Rantzau's report, the prison yard soon filled with a swarm of young National Socialists, many of whom were armed, and who vociferously demanded to be let into the prison. It had become seemingly impossible to pacify the crowd.[60] As the mob-like throngs of people got ready to storm the prison, according to his own testimony Rantzau had to give the order "to open the door in order to safeguard the lives of the prison guards."[61] Then about thirty to forty men stormed the prison, took hold of the keys to the cells, forced their way into Schumm's cell and killed him with about thirty bullets, of which

---

57. 2 April 1933, GStAPK Dahlem, Rep. 84a, no. 54897, "Rantzau an preußischen Innenminister," fols. 1–5, esp. 5. This constituted a grave breach of the peace.

58. 31 August 1945, Landesarchiv Schleswig-Holstein, Staatsanwaltschaft Kiel, Abt. 352, no. 4500, fol. 17. Schumm's shop was completely devastated. Since the perpetrators had also started a fire, the shop's inventory was damaged by fire extinguisher residue. See the 17-page list of damages at GStAPK Dahlem, Rep. 84a, no. 54897.

59. 2 April 1933 at GStAPK Dahlem, Rep. 84a, no. 54897, fol. 3. On this point Rantzau's report tallies with the statements of several police officials, who mentioned that there had been an attempt to get Schumm out of the building but that all of the exits were blocked. Of the thirty largest German cities, Kiel, pop. 218,325 (1933) had the highest percentage of NSDAP voters (46%), more than Königsberg (44%), Wuppertal and Breslau (each with 43%), and Chemnitz and Stettin (each 42%). See Thamer, *Verführung und Gewalt*, 258.

60. 2 April 1933, at GStAPK Dahlem, Rep. 84a, no. 54897, fol. 4. "The national-minded population of Kiel was seething with rage, since a Jew had spilled the blood of a German SS-man."

61. Ibid.

at least twelve might have been fatal.[62] Rantzau's report ends with the not quite accurate remark, "Popular fury set in explosively; less than four hours passed between Schumm's deed and his demise."[63] The post-war investigation then showed that there was no spontaneous popular frenzy. The throngs of SA and SS men, who had just destroyed Schumm's furniture shop, were intentionally directed to police headquarters, where they then committed the lynch murder as soon as Schumm's whereabouts became known.[64] The "breach of public peace," that is, the destruction of Schumm senior's furniture establishment by the Nazi mob and the lynching of Schumm, hardly fit the image the Prussian authorities wanted to convey of their state (Schleswig Holstein had become a Prussian province in 1866). Consequently, the public prosecutor's office, the police chief (who had played a pitiful role in all this), and the Prussian Minister of Justice made sure that the case would not come to court, where, in any case, only SA and SS men would have filled the benches of the accused. They did their best to nip it in the bud. This was already accomplished by 14 August 1933.[65] The furniture merchant Schumm not only saw his furniture establishment wrecked and his son killed. In 1934 he was sentenced to pay the very substantial sum of 25,000 Reichsmarks as compensation for the personal suffering of the SS man Asthalter, meanwhile restored to good health.[66]

The Schumm case was reopened immediately after the end of the war. It triggered a veritable avalanche of trials that lasted well into the 1950s, involving mostly persons who had been part of the crowd that forced their way into the prison at police headquarters. A 1946 report of the German public prosecutor to the British occupation authorities included

---

62. See the pathologist's report of Schumm's body with photographs, in GStAPk Dahlem, Rep. 84a, no. 54897.
63. 2 April 1933, ibid., fol. 4.
64. 31 August 1945 at LASH, Staatsanwaltschaft Kiel, Abt. 352, no. 4500, fol. 17.
65. 17 May, 23 May, 28 June, 7 July, 14 August 1933 at LASH, ibid., fols. 6–10.
66. 9 Mai 1934 at LASH, ibid., fol. 19. This corresponds roughly to 100,000 euros (insurance companies usually equate 1 Reichsmark (in 1933) to €4).

eleven names.[67] The trial against one of the main suspects, SS man Karl Wagner, who remained in Norwegian captivity and was at first believed missing and presumed dead, extended into the early 1950s. In 1951 the case had to be dropped, since prosecution witnesses revoked their earlier statements and freely conceded that they had incriminated Wagner only because they thought he had been killed in the war.[68] On 11 November 1947, three people received prison sentences of between one year and one year and eight months. One of them was the SS man Walter Köhler, who had loudly boasted before 1945 that he had killed Friedrich Schumm.[69] In 1959, Friedrich Schumm's widow, Irma Levy, and her second husband, Max Levy, tried to track down Kiel's former police chief, Count von Rantzau. Since he had opened the prison gates to the Nazi mob in 1933, the Levys now wanted to see him tried as an auxiliary to murder. The fall of 1959 thus saw a nationwide search operation for Rantzau in West Germany. It was finally established that he had already passed away in 1946 in Nierstein on the Rhine. The final legal proceedings in the Schumm murder were thus dismissed on 12 January 1960.[70]

Murder while in Custody

There were numerous murders of Jews, businessmen, politicians, and others in 1933 while they were in SA custody or in concentration camps. Here, too, the estimated number of unknown cases is high, so that it is

---

67. 16 October 1946 at LASH, Abt. 352, no. 4501. One of the main culprits, *SS-Sturmbannführer* (Major) Fritz Jahnke, who had organized the destruction of the furniture store and then directed the mob to the police prison, was killed by a lightning strike in 1936.

68. 9 November 1951 at LASH, Abt. 352, no. 4501, fols. 76–80. Most of the suspects survived the war but then disappeared.

69. LASH, Abt. 352, no. 1697. After the war Köhler denied having killed Schumm and testified that he was only "boasting" to make a name for himself. It could eventually be proven that he and the other defendants belonged to the crowd that had gathered outside the police presidium. As an SS member, Köhler had a firearm on him at the time of the incident. See also LASH, Abt. 352, no. 879.

70. LASH, Abt. 352, no. 879, "Rantzau, Graf zu, geb. 14.7. 1888, ehemaliger Polizeipräsident in Kiel."

impossible to calculate precise figures. Post-war trials and a few surviving contemporary documents have made the details of some significant cases known. The "shot while trying to escape" murder, which is central to this category, was also widespread in 1933 and remained so until 1945. It affected mainly political prisoners in the widest sense, including Jews.

A characteristic example is the murder of Felix Fechenbach, editor of the Social Democratic *Volksblatt* in Detmold in the small northern German state of Lippe. Fechenbach had already been taken into "protective custody" by the SA on 11 March.[71] In the ranks of the nationalist right, he had long been a hated figure, since he had been the secretary of the socialist Bavarian Minister-President Kurt Eisner, who precipitated the fall of the Wittelsbach dynasty in Munich in 1918. In 1922, Fechenbach was sentenced to a long spell in prison for alleged treason in the so-called Fechenbach affair (the judgment was overturned and annulled in 1924), and after 1929 he turned the Detmold *Volksblatt* into an effective propaganda weapon against the Nazis.[72] In August 1933, Fechenbach was to be transported from northern Germany to the Dachau concentration camp near Munich. He sensed what might be in store for him on the way. Before being moved, he remarked to fellow prisoners that he would certainly make no attempt to escape for fear of being shot. During the post-war investigation of his murder, it emerged that during the transport on 7 August 1933 the vehicle conveying Fechenbach stopped in a

71. Already before 1933, persons could be taken into "protective custody" for up to twenty-four hours for their own protection, for the preservation of public order, or for defense against a political danger. The "Decree for the Protection of the German People" of 4 February 1933 had extended the length of imprisonment to up to three months, whereby those taken into custody initially had the right to appeal; that right fell by the wayside with the Reichstag Fire Decree of 28 February. At first held in prisons, those in "protective custody" were later detained in camps. According to estimates, 25,000 people were taken into protective custody in March and April 1933 in the state of Prussia alone. "Protective custody" was an important instrument for the establishment of the dictatorship. See Klaus Drobisch and Günther Wieland, *Das System der NS-Konzentrationslager 1933–1939* (Berlin: Akademie, 1993); Hans Buchheim, Martin Broszat, and Hans-Adolf Jacobsen, *Anatomie des SS-Staates*, 6th ed. (Munich: DTV 1994); Wachsmann, *Nazi Concentration Camps*, 23–136.

72. BA Koblenz, Z38, no. 239, "Tötung eines jüdischen Hauptschriftleiters des sozialdemokratischen *Volksblatts* in Detmold." Detmold, in Lippe, pop.16,051 (1925); *Statistisches Jahrbuch* (1933), 11. On Fechenbach's role in Munich, see Mitchell, *Revolution in Bavaria*, 76–110.

remote forested area where Fechenbach was dragged out, at gunpoint forced to run away, and then "shot while trying to escape."[73] The driver of the car, SS man Paul Wiese, who already had a number of previous convictions but was clearly not the main instigator of the conspiracy to murder Fechenbach, freely conceded in the course of the trial that Fechenbach had been arrested only because he was a political opponent and a Jew. Wiese was sentenced to five years' imprisonment for complicity to manslaughter. The trial also made it clear that earlier plans to eliminate Fechenbach had failed. His transfer to Dachau had provided the desired opportunity to kill him. An earlier criminal investigation into Fechenbach's death had already been terminated on 15 September 1933.[74]

In 1933, being "shot while trying to escape" (auf der Flucht erschossen) had become proverbial. Fechenbach was by no means the only one who had heard of it. Rudolf Ditzen, better known throughout Germany as a novelist who wrote under the pseudonym Hans Fallada, came within an inch of meeting the same fate.[75] Fallada had been wrongfully denounced to the local Nazi authorities by the couple who owned his rented house for allegedly hatching a plot "against the person of the Führer." Both stood to profit from the denunciation and reap substantial financial advantages from Fallada's arrest.[76] After an extended search of

73. BA Koblenz, Z 38, no. 239 "Tötung eines jüdischen Hauptschriftleiters des sozialdemokratischen Volksblatts in Detmold." The post-mortem examination revealed bullet wounds of different calibers in the back, both arms, and neck. See also Hermann Schüler, Auf der Flucht erschossen. Felix Fechenbach 1894–1933 (Cologne: Kiepenheuer & Witsch, 1981).

74. A total of four SA and SS members from Detmold counted as suspects. Hans-Joachim Riecke, who had been named Reichskommissar of Lippe in 1933, was accused in the 1960s of having given the order for the transport. While Riecke had actively persecuted Fechenbach, it could never be proved that he gave the order to murder him. The trial dragged on until 1970, when the case against Riecke was dismissed. See BA Koblenz, Z38, no. 239, "Tötung eines jüdischen Hauptschriftleiters . . . ;" Wigbert Benz, Hans-Joachim Riecke, NS-Staatssekretär: Vom Hungerplaner vor, zum "Welternährer" nach 1945 (Berlin: Wissenschaftlicher Verlag, 2014).

75. Rudolf Ditzen (1893–1947) had become well known in the last years of the Weimar Republic for his novels Bauern, Bonzen und Bomben (1931) and Kleiner Mann – was nun? (1932), which colorfully depicted the zeitgeist of the late Weimar period. His other novels, Wer einmal aus dem Blechnapf frist (1934), Wolf unter Wölfen (1937), and Jeder stirbt für sich allein (1947), were very successful in post-war Germany and, after 2003, also in Britain and the USA.

76. Fallada's landlords had denounced him in order to regain full possession of their house. Fallada had leased parts of it for a longer period and paid the rent in advance. Fallada's biographer, Jenny Williams, aptly commented: "With the abolition of the Rechtsstaat,

his house that yielded no results, Fallada was packed into an old car to be conveyed to the prison in Fürstenwalde about 8 miles away.[77] The car suddenly stopped en route in an isolated part of the forest, where Fallada was told to get out. Knowing what might happen, he desperately clung to the frame of the car. There can be little doubt that he would also have been "shot while trying to escape" if the local village doctor, who was a friend of Fallada's, had not happened to be driving along the same lonely road. Immediately grasping the situation, the doctor insisted on following Fallada's car at a short distance on the way to Fürstenwalde. According to his own narrative and assessment of events, Fallada would have been shot if he had not forcefully resisted leaving the car and were it not for the unforeseen circumstance that his friend happened to be driving along the isolated road.[78]

The weeks after the election of 5 March 1933 saw a number of *Gleichschaltungsaktionen*—actions to eliminate political dissent—which were directed mostly against strongholds of the leftist parties and the trade unions. One such action took place between 9 and 26 March in the state of Braunschweig on the order of Braunschweig's National Socialist Interior Minister Dietrich Klagges.[79] It was carried out by the SA *Standartenführer* (Colonel) Sauke, whose men descended on several towns in the Harz Mountains, such as Blankenburg, Gandersheim, and Seesen, where they arrested members of the SPD and trade unions, mistreated them, and threatened some of them with execution. As Sauke stated in his

NSDAP members at all levels were emboldened to give free vent to a whole range of base feelings, such as cruelty, envy, and a desire for revenge in the firm knowledge that the normal sanctions of a civilized society no longer applied." See Jenny Williams, *Mehr Leben als eins. Biografie* (Berlin: Aufbau, 2011), 191.

77. Fürstenwalde, town in Brandenburg, pop. 23,278 (1925); *Statistisches Jahrbuch* (1933), 11.
78. Hans Fallada, *In meinem fremden Land. Gefängnistagebuch 1944* (Berlin: Aufbau, 2009), 33–52.
79. GStAPK Dahlem, Rep. 90 P, no. 71, Heft 1, fols. 34–36. Toward the end of this "action" there were numerous attacks in the city of Braunschweig, including one in which the city's Lord Mayor Ernst Böhme was led through the city streets in a "pillory march." Ibid., fol. 36. See also Hedda Kalshoven, *Between Two Homelands. Letters Across the Borders of Nazi Germany*, trans. and with a preface by Peter Fritzsche (Urbana: University of Illinois Press, 2014), 66–69.

post-war trial, "Intimidation was the desired outcome of these actions."[80] In Seesen, all Jewish tradesmen were arrested, and some of them—the merchants Hamm and Simon—beaten up and tortured.[81] The Jewish merchant Bremer, who was the target of special animosity by the SA because of an alleged sexual molestation of an underage girl, was also arrested and maltreated. Since there were no concrete charges against him, he was to be set free on 18 March. During the night before his scheduled release, he was again beaten by a number of SA men who had broken into the local jail. On the morning of the 18th, he was found in his cell hanging by a piece of packing string. Contemporaries doubted that Bremer would commit suicide on the eve of his release.[82]

In the post-war trial it was established that the original files in the Bremer case had been destroyed. Witnesses to the raid in the early hours of 18 March had heard Bremer calling out repeatedly, "Ich hab's ja nicht gemacht!" ("But I didn't do it!"), which seemed to indicate a connection between his murder and the alleged sexual offense. In the files it is noted that the package string would hardly have been strong enough to support Bremer's weight and that suicide was unlikely in view of his impending release.[83] In Bremer's case both contemporaries and the post-war trial officials concurred that he was murdered. They were, in all likelihood, correct in their assessment, as is shown by other cases from the period, since throttling victims to death and then making it look like suicide seems to have been a common method of killing by the SA and SS during the Nazi takeover.

On 28 March 1934, the prominent Jewish Baden SPD deputy Ludwig Marum, who had served his party in Baden's *Landtag* as well as in the Reichstag (1928–33), was murdered in the Kislau concentration camp near

---

80. BA Koblenz, Oberster Gerichtshof für die Britische Zone, Z 38, no. 216, "Freiheitsberaubung und Misshandlungen von Angehörigen links gerichteter Parteien und Juden," fol. 14. In 1949 Sauke was sentenced to six years in prison.
81. BA Koblenz, Z 38, no. 216; GStAPK Dahlem, Rep. 90 P, no. 71, Heft 1, fol. 34, and Heft 2, fol. 11.
82. GStAPK Dahlem, Rep. 90 P, no. 71, Heft 1, "Ein jüdischer Kaufmann Namens Bremer soll an den Misshandlungen gestorben sein. Der Fall wird anscheinend von der braunschweigischen Staatspolizei untersucht," fol. 34.
83. BA Koblenz, Z 38, no. 216.

Bruchsal in very much the same way.[84] Marum (1882–1934) was arrested as early as 10 March 1933 and transferred to the new camp in Kislau after having been being put on a truck and paraded through the Baden capital of Karlsruhe on 16 May. In this procession through Karlsruhe's busiest shopping streets, Marum was accompanied by other arrested SPD leaders and subjected to the jeers and catcalls of the onlookers—much like the humiliating pillory marches that took place during the spring and summer of 1933. The provisionary Minister-President of Baden and (since May 1933) Reich Governor Robert Wagner was Marum's bitter enemy, since Marum had publicly exposed Wagner's financial irregularities by demonstrating that he had charged his parliamentary attendance allowance to the Baden treasury even for the days he had been absent.[85] In a post-war trial, the *Landgericht* in Karlsruhe established that Wagner had ordered the Kislau deputy camp governor, Karl Sauer, to kill Marum.[86] The court record of 14 June 1948 indicates that Sauer, aided by two accomplices, stole into Marum's cell on 28 March 1934, throttled the sleeping Marum, strung him up at the window of his cell, and toppled over the stool in the cell to feign suicide.[87] The other SPD deputies from Baden who had been arrested alongside Marum, including the longtime (1919–31) Interior Minister Adam Remmele (1877–1951), had long been released by then. Only the Jewish Marum was murdered.

The same fate befell the Social Democratic local politician and editor of the *Lübecker Volksbote* Fritz Solmitz (1893–1933). Solmitz was also arrested in March 1933, paraded through Lübeck with a sign around his neck reading "Jude," then carted off to a Lübeck prison and transferred to the Hamburg concentration camp Fuhlsbüttel in May 1933.[88] At first Solmitz

84. Generallandesarchiv Karlsruhe (now Landesarchiv Baden-Württemberg), Bestand 480, no. 7700, vol. 1–2; Bestand 309, no. 4806–4824; Pohl, *Ludwig Marum*, 107–120; Ludwig Marum, *Briefe aus dem Konzentrationslager Kislau*, ed. Elisabeth Marum-Lanau and Jörg Schadt (Karlsruhe: Müller, 1984), 141–162.
85. Marum, *Briefe*, 142.   86. Ibid.
87. See "Urteil des Landgerichts Karlsruhe," ibid., 155.
88. Landesarchiv Schleswig-Holstein, Abt. 352.4, no. 540, vols. 1 and 2.; Martin Wein, *Willy Brandt, Das Werden eines Staatsmannes* (Berlin: Aufbau, 2003), 80–85, esp. 83; Christian Jürgens, *Fritz Solmitz: Kommunalpolitiker, Journalist, Widerstandskämpfer und NS-Verfolgter aus Lübeck* (Lübeck: Schmidt-Römhild, 1996).

was treated very much like other prisoners and housed in a communal cell. This changed when Lübeck's National Socialist police chief, Walter Schröder, visited the camp in September and recognized his old political adversary.[89] Solmitz was put into solitary confinement and, according to the testimony of fellow prisoners, submitted to bestial torture. Yet relief seemed near when the Lübeck Senate granted his release on bail. According to the post-war witness testimony of Solmitz's widow, her husband had then been murdered on Schröder's instructions shortly before his intended release.[90] As other witnesses confirmed, Schröder was behind the torture to which Solmitz had been subjected and then contacted the president of Hamburg's prison administration, Lahts, to have Solmitz murdered. According to Karolina Solmitz, in whose opinion antisemitism coupled with revenge on a political opponent had been the main motives, this was done as a kind of "favor" among old Party comrades. Witness statements of Solmitz's former fellow inmates confirm that, after having been subjected to protracted torment, he was killed by two henchmen at the Fuhlsbüttel concentration camp only days before the date of his envisioned release.[91] In the post-war trial, when the two main suspects were put on the stand, the crime could not be directly laid at their feet. The prime suspect, Ludwig Zerbes, who was accused of countless other atrocities, was formally charged with "having committed, as an official, fifty-five, either on his own or together with others...bodily injuries, willfully and with malice aforethought" and was sentenced to ten years' *Zuchthaus*. His partner in crime, Hans Lehmann, received three years.[92]

The presumed instigator of the murder, Walter Schröder, got off scot-free. Fritz Solmitz himself accused Schröder, in collusion with Lahts, of intending to have him killed; he wrote his accusations on cigarette papers that he hid in his pocket watch, which was given to Karolina Solmitz

---

89. According to concurring statements of former concentration camp prisoners in the post-war trial of Solmitz's torturers: 16 and 23 December 1947; 24 January, 17 March, 18 August 1948; 15 February 1949 at LASH, Abt. 352.4, no. 540, vol. 1, fols. 35–74.
90. 17 January 1960 at LASH, Abt. 352.4, no. 540.
91. LASH, Abt. 352.4, no. 540, vol. 1, fols. 35–74.
92. 24 March 1949 at LASH, no. 540, vol. 1, fols. 75–109.

soon after his death. Solmitz also recorded on the cigarette papers the countless antisemitic invectives his tormentors had hurled at him while torturing him.[93] Even though Solmitz's death had been the subject of several lawsuits at the end of the 1940s, Karolina Solmitz reopened the case against Schröder and Lahts on 16 January 1960 on the basis of the evidence provided by Solmitz on the papers hidden in his pocket watch. Members of Lübeck's former National Socialist government were again summoned to appear in court. Yet, as was to be expected, both Lahts and Schröder disavowed any collusion or verbal pact to harm Solmitz, and they denied having been in Fuhlsbüttel at the time of Solmitz's murder.[94] In the absence of further evidence or of direct witnesses contradicting their statements, the case against them had to be dropped.[95] The communist writer Willi Bredel, who was also an inmate in Fuhlsbüttel in 1933, published a novel in London the following year, *Die Prüfung*, in which Solmitz appears as the Lübeck newspaper editor Dr. Fritz Koltwitz. Even though Bredel in his novel originally proceeded on the assumption that Solmitz had committed suicide, he later revised this and wrote that it had transpired that "the SA murderers beat him to death and—in order to feign suicide—strung up the dead body."[96]

The Planned Murder

The third category of murder was the planned revenge murder committed against Jewish political opponents or personal enemies. Envy, professional

---

93. 5 September 1960 at LASH, Abt. 352.4, no. 540, vol. 2, fols. 7–13.

94. 23, 24 June 1960 at LASH, Abt. 352.4, no. 540, vol. 2, "Schröder, Walter, geboren 26.11.1902, ehemaliger Polizeipräsident von Lübeck; Verdacht eines Verbrechens gegen die Menschlichkeit," fols. 133–138.

95. 25 August 1960 at ibid., vol. 2, fols. 1–6. In his communication with Karolina Solmitz, who lived in Bryn Mawr, Pennsylvania (USA) in 1960, the Lübeck attorney general expressed his regret that the legal proceedings had to be terminated. He mentioned that Solmitz's death had already been the subject of several criminal proceedings at the end of the 1940s, in which the former commander of the Fuhlsbüttel concentration camp, among others, had been sentenced to twelve years in a penitentiary (albeit for different crimes).

96. Willi Bredel, *Die Prüfung. Roman aus einem Konzentrationslager* (Berlin: Aufbau, 1968), 345.

jealousy, malevolence, and antisemitic hatred often played a major role. In the murder of the prominent Social Democratic lawyer and city alderman Wilhelm Spiegel (1876–1933) in Kiel, political antagonism and antisemitism came together as motivating forces. As a 38-year-old father of three small children, Siegel joined the German army as a volunteer in August 1914 and was decorated during the war; in 1920, he played a leading role during the Kapp Putsch as head of the democratic forces opposing the coup attempt, and in the early 1920s he chaired Kiel's municipal council. In 1932, he was legal counsel to the editor-in-chief of the *Schleswig-Holsteinische Volkszeitung* in the "Wurbs–Hitler Prozeß," in which Hitler was the complainant and Ernst Röhm appeared as a witness, and in the course of which Spiegel argued that Hitler was preparing a civil war and had given instructions for a coup. It was therefore not surprising when an SS leader called for Spiegel's murder not long after Hitler had come to power.[97] On 11 March the NSDAP took over the city government of Kiel and installed the Nazi *Kreisleiter* Walter Behrens (who also played a role in the murder of Friedrich Schumm on 1 April) as the new mayor. As the post-war investigation brought to light, in the early hours of Sunday, 12 March (the day on which the last Prussian local elections were to take place), five men in SA and SS uniform met outside Spiegel's house. During the previous night, they had already reconnoitered the route to the suburb in which Spiegel lived to make sure that their escape would meet with no obstacles. Since they claimed to belong to the auxiliary police, Spiegel let two of them into his home. There, in the hall between the entrance door and his study, they shot Spiegel in the neck, killing him instantly.[98] Spiegel's housekeeper later testified that one of the perpetrators had worn a uniform.

A criminal investigation launched immediately after Spiegel's murder was dropped on 31 August 1933 under pressure from the Prussian Interior

97. Volker Jakob, "Wilhelm Spiegel: Jude-Anwalt-Sozialist. Das erste Mordopfer der antisemitischen Gewalt," in Gerhard Paul and Miriam Gillis-Carlebach, eds., *Menora und Hakenkreuz. Zur Geschichte der Juden in und aus Schleswig-Holstein, Lübeck und Altona 1918–1998*, (Neumünster: Wachholtz, 1998), 205–213, esp. 206–210.
98. 9 June 1945, at LASH, "Staatsanwaltschaft Kiel," Abt. 352.3, no. 4498, fols. 4–5.

Minister, because "the perpetrators could not be traced."[99] Soon after the end of the war a number of suspects were identified, some of whom were still in the custody of the British occupation authorities and could therefore not be interrogated.[100] In 1946, German authorities presented the British military government with a list of suspects and possible accessories, wherein bitter political antagonism was emphasized as the main motive.[101] In the late 1940s several trials were conducted against those, such as the SS men Kurt Kanthak and Wilhelm Schneekloth, who had bragged during the Third Reich that they had "finished off" Spiegel. But no murder sentences were passed; in the case of Schneekloth the proceedings were discontinued for lack of evidence.[102] The famous Kiel sociologist Ferdinand Tönnies, who knew Spiegel well and held him in high regard, had emphasized the essentially anti-Jewish motivation already a few days after the murder: "This is such a misdeed as I have rarely experienced. But then Spiegel was a Jew from the Rhineland."[103]

There are few crimes that reveal as clearly as this obviously planned murder of a local personage the utter lawlessness that already held sway in Germany by mid-March 1933. Everyone in Kiel who was politically aware knew who was responsible for Wilhelm Spiegel's murder. Nevertheless, the criminal investigation came to a quick end. Already at the very beginning of the Third Reich, the murder of a Jew was not a grave

99. 28 July and 31 August 1933, ibid., fol. 3. This was an unusual procedure in murder cases, especially since here a connection with "crimes committed during the National Socialist revolution" (and thus subject to the amnesty) was not assumed.

100. 31 August 1945, ibid., fol. 8. These included the former Lord Mayor of Kiel, Walter Behrens, and the NSDAP *Gauleiter* for Schleswig-Holstein, Hinrich Lohse, who were accused of being accessories to the crime.

101. 28 August 1946 at LASH, Abt. 352.3, no. 4499, fols. 29–30v. In 1933 no one had been charged, since the SA and SS gave the perpetrators false alibis. See 20 March 1946, ibid., fols. 19, 20.

102. LASH, Staatsanwaltschaft Kiel, Abt. 352.3, no. 885, "Schneekloth, Wilhelm, geb. 08.08.1902 aus Preetz, Verdacht des Mordes." Schneekloth had been awarded the "Golden Party Badge of the NSDAP."

103. Uwe Carstens, *Ferdinand Tönnies. Friese und Weltbürger. Eine Biographie*, 2nd ed., (Bredstedt: Nordfriisk Instituut, 2013), 290. Ferdinand Tönnies (1855–1936) was known mostly through his major work *Gemeinschaft und Gesellschaft*, which played a role in the ideological debates at the beginning of the First World War. The long funeral march of Kiel's workers on 15 March 1933 demonstrated that it was generally known who was responsible for the murder.

offense, as it was, after all, in keeping with the program of the Party that was now in full command of the State. Those who participated in the crime thus felt sufficiently safe that they freely bragged of the murder as a patriotic deed. The thoroughly criminal character of the SA and SS is rarely more evident than in this contract killing. In Spiegel's case, too, the antisemitic motivation is central. By the winter and spring of 1933, non-Jewish Social Democrats were carted off in the thousands to concentration camps, where they were beaten and mistreated but rarely deliberately murdered.[104] Ludwig Marum's non-Jewish fellow sufferers, who like him were members of Baden's Social Democratic Party leadership, had long been released by the time Marum was murdered. And in the Fuhlsbüttel concentration camp, where brutality seems to have been even more wanton than in Kislau, Communists and Social Democrats were beaten, maltreated, and tortured, but rarely singled out for killing. It was Spiegel's and Solmitz's Jewish background that sealed their fate.

Another planned homicide, the prelude to which took place in full public view, was the brutal slaying of the successful Wuppertal dentist Dr. Alfred Meyer during the night of 16/17 May 1933.[105] The meticulously conducted post-war investigation showed that Meyer had a flourishing dental practice and that he had possessed "a large circle of friends and acquaintances, all of whom cherished him as a human being and respected him as a professional, and he was also active in helping the poor."[106] His opponents and those who begrudged him his success, including his fellow dentist Dr. Viering, whose practice was in the same section of Wuppertal as Meyer's, accused him of holding "illegal communist meetings" and of being guilty of numerous "sexual misdemeanors."

104. There were notable exceptions: Georg Landgraf, the publishing director of the *Chemnitzer Stimme,* was killed by SA men because he refused to reveal where the party funds were hidden. In Braunschweig the Social Democratic city alderman, Matthias Theisen (occasionally spelled Theissen), was beaten to death. See Winkler, *Weg in die Katastrophe,* 891.

105. GStAPK, Rep. 84a, no. 53389, "Ermittlungsverfahren gegen Unbekannt wegen Ermordung des jüdischen Zahnarztes Dr. Alfred Meyer, Kommunist in Wuppertal-Barmen am 16. Mai 1933."

106. 8 December 1949 at HStA Düsseldorf, Gerichte Rep. 372, Staatsanwaltschaft Düsseldorf, no. 461, fol. 74.

Viering, who led an SA *Sturm* (a company-sized unit) had also claimed that Meyer was a dangerous opponent of the SA who had put a bounty of 50 Reichsmarks on the head of SA members. And Dr. Meyer's neighbors, the patent attorney Fischer and his wife, who were patients of Dr. Viering, spread rumors that Dr. Meyer had hosted communist meetings and had "indecently assaulted young patients in his office;" they claimed that he was known for the great "rate by which he goes through women."[107] As in Bremer's case in Seesen, there were also insinuations of offenses against minors. Such accusations were the stock-in-trade of Nazi propaganda. There was method in even the most far-fetched calumnies, for these often corresponded to current prejudices. The post-war investigation consigned all these rumors to the realm of legend—"the alleged secret communist conspiracies in his home" turned out to be political "literary evenings in a circle of friends." Since Meyer was happily married to another dentist, talk of "sexual misdemeanors" also seemed far-fetched. In addition, Meyer's entire biography was that of a national-minded patriot: born in March 1898, he volunteered for military service in February 1915, served until the end of the war as a frontline soldier, and was decorated for bravery. After World War I he fought with a *Freikorps* in the Baltic States against the spread of communism and took part in quelling communist uprisings at home. His was a kind of nationalist biography even an ardent National Socialist would have to admire. But different yardsticks were applied to Jews.[108]

Immediately after the 5 March 1933 elections, Meyer's opponents embarked upon a defamation campaign against him within the SA, spreading rumors to the effect that Meyer was a KPD functionary, that his apartment had been turned into a weapons depot, and that he had eluded impending arrest by escaping abroad.[109] This last charge was

---

107. 19 April 1933 at GStAPK Dahlem, Rep. 84a, no. 53389, fols. 38–40. As had already been brought to light in the 1933 murder investigation, Fischer and his wife had attempted to intimidate the Meyer family with nightly threats of terror (*Terroranrufe*).
108. Ibid.; 8 December 1949 at HStA Düsseldorf, Gerichte Rep. 372, no. 461, fols. 74–80.
109. 19 April 1933 at GStAPK Dahlem, Rep. 84a, no. 53389, fols. 38–40.

based on the fact that on 4 March Meyer left Germany for a cruise in the Mediterranean that lasted until early April. Whether he did so to take a vacation or to escape from anticipated unpleasantness cannot be elucidated from surviving documents. The fact that he left his wife behind indicates a purpose other than a mere holiday. In Meyer's absence, a number of attacks were made against his dental practice: the window panes of the practice were smashed on several occasions, the signs were removed four times, and his female medical assistant was beaten and, on one occasion, briefly arrested. After his return, Meyer voluntarily turned himself in to "protective custody," in order to have the charges levied against him investigated.[110] These turned out to be sheer inventions, as the post-war inquiries showed, even though the SA maintained in April 1933 that they had proof of his communist activities. When no incriminating materials could be produced after several weeks, Meyer was released on 6 May 1933. About a week earlier, during the night of 29/30 April, Meyer's apartment had been ransacked and devastated by the SA, who caused such noise and tumult that "the entire neighborhood was woken up within a wide radius" and "a large crowd" gathered in front of Meyer's apartment house. In the words of a (post-war) witness who had seen the destruction in 1933, his apartment looked "as if it had been hit by a bomb attack."[111] In 1949, the court spoke of a "savage furor against the Jew Meyer...which vented itself in the demolition of his surgery and apartment."[112]

After his discharge from protective custody, Meyer went into hiding in the house of a fellow dentist and friend of his in Düsseldorf, since the police had advised him to leave Wuppertal. In mid-May, Meyer's apartment and dental practice were again ransacked by the SA, in the course of which several articles went missing. In order to report this incident and

110. 19 April at GStAPK Dahlem, ibid.; 8 December 1949 at HStA Düsseldorf, Rep. 372, no. 461, fols. 74–76.
111. 8 December 1949 at HStA Düsseldorf, Gerichte Rep. 372, no. 461, fol. 79. The citizens of Wuppertal (pop. 408,602 in 1933; Thamer, *Verführung*, 258) had experienced many air raids during the war, as a consequence of which more than 6,500 people died.
112. Ibid., fol. 78.

claim damages for compensation, Meyer's wife went to the Wuppertal SA *Standarte* (regiment) that was connected with the raid and robbery. On this occasion, she accidently disclosed the hitherto secret location of Meyer's whereabouts in Düsseldorf.[113] As several witnesses later testified, Meyer was dragged out of the house of his Düsseldorf friend by four people only hours later, at 3:00 p.m. on 16 May, forced into a car, and carried off. The kidnapping attracted a great deal of public attention. On 17 May, several eyewitnesses identified the car's license plate to the police, and a local radio station issued a special announcement on account of the highjacking, which had taken place in full public view.[114] A detailed description of the four men who had abducted Meyer was also provided, so that it should have been quite easy to apprehend them there and then.[115] As was established later during the post-war trial of one of the main suspects, Hermann Birkenstock, Meyer was brought to the Düsseldorf SA headquarters "Schloss Jägerhoff," where he was "bestially murdered" during the night of 16/17 May. "[A]mong other things, his feet had been squashed in a printing press and he had been shot three times in the neck. The corpse was brought in a bedsheet to the Bevertal Dam" and thrown into the water.[116] On the morning of 18 May, a forester discovered the corpse there. It was weighed down with a printing press to keep it under water and the head was covered with a sack. It was a pure accident that the dead body had floated to the surface.[117]

In order to make sure that the perpetrators would not have to face trial, the Düsseldorf police chief contacted Roland Freisler in the Prussian Ministry of Justice, where Freisler saw to it that the case was dropped as early as 11 August 1933.[118] In the post-war trials against those

113. 8 December 1949 at HStA Düsseldorf, Gerichte Rep. 372, no. 461, fol. 77.
114. 17 May 1933 at GStAPK Dahlem, Rep. 84a, no. 53389, fols. 34–37, 42, 43, 48.
115. Ibid., fols. 44–45.   116. HStA Düsseldorf, Gerichte Rep. 372, no. 121, fol. 2.
117. GStAPK Dahlem, Rep. 84a, no. 53389; HStA Düsseldorf, Gerichte Rep. 372, nos. 121 and 122.
118. 25 May 1933 at GStAPK Dahlem, Rep. 84a, no. 53389, fols. 6, 12. The note of Düsseldorf's Chief of Police to Freisler is marked "Top Secret! Personal." He sent the Meyer case record with his own letter to *Ministerialdirektor* (ministry section head) Freisler in Berlin and requested that the case be handled in accordance with the telephone consultation of 27 May.

implicated in Meyer's murder and apartment demolition, it was established that the Düsseldorf crime squad and the prosecutor's office had to relinquish the case in 1933:

> The Meyer case was then only briefly in the hands of the criminal police, who had to hand over the investigation to the public prosecutor's office at the instigation of higher authorities. The local prosecutor's office could not clear up the case, as these particular records had to be passed on to the *Zentralstaatsanwaltschaft* [central prosecution authority] in Berlin.[119]

Such a procedure was rare, even by the standards of 1933, since anti-Jewish crimes fell under the amnesty and were thus dropped in any event. In cases where everything pointed to National Socialists as perpetrators and where enough was known to identify the murderers, as in Meyer's case, "vital national interests" could be used as a pretext to nip further investigations in the bud. What is striking in Meyer's case is that a generally well-known, national-minded, and respected professional was defenseless and doomed when confronted with professional jealousies, vendettas, and mere lust for revenge, and that the murderers got off scot-free even though parts of the crime had taken place in full public view. In 1933 this was possible because the victim was Jewish.

The investigation into Meyer's murder was reopened by his surviving friends in May 1945 and advanced by the British military government, under whose aegis the German criminal police acted. Dozens of witnesses were heard and several people arrested. Before 1945, some had bragged that they had participated in the Meyer killing. In 1943, for example, a certain Engels, in a state of complete inebriation, had called out in the street, "I am the murderer of Meyer," whereupon he was taken

---

119. 8 December 1949 at HStA Düsseldorf, Gerichte Rep. 372, no. 461, fol. 94. The proceedings were then officially closed with the usual formula: "The proceedings against unknown for murder – 6aJ765-33 – are dismissed, according to the decree of 12 August 1933, based on the decree of the Prussian *Ministerpräsident* of 22 July 1933 in connection with the general order of 25 July 1933 referring to 'Bestowal of mercy on the occasion of the ending of the National Socialist revolution.'" Signed: Prussian Minister of Justice. Berlin, 16 August 1933 (see also HStA Düsseldorf, Gerichte Rep. 372, no. 462, fol. 3).

to a police station for disturbing the peace. Such boasting could have disagreeable consequences after the war, when obvious scapegoats for the crimes of the regime were welcome, especially if they already had a police record. Those suspected of having taken part in the wrecking of Meyer's apartment were also subpoenaed after the war. Altogether, eight people were accused of pillage and murder.[120] During the following years, the investigation was expanded, so that by 1948 a total of ten potential perpetrators who might be charged for the crimes had been identified. While the investigation was carried out meticulously, in the absence of proof its success depended on some of the offenders contradicting or possibly even incriminating each other.

Finally, on 8 December 1949, after more than four years of investigation and witness interrogations, custodial sentences were pronounced against four of those implicated in Meyer's murder and the wrecking of his apartment. The SA *Sturmführer* Hermann Noelle, who identified Meyer in Düsseldorf when he was abducted, received a prison sentence of four and a half years. Hermann Birkenstock was sentenced to ten months, while others involved in the demolition of Meyer's apartment got off lightly, with prison sentences of only a few months.[121]

The cases of anti-Jewish violence and murder discussed here naturally are only the tip of the iceberg. Others—and we shall never know how many—will remain shrouded in obscurity. Speculations, even informed guesses, as to their number are bound to be too inaccurate to be put forward. The high volume of violence unleashed by the SA and SS and ranging from street attacks to murder was tolerated by the political climate prevailing in the late winter and spring of 1933. It is striking that murderers felt free to brag about their deeds and that they could be wholly confident in not being held to account. Police, the bureaucracy,

---

120. 8 November 1946 at HStA Düsseldorf, Gerichte Rep. 372, no. 122, fol. 38.

121. HStA Düsseldorf, Gerichte Rep. 372, no. 461, fol.6. It was established that behind the attack against Meyer lay a conspiracy by Dr. Viering and the SA *Sturmbannführer* Hans Pfeiffer, who wanted to get Meyer out of Wuppertal. Both imputed criminal acts to Meyer for which there was no foundation.

and the courts afforded no protection. As will be shown when dealing with the reaction of the administrative and judicial bureaucracy,[122] officials did all they could to minimize and belittle the crimes of the perpetrators, all of whom got off scot-free. There was also no more concerted opposition to the regime in the spring of 1933. Only individual acts of protection could help the persecuted, such as those of the doctor who saved Rudolf Ditzen's life by following the car on the forest road or the dentist Meyer's friend who hid Meyer in Düsseldorf. Parties and institutions formerly potentially capable of concerted resistance, such as the SPD or the Protestant Church, were either persecuted themselves, as was the case with the Social Democrats, silenced by their own anti-semitism, or intimidated into inactivity by the powerful dictate of a zeitgeist that portrayed as unpatriotic any assistance to even those Jews who had volunteered to go to war for Germany—a country they had considered to be their homeland.

122. See Chapter 13.

7

BOYCOTT

Boycott Movements before 1 April 1933

B oycotts against Jewish shops had a long tradition in Germany.
Already in the nineteenth century handbills urged customers not
to "buy with the Jew." In the early years of the Weimar Republic when the
anti-Jewish mood reached a first climax, the antisemitic *Deutschvölkischer
Schutz- und Trutzbund* (German *Völkisch* Protection and Defense League)
championed the boycott of Jewish shops.[1] Boycotts became even more
widespread after the onset of the Great Depression at the end of the
Republic. By then, they were systematically used as a weapon to bank-
rupt Jewish retailers and department stores.[2] Already before 30 January
1933, some National Socialist town councils or mayors' offices excluded
Jewish firms from the award of public orders, and strident Nazis called
for the boycott of Jewish lawyers and doctors. At the behest of the
Centralverein deutscher Staatsbürger jüdischen Glaubens such summons for
boycott actions could usually be quickly nipped in the bud by the
authorities while the Republic was in place.[3]

---

1. Wildt, *Volksgemeinschaft*, 145–152; Henry Wassermann and Eckhart G. Franz, "'Kauft nicht
beim Juden.' Der politische Antisemitismus des späten 19. Jahrhunderts," in Eckhart
G. Franz, ed., *Juden als Darmstädter Bürger* (Darmstadt: Roether, 1984), 123–136. In 1922 the
Deutschvölkische Schutz- und Trutzbund had 170,000 members.
2. Ahlheim, "*Deutsche, kauft nicht bei Juden!*" 106–205.
3. Paucker, "Jüdischer Abwehrkampf," 405–499, esp. 442–443; Sybille Morgenthaler,
"Countering the pre-1933 Nazi Boycott against Jews," *Leo-Baeck-Institute Yearbook*, 36 (1991),
127–149; Wildt, *Volksgemeinschaft*, 145–152; Stefanie Schüler-Springorum, *Die jüdische
Minderheit in Königsberg/Preußen* (Göttingen, Vandenhoeck & Ruprecht, 1997), 285–287;
Barkai, "*Wehr Dich!*"

Before the Holocaust: Antisemitic Violence and the Reaction of German Elites and Institutions during the Nazi Takeover.
Hermann Beck, Oxford University Press. © Hermann Beck 2022. DOI: 10.1093/oso/9780192865076.003.0008

Since 1928–9, National Socialist calls for boycotts of Jewish department stores had become increasingly widespread.[4] Boycott actions in smaller cities and towns were nothing out of the ordinary, especially during the run-up to Christmas. A handbill from Elbing in East Prussia from December 1932 calling for the boycott of Jewish shops epitomized typical resentments against Jewish tradesmen, as well as "arguments" not to frequent their shops. First, the increasing destitution of the small trades-men and merchant class is explained by the overpowering competition of Jewish department stores and the attitudes of non-Jewish Germans who patronized Jewish shops. Then the writer of the handbill comes to the point:

> Why bother about the dirty Jew? He has no business in your Fatherland. Hold him in contempt and don't let him make any money, then he'll disappear all by himself and your German brother can live again…Have you ever heard of the "Stab in the Back?" In 1918 scoundrels with Galician names stabbed the men at the front from behind. You have spoken with a sense of outrage of this Stab in the Back. Yet, you yourself wield the knife if you betray the German people's community by spending your money in Jewish shops. German People's Comrade, think better of it! Don't buy with Jews, buy with Germans.[5]

In 1932, the centers of boycott actions lay in northern Germany, espe-cially in areas where the NSDAP was strong, such as East Prussia, Pomerania, Schleswig-Holstein, and parts of Saxony.[6] With the onset of antisemitic attacks all over Germany after 5 March 1933, targeted boycotts set in with added vigor, better organization, and more violence. Now SA guards prevented customers from entering shops (occasionally not only with verbal exhortations), which subsequently were often forced to shut

---

4. Uhlig, *Warenhäuser*, 36–39; Ahlheim, *"Deutsche, kauft nicht bei Juden,"* 155–205; Christoph Kreutzmüller, *Final Sale in Berlin. The Destruction of Jewish Commercial Activity 1930–1945* (New York: Berghahn, 2015).
5. Wildt, *Volksgemeinschaft*, 147–148. The heading on the handbill read: "Christmas: a German holiday or a way to make a financial killing for the Jews?" Elbing, town in East Prussia with 76,000 inhabitants (1933), *Statistisches Jahrbuch* (1933).
6. Morgenthaler, "Countering," 134–136; Wildt, *Volksgemeinschaft*, 148–152.

down. As in cases of violent attacks against *"Ostjuden,"* the police did not intervene, but dismissed boycott actions as mere "protest demonstrations."[7] In the "revolutionary" atmosphere of March 1933, when courts of law were under siege by the SA, legal redress was not feasible. The geographical center of this new wave of boycotts between 7 and 9 March lay in the Prussian Rhine province, especially in the Rhenish-Westphalian industrial centers around Düsseldorf, Dortmund, Essen, Cologne, and Wuppertal.[8] Roused by warnings from the Ministry of Economics and alarming telegrams from commercial organizations such as the Central Organization of German Consumer Cooperatives, Hitler turned to Nazi Party members, the SA, and SS, asking them to refrain from "individual actions" and to keep calm. He explained that "unscrupulous subjects, mostly communist informers, have attempted to compromise the [National Socialist] Party through isolated transgressions, which have no relationship at all to the great achievement of the national uprising, result only in damage, and belittle the accomplishments of our movement."[9] These appeals for moderation, reprinted in the entire German press, and then reiterated twice with great urgency in the second half of March, had little effect.[10] Further boycott measures, accompanied by violent acts in Würzburg, Rostock, Schwerin, and other cities, occurred on and after 11 March 1933.[11]

Just as in the case of antisemitic violence following the elections of 5 March 1933, the March boycotts were initiated from below by local SA, SS, or Nazi party units. After the March elections the feeling was widespread among Nazi Party cells and affiliated organizations that the road

7. On the passivity of the police, see 15 March 1933 at BA Berlin, R43 II, no. 1195, "Auswärtiges Amt an Preußisches Ministerium des Innern," Akten der Reichskanzlei, NSDAP, fol. 107; and 23 March 1933, R 43 II, no. 1195, fol. 173; also Wildt, *Volksgemeinschaft,* 115–123, esp. 115.
8. Pätzold, *Judenverfolgung,* 47–52; Wildt, *Volksgemeinschaft,* 115–120.
9. BA Berlin, R43 II, no. 1195, "Reichskanzlei, NSDAP," fols. 58–64.
10. BA Berlin, R43 II, no. 1195, *Berliner Lokalanzeiger,* "Hitler gegen Einzelaktionen," fol. 63. Violent attacks, especially against *"Ostjuden,"* continued well into the month of April. On the futility of Hitler's appeals, see Beck, *Fateful Alliance,* 185–186, and Pätzold, *Faschismus,* 48–50.
11. Wildt, *Volksgemeinschaft,* 118.

was clear and they could now freely vent their hatred on the "Jewish enemy" so often conjured up in Nazi propaganda. These grassroot actions stood in sharp contrast to the April boycott that was organized by the Nazi party leadership and, to all intents and purposes, appeared as an initiative of the German State. Hitler's numerous appeals and injunctions after 10 March to "desist from individual actions" indicate that antisemitic actions in March ran counter to the image the newly installed NSDAP–DNVP coalition government wanted to project. At this point in time, it was interested mainly in presenting the image of an ordered and stable State in contrast to the turmoil of Weimar's last years. The officially sanctioned boycott of 1 April 1933, organized to counter criticism of Germany and the boycott of German goods abroad, then served two functions: first, to counteract the alleged "horror propaganda" against Germany abroad, and secondly, to appease local SA, SS, and Nazi Party units by adopting their earlier "wild" measures and channeling them into official policies. Depending on the respective neighborhoods in which they were conducted, the local boycotts in March may have been more or less successful and met with some enthusiasm on the part of participants. The April boycott met with a very different reception. Official and private reports concur that during the boycott on 1 April 1933 the vast majority of the population showed no enthusiasm, mostly quietly turned away, and in some districts even supported Jewish shop owners.

Global Protests and Boycotts against Germany

The violent antisemitic attacks after 5 March were taken up by the press of the Western powers and led to a worldwide wave of protests against Germany. Foreign voices of protest were first raised in response to harsh measures against socialists and communists following the Reichstag Fire Decree of 28 February; by mid-March they were directed against anti-Jewish attacks. Protests were especially widespread in Britain and the US, where reporting was more detailed than elsewhere, but there were anti-German protests in France and Poland as well.[12] In fact, protests and boycotts of German goods as a direct response to Nazi anti-Jewish attacks did indeed span the globe, as can be seen from complaints of firms in Hamburg to the city government. According to a meticulous report by Hamburg's Chamber of Commerce that summarized actions against German goods, boycott initiatives came from all continents with the exception of parts of South America. There were appeals to refuse booking passage or loading and unloading freight for Atlantic crossings on ships flying under the German flag. In the Cabinet meeting of 31 March 1933, the Reich Transportation Minister mentioned that "all ocean crossings on the [ocean liners] 'Europa' and 'Bremen'... have been canceled."[13] And not only commercial goods and passenger ships were affected. As the scholarly publication house Steinhoff Verlag in Dresden reported to the Saxon authorities, virtually all of their invitations sent abroad to subscribe to its publications had been rejected.[14] Already endangered as a stronghold of science and research by the expulsion of Jewish scientists and scholars, Germany was now in peril of becoming totally isolated in the world of scholarship and learning.[15]

German reactions to foreign protests were shaped partly by the experience of World War I and the international isolation that conflict brought in its wake. Gustav Stresemann's foreign-policy successes after 1925 and Germany's subsequent entry into the League of Nations were but first tentative steps toward an international rapprochement that had been cut short with Stresemann's untimely death in October 1929 and the

12. On protests in Britain, see BayHStaA, 5. Hauptabteilung, Sammlung Varia, no. 231, "Zur Judenfrage," esp. "The Persecution of Jews in Germany." On reactions in the USA: BA Berlin, R43 II, no. 602 and R 72, no. 1477; in Poland: BA Berlin, R43 II, no. 1480. See also Walter Tausk, *Breslauer Tagebuch*, ed. Ryszard Kincel (Berlin: Siedler, 1988), 47–61, and Chapter 9 below.
13. Staatsarchiv Hamburg, Bestand 132–1, "Reichs- und auswärtige Angelegenheiten," no. 828, "Boykottbewegung im Ausland als Gegenbewegung zu antisemitischen Bewegungen in Deutschland;" Pätzold, *Judenverfolgung*, 66–69. *Akten der Reichskanzlei, Regierung Hitler*, vol. I, 277.
14. Pätzold, *Faschismus*, 68.
15. See also Saul Friedländer, "The Demise of the German Mandarins. The German University and the Jews," in *Von der Aufgabe der Freiheit. Politische Verantwortung und bürgerliche Gesellschaft im 19. und 20. Jahrhundert. Festschrift für Hans Mommsen* (Berlin: Akademie: 1995), 69–82.

new harsh realities of economic nationalism that came with the Great Depression. The German reaction to international disapprobation therefore led to a united front that was joined even by opponents of the new government. Across the board, the by then largely censored German newspapers dismissed foreign reports of antisemitic attacks as lies and misrepresentations, whereby the present "campaign of defamation" was equated with the alleged anti-German "atrocity propaganda" concerning German war crimes during World War I.[16] Even prominent papers, such as the *Deutsche Allgemeine Zeitung*, the *Hamburger Fremdenblatt*, and the *Frankfurter Zeitung*, which had preserved a certain measure of independence, wrote of "propaganda hostile to Germany" and "atrocity reports and unscrupulous sensationalist news items that did not correspond to the truth."[17] The *Berliner Börsenzeitung*, another respected paper, pointedly entitled its article "War Atrocity Propaganda Revived."[18] This unanimity, which encompassed even internationally respected newspapers, coupled with a request by major Jewish organizations such as the *Centralverein* and the Reich Association of Jewish Frontline Soldiers to lift the international boycotts directed against Germany, bestowed a certain measure of legitimacy and persuasiveness on German protests.[19]

The united defensive front, spanning all political persuasions; the unifying feeling of having to confront an overpowering host of enemies; the uplifting sentiment of domestic unity, of another "*Burgfrieden*" that was reminiscent of 1914; and the continual comparison of current events with Allied reproaches of war atrocities did not fail to leave their mark.[20]

---

16. See Chapter 9 for more details. For an overview of reactions in Germany's most important daily newspapers, see BA Koblenz, Zeitgeschichtliche Sammlung 103, Presseausschnitts-Sammlung Lauterbach, no. 3101, "Boykott gegen jüdische Geschäfte."
17. See the *Frankfurter Zeitung*, "Gegen die Greuelpropaganda;" *Hamburger Fremdenblatt*, "Der Wahrheit die Ehre;" *Deutsche Allgemeine Zeitung*, "Boykott gegen deutsche Waren, eine englische Fehlrechnung," at BA Berlin, NS 5, VI, no. 17208.
18. 27 March 1933 at BA Berlin, NS 5, VI, no. 17208.
19. The *Centralverein* was the most influential Jewish organization in the Weimar Republic, claiming to represent 300,000 German Jews. Niewyk, *Jews in Weimar*, 86; Barkai, "*Wehr Dich!*"
20. The original accusations about German war crimes in August 1914, involving the shooting of Belgian civilians considered to be guerrillas, were basically accurate. Later, however, there were exaggerations in the English and French press, such as claims that German

Having been subjected to considerable political pressure, the *Centralverein* declared on 26 March (the day the anti-Jewish boycott scheduled for 1 April was decided upon): "For weeks now the German nation finds itself in a gigantic political upheaval. In this context there have been encroachments also against Jews. The Reich and state governments have successfully attempted to restore law and order. The order of the Reich Chancellor to desist from individual actions has produced results."[21] At the behest of Hamburg companies the board of Hamburg's German Israelite community declared in a telegram:

> Rumors spread abroad regarding pogroms and massacres of Jews in Germany are not true. In the political struggle of the last few weeks there has been violence, in some cases also against Jews, but not to the extent that these rumors allege. After the energetic intervention of the government, which strictly forbade any such actions, peace and order have been secured across the land. We request that there be no obstruction of German commerce; with God's help, German Jews will succeed in overcoming antisemitism.[22]

Apart from the fact that declarations of Jewish organizations had been prompted by threats and vain hopes of ameliorating the fate of Jewish Germans, they had also been boosted by gross exaggerations of the facts. On 24 March 1933, for example, the London *Daily Mail* reported on its front page, "1400 Jews slain," continuing in the text, "1400 Jews have been

soldiers would maim children. See Horne and Kramer, *German Atrocities 1914*, and Rainer Rother, ed., *Die letzten Tage der Menschheit. Bilder des ersten Weltkrieges* (Berlin: Deutsches Historisches Museum, 1994) for examples of anti-German propaganda.

21. *Frankfurter Zeitung*, no. 229, 26 March 1933, "Der Centralverein gegen ausländische Greuelmeldungen." The *Reichsbund jüdischer Frontsoldaten* declared: "We believe it to be our duty, not only in our national interest but also in the interest of the truth, to take a position on these actions. Mistreatments and violent excesses have occurred, the minimizing of which is most definitely far from especially our intent.... We know that the government and all leading state bodies most vehemently object to the violent acts that have occurred." Ibid. See also Barkai, *"Wehr Dich!,"* 270–284.
22. Staatsarchiv Hamburg; Bestand 132–1, "Reichs- und auswärtige Angelegenheiten," no. 828, "Boykottbewegung im Ausland als Gegenbewegung zu antisemitischen Bewegungen in Deutschland." This telegram was to be distributed in Tangier and Casablanca since it was here that boycotts of German ships had been initiated.

tortured and murdered in the city of Hamburg alone during the Hitler terrorism now sweeping Germany."[23] Even though the essence of the report on "Hitler terrorism" was accurate, it was partly due to such wanton exaggeration that foreign reports could be dismissed in toto as "atrocity propaganda." In this spirit of wounded respectability, Vice Chancellor Franz von Papen replied to a protest telegram by the German-American Chamber of Commerce in New York on 18 March that the news about alleged attacks lacked any foundation. The national revolution, whose goal it was to free Germany of communist elements, had been carried out with remarkable order: "News circulating in America about alleged torture of political prisoners and maltreatment of Jews has been met here with a storm of indignation and merit the strongest repudiation. Hundreds of thousands of Jews irrespective of nationality, who are not politically active, live here completely undisturbed."[24] Even though Papen conceded that "some deplorable encroachments" had occurred, the self-satisfied tone of his telegram leaves no doubt that he considered Germany the victim of foreign machinations. It was in the context of this mood of seeming self-defense against an international conspiracy that Hitler announced the Reich-wide boycott of Jewish shops and lawyers' and doctors' offices as an essentially defensive act of resistance forced upon his government.[25] The planned boycott fit in well with the image of a Germany surrounded by enemies that was once again exposed to the calumnies of an atrocity campaign reminiscent of the First World War. Parallels to 1914 and to a world of enemies who malevolently disseminated false rumors were conjured up on all levels.[26] The war analogy made it easy for the regime to rope in the non-Nazi press for its campaign. As Peter Longerich notes, the message conveyed to the

23. Ibid.
24. *Akten der Reichskanzlei*, Part I, vol. 1, 260–261. Papen knew all too well that this did not correspond to the truth, since by March 1933 his Vice Chancellor's office had been turned into an unofficial *"Reichsbeschwerdestelle"* (Reich Complaints Center) that was flooded with reports of antisemitic attacks and requests for help (among other things); see also Chapter 14 below.
25. For the precise timing, see Friedländer, *Nazi Germany*, 14–21, and Pätzold, *Faschismus*, 26.
26. On the World War I analogies, see Chapter 9 on the Protestant Church.

average newspaper reader in Germany was that foreign agitation amounted to an unfair disparagement of their country against which Germans had to defend themselves.[27] Worst of all, readers were made to believe that antisemitic attacks never took place. But then many knew from their own personal experience that this was a manifest lie.

The Boycott of 1 April 1933

The official announcement on 26 March of a nationwide boycott was like a clarion call for the SA to pursue new and more vigorous actions despite the intentions of the NSDAP–DNVP coalition government to curb so-called "independent actions." It was first scheduled to last for four days, then at the last moment, on 31 March, was limited to one day.[28] Already on 28 March, there were numerous boycotts of Jewish shops and department stores as well as forcible closings of Jewish retailers in the Ruhr area, especially in Essen, Herne, Mülheim, Witten, and Oberhausen; in Glogau and Liegnitz in Silesia, Ludwigshafen in the Bavarian Palatinate, neighboring Mannheim in northern Baden, and in Stettin in Pomerania.[29] Though it was a quasi-official governmental undertaking, the boycott was not organized by the Reich Interior Ministry but by the NSDAP. The four National Socialists in the Cabinet—Hitler, Frick, Göring, and Goebbels—kept themselves in the background. The organization of the boycott lay in the hands of a committee headed by Julius Streicher, publisher of *Der Stürmer* and *Gauleiter* of Franconia, a semi-criminal figure and rabid antisemite who would lose his Party positions due to corruption and graft in 1940. Also taking part were the various Nazi trade and

---

27. Longerich, *"Davon haben wir nichts gewusst!"* 60–64.
28. On the evening of 31 March 1933 Goebbels suddenly announced that the *"Greuelhetze* [rabble-rousing atrocity propaganda] abroad [is] in the process of dropping off" and that the boycott would start on Saturday, 1 April 1933, to be adjourned until 5 April on the condition that "atrocity propaganda" cease; Genschel, *Verdrängung*, 51.
29. Pätzold, *Faschismus*, 65; Wildt, *Volksgemeinschaft*, 120–122.

professional organizations,[30] in particular the leaders of the Fighting League of the Artisanal *Mittelstand*, whose members felt threatened by department stores and Jewish tradesmen and hoped to weaken both through the boycott; the National Socialist Factory Cell Organization (NSBO); the NS War Victims Provisions Service; the NS Civil Servants Organization; NS agrarian organizations; the NS Reich Youth Association; and the NS Jurists and NS Physicians Leagues; as well as Dr. Achim Gercke, who had compiled a detailed card index of "more than 500,000 Jews" living in Germany, put together under racial criteria and including ancestors.[31]

The boycott was carried out by the National Socialist Party apparatus at the county and provincial (*Gau*) levels.[32] This was done to ensure that the special interests of some Nazi organizations, such as the Fighting League of the Artisanal *Mittelstand*, would not become too dominant. According to instructions, foreign Jews were to be exempt from the boycott.[33] When it was put into operation on 1 April, however, SA mobs did not always heed this exemption, so that some foreign Jews were boycotted as well. While the NSDAP naturally claimed supreme authority over boycott actions, its smaller German National coalition partner had created its own modest organization to support the boycott, and did its best not to be considered too "*judenfreundlich*." Toward this end,

30. Julius Streicher became head of the "Central Committee for the Defense against Jewish Atrocity Propaganda and Boycott Campaign" on 28 March 1933. A grade-school teacher, he promoted an antisemitic picture book for children entitled *Der Giftpilz* (*The Poisonous Toadstool*), that was distributed free of charge to grade schools in his district of Franconia. Roos, *Julius Streicher*, 235–282.
31. Saul Friedländer, *Das Dritte Reich und die Juden*. Vol. I: *Die Jahre der Verfolgung, 1933–1939* (Munich: Beck, 1998), 28–31, Genschel, *Verdrängung*, 44–51; Barkai, *Vom Boykott zur "Entjudung*," 21–24; Pätzold, *Faschismus*, 53–56; Longerich, *Politik der Vernichtung*, 24–27; Uhlig, *Warenhäuser*, 77–78.
32. The Nazi Party bureaucracy virtually mirrored the State bureaucracy, so that State functionaries usually had a rival Party functionary at the same administrative level. The National Socialist *Kreisleiter* (county leader), for example, was often in charge of the same administrative area as the Prussian *Landrat* (or Saxon and Austrian *Kreishauptmann*). The National Socialist *Gauleiter* roughly corresponded to the administrative office of *Oberpräsident* (who was in charge of a Prussian province, such as Pomerania or East Prussia). Only on the district level (presided over by a *Regierungspräsident* in the civilian bureaucracy) was there no Nazi equivalent.
33. Pätzold, *Faschismus*, 56–57.

the DNVP main office in Berlin sent telegrams to twenty-five regional associations, demanding that they take part in the boycott.[34] The boycott of 1 April was thus not carried out solely by Nazi organizations.

Since Nazi Party circles feared that non-Jewish employees who worked in Jewish shops or department stores might sustain financial losses or even lose their employment, the leadership of the NSBO of Greater Berlin demanded that all non-Jewish workers and white collar employees be paid for two months in advance.[35] In a similar attempt to shield non-Jews, the leadership of the *Gewerkschaftsbund der Angestellten* (Union of White Collar Employees) emphasized in a letter to the Reich Economic Ministry of 30 March that the boycott also harmed Christian and national-minded employees. There was no word of regret about its effect on Jewish business owners, though this omission may have been due to fear of running counter to the prevailing zeitgeist and the possible attendant consequences.[36] Conservative members of the Reich Cabinet behaved in a similar way. Some raised concerns specific to their ministerial departments, but never broached the mind-boggling injustice of the anti-Jewish boycott. Minister of Transport Paul von Eltz-Rübenach drew attention to economic disadvantages, as foreigners had cancelled crossings on Germany's large transatlantic ocean liners; Minister of Finance Schwerin von Krosigk emphasized that the boycott might mean losses in sales taxes; and Foreign Minister Konstantin von Neurath, the most outspoken opponent of the boycott in the Cabinet, suggested that Western governments might be prevailed upon to repudiate the "atrocity campaign" if the boycott were to be cancelled.[37] In response to Krosigk's objection, Hitler declared that sales would simply shift from Jewish to Christian shops, and with regard to Neurath's proposal, he declared his

---

34. BA Berlin, R 8005, no. 48, fols. 104–106. See also Chapter 13 below.
35. Uhlig, *Warenhäuser*, 77–85; Genschel, *Verdrängung*, 51–59. Such demands were made when it was not clear how long the boycott would last. See Pätzold, *Faschismus*, 68–70, and Klemperer, *Zeugnis*, 16–17.
36. Pätzold, *Faschismus*, 68–70.
37. *Akten der Reichskanzlei*, Part I, vol. 1, 276–277. The devout Catholic Eltz-Rübenach later refused to accept the *Goldenes Parteiabzeichen* ("Golden Party Badge") because of the attacks on the Catholic Church and resigned his position on 30 January 1937.

willingness to postpone the boycott until Tuesday, 4 April, if the British and American governments "took a satisfactory stand against the atrocity campaign."[38] In the end, the envisaged date, Saturday, 1 April, remained in place, despite intense deliberations within the United States Department of State and hectic telephone calls between American diplomats in Berlin and the State Department in Washington. No satisfactory solution to avert the boycott could be found.

On Saturday, 1 April, SA guards took up their positions in front of department stores and Jewish-owned shops, while others smeared shop windows with swastikas and slogans—"It is forbidden to enter this shop" or "Achtung Jude! Entry prohibited!" In cases where members of the local SA harbored personal grudges against shop owners, slogans were more aggressive, such as the virtually omnipresent "Juda verrecke!" ("Go to hell, Jews!"). In Berlin there were posters in German as well as in English. Handbills and banners warned: "Steer clear of Jews! Don't shop in department stores!" and "Whoever supports the national government does not shop in department stores!" Lawyers' offices and doctors' practices were also affected by the boycott; banks were exempt. To safeguard against mixups and cases of mistaken identity, some shop owners hung signs in their shop windows reading "German Business," or "Recognized Christian German Enterprise," framed in the old Imperial colors, black-white-red.[39]

In Breslau, one poster read: "Juda has declared war on Germany, give them a suitable answer." The articled clerk (legal trainee) Sebastian Haffner, who travelled through the eastern parts of Berlin on the morning of 1 April, encountered the following scenes: "Jewish shops – there were many in the eastern streets – were open, but SA men, legs straddled wide, stood in front of open shop doors. Filth was scribbled on shop

---

38. *Akten der Reichskanzlei*, Part I, vol. 1, 277; *Documents on British Foreign Policy, 1919–1939*, 2nd series, vol. V, 1933 (London, 1956), 11–18; *Foreign Relations of the United States. Diplomatic Papers, 1933*, vol. II (Washington, D.C.: Government Printing Office, 1949), 338–347.

39. Genschel, *Verdrängung*, 51–59; Uhlig, *Warenhäuser*, 81–85; Schleunes, *Twisted Road*, 82–92; Friedländer, *Drittes Reich*, 32–35; Adam, *Judenpolitik*, 46–48; Longerich, *Politik der Vernichtung*, 26–28; Barkai, *Vom Boykott zur Entjudung*, 23–25; Wehler, *Deutsche Gesellschaftsgeschichte*, vol. IV, 653–659. Similar signs had also appeared in the *Scheunenviertel* riots of 1923.

windows; the owners had made themselves scarce. Curious onlookers hung about in front of the stores, partly fearful and partly *schadenfroh*."[40] Those who were not intimidated and wanted to make their purchases were often forcibly prevented from entering, as reported by Walter Tausk, a Jewish salesman from Breslau who posed as a sales representative from Paris in order to visit the shops he knew.[41]

From the point of view of the government, the boycott was not a success, since the population at large showed no enthusiasm. Overall, griping discontent prevailed; in working-class districts Jewish shops were even more frequented than usual. In Munich, the SA felt it necessary to reschedule the boycott to Friday afternoon, since, as the *Völkischer Beo-bachter* reported, "parts of the public... virtually forced their money on these enemies of the people and insidious slanderers."[42] In Breslau Walter Tausk observed that on the eve of the boycott Jewish shops were "frequented by buyers in such a way that some stores had to close temporarily, others posted signs: 'Sold Out.'" On the day of the boycott small groups formed all over Breslau "engaged in eager debate mostly opposed to the boycott! Mind you: it is rejected by Christians! And the gist of what one hears in the street – from the 'little people' all the way up to the affluent bourgeois – is: 'And we'll go back there to make our purchases.'"[43] Marta Appel, a rabbi's wife in Dortmund, reported expressions of vexation and disapprobation: "There were nevertheless many who had the courage to enter shops, even though they were badly abused by the Nazi patrols and also photographed in order to brand them as enemies of the German people in the newspapers."[44] The physician

40. Pätzold, *Faschismus*, 75; Sebastian Haffner, *Geschichte eines Deutschen: die Erinnerungen 1914–1933* (Munich: DTV, 2002), 158.
41. Tausk, *Breslauer Tagebuch*, 52–57; Uhlig, *Warenhäuser*, 83.
42. Uhlig, *Warenhäuser*, 82–83; Genschel, *Verdrängung*, 51–54; Schleunes, *Twisted Road*, 89; Friedländer, *Drittes Reich*, 33–35.
43. Tausk, *Breslauer Tagebuch*, 52–53. In Breslau, 3.2% of the 625,198 inhabitants (1933)—about 20,000—were Jewish; Thamer, *Verführung*, 258. See also Till van Rahden, *Juden und andere Breslauer. Die Beziehungen zwischen Juden, Protestanten und Katholiken in einer deutschen Großstadt von 1860 bis 1925* (Göttingen: Vandenhoeck & Ruprecht, 2000).
44. Marta Appel's report is reprinted in Monika Richarz, ed., *Jüdisches Leben in Deutschland. Selbstzeugnisse zur Sozialgeschichte, 1918–1945*, vol. III (Stuttgart: DVA, 1982), 231–243, esp. 231–233.

Henriette Necheles-Magnus (1898–1977), who had her own practice in Wandsbek (near Hamburg) and was also subjected to the 1 April boycott, mentions the many visits by patients and friends who wanted to express their solidarity and show her that she was not alone. The Jewish egg vendor on the other side of the street, whose husband had been killed in the war, had a similar experience: "She said that she had never sold so many single eggs as during that day, since the poor folks who only had money to buy one egg somehow wanted to show her a feeling of solidarity."[45] In addition to being unpopular with a majority of the population, the boycott had also failed to significantly weaken Jewish competition from the perspective of the National Socialist trade and professional associations, while the negative reporting on Germany continued unabated in the Western news media.[46] There were also hints of criticism in some of the newspapers that had not yet been fully "brought into line" with Nazi policy. The conservative *Deutsche Allgemeine Zeitung* commented on its 4 April front page that, "in their heart of hearts, the German people have little sympathy for such violent measures. Their powers of discernment do not lump together those who came from Galicia the day before yesterday with indigenous Jews who have done their duties as citizens in times of war and peace." And the formerly liberal *Frankfurter Zeitung* defended the principle of civic equality of German Jews with other Germans and reminded its readers of the history of Jewish emancipation in Prussia.[47]

The view, spread by the Reich government and generally accepted abroad, that the day of the boycott passed without major incidences is not accurate. It is striking that, precisely on the day of the boycott, numerous abductions, assaults, and other offenses against foreign and German Jews took place. Despite all the protestations of the German press to the contrary, the day of the boycott was not as calm and

---

45. Wandsbek, like Altona and Harburg-Wilhelmsburg, became part of Greater Hamburg only in 1937; Gruner, ed., *Verfolgung*, 109.
46. Genschel, *Verdrängung*, 50–51.
47. Longerich, *"Davon haben wir nichts gewusst,"* 62–63.

bloodless as German newspapers and western diplomats reported to their governments.[48] In addition to the well-known *cause célèbre*—the murder of the Königsberg lawyer Friedrich Schumm in the Baltic seaport city Kiel—there were numerous other violent incidents.[49] The Polish Diplomatic Mission, for example, reported two abduction cases in Berlin, where Mojzeszoni Ehrlich was carried off to Nazi Party headquarters in General-Pape-Straße, robbed, and badly beaten up with rubber truncheons, after which he was forced to sign a statement that he had been treated well.[50] A similar fate befell Emanuel Weiss, who was taken on that same day to an SA meeting place in Linienstraße in Berlin, where he was first roughed up and then, along with others, forced to sing nationalist songs.[51] National Socialist gangs obviously took advantage of the day of the boycott to attack or jail Jews throughout the Reich. Several such cases that took place on 1 April are also reported in the Hessian compensation claims files.[52] As David Abramowicz confirmed in his compensation claim file, he was attacked by three National Socialists in Hesse on the day of the boycott and badly injured—in addition to nose and sinus injuries, he suffered a concussion. Paul Aron from Frankfurt was arrested on the same day on the charge of high treason for allegedly taking photos with the intent of supporting the propagation of "horror propaganda" abroad.[53]

---

48. *Documents on British Foreign Policy 1919–1939*, Series 2, vol. V, ed. E. L. Woodward et al. (London: HMSO, 1956), 1–55; *Foreign Relations of the United States*, vol. 2, 320–354; Abraham Ascher, *Was Hitler a Riddle? Western Democracies and National Socialism* (Stanford: Stanford University Press, 2012), 15–144.

49. On the specific circumstances that led to the lawyer Friedrich Schumm's murder, see Chapter 6 above.

50. 5 April 1933 at BA Berlin, R43 II, no. 603, "Polnische Gesandtschaft an Auswärtiges Amt," fol. 20.

51. Ibid., 20–21.

52. Of a total of 110,000 compensation claim files in Hesse, 6,000 were examined in detail in the 1990s for a research project of the Hauptstaatsarchiv Wiesbaden on "Opposition and Persecution under National Socialism in Hesse." The databank set up for the purpose lists about twelve compensation claim files of claimants who were persecuted between March and May 1933. I am grateful to Dr. Eichler of the Hessisches Hauptstaatsarchiv in Wiesbaden for this information.

53. Hessisches Hauptstaatsarchiv Wiesbaden, Entschädigungsakten, Abt. 518, no. 76, David Abramowicz; Abt. 518, no. 2980, Paul Aron.

In many Saxon cities, in Berlin, and in the Prussian Rhein province, "*Ostjuden*" were subjected to brutal attacks and instances of mistreatment. All over the Reich, Jews were taken into "protective custody;" in Hesse, numerous assaults occurred on the day of the boycott; in Regensburg the SA set up a machine gun in the market place that was aimed at a department store and took 107 Jewish businessmen into "protective custody;" near Chemnitz, goods were first confiscated and then burned; the shop windows of the Tietz department store in Düsseldorf and those of the Wertheim department store in Breslau were smashed; in Dresden, students proclaimed that "it goes against the honor of German students to have contacts with Jews;" and in some of the smaller towns of Silesia, such as Oels, "open anarchy" was the order of the day.[54] Kurt Sabatzky, legal advisor to the *Centralverein* in East Prussia and bitter enemy of the East Prussian *Gauleiter* (provincial governor) Erich Koch, reported:

> On the day of the boycott, terrible things happened in some Saxon towns.... In Plauen, a Jewish commercial agent was murdered by an SA mob and in Chemnitz, it was the attorney Dr. Weiler, the local leader of the Reich Association of Jewish Frontline Solders [who was killed]... In Zittau, the preacher of the Jewish community, Leo Elend, was arrested and taken into protective custody. There he was bestially tortured.[55]

These were no isolated regional cases. Rudolf Diels, head of the political police force in the Prussian Ministry of the Interior and, beginning in April, of the Prussian Secret State Police Office, reported that police officials had told him of "canings and underhanded robberies that have taken place in Jewish shops." Walter Tausk related the following from Breslau:

54. On the attacks against East European Jews on 1 April 1933, see Chapter 1 above. On Regensburg, see Uhlig, *Warenhäuser*, 83–84, and Genschel, *Verdrängung*, 52–53; on Düsseldorf, see Pätzold, *Faschismus*, 75; on Breslau and Oels, see Tausk, *Breslauer Tagebuch*, 56, 58, 61; on Dresden, see Klemperer, *Zeugnis*, 18.
55. See Kurt Sabatzky's (1892–1955) report in Richarz, ed., *Jüdisches Leben*, 292–300, esp. 293. On Sabatzky's hostility toward Koch, see Schüler-Springorum, *jüdische Minderheit*, 282–287.

Here we have arrived in the second German Middle Ages, whereby the 'Margoniner case' shall be recorded as an illustration. Margoniner is a livestock dealer. At the time of the boycott, he fell into the hands of the SA, whose members did the following to him at the SA headquarters: they beat him with rubber truncheons until he was disfigured; they shaved the hair off his head, cut into his back a flesh wound in the shape of a swastika, rubbed salt into it, put the cut off hair into this wound, and sewed it up. In this half-dead condition, Margoniner was taken to the Jewish hospital. The head physician, Prof. Dr. Gottstein, summoned the police president Heines to show him this half-dead man.[56]

As a consequence of the boycott three to four hundred Jewish Germans took their own lives.[57]

According to Walter Tausk, the boycott "had turned into a frenzy of bloodlust all over Silesia, into open pillage, acts of violence and revenge. Government orders and those of boycott organizers have not been respected and references to them are answered by: 'We don't give a shit what the government in Berlin says, we only do what our Silesian leadership tells us.'"[58] Yet, even though they ran counter to the exhortations of the Reich government, these attacks and violent excesses were hardly seen as breaches of the law by SA perpetrators. Even when committing the most brutal outrages, they knew themselves to be in tacit agreement with their leaders and ultimately also with Hitler's long-term goals. His injunctions from 10 and 11 March had little effect; SA troopers knew that these had partly been prompted by foreign protests. They felt perfectly justified in committing violent acts, thereby only translating Hitler's "teachings" into direct action.

56. Rudolf Diels, *Luzifer ante Portas: Zwischen Severing und Heydrich* (Stuttgart: DVA, 1950), 205; Tausk, *Breslauer Tagebuch*, 61–62: "What Heines said, no one knows. But in the hospital, the poor man was photographed and they hope to save his life. But Adolf Hitler unabashedly lies: 'In Germany not a hair of any Jew is being touched.'"
57. Christian Goeschel, "Suicides of German Jews in the Third Reich," *German History*, 25 (2007), 22–45, esp. 23.
58. Tausk, *Breslauer Tagebuch*, 57.

Psychological Implications of the Boycott

The first day of April 1933 thus was more of a Reich-wide pogrom than a targeted commercial or professional boycott. In the context of the National Socialist takeover of power, it had a stabilizing function as a kind of domestic entrenchment and consolidation of Nazi rule. For the first time the German population had been caught in the net of Nazi crimes as jointly responsible, including even those who quietly turned away, thereby meaning to express their disapproval and disgust. Their "noble silence"—the genteel overlooking of unpleasantness so often practiced by the German upper classes—had become a corrupting silence that covered up political crimes. As Fritz Stern noted, the passivity and silence of the "decent" segment of the German population thus contributed as much to the success of National Socialism as the roaring enthusiasm of its supporters.[59] Whoever did not ostentatiously take a stand on 1 April and demonstratively venture into a Jewish shop was thus automatically complicit. Potential opponents of the regime who remained silent when confronted with situations such as the boycott also became psychologically weakened in that they lost credibility—internally as well as externally. Kurt Pätzold correctly pointed to the fact that 1 April 1933 marked the beginning of a moral decline, even for those who inwardly objected to the boycott: "Convictions and sentiments that are not translated into actions possess no historical relevance and are constantly in danger of being lost."[60] In promulgating actions such as the boycott, even though it was by no means popular or universally accepted, the National Socialist regime succeeded in having its doctrines acknowledged as the prevalent opinion in Germany.

On the other hand, there was, as pointed out above, a significant minority of Germans who opposed the boycott by ostentatiously buying

---

59. Fritz Stern, *Das feine Schweigen. Historische Essays* (Munich: Beck, 1999), 158–173, esp. 159, 173.
60. Pätzold, *Faschismus*, 79.

in Jewish shops. Apart from grumbling, there was also some opposition to the boycott. But protests and resistance, even when they came from within the ranks of the NSDAP, had their price. The Bremen attorney Wilhelm Cramer, an NSDAP member since 1931 and, as the son of Bremen's cotton exchange chairman, part of the patrician upper crust, protested against the boycott in a letter to the mayor of the Hanseatic city. Cramer complained that every principle of justice had been violated by the boycott: "Even if it were correct, for which we still lack conclusive proof, that the anti-German propaganda abroad is based on Jewish elements in foreign countries (and not, as I suspect, on political opponents), it still would not be justified to hold Jews living here in the country responsible for it." Cramer was declared of unsound mind and consigned to a psychiatric clinic.[61]

Through the boycott the National Socialist leadership had reached its goal of forcing Jewish Germans to realize that they were excluded from both the German State and German social life, of which most of them had felt a part up to the spring of 1933. This was a bitter realization for the vast majority of Jewish Germans, who were fully assimilated, had fought for Germany in the First World War, had lost close relatives in that conflict, and had been firmly established for generations in the cities and towns in which they had lived, where many had become local benefactors.[62] Already during the Empire, they were strongly represented in the middle and upper middle classes and had comprised a small wealthy elite accustomed to paying heed to State authorities and submitting to their directives. This included shouldering a disproportionate

---

61. Markus Meyer, "Ein schwieriger Patient. Ein Bremer Rechtsanwalt und der 'Judenboykott' im April 1933," *Arbeiterbewegung und Sozialgeschichte. Zeitschrift für die Regionalgeschichte Bremens im 19. und 20. Jahrhundert*, 11 (2003): 16–29.
62. Thomas Nipperdey, *Deutsche Geschichte 1866–1918*. Vol. I: *Arbeitswelt und Bürgergeist* (Munich: Beck, 1990), 396–414; esp. 399. In 1910, twenty-nine Jews were among the one hundred wealthiest men in Prussia. Many were considered pillars of the community who made generous public endowments, such as libraries and hospitals. On the social stratification of Weimar Germany's urban Jewish community, see the well-informed assessment of Niewyk, *Jews in Weimar*, 16–17.

tax burden.[63] The sudden transformation from upstanding citizen to social outcast thus must have come as a particular shock. The merchant and traveling salesman Walter Tausk, whose family had been long-term residents of the Silesian capital Breslau, felt "as if in tsarist Russia;" the Professor of Romance Languages and veteran of World War I Viktor Klemperer reported "a mood of all-pervasive fear as it must have been prevalent in France under Jacobin rule. One does not yet fear for dear life – but for bread and freedom."[64] For Edwin Landau, a highly decorated World War I veteran from Deutsch Krone, a West Prussian city with 16,000 inhabitants, 1 April stood for "the parting from German civilization, my inner separation from the Fatherland that once existed...I was internally broken." Landau was head of the Jewish community in Deutsch Krone, where he had founded a local chapter of the Reich Association of Jewish Frontline Soldiers. Later his spirits rallied as he turned to Zionism and emigrated to Palestine in November 1934. But on 1 April he asked himself, as did so many others, "And for these people, we young Jews suffered in the rain and cold in the trenches and shed our blood to protect the country from its enemies. Aren't there any of our comrades left from those days who are now appalled by what's going on?"[65] A Berlin merchant and decorated World War I veteran, whose forefathers had fought in the war against France in 1870–1, had the same feeling of alienation toward Germany because of the pervasiveness of anti-Jewish agitation. He saw himself caught among all fronts, since he also rejected help from the West. In its anti-German propaganda, he saw "the same elements at work that instigated the defamation and

---

63. In 1905, for example, the Jewish population of Berlin, which amounted to 5.1%, carried 30.7% of the tax burden; in Mannheim the Jewish population of 3.2% paid 28.7% of the taxes; and in the small Baden city of Bruchsal the Jewish population of 1.1% paid 17.6% of the taxes (Nipperdey, *Deutsche Geschichte 1866–1918*, 399). According to Peter Pulzer, the average amount of taxes paid by Jews was seven times as high as that paid by Catholic Germans and three and a half times as high as that paid by Protestants. See Pulzer, "jüdische Beteiligung, " 143–241, esp. 189.
64. Tausk, *Breslauer Tagebuch*, 48; Klemperer, *Zeugnis*, 14.
65. Excerpt from Edwin Landau's autobiographical *Aufzeichnungen*, "Mein Leben vor und nach Hitler," in Richarz, *Jüdisches Leben*, 99–108, esp. 105, 104.

atrocity propaganda against us during the War and that are now stirring things up again."[66]

Continuation of the Boycott Movement

The boycott of 1 April 1933 was not a one-day event, as depicted to the contemporary German and Western public; it extended into ongoing boycott activities (albeit regionally different) throughout the entire Reich. (For forcible shop closures and boycotts before and after 1 April 1933, see the map on page 44). As a majority of German Jews were self-employed in the retail trade, continuing boycotts were bound to lead to severe financial losses and gradual ruin, quite apart from their destructive psychological effects.[67] Yet, since open-ended local and regional boycott actions directly contravened the declared policy of the Reich government, occasional protests by Jewish organizations (such as the *Centralverein*) against them had some success with the authorities.[68] Specific boycotts were frequently announced through ads in newspapers, and local Nazi leaders often enacted additional prohibitions against buying in Jewish shops for civil servants and Nazi Party members, so that the efficacy of the Reich authorities was limited and more in the order of

---

66. 27 March 1933 at BA Berlin, R 8005, no. 19, "DNVP, Politischer Schriftwechsel," fols. 57–58.
67. Barkai, *Vom Boykott zur Entjudung*, 11–18, esp. 12. According to Barkai, more than 60% of all gainfully employed German Jews were concentrated in trade and commerce, with a large majority of these in the retail trade. Many of the German Jewish businesses were artisanal enterprises (*mittelständische Handwerksbetriebe*). See also Bennathan, "Struktur," 87–131, esp. 104–108. According to Bennathan, 61.3% of German Jews (18.4% of the total population) were active in *Handel und Verkehr* (the commerce and trade services sector), of which 47.7% (8.4% of the total population) were engaged in commerce and the finished product trades.
68. Longerich, *Politik der Vernichtung*, 597, provides as an example the successful intervention on the part of the *Centralverein* in East Prussia at the beginning of June 1933, when, as a result of complaints to the *Regierungspräsident*, guards were recalled from their posts in front of Jewish shops. Longerich may tend to overestimate the effectiveness of protests against arbitrary measures when he writes, "Such open blockades through local [Nazi] party organs could be sustained for only a few days, since they ran counter to the official policies of the Reich government" (39). Depending on the region, local Nazi leaders could wield their power pretty much unchecked in the spring and summer of 1933.

needle pricks against local boycotts. They were in any case unable to put a definitive stop to an ongoing phenomenon. Those who initiated boycotts (often to eliminate local competition or get back at an old adversary) also knew themselves to be in sync with the Party, so that it mattered little if their actions occasionally met with sanctions by the State bureaucracy, whose image was still shaped by the negative idea of the Weimar "*Systemzeit*," the Nazi term of execration for the governments of the Weimar Republic. It would take time before this was replaced by the more positive image of the "*Führerstaat.*"

Thus, notwithstanding governmental orders to end the boycott on the evening of 1 April, it continued in several cities, in particular and with special vehemence and endurance in Pforzheim.[69] As late as September 1933, the *Pforzheimer Anzeiger* appealed to the population, under the headline "Achtung! People's Comrades in Pforzheim," not to participate in clearance sales in Jewish shops.[70] In the fall of 1933 there were comparable proclamations from virtually all regions of the Reich: the *Bamberger Tageblatt* in northern Bavaria wrote on 10 October, "We frown upon purchases in the shops of even the so-called decent Jews.... Away with all false compassion! The catchword must be: No German makes his purchases from Jews...;" and *Die Deutsche Frau* from the *Gau* Rheinpfalz added that no prohibitions were necessary, since for German women it was a matter of course "to avoid anything Jewish. The Jew is and remains the mortal enemy of our people, and whoever supports him in the least is the enemy of his own people."[71] Here it is already suggested that in the eyes of the Party it could no longer be tolerated to shop in Jewish

---

69. Pforzheim, a city in central Baden known for its gold work, pop. 78,937 (1925); *Statistisches Jahrbuch* (1933), 13; Uhlig, *Warenhäuser*, 85.
70. 14 September 1933 at BA Berlin, R43 II, no. 594, "Schrift der Reichsvertretung," *Pforzheimer Anzeiger*, fol. 85.
71. 1 November 1933 at BA Berlin, R43 II, no. 594, "Schrift der Reichsvertretung...," *Bamberger Tageblatt*, 10 October 1933; *Die deutschen Frauenfront*, Beilage der NS-Frauenschaft, *Gau* Rheinpfalz, fols. 85–86. Bamberg, city in Upper Franconia, pop. 50,152 (1925); the Nazi-era *Gau* of the Rheinpfalz roughly corresponded to the Bavarian Palatinate on the left bank of the Rhine, with about one million inhabitants; *Der Neue Brockhaus*, vol. III (Leipzig: Brockhaus, 1937), 528.

establishments at all. In Zittau, in Saxony, the *Zittauer Nachrichten und Anzeiger* proclaimed in a headline on 23 November 1933: "Yes! Now all Zittauers buy only in Christian shops;" and the *Beuthener Stadtblatt*, the official gazette of Beuthen in Upper Silesia, proclaimed in a headline on 15 October 1933, "German People's Comrade, stay away from Jewish shops!" The *Bayerische Ostwacht* in Straubing lectured its readers directly on 3 November 1933, under the headline "A Serious Admonition!," "It ought to be clear to all German women that if they buy from the Jew, they support alien intruders.... You ought to be too proud to go to the Jew at all." The *Märkisches Tageblatt*, the official Party gazette of the *Gau* Kurmark in Brandenburg, wrote on 11 October: "Germans, stay away from Jewish goods and Jewish shops! In our newspaper, you find ads only from purely Aryan enterprises."[72] Further calls to boycott shops were reported from Magdeburg, Hanover, Weiden in the Bavarian Upper Palatinate, and Weißenburg, also in Bavaria, where the National Socialist county leadership published an appeal in the *Weißenburger Tageblatt* on 7 December that concluded with the phrase, "Whoever as a German makes his Christmas purchases from the Jews is not only no Christian but also a traitor to his people."[73] One can only imagine the courage and resolve it must have taken to enter a Jewish-owned shop in the second half of 1933 in any of the above-mentioned cities and to withstand the insidious social pressure, occasionally coupled with the threat of professional disadvantages, that was exerted on those who did.

The *idée fixe* that it was morally reprehensible to buy in Jewish shops was thus propagated in all walks of life already by the end of the first year of Nazi rule. In Rennertehausen in Hesse, for example, an elementary school

---

72. BA Berlin, R43 II, no. 594, "Schrift der Reichsvertretung...," fols. 86–87. The *Märkisches Tageblatt* hinted at the increasingly widespread practice of refusing to publish advertisements from Jewish firms. Zittau, city in Saxony, pop. 38,353 (1925); Beuthen in Upper Silesia, pop. 86, 881 (1925); Straubing in Lower Bavaria, pop. 23,593 (1925); *Statistisches Jahrbuch* (1933), 11–13.
73. BA Berlin, R43 II, no. 594, "Schrift der Reichsvertretung...," fols. 87–89. Magdeburg, pop. 297,151 (1925); Hanover, capital of the eponymous Prussian province, pop. 425,274 (1925); Weiden, pop. 19,536 (1925); Weißenburg in Bavaria, a Free Imperial City until 1803, pop. 8,500 (1933); *Statistisches Jahrbuch* (1933), 11–13; *Neuer Brockhaus*, vol. IV, 677.

teacher asked his pupils which *Eintopfgericht* (meat or vegetable stew) they had eaten on Sunday. He then explained that all those families who had bought food in a Jewish store were not national-minded.[74] To make sure that people did not do their Christmas shopping in Jewish shops, between 20 December 1933 and the end of the year placards in Worms were fixed to the buildings that housed Jewish stores warning: "Whoever buys from the Jew is a traitor to the people."[75] And in Schivelbein, a small town in the Pomeranian district of Köslin, gangs led by SS men roamed through the streets and drove customers out of Jewish shops.[76]

In addition, special local directives prohibited civil servants and Nazi Party members from buying in Jewish shops. On 13 October 1933, for example, the city of Gießen in Hesse sent a circular letter to civil servants admonishing them "not to make their purchases in Jewish shops, department stores, etc. in the future, lest they incur disagreeable consequences." In November Gießen's mayor repeated the prohibition per decree. Similar orders were issued in Wesel on the Lower Rhine on 24 October, while in the Westphalian city of Paderborn officials were even bound by their signature not to buy in Jewish shops. In Delmenhorst in the neighboring state of Oldenburg, the mayor demanded on 7 August that "all civil servants, teachers, white collar employees, and workers in the city administration make their purchases only in German shops."[77]

Jewish shops were also frequented by Nazi Party members, to the point where numerous Party agencies deemed it necessary to pronounce

74. BA Berlin, R43 II, no. 594, "Schrift der Reichsvertretung...," fol. 90. Starting in 1933 the regime propagated the idea that Germans should replace their usual big Sunday dinner with a simple beef and vegetable stew, and then donate the money saved to (winter) relief organizations. To promote this idea, prominent culinary experts participated in preparing such stews in newsreels of the day. Friedemann Bedürftig, *Taschenlexikon Drittes Reich* (Munich: Piper, 1997), 92.

75. BA Berlin, R43 II, no. 594, "Schrift der Reichsvertretung...," fol. 90. Worms in Rhine-Hesse, pop. 47,015 (1925); *Statistisches Jahrbuch* (1933), 13.

76. Wildt, *Volksgemeinschaft als Selbstermächtigung*, 152; Schivelbein, pop. 9600 (1933); *Neuer Brockhaus*, vol. IV, 82.

77. BA Berlin, R43 II, no. 594, "Schrift der Reichsvertretung...," fols. 91–92. Gießen in Upper Hesse, pop. 33,600 (1925); Wesel in the Prussian Rhine province, pop. 24,136 (1925); Paderborn in Westphalia, pop. 33,719 (1925); Delmenhorst in Oldenburg, pop. 24,700 (1925); *Statistisches Jahrbuch* (1933), 11–13.

drastic bans. In this context, the Mannheim *Hakenkreuzbanner*, the Silesian *Niederschlesische Tageszeitung*, and the *Würzburger Generalanzeiger* threatened all those who procured their goods from Jewish shops with expulsion from the Party.[78] In Horhausen in the Prussian province of Hesse-Nassau, local Nazi officials even imposed monetary fines of 300 Reichsmarks for those caught shopping for the first time, and 500 Reichsmarks for a second infringement; a third would entail immediate arrest.[79]

Boycott proponents did everything they could to involve the general public and sanction those who refused to participate. Unbounded manhunts sought to identify those who violated boycotts and public denunciations followed in their wake. Whereas murders were carried out mostly without witnesses and perpetrators in general sought concealment and shied away from the light of day,[80] boycotts thrived on public participation. To be successful, boycott measures had to be announced in newspapers and on posters, or spread by word of mouth. Thus informed, the general public was encouraged, even bullied, into playing a role in the branding and denunciation of those who made their purchases in Jewish shops. Their names were bandied about as *Volksschädlinge* (people's parasites) or *Volksverräter* (traitors of the people) at public meetings, in newspapers, and on noticeboards outside town halls, and photographs were published of those who had been observed violating the directive. Since boycotts were by no means universally accepted among the German public, they brought in their wake a manhunt against those Germans who were unwilling to participate in antisemitic discriminatory actions. Just as the soldier who deserted in wartime was shot, those who refused to participate in boycotts were branded, usually resulting in the ruination of their social status. Social pressure to join in antisemitic smear campaigns was high.

78. BA Berlin, R43 II, no. 594, "Schrift der Reichsvertretung...," *Hakenkreuzbanner*, 8 September 1933; *Niederschlesische Tageszeitung*, 10 October 1933; *Würzburger Generalanzeiger*, 14 December 1933, fol. 134; pop. Mannheim, 260,871 (1925);; Würzburg in Lower Franconia, pop. 95,113 (1925).
79. BA Berlin, R43 II, no. 594, "Schrift der Reichsvertretung..." fol. 94.
80. On murders see Chapter 6 above.

Though boycotts may on the surface appear to result in less harm to its victims than violent attacks, this was not always the case. Boycotts entailed a slow but steady and ultimately complete destruction of the material existence of their target. For those affected, it was a kind of creeping death, accompanied by long-standing social leprosy and the existence of a pariah. Boycotts of Jewish shops, in one form or another, had begun long before 1 April 1933; in their 1933 versions, regardless of their level of support, they succeeded in branding German Jews as an unwelcome foreign body and anathema to the German people's community. In 1933, Jewish boycott victims suffered devastating psychological and material consequences as they were increasingly ostracized; by 1938, German Jews were completely eliminated from the German economy—and the worst was yet to come.

8

LEGAL AND ECONOMIC DISCRIMINATION

The year 1933 marks the decisive caesura in the history of German Jews. As Leo Baeck emphasized in his speech on the occasion of the founding of the *Reichsvertretung der Juden in Deutschland* (Reich Representation of Jews in Germany; hereafter *Reichsvertretung*) in the fall of 1933, the thousand-year-old history of German Jews had come to an end with the measures taken by the National Socialist government.[1] In addition to the Reich-wide 1 April boycott of Jewish shops and lawyers' and doctors' offices, followed by the antisemitic legislation of April 1933, German Jews were affected by a multitude of other discriminatory measures, such as continuing local boycotts after 1 April, additional hurdles in professional training for agriculture and the trades, countless public defamations, local prohibitions on the use of public services such as bathing facilities and spas, and the wanton destruction of property solely because it belonged to Jews. The attempt to banish Jewish Germans from public life—legally, professionally, economically, and socially—began in earnest already in the early spring of 1933.

The Antisemitic Legislation of April 1933

The national antisemitic legislation of April 1933, just as the 1 April boycott, has received some attention by previous historiography.[2] The

---

1. Zimmermann, *Deutsche Juden*, 57; Wistrich, *Who's Who*, 7.
2. Friedländer, *Nazi Germany*, 9–40; Adam, *Judenpolitik*, 46–71; Schleunes, *Twisted Road*, 62–114; Pätzold, *Faschismus*, 35–113.

Before the Holocaust: Antisemitic Violence and the Reaction of German Elites and Institutions during the Nazi Takeover.
Hermann Beck, Oxford University Press. © Hermann Beck 2022. DOI: 10.1093/oso/9780192865076.003.0009

discussion here is related to one aspect of the legislation's intent, namely to control the wanton acts of violence against Jewish Germans, as well as its overall inability to moderate more radical antisemitic measures at the *Land* and local levels throughout the remainder of 1933. The first of the antisemitic laws was euphemistically named Law on the Restoration of a Professional Civil Service (7 April), accompanied by the Law on Admission to Legal Practice of the same day, followed by the Decree on Physicians and the Statutory Health Insurance System (22 April), and the Law against the Overcrowding of German Schools and Universities (25 April).[3] As a memorandum by the *Reichsvertretung*, addressed to Hitler personally and dated 16 January 1934, noted:

> The [1933] legislation excluded Jews in principle, with known exceptions, from the administration of justice and from public positions on the level of Reich, cities, communities, and other public corporations. The reason given for this was that in a Reich newly constructed along racial lines Jews could not occupy positions representing national sovereignty. In addition, the percentage of Jews in all the professions has been reduced or even eliminated.[4]

If the purpose of the eighty-page memorandum, which listed many hundreds of regionally different discriminatory measures that went beyond the April legislation, was to appeal to Hitler to moderate the effects of antisemitic measures throughout Germany, it inevitably missed its mark, for it is doubtful whether Hitler ever read it.

---

3. On the civil service legislation, see "Gesetz zur Wiederherstellung des Berufsbeamtentums. Vom 7. April 1933," paragraph 7, point 2, *Reichsgesetzblatt* (hereafter RGB), Part I, no. 34 (1933), 175–177 at ALEX/Österreichische Nationalbibliothek; Jane Caplan, *Government without Administration. State and Civil Service in Weimar and Nazi Germany* (Oxford: Oxford University Press, 1988), 141–149; Horst Göppinger, *Juristen jüdischer Abstammung im "Dritten Reich." Entrechtung und Verfolgung*, 2nd ed. (Munich: Beck, 1990), 69–76.

4. 16 January 1934 at BA Berlin, R43 II, no. 594, "Jüdische Angelegenheiten im Allgemeinen," Vol. II, "Stellung der Juden in Deutschland," fols. 59–142. It is not clear if Hitler ever saw the memorandum, which was signed by Leo Baeck. On 19 January 1934, Baeck offered to personally hand over the memorandum with the relevant documents to Hans Heinrich Lammers, Hitler's *Staatssekretär* in the Reich Chancellery. Ministerial Councilor Richard Wienstein then requested that he himself be given the memorandum.

The Law on the Restoration of a Professional Civil Service

The *Reichsvertretung* observations and Leo Baeck's comment about the impact of the April legislation were no exaggeration. The civil service law was unprecedented and unique of its kind. Depending on the type of public authority, German civil service legislation up to this point had distinguished among civil servants owing allegiance to the Reich, the *Länder* (German states), municipalities (cities and towns), and the Churches. Even though the latter category was exempted in the April 1933 law, it still affected more than two million officials of the German civil service.[5] Due to the long-standing Prussian civil service tradition, service for the State had been endowed with a special aura since the late eighteenth century, for the respect citizens showed the power of the State also applied to its representatives. Traditionally, public office carried with it the honor that the office bestowed on its holder, the *Amtsehre*; its violation, in the form of a *Beamtenbeleidigung* (offending a civil servant), could meet with severe punishment. Therefore, only a person of unblemished reputation was allowed to hold public office. German officials were thus under considerable pressure to conduct themselves impeccably, even in their private lives.[6] Given the central position of the German civil service, the National Socialist rulers made it a priority to quickly conquer the bureaucracy and purge from it elements they deemed

---

5. Friedländer, *Nazi Germany*, 26–32; Mommsen, *Beamtentum*, 39–61; Günter Neliba, *Wilhelm Frick. Der Loyalist des Unrechtsstaates. Eine politische Biographie* (Paderborn: Schöningh, 1992), 168–172; Schleunes, *Twisted Road*, 102–105; Adam, *Judenpolitik*, 51–64; Pätzold, *Faschismus*, 81–112. At the time, German civil servants were divided into three basic rankings, "einfacher" (lower), "mittlerer" (middle), and "höherer" (upper). Judicial and administrative officials were separately ranked according to the types of their duties. See Rainer Fattmann, *Bildungsbürger in der Defensive. Die akademische Beamtenschaft und der "Reichsbund der höheren Beamten" in der Weimarer Republik* (Göttingen: Vandenhoeck & Ruprecht, 2001).
6. Criminal offenses committed by officials were accordingly severely punished. See Tibor Süle, *Preußische Bürokratietradition* (Göttingen: Vandenhoeck & Ruprecht, 1988); Hermann Beck, *The Origins of the Authoritarian Welfare State in Prussia: Conservatives, Bureaucracy, and the Social Question, 1815–1870* (Ann Arbor: University of Michigan Press, 1995), 125–149; Otto Hintze, "Der Beamtenstand," in Otto Hintze, *Soziologie und Geschichte, Gesammelte Abhandlungen*, 3rd ed., vol. 2, ed. Gerhard Oestreich, (Göttingen: Vandenhoeck & Ruprecht, 1982), 66–126.

hostile, in order to obtain and maintain absolute power, especially since the influence of the bureaucracy had grown during Heinrich Brüning's years in office, when parliament was significantly weakened and civil servants played an increasingly important role in running the State.[7]

The Law on the Restoration of the Civil Service was designed to remove officials of "non-Aryan" descent as well as political opponents, especially Communists, but also Social Democrats and occasionally even Center Party officials. The First Ordinance on the Implementation of the 7 April law defined "non-Aryan" as those with even only one Jewish parent or grandparent.[8] The ordinance introduced the idea of "racial proof:" "If Aryan heritage is in doubt, then a certificate [proving "Aryan" heritage] by an expert on racial research ordered by the Reich Interior Ministry is to be obtained."[9] All those concerned had to fill out a seven-page questionnaire. For question number 4C—"Are you of Aryan descent?"— birth and marriage certificates, as well as military papers and other documents, had to be submitted in order to provide documentary evidence regarding one's parents, grandparents, party membership, military career, and professional positions.[10] A kind of semi-totalitarian supervision thus went into effect already in April 1933, with Hitler barely three months in office. The law applied to an enormous number of people: Saul Friedländer writes of more than two million Reich, *Länder*, and municipal officials who were potentially affected by its exclusionary

7. Hans Mommsen, "State and Bureaucracy in the Brüning Era," in Hans Mommsen, ed., *From Weimar to Auschwitz* (Princeton: Princeton University Press, 1991), 79–118; on the background of the law, see Adam, *Judenpolitik*, 51–64, and Mommsen, *Beamtentum*, 39–50. On the NSDAP's attitude toward the civil service before 1933, see Caplan, *Government*, 102–130.
8. Walk, *Sonderrecht*, 12; Michaelis and Schraepler, eds., *Ursachen und Folgen*, vol. IX, 283–288. On the definitional and political difficulties of attempts to define "Aryan," "non-Aryan," and mixed-race (*Mischlinge*), see "Definition by Decree," in Raul Hilberg, *The Destruction of the European Jews*, vol. 1, 3rd ed. (New Haven: Yale University Press, 2003), 65–80.
9. "Erste Verordnung zur Durchführung des Gesetzes zur Wiederherstellung des Berufbeamtentums. Vom 11. April 1933," *RGB*, Part I, no. 37 (1933), 195, at ALEX/Österreichische Nationalbibliothek.
10. See BA Berlin, R43 II, no. 1374, fols. 51–55 for the original questionnaire. Other questions pertained to membership in a "Free Mason Lodge, the Rotary Club, or a similar secret organization." Initially, this information was requested only from officials, not from lower-level public service workers.

measures. Martin Broszat writes that 1–2 percent of all civil servants were pensioned off for racial or political reasons.[11] Actual numbers were even higher, since an almost equal number of salaried employees (*Angestellte*) and workers in the public service sector were included after 4 May.[12] The material existence and professional future of millions of people were on the line.

As a consequence of Hindenburg's intervention during the deliberations about the law, paragraph 3 (known as the "Aryan clause") was toned down and suspended for those officials "who were in office on 1 August 1914, who fought at the front for the German Empire or its allies, or whose fathers or sons were killed in action during the World War."[13] Hindenburg had written to Hitler on 4 April that in his opinion "civil servants, judges, teachers, and attorneys who had been disabled during active duty, and frontline soldiers or sons of war casualties or those who had lost sons in the field" must be allowed to stay in office.[14] In his respectful response, Hitler claimed that "here an alien body that was never fully integrated into the German nation" had forced its way into State positions, constituting "the mustard seed of corruption," the extent

---

11. Friedländer, *Nazi Germany*, 27; Broszat, *Staat Hitlers*, 306. Dismissals affected mostly those in the upper echelons of the civil service.
12. Mommsen, *Beamtentum*, 39; Bracher, Sauer, and Schulz, *Nationalsozialistische Machtergreifung*, 480–481. Gerhard Schultz (who dealt with the *Beamtentum*) calculated the following totals for the year 1931: of the personnel in the entire public administration (936,268), 761,972 were tenured civil servants (96,681 at the level of the Reich, 362,891 at that of the *Land*, 302,400 at the municipal level); 174,296 were public employees without tenure. Another 1.3 million worked for the Reich rail and post office services (of which slightly more than half were tenured civil servants). Of the Reich civil servants, 72,958 worked in the finance, tax, and debt management administrative offices. Of the civil servants in the various German *Länder*, 130,166 worked for the police, 91,987 for the school system, and 63,705 for the judicial administration. Of the 362,891 state officials, 150,298 were employed in Prussia. See *Statistisches Jahrbuch für das deutsche Reich*, 49 (Berlin: Statistisches Reichsamt, 1930), 510–511 and 514–515. See also Caplan, *Government*, 144–148.
13. Michaelis and Schraepler, eds., *Ursachen und Folgen*, vol. IX, 284; Walk, *Sonderrecht*, 12.
14. Hindenburg's exchange of letters with Hitler of 4 and 5 April 1933, in Michaelis and Schraepler, eds., *Ursachen und Folgen*, IX, 393–395; Hitler's reply is reprinted in full in *Akten zur Deutschen Auswärtigen Politik 1918–1945*, Serie C: 1933–1937, Vol. I, 30 January to 15 May 1933, 253–254. In the Old Prussian state and during the Empire, Jews were excluded from the officer corps and from higher administrative positions, so that their number in the Reich bureaucracy was relatively low. See also Werner Angress, "Prussia's Army and the Jewish Reserve Officer Controversy before World War I," in James Sheehan, ed., *Imperial Germany* (New York: Watts, 1976), 93–116.

of which, he continued, was still unknown. Hitler also denigrated the military contribution of Jewish Germans in World War I by remarking that Hindenburg generously "stood up for members of the Jewish people who had been forced into active duty on account of general conscription."[15] By focusing on the requirement to serve, Hitler's line of reasoning deliberately negated the high number of German Jews who volunteered for duty in 1914. Still, the "Hindenburg Exemptions," as they came to be known, remained legally in place—although violated in actual practice—until Hindenburg's death in 1934.[16]

The civil service law had been in preparation since mid-March 1933 as the NSDAP–DNVP coalition government tried to put a break on local anti-Jewish administrative measures, decrees, and actions by introducing nationwide legislation to standardize rules and exemptions throughout the country. [17] Already in March, local ordinances that mandated harsh measures against Jewish lawyers and doctors had often been accompanied by acts of violence, and in early April German cities and states issued sweeping hiring and employment prohibitions directed against ethnic Jewish Germans and their spouses.[18] On 2 March, the *Land* government of Thuringia mandated that public contracts be awarded only to "good old *Mittelstand*" firms and Christian businesses; on 18 March, the city administration of Berlin forbade Jewish lawyers and notaries from

---

15. *Akten zur Deutschen Auswärtigen Politik*, Serie C: 1933–1937, Vol. I, 253–254. When Hitler remarked that he appreciated Hindenburg's motives and himself "often suffered from the harshness of fate that compels one to make certain decisions that one would prefer a thousand times to avoid on grounds of humanity," the hypocrisy of this phrase must even have struck Hindenburg.
16. Gruchmann, *Justiz*, 134–138.
17. Caplan notes that "[t]he preparation of such a measure was agreed at the cabinet meeting on 24 March 1933, the day after the adoption of the Enabling Act" (Caplan, *Government*, 141 n.). Friedländer confirms the Cabinet agreement but goes further back for the origins of the law: "Wilhelm Frick was at the immediate origin of the Civil Service Law; he had already proposed the same legislation to the Reichstag as far back as May 1925. On March 24, 1933, he submitted the law to the cabinet. On March 31 or April 1, Hitler probably intervened to support the proposal" (Friedländer, *Nazi Germany*, 28).
18. Schleunes, *Twisted Road*, 72; Irene Mayer, "Berlin-Tiergarten," in Wolfgang Benz and Barbara Distel, eds., *Der Ort des Terrors. Geschichte der nationalsozialistischen Konzentrationslager*. vol. 2 (Munich: Beck, 2005), 64; Gruchmann, *Justiz*, 142; "Nazis Hunt Arms in Einstein Home. Ousting of Jews Goes on," Special Cable, *New York Times*, March 21, 1933, 10.

handling any of its legal matters; on 27 March the city administration of Cologne decreed that no public contracts be awarded to Jewish-owned firms; and on 31 March, Bavaria's Interior Ministry demanded the immediate resignation of all Jewish school doctors.[19] On 1 April a memorandum of the new Lord Mayor of Cologne (Konrad Adenauer had been forcibly retired in mid-March) decreed a ban on employing Jews, converted Jews, and all those who were married to Jews in the city of Cologne. On the same day, the acting (*kommissarisch*) Superintendent of Berlin's schools suspended or furloughed "all teachers of Jewish blood employed in municipal schools," and on 6 April the Ministry of Culture of the state of Baden decreed that all Jewish teachers and employees in public schools were immediately to be furloughed.[20]

The pogrom-like mood that lay in the air during the boycott of 1 April (a day which, as has been shown above, was characterized by many violent attacks), as well as the uncertainties, disruptions, and general atmosphere of fear caused by local antisemitic measures, accelerated the swift implementation of the antisemitic legislation of April 1933. The national legislation in April, once enacted, was designed to curb the interference of Nazi revolutionary actions with the working of the State administration.[21] The civil service legislation, in particular, sought to curb the autonomy of the *Länder* and centralize the Reich government's control over the bureaucracy.[22] By standardizing discriminatory criteria, the government also intended to stem local measures, though this was only partially successful, since Nazi officials at the *Land* and local

---

19. Walk, *Sonderrecht*, 4, 5, 6, 8.   20. Ibid., 8, 9, 11.
21. Broszat, *Staat Hitlers*, 250, 306; Mommsen, *Beamtentum*, 56.
22. Caplan, *Government*, 141–149. Centralization had begun with the "Preliminary Law for the Co-Ordination of the Länder with the Reich" of 31 March, according to which the respective strength of political parties in state parliaments was reproportioned to correspond to the 5 March Reich election results. On 7 April, the law was supplemented by the *Reichsstatthaltergesetz*, stipulating the appointment of Reich governors, whose task it was to bring the policies of the *Länder* in line with those of the central government, thus annulling the century-old rights and prerogatives of the states with the stroke of a pen and with it the federal principle so deeply engrained in German history. See Hermann Beck, "The Nazi Seizure of Power," in Robert Gellately, ed., *The Oxford Illustrated History of the Third Reich* (Oxford: Oxford University Press, 2018), 51–84, esp. 69.

levels would continue to test the limits of the April legislation by constantly introducing local exceptions which, as will be shown below, continued to undermine the livelihood of German Jews.

The Law on Admission to Legal Practice

The Law on Admission to Legal Practice that accompanied the new civil service legislation on 7 April extended the "Aryan clause" to members of the legal profession.[23] It outright denied "non-Aryans" admission to the bar with the exemptions noted in the civil service legislation, and established guidelines for deciding on expulsion and retention policies for established lawyers and jurists. Even though the law was initially meant to be temporary, there was a consensus during the Reich Cabinet discussion on 7 April that "the introduction of a *numerus clausus* for lawyers...will not be considered for the time being."[24] There had been decades-long discussions of a general *numerus clausus* in the legal profession as a way to reduce overcrowding and to address its threatened proletarianization, and in December 1932 the German Bar Association (Deutscher Anwaltverein, DAV) voted to petition the government to impose a ban on new admissions to the bar and draft a plan for a *numerus clausus* for lawyers.[25] With the removal of Jewish lawyers such a *numerus clausus* was now no longer necessary, calling into question the "temporary" nature of the law. The supplementary Law on Admission to Patent Law Practice and to the Bar of 22 April that mandated expunging the names of "patent

23. The law was hastily put together in part because of the harsh anti-Jewish measures that Hanns Kerrl, Reichskommissar in the Prussian Ministry of Justice, and Hans Frank, Acting Bavarian Minister of Justice, had introduced in Prussia and Bavaria since March. Once Kerrl and Frank started to "cleanse" the justice administrations in their states, the Reich Justice Ministry found it necessary to quickly put together a Reich law that would standardize procedure. See Gruchmann, *Justiz*, 124–143.
24. *Akten der Reichskanzlei*, part 1, vol. I, 324. For a discussion regarding a *numerus clausus* in the legal profession, see Konrad Jarausch, "The Crisis of German Professions 1918–1933," *Journal of Contemporary History*, 20 (1985), 379–398, esp. 388–390; Kenneth Ledford, "German Lawyers and the State in the Weimar Republic," *Law and History Review*, 13 (1995), 317–349, esp. 342–346.
25. Kenneth Ledford, *From General Estate to Special Interest. German Lawyers 1978–1933* (Cambridge, Cambridge University Press, 1996), 270–271; Adam, *Judenpolitik*, 66, n. 218.

lawyers of non-Aryan descent" from the rolls of patent lawyers by 30 September 1933, and the fact that cities and some states continued to violate the more lenient retention rules of the 7 April national legislation, proved to be the writing on the wall: there would ultimately be no lifelines for Jewish professionals.[26] The national legislation appeared to be more moderate than local measures, but without strict enforcement many local and *Land* Nazi government officials continued to make and implement their own rules, often tolerating associated violence and technical violations of the law.

The 7 April legislation on admission to the legal profession had been preceded by a multitude of sweeping anti-Jewish local and state ordinances, often accompanied by violent attacks on Jewish judges, lawyers, and public prosecutors, including SA occupations of law courts in various cities.[27] The perpetrators of these actions often claimed that they were being taken "in the name of the people" or "according to the wishes of the people."[28] On 11 March the main Nazi Party press organ, *Völkischer Beobachter*, published a statement by Hitler's legal advisor and (since 10 March) acting Bavarian Minister of Justice, Hans Frank. In order to fulfill a central tenet of the National Socialist government, Frank declared that justice was now to be administered to Germans only by "German people's comrades." On the same day, armed SA men forced their way into the Breslau law courts and violently expelled all Jewish jurists.[29] The Chemnitz law courts had already been occupied on 9 March; further attacks on Jewish members of the legal profession took place in law courts in Gleiwitz in Upper Silesia, Görlitz, Cologne, Berlin,

26. *Walk, Sonderrecht*, 12, 16; Friedländer, *Nazi Germany*, 28–29; Schleunes, *Twisted Road*, 100–110; Adam, *Judenpolitik*, 65–67.
27. See, for example, 3 April 1933, BA Berlin, R 8005, no. 19, "DNVP, Politischer Schriftwechsel," fols. 63–64.
28. Gruchmann, *Justiz*, 124–125.
29. On the details of the Breslau attack, see Göppinger, *Juristen*, 49–50; Angelika Königseder, *Recht und nationalsozialistische Herrschaft. Berliner Anwälte 1933–1945* (Bonn: Deutscher Anwaltsverlag, 2001), 22–25; Benjamin Lahusen, "Die Selbstermächtigung des Rechts: Breslau 1933. Zum 'Stillstand der Rechtspflege' in der Juristischen Zeitgeschichte," *Studies in Contemporary History*, 2 (2019), 258–277.

Dresden, and Frankfurt am Main.[30] Roland Freisler, who had been appointed Section Head in the Prussian Ministry of Justice in March 1933, contributed to the pogrom-like climate through his incendiary anti-Jewish speeches at the end of March, transmitted by loudspeakers and resulting in the expulsion of all Jewish members of the legal profession from the High Appellate Court in Frankfurt.[31] On 18 March, Berlin's municipal administration ruled that Jewish lawyers and notaries could no longer represent the city of Berlin in legal matters; on 31 March the acting (*kommissarisch*) Bavarian government ordered the suspension of all Jewish judges and public prosecutors, effective 1 April; and, on the same day, the *Reichskommissar* for the Prussian Ministry of Justice, Hanns Kerrl, published a temporary injunction according to which Jewish judges and other Jewish members of the judiciary employed at law courts were to be forcibly furloughed.[32]

To some, the new situation created by the national law may have appeared initially as an easing of conditions when compared to late March, especially in view of the exemptions for frontline service in the First World War. Of the 4,585 Jewish lawyers affected by the legislation, 3,167 (about 70 percent) could continue to practice for the time being, and of the 717 Jewish judges and public prosecutors 336 (46.8 percent) were allowed to remain in office for the next two years.[33] But it was obvious that this was a temporary solution, for Jewish lawyers remained excluded

30. Attacks against Jewish judges and defense attorneys in March 1933 are among the best documented. See also Friedländer, *Nazi Germany*, 28–29; Schleunes, *Twisted Road*, 97–99; Pätzold, *Faschismus*, 42–47; Adam, *Judenpolitik*, 46–51; Göppinger, *Juristen*, 49–55.
31. 3 April 1933 at BA Berlin, R 8005, no. 19, "DNVP, Politischer Schriftwechsel," fols. 63–64.
32. Walk, *Sonderrecht*, 5, 7; Schleunes, *Twisted Road*, 97–100; Adam, *Judenpolitik*, 50–51; Gruchmann, *Justiz*, 127–128.
33. Dirk Blasius, "Zwischen Rechtsvertrauen und Rechtszerstörung: Deutsche Juden 1933–1935," in Dirk Blasius and Dan Diner, eds., *Zerbrochene Geschichte: Leben und Selbstverständnis der Juden in Deutschland* (Frankfurt: Fischer, 1991), 130; Friedländer, *Nazi Germany*, 29. In a report of the Prussian Interior Ministry of 11 May 1933, the following numbers were given for Prussia: 11,814 lawyers had been admitted to practice (by the date of the Civil Service law), 8,299 of them "Aryan" and 3,515 Jewish. Of the latter, 1,383 were accorded the status of "*Alt-Anwälte*" (those who had been admitted prior to 1 August 1914) and 735 of "*Frontkämpfer*." Denial of admission was issued to 923 Jewish and 118 communist applicants. A total of 2,158 Jewish lawyers were henceforth admitted to the legal profession. *Akten der Reichskanzlei*, vol. I, 324.

from the DAV professional umbrella organization and subjected to other professional slights and disadvantages.[34] Numerous local discriminatory measures and attacks, coupled with state-wide ordinances in Bavaria and Prussia, had created a situation of hopeless despondency for many Jewish members of the legal profession. Like other Germans, most of them had lost their savings in the inflation of 1923 and were penniless without their professional income, so that many felt pushed to the brink of suicide, as the Vice-President of the Frankfurt High Appellate Court wrote in a confidential letter to Oskar Hergt, Chairman of the DNVP in the early 1920s.[35] The attacks in Breslau, Frank's injunction that Jewish judges could not pronounce sentence in criminal cases, and the local measures in Berlin were all commented upon by the foreign press and reported in detail in *The Times* and *The Manchester Guardian*.[36] The interested public in Britain and elsewhere was thus well informed about antisemitic transgressions in Germany from the very beginning.

Reich Justice Minister Franz Gürtner was concerned that some states might not recognize the new law of 7 April, so he asked Hitler to see to it "that this directive of the government is to be respected by everybody."[37] For Gürtner, the active opposition to Reich law from Kerrl in Prussia and Frank in Bavaria meant that the implementation of the Law on Admission to Legal Practice "concerned not simply a matter of the justice administration, but rather 'a question of the authority of the State, the authority of the Reich government in and of itself.'"[38] Gürtner had cause for concern. In their own administrative purviews, Frank, Kerrl, some *Länder* justice ministers, and the National Socialist Association of German Jurists (BNSDJ) applied "administrative obstructionism" to try to circumvent the Reich

---

34. Their names were not listed in the German Bar Association Yearbook, but in a separate directory. See Friedländer, *Nazi Germany*, 29.
35. 3 April 1933 at BA Berlin, R 8005, no. 19, "DNVP, Politischer Schriftwechsel," fols. 63–64.
36. *Manchester Guardian* 14 March 1933, 27 March 1933, 7 April 1933; *Times*, 3 April 1933 at BayHStaA, V. Hauptabteilung, Sammlung Varia 231, "The Persecution of Jews in Germany."
37. Adam, *Judenpolitik*, 66, n. 215. In the Cabinet meeting of 7 April 1933, Franz Schlegelberger, *Staatssekretär* in the Ministry of Justice, mentioned that the heads of the administrations of justice of the different German states had more far-reaching plans. *Akten der Reichskanzlei*, part 1, vol. I, 323.
38. Gürtner quoted in Gruchmann, *Justiz*, 148.

legislation.[39] On 18 April, for example, Kerrl issued an overall denial of promotion for Jewish civil servants; on 28 April 1933 he imposed a ban on elevating newly minted Jewish attorneys (*Referendare*) to probationary positions in the civil service (*Assessoren*), and on 31 May 1933 Jewish judges who dealt with criminal and administrative law were reassigned to courts dealing exclusively with civil law cases. In Prussia, the new section head in the Ministry of Justice, Roland Freisler, initially even refused to countenance exceptions made for frontline soldiers.[40] There were additional professional restrictions on Jewish lawyers, not provided for in the Law on Admission to Legal Practice, that were technically illegal: following orders from the Prussian Ministry of Justice of 31 March and 31 May 1933, "non-Aryan" lawyers were regularly excluded from handling *Armenrechtssachen*, legal actions relating to poor relief.[41] In Thuringia, Hesse, and the Hanseatic cities, the same conditions prevailed. As a result of resolutions of the Reich Chamber of Lawyers (Reichs-Rechtsanwaltskammer) of 12 July and 27 October 1933, *Bürogemeinschaften* (law firms) employing a mix of "Aryan" and "non-Aryan" lawyers were to be denied admission to the professional organization, while the *Juristische Wochenschrift* had already made it known on 5 August that it would no longer accept contributions from "non-Aryans," review the works of "non-Aryan" authors, or even list them in its columns, and in November 1933 the German Bar Association completely banned "non-Aryan" members from its ranks. In December 1933 readers of *Der Stürmer* were informed that Nuremberg firms represented by Jewish lawyers would find their names published *en clair* in the paper, to be branded as a warning to others.[42] As local and state NSDAP satraps and professional organizations openly challenged the Reich-wide law in their own domains, it almost seemed that the Reich Cabinet had lost control over the content and implementation of its anti-Jewish policies.[43]

39. Gruchmann, *Justiz*, 141: Königseder, *Recht*, 33.
40. Adam, *Judenpolitik*, 65–67; Pätzold, *Faschismus*, 109–110.
41. Gürtner tried in vain to convince Kerrl to stop this exclusion; Königseder, *Recht*, 42; Gruchmann, *Justiz*, 148–149.
42. 16 January 1934 at BA Berlin, R 43 II, no. 594, "Denkschrift der Reichsvertretung," fol. 67.
43. See Adam, *Judenpolitik*, 65–67, and Pätzold, *Faschismus*, 109–110.

The Decree on the Admission of Physicians
to the Statutory Health Insurance System

In the same 7 April Cabinet meeting at which the legislation for the civil service and legal profession were discussed, Hitler stressed that "legal regulations" for Jewish doctors were not yet necessary; this should be preceded by "a comprehensive educational campaign."[44] It was widely known that many Germans had a close relationship with their doctors, and since almost 11 percent of German physicians were Jewish, this would have meant disrupting ties between thousands of German doctors and tens of thousands of their patients, causing unnecessary discontent, as Saul Friedländer pointed out.[45] Despite initial caution on the part of Hitler and the Reich government, pro-Nazi physicians themselves were taking the lead in undermining their Jewish colleagues by trying to convince patients that they should not consult doctors of "foreign origin."[46] On the whole, German doctors tended to exhibit stronger and more explicit antisemitic orientations than lawyers;[47] their license to give vent to their prejudice after 30 January led to a more pronounced effort to undermine their Jewish colleagues than was the case with lawyers, some

44. *Akten der Reichskanzlei*, part 1, vol. 1, 325.
45. Friedländer, *Nazi Germany*, 30. On the percentage of Jewish doctors in 1933, see also Siegfried Ostrowski, "Vom Schicksal Jüdischer Ärzte im Dritten Reich. Ein Augenzeugenbericht aus den Jahren 1933–1939," *Bulletin des Leo-Baeck-Instituts* 6:24 (1963): 313–351; Robert Proctor, *Racial Hygiene. Medicine under the Nazis* (Cambridge: Harvard University Press, 1988), 147; Claudia Huerkamp, "Jüdische Akademikerinnen in Deutschland 1900–1938," *Geschichte und Gesellschaft*, 19 (1993), 319.
46. Ostrowski, "Vom Schicksal," 317–318; Michael H. Kater, *Doctors Under Hitler* (Chapel Hill: University of North Carolina Press), 184–185, 188.
47. On this point see Michael H. Kater, "Hitler's Early Doctors: Nazi Physicians in Predepression Germany," *Journal of Modern History*, 59 (March 1987), 25–52, esp. 51: "What makes the case of the physicians a special one and probably singles them out as a natural vanguard for Hitler in the Weimar social elite is that certain of these already disillusioned young men found, in National Socialist ideology, welcome complements to the social Darwinian notions that had informed the medical Zeitgeist for some time." See also Konrad Jarausch, *The Unfree Professions* (Oxford: Oxford university Press, 1990), Table 4.1, "Nazi Proclivity of Professions, 1925–1945," 101.

of whom continued to exhibit at least a rudimentary regard for the rule of law in the early months of Nazi rule.[48]

Local and regional administrative measures also compelled the government to act. Already on 21 March the Bavarian Interior Ministry had suspended "all school doctors who belonged to the Jewish race;" on 4 April Munich's Lord Mayor ruled that Jewish doctors in Munich hospitals had to confine their treatment to Jewish patients and were forbidden from performing post-mortem examinations on "Aryan" cadavers; on 7 April the Bavarian Interior Ministry halted university admissions for Jewish medical students; and on 11 April Cologne's municipal administration ruled that bills issued by Jewish doctors no longer had to be honored.[49] Beginning in mid-March, local and regional medical and insurance fund doctors' associations expunged Jewish physicians from their leadership positions in the professional associations throughout Germany, and during the April boycott and the weeks following it, acts of character assassination and physical violence were carried out against Jewish physicians in the whole country.[50]

In response to these haphazard local rulings, the Reich Ministry of Labor issued the Decree on the Registration of Doctors for Participation in the Statutory Medical Insurance Funds on 22 April, which revoked the right of "non-Aryan" doctors to register with statutory health insurance funding bodies (Krankenkassen), with the Hindenburg exemptions remaining in place.[51] As a result of the decree, patients insured under the

48. On the numbers and percentages of German doctors who joined the NSDAP and the National Socialist Physicians League, both before and after the Nazis came to power, see Michael H. Kater, "Medizin und Mediziner im Dritten Reich," Historische Zeitschrift, 244:2 (April 1987), 299–352, esp. 311–315; Proctor, Racial Hygiene, 65–66; on the support of the NSDAP among university medical faculties in March 1933, Proctor, Racial Hygiene, 94.
49. Walk, Sonderrecht, 8, 10, 13. The Times and The Manchester Guardian also commented on these measures; see also 3 April 1933 at BayHStaA, V. Hauptabteilung, Sammlung Varia 231, "The Persecution of Jews in Germany."
50. Kater, Doctors under Hitler, 183–185.
51. "Verordnung über die Zulassung von Ärzten zur Tätigkeit bei den Krankenkassen vom 22. April 1933," RGB, Part I, no. 42 (1933), 222-223, at ALEX/Österreichische Nationalbibliothek; Kater, Doctors under Hitler, 185–186; Adam, Judenpolitik, 67–68; Walk, Sonderrecht, 16. A change in the statutes of the German Pharmacists' Association led to the application of the "Aryan clause" for pharmacists on 22 April 1933. See Walk, Sonderrecht, 17.

Krankenkassen would not be reimbursed for expenses incurred with a "non-Aryan" physician, thus gradually compelling non-Jewish Germans to abandon their Jewish doctors for economic reasons. Those Jewish doctors who were not exempted were henceforth confined to serving the small number of privately insured patients. This, too, was beset with complications, since private insurance funds usually conformed to public insurance fund practices. The Association of Private Health Insurance Companies, for example, compiled lists of doctors who were to be excluded from the funds on the basis of race and alleged political activities.[52] After the passing of the 22 April decree, all of Germany's 32,000 *Krankenkassen* doctors received a detailed questionnaire designed to determine the "qualifications" of the recipient based on the new racial categories and political affiliations and activities, including questions about the recipients' ancestors and their spouses' ancestors. Questionnaires were to be returned within a week (later submissions would incur a penalty of 20 Reichsmarks a day), and doctors were warned that false or misleading answers would result in criminal penalties and might lead to a revocation of their license to practice medicine.[53] As in the case of Jewish lawyers, Jewish doctors were expected to self-identify as "non-Aryan" and face the consequences of the new laws.

Local measures against Jewish doctors in 1933 soon went beyond the provisions of the Ministry of Labor's decree. The list of local restrictions and discriminations was long: on 16 May a ruling by the National Socialist faction in Bad Nauheim's (Hesse) town council mandating that benefit recipients must henceforth consult only doctors and dentists of "Aryan" ancestry was endorsed, and in Frankfurt, Cologne, and Duisburg only "Aryans" could serve as welfare service medical officers. Here even

---

52. See Stephan Leibfried and Florian Tennstedt, *Berufsverbote und Sozialpolitik 1933. Die Auswirkungen der nationalsozialistischen Machtergreifung auf die Krankenkassenverwaltung und die Kassenärzte*. 2nd ed. (Bremen: Universität Bremen, 1980), 241–247. The fate of Jewish doctors from the perspective of one of those concerned is vividly portrayed by Hertha Nathorff, in her *Tagebuch*. On 2 June 1933 the decree was expanded to include dentists and dental technicians. Walk, *Sonderrecht*, 28; Adam, *Judenpolitik*, 67.
53. Leibfried and Tennstedt, *Berufsverbote*, 76–86.

verified frontline service in the war had ceased playing a role. After 20 May the Prussian province of Brandenburg and the city of Berlin accepted medical certificates attesting to illness or applications for sick leave only from non-Jewish doctors. In the state of Baden, several specialized health care providers, such as the Teachers' Health Care Insurance of Baden, the Relief Fund for Upper Echelon Employees, and the Insurance Fund for National Railroad Officials refused to honor bills issued by Jewish doctors, even if they had served as frontline soldiers in World War I. After 30 September Jewish doctors in Berlin were excluded from ambulance and rescue operations (*Rettungswesen*) of all kinds.[54]

At the national level, Dr. Gerhard Wagner, leader of the National Socialist Physicians' League since 1932, had been active in placing National Socialist sympathizers in leading positions in the two leading medical professional associations—the Hartmannbund and the German Medical Association.[55] On 9 July 1933 Wagner, now *Reichärzteführer*, chastised the Reich Ministry of Labor for refusing to countenance attempts to go beyond the 22 April decree and expel more Jewish physicians from the medical insurance funds, claiming that the Labor Ministry's decisions to reinstate some physicians who had been ousted had led to "outrage within the medical profession."[56] Weeks later he admonished the Ministry again:

> It is unfortunately sufficiently known to us that the Ministry of Labor abides by the provisions of federal law. We National Socialists, however, believe that the meaning of the National Socialist revolution cannot be exhausted in these provisions of federal law. In the final analysis the benefit of the German people stands once again above all as the supreme law.[57]

54. 16 January 1934 at BA Berlin, R43 II, no. 594, "Denkschrift der Reichsvertretung," fols. 68–70.
55. Kater, *Doctors Under Hitler*, 20–21.
56. Thomas Gerst, "Vor 80 Jahren: Ausschluss jüdischer Ärzte aus der Kassenpraxis." *Deutsches Ärzteblatt* 110:16 (2013), 772.
57. Stephan Leibfried and Florian Tennstedt, "Health Insurance Policy and Berufsverbote in the Nazi Takeover," in Donald W. Light, ed., *Political Values and Health Care. The German Experience* (Cambridge, MA: MIT Press, 1986), 127–184, quotation, 168.

On 10 August 1933 Wagner issued a decree forbidding "doctors of German and alien blood from deputizing for each other," transferring patients to Jewish doctors, consulting "non-Aryans" for professional advice, and including them in common doctors' practices.[58] Wagner thus tried to negate the limits set by the decree on *Krankenkassen* physicians in the same way Hans Frank and Hanns Kerrl had attempted to go beyond the confines of the lawyers' legislation and vociferously criticized Reich Justice Minister Gürtner for wishing to adhere to the letter of the law. Even though the Hindenburg exemptions limited the number of Jewish doctors expelled from the insurance funds in 1933, the wheels were now set in motion by Nazi activists such as Wagner to expel Jewish doctors not only from the growing national health insurance funds but eventually from the medical profession altogether.[59]

The Law against the Overcrowding of German Schools and Universities

On 25 April, the Hitler Cabinet issued the last portion of the antisemitic legislation of April 1933, the Law against the Overcrowding of German Schools and Universities (*Gesetz gegen die Überfüllung deutscher Schulen und Hochschulen*), as it was euphemistically labelled, which introduced a quota system for Jewish *Gymnasium* and university students. In the aftermath of the First World War "a wave of antisemitism suddenly welled up in the Reich" among university students, who blamed the "Jewish revolution," the "Jewish constitution," "Jewish government," and an influx of "*Ostjuden*" on the overcrowding of universities and the concomitant decline in their

---

58. BA Berlin, R43 II, no. 594, "Praxisgemeinschaften," fol. 68.
59. Kater, *Doctors Under Hitler*, 187–189. By the beginning of 1934, 2,600 physicians (most of them Jewish) were expelled from the insurance funds in the Reich as a whole because of either race or political activities, lowering the percentage of Jewish national insurance fund doctors from 16.5% to 11.5%. Female physicians were hit even harder. More than 50% of their total number in the Reich were signed on to the statutory insurance funds, and a majority of those were expelled (Huerkamp, "Jüdische Akademikerinnen," Table 3: Jüdische Ärztinnen und Ärzte, 1925 und 1933, 325). In June 1933, of the 4,367 female doctors in Germany, 587 (13.4%) were Jewish (Huerkamp, 319). More female than male physicians emigrated.

career prospects.[60] The rise of the NSDAP radicalized this already rampant antisemitism and gave it institutional support with the establishment of Nazi student and professional groups.[61] By the spring of 1933, random local violence and indiscriminate expulsions in educational institutions and student organizations provided a pretext for the Interior Ministry to introduce standardized regulations for antisemitic discrimination.[62]

In earlier drafts the title of the law was designated "against *Überfremdung*," that is, "foreign infiltration" (instead of "overcrowding"), a reflection of the Nazis' attempt to categorize German Jews as "foreigners" in their own land as a legitimation for reducing their numbers in public life. The change in the wording served two purposes. First, it allayed concerns that Germany would violate its 1922 treaty obligations with Poland concerning the rights of Poles in the German parts of Upper Silesia, thus risking Polish reprisals against the German minority in Poland.[63] Secondly, as with the legal and medical professions, overcrowding had also led to calls for limiting numbers of students in teaching faculties, so that the term "overcrowding" spoke more pointedly to the academic community's fears of an overabundance of university graduates and teachers that made it difficult for newcomers to find employment and had established professionals and teachers concerned about the security of their jobs.[64] Accordingly, the first three

60. Thomas Nipperdey, "Die deutsche Studentenschaft in den ersten Jahren der Weimarer Republik," in Thomas Nipperdey, ed., *Gesellschaft, Kultur, Theorie* (Göttingen: Vandenhoeck & Ruprecht), 390–416, esp. 408; Hans Peter Bleuel and Ernst Klinnert, *Deutsche Studenten auf dem Weg ins Dritte Reich* (Gütersloh: Mohn, 1967), 132.

61. Michael H. Kater, *Studentenschaft und Rechtsradikalismus in Deutschland 1918–1933* (Hamburg: Hoffmann & Campe, 1975).

62. Bleuel and Kleinnert, *Studenten*, 246–247; Grüttner, *Studenten*, 213; Béla Bodo, "The Role of Anti-Semitism in the Expulsion of non-Aryan Students, 1933–1945," *Yad Vashem Studies*, 30 (2002), 189–227, esp. 193–198.

63. Albrecht Götz von Olenhusen, "Die 'nichtarischen' Studenten an den deutschen Hochschulen: Zur nationalsozialistischen Rassenpolitik 1933–1945." *VJHZ*, 14:2 (April 1966), 175–206, esp. 177.

64. Marjorie Lamberti, "German Schoolteachers, National Socialism, and the Politics of Culture at the End of the Weimar Republic," *Central European History*, 34:1 (2001), 53–82, esp. 62–63; Jarausch, "Crisis," 390, and Jarausch, *Unfree Professions*, 57–58, 81–82. On antisemitism among students and some faculty, see Kater, *Studentenschaft*, and Geoffrey Giles, "Die Fahne hoch, die Reihen dicht geschlossen: Die Studenten als Verfechter der

paragraphs of the law refer to the goal of redressing the imbalance between students enrolled in professional programs and the jobs available in a given profession, mandating that *Länder* governments establish the relevant quotas.[65]

The antisemitic intent of the law is laid bare in article 4 and in the first ordinance on the implementation of the law, where precise figures are issued: the percentage of "non-Aryans" among enrolled students should not exceed 5 percent of their total number, and new enrollments of Jewish students were possible only if the percentage of "non-Aryans" remained below 1.5 percent. Students would not be allowed to transfer to a different school to avoid expulsion.[66] Jewish students who had just matriculated in 1933 were not spared—they were considered "not yet accepted" and thus subject to the stricter 1.5 percent limit. The law did not significantly affect numbers of Jewish students in 1933, but within a year, numbers of Jewish students at German universities fell sharply from 3,326 in the winter semester 1932–3 to 812 a year later, not only because German states and individual universities arbitrarily introduced stricter quotas but also because new Jewish students stayed away given the vanishing career prospects and increasingly perilous conditions for them at German universities.[67] Those Jewish students who could afford it chose to study abroad, while those whose fathers had been frontline soldiers in the war and were thus exempted from the law were allowed to remain in *Gymnasium* or university, though in Hitler's Germany exemptions for German Jews would prove neither reliable nor long-lasting.[68]

völkischen Universität?" in Eckhard John et al., eds., *Die Freibrger Universität in der Zeit des Nationalsozialismus* (Freiburg and Würzburg: Ploetz, 1991), 43–56.

65. "Gesetz gegen die Überfüllung deutscher Schulen und Hochschulen. Vom 25. April 1933," *RGB*, Part I, no. 43 (1933), 225, at ALEX/Österreichische Nationalbibliothek.
66. Ibid, 225–226. Grüttner, *Studenten*, 213–214.
67. Grüttner, *Studenten*, 214–217; von Olenhusen, "nichtarische Studenten," 179.
68. For an example of an exemption, see Peter Gay, *My German Question* (New Haven: Yale University Press, 1997), 60–61.

Impact of the April Legislation

The exemptions from the new laws based on frontline military service were not uniformly applied. Officers in the Reichswehr Ministry ultimately decided whether someone could claim that he had served on the front line (and was thus eligible for an exemption), or else spent the war in the rear with no direct contact with the enemy—and was thus subject to dismissal. The Undersecretary of State in the Ministry of the Interior, Hans Pfundtner, in whose jurisdiction the antisemitic legislation lay, noted that different countries offered differing interpretations as to who fell into the category of the *fechtende Truppe* (fighting troops). If one defined the term of "*fechtende Truppe*" too narrowly (the term went back to the Imperial Army), one might even decide "not to consider members of the Army High Command as *Frontkämpfer*, since they did not actively participate in combat."[69] Due to these ambiguities, countless petitioners pleading to be recognized as *Frontkämpfer* were directed to the *Allgemeines Wehrmachtsamt* (Reichswehr Ministry Main Office). In this way, officers, assuming the role of de facto judges, became implicated in the machinery of the antisemitic legislation, as they decided upon the weal and woe of the "non-Aryan" population.[70]

The April laws also elevated hundreds of archivists, municipal employees, and administrators of Church documents into the position of researchers with the de facto power of judges. After all, the results of their investigations could decide the fate of individuals and families.[71] There was hardly a Catholic or Protestant clergyman, archivist, or civil magistrate who, by the summer of 1933, "had not become a functioning wheel in the machinery of the search for Jews."[72] Merely months after the

---

69. Quoted in Pätzold, *Faschismus*, 107; Mommsen, *Beamtentum*, 48, 52, 59–60.
70. See Bundesarchiv-Militärarchiv Freiburg, Allgemeines Wehrmachtsamt, RW 6, nos. 73a and 73b.
71. Manfred Gailus, "Kirchenbücher, Arier-Nachweise und kirchliche Beihilfen zur Judenverfolgung. Eine Einführung," in Manfred Gailus, ed., *Kirchliche Amtshilfe* (Göttingen: Vandenhoeck & Ruprecht, 2008), 7–27.
72. Pätzold, *Faschismus*, 105.

National Socialist takeover, thousands of Germans had thus turned into active participants in the machinery of the antisemitic apparatus as part of their professional duties, even if it was merely a matter of documenting whether the grandfather of the person under scrutiny had been "Aryan" or "non-Aryan." By their active participation in certain actions, if only as part of their professional duties for which they were duly remunerated, they had become an instrument of antisemitic ideology. Possibly without fully realizing it, they vindicated this ideology because their actions supported it. From very early on, through the activities of State officials, civil servants, municipal employees, and archivists, the antisemitic laws were thus endowed with implicit legitimacy on the basis of a bureaucratic machinery that excluded questions of principles, values, or conscience.[73]

As we have seen, in the first revolutionary phase of the Nazi takeover the legal provisions of the national antisemitic legislation of April 1933 were only partially applied. Despite the blatant discrimination and hardships that the new laws entailed, they were often more lenient than local laws that determined the actual reality of anti-Jewish actions in regions and cities throughout Germany. In many instances radical local Nazi leaders had gone well beyond the statutory rules of the April laws to make life even more unbearable for the local Jewish population. Paradoxically, the legislation of April 1933 thus appeared occasionally more moderate than the more or less spontaneously conceived local measures. In some instances, this may well have had the equally paradoxical corollary of giving some German Jews a false sense of security with regard to the position of the Reich government, especially in conjunction with Hitler's repeated warnings to stop spontaneous violence. In response to the violent disruptions of public life, complaints concerning the disruption of the economy, and protests by foreign consulates and

---

73. Louis Althusser, *Ideologie und ideologische Staatsapparate* (Hamburg: VSA, 1977). Althusser shows, using the example of the Catholic Church, how an organization's staff reproduced an ideology simply by virtue of their practical participation in certain actions. Many Germans were implicated in this way from the very beginning.

embassies about the antisemitic attacks against foreign Jews that swept over Germany after the 5 March elections,[74] Hitler promulgated a series of exhortations to Nazi Party members, SA, and SS men to maintain peace and order, and cease violence immediately, so that Germany's reputation abroad would not be harmed.[75]

Hitler's repeated appeals to put an immediate stop to "independent actions" were obviously not inspired by humanitarian motivations but meant to protect his government both domestically and in terms of its standing abroad.[76] If Party radicals and the SA seemed to be getting the upper hand, Hitler's own position might be jeopardized. While Hitler welcomed terror in general as it reduced the capacity of his communist and socialist opponents to organize, it had to be clear that he was firmly in control. If his grasp on government appeared to be tenuous, excessive terror by the SA could only be harmful to his own position.[77] To German Jews and Jewish organizations, on the other hand, such appeals may have been indicative of signs of moderation. In the context of the 1 April boycott, this supposed "moderation" even allowed German Jewish organizations to downplay antisemitic excesses in Germany vis-à-vis foreign powers, to the point that some called on foreign powers to end their boycotts of German goods and services. In turn, this could have a significant impact on foreign countries: if German Jewish organizations

74. BA Berlin, R43, II, no. 1195, "Reichskanzlei, NSDAP," fols. 23–24, 30–53, and 67–79.
75. For Hitler's exhortations see "Ermahnungen des Reichskanzlers," at BA Berlin, R43, II, no. 1195, "NSDAP," fol. 13 (from 22 February 1933) and fols. 61–62 (from 11 March 1933). Hitler's appeal to the SA and SS of 11 March 1933 reads as follows: "Party members, SA and SS men: Germany has undergone an immense cataclysm. It is the result of the most acrimonious battles, the most tenacious perseverance, but also of the highest discipline. Unscrupulous elements, mostly communist spies, are trying to compromise the party through isolated actions that bear no relation to the great feat of the national awakening, but instead besmirch and debase our struggle. In particular, by harassing foreigners in cars flying foreign flags, they attempt to bring the Party and Germany into conflict with foreign powers. SA and SS men! You must stop and detain such creatures immediately and call them to account. Hand them over to the police immediately, no matter who they may be."
76. See also the Berlin Lokal-Anzeiger, 11 March 1933 at BA Berlin, R43 II, no. 1195, "Akten der Reichskanzlei, NSDAP," "Hitler gegen Einzelaktionen," fol. 63. Toward his colleagues in the Cabinet, Hitler maintained that the attacks had been committed mainly by communists in SA uniforms (ibid., 84).
77. Karl Schleunes, Twisted Road, 68–69.

communicated that antisemitic measures could be held in check, they were less likely to intervene. But in the winter and spring of 1933, the actual effect of Hitler's appeals was negligible. Intra-ministerial correspondence among Interior Minister Frick, Foreign Minister Neurath, and Hitler's Undersecretary in the Reich Chancellery, Lammers, make it clear that Hitler's appeals had been unsuccessful in preventing further attacks, let alone flushing out their perpetrators as a warning to stem the violence.[78] After the April legislation was passed, the power of Nazi officials to interpret the law, as well as the numerous local interventions that ignored frontline service exemptions, showed that the April laws were utterly unsuccessful in standardizing discriminatory measures and in preventing more radical measures at the local level.

Due to the Aryan clause in the April legislation, tens of thousands lost their positions and income, hundreds of thousands were stigmatized and excluded from society, and millions were forced to document their "Aryan" ancestry or lack thereof. It is difficult to assess the reaction of the German population to the April laws and their consequences. Before 30 January 1933, only the NSDAP had demanded that Jewish Germans be forcibly dismissed from State service. Hitler's German National alliance partner supported this policy in April 1933, but it was not part of the DNVP's own program. Peter Longerich has argued that it is impossible to judge the extent to which the April laws were welcomed by those who did not support the NSDAP. In his view, it is inappropriate to conclude from the absence of protest that the population at large actively favored the dismissal of German Jews from the civil service and other influential positions.[79] David Bankier maintained from the evidence he gathered that large sections of the population found the violent persecutions and the boycott abhorrent and that there were misgivings about the brutal methods employed, while the professional dismissals resulting from the April legislation met with some approbation on the part of the German

---

78. BA Berlin, ," R43 II, no. 1195, "Akten der Reichskanzlei, NSDAP," fols. 67, 33, 29–32, 91–94, 177.
79. Longerich, *"Davon haben wir nichts gewusst!"* 66.

population, since the few existing sources (mostly personal recollections) suggest that "the removal of Jews from influential positions was consonant with the wishes of the great majority of the public."[80] This seems accurate given that even Nazi opponents, such as Thomas Mann, agreed to a certain extent with the legislative measures. In April 1933 he confided to his diary: "it is no great misfortune...that the Jewish presence in the judiciary has been ended."[81] These sentiments were shared by the great majority of the Protestant Church leadership, as will be shown below. The passivity and silent approval of the measures by a majority of the German population, whatever its causes, also made it possible that subsequently even the stringent antisemitic laws could not rein in more radical attempts to purge Jewish Germans from public life. This passivity and occasional willing complicity was already noted by Jewish professionals as the new laws were being promulgated: "In general, however, the great mass of the population remained apathetic and mute and showed itself fearful and timorous except for those, influenced by Nazi propaganda, who displayed thrill at the brutal actions against Jews."[82]

Economic Discrimination

Legislative measures did not tell the whole story. The reality of daily life was more cruel than the letter of the law led one to expect: discrimination was more manifold and violence more frequent in many walks of life— from continuing boycotts to destruction of property, robbery, blackmail, intimidation, rituals of humiliation, abductions, and outright murder. Laws had the function of sanctioning conditions that already prevailed in some regions of the Reich, putting in place uniform regulations for all

80. Bankier, *Germans and the Final Solution*, 68–69, esp. 69.
81. Thomas Mann, *Tagebücher 1933–1934*, ed. Peter de Mendelssohn (Frankfurt: Fischer, 1979), 46; also quoted in Fritz Stern, "National Socialism as Temptation," in *Dreams and Delusions. National Socialism in the Drama of the German Past* (New York: Vintage, 1989), 180.
82. See Ostrowski, "Vom Schicksal," 321. In 1933, Ostrowski was a chief surgeon in a municipal hospital in Berlin. See also the remarks by banker Georg Solmssen below.

of Germany, and softening the image of revolutionary anarchy that had captured headlines abroad. But uniformity and *Rechtssicherheit*, (legal certainty) even in the context of the harsh and inhuman antisemitic legislation, remained elusive.

The Reich government had emphasized that the April laws would pertain solely to the public realm and that the Aryan clause would play no role in the private sector of the economy. This was not the case in actual practice. The public sector dovetailed in many ways with the private economy, since the ministries of the Reich and the different German states continually awarded orders to companies in private industry and commerce, such as those to the *Reichspost* and *Reichsbahn*, and municipal governments contracted out to private commercial firms. Due to these interconnections between State and private industry and commerce, the "Aryan clause" was effectively introduced into the non-public sector of the economy. Already by the late spring and early summer of 1933, orders and contracts became dependent on whether the firms in question were *"judenrein,"* that is, free of Jewish influence. Even public authorities, such as the Reich Ministry of Finance, extended their anti-Jewish provisions without any prior warning.[83]

The detailed eighty-page memorandum that Leo Baeck sent to Hitler in January 1934 in the name of the *Reichsvertretung* lists the discriminatory measures introduced in the private sector of the economy in all of their regional diversity.[84] From the first, Jewish firms were disadvantaged when it came to orders from public authorities. On 14 July 1933 the Reich Cabinet decreed that in cases of equally good offers, "firms of

83. Pätzold, *Faschismus*, 110–111. By an edict of the Reich Finance Minister, commercial employees were required to submit declarations concerning their "Aryan" heritage if they furnished customs declarations on behalf of their firms or if they wanted to obtain customs information. All matters involving foreign countries were to be reserved to "Aryans."

84. BA Berlin, R43 II, no. 594, "Schrift der Reichsvertretung..." 59–137. The *Reichsvertretung der deutschen Juden* was the first umbrella organization to represent German Jews. A forerunner was the *Arbeitsgemeinschaft der Landesverbände der deutschen Juden* (1928), renamed *Reichsvertretung der Landesverbände der deutschen Juden* in 1932, which represented Jewish interests vis-à-vis the Reich government. Zimmermann, *Deutsche Juden*, 18; Max Gruenewald, "The Beginning of the 'Reichsvertretung,'" *Leo Baeck Institute Year Book*, 1:1 (1956): 57–67; and Friedländer, *Nazi Germany*, 60–61.

German blood" had to be given preference over those in which owners or members of the management were of "non-Aryan" descent.[85] Since prices of materials for public use needed by city or regional governments were often fixed, this amounted to the effective exclusion of "non-Aryan" firms.[86]

Economic discrimination against Jews also affected those who owned local stores dependent on private and municipal government customers. In its struggle against unemployment, on 1 June 1933 the Reich Cabinet passed the Law on the Reduction of Unemployment, the so-called Reinhardt Program. The law provided for government loans to young married couples. To increase general consumption, the money was not distributed in cash but in the form of vouchers for furniture and household articles, referred to as *Bedarfsdeckungsscheine* (personal needs certificates), intended as welfare support or as a supplement to wages.[87] According to the directions issued by municipalities, these certificates could not be redeemed in "non-Aryan" stores.[88] In addition, many towns issued guidelines that municipal vouchers provided to welfare recipients could be accepted only "by local, Christian German, and non-Marxist enterprises." The city of Meissen in Saxony, for example, ruled in October 1933 that a company stamp had to be punched on the front side of the voucher as proof that the purchase had not been made in a Jewish shop.[89] Other city governments and individual departments issued even more sweeping discriminatory measures: in the summer of 1933,

---

85. Walk, *Sonderrecht*, 37; *Akten der Reichskanzlei*, part I, vol. I, 676–678.

86. BA Berlin, R43 II, no. 594, "Schrift der Reichsvertretung ...," fol. 74.

87. The program was named after the Undersecretary of State in the Ministry of Finance, Fritz Reinhardt. See Michael Schneider, "The Development of State Work Creation Policy in Germany, 1930–1933" in Peter Stachura, ed., *Unemployment and the Great Depression in Weimar Germany*, (London: Macmillan, 1986), 163–186; Schneider, *Unterm Hakenkreuz*, 255–263, esp. 261; Lisa Pine, *Nazi Family Policy, 1933–1945* (Oxford: Oxford University Press, 1997).

88. BA Berlin, R43 II, no. 594, fol. 75. Since hundreds of thousands of *Ehestandsdarlehen* (marriage loans) were eventually granted, the potential financial loss to Jewish store owners was considerable.

89. BA Berlin, R43 II, no. 594, fol. 76. Meissen, pop. 45,485 (1925); *Statistisches Jahrbuch* (1933), 12. In Berlin, Hamburg, Duisburg, and several smaller cities, such as Cottbus and Insterburg in East Prussia, the certificates issued by city welfare offices bore the stamp, "Department stores and Jewish businesses are excluded from redemption of this certificate."

the police chief of Recklinghausen in the Prussian Rhine province wrote to a firm in neighboring Gelsenkirchen that its offer of services to the police department had to be accompanied by a certificate attesting that "your enterprise is Christian and national-minded." And the city government of Speyer in the Bavarian Palatinate officially announced in the same time period that for orders and deliveries to the city only purely "Aryan" firms could be considered.[90]

The discriminatory measures were designed to weaken the economic prospects and destroy the financial foundation of Jewish individuals and firms from a multitude of angles. Already in the very first year of Hitler's rule, malice and chicanery were extended into every corner of daily life. An August 1933 decree of the National Socialist *Rundfunkkammer* (Wireless Supervisory Board), for example, prohibited Jewish retail and wholesale merchants from selling the new inexpensive *Volksempfänger* (people's receiver) radio set, which cost a mere 76 Reichsmarks instead of the 200–400 Reichsmarks for conventional sets, in an attempt to deprive them of customers.[91] And credit institutions, such as the co-operative Raiffeisenbanken, withdrew loans from Jewish lenders, just as many cities and some German states no longer accepted advertisements from Jewish business owners.[92] Such bans on advertisements from Jewish firms were indeed widespread: following a 24 June 1933 decree of Braunschweig's Nazi government, all newspapers published in the city and state of Braunschweig rejected ads from Jewish firms. This was also the case for newspapers in the state of Mecklenburg/Schwerin and the city of Chemnitz. In December 1933 bans on ads from Jewish firms extended to

90. BA Berlin, R43 II, no. 594, fol. 74. Recklinghausen, pop. 84,609 (1925); Gelsenkirchen, pop. 327,703 (1933); Speyer, pop. 25,609 (1925); *Statistisches Jahrbuch* (1933), 7, 13.
91. BA Berlin, R43 II, no. 594, fol. 77. The production of "people's receivers" was ordered by the Propaganda Ministry so that radio broadcasts could be used to influence public opinion more easily. Since *Volksempfänger* sets could receive broadcasts only on the medium waveband, foreign radio stations, which used shortwave bands, could not be received on these devices. Due to the production of "people's receivers," 65% of all households had a radio set by 1941; in 1933 the percentage had been 25%. See Hilde Kammer and Elisabeth Bartsch, eds., *Nationalsozialismus. Begriffe aus der Zeit der Gewaltherrschaft 1933–1945* (Hamburg: Rowohlt, 1992), 221.
92. BA Berlin, R43 II, no. 594, "Schrift der Reichsvertretung," fol. 79.

newspapers in about one hundred German cities.[93] And there were further instances of subtle discrimination: some artisan guilds, such as the *Tapezierer-Innung* (Paperhangers' Guild) of Greater Berlin, put together lists of suppliers from which Guild members could order raw materials or finished products. These *Bezugsquellenverzeichnisse* (lists of supply sources) included only "Aryan" providers, as did supply lists distributed from firms in Berlin-Schöneberg, Gleiwitz in Upper Silesia, Dresden, and Königsberg.[94]

Demands for continued boycotts of Jewish firms, bans preventing officials and Nazi Party members from buying in Jewish shops, and the innumerable discriminatory economic measures all sprang from one source: overzealous Party leaders, members, functionaries, and hangers-on who wanted to demonstrate by their anti-Jewish activism that they stood fully behind the declared goals of the Party. Through ideological zeal and violent actions directed against Jews, they meant to strengthen their own position and prove themselves active members fit for higher office in the Party. Those belonging to Nazi organizations used antisemitic attacks to excel within their peer group by dint of their brutality, thus demonstrating their allegiance to the movement. A contemporary observer, Sebastian Haffner, emphasized that antisemitic violence functioned as a test of courage, a means of selection, and a bonding of the Nazi in-group "through the iron trammels of jointly committed crimes."[95] Perpetrators also did not need to fear that they were antagonizing the population at large through their actions. Georg Solmssen, speaker of the Executive Board of Deutsche Bank, who had converted

---

93. BA Berlin, R43 II, no. 594, fols. 80–82. The established National Socialist press frequently threatened newspapers that published advertisements of Jewish firms with branding and denunciation. The *Liegnitzer Tageblatt*, for example, refused to publish ads of Jewish firms because its publisher feared retaliatory measures from the National Socialist press. In Bochum, Herne, and Duisburg the city administrations openly came out against accepting advertisements from Jewish firms. In Chemnitz the ban went so far that newspapers refused to print an appeal by the *Reichsvertretung der deutschen Juden* to vote "yes" (i.e., with the government) in the November 1933 plebiscite about Germany leaving the League of Nations.
94. BA Berlin, R43 II, no. 594, fol. 83.   95. Haffner, *Germany: Jekyll & Hyde*, 69–70.

to Protestantism, wrote a letter to fellow banker Franz Urbig on 9 April 1933, in which he pointed to Nazi attempts to destroy the economic livelihoods of Jews in Germany and the dangers posed by the passivity and silence of the German population:

> The expulsion of Jews from State service, now accomplished by law, forces us to consider the question of what consequences these measures, which were accepted even by the educated section of the population virtually as a matter of course, will have on the private sector.... The complete passivity of those not belonging to the National Socialist Party, the absence of any feeling of solidarity shown by those who hitherto worked shoulder to shoulder with their Jewish colleagues in the firms in question, the ever more evident urge to take advantage of positions becoming vacant, the covering up with a veil of silence the shame and mortification indelibly inflicted upon all who, though without any guilt, have lost the foundation of their material existence and honor from one day to the next – all this reveals such an utterly hopeless situation that we must brace ourselves and view things as they are.[96]

Other Discriminatory Measures

Beginning already in the late summer of 1933, some small towns and villages banned Jews from entering their confines. Signs to this effect are well known for a later period, just as it is known that most of these signs were taken down temporarily for the Olympic Games in 1936.[97] Less known is that signs barring Jews from German towns were put up as early as 1933. As the *Würzburger General-Anzeiger* reported on 20 September 1933, the Community Council of Rödelsee, a village in the Bavarian district of Lower Franconia, made it known that "non-resident Jews are banned from entering this locality;" signs had been put up at entrances

96. Quoted in Harold James, "Die Deutsche Bank und die Diktatur 1933–1945," in Lothar Gall, Gerald Feldman, Harold James, Carl-Ludwig Holtfrerich, and Hans E. Büschgen, *Die Deutsche Bank, 1870–1995* (Munich: Beck, 1995), 337.
97. See also Bajohr, *"Unser Hotel,"* 116–134; Burleigh, *Third Reich*, 281–322.

to the village.[98] The *Fränkische Tageszeitung* reported in September and October that comparable notices had been put up in many small towns and villages at the behest of local authorities.[99] Violations were met with threats. The Mayor and Town Council of Behringersdorf, for example, wrote to a gentleman in Nuremberg who had contravened the ban:

> Despite the public notices that Jews are not wanted in Behringersdorf, you have the audacity to come here day after day to conclude commercial deals. In the interest of your physical well-being, we advise you to stay away from the Behringersdorf area and desist from even indirect business contact with local farmers. Otherwise you might become permanently disabled.[100]

Apart from threats, there were no legal provisions to implement these prohibitions. In the case of admittance to spas and resort towns, the first Reich-wide regulations for "Jewish visitors in spas and health resorts" were passed by the Reich Interior Ministry in July 1937. But "spa and seaside resort" antisemitism was in evidence already long before this, illustrating that National Socialists were taking up a tradition of discrimination that had begun in Imperial Germany.[101] Before 1933, however, the initiative came from spa resort tourists, who exerted pressure on hotel owners and spas not to admit Jewish guests. In 1933 the initiative shifted to the local Nazi leadership and National Socialist town administrations, which now showed great eagerness to keep their seaside resorts *"judenfrei."*[102]

Already in June 1933 signs appeared indicating that Jewish resort visitors were not wanted on Norderney, a North Sea island where many Jewish guests traditionally spent their holidays. In the late fall of 1933 the Norderney resort administration had thousands of official letter-sealing stamps

---

98. BA Berlin, R43 II, no. 594, fol. 102. The small village of Rödelsee, pop. 734 (1905), had one Protestant and one Catholic church, as well as one synagogue. Villagers lived mainly from the wine trade. *Meyers Großes Konversations-Lexikon*, 6th ed., vols. 17, 45.

99. BA Berlin, R43 II, no. 594, fol. 102. For more examples from Lower Franconia see also Gellately, *Gestapo*, 102–106.

100. BA Berlin, R43 II, no. 594, fol. 103.   101. Bajohr, "*Unser Hotel*," 11–52.

102. Bajohr, "*Unser Hotel*," 116–117.

printed and distributed, with the inscription, "North Sea Spa Norderney is *judenfrei*."[103] Yet the legal preconditions for exclusion and expulsion from the island were conspicuously lacking, so that in June 1934 the Prussian Interior Minister had to confirm that resident bans were incompatible with the Reich Constitution and that police protection had to be granted to all resort guests, "irrespective of racial affiliation." Unimpressed, the Norderney resort administration continued to make it known that Jews would not be welcome on Norderney or other islands.[104] These yawning contradictions between state law and local practices were not limited to Norderney—they extended throughout the Reich. But in 1933, local Nazi leaders and supporters knew only too well that their violations of existing law would go unpunished.

German Jews had to fight an uphill battle even when it came to obtaining training positions in agricultural and artisanal trades. Due to increasing difficulties in attending *Gymnasien* and universities, and thus faced with the danger of exclusion from the professions, some Jews sought to acquire training in agriculture and the trades, especially since expertise in the fields of farming and the crafts would be necessary in case of emigration.[105] Even though such training would have promoted Jewish emigration and was thus grist for the mill of the Nazi emigration

---

103. BA Berlin, R43 II, No. 594, "Schrift der Reichsvertretung . . . ," fol. 137; Bajohr, "*Unser Hotel*," 117. The Norderney spa administration sent Jewish newspapers a press release declaring that "Jewish resort guests are not welcome on Norderney. . . . Should Jews nevertheless come to Norderney this coming summer, they must bear the consequences. Should conflicts arise, the spa administration would immediately have to expel Jews who are present from the island in the interest of the spa and the German guests." *C.V. Zeitung*, 14 December 1933, in Bajohr, "*Unser Hotel*," 117–118.
104. Bajohr, "*Unser Hotel*," 118. In March 1934 the mayor of Westerland on the island of Sylt supported an entry ban there. This had little impact since some Bed and Breakfast owners continued to accept Jewish guests. The mayor's call for an entry ban was not met with universal agreement amongst the spa authorities. To the inquiry of a Jewish traveler who wanted to visit Westerland, the spa administration answered that while, according to the local council, Jews were "not welcome" in Westerland, "there is no known legal lever to keep Jews away from Westerland. . . . We would be pleased to be able to welcome you to Westerland." See Bajohr, "*Unser Hotel*," 122, 213.
105. Such attempts were often supported by Zionist groups, since agricultural experts and artisans were needed in Palestine and in countries such as Argentina and Brazil, which welcomed trained artisans. See Schleunes, *Twisted Road*, 181–190; Friedländer, *Drittes Reich*, 75–79.

policy, local Nazi Party officials often pointedly hampered training by refusing to tolerate Jewish trainees in their districts, or put a stop to instruction because National Socialist Chambers of Commerce lodged protests against it. In November 1933, for example, the *Nationalsozialistische Landpost* heaped scorn on the idea of Jewish farm labor: "Already the fact that Jews own German soil and pass themselves off as farmers is a provocation. German soil belongs solely in the hands of Germans."[106] In June 1933 the Reich Association for Jewish Settlement set up an instruction course for Jewish farmers on an estate near Rathenow in Brandenburg. The beginning was promising, but due to objections from the local SA, the course soon had to be discontinued. On the Silberberg estate near Saarow (also in Brandenburg) about 3,000 acres were leased from the local NSDAP *Kreisleiter* for a similar purpose. Fifteen Jewish trainees began their instruction under the guidance of "a well-intentioned inspector" so that "both sides were well satisfied" with the arrangement. Faced with the choice of either relinquishing his office as *Kreisleiter* or cutting short the training of the Jewish apprentices, the Nazi Party official opted for the latter and the agricultural trainees were forced to leave the Silberberg estate.[107]

In Karlsruhe, the capital of Baden, the *Oberrat der Israeliten* (Superior Council of Israelites), a corporation under public law, had received permission from the Nazi county leadership and the Baden Ministry of Labor to offer courses in metalworking for young Jewish Germans under the guidance of local trade-school teachers. But even these modest attempts came to naught when local artisan guilds objected to the training and the courses could not be held.[108] In mid-November 1933 the Jewish Welfare Association of southern Saxony-Thuringia in Erfurt complained that it was impossible to implement plans for vocational

106. *Nationalsozialistische Landpost*, no. 47, 18 November 1933 at BA Berlin, R43 II, no. 594, "Schrift der Reichsvertretung," fol. 123,
107. BA Berlin, R43 II, No. 594, "Schrift der Reichsvertretung," fols. 124–125. Rathenow in the Prussian *Regierungsbezirk* of Potsdam, pop. 27, 588 (1925); *Statistisches Jahrbuch* (1933), 13.
108. BA Berlin, R43, no. 594, fol. 127.

retraining. Attempts to place potential trainees with master artisans failed due to the resistance of artisan guilds, which argued that, according to a directive of the *Reichsstand des Deutschen Handwerks*, "Jews must not be trained, so as to keep them away from the artisan trades." When asked whether this was lawful, the government of Thuringia became evasive: "Just now things are still in the process of development...."[109] There were also cases in which training programs begun before 1933 came to a sudden end. Ernst Fuchs, who had started his training program with the *Reichsbahn* with a two-year contract in early October 1932, received a registered letter from the national railroad training center in Tempelhof on 30 September 1933: "We are terminating your apprenticeship with the Reichsbahn, effective 31 October 1933 due to your non-Aryan descent."[110]

Discrimination abounded in all sectors of the economy, though it was probably most evident in agriculture. Farmers were frequently forbidden from "doing business with non-Aryan traders," which meant that they could not sell agricultural produce or livestock to them.[111] Violations were severely punished. In this context, the head of a local Farmers' Association in Prussian Friedland wrote to a peasant: "Infringements against this ruling will have the consequence that you will not receive any further official support from the authorities and even the refinancing of your liabilities might fail."[112] This was an effective means of exerting pressure, given that farmers were so frequently in debt that their survival might depend on refinancing their debt payments. In Schivelbein, located in the Pomeranian county of Belgard, the Nazi head of the local Farmers' Association requested a list of all farmers who still entertained "business connections with Jewish firms" on 30 September 1933; in neighboring Neustettin, the Farmers' Association wrote to a farmer who still entertained Jewish business contacts that "farmers who do business with Jews cannot be considered honorable," and in Stolp in eastern Pomerania the *Kreisbauernführer* (county Farmers' Association leader) threatened to

---

109. BA Berlin, R43 II, no. 594, fol. 130.   110. Ibid., fol. 131.
111. Ibid., fols. 104–118.   112. Ibid., fol. 104.

"publicly denounce every farmer who continues or initiates trade with Jewish firms."[113] On 10 December 1933 the Electoral Hesse Rural Association in Kassel threatened to bring those farmers who belonged to the NSDAP and traded with Jews before a committee of inquiry.[114] Comparable prohibitions coupled with sanctions were widespread throughout the Reich, with geographic centers in Hesse and East Elbian Prussia. The *Deutsche Getreidezeitung* wrote in September 1933 that "trade in the nutritional foundation of the German people [i.e., grain]" was the sole remit "of men of German blood," and that the hour was not far off "in which Jewry will be eliminated altogether from the trading of goods."[115]

Beginning in August 1933, efforts were also made to drive Jewish merchants out of the barley and hops trades, in which they had hitherto played a leading role. According to a memorandum by the German Rural Commerce Association of 31 August 1933, "the brewery industry had hitherto bought the lion's share of its supply of barley from non-Aryan merchants." Now the barley trade was to be transferred "into Aryan hands." The same was to happen with the hops trade, which hitherto had "equally been dominated by Jewish firms," as stated in a letter from the *Deutscher Landeshandelsbund* to the *Deutsche Brauindustrie* dated 8 September 1933.[116] Also on 8 September the *General-Anzeiger* of Dortmund— one of the centers of the German brewing industry—wrote that hops growers would have to conduct their business in future without Jews, and should sell their harvest directly to the brewery owners to eliminate the Jewish commission business.[117]

Dairy co-operatives also exerted pressure on farmers not to conduct business with Jewish firms. In Ober-Mockstadt near Friedberg in Hesse, it was publicly proclaimed that farmers who continued to do business with

---

113. Ibid., fols. 106, 108.   114. Ibid., fol. 109.
115. *Deutsche Getreidezeitung*, no. 224, 26 September 1933, at BA Berlin, R43 II, no. 594, fol. 105. Here the intention of completely excluding German Jews from the business world is suggested as early as September 1933.
116. Ibid., fols. 111–112.
117. Ibid., 113. With its numerous large breweries, Dortmund was a center of the German hops trade and beer production.

Jews would no longer be able to sell "milk to the dairy cooperative." This would be tantamount to economic ruin. The dairy co-operative in Apen in the state of Oldenburg used uncommonly blunt speech in its communication "to our honored representatives" on 4 October 1933. After announcing a ban on business with Jewish firms and mandating that deliveries be stopped and contracts cancelled immediately, it stated: "You may well imagine that we do not want to be candidates for a concentration camp and therefore ask you that wherever ties to Jewish firms exist, you dissolve them immediately. It is out of the question that we continue deliveries under some phony cover."[118]

In contrast to the grassroots nature of antisemitic violence that sprang up spontaneously and was mostly unorganized, the boycott and the April legislation were acts of State that made it plain that ostracization had become official State policy. In view of the fact that officials and judges had already been put on furlough in March and early April, the laws regulated an already existing practice by conceding retroactive legality. Standardizing regulations for the Reich as a whole for an already existing state of affairs was in effect a *justificatio post eventum*, since the new legal stipulations merely reflected existing practices and now simply legalized previous infractions of existing laws.[119] This chapter has also shown that the April legislation was often violated by Nazi activists and bureaucrats who took advantage of its ambiguously worded provisions to the detriment of its Jewish targets. The Aryan clause, first introduced with the civil service legislation, also did not remain confined to the public realm but was widely applied within the private sector of the economy.

In contrast to antisemitic violence and the April boycott, which seems to have been met with widespread disapprobation, especially among the educated bourgeoisie, there was little public disgruntlement when it came

---

118. BA Berlin, R43 II, no. 594, fols. 116, 115.
119. See also Adam, *Judenpolitik*, 67–68. Adam rightly considers this a hallmark of Nazi rule, since frequent violations of existing laws often compelled authorities to bestow *post factum* legality on legal breaches by introducing new legislation.

to removing high-ranking officials and other Jewish professionals and denying them access to the professions.[120] The educated sections of the population in particular appear to have condoned these policies, not least because they created increased opportunities for their own advancement. But even those who were not directly affected, such as the Protestant Church hierarchy (see Chapters 9, 10, and 11 below), wholeheartedly endorsed the spirit of the April legislation. As Thomas Mann wrote in the spring of 1933, "I could to some extent go along with the rebellion against the Jewish element, were it not that the Jewish spirit exercises a necessary control over the German element, the withdrawal of which is dangerous."[121] As shown in Part III of this book, in the spring of 1933 most members of the German elite might have agreed with the first part of that sentence.

120. Bankier, *Germans and Final Solution*, 69.
121. Mann, *Tagebücher 1933–1934*, 54. Mann continued (perhaps a little self-servingly), "Left to themselves the German element is so stupid as to lump people of my type in the same category and drive me out with the rest."

PART III

REACTIONS TO ANTISEMITIC VIOLENCE

9

THE PROTESTANT CHURCH AND THE "JEWISH QUESTION"

The Church as Conscience of the Nation

During the nineteenth century, German Protestants had helped to advance the process of unification. In fact, their very identity was so closely interwoven with the fate of the nation that the German Protestant Church considered itself a kind of German National Church.[1] This identification was all the more instinctive since, as Ralf Dahrendorf wrote, "in its essential character, [German] society was Protestant," a fact that was accentuated by the relatively low percentage of Catholic university students in the law faculties before and after the First World War.[2] During World War I the Protestant Church had wholeheartedly supported the German war effort and was unshakeable in its interpretation of the conflict as a defensive war. Moral right was clearly on Germany's side. Spiritual support went so far as to equate the German "mission" with the will of God, so that the hoped-for German victory would be interpreted as the realization of divine justice. Protestants held fast in their belief in the superiority of German intellectual and scientific achievements, as well as of ethical standards and piety, as compared to

---

1. Jonathan R. C. Wright, *"Über den Parteien." Die politische Haltung der evangelischen Kirchenführer 1918–1933* (Göttingen: Vandenhoeck & Ruprecht, 1977), 103–104. Adolf Stoeker, the Protestant court preacher from Berlin who was notorious for his antisemitism, wrote in 1871: "The Holy Evangelical Reich of the German nation has now been fulfilled; ... in this we recognize the hand of God from 1517 to 1871." Quoted in Walter Frank (a leading National Socialist historian), *Hofprediger Adolf Stoecker und die christliche Bewegung*, 2nd ed. (Hamburg: Hanseatische Verlagsanstalt, 1935), 27–28.
2. Ralf Dahrendorf, *Gesellschaft und Demokratie in Deutschland*, 5th ed. (Munich: DTV, 1977), 131.

Before the Holocaust: Antisemitic Violence and the Reaction of German Elites and Institutions during the Nazi Takeover.
Hermann Beck, Oxford University Press. © Hermann Beck 2022. DOI: 10.1093/oso/9780192865076.003.0010

(as they saw it) shallow West European civilization. Through the experience of war, the Protestant Church thus found itself all the more internally united with and bound to the monarchy, to the point where German defeat in the war felt like a psychological catastrophe. In a certain sense religious belief itself was hallowed out for those Protestants who attributed so much spiritual meaning to the German war effort, for the defeat left many in despair and doubting divine justice.[3]

The collapse of the Empire and monarchical government in 1918 meant that the German Protestant churches had to reorient themselves. Until 1918, the prince of a German state had also been the head of its Protestant *Landeskirche,* (*Land* Church) so that all important decisions were made in his name. The Protestant Church in Prussia, for example, recognized this tight connection in Sunday prayers for the sovereign. For German Protestants the removal of the monarchic sovereign as *sumus episcopus* was an especially grave loss, since Protestants had no political party to defend their interests, while German Catholics could always turn to the Center Party for protection.[4] In a revolutionary State inimical to the Church (into which the Weimar Republic threatened to turn at its very beginning), financial support would also have been uncertain, since the *Landeskirchen* were financially dependent on the State (in 1918, the Prussian state accounted for 50 percent of the Church's budget, about 28 million marks, of which most was used for ministers' salaries).[5]

---

3. Karl Hammer, *Deutsche Kriegstheologie 1870–1918* (Munich: DTV, 1974); Scholder, *Kirchen und Drittes Reich,* 13–37.
4. After the Reformation the territorial rulers in the Protestant regions had the right to control all external Church matters. In the "religious peace" at Augsburg (1555), control over territorial jurisdiction was transferred from bishops to territorial princes. The latter possessed the *ius reformandi*—the right to determine the confession of their subjects. On the Prussian background, see Robert M. Bigler, *The Politics of German Protestantism. The Rise of the Protestant Church Elite in Prussia, 1815–1848* (Berkeley: University of California Press, 1972); Thomas Nipperdey, *Deutsche Geschichte 1800–1866. Bürgerwelt und starker Staat* (Munich: Beck, 1983), 423–440.
5. Gottfried Mehnert, *Evangelische Kirche und Politik. Die politischen Strömungen im deutschen Protestantismus von der Julikrise 1917 bis zum Herbst 1919* (Düsseldorf: Droste, 1959); Jochen Jarke, *Kirche zwischen Monarchie und Republik. Der preußische Protestantismus nach dem Zusammenbruch von 1918* (Hamburg: Hans Christians, 1976); Sun-Ryol Kim, *Die Vorgeschichte der Trennung von Staat und Kirche in der Weimarer Verfassung von 1919. Eine Untersuchung über das*

On account of the Church's traditional interconnectedness with the State, Protestant Church leaders considered it their duty to continue their unconditional support of German interests during the Weimar Republic (especially in the face of foreign adversaries), to get involved in politics, and, if necessary, to issue proclamations on the pressing political concerns of the day. In 1918–19 they condemned the Allied blockade, which had led to widespread starvation, and the continued incarceration of German prisoners of war following the 11 November armistice. Protestant Church leaders voiced their disapproval of the injustices of the Versailles Peace Treaty (as they perceived them); even the tenth anniversary of the signing of Versailles was observed as a day of national mourning, with nationwide ringing of bells and flags at half-mast. Church leaders also denounced the Allied prohibition of Austria joining the Reich as violating Wilson's principle of self-determination of nations, and they took exception to the forcible transfer of parts of Upper Silesia to Poland after the 1921 plebiscite had resulted in 60 percent of the eligible voters voting in favor of remaining with Germany.

In their meetings with foreign Church leaders, German Protestants defended the goals of German foreign policy. In the 1924 meeting of the German chapter of the World Alliance for International Friendship Through the Churches, the issue of war guilt was thus a prominent theme. In 1926, the American Council of the World Alliance expressed sympathy and support for the German point of view.[6] The feeling that Germany was treated unfairly and dishonorably by the Allies also influenced the attitude of the Church toward the rise of National Socialism. Before 1933 a majority of Protestant Church leaders considered the

---

Verhältnis von Staat und Kirche in Preußen seit der Reichsgründung von 1871 (Hamburg and London: LIT, 1996); and Scholder, *Kirchen und Drittes Reich*, 16.

---

6. The American Council of Churches positioned itself as follows: "Surely no sane person today believes that the entire responsibility for that awful catastrophe rests exclusively on one nation and that all the other nations are absolutely guiltless. All fair-minded persons now realize that Article 231 of the Treaty of Versailles was dictated by the war spirit at a time when passion ran high and that such an Article would not be framed today" (Wright, *Parteien*, 104–120, esp. 112).

rise of the Nazi movement to be a reaction to the ongoing humiliation of their country by foreign powers. This view tended to generate a certain elective affinity and sympathy for the nationalist aims of the movement. And once the National Socialist party had come to power, this became translated into a reluctance to criticize a political party with whose essential foreign policy goals most Church leaders were inclined to agree.

Fragmentation and Efforts to Form a Unified Organizational Structure

In stark contrast to German Catholicism, the Protestant Church during the Weimar Republic did not speak with one voice. It was divided into twenty-eight *Landeskirchen*, of which the Protestant Church of the Old Prussian Union was the most important. Founded in 1817, the Protestant Church of the Old Prussian Union included the Lutheran and Reformed Churches of all provinces that had formed part of Prussia in 1817: East Prussia, Brandenburg, Berlin, Pomerania, the *Grenzmark* Posen-West Prussia, Silesia, Saxony, Westphalia, Rhineland, and Hohenzollern. In 1932 it comprised about 19 million Protestants; in conjunction with Protestants in the ceded territories of Memelland, Danzig, West Prussia, and Upper Silesia, roughly 20 million.[7] In 1866, when Prussia annexed the new territories of Schleswig-Holstein, Hesse-Kassel, Nassau, Frankfurt, and the Kingdom of Hanover, Bismarck made sure not to tamper with

---

7. The regional distribution of members of the Protestant Church of the Old Prussian Union in 1932 was as follows: East Prussia (82% Protestant), 1,851,167; Mark Brandenburg (91% Protestant), 2,363,027; Berlin (75.5% Protestant), 3,039,390; Pomerania (93.8% Protestant), 1,761,956; Grenzmark Posen-West Prussia (61.8% Protestant), 205,517; Silesia (49.6% Protestant), 2,236,256; Saxony (with Roßla und Stolberg, 88.5% Protestant), 2,901,977; Westphalia (46.2% Protestant), 2,222,538; Rhineland (29.4% Protestant), 2,337,000; Hohenzollern (5% Protestant), 3,572. In total: 18,917,975. In addition, there were 702,036 Protestants in the territories ceded after 1918: Memelland, Danzig, West Prussia and Upper Silesia. See *Kirchliches Jahrbuch für die evangelischen Landeskirchen Deutschlands*, ed. Hermann Sasse (Gütersloh: Bertelsmann, 1932), 558–585; Siegfried Hermle and Jörg Thierfelder, *Herausgefordert. Dokumente zur Geschichte der evangelischen Kirche in der Zeit des Nationalsozialismus* (Stuttgart: Calwer, 2008), 26–27.

their confessional status (*Bekenntnisstand*) in order to avoid disputes between Lutheran and Reform Churches, which had erupted in 1817.[8] On the eve of the Nazi seizure of power, another 20 million Protestants can be added to the count with the *Landeskirchen* that were included in Prussia as of 1866, together with the non-Prussian Protestant churches in Waldeck-Pyrmont (Uniate), Bavaria (Lutheran), the Palatinate (Uniate, headquarters in Speyer), the Free State of Saxony (Lutheran), Württemberg (Lutheran), Baden (Uniate), and other localities with smaller Protestant *Landeskirchen*.

Throughout the nineteenth century, issues surrounding the formation of a united German Protestant Church had been hotly debated, but confessional antagonism and friction between Lutherans and members of the Reformed and Uniate Churches remained irreconcilable, and especially the smaller *Landeskirchen* clung to their independence. After 1918, renewed demands for the unification and centralization of German Protestantism were raised, but after overcoming initial problems and threats from the revolutionary governments in Prussia, Saxony, Thuringia, and Braunschweig, the individual *Landeskirchen* emerged from collapses and revolution stronger and more independent than before.[9] It was only in 1933 that another serious effort was made to create a unified Protestant Reich Church.

On the other hand, already since 1903 the German Protestant Church possessed an all-embracing executive organ—the *Deutscher Evangelischer Kirchenausschuss* (Executive Committee of the German Protestant Church).[10] In 1922, the *Evangelischer Kirchenbund* (Protestant Church

---

8. Rudolf von Thadden, "Die Geschichte der Kirchen und Konfessionen," in Wolfgang Neugebauer, ed., *Handbuch der preußischen Geschichte*, vol. III (Berlin and New York: Walter de Gruyter, 2001), 547–711, esp. 579–596. There was a Lutheran Protestant Church and a Reformed Protestant Church in Hanover, a Lutheran Protestant Church in Schleswig-Holstein, Uniate Churches in Hesse-Kassel and Nassau, and Lutheran, Reformed, and Uniate *Landeskirchen* in Frankfurt.

9. Wright, *Parteien*, 11–36; Scholder, *Kirchen und Drittes Reich*, 13–59. In Prussia, the politics of the radical leftist Minister Adolf Hoffmann (USPD) at first seemed to undermine the position of the Church and, in Saxony, Thuringia, and Braunschweig, radical-leftist governments remained in power beyond the constitutional convention.

10. Scholder, *Kirchen und Drittes Reich*, 50–55; Wright, *Parteien*, 38–42.

Federation) was founded in the famous *Schlosskirche* in Wittenberg, where Luther had nailed his ninety-five theses to its entrance door. The *Kirchenbund*, charged with overseeing all matters relating to German Protestantism as a whole, was comprised of three main institutions: the *Kirchentag* (Church Diet), a kind of Church Federation parliament with 210 members; the *Kirchenbundesrat* (Federal Church Council), comprised of representatives of the twenty-eight *Landeskirchen*, and the aforementioned *Kirchenausschuss*, the main executive body, whose members made all crucial decisions important to the Church as a whole.[11] This Executive Committee and its president thus formed the most important representative body of German Protestantism. Half of its members were elected by the *Kirchentag*; the other half were dispatched by the *Kirchenbundesrat*. The leadership of this crucial committee lay in the hands of the president of the Prussian *Oberkirchenrat* (Supreme Church Council). Financially, the Protestant Church Federation was dependent on the *Land* churches that were represented in it. The independence of the *Land* churches was guaranteed by the fact that they could always leave the Federation. The pivotal position of Head of the Protestant Church Executive Committee was occupied by Hermann Kapler from 1925 to June 1933. He was thereby destined to play an important role during the first phase of the Nazi seizure of power.[12]

The Church as a Moral Authority

The Protestant Church considered itself a moral authority and was seen as such by German Protestants. This was increasingly the case after the

11. Connected with the *Kirchenausschuss* was the *Kirchenbundesamt* in Berlin.
12. Hermann Kapler (1867–1941); see also Hannelore Baum and Gertraud Grünzinger, eds., *Personenlexikon zum deutschen Protestantismus 1919–1949* (Göttingen: Vandenhoeck & Ruprecht, 2006), 129; Heinz Boberach, Karsten Nicolaisen, and Ruth Papst, eds., *Handbuch der deutschen evangelischen Kirchen 1918–1949: Organe-Ämter-Verbände-Personen*, vol. 1 (Göttingen: Vandenhoeck & Ruprecht, 2010), 15–69. Meetings of the Church Executive Committee took place at least once every six months.

removal of princely sovereigns in 1918. In his 1925 bestselling book *The Century of the Church*, Otto Dibelius characterized the role of the Church as the conscience of the State and nation.[13] Dibelius, "General Superintendent" of Brandenburg since 1925, the youngest and, according to Klaus Scholder, most talented Protestant Church leader of his day, considered the new Weimar Republic to be devoid of religion and universally binding norms and standards.. As the conscience of the nation, the Church was responsible for the introduction and upholding of Christian values and moral norms in society; one of its tasks was to judge what constituted "good" and "bad," as well acceptable and unacceptable behavior, in the daily lives of Germany's citizens.[14] Dibelius's work was in sync with the mental climate of the age. The dissemination of ethical norms (*sittliche Gedanken*) was seen as the central concern of German Protestantism before and after World War I. Despite significant differences between conservative and liberal theology, there was agreement about the moral mission of German Protestantism. While the exact substance of ethical religious norms and standards was in dispute among conservative, national-minded, and liberal theologians, there was a broad consensus among them that religion was the decisive propelling force of moral development and renewal.[15] This connection between religion and moral behavior was the mainspring of German Protestantism—the nucleus and common denominator of the German Protestant *Weltanschauung*. In the tradition of German Idealism, the meaning of an individual's life, and of mankind as a whole, was considered to lie in the quest for ever-higher levels of morality. German Protestants were familiar with this striving for ethical perfection as a heritage of German Idealism and the central

13. By 1928 five editions of the book had been published. "Otto Dibelius, 1880–1967," in Baum and Grünzinger, eds., *Personenlexikon*, 58; Hartmut Fritz, *Otto Dibelius. Ein Kirchenmann in der Zeit zwischen Monarchie und Diktatur* (Göttingen: Vandenhoeck & Ruprecht, 1998); Robert Stupperich, *Otto Dibelius. Ein evangelischer Bischof im Umbruch der Zeiten* (Göttingen: Vandenhoeck & Ruprecht, 1989). Otto Dibelius, for all his faults, was probably the most eminent figure of German Protestantism in the twentieth century.
14. Otto Dibelius, *Das Jahrhundert der Kirche*, 2nd ed. (Berlin: Furche, 1928), 227–229; Scholder, *Kirchen und Drittes Reich*, 56–59.
15. See also Scholder, *Kirchen und Drittes Reich*, 60–80.

element in the works of Schiller and Goethe, which were well known to educated Germans.[16] This causal connection between religion and ethical behavior was convincingly explained by the Protestant moral theologian Wilhelm Herrmann in his *Ethik* on the eve of World War I.[17]

According to Herrmann, *Sittlichkeit*—morality—constitutes a set of standards "by which individual human life is meant to transcend the limitations of its own nature and attain a higher way of being by virtue of creative activity."[18] This Protestant concept of morality is characterized (according to Klaus Scholder) "by the harsh demands of 'you ought to,'" regardless of human weakness. Hermann makes this very clear in his *Ethik*:

> Only in transcending the existing barriers of our own personal life is the moral good [to be realized]. For in every moment the demands of the absolute command us to be different from what we are on the basis of our emotions, interests, and sensual desires. In what we find agreeable, what we involuntary covet and crave, we are moored in [a] current reality [that is] connected with present conditions. The moral imperative, on the other hand, always directs us to a future that we do not yet fully comprehend. From the point of view of natural instincts and desires, the attainment of moral behavior therefore means not self-realization or development, but self-denial.[19]

16. According to Schiller's famous formulation, every individual carries the "Anlage und Bestimmung nach einem reinen, idealistischen Menschen in sich, mit dessen unveränderlicher Einheit in allen Abwechslungen übereinzustimmen, die große Aufgabe seines Daseins ist" ("the conception of and destiny toward a pure, idealistic *Mensch*; it is the most important purpose of his existence to reconcile all of life's changes and bring them into harmony with this ideal"). Central to Schiller's thought was the proposition that it is only through *Bildung* and striving for perfection that we come into our own as human beings. As he once famously put it, "He who through his own efforts does not make a name for himself or strive toward noble objectives belongs to the basest elements." Yet striving for knowledge was connected with the pain of searching and struggling. As Goethe comments on the unending quest of his hero *Faust*, "But you'd better understand, happiness plays no role in this." Franz Schnabel, *Deutsche Geschichte im 19. Jahrhundert*, 4th ed., vol. I (Freiburg: Herder, 1948), 204–234.
17. Wilhelm Herrmann, *Ethik*, 5th ed., (Tübingen, 1913); Scholder, *Kirchen und Drittes Reich*, 60–63.
18. Herrmann, *Ethik*, 12; Scholder, *Kirchen und Drittes Reich*, 61.
19. Herrmann, *Ethik*, 139–140; Scholder, *Kirchen und Drittes Reich*, 61.

A sharper contrast between this strict moral dogma of German Protestantism, on the one hand, and the Anglo-Saxon and American ideal of the "pursuit of happiness" with its inherent eudemonism, on the other, can hardly be imagined.[20]

Yet the religion-based ethical worldview of German Protestantism also called for social activism and the testing of believers' mettle; the State was considered to be an important realm of this kind of activity. As Scholder argued, in the political field it was necessary to demonstrate "what religiously grounded morality based on self-denial could do for society."[21] In a similar context, Ralf Dahrendorf pointed to "an affinity between certain Protestant values and the ethos of service for the State."[22] Within this frame of reference, Herrmann mentions the "justification of the struggle for better working conditions" as an ethical imperative. With keen perspicacity as to the future, he wrote already before the First World War: "In a State in which, for example, a general antisemitism holds sway, a human being who wishes to follow Jesus Christ or one who possesses any moral worth will find no Fatherland."[23] Herrmann, though a liberal theologian himself, expressed a belief that was common to all of German Protestantism: Given the emphasis placed on its moral foundation, the Protestant Church should have felt compelled to raise its voice against flagrant injustices and become politically active regardless of possible dangers into which political protests might lead. The code of strict self-denial of the individual's own interests in conjunction with the Church's

20. Thomas Mann masterfully characterized this clash of beliefs between a Protestant sense of duty and self-denial in the pursuit of transcendental qualities and Anglo-American "common sense" and the pursuit of happiness in the here and now in his novel *Königliche Hoheit* (Frankfurt/Main: Fischer, 2001).

21. Scholder, *Kirchen und Drittes Reich*, 60–63.   22. Dahrendorf, *Gesellschaft*, 271.

23. Herrmann, *Ethik*, 177; Scholder, *Kirchen und Drittes Reich*, 61–62. National Socialism also demanded that behavior be based on moral guidelines, though these were diametrically opposed to the values of the Church. Whereas Kant saw morality as the basic demand of reason (*Grundforderung der Vernunft*), National Socialism viewed it in an ideological light: "The German moral credo of the present time seeks in a new consciousness of community the main prerequisite for a renewal of moral life and moral philosophy; it stands for the concepts of race, *Volkstum*, honor, blood and soil, and 'a common good that transcends self-interest.'" *Neuer Brockhaus*, IV (Leipzig, 1938), 224.

self-declared role as the "conscience of the nation" dictated such a course of action. Failure to act would mean disavowal and renunciation of the Church's very identity.

The Church in Politics: Interconnections with the DNVP

In order to defend Church interests, theologians and other Protestant notables were called upon to participate actively in political life. The Church's natural ally in the political arena was the German National People's Party (DNVP), in accordance with the slogan: "The Church is politically neutral, but it votes German National."[24] In 1919, four Protestant *Generalsuperintendenten* (an office comparable to that of Bishop) sat in the Prussian Diet as DNVP deputies, and in Bavaria, Saxony, Württemberg, Baden, and Lippe-Detmold Protestant theologians were DNVP deputies in the state legislatures.[25] In the Constitutional National Assembly that met in Weimar in 1919 the Protestant clergy had also been strongly represented in the German National parliamentary faction.[26] The DNVP was attractive to Protestants since it supported similar political goals: it stood up for the monarchy (until 1928), advocated Christian education and the importance of Christianity in general, and appealed to the strong nationalism among Protestant Church leaders by championing the resurrection of German might. Throughout the Republic, but especially in its middle years, Protestant notables were thus also well represented in the DNVP Reichstag faction.[27] The involvement of the

---

24. Karl Wilhelm Dahm, *Pfarrer und Politik. Soziale Positionen und politische Mentalität des deutschen evangelischen Pfarrerstandes zwischen 1918 und 1933* (Cologne: Westdeutscher Verlag, 1965), 104.
25. Mehnert, *Evangelische Kirche*, 237–240; Wright, *Parteien*, 66–69.
26. Mehnert, *Evangelische Kirche*. Protestant theologians also sat as representatives of the DVP, DDP, and other parties in the National Assembly and in the German state parliaments, although in lesser numbers.
27. In the middle years of the Weimar Republic a series of prominent Church representatives were active in the DNVP Reichstag faction: the theology professor Hermann Strathmann; deputy chairman of the Protestant Workers' Association Wilhelm Koch; the *Domprediger*

Protestant Church leadership in politics was multifaceted and direct. This manifested itself when the Church raised a warning voice in its numerous declarations on political events of the time.

As conservative pillars of the State, Protestant Church leaders felt responsible for the political climate in society and for the wider political culture as a whole. They thus condemned the political murders at the beginning of the Republic, in particular that of Foreign Minister Walter Rathenau in June 1922 as a "vile and treacherous assassination." But the decline of political culture that was reflected in this and other politically motivated murders was blamed mainly on the vindictiveness of the Western powers.[28] Already in the second half of the 1920s, antisemitic voices came to the fore, as on the occasion of the 1927 Königsberg *Kirchentag* (Church Congress), when the Erlangen theologian Paul Althaus declared that "everywhere today a mindset created by Jewish influence in the economy, press, art, and literature runs counter to the adoption of the forces of the Gospel by our people." Althaus intimated that he was not advocating a race-based antisemitism but rather warning of "the danger emanating from the peril of an undermining and corrosive intellectualism that is upheld first and foremost by Jews."[29] This distinction between racist and cultural antisemitism would effectively be rendered irrelevant after Hitler came to power.

When, with increasing unemployment and the rise of the NSDAP and KPD, political violence became rampant after the summer of 1930,

---

(Canon) Ernst Martin; chairwoman of the German Evangelical Womens' League Paula Müller-Otfried; managing director of the *Kirchlich-Sozialer Bund* Reinhard Mumm; after 1928, Canon Bruno Doehring; Head of the Westphalian provincial Synod Karl Koch; chairwoman of the Federation of Evangelical Womens' Associations Magdalena von Tilling; and member of the Protestant Church of the Old Prussian Union Senate Detlev von Arnim. See Günther van Norden, *Kirche in der Krise. Die Stellung der evangelischen Kirche zum nationalsozialistischen Staat im Jahre 1933* (Düsseldorf: Presseverband der Evangelischen Kirche, 1963), 19, 174.

---

28. Wright, *Parteien*, 84. "We condemn our enemies for their blindness, which plunges our people into disgrace, ignominy, and distress, out of which all the ghosts of the darkest depths rise up."
29. Wright, *Parteien*, 76–77; Robert Ericksen, *Theologians under Hitler: Gerhard Kittel, Paul Althaus, Emmanuel Hirsch* (New Haven: Yale University Press, 1985).

Church leaders warned of the growing barbarization of public life, condemned violent excesses, and demanded that law and order be respected. In 1931 they issued numerous declarations "against the degeneration of mores in public life" and exhorted their congregations to help redress public grievances.[30] But they strenuously avoided naming the guilty party. After the *Kurfürstendammkravall* on 12 September 1931, when roughly 500 SA men attacked Jewish-looking pedestrians on the Kurfürstendamm in the western part of Berlin, the Church Executive Committee decided against a blanket denunciation of the violent attacks, as this might have appeared as an exclusive branding of the Nazi Party.[31] In the spring of 1931, the Prussian Superior Church Council had rejected a request from Jewish circles to publicly condemn the desecration of Jewish cemeteries. The specious excuse was that Protestant Christians had not taken part in this sacrilege.[32] In December 1931, Interior Minister Wilhelm Groener asked Hermann Kapler to "assist the State in the prevention of public violence," a request that Kapler then passed on to the various *Landeskirchen*. Already in March 1932, Kapler transmitted to Groener the affirmative answer of nine *Landeskirchen*, which demonstrated that their leadership was prepared to get involved in the political arena.[33]

The Church and Politics at the End of the Weimar Republic

During the course of 1932 the Church spoke out publicly on three separate occasions. In doing so, it did not shy away from openly criticizing National Socialism. The first occasion was the *Altonaer Blutsonntag* of 17 June 1932, the event that provided the pretext for Papen's coup against

---

30. Scholder, *Kirchen und Drittes Reich*, 258; Wright, *Parteien*, 166–169.
31. Walter, *Antisemitische Kriminalität*, 211–221; Wright, *Parteien*, 166–167.
32. Wright, *Parteien*, 167.   33. Scholder, *Kirchen und Drittes Reich*, 258–259.

the Prussian government on 20 July 1932 in the so-called *Preußenschlag*.[34] During an SA rally marching through a communist working-class district of Altona, eighteen persons had been killed and more than one hundred seriously wounded.[35] The attack was begun by communist snipers, who fired at the rally from neighboring balconies and rooftops. Ensuing gunfights and skirmishes took place near Altona's main Protestant church, in which a Sunday afternoon service was being held at the time. The Church's reaction to the bloodbath was a series of special religious services in the Altona church district on 21 July 1932 and, half a year later, the so-called Altona Confession on 11 January 1933, in which local church leaders rejected National Socialism's claim for total power and proclaimed the right to political resistance.[36]

Church leaders spoke out again after the second notorious murder of that summer. During the night of 9/10 August 1932, five SA men assaulted the communist laborer Konrad Pietczuch in his home in Potempa in Upper Silesia, beating and kicking him to death in the presence of his mother. Immediately prior to this bloody deed, the Papen government had passed an emergency decree responding to the rise of violence that made political murder punishable by death. On 22 August the five murderers of Potempa were therefore sentenced to death by a special court in Beuthen in Upper Silesia. The following day Hitler proclaimed his unshakeable solidarity with the five murderers in a public telegram: "In view of this monstrous blood sentence I feel tied to you in boundless loyalty. From this moment on your freedom becomes a matter of our honor."[37]

34. A. McElligot, "Street Politics in Hamburg 1932–1933," *History Workshop*, 16 (1983): 83–90; Wolfgang Kopitzsch, "Der 'Altonaer Blutsonntag,'" in Arno Herzig et al., eds., *Arbeiter in Hamburg* (Hamburg: Erziehung & Wissenschaft, 1983), 509–516; Winkler, *Weg in die Katastrophe*, 650–652.
35. Altona, near Hamburg, was then still part of the Prussian province of Schleswig-Holstein; pop. 227, 433 (1925); *Statistisches Jahrbuch* (1933), 11.
36. For the text of the Altona Confession, see Hermle and Tierfelder, *Herausgefordert*, 64–67; Scholder, *Kirchen und Drittes Reich*, 259–260; 267–272; Richard Bessel, "The Potempa Murder," *Central European History*, 10 (1977), 241–254.
37. Paul Kluke, "Der Fall Potempa," *VJHZ*, 5 (1957), 279–297; Hans Mommsen, *Aufstieg und Untergang der Republik von Weimar 1918–1933* (Berlin: Ullstein, 1998), 534–535; Winkler, *Weg in*

Following this event, Otto Dibelius pointedly criticized Hitler's declaration of solidarity with the SA murderers. In his weekly column in the conservative daily paper *Der Tag*, Dibelius underlined the importance of maintaining legal norms:

> It must never be doubted that murder remains murder regardless of the political attitude on the basis of which it was committed.... Only in a State built on the rule of law can a citizen look up with pride to the Fatherland. Law is the precondition for freedom. It is only in a State where the Christian norms of morality remain untarnished that a Christian can develop a feeling of belonging.[38]

The Württemberg church president Alois Wurm wrote to the Tübingen pastor Wilhelm Pressel, himself a member of the NSDAP, that "a word of condemnation about such National Socialist misdeeds must not be omitted."[39] Wurm also mentioned that he had expected a declaration from the Church leadership protesting against violent Nazi attacks and that the "omission of an expression of disapprobation" would discredit the Church.[40] According to Wurm, those Protestant pastors who sympathized with National Socialism were now called upon to issue a declaration of caution and reprimand, so that Protestantism could demonstrate that it possessed the courage "to also oppose a movement it endorses in its goals and objectives if that movement finds itself on the wrong path."[41] Pastor Pressel followed the advice of his superior and

---

die Katastrophe, 699–702; Beck, *Fateful Alliance*, 81–82. The five murderers were given a reprieve of lifelong imprisonment and released soon after 30 January. Not long after their release, three of them were implicated in another assault case. See GStAPK Dahlem, Rep 84a, no. 54858.

38. *Der Tag*, 4 September 1932, "Sonntagsspiegel." See also, Fritz, *Dibelius*, 395; Wright, *Parteien*, 136–137.
39. Gerhard Schäfer, *Die evangelische Landeskirche in Württemberg und der Nationalsozialismus. Eine Dokumentation zum Kirchenkampf*, vol. I (Stuttgart: Calwer, 1971), 154–172, esp. 154–156.
40. Ibid., 155.
41. Ibid., 156. Scholder estimates that in 1931 about 100 out of 18,000 Protestant ministers were members of the NSDAP (*Kirchen und Drittes Reich*, 279); Jeremy Noakes calculates that there were 17 NSDAP members among the Protestant ministers in Hanover-South Braunschweig; and the Berlin *Generalsuperintendent* Emil Karow reported in July 1932 that there

lodged a protest against Hitler's action with his fellow National Socialist pastors and the regional Nazi leadership in Stuttgart. As a consequence of his complaint, which was qualified since Pressel had made it clear that he too was opposed to the sentence passed in the Beuthen case, the Württemberg *Gauleiter* Wilhelm Murr expelled him from the Party on account of mutiny.[42] The exchange of letters between Pressel and his fellow National Socialist pastors makes it clear that most of them defended Hitler's declaration of solidarity and considered the judgment of Beuthen to be "the justice of dead legal clauses," while they endorsed Hitler's stand as an "elementary outcry of one's very being."[43] This was an ominous sign for the future.

Another incident in the small northern German state of Oldenburg, which had been governed by the NSDAP since June 1932, shows how tenaciously the Church was able to defend its rights on the eve of the Nazi seizure of power.[44] The occasion was a lecture tour by Robert Kwami, the African *Präses* of the Protestant Church of the former German colony of Togo.[45] On his tour, Kwami was scheduled to speak at two

were approximately 30 NSDAP members among the Protestant ministers in the capital. See Jeremy Noakes, *The Nazi Party in Lower Saxony 1921–1933* (London: Oxford University Press, 1971), 208; Wright, *Parteien*, 140, n. 75; and, in general, Manfred Gailus, *Protestantismus und Nationalsozialismus. Studien zur Durchdringung des protestantischen Sozialmilieus in Berlin* (Cologne: Böhlau, 2001), 89–196.

42. Schäfer, *Kirchenkampf*, vol. I, 158, 171–172. After the NS Student League lent its support to Pressel and communicated this to Murr, the latter withdrew Pressel's expulsion from the Party on 3 March 1933. On 12 December 1934 Pressel was then banned from the NSDAP once and for all.

43. Schäfer, *Kirchenkampf*, vol. I, 157, 161.

44. With only 581,296 inhabitants (1933) and an area of 6,424 square kilometers, Oldenburg was one of the smallest German *Länder*. In this mostly Protestant state the Lutheran Church had 321,134 members (1932). In the 29 May 1932 state parliamentary elections, the NSDAP received 48.4% of the votes and had an absolute majority in the state legislature, with 24 out of 46 representatives. The National Socialist *Gauleiter* of Weser Ems, Carl Röver (1889–1942), became *Ministerpräsident* of the state in June 1932; *Statistisches Jahrbuch* (1933), 5; Hermle and Tierfelder, *Herausgefordert*, 28; Albrecht Tyrell, *Führer befiel … Selbstzeugnisse aus der "Kampfzeit" der NSDAP* (Düsseldorf: Droste, 1969), 383; Hermann Weiß, ed., *Biographisches Lexikon zum Dritten Reich* (Frankfurt: Fischer, 2002), 384.

45. In the Protestant Church the *Präses* was the elected chairman of a provincial or state synod; in the Rhineland and Westphalia, the *Präses* could also be the head of the *Kirchenleitung* (Church leadership).

events in the Oldenburg St. Lamberti Church on 20 September 1932. When this became public, the National Socialist leadership of Oldenburg made it known through the press that it had instructed the Ministry of Culture to put an end to "such a crime against civilization." The Ministry of Culture, in turn, declared that this did not fall within its sphere of competence and referred the issue to the Oldenburg Superior Church Council, which vehemently rejected the protestations of the NSDAP. Both events took place as planned before large audiences.[46]

As was to be expected, the National Socialist *Gau* leadership did not let the matter rest there. *Gauleiter* Röver called the Oldenburg Church Council's actions "a stupidity... that ought to be punished with incarceration," since "the House of the Lord... had been defiled by a man of the lowest race."[47] The Oldenburg Church then reacted decisively to such blatant racism. The pastor of the St. Lamberti church, who had appeared together with Kwami, publicly called on Röver to take back his words "with a clear expression of regret." Since no apology was forthcoming, the Oldenburg Supreme Church Council instituted proceedings against Röver on 7 October, "on account of gross public insults." Even though this action was ultimately unsuccessful, it was a sure sign that the Church (in this case through the Oldenburg *Landeskirche*) was determined to resist National Socialism. Subsequent to the affair, the Oldenburg *Landeskirche* cautioned "against a racial hatred that cannot be reconciled with 'positive Christianity,'"[48] and in early December the Oldenburg *Kirchenblatt* published nine theses on "Christian Belief and Racial Research," which made it clear that Christianity was irreconcilable with any kind of racial

---

46. According to Scholder, *Kirchen und Drittes Reich*, 263–267, the large public turnout was meant as a demonstration against Nazi protests.
47. Scholder, *Kirchen und Drittes Reich*, 264.
48. Ibid., 265. "Positive Christianity" was the National Socialist expression of its ideology-infused "Christianity." Hitler knew it was inopportune to openly oppose Christianity at this stage and he wanted to avoid committing his movement to the support of only one of the two great denominations. See Richard Steigmann-Gall, *The Holy Reich. Nazi Conceptions of Christianity 1919–1945* (Cambridge: Cambridge University Press, 2003), 13–86.

discrimination.[49] The president of the Oldenburg Church Council, Heinrich Tilemann, published a critique of Nazi conduct in the Kwami case in the main Protestant press organ, *Das Evangelische Deutschland*, in which he expressed regret for National Socialists' "disrespect of personal freedom and legal norms."[50] Tilemann explained that it was the responsibility of the Church "to lend succor and understanding to those who suffer under terror." The duty that the Church owed the State was to protect personal freedom, oppose the violation of legal standards, and show the State the limits of its powers.[51] These were prophetic words that would soon gain new relevance. From Tilemann's courageous stand it seemed as if the rise of National Socialism had compelled the Protestant Church leadership to change its emphasis: from duty and obedience to the State, to individual freedom and the limits of State power. Would this still be the case once Hitler was in power?

Political Groupings within the Church

While it was possible for a small *Landeskirche* to oppose National Socialism in its regional framework, matters were more complicated at the national level. On the eve of the transfer of power to Hitler, the Protestant Church was not only divided into twenty-eight *Landeskirchen* of diverse confessional status; it was also separated into different political groupings, all of which made concerted political action difficult. With regard to

49. *Oldenburgisches Kirchenblatt*, no. 12, 7 December 1932, in Kurt Dietrich Schmidt, ed., *Die Bekenntnisse und grundsätzlichen Äußerungen zur Kirchenfrage des Jahres 1933* (Göttingen: Vandenhoeck & Ruprecht, 1934), 18–19. In these theses it is argued that "the different races are called to the service of one another" (no. 2); "every arrogant condescension of one race to another is incompatible with the Christian faith" (no. 3); and a true Christian fights against "the science of racial research being robbed of its strictly scientific character and turned into an ideology." With this, "scientific racial research" was recognized as a legitimate field of study.
50. Heinrich Tilemann (1877–1956), from 1920 to 1934 *Oberkirchenratspräsident* of Oldenburg. Baum and Grünzinger, eds., *Personenlexikon*, 258. *Das Evangelische Deutschland* covered the entire area of the German Protestant Church Federation (circulation: 20,000 copies); *Handbuch der Evangelischen Presse* (Leipzig: Wallmann, 1929), 32.
51. *Das Evangelische Deutschland*, 10, 1933, 10–12.

the events unfolding in 1933, the most significant grouping was the *Glaubensbewegung Deutsche Christen* (German Christians' Faith Movement, hereafter German Christians), created by the Brandenburg *Gauleiter* Wilhelm Kube in 1932 to ensure that the Nazi Party had a sympathetic Church faction that could participate in the Church elections of November 1932.[52] Since the German Christians could count on the support of leading National Socialists and the Nazi Party, they immediately won one-third of the seats in the November 1932 Church elections, even though the regional distribution of votes was quite uneven.[53] According to their guidelines of 26 May 1932, the German Christians advocated a union of the twenty-eight *Landeskirchen* into one *Reichskirche*, rejected parliamentarianism, propagated the struggle against "an anti-religious Marxism that is hostile to the people," and considered "race, *Volkstum* (national traditions and culture), and nation as God-given principles of life." The attempt to convert Jews to Protestantism was considered to be "a grave danger to our *Volkstum*."[54] Given this emphasis, German Christians thus propagated a Church that was rooted in national traditions and culture, as well as a racial approach to the "Jewish Question."

The German Christians could play an important role in 1933 because they managed to integrate intellectual currents that had a long tradition reaching back to the nineteenth century. The *Christlich-Deutsche Bewegung* led by Pastor Werner Wilm, for example, gathered those who championed a national-minded Protestantism, including its cultural and

---

52. Wilhelm Kube (1887–1943) became a member of the DNVP in 1919 and of the NSDAP in 1928. NSDAP *Gauleiter* of the "Gau Ostmark" since September 1928, his *Gau* merged with the "Gau Brandenburg" under his leadership into the "Gau Kurmark" in May 1933; Weiß, ed., *Lexikon*, 285–287. Already in 1930 Kube had charged two National Socialist pastors, Karl Eckert (Neumark) and Friedrich Wienecke (Soldin), with looking after Nazi interests.
53. In East Prussia, Pomerania, and the "Grenzmark Posen-West-Prussia" the German Christians received almost half of the votes, whereas in the Rhineland and Westphalia they received only about one-fifth. Kurt Meier, *Die Deutschen Christen. Das Bild einer Bewegung im Kirchenkampf des Dritten Reiches*, 2nd ed. (Halle: Niemeyer, 1965), 1–17; Wright, *Parteien*, 146–164; van Norden, *Kirche*, 22–40; Doris L. Bergen, *The Twisted Cross. The German Christian Movement in the Third Reich* (Chapel Hill: University of North Carolina Press, 1996), 1–20.
54. "Richtlinien der Glaubensbewegung 'Deutsche Christen,'" in Hermle and Thierfelder, *Herausgefordert*, 47–48.

political orientations. Apart from *völkisch*-minded Christians, it included traditional conservatives, such as Ewald von Kleist-Schmenzin and Canon Bruno Doehring, as well as the German National professors Paul Althaus, Emanuel Hirsch, and Heinrich Bornkamm.[55] The two National Socialist pastors Julius Leutheuser and Siegfried Leffler had already founded a *Kirchenbewegung deutsche Christen* (German Christians' Church Movement) in 1929.[56] This group later joined the German Christians' Faith Movement to create a united German National Church. Both groupings seem to have subscribed to the belief that the emergence of Adolf Hitler and his movement constituted a kind of divine intervention to save the chosen German people in order to lead mankind to even greater perfection.[57]

The oldest precursor of the German Christians was the *Bund für deutsche Kirche* (League of German Churches), founded in 1917 by the Flensburg pastor Friedrich Andersen, the literary historian Adolf Bartels, and Hans von Wolzogen, who formed part of Richard Wagner's Bayreuth circle, and whose mother was the daughter of the famous Prussian architect Karl Friedrich Schinkel. Its members welcomed the formation of the German Christians, hoping that it would help disseminate its *völkisch* ideals. After 1932, the *Bund* continued to exist as its own separate organization but henceforth supported the German Christians in Church elections and renounced lists of its own. Just as the German Christians, it advocated the creation of a national German Church focused on a deep inner bond to German national traditions and culture, and opposed anything "Jewish" in State and religious life. The ideology of the *Bund für deutsche Kirche* was based on the writings of Max Maurenbrecher and Houston Stewart Chamberlain, whose works appeared in mass

---

55. Meier, *Deutsche Christen*, 10–12; Wright, *Parteien*, 149–50; van Norden, *Kirche*, 24–26; Ericksen, *Theologians*.
56. Scholder characterizes the movement as "the ideal-type of a *völkisch*-Christian movement," in which "[there exists] no more difference among ecclesiastical, cultural, and political concerns, since everything emerges from the same life-force and serves the same goal—the Christian-*völkisch* renewal of the German nation." Scholder, *Kirchen und Drittes Reich*, 280; Van Norden, *Kirche*, 24–26.
57. Van Norden, *Kirche*, 22–33.

circulation and were widely read.[58] Maurenbrecher propagated the idea that God speaks to different peoples through their history and that the purpose of the individual is to serve the larger whole. On a political level, he argued that Germany needed a new State ideology that was based on a fusion of socialism and militarism.[59] Maurenbrecher also took up ideas and concepts of Paul de Lagarde and Houston Stewart Chamberlain; these were then passed on to the German Christians.[60] Chamberlain espoused the "liberation" of the Old Testament from anything "Jewish," and argued for the realization of an all-encompassing "*völkisch* Weltanschauung of the Church."[61]

The leadership of the various *Landeskirchen* usually refrained from commenting on everyday political events and claimed to be neutral in party politics. On 21 November 1931 the Superior Council of the largest *Land* Church, the "Old Prussian Church," proclaimed absolute neutrality: political struggles should be left outside church buildings and the Church should not become enmeshed in party politics.[62] In Württemberg, members of the Protestant clergy were expressly forbidden to take part in campaigns for the 1932 Reichstag elections, to wear Party badges, or to take part in political parades.[63] It is not without irony that, of all people, the head of the Executive Committee of the Protestant Church, Hermann

---

58. Ibid., 26–33. In particular, Maurenbrecher's *Der Heiland der Deutschen* and Houston S. Chamberlain's *Die Grundlagen des 19. Jahrhunderts* were very popular.
59. Max Maurenbrecher (1874–1930), Protestant theologian and journalist. In 1903 he joined the SPD and remained a member until 1916; in 1917 he joined the "German Fatherland Party." Lothar Bily, "Max Maurenbrecher," in *Biographisch-Bibliographisches Kirchenlexikon*, vol. V (Herzberg: Bautz, 1993), 1051–1055; Wolfgang Heinrichs, *Das Judenbild im Protestantismus des deutschen Kaiserreiches*, 2nd ed. (Gießen: Brunnen, 2004); Mehnert, *Evangelische Kirche*, 24–25.
60. Maurenbrecher argued that Lagarde was the first for whom the feeling of belonging to a people was consciously experienced as religion. According to Lagarde, no people would crucify their ideal on the cross; Jesus could therefore not be a Jew. Lagarde also advocated a national religion in order to avoid the collision between the claims of religion and fatherland, both of which demanded unlimited authority. In this national religion the interests of the fatherland and of religion would coalesce. Lagarde thus also proposed the formation of a national German Church. See the perceptive remarks in van Norden, *Kirche*, 26–33, and Fritz Stern, *The Politics of Cultural Despair. A Study in the Rise of Germanic Ideology* (Berkeley, Los Angeles, and London: University of California Press, 1974), 3–94.
61. Van Norden, *Kirche*, 26–33; Wilhelm Laible, "'Deutschkirche' und 'Deutsche Christen,'" *Allgemeine Evangelisch-Lutherische Kirchenzeitung*, 66:34 (25 Aug. 1933), 786–788.
62. Wright, *Parteien*, 169; Dahm, *Pfarrer*, 81–87.   63. Schäfer, *Kirchenkampf*, 225.

Kapler, violated this neutrality commandment by participating in the so-called Sahm Committee, where, together with other national-minded liberal and conservative Church leaders, he supported Hindenburg's re-election against Hitler and the DNVP candidate Duesterberg.[64] Other Protestant notables on the *Sahm Ausschuss* included Georg Burghart, Vice-President of the Prussian Church Council, the Nassau bishop August Kortheuer, and the *Generalsuperintendenten* of Berlin and East Prussia, Emil Karow and Paul Gennrich.[65] Since Hindenburg's re-election in the spring of 1932 was supported mainly by political parties close to the Republic, such as the SPD and Center Party, Kapler's support for Hindenburg caused protests among more rightist Church leaders, including the Mecklenburg bishop Heinrich Rendtorff, who was mollified only when Kapler informed him that he had merely exercised his right as a private individual.[66]

To the left of this small moderate conservative–liberal group around Kapler was the grouping of religious socialists, equally small in number, that uncompromisingly opposed National Socialism.[67] The most significant representative of this group, Paul Tillich, had published his "Ten Theses" in 1932, in which he had argued that if Protestantism were to open itself to National Socialism, it would "betray its mission to the world."[68] The attitude of religious socialists toward the NSDAP was also determined by their political ties to the SPD. Already years earlier, there had been an open conflict between National Socialism and a member of

---

64. The Sahm Committee, named after its founder Heinrich Sahm, Lord Mayor of Berlin from 1931 to 1935. It was meant to be above parties and aimed to facilitate Hindenburg's re-election. See Larry E. Jones, *Hitler versus Hindenburg. The 1932 Presidential Elections and the End of the Weimar Republic* (Cambridge: Cambridge University Press, 2016), 154–177.

65. Van Norden, *Kirche*, 34–35; Wright, *Parteien*, 174–175.

66. Wright, *Parteien*, 174. According to Kapler's son, the Protestant minister Albrecht Kapler, his father was closest to Stresemann and the DVP; ibid., 67.

67. See Stefan Vogt, *Nationaler Sozialismus und soziale Demokratie. Die sozialdemokratische Junge Rechte 1918–1945* (Bonn: Dietz, 2006), 67–78; 234–238.

68. Paul Tillich (1886–1965) was Professor of Theology in Marburg, Dresden, and Frankfurt before he emigrated to the United States in 1933. Baum and Grünzinger, eds., *Personenlexikon*, 259. Tillich's "Ten Theses" are reprinted in Leopold Klotz, ed., *Die Kirche und das Dritte Reich. Fragen und Forderungen deutscher Theologen*, vol. I (Gotha: Leopold Klotz, 1932), 126–128; Hermle and Tierfelder, *Herausgefordert*, 57–58.

the religious socialism group in the so-called Dehn case. Günther Dehn, a well-known religious socialist, had condemned the glorification of war and the equation of Christian sacrificial death with death of the Fatherland in a 1928 public lecture. Because of this supposed anti-national attitude, he soon became a target of the political Right. In December 1930, Dehn was awarded a chair in practical theology at Heidelberg University. Yet the Heidelberg faculty, which feared right-wing protests, refused to grant the desired endorsement. This, in turn, prompted Dehn to renounce his claim to the chairship. When Dehn was subsequently offered a chair at Halle University, Nazi students at Halle protested against his appointment. Once Dehn had begun teaching at Halle, students continued to disrupt his lectures to the point that he felt compelled to apply for a year-long sabbatical. In November 1933 he was dismissed from his post by the Nazi regime.[69]

Apart from these groupings, the Protestant Church counted several prominent personalities in its ranks who rejected National Socialism for religious reasons and who were in turn supported by groups of Protestant theologians. Two central personages in this context were Walter Künneth, head of the *Apologetische Zentrale* in the Protestant Johannesstift in Berlin-Spandau, and Hermann Sasse, the editor of the *Kirchliches Jahrbuch*. Künneth published a programmatic statement in April 1931 that amounted to a qualified rejection of National Socialism. While he commented favorably on the will to carry out a "social restructuring" and the principle that "the common good comes before the individual good," Künneth pointed out "the danger of an overvaluation of racial principles" and of "an exaggerated nationalist idealism of an almost metaphysical character."[70] According to Künneth, Christianity and the Church could

69. Christian Jansen, *Professoren und Politik* (Göttingen: Vandenhoeck & Ruprecht, 1992), 232–233; 238–239; 246; Scholder, *Kirchen und Drittes Reich*, 249–250; Gunther Dehn, *Die alte Zeit, die vorigen Jahre. Lebenserinnerungen* (Munich: Kaiser, 1962), 260–278; Anselm Faust, *Der nationalsozialistische Studentenbund*, vol. II (Düsseldorf: Schwann, 1973), 62–73; Fritz, *Dibelius*, 350–354.
70. Walter Künneth (1901–97), head of the *Apologetische Zentrale* of the Internal Mission of the German Protestant Church in Berlin-Spandau from 1932 to 1937. Hermann Sasse

well be misused "for national purposes," and in view of the nature of the political struggle—"the unscrupulous indoctrination, the boundless hatred, the recklessness in the selection of means"—it was clear that "demonic chasms of public life" had opened up.[71] In 1932 Hermann Sasse criticized the Nazi Party program in his *Kirchliches Jahrbuch* by denying the existence of "a positive Christianity that people can support without binding themselves to a specific confession."[72] A dialogue with National Socialism was impossible since the Protestant Church would have to begin with the admission that National Socialist "teachings are an intentional and permanent insult to the moral sense of the Germanic race."[73] Sasse was thus particularly opposed to National Socialism's emphasis on race.

After 30 January 1933: a "Church-friendly National Socialism"

During the weeks after 30 January 1933 the new regime was more accommodating toward the Church than at any other time before 1945. Together with its German National coalition partner, the Hitler government made every effort to publicly support the Church. The first important emergency decree of the new regime, "For the Protection of the German People" of 4 February, designed to curb freedom of assembly and the press and to ban newspapers hostile to the government, also

(1895–1976), editor of the *Kirchliches Jahrbuch für die Evangelischen Landeskirchen Deutschlands* from 1931 to 1934. See Baum and Grünzinger, eds., *Personenlexikon*, 149; 212–213.

71. Walter Künneth, *Was haben wir als evangelische Christen zum Rufe des Nationalsozialismus zu sagen?* (Dresden: Landesverein für innere Mission, 1931), 6–8. Excerpts are reprinted in Hermle and Tierfelder, *Herausgefordert*, 42–47.

72. In their 1920 party program, the NSDAP subscribed to a *positives Christentum*, close to neither the Protestant nor the Catholic Church. See Claus-Ekkehard Bärsch: *Die politische Religion des Nationalsozialismus: Die religiösen Dimensionen der NS-Ideologie in den Schriften von Dietrich Eckart, Joseph Goebbels, Alfred Rosenberg und Adolf Hitler*, 2nd ed. (Munich: Fink, 2002), Steigmann-Gall, *Holy Reich*, 13–50.

73. *Kirchliches Jahrbuch 1932*, 65–67; reprinted in Hermle and Tierfelder, *Herausgefordert*, 62–63.

threatened punishment for disparagement of religious institutions and rituals. Hitler's speech in the Berlin Sportpalast of 10 February ended with a loudly proclaimed "Amen" (intended for maximum effect), as did several other of his speeches during his first months in office. In these Hitler presented the Church as the basis of popular morality and seemed to back the Christian state without reservation. Never before or later did Hitler and his party profess such unconditional support for Christianity as in February and March 1933. Already in his government's first appeal to the public that was read over the radio on 1 February there had been talk of "reverence for our great past," "pride in our old institutions," and the intent of the new government to put Christianity under its protection "as the basis of our entire moral system."[74]

On 16 February Hitler emphasized that "Christians and not inter-national atheists" were at the helm in Germany, and that he himself wished to imbue "our culture again with Christian spirit." In his Königsberg speech of 4 March on the eve of the elections, Hitler intimated that Christian values formed the guiding principles of his actions: "God will help only those who deserve to be aided." High unemployment appeared to him as "an all-powerful scourge of God," and he proclaimed in conclusion that "in past decades the others have not had the blessing of the Almighty who, transcending all human effort, holds the ultimate decision in his hands. We beg: Lord, let us never falter and be cowardly and let us never forget the duty we have taken on."[75] Hitler's fervent speeches, bombastically produced press reports about the solemn State funeral of an SA *Sturmführer* in Berlin's cathedral on 6 February, and reports of church attendance by entire Party formations in Protestant Lower Saxony, all conveyed the idea that the NSDAP would continue to

---

74. Hitler's speeches of February and March 1933, in Domarus, ed., *Hitler*, 190–252, esp. 191–194, 204–207.
75. Georg Kretschmar and Carsten Nicolaisen, eds., *Dokumente zur Kirchenpolitik des Dritten Reiches*, vol. I: *Das Jahr 1933* (Munich: Kaiser, 1971), 1; 8–10; 13–14. This passage of Hitler's Königsberg speech was left out of the reprint in the *Völkischer Beobachter* of 6 March (ibid., 14, n. 1).

stand firmly behind the Protestant Church.[76] This impression was reinforced by statements of prominent Nazis, such as the new Prussian Minister of Culture, Bernhard Rust, who, upon assuming office on 7 February, spoke of a "fierce struggle for existence against Bolshevism" and called on "the Christian churches of both confessions ... to exert their living values of belief and morality together with us in the struggle against this enemy."[77]

The threat posed by communism seemed all too real given the growing strength of the Communist Party: its numbers had increased from 77 deputies (13.1 percent of the vote) to 89 (14.3 percent) and finally 100 (16.9 percent) in the Reichstag elections of September 1930 and July and November 1932. KPD propaganda was openly hostile to the Church, whose members were well aware of the fate of the Orthodox Church in Russia. The Nazi version of the Reichstag fire as the beginning of a communist conspiracy therefore tended to be believed by Protestants and Catholics alike. The theme of rescue from the mortal danger of an imminent communist coup d'état through the vigorous actions of the new government thus also played a role in the outlook of both Christian Churches. In the words of a Württemberg Protestant organization, "The developments of the last months have made it clear to everyone who is willing to see reality as it is that we were facing a yawning abyss."[78] On 1 March 1933 the practicing Catholic Franz von Papen told the alarmed Munich Archbishop Cardinal Michael von Faulhaber about the abominations they had just escaped: communist revolutionaries would not,

76. Ibid., 2–4; 6–8. The funeral in Berlin's cathedral was also attended by Crown Prince Wilhelm (1882–1951) in the uniform of a general.
77. Rust's speech was entitled "Our Declaration of Belief in Christianity," Kretschmar and Nicolaisen, eds., *Dokumente zur Kirchenpolitik*, vol. I, 4–6. Bernhard Rust (1883–1945) was *Gauleiter* of Hanover-North (from 1925) and South Hanover-Braunschweig (from 1928); from 4 February 1933 he was the acting Minister of Science, Art, and National Education (*Volksbildung*) in Prussia.
78. According to the "*Evangelische Volksbund* of Württemberg;" see Scholder, *Kirchen und Drittes Reich*, 879, n. 29.

as in former times storm government buildings, but wear down the people, set fire in a hundred places at the same time, burn down farmsteads, tear up railroad tracks, kidnap the children of civil servants on their way to school and use them as living shields during strike actions, poison food supplies, invade homes, and shoot down doormen and domestic staff.[79]

In the winter of 1933 such a scenario was not completely unthinkable to some. Deliverance from such a fate and genuine gratitude for the energetic measures of the government thus played an important role in the events of March 1933.

Another key factor in the Church's changing attitude toward National Socialism was the almost paradoxical overestimation of the position of the DNVP in the government which, in turn, made the NSDAP seem less dominant and threatening. Faulhaber, for example, mentioned in his conversation with Papen that his "mistrust was directed mostly against Hugenberg, and his possible overpowering might over the [Catholic] Church."[80] Konrad Adenauer, Center Party politician and Lord Mayor of Cologne (until 17 March 1933), considered the German Nationals to be the more experienced and seasoned politicians, who set the tone in the coalition government. The political Left promoted the idea that "Hitler is the figurehead – Hugenberg and Papen the proprietors of the firm," widespread also in Center Party circles.[81] It was part of the political Left's ideology that the conservative capitalist Hugenberg was the dominant figure in the Cabinet. The SPD deputy Kurt Schumacher, who emerged as the leader of the SPD after World War II, for example, argued in a speech on 4 February that Hitler could claim only "the illusion of power:" "He used to be a decorator, today is just a piece of decoration. The Cabinet is headed by Adolf Hitler, but it is (in reality) Alfred

---

79. Ludwig Volk, ed., *Akten Kardinal Michael von Faulhabers 1917–1945*, vol. I: *1917–1934* (Mainz: Grünewald, 1975), 651–652.
80. Volk, ed., *Akten von Faulhabers*, 651–652. Here Faulhaber naturally referred only to the Catholic Church.
81. Rudolf Morsey, "Die Deutsche Zentrumspartei," in Matthias and Morsey, eds., *Ende der Parteien*, 281–453, esp. 346.

Hugenberg's. Adolf Hitler may talk, Alfred Hugenberg will act."[82] And the future Nobel Prize winner Carl von Ossietzky wrote in the *Weltbühne* on 7 February that National Socialists "merely supply the foot soldiers of the government."[83] Given this mood in the ranks of democratic parties, and in the absence of as yet dramatic national transformations, exaggerated concern was quickly interpreted as political fearmongering within the Churches as well. A letter by the Swiss theologian Karl Barth, the founder of dialectical theology and one of the more prominent figures among the academic opponents of Hitler in 1933, was characteristic of this wide-spread insouciance during the first weeks of Hitler's reign. On 10 February Barth wrote that Hitler's chancellorship would not change much in the country at all: "Germany is, from the inside out, far too lethargic a body for movements on its periphery to change much. The people involved are altogether too mediocre. And there is too little in the German people of that élan vital [*Lebensmut*] that is needed to set up a Mussolini-like regime or a counter-revolution."[84] At this point it still seemed unthinkable that precisely this new regime would furnish parts of the German population with the misdirected dynamism that would alter the country for good.

In view of the new government's overwhelmingly friendly attitude toward the Protestant Church, the position of the Church leadership toward the regime until the elections of 5 March 1933 remained one of essential optimism, tempered with a note of concern that the liberties newly acquired during the Republic would again be lost to an over-powering State.[85] Since early February, the leadership of the Church,

---

82. Becker and Becker, eds., *Machtergreifung*, 45. Kurt Schumacher (1895–1952).
83. Becker and Becker, eds., *Machtergreifung*, 53.
84. Quoted in Scholder, *Kirchen und Drittes Reich*, 318; Becker and Becker, eds., *Machtergreifung*, 35. Barth, who had a professorship at the University of Bonn, had to resign his position after 1933 for refusing to swear allegiance to Hitler.
85. A typical expression of this concern was the declaration of the Kassel Ecclesiastical Convention (*Pfarrkonvent*) of early February 1933: "The Church is here for everyone, and her Word should be directed toward all people in all walks of life and all parties. Whoever wants to have the Church represented at military, state, party—or also even at family celebrations—solely in order to increase the festive atmosphere of the celebration misuses the Church." See EZA Berlin, Bestand 1, no. 2867, fol. 36.

notably Theophil Wurm, head of the Württemberg *Landeskirche*, struggled to find a "trend-setting word [*richtungsgebendes Wort*] of the Church" vis-à-vis the new government.[86] Wurm had been preparing various drafts of a manifesto by the Church Executive Committee. On 2 February he noted that "the understanding between Hindenburg, Hitler, and Hugenberg" had created a new situation: "The reconciliation among them provides at least 80 percent of those who consider themselves to be Protestants with clear marching orders."[87] The draft discussed in the meeting of the Executive Committee on 2 March, as well as the entire tone of deliberations concerning the new government, were not without criticism: "The most terrible danger threatening us at the moment is that what we have fought for – a certain freedom of movement toward Reich and State – might be lost! We have to take care that we do not lose this independence again."[88] There were other critical statements toward the regime, such as a petition by Agnes von Zahn-Harnack (daughter of the eminent theologian Adolf von Harnack), who complained that "God's name and well-established phrases that are part of Christian religion and life are being used in election campaigns and election speeches, which are concluded with the word 'Amen.'" She also deplored "the struggle against our Jewish compatriots, which destroys the community of our people and constitutes a continual transgression against the highest commandment of Christianity."[89] Following intensive discussions, an internal recommendation of the *Landeskirchen* was passed. Point 2 of this resolution of the German Protestant Executive Committee emphasized: "The duty of a

86. Schäfer, *Kirchenkampf*, 234–255. Theophil Wurm (1868–1953), from 1929 the *Kirchenpräsident* (Church president) of Württemberg, held the title of *Landesbischof* from 1933 to 1949. In 1919–20, he was a representative for the conservative *Württembergische Bürgerpartei*, the regional branch of the DNVP in the Württemberg state parliament; Baum and Grünzinger, eds., *Personenlexikon*, 280.
87. Schäfer, *Kirchenkampf*, 234.   88. Ibid., 250.
89. For the minutes, see ibid., 250. Agnes von Harnack requested that the Deutscher Evangelischer Kirchenausschuss (DEKA) "very publicly raise its voice against these abuses." See also Gisa Bauer, *Kulturprotestantismus und frühe bürgerliche Frauenbewegung in Deutschland: Agnes von Zahn-Harnack, 1884–1950* (Leipzig: Evangelische Verlagsanstalt, 2006).

pastor toward a political organization may never take precedence over his loyalty to the Church."[90]

At the suggestion of the conservative Bavarian Lutheran Wilhelm von Pechmann, the Church published a manifesto to all its members.[91] Pechmann had presided over several Protestant Church conventions in the 1920s and also made his political position clear in the meeting of 2 March by castigating "the sea of hatred and lies" in the face of which the Church could not remain silent. The manifesto had an obvious relevance for current politics and was clearly critical of National Socialist rule, stating that the Church had "the right and duty to administer spiritual guidance to all its members, regardless of party affiliation: 1. The greater the hatred, the stronger the love (Romans 12:21)! 2. The more lies, the stricter the veracity! Take seriously the 8th commandment!"[92] This resolution was published in the German press on the day before the elections. But even this last exhortation was so generally worded that not only Nazis had reason to believe that it was directed toward them.[93]

The initial reserve of the Church leadership toward the regime should not obscure the fact that there was fundamental agreement with National Socialism about the course of recent German history. In his first draft for the Church Executive Committee meeting, Theophil Wurm wrote that "the World War was caused, not by the German government, but by the decision of the [other] powers to push the German people back to the

---

90. EZA Berlin, Bestand 1, no. 2867, fol. 27.
91. Scholder, *Kirchen und Drittes Reich*, 330. Wilhelm von Pechmann (1859–1948), member of the DEKA from 1929 to 1933. In 1934 he left the DEKA because of the persecution of Jews; Baum and Grünzinger, eds., *Personenlexikon*, 192–193. A public protest rally, as proposed by Pechmann, was rejected, since it would be seen to be directed toward the upcoming Reichstag elections. See also Wolfgang Sommer, *Wilhelm Freiherr von Pechmann. Ein konservativer Lutheraner* (Göttingen: Vandenhoeck & Ruprecht, 2010), 129–180.
92. EZA Berlin, Bestand 1, no. 2867, fol. 28. The Eighth Commandment in the Bible mandates: "Thou shalt not bear false witness against thy neighbor."
93. In addition to the German Christians and the Württemberg NS-Pastors' League, it was in particular the *Evangelischer Bund zur Wahrung der Deutsch-Protestantischen Interessen* (Protestant League for the Protection of German-Protestant Interests) that unconditionally supported the NSDAP before the 5 March 1933 elections. The latter had backed the creation of a Protestant Reich Church ever since its foundation in 1886, to overcome the fragmentation of the *Landeskirchen*. Scholder, *Kirchen und Drittes Reich*, 48–49.

times when their State was powerless and the economy backward, in which purpose they unfortunately largely succeeded." Signs of current decadence, such as "the decline of the economy," "unemployment," and the "desolate situation of large parts of the population," were also blamed on Germany's wartime enemies. Inevitably, mention is also made of "the struggle against the war guilt lie and the reparations connected with it."[94] There was thus broad consensus with the National Socialist regime that a conspiracy of the former Entente powers was responsible for Germany's current plight. In the second draft of his manifesto, Wurm cites "the struggle for the liberation from the oppressive shackles of Versailles" as "one of the main reasons for the current predicament" and emphasizes the need for a "cleansing...of literature and art, of the corroding and poisonous influences of cultural Bolshevism, and the purging of the public service administration of corruption of any kind."[95] Within a matter of years Wurm would become a thorn in the side of National Socialist potentates; during the war he bravely protested against euthanasia and the deportation of Jews. Yet the above-quoted lines might well be taken from a Nazi newspaper. In March 1933, commonalities still prevailed.

Another example of how similar ideas about recent political history did not necessarily forestall criticism is illustrated by a confidential memo written by Otto Dibelius to the pastors in the Mark Brandenburg on 8 March. Dibelius began by expressing his satisfaction that the elections of 5 March "have, for the first time since the [1918] Revolution, led to an intensely national-minded parliamentary majority" that formed a welcome contrast to the Weimar National Assembly: "There are few among us who do not wholeheartedly embrace this turn of events."[96] Yet even in this new situation it was important to preserve the "responsibility of the

94. Schäfer, Kirchenkampf, vol. I, 237; see also Rainer Hering, "From Collegiality to the Führerprinzip: The 1933 Introduction of the Episcopacy in the Hamburg Landeskirche," in Beck and Jones, eds., Weimar to Hitler, 281–309.
95. Schäfer, Kirchenkampf, vol. I, 239.
96. Becker and Becker, eds., Machtergreifung, 129–133, esp. 130; Scholder, Kirchen und Drittes Reich, 333–335.

Church for the entirety of our people," be they "National Socialists or Social Democrats, members of the [nationalist] *Stahlhelm* or the [Republican] *Reichsbanner*." And, he continued, "Even if politics digs ditches, statesmen speak of destruction, extermination and knockdowns, even if hate speech draws unending applause in mass rallies, we subscribe to a different spirit!"[97] According to Dibelius, it was essential that "the Church remain the conscience of the State," and it must never happen that "pastors march through their congregation with Party badges and greet its members with the Party salute." Then Dibelius expressed a truism that was rarely stated in such clarity in March 1933: "...unless we resist in these points, we will find ourselves again in the position of a State Church, but this time in a much more oppressive way than was the case under a *sumus episcopus*." This clear and unambiguous warning shows that Dibelius was aware from early on of the danger posed by National Socialism.[98] Shortly afterwards, the National Socialist press agency pronounced Dibelius's memo to be "high treason against the Church," and *Gauleiter* Wilhelm Kube's paper, the *Märkischer Adler*, which reprinted Dibelius's memo, characterized it as an "unprecedented diatribe against National Socialism."[99] Throughout these and subsequent Nazi attacks in March and April 1933, his pastors and subordinate Protestant *Superintendenten* in the Kurmark uniformly rejected all attacks and staunchly supported Dibelius, emphasizing "his burning love for our people in dire times" and their belief that "only a strong and independent Church...can successfully support the national cause."[100]

Except for declarations by the *Landeskirchen* of Nassau and Bavaria on 9 and 15 March 1933, in which they stressed the independence of the

---

97. Becker and Becker, eds., *Machtergreifung*, 130, 131.
98. In his conclusion, Dibelius exposed the unwelcome truth that the bells heard during Hitler's Königsberg speech that was broadcast on the radio and concluded the election campaign "were not those of the Königsberg Cathedral chiming in the background, as Herr Dr. Goebbels claimed....In the radio broadcast a record was played with the peeling of bells, and listeners were persuaded that this was the Königsberg cathedral." Ibid, 133.
99. Scholder, *Kirchen und Drittes Reich*, 336–337, 414; on Dibelius see also Marikje Smid, *Deutscher Protestantismus und Judentum 1932/33* (Munich: Kaiser, 1990), 346–353.
100. EZA Berlin, Bestand 7, no. 989, fols. 186–187.

Church, Dibelius's memo would remain the last critical statement from an official Church leader for some time.[101] In the weeks after the elections, when the triumphal march of National Socialists' success seemed unstoppable, a change in the political and mental climate took place throughout the Reich that carried away the Protestant Church as well. Between 5 and 10 March, the NSDAP rapidly took over those German states in which it had not yet formed governments, such as Hamburg, Bremen, Lübeck, Schaumberg-Lippe, Hesse-Darmstadt, Saxony, Baden, Württemberg, and Bavaria. Except for Bavaria, the takeovers were carried out without encountering much resistance. The fact that political opponents such as the SPD, the Center, and the 400,000-strong Republican paramilitary organization *Reichsbanner* retreated without putting up a fight left the populations in the usurped states with the impression that further resistance was futile.[102] This iniquitous surrender was followed by the unexpectedly rapid willingness of trade unions, especially the *Allgemeiner Deutscher Gewerkschaftsbund* (ADGB) under Theodor Leipart, which was close to the SPD, to co-operate with the new masters.[103] Dispirited, demoralized, and worn down by countless Nazi acts of violence after the Reichstag fire at the end of February, to which its members had been exposed without physical protection or recourse to the law, the most powerful of trade union organizations distanced itself from the SPD on 20 March, even before the passing of the Enabling Act, and declared its readiness to work with the new government.[104] In the second half of

---

101. Martin Hoffman, Hans Friedrich Lenz, Paul Gerhard Schäfer, and Johannes Stoll, eds., *Dokumentation zum Kirchenkampf in Hessen und Nassau*, vol. I. *Jahrbuch der Hessischen kirchengeschichtlichen Vereinigung*, no. 25 (Darmstadt: Verlag der Hessischen kirchengeschichtlichen Vereinigung, 1974), 203; Helmut Baier, *Die Deutschen Christen Bayerns im Rahmen des bayerischen Kirchenkampfes* (Nuremberg: Selbstverlag des Vereins für bayerische Kirchengeschichte, 1968), 42.

102. The National Socialist takeover in the German states was made easier given that Hamburg, Hesse, Saxony, Württemberg, and Bavaria had only *geschäftsführende* (caretaker) minority governments. See Broszat, *Staat Hitlers*, 130–140; Bracher, Sauer, and Schulz, *NS Machtergreifung*, 136–144; Thamer, *Verführung*, 260–263.

103. William L. Patch, Jr., "Nationalism, Socialism and Organized Labor's Response to the Dissolution of the Weimar Republic," in Beck and Jones, eds., *Weimar to Hitler*, 248–280.

104. The ADGB had 7.8 million members in 1922; by 1932 their number had declined to 4.1 million. Klaus Schönhoven, *Die deutschen Gewerkschaften* (Frankfurt: Suhrkamp, 1987),

March, members of the *Reichsbanner* flocked into the *Stahlhelm* and the *Kampfstaffeln* (fighting squads) of the DNVP, where they sought sanctuary from SA persecution. Throughout March, many tens of thousands of formerly long-standing and loyal members of the SPD relinquished their party membership out of fear for their careers and families, or simply to ensure personal safety.[105] In March 1933 the dominant individual reason for jumping on the Nazi bandwagon was a mixture of enthusiasm and fear, whereby most people hardly knew which motivation was decisive. Since few liked to admit voluntarily that they were afraid, it was easier to feign enthusiasm about domestic unification and the renewed vigor that the regime promised and radiated. Legislation, such as the *Heimtücke-Verordnung*, and the new oppressive psychological climate quickly convinced many that it was better to join and follow than to stand aloof.[106] Apart from naked fear, it was mostly opportunism that accounted for the defeatism and for the large number of converts and defectors into the Nazi camp. Terror against the KPD, SPD, trade unions, and *Reichsbanner* set in immediately after the Reichstag fire. It was systematic and all-encompassing. By the summer of 1933 about 27,000 political opponents were held captive in concentration camps, and about 100,000 in the "wild" camps and torture cellars of the SA; more than 600 people had been murdered.[107] Since the existence of camps, such as Dachau, was well known and violent crackdowns often took

179–183; Winkler, *Weg in die Katastrophe*, 893–898; Broszat, *Staat Hitlers*, 113–114; Dirk Erb, ed., *Gleichgeschaltet. Der Nazi-Terror gegen Gewerkschaften und Berufsverbände 1930–1933* (Göttingen: Steidl, 2001).

105. NHStA Hannover, Hann 310 II A, no. 41. Party membership resignations were occasionally accompanied by explanations. In addition to fear for life and limb, the conduct of party leaders is mentioned as a reason. Some withdrawals were explained by a newfound belief: "A deciding factor for me was the idea that service to the people is more important than supporting a political party" (O. [abbreviated name], 21 March). See also Matthias, "Sozialdemokartische Partei," 101–278, esp. 238–242.

106. On the peculiar mixture of motivations, see Haffner, *Geschichte*, 122–133; on the *Heimtücke-Verordnung*, see Chapter 7 above.

107. Winkler, *Weg in die Katastrophe*, 898; Michael Schneider, *Unterm Hagenkreuz*, 455; Broszat, "Nationalsozialistische Konzentrationslager," 323–449, esp. 336; Beck, "Konflikte," 645–681. For examples of terror, see Diels, *Luzifer*, and Erb, *Gleichgeschaltet*.

place in public, people quickly learned to guard their tongues, even though the bulk of the middle and upper classes endorsed the settling of scores with the "Marxist parties."

A central event and first catalyst responsible for the increasing approval of the new regime among Protestants was the "Day of Potsdam" on 21 March 1933, with its marches, processions, and church services. The well-orchestrated pageant in Potsdam made many critics, especially in the ranks of the national-minded bourgeoisie, fall silent. The non-Nazi sections of the nationalist middle and upper classes wholeheartedly welcomed the apparent fusion of the radical Nazi movement with conservative Prussian traditions. At Potsdam, National Socialists gave the impression of being domesticated, apparently justifying the old elites' calculation that the attempt to tame Hitler had come off successfully after all. As Hitler put it in his speech in the Potsdam Garrison Church: "In an unprecedented ascent [the German people] has, within weeks, restored its national honor...and carried out the union between the symbols of the old grandeur and the young vigor."[108] The latter was an obvious reference to the Nazi movement. The leadership of the Protestant Church was especially impressed: time and again internal memoranda stressed that the Day of Potsdam had been the crucial event in convincing them that National Socialism would, on the whole, have a beneficial effect on Germany's future.

The larger change in attitude that took place in March was also reflected in Dibelius's sermon in the Nikolaikirche on 21 March. It was based on the same verse in the Bible as the sermon by Ernst von Dryander at the onset of World War I on 4 August 1914. Dibelius reminded his audience of the commonalities with the earlier occasion:

It was a day on which the German people experienced the most sublime event a nation can undergo – a surge of patriotic feeling that swept all and everyone away; a blazing up of a new belief in millions of hearts, a fervent

---

108. Klöss, Erhard, ed., *Reden des Führers. Politik und Propaganda Adolf Hitlers 1922–1945* (Munich: DTV, 1967), 91.

readiness to sacrifice one's own life, so that Germany [can] live: One Reich, one people, one God! On such a day of fervent collective upsurge this phrase forced itself on to us, this phrase filled with defiant belief and confidence in victory: "If God is for us, who may be against us?" What we experience today is similar to what people felt then.

Though Dibelius's speech was not free of critical undertones—he warned, for example, not to confuse "the official authority of office" with "wanton personal despotism"—national pathos prevailed: "through North and South, East and West, there is a new desire [to create] a German State, a longing, to say it with Treitschke, no longer 'to do without the most noble sentiment in the life of a man, namely to admiringly look up to one's own State.'"[109] Dibelius also meant to utilize the pregnant symbolism of the location. Already on 5 March he had written, "The Paulskirche in 1848; the theatre in Weimar in 1919; the Garrison Church in Potsdam in 1933 – such symbols leave a deeper imprint on the memory of a people than all speeches. They usher in a new chapter of history under an unmistakable sign."[110]

Two days later, in his policy statement about the Enabling Act, Hitler revealed that he was determined to carry through "the political and moral decontamination of our public life" and to create the preconditions for a "truly deep inner religiosity." It was with approval and relief that leading Church circles noted statements such as this, as well as Hitler's promises to honor existing treaties and not to touch the rights of the Church with respect to its position on the State, and his assurance that the Christian confessions would continue to be "the most important factors in the safeguarding of our people."[111] Five days after the Enabling Act, on 28 March, the Catholic Church underwent a complete reversal in its attitude toward National Socialism. Cardinal Bertram, Archbishop of Breslau and *primus inter pares* of the five German archbishops, proclaimed

---

109. *Das Evangelische Deutschland. Kirchliche Rundschau für das Gesamtgebiet des Deutschen Evangelischen Kirchenbundes*, 26 March 1933, 101–102.
110. Stupperich, *Dibelius*, 203.
111. Kretschmar and Nicolaisen, eds., *Dokumente zur Kirchenpolitik*, 23–24.

that from now on he no longer regarded the earlier prohibitions and warnings directed against National Socialism as necessary. Given the prevailing rivalry between the Protestant and Catholic Churches in Germany, the Catholic Church hierarchy naturally did not want the Protestant Church to be the beneficiary of the consequences of its own critical position toward the new regime and thus felt under pressure to revise its previous stance within a matter of days.[112] And this, despite all of the SA violence targeting Jews, the storming of law courts, and the "racial cleansing" in Prussia and Bavaria. The sea change in German Catholicism was attentively observed by Protestants and contributed to further positive feelings toward the new government on the part of the Protestant Church. It was in the midst of this ongoing revolutionary change in the nation's mental climate that the first news of assaults and random attacks on Jews began to dispel illusions. Later in March, when the reports had swelled into an avalanche, foreign Churches started making inquiries, demanding that German Church leaders speak out against the unprovoked attacks against Jews. Would the German Protestant Church be able to live up to its self-proclaimed image and identity by fulfilling its role as guardian of the conscience of the nation?

112. Hubert Gruber, *Katholische Kirche und Nationalsozialismus 1930–1945* (Paderborn: Schöningh, 2006), 40–41. This change in thinking in German Catholicism was accelerated by Hitler's public declaration of 21 March 1933, in which he explained via Wolff's Telegraph Bureau, that he did not attend Catholic mass in Potsdam because the Catholic clergy characterized "leaders and members of the NSDAP as apostates of the Church, who may not have the privilege of receiving the sacraments. Until today, these declarations have not been revoked and the Catholic clergy continues to act in accordance with them." Kretschmar and Nicolaisen, eds., *Dokumente zur Kirchenpolitik*, 22–23.

10

PROTESTANT CHURCH LEADERS AND THE "JEWISH QUESTION"

Conscience Betrayed

Foreign Reactions

In the second half of March, the Protestant Church was indeed galvanized into action, but not on behalf of the victims. In the face of increasing reports of attacks against German and foreign Jews, Church officials made concerted efforts to defend the Church's position and reputation, often justifying their own inaction by downplaying the significance and potential consequences of the racial policies and anti-Jewish attacks of the new regime. Once antisemitic violence had burst forth on a national scale in early March, the Western democratic press took up the issue and published detailed reports about events in Berlin and other German cities. Numerous diplomatic communications also focused on the problem, especially in the days before the 1 April 1933 boycott.[1]

There were also widespread protests in British and American Church circles. The Bishop of Liverpool spoke of a "flagrant breach of moral law in Germany," there were protests in the House of Lords and letters by

---

1. *Foreign Relations of the United States 1933. Diplomatic Papers*, vol. II, 320–365; *Documents on British Foreign Policy 1919–1939*, 2nd series, vol. IV, 395–481, vol. 5, 1–55. A synopsis of British press reports can be found in BayHStaA, V. Hauptabteilung. Sammlung Varia 231, "The Persecution of Jews in Germany." For an analysis of diplomatic reports, see Ascher, *Hitler*.

Before the Holocaust: Antisemitic Violence and the Reaction of German Elites and Institutions during the Nazi Takeover. Hermann Beck, Oxford University Press. © Hermann Beck 2022. DOI: 10.1093/oso/9780192865076.003.0011

prominent personalities to *The Times* of London, and in the House of Commons Austen Chamberlain declared that "the anti-Semitic statements of men in authority in Germany... reveal a spirit which we had hoped had departed from this world." Other British deputies sent letters of complaint to President Hindenburg. During a protest meeting in Liverpool on 5 April one complainant, Eleanor Rathbone, uttered prescient (though unheeded) words: "We must recognize... that even if this persecution does cease... we have learned to see in the present temper of the German people a great menace to the world. It is possible that the sufferings of the Jews now may save the world from future suffering by putting us on our guard."[2] The unanimous condemnation of political developments in Germany, from the establishment of the dictatorship to the pogrom-like antisemitic attacks, diminished Germany's reputation worldwide within a matter of weeks and also had serious repercussions for German exports.

In the United States, the American League for the Defense of Jewish Rights, led by Samuel Untermyer of New York, organized embargoes of German goods. Untermyer put together extensive registers of all articles imported from Germany to identify them more easily and to achieve maximum effect. The inventory of imported goods stretched from "home furnishings" and "drugs and chemicals" to "optical goods."[3] Untermyer correctly assumed that boycotts of pharmaceutical products would hit Germany especially hard; his organization thus published detailed listings of German drugs and their American equivalents, so that consumers could switch to other products: "German drugs, chemicals, instruments, laboratory supplies and equipment, optical goods, cameras – in short, everything produced in Germany is produced in a spirit of intolerance, hatred, and terror."[4] In addition, a list of European spas outside Germany was published under the admonition, "Do not

2. BayHStaA, "The Persecution of Jews in Germany," fols. 35, 40, 42.
3. BA Berlin, R72, no. 1477, including Untermyer's lists of goods, fols. 115–139, esp. 137–139.
4. BA Berlin, R43 II, no. 602, fols. 55–63, esp. 58.

patronize German spas," so that American visitors who wanted to visit a health resort could avoid Germany altogether.[5]

This boycott of German goods and health resorts had its most far-reaching and long-lasting effects in England and the United States. German press reports used occasional exaggerations in accounts of attacks to make the claim that all reports were based on *Greuelmärchen* (invented atrocity tales). On 23 March, for example, a German diplomat reported from Chicago on false rumors circulated there that 1,400 Jews had been murdered in Hamburg.[6] On Friday, 24 March, London's *Daily Mail* carried an emblazoned headline on its front page: "Fourteen hundred Jews slain. Fourteen hundred Jews have been tortured and murdered in the city of Hamburg alone during the Hitler terrorism now sweeping Germany."[7] Even though overall concern about antisemitic attacks was correct, the—at this point in time—grotesquely exaggerated figures played into the hands of the German press and provided a believable pretext for the German media to reject foreign press reports about anti-Jewish transgressions altogether.

A long letter of 4 May 1933 from the Hamburg Chamber of Commerce to the city government—the Hamburg Senate—made it clear that boycotts of German goods were by no means limited to Western Europe and the United States. The embargo was global. Based on reports of Hamburg firms, whose connections stretched to all five continents, the centers of boycott actions lay in French and Spanish Morocco, South Africa, Egypt (though Muslims there reportedly did not participate), and Syria-Palestine. From Rumania, Spain, and Czechoslovakia numerous communications about protests against "German atrocities" had also been received, while in Warsaw posters advertised the recruiting of volunteers

---

5. Ibid., fol. 62. According to a note from the German Consul General to Undersecretary of State (*Staatssekretär*) Lammers of 11 May 1933, the register of German pharmaceuticals was sent to "all physicians in the United States." They were urged to replace German drugs and medications with non-German equivalents. (Ibid., fol. 54.)

6. StA Hamburg, Bestand 132–1, no. 828, "Boykottbewegung im Ausland als Gegenbewegung zu antisemitischen Bewegungen in Deutschland."

7. StA Hamburg, Bestand 131–4, A 35/34, "Boykottmaßnahmen gegen Juden wegen der Veröffentlichung in ausländische Zeitungen 1933."

to defend Polish soil from threats, fanning the flames of anti-German hostility. In France and Belgium, goods from Germany were turned back, while in Holland "a more sensible judgement of conditions ... seemed to prevail;" and in Scandinavia, "the unfriendly mood toward Germany ... was about to disappear." In England "instructional leaflets had not yet found the necessary appreciation" and boycotts continued, whereas in Latin America, "the smear campaign" against Germany had remained without significant influence.[8] This boycott movement had a marked effect on German exports.[9] In conjunction with the detailed reporting on conditions in Nazi Germany, it is a clear indication that, already during the first months of Nazi rule, large parts of the world knew quite well what to expect from Hitler's Germany.

Church Reactions to Foreign Protests

This general and almost worldwide censure of German behavior reminded many Germans of their country's international isolation during the First World War and almost instantly created a unified defensive front. The categorical rejection of foreign reports as "a tissue of lies and atrocity propaganda" was not confined to supporters of the government.[10] Many now equated foreign reporting about events in

---

8. 4 May 1933 at StA Hamburg, Bestand 132–1, no. 828. The Chamber of Commerce also requested that the Foreign Office disseminate information to alleviate the situation and "come out against false rumors" in the press.

9. Between the last quarter of 1933 and the second quarter of 1934, German exports decreased by 1.26 billion Reichsmarks. German exports in 1929 had amounted to 13,486 billion Reichsmarks; in 1934 they amounted to merely 4,178 billion Reichsmarks. The main reason for the overall decrease in exports was the worldwide depression, though the boycott movement against German goods was chiefly responsible for the decline from 1932. In 1925, the percentage of German exports to the USA was 7.4% of all exports; by 1938 it had fallen to 2.8%. Dietmar Petzina, Werner Abelshauser, and Anselm Faust, *Sozialgeschichtliches Arbeitsbuch. 1914–1945* (Munich: Beck, 1978), 74–75; Richard Evans, *The Third Reich in Power* (New York: Penguin, 2005), 354–355.

10. This expression (*Lügenmärchen und Greuelpropaganda*) was used by Church leaders at their 25–26 April 1933 meeting when the "Jewish Question" was discussed. EZA, Berlin, Bestand 1, no. 2411, "Niederschrift der Verhandlungen...," fols. 1–17.

Germany with Allied war propaganda about German war crimes in Belgium and northern France at the beginning of World War I. In Belgium, the German army had actually carried out mass executions of civilians who had allegedly been mistaken for *Franktireurs*, that is, snipers without proper military affiliation who ambushed military personnel.[11] In August 1914 alone, about 4,200 civilians were shot on the basis of often not very convincing charges; cultural monuments and memorials of national identity, such as the library at Leuven, were reduced to rubble.[12] Since it quickly became clear to French and especially British propagandists that German atrocities could be effectively instrumentalized to motivate their own troops, Allied war propaganda soon indulged in flagrant exaggeration. Germans were said to have indiscriminately murdered women, children, even priests, and the "lurid theme of hacked-off children's hands" soon became a staple of Allied propaganda.[13] There were reports of everything from mass rape to cannibalism. The unimaginably gruesome consequences for the people and societies in France and England—in case Allied armies were to succumb to this inhuman foe—were conjured up in stark and wrenching images.

After the war, British politicians, including David Lloyd George, conceded exaggerations in the reporting, and in 1928 the former diplomat and Labour deputy Arthur Ponsonby published his *Falsehood in Wartime*, which dealt with "the exaggeration and invention of atrocities...[as] the main staple of propaganda." Ponsonby's book was swiftly translated into

---

11. Horne and Kramer, *German Atrocities*. During the Franco-Prussian War of 1870–1, *Franktireurs*, from the French *"Francs-tireurs"* (*Freischützen* or sharp-shooters), were Free Corps under self-elected leaders; they tried to disrupt German army supply lines and posed a danger to reconnoitering cavalry and small, unprotected units. See *Meyers Großes Konversations-Lexikon*, 6th ed., vol. 6, 824.

12. Klaus-Jürgen Bremm, *Propaganda im 1. Weltkrieg* (Darmstadt: Theiss, 2013), 39–44. German military authorities placed the responsibility for the destruction in Leuven on the city's residents, who allegedly had taken potshots at German troops from their houses.

13. Deutsches Historisches Museum Berlin, *Die Letzten Tage der Menschheit. Bilder des ersten Weltkrieges* (Berlin: DHM, 1994), 177–197. Bremm, *Propaganda*, 41–42. According to the *Daily Express*, on 31 August 1914 German soldiers near Tournai had ripped a child from the arms of his mother and cut off both his hands. See Michael Schramm, *Das Deutschlandbild in der britischen Presse 1912–1919* (Munich: De Gruyter, 2007), 381.

German and went through several editions.[14] Quickly made popular by the press, it helped foment the conviction among the national-minded public that all reports of German war atrocities were fictional, based on tales spun by the enemy. In the late 1920s and during the 1930s, skepticism about the veracity of Allied propaganda became common not only in Germany but also in England and the United States, where it was part of a generally negative reaction to U.S. participation in World War I, which would soon find its reflection in the American policy of neutrality of the late 1930s.[15]

In Germany the admission of certain exaggerations of Allied war propaganda was interpreted as the confirmation of what parts of the nationalistic public had always wanted to believe: namely, that all tales of German war atrocities were filthy lies. March 1933 thus saw a spontaneous gut-level reaction against foreign newspaper reports dealing with Germany. Many who should have known better rejected all of them without differentiating truth from lies. Protestant Church leaders who, after the Versailles Treaty blamed the West for Germany's plight, were now on the front line when it came to repelling "atrocity propaganda." The Protestant Church fought against the purported exaggerations with all its moral authority, just as it had earlier combatted the "ignominious dictate of Versailles" and the "war guilt lie." In reaction to protests by

14. Arthur Ponsonby, *Falsehood in Wartime: Containing an Assortment of Lies Circulated throughout the Nations during the Great War* (London: E. P. Dutton, 1928). Ponsonby emphasized cases of deliberate fabrication, such as the "corpse factory," a 1917 report that "the Germans were rendering the bodies of their dead soldiers for use in various kinds of war production." See Horne and Kramer, *German Atrocities*, 368–370; Michael Sanders and Philip Taylor, *British Propaganda during the First World War, 1914–1918* (London: Palgrave Macmillan, 1982), 146–148.
15. Harold Laswell, *Propaganda Technique in the World War* (Cambridge, MA.: Harvard University Press, 1927), esp. ch. 4; James Morgan Read, *Atrocity Propaganda 1914–1919* (New Haven: Yale University Press, 1941); Klaus Schwabe, *Weltmacht und Weltordnung. Amerikanische Außenpolitik von 1898 bis zur Gegenwart* (Paderborn: Schöningh, 2006), 95–104. At the beginning of the 1930s, the often brutal German occupation policies and the 1914 shooting of civilians appear to have been forgotten: "Some people, having become so thoroughly convinced of the non-existence of Belgian babies without hands, have forgotten that the treatment of Belgians was, in the words of General Moltke himself, 'certainly brutal'" (Read, *Atrocity Propaganda*, 82–83).

American Churches, German Protestant Church leaders responded during the second half of March with their own indignant denunciations.

The frantic activities were triggered by the Baden *Kirchenpräsident*, Klaus Wurth, who sent a telegram to the *Kirchenausschuss* on 24 March in which he demanded "immediate action of the German *Kirchenausschuss* [including that] Churches outside Germany be informed about the actual state of things."[16] The next day this telegram was published in the main Nazi press organ, *Völkischer Beobachter*. Now under considerable pressure, Hermann Kapler, president of the DEKA, sent the following telegram to the American Church leader Dr. Samuel Cadman:

> Press here reports about participation of American Church circles in protests against alleged persecution of Jews in Germany. Urgently request that you bring to bear your influence lest demonstrations against Germany be staged that are based on false reports and will seriously damage cooperation between our Churches. Reich government ensures order and security. Impartial examination of conditions here is always possible and welcome.[17]

On 30 March, Kapler sent copies of his telegram to other foreign Church leaders, including the Bishop of Chichester and the General Secretary of the World Alliance for International Friendship Through the Churches, Henri-Louis Henriod, in Geneva. *Oberdomprediger* (Canon) Georg Burghart, a member of the *Kirchenausschuss* and president of the German branch of the World Alliance, cabled the American Lutheran Council: "Warn urgently not to believe exaggerated and invented reports about terror in Germany."[18]

---

16. 24 March 1933 at EZA Berlin, Bestand 5, no. 802. Hermann Kapler immediately protested against the pressure that was being put on him through the press; 30 March 1933 at EZA Berlin, Bestand 5, no. 802; Hermann Rückleben and Hermann Erbacher, eds., *Die evangelische Landeskirche in Baden im "Dritten Reich." Quellen zu ihrer Geschichte*, vol. 1 (Karlsruhe: Evangelischer Presseverband, 1991), 549–550.

17. 30 March 1933 at EZA Berlin Bestand , no. 802. Samuel Parkes Cadman (1864–1936).

18. 27 March 1933 at EZA Berlin Bestand 5, no. 802; Georg Burghart (1865–1954), Baum and Grünzinger, eds., *Personenlexikon*, 49.

These telegrams by Protestant Church leaders quickly found their way into the German press, where conservative dailies, such as *Der Tag* and the *Kreuzzeitung*, published detailed reports.[19] The German section of the *Protestantisher Weltverband* cabled to several international church organizations, including the American Federal Council of Churches: "We declare upon our honor and conscience that no pogroms against Jews have taken place. We ask insistently that the misleading of public opinion through erroneous propaganda concerning horrific acts be prevented and that Christian justice and veracity be respected."[20] Erich Stange, the Reich Leader of the Protestant German Youth, alluded to the recent past in his declaration before the managing board of the Young Men's Christian World Alliance in Geneva:

> Once again a wave of dirty calumnies about Germany goes through the press of large parts of the world. Based on free invention and scooped up from murky sources, they poison in outrageous fashion the mutual trust among peoples. Here a State and a government, to which the Protestant Church and the Protestant youth of Germany have gratefully and joyfully expressed their loyalty in public declarations, are being slandered. Yet, in spite of this, even Christian groups abroad are misled to the point that they protest against atrocities that have nowhere taken place in Germany."[21]

German Protestant Church leaders veritably outdid each other in making patriotic declarations and in repudiating the "propaganda of lies." In the second half of March 1933 their voices thus chimed in with the (at this point in time) largely censored German press. Direct comparisons between "supposed" German atrocities in Belgium and present "slanders," whose main objective, it was said, was to find a pretext for boycotting

---

19. The corresponding articles can be found at EZA, Berlin Bestand 7, no. 3688, fols. 16–18.
20. 29 March 1933 at EZA Berlin, Bestand 5, no. 802. The awkwardly worded English text as sent to Beaven (possibly Kapler's own translation); 25 March 1933, ibid.
21. EZA Berlin, Bestand 7, no. 3688, fol. 21 (from *Der Reichsbote* of 29 March 1933). Erich Stange (1888–1972) became a member of the NSDAP in 1933 but soon got into trouble with the new regime and was expelled from the Party in 1934; Baum and Grünzinger, eds. *Personenlexikon*, 244–245.

German goods, were a recurring theme.[22] Headlines such as "Hands Off Germany" (24 March, *Der Tag*), "Atrocity Campaign Hostile to Germany" (23 March, *Kölnische Zeitung*), "Hitler against the Jewish Atrocity Campaign" (25 March, *Der Tag*), "Foreign Smear Campaign by Jews along Well-Trodden Lines," (25 March, *Völkischer Beobachter*), and "Pogroms Never Happened" (25 March, *Der Reichsbote*) set the tone and shaped the public discourse.[23] For many Germans, press reports conveyed the message that they were in a fortress under siege and that national unity was now more important than ever.

The Church and the Boycott of 1 April 1933

On the day of the boycott, Saturday, 1 April 1933, Hermann Kapler explained in a letter to Church authorities how, "in the midst of political events following hot upon the heels of each other," he safeguarded "general Protestant interests" via-à-vis the new Reich government.[24] Kapler recapitulated what he had done to counter "foreign atrocity propaganda," emphasizing, in particular, his own telegram,[25] but he failed to mention a letter of 24 March by Albert W. Beaven, President of the Federal Council of Churches of Christ in America, in which Beaven expressed his "concern over the reports which come to us of Nazi anti-

22. For examples from the German press, see BA Koblenz, Zeitgeschichtliche Sammlung (ZSg) 103, no. 3101, "Boykott gegen jüdische Geschäfte." Comparisons between "invented atrocity tales" (*Lügenmärchen*) about German violence in Belgium during World War I and the current "defamation campaign" (the main goal of which was said to boycott German goods) are here a periodic theme.
23. The newspaper articles can be found at EZA Berlin, Bestand 5, no. 802 and Bestand 7, no. 3688.
24. 1 April 1933 at EZA Berlin Bestand 7, no. 3688, fols. 23–24v., and 1/2867, fols. 121–122v.
25. EZA Berlin Bestand 7, no. 3688, fols. 23v.–24. Kapler quoted the telegram from the American Federal Council of Churches: "The alarm of American Christians because of the reported German persecution of Jews does not mean in any way the abandonment of our esteem for the German people or reduced affection for our Christian brothers. We acknowledge the signs of new unity and the revival of hope in Germany and sympathize warmly with the German claim of equality in international relations." Undersigned by Cadman, Cavert, and Leiper. EZA Berlin, Bestand 7, no. 3688, fol. 23 v., and Bestand 1, no. 2867, fol. 120.

Semitism in Germany."[26] In it Beaven requested answers to two questions: "1) What positions are the German Christians taking regarding Hitler's anti-Semitic policies? 2) Do you think it would be possible or wise if the German Protestant Church Association and the American Federal Council of Churches jointly issued a manifesto denouncing anti-Semitism as un-Christian?"[27] Kapler took his time in getting back to Beaven. It was only in early June 1933 that the Protestant Church leadership prepared a nine-page manifesto for foreign consumption and transmitted it to all foreign Churches, albeit in general terms and without addressing Beaven's specific questions.[28] Germany's secular leaders, in the meantime, were grateful for the Protestant Church's support and quick to show their appreciation. On 8 April Hitler's chief of staff in the Reich Chancellery, Heinrich Lammers, passed on "the special thanks of the Reich Chancellor" that Kapler "energetically protested against the Jewish smear campaign and explained the true facts of the matter." The Reich Chancellor, Lammers continued, "is also very grateful for other measures taken by the Protestant Church to combat the atrocity campaign."[29]

It is difficult to believe that the entreaties by Kapler and other Church leaders to discount foreign "atrocity propaganda" were entirely sincere, since German Church leaders knew from appeals, pleas, and petitions addressed to them personally that foreign protests against the mistreatment of Jews were justified. Already well before the boycott of 1 April Kapler had received a number of complaints, some via telegram, demanding that the Church speak up on behalf of the victims. The most vehement demands came from the conservative Church leader Wilhelm von Pechmann, who had opposed National Socialist attempts to create a centralized National Church from early on. Pechmann would maintain his opposition to National Socialism throughout the Third

---

26. 24 March 1933 at EZA Berlin Bestand 7, no. 3688, fol. 116.
27. Ibid., fol 116.
28. Ibid., fol. 117; see the section "The Memorandum on the Judenfrage" in Chapter 11 below.
29. 8 April 1933 at EZA Berlin, Bestand 5, no. 802.

Reich.[30] Two days before the boycott, Pechmann urged that the Protestant Church, in conjunction with the Catholics, "speak a decisive word against the boycott of Jews in Germany now set in motion."[31] An "unequivocal step of the Protestant Church" would be "welcomed by many quarters with great joy as a decisive sign of the independence of the Church."[32] On 30 March Pechmann followed this up with a telegram to the Federal Church Office (*Kirchenbundesamt*) in Berlin, arguing that he "would consider it calamitous if our Church would decide to remain silent at such a time."[33] He was not alone in his protest. The Württemberg Church President Theophil Wurm recommended convening a special session of the *Kirchenausschuss* "to say something about the Jewish boycott. The church-going people of Württemberg are in no way in agreement with the boycott movement."[34] Wurm's request is less resolute than Pechmann's, but he, too, demanded that Kapler take action: "Every word of the President of the Church Council will be gratefully welcomed by all *Landeskirchen*."[35]

Another admonition to speak out against the persecution of Jews was put forward by the Frankfurt Church leader Johannes Kübel, who wrote to Kapler that all of the *Landeskirchen* suffer "terribly" because of "the treatment of Jews." He was "incessantly asked the question: What does the Church do?" The "honor of the Christian name and basic concepts of Christian ethics [are] distorted...wherever Jews are stigmatized," especially "when families have belonged to the Protestant Church for generations and are now suddenly incriminated with the stain of being

---

30. Wilhelm von Pechmann, a DNVP member, had been president of the Bavarian General Synod since 1919, as well as the head of several German Protestant Church conventions (1924 in Bethel, 1927 in Königsberg, 1930 in Nuremberg). See Friedrich Wilhelm Katzenbach, *Widerstand und Solidarität der Christen in Deutschland 1933–1945. Eine Dokumentation zum Kirchenkampf aus den Papieren des D. Wilhelm Freiherr von Pechmann*, reprint (Neustadt/Aisch: Landessynode der Evangelischen Kirche, 2000); Sommer, *Wilhelm Freiherr von Pechmann*.

31. EZA Berlin, Bestand 1, no. 2867, fol. 125.   32. Ibid., fol. 125.

33. Ibid., fols. 125a, 126–127. "As for the rest, I take the liberty...of repeating the belief, forcefully and with all the resources available to me according to my deepest convictions, that I would consider it calamitous if our Church would decide to remain silent at such a time."

34. Ibid., fol. 128.   35. Ibid., fol. 128.

Jewish."[36] Kübel maintained that the Protestant Church would appear "equally guilty" unless "we protest in the name of Christianity:"[37] "Even seemingly disinterested third parties whose outlook is not deeply Christian tell us that they are currently ashamed of being German and Christian!"[38] Kübel then enumerates flagrant injustices that he himself witnessed in Frankfurt and begged Kapler to consider steps by which "our Christian scruples can [be brought] before the leading men of the government." He was even prepared to act himself, "by putting forward a motion to the government" in his own Frankfurt Church Council, though he believed that ultimately his own small church was too insignificant to be successful with such a move, and besides, "no *Landeskirche* should proceed on its own."[39] In actual fact, it was often insistence on concerted action that nipped in the bud spontaneous individual actions, which otherwise might have been feasible. Thus, there was no shortage of demands to become active. Among the reprimands directed toward Hermann Kapler that he and the Church had failed to take action, Pechmann's and Kübel's were the loudest voices. On 3 June 1933, about a week before Kapler retired at his own request (he had turned 65 in December 1932), Kübel warned again that "the envisaged settlement of the Jewish Question [must not] violate the principles of Christian morality." It is unthinkable, Kübel maintained, that "citizens of Jewish background are subject to a different legal status...than other German citizens." As the "upholder of Christian moral principles," the Protestant Church had to make sure that "Jewish citizens suffer no un-Christian harm."[40]

After the boycott other prominent Church leaders contacted Kapler to convey their misgivings and urge action. The Bishop of Mecklenburg-Schwerin, Heinrich Rendtorff, who stood politically to the right of

36. Ibid., fols. 138–140, esp. 138.   37. Ibid., fol. 138.
38. Ibid., fols. 138–139.   39. Ibid., fol. 140.
40. 3 June 1933 at EZA Berlin, Bestand 1, no. 3069, fols. 41–42. Kübel counseled that the Church's "members of Jewish descent not be eliminated from the German-Christian *Kulturkreis* on account of their Jewish blood, and be labeled as second-class citizens." Kübel's Frankfurt Church was directly concerned, since 4.7% of Frankfurt's population of 555,857 (1933) were Jewish. See Thamer, *Verführung*, 258; Armin Schmid and Renate Schmid, *Frankfurt in stürmischer Zeit, 1930–1933* (Stuttgart: Theiss, 1987).

Kapler, warned on 5 April: "Before permanent measures are taken and special legislation for Jews is introduced, the Church will have to raise its voice in time."[41] According to Rendtorff, this issue also preoccupied the Schwerin Church Council, which expected "concerted action by the Church leadership."[42] In this instance, too, action was impeded because joint political activity was difficult to coordinate, given the differences among the twenty-eight *Landeskirchen*. In mid-April, the prominent Gießen theology professor and Privy Church Councilor (*Geheimer Kirchenrat*) Gustav Krüger protested to Kapler that "countless Protestant Christians" regretted the absence of open protest that was comparable to that voiced by Catholic bishops: "The excesses of an antisemitism run rampant" have been "conducive more than anything else to sowing hatred and discord."[43]

It had indeed been the case that German Catholic bishops had speedily reacted to the civil service legislation of 7 April, designed to eliminate political opponents and Jewish Germans from the bureaucracy, especially its upper echelons, since it introduced for the first time the so-called "Aryan clause." On 9 April the Archbishops of Cologne and Paderborn together with the Bishop of Osnabrück published a manifesto in which they deplored "with profound sorrow and concern" that "for many loyal citizens, including conscientious civil servants, the days of the national uprising have undeservedly also become days of severe and bitter suffering."[44] This Catholic manifesto was motivated mainly by concern for those officials who were close to the Center Party, many of whom feared being dismissed on political grounds; concern for German Jews was

41. 5 April 1933 at EZA Berlin, Bestand 1, no. 2867, fols. 141–142. Rendtorff stressed that priority must be given to protecting those Jews "who are part of our Church and as such have a right to our protection."

42. Ibid., fol. 141. Heinrich Rendtorff (1888–1960); Baum and Grünzinger, eds., *Personenlexikon*, 205.

43. 18 April 1933 at EZA Berlin, Bestand 1, no. 2867, fol. 172. Gustav Krüger (1862–1940), Professor of Protestant Theology in Gießen; Baum and Grünzinger, eds., *Personenlexikon*, 145–146.

44. Bernhard Stasiewski, *Akten deutschen Bischöfe über die Lage der Kirche 1933–1945*, vol. I, 1933–1934 (Mainz: Grünewald, 1968), 51.

secondary. The manifesto was preceded by professions of patriotism, namely that the bishops were "imbued with the warmest love for their Fatherland, whose national ascent they [wished] to promote with all their might," while keeping "strife and hatred" at bay.[45] On 12 April the Archbishop of Breslau, Cardinal Adolf Bertram, head of the Fulda Bishops' Congregation and spokesman for German bishops, endorsed the manifesto.[46] Bertram added that he had already communicated with Hindenburg on 6 April and complained that "many hardworking and proficient citizens" who were loyal to Church and State had been prevented from participating in the reconstruction of the nation.

All of these declarations were reprinted in the main Catholic newspapers, such as *Germania* and the *Kölnische Volkszeitung*. Yet, in his open letter to Hindenburg of 6 April, Bertram had used his influence exclusively on behalf of "exceptionally competent Catholic civil servants," whose material existence he considered to be in jeopardy; the exclusion of Jews was not mentioned.[47] Bertram spoke quite bluntly, arguing that "in wide circles among the most patriotic and order-loving citizens, especially in the Catholic community, deep concern and a mood of depression" predominated. In instances of "the base and brutal attacks on Catholic State officials in high positions," the "regular police [are said to be] ... often powerless ... in the face of frenzied threats from members of nationalist organizations, who demanded their immediate dismissal."[48] On 15 April Freiburg Archbishop Conrad Gröber followed with a declaration on behalf of his dioceses on the Upper Rhine. Gröber, too, mentioned "the unfortunate and growing expulsion of loyal citizens and respected hardworking men from their former positions." Possibly to assure the regime of his loyalty, he also asserted that the bishops of the Upper Rhine province greatly regretted the attacks "leveled at our people in slanderous fashion from beyond Germany's borders." Boycotts, attacks, and discrimination against Jews found no mention.[49]

45. Ibid., 51. 46. Ibid., 59.
47. Ibid., 49–50. 48. Ibid., 49–50.
49. Ibid., 60.

The response of the Protestant Federal Church Office by *Oberkonsistorialrat* Johannes Gisevius to the Gießen theology professor Gustav Krüger (who had lauded the action of Catholic bishops) followed only on 13 July 1933, after Kapler had already retired. It is revealing as to the mindset of the Protestant Church leadership.[50] After correctly pointing out that "the bishops…in their manifesto were concerned first and foremost with officials who are members of the Center Party," it is emphasized that Kapler, while making no public proclamations, "had expressed his serious concern about the harsh measures affecting so many people in his personal deliberations with leading personalities of the government." It must not be overlooked, Gisevius argued, that, "among the communists, aiming at a violent overthrow of the political order in Germany, Jewish elements were strongly represented, and…German citizens have been placed at a severe disadvantage because of the exaggerated preferences shown to Jews in State service, in science and scholarship, in the free professions, etc." Because of this, Gisevius maintained, it was wrong "to speak of the excesses of an antisemitism run rampant."[51] Given the "discrimination" against German citizens, "it had been necessary to remedy deeply felt defects and abuses, whereby it is to be stressed that no Jew was persecuted on account of his religion or in any way prevented from exercising his religious duties."[52] In the name of the Federal Church Council, Gisevius thus excused antisemitic violence and legislative measures with a set of arguments that were stock-in-trade of a conservative nationalist milieu. Here it becomes clear that the Protestant Church leadership and a conservative nationalism shared certain commonalities, in particular the argument that "Jewish elements" supported communists and that "excessive preference" was given to Jews in the professions and in the world of learning. The fact that merit may have played a role in the

---

50. EZA Berlin, Bestand 1, no. 2867, fol. 173. *Oberkonsistorialrat* Johannes Gisevius (1880–1955), an administrative official, signed the response instead of the DEKA president. See Baum and Grünzinger, eds., *Personenlexikon*, 88. EZA Berlin, Bestand 1, no. 2867, fol. 173.
51. EZA Berlin, Bestand 1, no. 2867, fols. 173–173v.
52. Ibid., fol. 173v.

latter did not enter Gisevius's mind. The silence of the Church leadership thus also had reasons that went beyond mere tactical considerations, such as opportunism or fear of the new Nazi masters. In Gisevius's argumentation antisemitic measures had acquired a certain moral justification.

Church Reactions to Pleas for Help and Reports of Discrimination

In addition to protests and complaints from members of the Church leadership, there were numerous reports from victims, pleas for help, complaints, accusations about flagrant injustices, and inquiries and petitions directed to individual pastors, Church administrators, and Church leaders. These vividly illustrate the tragedy of total exclusion and the flagrant injustice connected with it. The following letters were addressed to Kapler himself in his role as the head of the Old Prussian Church; most were written by Protestant Christians who had converted from Judaism and who now disbelievingly saw their shops boycotted and their families stigmatized. The lawyer Hans Bendix, who had converted as a child in 1908, and whose family had been living in Germany for centuries, was now in danger of losing his livelihood; he wrote: "I cannot understand that because of my Jewish descent I will now count as a Jew and not as a Christian, as a Jew and not as a German, as a Jew and no longer as a human being with equal rights."[53] Doctor Johannes Schupp from Neubabelsberg near Potsdam did not plead for himself but "for the men and women who entered marriages with Jews as well as ... their children." It simply could not be the case that "the Protestant Church permits the exclusion of these Christians and their children from the German *Volksgemeinschaft*." Schupp, who like other letter writers stressed his strictly

---

53. 13 April 1933 at EZA Berlin, Bestand 7, no. 3688, fols. 81–82. Bendix asked the Church to take up his case and to intervene with the Prussian Ministry of Justice, since his livelihood had been threatened by the "Law on the Admission to Legal Practice" of 7 April 1933.

national-minded attitude and emphasized that he "viewed the nationalist tendencies of our age with understanding" (such phrases were often used to protect the writer against accusations of not being national-minded), asked Kapler to "mobilize the entire influence of the Protestant Church to make sure that hectic overzealousness does not lead to results that would constitute a severe injustice."[54] A woman married to a Jewish German wrote to Kapler: "The sad fate of relatives and friends around me troubles me terribly.... And inwardly mortally wounded, I wait for a word from the Church...which raised no racial objections when we entered it, but administered the sacraments, baptized our children, and now repudiates us all." She continued,

> Does anyone realize what is being done to all of these thousands of children? Does anyone appreciate the sorrow of those declared outlawed and without a homeland?...Never before in history has what we are living through now happened, namely that the baptism of those people who received it, did not make them Christian....How can we continue to go on living when everything that is holy to us, faith and Fatherland, has been denied us?...And how can children honor their parents when these...are now openly boycotted? Do members of the cloth realize what spiritual and moral hardships the thousands of children whom they have baptized have been exposed to by living through the last weeks?[55]

Letters of this kind could hardly have left Kapler indifferent. On 16 May the merchant Richard Oppenheimer, who was faced with financial ruin due to the boycott, wrote: "Mister President! We who converted to the Protestant Church are affected doubly hard, since we now belong to no one. We are not Jews, but the State also does not count us among Christians; what then are we Mister President?"[56] Like others,

---

54. 7 April 1933, ibid., fols. 44–46. Schupp mentioned that he counted the well-known seventeenth-century preacher Johann Balthasar Schupp, who served as senior pastor in Hamburg, among his forefathers. See Percy Ernst Schramm, *Neun Generationen. Dreihundert Jahre deutsche Kulturgeschichte im Licht der Schicksale einer Hamburger Bürgerfamilie (1648–1948)*, vol. I (Göttingen: Vandenhoeck & Ruprecht, 1963), 44, 49.
55. 3 May 1933 at EZA Berlin, Bestand 7, no. 3688, fol. 99.
56. 16 May 1933, ibid., fols. 103–104.

Oppenheimer stresses his national-minded outlook and that he fought in the First World War and was decorated: "My father, who fought in the campaigns of 1864 and 1866, was a born Israelite, a born Jew...I was baptized Protestant in 1908....Despite my being Christian, pieces of paper were glued to the windows of my shops on the day of the boycott: 'Don't shop with Jews!'"[57] Oppenheimer appealed to the Church as the one institution that was still in a position to help. He concluded his letter with a question that must have preoccupied many in 1933: "Which Jewish-looking German dares to enter a public house today or even a public meeting?" The files contain no response. Since Kapler escaped into retirement at the beginning of June, Oppenheimer probably never received an answer from anyone.[58]

Church leaders could not plead ignorance, for on all its hierarchical levels the Church was well informed about the plight and suffering of Jewish Germans, as documented in letters and petitions that survived in archival holdings. Those were directed to individual pastors or the head of a *Landeskirche*. On 9 April the Hamburg pastor Hugo Johannes Poppe wrote to the Hamburg Church Senate:

> Last week I had several heart-to-heart discussions that affected me most deeply with members of my congregation who descended from Jewish parents or grandparents, were then baptized, confirmed, and also married and who have been loyal to our Church. They are depressed by the persecutions against the Jewish race, among which they are also counted, and they ask me: "Is the Protestant Church, to which we belong, prepared to protect us, its members, against the injustices we are facing?" I humbly venture to submit this question to the venerable Church Council and would be grateful for any information regarding whether Church governments are able and willing to protect individuals against the disregarding of the sacrament of baptism by authorities of State.[59]

57. 16 May 1933, ibid., fols. 103v., 104.
58. In another letter, the complaint was made to Kapler: "We are hanging in the air in that we belong to the Protestant Church but are labeled as Jews." 24 April 1933 at EZA Berlin, Bestand 1, no. 3069, fols. 15–16.
59. Nordelbisches Kirchenarchiv Kiel, Bestand 32.01, no. 2268, fol. 18. (I would like to thank Dr. Stephan Linck, Kiel, for his help in locating archival sources in this collection.)

Simon Schöffel, Hamburg's future *Landesbischof* (May 1933), also sought advice from the Hamburg Church Council and passed on an inquiry by a member of the Church as to "whether the Church [feels] no obligation to protect Jews baptized as Protestants," pointing out that this was an example of how much the *"Judenfrage"* "stirred the hearts of our Church members." He himself had been repeatedly asked about this problem and wanted to know if "there exists an answer" that "can be passed on as the official opinion of the Church."[60] Indecision, uncertainty, and hapless-ness were prevalent among all levels of the Church leadership. The Hamburg merchant Hans Lebenbaum, who had converted to Protestant-ism in 1917, surely vented a common sentiment when he wrote to Schöffel (now the new *Landesbischof*) on 19 June 1933: "Can we continue to belong to a Church that once accepted us into its fold but now not only fails to protect us but, quite to the contrary, doesn't even seem to want to have us anymore?"[61] In the southern German state of Baden the *"Judenfrage"* was also a sensitive issue, especially after the boycott. In this highly charged climate, the Weinheim *Pfarrer* Hermann Brecht wrote to Prälat Julius Kühlewein (who would become the new Baden *Landesbischof* in June) on 5 April: "What does the Church undertake to counter the current crime against civilization, the persecution of Jews?" The Church ought to say "a decisive word against the hate campaign directed against Jews."[62] Kühlewein responded evasively on 25 April, indicating that "the German Protestant Church Council will today deal with the burning problem of the Jews."[63] Yet, as will be shown below, even the assembled

60. Nordelbisches Kirchenarchiv Kiel, ibid.,. fols. 18–18v., 21; see also Rainer Hering, *Die Bischöfe Simon Schöffel, Franz Tügel.* Hamburgische Lebensbilder in Darstellungen und Selbstzeugnissen, no.10 (Hamburg: Verein für Hamburgische Geschichte, 1995).

61. Nordelbisches Kirchenarchiv Keil, ibid., fol. 6. On the Hamburg Church, see Hering, "Collegiality to *Führerprinzip*," 281–309.

62. Rückleben and Erbacher, eds., *Evangelische Landeskirche*, 572–573. Factory owner Walter Freudenberg posed this question in his church's parish council and then elaborated: "It would be all the easier for the Church to make such a comment given that she is so positively oriented toward the current State and its government.... But she must definitely say something because the virulent campaign against Jews has taken on forms that are immoral and un-Christian." See Joachim Scholtyseck, *Freudenberg: Ein Familienunternehmen in Kaiserreich, Demokratie und Diktatur* (Munich: Beck, 2016).

63. Rückleben and Erbacher, eds., *Evangelische Landeskirche*, 573.

group of the entire German Protestant Church could not bring itself to break its fateful silence.

Another request was made by the daughter of a professor at Freiburg University, Lilly R., who at the age of 15, "following an inner calling and not prompted by outward circumstances," converted to Protestantism and now found herself in danger of losing her position as a teacher. She turned to the head of her *Landeskirche* for support so that she could keep her position. Her request was met with an outright refusal. The Baden Church President Klaus Wurth replied (truthfully as it happened) that it was "completely out of the question that the Reich government would cancel legal restrictions against non-Aryan people's comrades [*Volksgenossen*]." Wurth followed this with an analogy that ran like a recurring theme through the argumentation of Church leaders:

> Just as the Church was unable to prevent the deprivation of rights of many hundreds of thousands of Germans who, after the war, were pushed back into their old Fatherland from all countries and continents after having been robbed of their fortunes and deprived of their material existence, in the same vein, the Church is currently unable to forestall measures against the infiltration of our people by foreign elements.[64]

Wurth here alludes to the expulsions of Germans from Alsace-Lorraine (in this case *Reichsdeutsche*," Germans not born in the Alsace, had to leave the province after it became French in 1919), as well as to the loss of German property in the former German colonies and in North and Central America when it was confiscated without compensation after World War I. In his response, Wurth virtually blamed the petitioner, Lilly R., for being part of an "infiltrating" foreign element. He equates the injustice suffered by Germans after World War I—to which the world remained silent, as there were no significant neutral powers that might have supported the vanquished country in its protests—with the

---

64. Ibid., 593–593. Wurth's formulation conveyed the idea that even if the Church could do something, it would nevertheless not be advisable to actually do it.

injustices suffered by Jews in 1933. He thus considers the anti-Jewish legislation of 1933 not as a moral wrong, but vindicates it as "measures against the infiltration of foreign elements." This comparison based on indiscriminate collective guilt permits him to look on and remain silent with a clear conscience and without feeling the obligation to protect an innocent individual citizen against an injustice he does not acknowledge.

Letter Exchanges between Wilhelm Menn and Ernst Stoltenhoff

With regard to the persecution of Jews, the most revealing exchange of letters within the Church took place between the Düsseldorf pastor for social concerns (*Sozialpfarrer*) Wilhelm Menn, who viewed the new regime with skepticism, and the Rhenish *Generalsuperintendent* Ernst Stoltenhoff.[65] In this exchange two polar opposite political viewpoints within the Church clashed: that of Menn, cosmopolitan and attuned to social problems because of his work in the international ecumenical movement, and—far more typical for the Protestant Church in 1933—the strictly conservative and national-minded Stoltenhoff. On the day of the boycott, Menn wrote to the *Generalsuperintendent*::

> There is no point in denying that with the boycott we have begun the first persecution of Jews in centuries. I am horrified by the cold hatred and the devilish sure-footed specificity of [the NSDAP's] methods, as reflected in the instructions of the Party. Here, everything used to great effect in the persecution of Marxists has been far surpassed....It is evident that you cannot let mobs yell '*Juda verrecke!*' for years without unleashing this brutal lust for persecution....Who will have the courage to say what is needed – to say that the Christian Church...considers it a conspicuous moral

---

65. Wilhelm Menn (1888–1956) was the head of the clergy's social office (*Sozialpfarramt*) of the Protestant Church in the Rhineland in Düsseldorf from 1926 to 1934; from 1934 to 1950 he was a pastor and *Superintendent* (regional head) in Andernach. Ernst Stoltenhoff (1879–1953) was *Generalsuperintendent* in Koblenz and Düsseldorf from 1928 to 1949. Baum and Grünzinger, eds., *Personenlexikon*, 170, 250.

injustice and anti-Christian to persecute and harm individuals because they form part of a group that, for some reason, people are told should be opposed and stigmatized.

Menn went further: "The freedom of public expression has been completely taken away from us. But the Church can still speak; at least to its members.... I cannot believe that what we are experiencing now in terms of violence and the maniacal rage in the pursuit of personal revenge is German."[66] In his answer Stoltenhoff conceded that the overall situation, "apart from the great joy about all that the revolution has brought us," also raises "serious concern." Trying to balance support for the regime with unease for its excesses, it is clear that for Stoltenhoff the positive aspects prevail. He expresses understanding that "the accumulated and justified resentment, also on the part of those who are not strictly antisemitic, about all that the Jewish-dominated press, stock exchange, and theatre have done to us, is finally bursting open."[67] He agrees with Menn that "the perennially howled-about 'Juda verrecke'" cannot be defended, but resignedly silences his doubts by arguing that "the individual can do nothing against the elemental power of this movement in our time."[68]

Stoltenhoff's criticism of Jewish influence in German public life, especially in the fields of journalism, finance, and culture, was pervasive among the leadership of the Protestant Church and frequently cited as an excuse for anti-Jewish discrimination. From this standpoint, the attackers were characterized as the victims and not as the perpetrators.

---

66. The exchange of letters is reprinted in van Norden, *Kirche in der Krise*, 59–62; 177–179; see esp. 59. As his source, van Norden refers to the "Dokumentensammlung des Landeskirch-enarchivs Düsseldorf II." During my visit to the Düsseldorf *Landeskirchenarchiv* in the fall of 2013, the local head archivist assured me that this document collection was not in his archive. It must therefore be assumed that after the appearance of van Norden's book in 1963 the collection of documents had somehow disappeared, been damaged, or was lost during the move of the archive to a new building in the 1990s. In his *Die Kirchen und das Dritte Reich* (which first appeared in 1977), Klaus Scholder also referred to van Norden's book rather than to the *Landeskirchenarchiv* in Düsseldorf as his source, even though Scholder usually preferred to go directly to the archive in question.

67. Van Norden, *Kirche in der Krise*, 60.   68. Ibid.

This motif of pernicious Jewish influence in German cultural life was so deeply rooted in the conservative milieu that even those few who energetically opposed antisemitic violence and legislation subscribed to it. Wilhelm von Pechmann, for example, a stalwart opponent of the National Socialist persecution of Jews who had fought for the independence of the Protestant Church in March and then initiated a petition protesting the treatment of German Jews in April,[69] was at one time himself critical of, as he put it, "Jewish predominance in public life." In a proclamation of 14 June 1920 addressed to his *Kirchenvorstand* (parish council) in Munich and to "our fellow Israelite citizens," in which he also condemned antisemitic excesses in Munich after the revolutionary upheavals of 1919 and praised the bravery of Jewish soldiers during the war, he wrote:

> German and Christian sensibilities, offended by the Jewish-influenced part of the German press, literature, etc. and its provocative lack of consideration, can and will never tolerate what they have been saddled with in terms of Jewish predominance in public life in these most shameful years of German history [after Germany's defeat in World War I and the revolutions of 1918–19 in Munich]. And the more sincerely we try to strive for a true and lasting peace in accord with our Jewish co-citizens, the more earnestly we have to ask the reasonable and well-meaning among them to insistently work toward the goal of making sure that the small Jewish minority exercise a befitting reticence and reserve in its relationship to the larger German people in whose midst it resides, a reserve that all too many members of that minority have ... thrown overboard.[70]

A majority of Protestant Church leaders would undoubtedly have agreed with Stoltenhoff's next comment: "For me," he wrote, "the 21st of March [the Day of Potsdam] was a great experience. In my heart and in my house the colors Schwarz-Rot-Gold [the colors of the Weimar flag] have never meant a thing. To this very hour, I have always stood very far to the

69. This was discussed in the executive committee meeting of 26 April 1933 (see below).
70. Quoted in Sommer, *Wilhelm Freiherr von Pechmann*, 155–156.

right politically."[71] In his response on 8 April, Menn freely vented his doubts about the legality of the "national revolution." With regard to the persecution of Jews, he argued that "the destruction of all legality driven by the demands of crowds, which have been incited for years," is "immoral and dangerous." According to him, "[t]he new Germany also needs legal foundations if it is not to plant the seeds of its own destruction."[72] Others who felt as he did had discussed this problem with him and were now asking, in bewilderment: "We, who have felt like this, are we to be just as lonely and isolated in our own Church as we are within the State?" Menn was also concerned that the Church attempted "to now act tactically and to allow itself to fold under the dictate of the State." It is "an irresponsible sacrifice of the Church to remain quiet about so many things today, when a Church that today could really count on being listened to seriously, should speak up."[73]

In another letter to Otto Dibelius, whose circular dispatch to Brandenburg pastors had quickly gained notoriety, and whom Menn thus regarded as a kindred spirit, he expressed his doubts about the role of the Church in the "national revolution." The *Osterbotschaft* (Easter message), in which the Prussian Church professed to support the regime unconditionally, left an especially bitter taste in his mouth. On the one hand, Menn maintained, "Of course, no one can doubt that the overwhelming part of our Church congregation, for whatever reason, joyously supports the revolution as the awakening of the deepest forces of our nation, harkening back to real patriotism, a genuine community of the people, and a religious renewal."[74] On the other hand, he argued, the Prussian *Oberkirchenrat* had to be aware that there were also many parishioners who did not share these sentiments:

> I am sure you will understand that we expect and demand...from the Church that she does not continue to violate our conscience through these completely superfluous declarations of loyalty that are unworthy of

---

71. Van Norden, *Kirche in der Krise*, 60.   72. Ibid., 177–178.
73. Ibid., 178.   74. Quoted in ibid., 61.

her.... A Church... that creates her own new inner organization amidst the delirious frenzy of a political revolution cannot expect that she will be met with trust and respect by earnest Christians. We have never needed the Church more than at this moment. But we need the Church – and not just another organ of the national revolution.[75]

Growing Consensus with the Regime

The *Osterbotschaft* to which Menn reacted so indignantly ran as follows:

In the conviction that the renewal of the nation and the Reich can be upheld and safeguarded only by these forces [of the Gospel], the Church understands herself [to be] gratefully bound to the leadership of the new Germany. It is with enthusiasm that she is prepared to work for the national and moral renewal of our people.[76]

This proclamation marked a first high point of the Protestant Church's growing enthusiasm for the new State. It was adopted at the Ephoren Conference of the Prussian Church Council with its thirteen *Generalsuper-intendenten* and eight *Konsistorialpräsidenten* (presiding administrative officers) on 11 April 1933 in Berlin. Both Stoltenhoff and Dibelius attended.[77] Those present at the meeting overwhelmingly favored the proposal that the Church leadership publicly support the new State, especially since it

---

75. Ibid., 61–62. Menn contrasted what was for him the undignified behavior of the Protestant Church with the courageous behavior of the Catholic bishops of the Upper Rhine region, who at Easter "spoke openly of the privations and injustices that are now occurring in the name of the 'new' Germany."

76. Hermle and Thierfelder, *Herausgefordert*, 92. The proclamation was reminiscent of that of the 1927 Church Congress in Königsberg, where it was proclaimed: "We are Germans and want to remain Germans. Our national heritage is given to us from God. Christianity and German-ness have been intimately bound up with each other for more than a millennium." Ibid.

77. EZA Berlin, Bestand 7, no. 1087, fols. 225–236. The text in this file is the provisional protocol with several added linguistic corrections. In a note of 16 July 1933, it was remarked that as a result of President Kapler's leave it had not been possible to produce a revised version (ibid., fols. 224–224v.). The Protestant *Oberkirchenrat* included, in addition to Kapler and the clerical and secular vice presidents Georg Burghart and Ernst Hundt (an NSDAP member), several Protestant ministers and thirteen *Konsistorialräte* or *Konsistorialpräsidenten*. The latter were legally trained administrative officers of the Church.

was believed that the younger generation of pastors was already well disposed toward National Socialism.[78] Conference attendees were painfully aware that "the future organization of things…will largely be influenced by the NSDAP as the main upholder of the renewal of the nation and the State."[79] The Church's promotion of the new regime was thus facilitated by a fair dose of opportunism. Hermann Kapler, who was also head of the Old Prussian Church, had long been haunted by the specter of the Protestant Church's loss of influence during the Weimar Republic. He now pointed out that the new German Chancellor could not fathom "the existing condition of fragmentation into twenty-eight Landeskirchen." Hitler desired "a Protestant bloc capable of concerted action as a counterweight to the unitary organization of Catholicism."[80]

Dibelius was alone in rejecting a programmatic endorsement of the new State. He argued that the Church should confine itself to commenting on "individual issues resulting from the new order of things," though he was quick to qualify: "It is not appropriate for the Church to take a public stand on the Judenfrage."[81] Kapler expressed agreement with this latter sentiment. Stoltenhoff urged the Church to "say 'yes' to this State, a 'yes' without qualification. The entire nation and the Church have been freed from an enormous danger, which was much closer at hand than commonly assumed."[82] The new State had cleared the way for the Church; "great things have been accomplished and occasional mistakes should be overlooked…a 'Gleichschaltung' of the twenty-eight German state churches is absolutely necessary."[83] There was a broad consensus among participants regarding the affirmative character of the Osterbotschaft. Some of them vied to rival each other in their professions of loyalty to the new regime: it was proposed, for example, that special church services be held, and church buildings decorated with flags; church bells could also possibly be rung on Chancellor Hitler's birthday

---

78. Ibid., fol. 228.
79. Ibid., fol. 225v. The German original is "Volk und Staat" ('Volk' is here rendered as nation).
80. Ibid., fol. 227.   81. Ibid., fol. 228v.
82. Ibid., fols. 225–226.   83. Ibid., fols. 228v.–229.

(20 April). In the ensuing discussion of the Church's official relationship toward the German Christians, anxious attempts were made to remain on a friendly footing with Hitler's preferred faction within the Church: it would be desirable "to integrate the German Christians into the Church and provide them with positions of responsibility."[84] It is astonishing that, after strenuously striving for independence in the first weeks after 30 January, Church leaders seemed to be in agreement already by early April that the Church needed a centralized unitary organization, thereby supporting the creation of a common Reich Church. Even Dibelius emphasized "the necessity of a union of all German Protestant churches that will then be capable of action."[85] Kapler summarized the result of the discussion, which took place "in a spirit of general agreement," by maintaining that there existed "unanimity among those present regarding the position of the Church in the new State." The Church was prepared "to participate in the reconstruction of the nation, but in order to assist in this task, she had to preserve her freedom vis-à-vis the State."[86] Here again the attempt was made to strike an impossible balance between taking part in the "reconstruction of the nation" and maintaining independence from the Nazi State.

In conjunction with the *Osterbotschaft*, this declaration amounted to a sea change in Church leaders' attitudes since their last official declaration at the beginning of March. The pressure of political events since the 5 March elections, the rapid and smooth takeover of German states not yet in Nazi hands, and the inglorious and complete collapse of those forces that had previously opposed Nazism undoubtedly played a role in this. For both the Protestant and Catholic Churches, the most important factors consisted in the well-staged *mise en scène* of the 21 March "Day of Potsdam" and Hitler's 23 March policy declaration, in which he promised to value both Churches as pillars of the preservation of the German *Volkstum*; the volte-face of the Catholic bishops on 28 March also had an impact. Apart from these alluring temptations to jump on the

---

84. Ibid., fols. 229–233v.   85. Ibid., fol. 233.   86. Ibid., fols. 235v.–236.

bandwagon of National Socialism, equally persuasive may have been the menacing aspects of the new regime, such as the continuing terror of the SA and other Nazi organizations, as well as the construction of concentration camps. At the end of March, it was publicly announced in the newspapers that a former munitions factory had been converted into the first concentration camp in Dachau.

Otto Dibelius's Position on Antisemitism and his Relationship to the New State

Wilhelm Menn was correct in his assessment of Dibelius as that of a fearless theologian who did not mince words. Undaunted, Dibelius confronted the new regime not only in his 8 March circular but also when he refused the government use of the Garrison Church in Potsdam for the opening of the new parliament (the Reichstag building in Berlin having been gutted by fire). And this despite the fact that it had been Hitler's expressed wish. As the burial place of Frederick the Great, the Garrison Church would have been ideally suited to bridge the gap between past Prussian glory and the rising national aspirations of the present.[87] Even though Dibelius was not receptive to the promises and inducements of National Socialism and ultimately showed himself to be an enemy of the new regime after the late summer of 1933, there were common political denominators. In addition to his intense patriotism, which he shared with most other Protestant Church leaders, Dibelius's decidedly anti-Jewish attitude may have made him initially appreciate some features of the new regime. Dibelius, like the National Socialists,

---

87. In his memoirs Dibelius mentions that Hitler had determined that the opening of the new *Reichstag* should take place in the Potsdam Garrison Church. When Dibelius spoke out against this (the church lay in his area of jurisdiction), the Potsdam Lord Mayor implored him again and again to change his mind, since he "would not want to let such a great event pass his city by." In the end a compromise was found: a Protestant service would be celebrated in the Nikolai Church, followed by an additional official act of State in the Old *Garnisonskirche*. Otto Dibelius, *Ein Christ ist immer im Dienst*, 2nd ed. (Stuttgart: Kreuz, 1963), 170–171.

blamed German Jews for what he considered the moral decline of Germany during the Weimar years, and used them as a scapegoat for a host of related problems. Dibelius later wrote in his memoirs about the first weeks of the new government: "There were positive signs. The entire moral sleaze, which had increasingly gained ground in Germany at the end of the Weimar period, disappeared in one fell swoop."[88] After the Second World War, Dibelius acknowledged his antisemitism with characteristic bluntness:

> I have never made any bones about my attitude: as was the case with most families of higher officials in the old Germany, we did not discuss the problem of the *Judentum* at home. But you did your shopping at Jewish shops only in emergencies, and it was a matter of course that you avoided personal dealings with them. This was not done with a hostile attitude, but still in a way that one sensed the foreignness in their manner. At home we knew very well that, on the one hand, the [positive] type represented by Bernhard Ehrental existed, but [on the other] also the [negative] type of Veitel Itzig, since *Soll und Haben* was then widely read among the younger generation. Both my brother and I have frequently met the Bernhard Ehrental type – but the other type as well, especially in Berlin's Bayerisches Viertel....[89]

Dibelius also conceded that "as a student in the VDSt (Association of German Students) I always advocated that the eastern borders should be closed to further Jewish immigration; in due course, the Jewish question would have then taken care of itself."[90] Yet, he qualified, "Since 1933, the situation changed. For it is understood that the place of the Protestant Christian is with those who suffer injustice and are violated. For me it has always been gratifying that I succeeded in protecting two Jewish families

---

88. Dibelius, *Ein Christ*, 169.
89. This is in a letter of 23 January 1965 from the almost 85-year-old Dibelius to Wolfgang Gerlach, who included the letter in his book *Als die Zeugen schwiegen. Bekennende Kirche und die Juden* (Berlin: Selbstverlag Institut Kirche und Judentum, 1987), 42. Bernhard Ehrental is the literature-loving positive Jewish figure in Gustav Freytag's novel *Soll und Haben* (1855), considered to be one of the most widely read novels in pre-World War I Germany; Veitel Itzig is the very negative, caricatured counterpoint.
90. Gerlach, *Als die Zeugen*, 42, n. 17.

during the entire period of persecution, and in doing so exposed myself to danger."[91] Here Dibelius refers to a situation during the Second World War, when he hid persecuted Jews on the premises of the Protestant Gustav-Adolf-Verein in Berlin, of which he was the head, thus saving their lives: "When the front bell rang, they went softly down the back stairs, in order to leave without being noticed, if it was the Gestapo. It was a do-or-die game for us all, but we were thankful that we could succeed in doing it."[92]

In December 1930 (before standing up for Jews became a matter of life and death) the then 50-year-old *Generalsuperintendent* advised the readers of the *Berliner Evangelisches Sonntagsblatt* to follow the example of his parental household: "It is here that we have to take a decisive stand. We have to spread the word from one house to the next: a decent woman buys German goods. The made-up and powdered rabble, which frequent the elegant nightclubs, may do what they please – the decent German woman buys in German shops."[93] Such phrases from a highly respected Protestant Church leader during the run-up to Christmas, the main shopping season of the entire year, could not fail to leave its mark on readers. It may seem astonishing how freely Dibelius dispensed his value judgments about the "made-up and powdered rabble." He believed he was on safe ground, assuming that the bulk of his readers shared the same predispositions, which were in keeping with the moral code of the German *Bürgertum* at the time. A few days after the April boycott, Dibelius again felt called upon to communicate his personal predilections to the pastors of his Brandenburg district. In a circular labeled "Confidential," written on the occasion of the Easter holiday, he wrote with provoking (and perhaps unnecessary) openness:

My dear brethren! All of us will not only understand but feel the fullest sympathy for the ultimate causes from which the *völkisch* movement sprang. Despite the negative connotation the word has acquired, I have

91. Ibid., 42.　　92. Dibelius, *Ein Christ*, 204.
93. *Berliner Evangelisches Sonntagsblatt*, 7 December 1930; Gerlach, *Als die Zeugen*, 42, n. 16.

always known myself to be an antisemite. It is impossible to fail to appreciate that in all the corroding phenomena of modern civilization, Jewry has played a leading role. God bless us Christians and our Easter Gospel.[94]

Reading these lines, one has the impression that Dibelius almost takes pride in his antisemitism. Even if he may have assumed that the majority of Protestant pastors in the Mark Brandenburg shared his cultural anti-semitism, it is still likely that there were some who did not and might have taken offense, especially in view of the bluntness with which it was presented. And there may well have been Protestant pastors who had converted from Judaism.[95]

This cultural antisemitism was widespread among middle- and upper-class Protestant Prussians. In his perceptive analysis of the mindset of Gotthard Heinrici, a Prussian general, whose father was an East Prussian parson and Protestant Church administrator (*Superintendent*) and who was himself steeped in the Prussian Protestant tradition, Johannes Hürter argues that cultural antisemitism was multifaceted: it often combined a religious anti-Judaism, widespread among East Elbian Protestants, with a political antisemitism that took for granted that Jews monopolized leftist politics (encapsulated in the concept of "Jewish Bolshevism"). Its propon-ents opposed Jewish assimilation with the goals of restricting Jewish influence, partially undoing emancipation, and erecting segregationist barriers.[96] Dibelius never used his antisemitism as a tactical device to curry favor with the regime, even during the first months before he became its avowed opponent. We may therefore believe him to be subjectively honest when he writes in his memoirs: "With the National

94. Ibid., 42.
95. In his memoirs Dibelius wrote that he saw the role of Protestant clergy as that of an advisor for vital questions about life in general, and that he unreservedly and unquestioningly did his best to give his life's work to fulfilling this role, possibly on the assumption that he could be a model and an example to the members of his parish and his flock of ministers. Dibelius, *Ein Christ*, 42–44.
96. See Johannes Hürter, ed., *Notizen aus dem Vernichtungskrieg. Die Ostfront in den Aufzeichnungen des Generals Heinrici* (Darmstadt, WBG, 2016), 15–16.

Socialists I never had anything in common. Their swaggering loud-mouthed propaganda repelled me." In his memoirs, Dibelius also mentions that already weeks after 30 January, "isolated pieces of news about the mistreatment of Jews...[reached] our ears, but they were far too unspecific to undertake anything against it."[97] Without doing him an injustice, one may safely assume that a person of Dibelius's political and ideological predisposition would not have assigned great urgency to such news.

In early April 1933, Dibelius became the unofficial spokesman for German Protestantism when he expounded on the boycott in a radio speech to American listeners. The Reich-wide boycott of Jewish-owned shops, department stores, doctors' surgeries, and lawyers' offices of 1 April had attracted enormous international attention and engendered dismay and misgivings, so that Dibelius's speech on 4 April via the new radio connection found an interested and receptive audience among Americans.[98] Germany had just experienced a second revolution, Dibelius maintained, but in contrast to the "revolution of 1918," during which "bloodshed and cruelties of all kinds" were commonplace, this second revolution came about "by the lawful decision of the German people." Reich Chancellor Hitler had assumed power "in a strictly legal fashion," and those who witnessed the official ceremony at Potsdam remained, like him, "under the strong impression that in Germany a new beginning was made on the path toward justice and legality."[99] Then Dibelius turned to what he considered the mortal danger Germany had just escaped through the determined crackdown by the government. In Russia, Bolshevism had "destroyed churches, dissolved families, annihilated property" and reduced "people to slaves of a cruel tyranny without rights." In Germany, where Bolshevik terror was known from the brief communist

97. Dibelius, *Ein Christ*, 169.
98. Deborah E. Lipstadt, *Beyond Belief. The American Press and the Coming of the Holocaust* (New York and London: Free Press, 1986), 13–63; Seul, "Herr Hitler's Nazis," 412–430.
99. 4 April 1933 at EZA Berlin, Bestand 51, E2e8,1, "Die nach Amerika gerichtete Rundfunkrede des Herrn General-superintendenten Dibelius vom 4. April 1933."

rule in Bavaria and Thuringia after World War I, "during which the communist rabble chased clergymen in front of them as protective shields," it was expected that "the decisive battle between occidental civilization and Bolshevism would be fought on German soil." Now the battle had been won without bloodshed or street battles; "especially in the first days, transgressions occurred," but overall the image of public life in Germany has been characterized by "order and discipline."[100] Dibelius thus maintained that "there is not a word of truth...in the atrocity tales about the cruel and barbarous treatment of communists in Germany." The communist leaders he visited in prison had all told him that "they were treated correctly." In view of what had actually occurred, it is indeed astonishing that Dibelius could say to his American audience with a seemingly clear conscience: "You will understand that it embitters a nation that has just carried out its revolution in perfect discipline that its people now must stand by and see that such news is spread and believed throughout the world."[101]

In the second part of his speech Dibelius fully adopted the National Socialist version of events: Based on misinformation and "false news... Jewry had now begun a campaign of agitation against Germany in several countries," coupled with appeals to boycott German goods. According to Dibelius, it was solely to break this (in his opinion unjustified) foreign boycott that National Socialists had initiated a purely defensive counter-boycott against Jews in Germany. There had been virtually no encroachments, save for one incident in Kiel.[102] In Dibelius's reading of the situation, the 1 April boycott thus appeared as a legitimate defense against the unjustified anti-German smear campaign. The violent occurrence he referred to was the previously mentioned murder of Friedrich Schumm, which he characterized as an act resembling lynch justice: "in the city of Kiel...a Jew shot down a young National Socialist and was then himself shot by an embittered crowd even before the police

---

100. Ibid., fol. 2.   101. Ibid., fol. 2.   102. Ibid., fols. 2–3.

could bring him to safety."[103] Finally, Dibelius appealed to "Christian friends" in America to use their influence "so that no more false news is spread and believed about Germany," especially since everybody knows "that we are a people of order, law, and discipline."[104] In concluding, Dibelius placed the National Socialist movement in the larger context of German history: the National Socialist government stood for "a return to the good German traditions." Because of it, the German Reich was now "as unified and firmly established as never before in our history." Out of the "decomposition" of the last fifteen years the path had now been forged to lead "to a Christian and truly German life for the people."[105] Taken as a whole, Dibelius's speech, which amounted to a justification of German policy since 30 January, was a rhetorical masterpiece. He repeatedly appealed to "the good in man" and may have convinced many skeptics that their view of the new Nazi government was unjust:

> Do not make things even more difficult in this hard time for the German people by lending an ear to sensationalist news! Have confidence! Once again, trust in us! You will see that what is happening in Germany now will lead to a result for which everyone who loves and honors German ways can be grateful! And it will be good not only for Germany, but will turn out to be a blessing for a whole world![106]

It probably did not take Dibelius very long to realize that this prediction would fail to materialize.

Those who could not counter Dibelius's words based on their own experience may have found it difficult to extricate themselves from the spell of his forceful rhetoric, in particular since he seemed to be convinced of the veracity of what he was saying. His persuasive attempt to

103. Ibid., fols. 2–3. On the Schumm murder, see Chapter 6 above.
104. Ibid., fol. 3.
105. Ibid., fol. 4. On the other hand, Nazi leaders continued to regard Dibelius as one of their detractors. At the Reich Conference of the German Christian Faith Movement (3–5 April 1933 in Berlin), Dibelius was sharply attacked by the Brandenburg *Gauleiter* Kube because of his candid comments and criticisms of the National Socialist movement.
106. Ibid., fol. 4.

explain away what had happened in March and early April emanated from patriotic solidarity with the country he felt was wrongly stigmatized, from which his antisemitic views could not be separated. Dibelius's own frankly admitted antisemitism explains a certain willful blindness toward anti-Jewish prejudice and violent attacks. Like millions of Germans, he too seems to have been affected by the promise of unity, a strong government capable of and willing to take decisive action, the successful crackdown against the political Left that eliminated the seemingly real danger of a communist revolution, the sweeping away of what many considered the loud, garish, vulgar, enfeebling, and wholly "un-German" culture of Weimar, and the return to "good" German traditions. Yet, in the spring of 1933, the hopes associated with these promises dissipated more swiftly with each passing day.

Dibelius did not yet realize that National Socialists intended a radically new beginning—a break amounting to a revolutionary change that was ultimately determined to destroy traditions, especially those connected with the Church, and eventually eliminate, not just disadvantage, Jews in Germany. According to his later testimony, Dibelius coldly dismissed Hitler and the Nazi movement after Hitler's declaration of solidarity with the murderers of Potempa in August 1932. A year later the Nazis removed Dibelius from office.[107] Yet the fact that an immensely energetic Church leader such as Dibelius, who was openly critical of National Socialism, could fall into such blind justification of Nazi crimes raises the question: How would those who were less critical and even more favorably predisposed toward National Socialism react?

---

107. Dibelius, *Ein Christ*, 169: "With Hitler's telegram to the National Socialist murderers in Beuthen, I had made up my mind on this movement."

11

THE PROTESTANT CHURCH BETWEEN ACTION AND SILENCE

The World Alliance for International Friendship Through the Churches and the Situation in Germany

Dibelius was not the only high-ranking German Church leader who tried to mollify the outside world and downplay the gravity of the situation in Germany, even though he was more forceful and convincing than others. Georg Burghart, a member of the Protestant Church Executive Committee, Clerical Vice-President of the Old Prussian Church since 1927, and head of the German branch of the World Alliance for International Friendship Through the Churches (hereafter, World Alliance), was also constantly in contact with foreign Church leaders.[1] When the president of the Alliance, Lord Dickinson, asked Burghart for his opinion on antisemitic discrimination and attacks in Germany, Burghart responded on 25 May that it was unnecessary "to fear that Germany would jeopardize world peace;" Germany wanted peace, as Hitler had

---

1. Georg Burghart, from 1927 the "Clerical Vice-President and *Oberdomprediger*" (Canon), retired in May 1933 at his own request; Baum and Grünzinger, eds., *Personenlexikon*, 49. German religious leaders were also active in the World Alliance for International Friendship Through the Churches, founded in 1914. In 1933, the English Church leader Willoughby Dickinson was president of the Alliance. The Alliance's German National Council sent eight members to the international Council, including Professor Friedrich Siegmund-Schultze, Berlin; former Reich Supreme Court president (*Reichsgerichtspräsident*) Walter Simons; and, as Youth Secretary, Dietrich Bonhoeffer. See Armin Boyens, *Kirchenkampf und Ökumene 1933–1939* (Munich: Kaiser, 1969), 17–18.

Before the Holocaust: Antisemitic Violence and the Reaction of German Elites and Institutions during the Nazi Takeover.
Hermann Beck, Oxford University Press. © Hermann Beck 2022. DOI: 10.1093/oso/9780192865076.003.0012

demonstrated in his recent speech on 17 May.[2] Danger could arise only "if Jews and Marxists sow strife and dissension." As far as the position of the Church on the "Jewish Question" was concerned, the president of the Church Executive Committee, Hermann Kapler, would soon put together a definitive commentary.[3] According to Burghart and the World Alliance's German Committee, "pushing back against the dominant Jewish influence on the culture and general outlook of the German people is imperative and justified by the Gospel." When judging the overall situation, Burghart continued, one should bear in mind that "we have experienced a unique revolution...which the best among the people and especially those of Christian outlook perceive as a great liberation from unprecedented domestic gloom."[4] This heartfelt defense of the "national revolution" by the 68-year-old Burghart and his assertion about "the necessity of pushing back against the dominant Jewish influence" are symptomatic of the mindset of the Church leadership. The injustice suffered by hundreds of thousands of Jewish Germans, many of whom had sacrificed much for their country and served it well during the First World War, does not even figure in this equation.

At the seat of the World Alliance in Geneva and also among foreign Churches it was well known that German Church leaders closed their eyes to what had been going on in Germany in March and early April 1933. But even though the facts were well known, out of consideration for what was seen as the precarious political predicament of the German Protestant Church, criticism was held in check.[5] There were some within the international ecumenical movement, such as the Swiss professor

---

2. 25 May 1933 at EZA Berlin, Bestand 51, E2e8,1, Politische Weltbundkorrespondenz. Hitler's foreign policy speech of 17 May 1933 was a masterpiece of political demagoguery; even SPD representatives applauded it. On Burghart's letter, see also Boyens, *Kirchenkampf*, 204.

3. 25 May 1933 at EZA Berlin, E2e8,1, fol. 3 of the letter. On Kapler's memorandum, see the section "The Memorandum on the Judenfrage" below.

4. Ibid., fols. 3–4.

5. 4 April 1933 at EZA Berlin, Bestand 51, E2e8,1, Politische Weltbundkorrespondenz. The French clergyman Jules Jézéquel wrote to the General Secretary of the Alliance, Henry-Louis Henriod: "The Churches in Germany, to judge by Dr. Kapler's telegram, appear to deny that there has been persecution of Jews in their country. I do not hide from you that such a viewpoint seems to us quite outrageous."

Adolf Keller, General Secretary of the European Center for Church Aid (Europäische Zentralstelle für *Kirchliche Hilfsaktionen*), who insisted that Germany's Churches issue a declaration about the boycott. But overall, the attitude of World Alliance leaders was divided.[6] On 7 April, General Secretary Henri-Louis Henriod even requested of the French representative, Pastor Jules Jézéquel, that French Churches first contact German Church authorities before issuing a declaration on antisemitic transgressions, since German Churches found themselves in a difficult situation. He was aware of the danger, on the one hand, that German Church leaders might be compelled to declare their solidarity with their government in the face of foreign interference; on the other hand, if no declaration was issued, they may assume that the "Christian conscience" of other countries countenanced the discriminatory measures passed by the German government.[7]

Thus, different factors, partly political and partly tactical in nature, coincided and had the effect that foreign Churches exhibited excessive restraint and failed to put pressure on German Protestants to speak out. The true mindset of the leaders of German Protestantism was partly misunderstood abroad, since fear was not the sole reason that the German Churches held back on protests against Nazi violence and antisemitic legislation. Their reserve was also due to the fact that they largely agreed with the legal measures, as well as with certain aims of National Socialist antisemitism as expressed in March and April 1933. On 18 and 19 April Henri-Louis Henriod spent two days in Berlin, where he met for talks with German Church leaders, including Kapler, Burghart, Dibelius, and the young Dietrich Bonhoeffer. Henriod wrote down the impressions he gathered during his visit in a detailed memorandum that

---

6. 7 April 1933 at EZA Berlin, Bestand 51, E2e8,1, Politische Weltbundkorrespondenz, fol. 2 of the letter. On 7 April 1933 Henriod wrote to Jézéquel that Keller "insists on the need for a declaration by the Churches in Germany concerning the boycott of Jews."
7. Ibid., fol. 3 of the letter. "Il me paraît y avoir d'une part, le danger de les forcer, en quelque sorte, de l'extérieur à se solidariser avec leur Gouvernement, ce qui serait tragique, d'autre part, par le silence, à leur faire croire que la conscience chrétienne des autres pays comprend et approuve des mesures de discrimination qui semblent devoir être adoptées par les autorités actuelles d'Allemagne."

he forwarded to other international dignitaries of the Church.[8] Henriod's report reveals that, while he understood the gravity of the situation that had arisen due to the establishment of the dictatorship and the concomitant centralization of the State, he also incorporated, in part, the political perspective of his German interlocutors and framed his report accordingly. In reviewing the situation in Germany, he adopted the argumentation patterns of German Church leaders with regard to anti-Jewish Reich legislation and faithfully recounted the rationalizations of conservative Protestants. These included bemoaning the large number of "Ostjuden" immigrants, who then "quickly gained great influence within communist and socialist parties," and the "predominant Jewish influence" in public service positions, law courts, hospitals, institutions of higher learning, social services, and the press: "Moral decline and corruption in the public service sector are said to be due largely to the destructive influence of Jews, and socialism and communism, where they play a dominant role."[9]

The reader of Henriod's report is thus under the impression that, based on what were conveyed as facts in the report, the German Churches had little inclination to protest against antisemitic measures. He goes on to advise caution "in view of the danger of reprisals by a revolution intoxicated with triumphant frenzy such as Germany has never seen before." And Henriod counsels the Churches of other countries not to form rash judgments about the situation in Germany and the silence of German Churches; to have confidence in Christians in Germany and to exert discretion in their correspondence with its representatives; and to base public declarations only on strictly proven facts. According to Henriod, attacks on Germany or on German Churches could have only negative repercussions.[10]

---

8. See Boyens, Kirchenkampf, 51–52; on the memorandum: 291–295; 440–445. Henriod's report about his visit to Berlin is classified as "strictly confidential."
9. Boyens, Kirchenkampf, 293. Henriod also mentioned that the average age of senior Church administrators was 64 years.
10. Boyens, Kirchenkampf, 295.

Henriod's appeal to foreign Churches for prudence and understanding regarding silence on the part of German Protestants about antisemitic discrimination undoubtedly helped World Alliance members to justify the inactivity of German Church leaders at a time when the Protestant Church leadership knew quite well what was really going on. On 31 March, for example, *Oberkonsistorialrat* August Wilhelm Schreiber noted: "D. Nuelson and I stayed from half past four until a quarter to six in the German branch of the Alliance. News came in about various attacks and mistreatments. D. Burghart pointed out that one must never forget the larger context in which these deplorable events occurred. I supported him in this."[11] And Hermann Kapler had been informed in a letter from Henriod dated 5 April that more than three thousand Jewish refugees from Germany had crossed the border into Switzerland by the beginning of April.[12] Ignorance can certainly not be used as an excuse. The "larger context" of which Burghart spoke illuminates the mode of reasoning of the Protestant Church leadership: "foreign infiltration," discrimination against the non-Jewish German population by the alleged Jewish monopolization of the professions, "moral decay," and a general decline in public morality—all factors that Henriod had listed in his memorandum—were frequently used to justify and excuse antisemitic attacks. Henriod completely failed to understand that it was also the grateful approval of the "accomplishments" of the national revolution and strong mental reservations about German Jews in general that were behind the silence of the Church leadership and not primarily fear of the new regime.

This is not to say that there were no protests at all or that such protests would have been free of risk. The case of Friedrich Siegmund-Schultze (1885–1969), Professor of Youth Welfare and Social Pedagogy in Berlin since 1926, clearly shows the risks involved in active dissent. Siegmund-Schultze complained to *Oberkonsistorialrat* Schreiber on 6 April that

11. August Wilhelm Schreiber (1867–1945), *Oberkonsistorialrat* and *Ökumenenreferent* from 1925 to 1933 in the *Kirchenbundesamt* (Federal Church Office) in Berlin; a member of the Protestant Mission Committee. Baum and Grünziner, eds., *Personenlexikon*, 228.
12. Boyens, *Kirchkampf*, 43.

Church leaders who voiced comforting and mollifying statements about the current situation in Germany barely believed those justifications themselves. He accordingly collected material for *Die Eiche*, the journal he edited, "so that we can provide our foreign friends with certain information on the situation in Germany," also with reference to anti-semitic attacks.[13] Siegmund-Schultze was arrested on 21 June and expelled from Germany because of aid to Jews in ninety-three cases.[14]

A public lecture presented by the German delegation of the World Alliance in Basel on the occasion of a meeting between French and German members of the organization shows to what extent German Protestantism was in agreement with the new State. The lecture encompasses the range of arguments in support of the National Socialist revolution, presented here as a synopsis of key points and justifications.[15] First, the threat to "the Christian culture of Germany," the erosion of any kind of authority, and the "spirit of inflammatory agitation, insubordination, and unruliness" are emphasized in stark colors. The specter of communism rattled at the gates: "Suicide in the face of communism was for many the only alternative."[16] The Church was powerless. Then Hitler came and saved the people from great suffering. He led Germans out of terrible self-alienation back to their true inner nature, for "the raiment of democracy was as ill-fitting for the German people as Saul's armor would have been for David."[17] Now the country was once again guided by the leadership principle, which was in sync with its inner makeup: "The German people are filled with touching blind confidence; they want a man at the top in whom they can confide, in whom they can believe: this

---

13. Boyens, *Kirchenkampf*, 45. When Schreiber heard about this, he was clearly alarmed and wrote to Kapler on 8 April: "Professor Siegmund-Schultze, with his investigations and eventual reports, causes me no end of worry;" ibid. On Siegmund-Schultze, see Baum and Grünzinger, eds., *Personenlexikon*, 237–238.
14. Boyens, *Kirchenkampf*, 45; John L. Conway, "Between Pacifism and Patriotism. A Protestant Dilemma: The Case of Friedrich Sigmund- Schultze," in Francis R. Nikosia and Lawrence D. Stokes, eds., *Germans against Nazism. Nonconformity, Opposition and Resistance in the Third Reich. Essays in Honor of Peter Hoffmann*, rev. ed. (Oxford and New York: Berghahn, 2015), 87–114. Siegmund-Schultze, his wife, and four children were expelled from Germany.
15. 8 and 9 June 1933 at EZA Berlin, Bestand 51, E2e8,1, Politische Weltbundkorrespondenz.
16. Ibid., fol. 1.   17. Ibid., fol. 3.

man will provide us with what is needed."[18] One could therefore not reproach the Church if it endorses "what other peoples have had for centuries: unity." With respect to the "Jewish Question," the emphasis was still on maintaining institutional independence from the consequences of racial ideology—the Church vehemently refused "to turn Jesus Christ into an Aryan." But there was no concerted effort to protect Jewish Germans, and racial ideology itself was minimized and ultimately rationalized: all that talk about the Nordic-Germanic race that was now so prominently characterized as the *"Edelrasse,"* the German delegation emphasized, should be seen as a reaction to "the disgrace and shame" that the German people had to endure. The Hitler movement had rekindled a sense of honor in the nation. The lecture reiterates the German delegation's assumption that the German Protestant Church could participate in the set of political goals put forth by National Socialism while retaining its institutional and theological independence. The expectation that the Church could successfully engage in such a precarious balancing act would soon turn out to be fatefully misguided.[19]

The Protestant Churches under Pressure: Prelude to the 26 April Meeting

Despite the restraint foreign Churches exerted with regard to the stubborn silence of German Church leaders, a number of urgent requests were sent to the Federal Church Office in Berlin: Henriod had asked Kapler for his opinion about the 1 April boycott a few days before his journey to Berlin on 4 April; the *Fédération protestante de Belgique* requested from Kapler that the Protestant Church support Jews in Germany; on 6 April the *Fédération des Eglises et Associations Protestantes de Genève* joined in with this request; on 10 April, the Council of Dutch Churches for Practical Christianity also wrote to Kapler, with the Association of

18. Ibid., fol. 4.   19. Ibid., fol. 4.

Protestant Congregations of Portugal following suit on 11 April. And on 20 April the Executive Committee of the World Alliance requested a report from Kapler for its meeting on 9 May.[20] In addition to these official requests for policy clarifications, there were further recommendations and open letters to large foreign newspapers by leading Church personalities abroad and "well-known dignitaries of the ecumenical movement," so that, taken as a whole, there was considerable pressure on Kapler and the Church leadership to finally issue a decisive statement.[21]

It was for this reason that, at long last, two separate meetings were scheduled for 25 and 26 April 1933. The first was to deal with the reorganization of the Church; the second with the *"Judenfrage."* Yet, in the days preceding these scheduled meetings, two events took place that decisively shaped developments. First, there was the attempted *Gleichschaltung* of the Mecklenburg *Landeskirche* in Schwerin. At 8:00 a.m. on 22 April members of the Mecklenburg *Oberkirchenrat* (Superior Church Council) were informed by Schwerin's National Socialist *Ministerpräsident*, Walter Granzow, that a commissar had been appointed for the Mecklenburg Church "for the purpose of coordinating the administration of the Church with the government of the *Land* and Reich."[22] At this point, neither the leadership of the Mecklenburg Church nor the Federal Church Office in Berlin knew that this was an isolated, albeit well-planned, action on the part of Granzow.[23] The Church leadership had to assume that this was just the beginning of a larger concerted action that would result in the *Gleichschaltung* of all Protestant *Landeskirchen.* In view of this seemingly dire threat, it is not surprising to see the determination and resolve with which the leadership of the Church protested the measure, not only with

---

20. Boyens, *Kirchenkampf*, 43–44.   21. Ibid., 44.

22. This was part of a well-coordinated preconceived operation. See Scholder, *Kirchen und Drittes Reich*, 380; 428–429. On the NSDAP in Mecklenburg, see Beate Behrens, *Mit Hitler zur Macht. Aufstieg des NS in Mecklenburg und Lübeck 1922–1933* (Rostock: Neuer Hochschul-Schriften Verlag, 1998).

23. Granzow, a Mecklenburg farmer, was encouraged in his move by Walter Darré, who had been Reich Farmers' leader (*Reichsbauernführer*) since 4 April 1933. On the run-up to this operation, see Scholder, *Kirchen und Drittes Reich*, 379–380; 427–428.

Interior Minister Frick and Hindenburg, but even with Hitler.[24] The Mecklenburg Bishop Heinrich Rendtorff immediately wrote a letter of protest to Granzow, which he then passed on to the press for publication.[25] Hitler, who had not been informed of the action, disapproved of the operation as soon as he heard about the protests and quickly instructed his Interior Minister Frick to find a solution that would permit all parties concerned to save face. The designated commissar for the Mecklenburg state Church resigned shortly thereafter on 27 April.[26] In late April, Hitler still had other plans for the Church. He hoped to amalgamate the Protestant *Landeskirchen* into one united Reich Church with the help of his spokesman, the Protestant *Wehrkreispfarrer* Ludwig Müller, who was close to the NSDAP.[27]

Indirectly, the Mecklenburg incident had repercussions for the Church as a whole, since on 22 April Kapler still had reason to fear that the *Gleichschaltung* of the entire Protestant Church was imminent. Under the Damocles sword of the Mecklenburg action, Kapler therefore decided to preempt a possible *Gleichschaltung* by the State through swift reform from within the Church. He and Johannes Hosemann, the Director of the *Kirchenbundesamt* (Federal Church Office), immediately telephoned the two theologians who had been selected to report on the intended *Reichsreform* of the Church—the Lutheran Bishop of Hanover, August Marahrens, and the Reformed Elberfeld pastor Hermann Albert Hesse.[28] Both spontaneously agreed to take on responsibility for a reform of the

---

24. On Kapler's protests, see BA Berlin, R 43 II, no. 161, "Evangelische Kirche," fols. 23–30.
25. 22 April 1933, 26 April 1933 at LHA Schwerin 5.12–1/1, no. 517.
26. Scholder, *Kirchen und Drittes Reich*, 429 (2000); 381 (1977); Kretschmar and Nicolaisen, eds., *Dokumente*, vol. I, 37–41. A detailed depiction of the Mecklenburg events is also found in Rendtorff's report at the beginning of the Church Executive Committee meeting of 25 April 1933; see 25 April 1933 at EZA Berlin, Bestand 1, no. 2411, "Niederschrift der Verhandlungen...," fols. 3–6.
27. Up until the autumn of 1933 it seemed as though he might be successful. In any case, Hitler wanted to avoid annoying the Reich President, who had also intervened in the Mecklenburg affair through his State Secretary, Otto Meissner. Müller was a military chaplain in East Prussia.
28. Scholder, *Kirchen und Drittes Reich*, 432 (2000); 383 (1977). Johannes Hosemann (1881–1947), Director of the Protestant Federal Office (*Kirchenbundesamt*); Baum and Grünzinger, eds., *Personenlexikon*, 117.

Church together with Kapler. The next day, 23 April, Kapler appealed to Church leaders to begin the unification process without delay, which, in turn, sparked a series of affirmative declarations from Protestants throughout Germany.[29] With his public appeal, Kapler intended to forestall further *Gleichschaltung* measures, such as the one threatened in Mecklenburg, as well as possible preemptive moves by the German Christians. At the same time, he was resolved to preserve the independence of the *Landeskirchen* and to salvage intact their own current confession of the Protestant faith (*Bekenntnisstand*)—Lutheran, Reformed, or Uniate—as they were incorporated into a new unified Church administrative structure.

The second event was Kapler's meeting with Hitler, initially scheduled for 8 April, but then postponed to 25 April, just hours before the important Executive Committee meeting on that same day.[30] In the meeting, Kapler then recounted in detail his discussion with Hitler. Two of the Church leaders present took copious notes, so that we know what transpired between Hitler and the Executive Committee's president, that is, at least Kapler's version of events.[31] First, the attempted takeover in Mecklenburg was broached, with Kapler emphasizing that the State must not involve itself in Church affairs, while Hitler asserted that he was interested mostly in having one coherent Protestant bloc as a counterweight to the Catholic Church. At this point, Kapler was able to

---

29. Scholder, *Kirchen und Drittes Reich*, 432 (2000); 383 (1977). Kapler's appeal ran as follows: "The hour demands the immediate launching of a reform of the constitution of German Protestantism. The goal of the reform is the [creation of a] United German Protestant Church, built on the foundation and under the full observance of the confession of faith." This reform should "grow out of vital, functioning Landeskirchen" and retain their full authority. It was precisely because of these factors—the observance of the confession of faith and the rights of the *Landeskirchen*—that every previous meaningful union of *Landeskirchen* failed. The various Lutheran, Reformed, and Uniate *Landeskirchen* jealously safeguarded their respective *Bekenntnisstand* (confessional status), and politicians were reluctant to enforce unity (just as Bismarck had been in 1866).

30. Hitler had delayed the meeting, since he wanted to first speak with Ludwig Müller; Kretschmar and Nicolaisen, eds., *Dokumente*, 39, n. 9.

31. Johannes Kübel and Wilhelm von Pechmann each took very detailed notes, which, on several points, corresponded verbatim. Scholder, *Kirchen und Drittes Reich*, 433–435; 896–897 (2000); 384–386; 810–811 (1977).

explain that the Protestant *Landeskirchen* were already on the verge of forming a cohesive union. Through his agreement with Marahrens and Hesse, and by virtue of his appeal of 23 April, Kapler had indeed anticipated any further *Gleichschaltung* measures through a kind of Church revolution from above.[32] Despite all the pleas and exhortations from foreign Churches, Kapler did not even mention the *"Judenfrage"* in his one-and-a-half-hour meeting with Hitler. Through informants from inside the Church, Hitler undoubtedly knew that this issue was on the agenda for the meeting of 26 April. He had finely honed sensibilities for such omissions and could thus safely assume (given that the head of the Church Executive Committee clearly did not want to disrupt the atmosphere by touching on this controversial subject) that this particular issue would not constitute a major problem in the relationship of his regime with the Protestant Church.

Church Leaders on the *"Judenfrage:"* Opinions and Comments

Every participant at the 26 April meeting received two mimeographed commentaries, each about three pages in length, on "The Church and the Jewish Question in Germany" and "The Protestant Church and its Judeo-Christians [Jews who converted to Protestantism]" as additional information.[33] "The Church and the Jewish Question in Germany" starts out with the theme of the "preponderance of Jewish influence" and then quickly comes to the conclusion that the new regulations in the April antisemitic legislation had "the character of a protective measure to safeguard the German people."[34] Then the focus shifts to the "obligation

32. According to Pechmann, Kapler mentioned that Hitler had first learned through Müller that there were twenty-eight *Landeskirchen*. On similar events on the state level in the Hamburg *Landeskirche*, see Hering, "Collegiality," 287–293.
33. The latter text had been prepared by the Baden *Landeskirche*; the former by Walter Künneth. Smid, *Deutscher Protestantismus*, 364–372.
34. 26 April 1933 at EZA Berlin, Bestand 1, no. 2411, Anlage 2, fol. 1.

of the Church" for its baptized Judeo-Christians, which seems to indicate their inclusion in the Church and thus calls for a "gradation of legislation" that would "differentiate between Jews and Judeo-Christians."[35] The State should be reminded to make a difference between Judeo-Christians who had converted to Christianity before 1914 "and those Jews who had immigrated since the November revolution."[36] It thus comes as no surprise when the argument is made that "unconditional Christian love that is not dependent on the national-political situation" should turn first and foremost to "the suffering Judeo-Christians as those nearest to our congregation." Finally, it is emphasized that "the Church should object to...any kind of violent persecution of Jews,"[37] without taking into consideration that there might be a connection between "the new regulations" and the violent attacks that preceded them. This draft commentary would not be discussed in the meeting and had little impact on its outcome, even though the call for further religious differentiation in State legislation was frequently made.

The second commentary, "The Protestant Church and its Judeo-Christians," is also revealing as to the mindset of parts of the Church leadership. It begins with an enumeration of oppression and inequities committed against Germans after World War I, concluding that "The propaganda of hatred against Germans from Prague to Memel creates a history of our nation written with blood and tears."[38] The antisemitic legislation of April 1933 is rationalized as "self-protection and preservation of one's own kind" and compared with the expulsions of Germans after World War I, when "hundreds of thousands of Germans...with ruthless brutality, deprived of their belongings, and their material existence, were driven back ruined into our Fatherland, merely because they

---

35. Ibid., fol. 2.
36. Ibid., fol. 3. As a reason for this it was mentioned that the "tight bond between the Christian faith and Germanness... [had brought] the Judeo-Christians into a close relationship with the German people and German culture."
37. Ibid., fol. 3.
38. 26 April at EZA Berlin, Bestand 1, no. 2411, Anlage 3, fol. 1.

were German."[39] This direct equation of two very different kinds of injustices, whereas to most contemporaries the expulsion of Germans was seen as far more iniquitous, thus serves as a central excuse for the hesitant attitude of the Church.[40] In the spring of 1933 one frequently encounters this pattern of argumentation, and the identification of two very different sets of constituent facts was widely accepted. During the implacable struggle of the First World War, which had ended less than fifteen years previously, contemporary Germans acquired the habit of thinking in "friend or foe" antagonisms, and the general political discourse was suffused with terms such as *"artfremd"* ("alien to our kind"), *"nichtdeutsche Elemente"* ("non-German elements"), and *"andersrassige Elemente"* ("members of a foreign race").[41] Contemporaries constantly heard and read tales of how badly Germans were treated in the Sudetenland, of mistreatment in (now Polish) West Prussia, of expropriated property in the former German colonies and in North and Central America, and of expulsions from the Alsace, so that these arguments did not fall on deaf ears. Even this second Commentary came to the conclusion that the Church should protect her "Protestant brothers of foreign race," though it was expected that "these, our fellow Christians of foreign race, should earnestly attempt to shed their characteristics inherited by their fathers that are alien to Germany, assimilate into our

39. Ibid. Many driven out of the Alsace after 1918 settled in neighboring Baden. This draft was prepared by officials of the Baden *Landeskirche*, many of whom had witnessed the expulsions.
40. On the "Expulsion and Deprivation of Rights of Germans" from Alsace-Lorraine, West Prussia, Upper Silesia (after 1921) and the Memel area, see David Allen Harvey, "Lost Children or Enemy Aliens? Classifying the Population of Alsace after the First World War," *Journal of Contemporary History*, 34:4 (1999), 537–554; Richard Blanke, *Orphans of Versailles: The Germans in Western Poland, 1918–1939* (Lexington: University of Kentucky Press, 2014); Hans Lukaschek, "The Germans in Polish Upper Silesia," in Otto Eduard Lessing, ed., *Minorities and Boundaries* (Dordrecht: Springer, 1931), 96–108; Martin Broszat, "Aussen- und innenpolitische Aspekte der preußisch-deutschen Minderheitenpolitik in der Ära Stresemann," in Kurt Kluxen and Theodor Schieder, eds., *Politische Ideologien und nationalstaatliche Ordnung* (Munich: Oldenbourg, 1968), 393–445; Ingo Esser, *"Volk, Staat, Gott!" Die deutsche Minderheit in Polen und ihr Schulwesen 1918–1939* (Wiesbaden: Otto Harrassowitz, 2010).
41. In this context see Thomas Pegalow Kaplan, *The Language of Nazi Genocide. Linguistic Violence and the Struggle of Germans of Jewish Ancestry* (Cambridge: Cambridge University Press, 2009), 58–102.

Volkstum, and observe a prudent restraint in public life."[42] Yet the observation was also made that, "In their understandable grief they ask for a word of ours – their Church, whose silence would be incomprehensible to them."[43] It is quite possible that it was this sentence that moved Kapler to rule out the entire draft in the meeting of 26 April with the words, "The Baden draft appears to me not to be appropriate, especially since a reduction of the problem to the Judeo-Christians is not legitimate."[44] Acceptance of the Baden draft would have necessitated concrete action.

In the Church Executive Committee meeting of 25 April, which followed Kapler's meeting with Hitler, Kapler received an unlimited mandate to act in the name of the Church as he saw fit.[45] At the beginning of the meeting Bishop Heinrich Rendtorff reported extensively on a local Nazi Party's attempt to "coordinate" the Mecklenburg Church with National Socialist policy and reassured those present at the meeting that "the Reich in no way stood behind these measures."[46] In the ensuing discussions on bestowing full powers on Kapler to act in the name of the Church, it quickly became evident that the vast majority of the (forty-four) Church leaders present supported the "idea of the Reich Church," that is, a program of centralization that had been at the top of the official Church's agenda since the Reich Congress of German Christians in early April. In mid-April, the (by then already retired) *Generalsuperintendent* of the Westphalian Church, Wilhelm Zöllner, had publicly called for the creation of a "Protestant Church of the German Nation." This attracted widespread attention and forced the hand of the official Church to react in some way.[47] The assembled Church leaders thus found themselves under considerable pressure to implement a union of the twenty-eight

42. 26 April 1933 at EZA Berlin, Bestand 1, no. 2411, Anlage 3, fols. 1–2.
43. Ibid.   44. EZA Berlin, Bestand 1, no. 2411, fol. 15.
45. 25 April 1933 at EZA Berlin, Bestand 1, no. 2411, 12 folios. This meeting focused on matters of organization.
46. 25 April at EZA Berlin, Bestand 1, no. 2411, "Niederschrift der Verhandlungen . . . ," fols. 3–6. He mentioned that the German Christian group had nothing to do with the matter: "Their theologians have strongly protested." Ibid., fol. 6.
47. Wilhelm Zöllner (1860–1937); Baum and Grünzinger, eds., *Personenlexikon,* 284; Wright, *Parteien,* 200.

Landeskirchen, as otherwise the State might step in and bring it about by forcible means, which might well mean that the Church would lose its independence and room for maneuver to make its own decisions. August Marahrens, the Hanover *Landesbischof*, undoubtedly spoke for many when he maintained that "among Protestant congregations there is a powerful longing for one [united] Church."[48] This desire on the part of many Protestants neatly dovetailed with the drive toward unity, centralization, and standardization of the new regime that was part of the National Socialist *Gleichschaltung* policy, as documented in the laws for the coordination of the German *Länder* with the Reich of 31 March and 7 April.[49] Alone among the assembled Church leaders, Wilhelm von Pechmann spoke out against giving Kapler an unrestricted mandate. While asserting that he trusted Kapler, Pechmann doubted his ability to resist Nazi pressure: "Who can guarantee the freedom of the Church, when thousand-year-old rights of the *Länder* are swept away with the stroke of a pen?"[50] But Pechmann remained the lone skeptic. Under the compelling force of events, the remainder of those assembled agreed to give Kapler unconditional authority to act in the name of the Church. In addition to Kapler, Bishop Marahrens and the Reformed Church pastor Hermann Albert Hesse were confirmed as members of the committee charged with working out a centralizing *Reichsreform* of the Church.[51]

---

48. 25 April 1933 at EZA Berlin, Bestand 1, no. 2411, fol. 11.
49. According to the "Vorläufiges Gesetz zur Gleichschaltung der Länder mit dem Reich" of 31 March 1933, the composition of the *Länder* parliaments had to be shifted to correspond to the 5 March election results (with KPD seats eliminated). This gave the NSDAP an automatic majority. The "Zweites Gesetz zur Gleichschaltung der Länder mit dem Reich" of 7 April 1933 made provisions for the appointment of *Reichsstatthalter* to bring the policies of German states in line with those of the Reich.
50. 25 April 1933 at EZA Berlin, Bestand 1, no. 2411, fol. 9. Pechmann also argued that precipitate action might give the impression that "the Church acted under outside pressure" (i.e., pressure from the Nazi government).
51. The Thuringian *Landesbischof* Wilhelm Reichardt, who was also present, reported that during Kapler's report about his meeting with Hitler, an assistant handed him a telegram as he was making his remarks. As Kapler read it, "his hands began to shake convulsively and his usually pale face became ashen." In the telegram Hitler apparently demanded that Ludwig Müller should be brought into the three-person committee (Kapler, Marahrens, and Hesse) as the fourth man to work out a constitution for a future Reich Church; Scholder, *Kirchen und Drittes Reich*, 384–385 (1977). Scholder rejects Kretschmar's version that

Throughout the meeting Kapler showed himself to be a shrewd tactician with a sure instinct for getting what he wanted and cleverly directing opinions in such a way that his mandate remained unrestricted. He masterminded the course of discussion and knew how to nip critical inquiries in the bud. According to Klaus Scholder, the greatest authority on the Protestant Church in these critical years, no other Church leader equaled Kapler in reputation and influence.[52] As one of the politically more moderate conservative Church leaders who supported Hindenburg's re-election in 1932 against Hitler and the German National candidate Duesterberg, Kapler could be expected to stand up to direct NSDAP strong-arm tactics to undermine Church independence. When Wilhelm Kube, the Nazi patron of the German Christians, in his opening speech at the German Christian Reich Congress on 3 April, threatened to use State power in the field of Church policy, Kapler immediately launched a written protest with the Prussian Ministry of Culture. Yet, despite his distance to National Socialism, Kapler concurred with some of the basic tenets of the national revolution: the renewed emphasis on pride in the nation, the fight against "materialism" (anathema to most Church leaders as a hallmark of Weimar democracy), and the general trend toward a more "unified formation of the will of the nation," as it was put in the jargon of the time.[53] If Kapler had favored an official statement by the Church in support of the persecuted Jewish minority, it would have been passed. Why Kapler avoided taking a stand—whether for the purely tactical reasons of not offending an increasingly popular and powerful regime and protecting the position of the Church, or for personal reasons stemming from his own beliefs and orientations concerning the Jewish part of the German population, mixed with a "cultural antisemitism"

Hitler had broken the news of Müller's appointment as his authorized representative during his meeting with Kapler; Kretschmar and Nicolaisen, eds., *Dokumente*, vol. I, 39, n. 9.

---

52. As Scholder wrote in connection with Kapler's resignation on 8 June 1933, there was no one who came close to him in terms of standing, prestige, and influence; Scholder, *Kirchen und Drittes Reich*, 442 (1977); 497 (2000).

53. See also Wright, *Parteien*, 189.

(shared with several of the more conservative Church leaders, including Dibelius)—cannot be stated with certainty. In the decisive Church Executive Committee meeting of 26 April that focused exclusively on the issue of the *"Judenfrage,"* Kapler asserted that he had felt "heavy pangs of conscience" about some of the measures taken by the new government. In his meeting with Hitler's Undersecretary of State Lammers on 8 April, he had emphasized in the same vein that "the planned legislation against non-Aryan civil servants, lawyers, and doctors weighs heavily on the Christian conscience."[54] On the other hand, Kapler openly affirmed during the meeting of 26 April that the State "was justified and obliged to take protective measures for our *Volkstum,* given that the German nation is increasingly jeopardized by the economic, political, and cultural advances of the *Judentum.*"[55] In its unambiguous clarity this sentence goes well beyond anything that might be seen as a mere concession to the new government. It was thus probably no accident that Kapler was "absent due to official duties" at the beginning of the all-decisive 26 April meeting and unable to hear Pechmann's passionate plea to the Church leadership, demanding that they drop their reserve and issue a proclamation "on behalf of the persecuted Jewish minority."[56]

The entire session of 26 April was devoted to the discussion of the *"Judenfrage."* For weeks prior to the meeting, Pechmann had been urging the Church leadership to finally speak out. Since he himself had the opening word and would use it for a beseeching recommendation in favor of a public statement by the Church, Kapler knew quite well that it was easier to thwart Pechmann's effort and oppose it if he were not present at the beginning of the meeting. The meeting started

54. 26 April 1933 at EZA Berlin, Bestand 1, no. 2411, "Auf der Tagesordnung steht die Behandlung der Judenfrage," fols. 13–17, esp. 14; Johannes Kübel, *Erinnerungen: Mensch und Christ, Theologe, Pfarrer und Kirchenmann,* ed. Martha Frommer (Villingen-Schwenningen: Selbstverlag, 1973), 89; Wright, *Parteien,* 93, n. 43.
55. 26 April 1933 at EZA Berlin, Bestand 1, no. 2411, fol. 14.
56. Ibid., fol. 13. From the original, unedited minutes of the *Kirchenausschuss* meeting of 26 April it becomes clear that Pechmann's comments were significantly shortened and "smoothed over" for the final summary. See 26 April 1933 at EZA Berlin, Bestand 1, no. 3210, "Kirchenkanzlei, Sitzung des DEKA," fols. 271v.–276.

auspiciously. All participants had a copy of Pechmann's planned petition, affirming that

> the Protestant Church continues to regard its members of Jewish back-ground as her own, feels with them, and continues to support them to the limits of what is practically possible. The Church Executive Committee also feels compelled to direct a word of Christian exhortation to the powers of State not to disregard the laws of justice and Christian love in the remedy of justified wrongs.[57]

While the latter phrase was a concession to the zeitgeist, Pechmann depicted the situation without mincing words: "Cries for help from people with Jewish ancestors who have become convinced Christians" had reached him. They were marked by "deep inner pain" and should not be abandoned "without a word in this hour of terrible suffering."[58] With unsparing bluntness he addressed the Church's recent defense of govern-ment behavior:

> I ask you, gentlemen, whether among all our friends abroad – we don't have many – there is one who would not turn away in disgust when confronted with the injustices committed here against Jews. Nothing is easier than to reproach other countries with their own wrongdoings... what has been happening here would be unthinkable in any other civil-ized state.

Such unusually forthright and self-critical words were rarely uttered in Church meetings. In the official version of the minutes that was sent to the *Landeskirchen* on 26 July they were omitted. They survived only in the draft version of the initial unedited protocol.[59] Pechmann's next sentence also fell victim to the censors: "I have the feeling that our Church will

---

57. 26 April 1933 at EZA Berlin, Bestand 1, no. 2411, fols. 13–17, esp. 14.
58. 26 April 1933 at EZA Berlin, Bestand 1, no. 2411, fol. 13.
59. See the original, unedited text of the minutes, 26 April 1933 at EZA Berlin, Bestand 1, no. 3210, fol. 272. In the "smoothed over" summary, which was sent to Church Executive Committee members and the senior authorities of the *Landeskirchen* only on 26 July 1933—that is, after significant changes in the political situation—this sentence was omitted. See 26 April 1933 at EZA Berlin Bestand 1, no. 2411, fol. 13.

have to be ashamed of itself if it does not finally express a sincere consoling word of protection on behalf of its own loyal members."[60] Up to now, the Church had failed to make such a statement: "It would be irresponsible if the Executive Committee disbands without having spoken such a word."[61]

Pechmann's powerful and unvarnished indictment fell on deaf ears. Despite some meaningless concessions,[62] the initial discussion revealed that the general mood of the assembly was vehemently opposed to Pechmann's petition. The first four speakers raised strong objections to a public statement, using the stock-in-trade arguments of conservative Church leaders. Klaus Wurth, president of Baden's Protestant Church, deplored that "in this way people who have adopted the Christian faith are expelled from the people's community," but his doubts and misgivings prevailed, given "that there has been a foreign infiltration of the most terrible kind in certain professions."[63] With this he implied that Jewish Germans who had lived in the country for centuries were now considered "foreign." *Oberkonsistorialrat* Hans Wahl, who was to be the main collaborator in Kapler's official memorandum on the *"Judenfrage,"* which would be sent to foreign Churches in June, downplayed the urgency of taking action by pointing out that foreign Church interventions ran the gamut from merely reflecting public opinion in their countries to "more or less clear protests." A matter-of-fact memorandum regarding the origins of and solutions to the "Jewish problem," soon to be composed, would ostensibly satisfy foreign Churches. The Berlin theology professor Arthur Titius contended that the opinion of foreign countries should be disregarded; for him, "the disclosure of figures regarding Jewish infiltration has occasioned ... a strong inner transformation," so that he

60. EZA Berlin, Bestand 1, no. 3210, fols. 272–272v. After participants had decided to remain silent about Nazi crimes, this sentence was also stricken from the official meeting minutes.
61. 26 April 1933 at EZA Berlin, Bestand 1, no. 2411, fol. 13.
62. Church Executive Committee member Professor Arthur Titius (1864–1936) said that it went without saying that "one should accommodate Judeo-Christians when possible, and that one should demonstrate Christian love, as expressed by Freiherr von Pechmann." Ibid., fol. 14.
63. Klaus Wurth (1861–1948); see also Baum and Grünzinger, eds., *Personenlexikon*, 280–281.

could never endorse a public statement. He also opposed privileged treatment for Judeo-Christians, as this might "intensify their influx into Christianity in the most fateful way."[64] Ernst Hundt, Vice President of the *Oberkirchenrat* of the Old Prussian Church (who was already a member of the NSDAP at the time of the meeting), cast doubt on whether the Church had the authority to issue a public declaration that, after all, might be misused by Germany's enemies abroad.[65] At this point Kapler rejoined the meeting. The ground had been well prepared for his comments. Kapler again professed that in his meeting with Hitler on the previous day he had not "mentioned the *Judenfrage* as such." But he had insisted that whatever State leaders "considered essential for the well-being of the people and the nation," the Church would want to see implemented with forbearance. He had not "considered [it] prudent at this first official meeting" to say more.[66] Kapler then also came out against Pechmann's petition, not only with his worn argument that Germany was being "increasingly jeopardized by the economic, political, and cultural advances of the Judentum" but also by emphasizing that "a public manifesto on the Judenfrage invokes the danger that it may be misused by foreign propaganda directed at the new Germany."[67]

With Kapler's unambiguous stand, the weighty arguments concerning potential perils for Germany's own position, and the temper of the meeting so clearly against him, Pechmann was fighting a losing battle. He did his best by reiterating the need for a public declaration and his conviction that "a grateful sigh of relief will spread through many Christian houses if the *Kirchenausschuss* speaks a courageous word dictated by conscience," but all to no avail. Doubts, second thoughts, and

---

64. EZA Berlin, Bestand 1, no. 2411, fol. 14. Titius clearly considered efforts to convert Jews to Christianity, the so-called *"Judenmission,"* a mistake.

65. Ibid., fols. 13–14. Ernst Hundt (born 1877; committed suicide on 27 April 1945); from 1929 to 1933, secular Vice President of the Protestant *Oberkirchenrat* in Berlin.

66. EZA Berlin, Bestand 1, no. 2411, fols. 14–15. In Kapler's absence the session had been chaired by Friedrich Seetzen (1868–1945), president of the Saxon Consistory, the administrative body of the Protestant Church of Saxony in Dresden. After Kapler's resignation, Seetzen became acting president of the DEKA until 1 July 1933. Baum and Grünzinger, eds., *Personenlexikon*, 235.

67. EZA Berlin, Bestand 1, no. 2411, fol. 15.

misgivings prevailed. Church leaders who spoke after Kapler also opposed a public statement. Even Johannes Kübel and Theophil Wurm, the heads of the Frankfurt and Württemberg Churches who had supported Pechmann in the past and argued along similar lines, remained silent. Pastor Walter Michaelis of Bethel went so far as to argue that nations had "misunderstood God's counsel about this people [i.e., the Jews] when they bestowed full citizenship on them." Silence was also justified, according to Michaelis, by Church leaders' interpretation of the political situation; in view of "the immense peril in which the Church currently finds itself, its tongue is tied. It is false to assume that one must always say everything at any given moment."[68]

Others followed Michaelis's expostulation; even the Mecklenburg Bishop Heinrich Rendtorff, despite the recent Nazi attempt to take over his *Landeskirche*, professed his loyalty to the new regime: the Church "gratefully acknowledges that we finally have a legitimate political authority (*Obrigkeit*) again." Besides, the *"Judenfrage"* was "the central point in the program of National Socialism."[69] For 1700 years (that is, before emancipation), Rendtorff intoned, Jews had lived in the country under special legislation with the full endorsement of the Church. The fact that this special (pre-emancipation) legislation fell by the wayside must be seen in the context of "the progress of an enlightened way of thinking" and must not be "identified with Protestant norms." Rendtorff here clearly implied that he was not opposed to a new kind of special legislation for Jews; he continued to make it clear that he rejected an "enlightened way of thinking," with its emphasis on individual rights, but instead preferred "the preponderance of the State," which pushes "to the foreground the interests of the community." Rendtorff thus rejected a public declaration on philosophical grounds. Only Rendtorff's father,

68. Ibid., fol. 15. Walter Michaelis (1866–1953), theologian and missionary. Michaelis later resigned his chairship of the Association for Community Care and Evangelization (*Gnadauer Verband*) in protest against the "Aryan clause." Baum and Grünzinger, eds., *Personenlexikon*, 174.
69. This is how it read in the original draft of the minutes (EZA Berlin, Bestand 1, no. 3210, fol. 275); for the edited version, see EZA Berlin, Bestand 1, no. 2411, fol. 16.

the Privy Church Counselor and Leipzig university professor Franz Rendtorff, who was also a member of the *Kirchenausschuss*, thought a public declaration was worth considering, given his apprehension that "due to the treatment of Jews in Germany new legislation on minorities will come into being abroad." His motivation was mainly to protect German minorities in Eastern and Southeastern Europe.[70] In the end, Pechmann's intended manifesto was referred to as "material to the president," which meant that Kapler alone could decide what to do with it. The final result was that the Protestant Church would make no public declaration against antisemitic legislation and the persecution of Jews in Germany.

It is noteworthy that it was the traditional Protestant Church leadership from the days of the Weimar Republic, led by the moderate conservative Hermann Kapler (as opposed to pro-National Socialist German Christian theologians) who decided not only to refrain from criticizing antisemitic attacks and legislation but also to justify them, despite international pressure and complaints from within the German Protestant Churches.[71] Theologians born between the 1860s and 1880s, shaped by the values of the Empire, were responsible for this momentous failure to offer protection to German Jews. Even though participants were fully aware of what was going on, there had been no open debate concerning antisemitic attacks and blatant discrimination. The discussion focused mainly on Jews who had converted to Protestantism, that is, on members of the Protestant Church. Even Pechmann's intended petition was designed primarily to help converted Jews—"[the Church's] own members of the Jewish tribe," as it was phrased in the petition. The refusal of Protestant Church leaders to countenance Pechmann's petition meant that they were not even prepared to lodge a protest on behalf of their own brethren who were members of the Protestant congregation and

---

70. EZA Berlin, Bestand 1, no. 2411, fol. 16. Franz Rendtorff (1860–1937) maintained extensive contacts after the First World War with German minorities in Rumania, Poland, and Yugoslavia; from 1916 to 1932 he led the DEKA's foreign association. Baum and Grünzinger, eds., *Personenlexikon*, 204–205.

71. Rainer Hering makes a similar point in "Collegiality."

paid Church taxes.[72] Apart from Pechmann himself, no one said a word about the suffering of the persecuted victims. The precarious position of baptized Jews is merely alluded to in vague wording. Instead, tactical considerations prevailed: the effect on foreign countries, potential repercussions for German minorities in Eastern Europe, and the possible negative implications of a protest manifesto for the current regime and Germany's reputation abroad. Old prejudices were voiced without scruples and in the certain knowledge that in the charged political climate this was not only permitted but expected. Even the emancipation of German Jews was called into question. The subliminal comparison with what was perceived as the far greater injustice committed against Germans after the First World War always resonated underneath as an extenuating circumstance. Rendtorff's remark that the "Jewish Question" was of central concern for the new government, thus making it inadvisable "to stay the hand of the secular sword," betrays tangible fear of retaliatory measures by the regime.[73] The behavior of those members of the Church Executive Committee who had received pleas for help from converted Jewish members of Landeskirchen, and thus possessed first-hand knowledge of the persecution, yet still opposed a making a public statement, defies comprehension and can hardly be excused. The Baden Landeskirche President Klaus Wurth, Hermann Kapler, and the Head of the Hamburg Landeskirche Karl Albert Horn, fall into this category; it can safely be assumed that most of those present had received similar petitions.[74] Those who had

72. In the mid-1920s income from the Church tax amounted to about 130 million Reichsmarks. It fell after that until 1933 to about 60 million Reichsmarks due to the Great Depression, and then rose again in the course of the 1930s. See "Die Finanzen der Evangelischen Kirche in Deutschland," LAKA Dresden, Bestand 36, no. 113.

73. 26. April at EZA Berlin, Bestand 1, no. 2411, fol. 15.

74. Karl Albert Horn, (1869–1942), president (Senior) of the Hamburg Landeskirche from 1929 to 1933; a DEKA member, he also participated in the World Alliance. See Heinrich Wilhelmi, Die Hamburger Kirche in der nationalsozialistischen Zeit 1933–1945. Arbeiten zur Geschichte des Kirchenkampfes, vol. 5 (Göttingen: Vandenhoeck & Ruprecht, 1968); Rainer Hering, "Auf dem Weg in die Moderne? Die Hamburgische Landeskirche in der Weimarer Republik," Zeitschrift des Vereins für Hamburgische Geschichte, 82 (1996), 127–66; Klaus Wurth ceded his position as president of the Baden Landeskirche to Julius Kühlewein in July 1933. Baum and Grünzinger, eds., Personenlexikon, 116; 280–281. For letters to Horn, see NEKA Kiel, Bestand 32.01, no. 2268, fols. 1–2; 14–14v.; letters to Wurth in Rückleben and Erbacher, eds., Evangelische Landeskirche, 532–594.

earlier demanded that the Church speak out against the treatment of Jews and now chose to remain silent, such as Württemberg's Theophil Wurm and the head of the Frankfurt *Landeskirche* Johannes Kübel, may have lacked the courage to break ranks with the overwhelming majority and oppose the prevailing mood. The gathering of Church leaders on 26 April would have been the moment to speak. By ultimately remaining silent they squandered the final opportunity for the Church to speak up publicly with one voice.[75]

The reactions of Protestant Church functionaries to the regime's anti-semitic measures—including the verbal pronouncements in the 26 April session and the various memoranda dealing with the issue—reveal shared underlying assumptions, rationalizations for remaining inactive, and a common mindset, the components of which can be identified as follows:

I) Participants in the meeting of 26 April compared the reporting of antisemitic attacks and other transgressions to the Allied *"Greuelmärchen"* and *"Lügenpropaganda"* during World War I. They alleged that these were either fabrications or else gross exaggerations. Who, some asked, cared about the manifold injustices committed against the German minorities in Poland and Czechoslovakia? In this mindset, vastly exaggerated reports about anti-Jewish attacks constituted just another anti-German plot. Vice President Ernst Hundt of the *Oberkirchenrat* in Berlin averred that foreign comments on the issue could hardly be taken at face value—given their innate anti-German bias, doubts regarding their honesty were justified. Public statements in favor of German Jews could thus be misconstrued by Germany's enemies abroad, an opinion also advanced by Hermann Kapler,

---

75. In his essay "Das Feine Schweigen," 158–173, Fritz Stern writes of the disastrous conse-quences of a "high-minded" purposeful silence, whose (mostly upper-class) adherents often disregard injustice out of considerations of convenience and expediency, and remain silent even in the face of crimes out of regard for their own country. Stern also argues that there is a dialectical relationship between silence and concealment, on the one hand, and disclosure or polemical rectification on the other. As Stern writes, "the passivity, the silence of the respectable people . . . [was] just as important for the success of National Socialism as the bellowing of the enthusiasts" (173).

who argued that proclamations of protest might well be used as a propaganda tool against the new Germany.

II) A second set of objections address the concern that public pronouncements criticizing government conduct might ultimately rebound upon the critics themselves. The "Jewish Question" was, after all, a "pivotal issue" for the new government. Thus, fear of alienating the authorities, that is, prudence alone, mandated silence. *Kirchenpräsident* Kapler admits that in his audience with Hitler he had refrained from mentioning the issue. As a way of further rationalization, Kapler raised the question of whether, from a religious viewpoint, the Church had any moral right to intervene on behalf of those Jews who had converted to Christianity to help them retain their State positions in the civil service. In the course of the debate among Protestant Church leaders it became increasingly clear that outright fear of incurring Nazi wrath was a powerful factor behind the silence. In a characteristic statement, Pastor Michaelis from Berlin held forth that "given the enormous danger in which she found itself, the tongue of the Church is tied."

III) A third cluster of rationalizations is especially revealing. It focuses on the putative "injustices" that Jews (now viewed as "aliens," even if they were born in Germany) allegedly committed against the Germans, thereby necessitating measures to actively "contain" them. The *Kirchenpräsident* of Baden, Wurth, speaks of a "foreign infiltration of a most terrible kind" to the point that Jews had completely monopolized certain professions. Another member of the Executive Committee, Professor Titius of Berlin, professes that "the figures on the Jewish infiltration in Germany" occasioned within him "a strong change of heart." He thus found himself unable to support declarations that were opposed to "a legal solution of the problem." Any kind of public stand against the discriminatory treatment of Jews would be "extraordinarily difficult," especially since nothing could be said on their behalf "that would not be contested." *Präsident* Kapler goes so far as to maintain that given the advances of "Jewry" (*Judentum*) since 1918 and the danger consequently posed to the inner cohesiveness of German *Volkstum*, the State was "justified and obligated" to resort to protective measures.

IV) Another implicit rationalization for lack of action was the all too obvious contentment and complacency when it came to National Socialist policies. Time and again it was emphasized that the "national government" saved the country from communist rule. Mecklenburg Bishop Rendtorff argued that "one could hardly call the manner in which the *Judenfrage* is handled *unevangelisch*," given the Church's historical orientation to Jews in Germany. In other words: there was no need for the Church to take any kind of action. Finally, the memorandum "The Church and the Jewish Question in Germany" begins with the ominous sentence, "The self-realization of the national State and the specific character of the *Volkstum* forces us to take on the task of having to regulate the *Judenfrage* anew." Far from being opposed to the new regulations, the Protestant Church thus actually endorsed them.

The Memorandum on the *"Judenfrage"*

The last and most detailed commentary on the "Jewish Question" issued in the name of the *Kirchenausschuss* and its departing president, Hermann Kapler, was a nine-page memorandum, meant mostly for foreign consumption. Though completed and sent out only in early June, it had been in preparation for some time. The detailed execution of the memorandum owed much to the requests of the German Foreign Office and the Propaganda Ministry, which had demanded that the *Kirchenausschuss* decisively intervene with foreign Churches to expound upon the treatment of Jews in Germany.[76] It was understood that this would be done in

---

76. On 23 May, Baron von Reibnitz, affiliated with the German Foreign Office and Reich Propaganda Ministry, spoke to Kapler and requested that the Church issue a statement along these lines for foreign audiences, since Germany would otherwise run the danger of becoming politically isolated due to its treatment of Jews. See Boyens, *Kirchenkampf*, 54–55; Wright, *Parteien*, 194–195.

such a way that justified the government's actions. When this request was initially brought before Kapler by a representative of the German Foreign Office on 23 May 1933, he prevaricated and explained that he "felt oppressed in his conscience when he saw the indiscriminate treatment of Jews in Germany.... Regardless of whether established or recently immigrated from the East ... the sudden deprivation of the livelihood of thousands is not compatible with the Christian conscience."[77] In the end, he nevertheless declared that "it is understood that the Church Executive Committee will do what is useful for the German Reich."[78]

The result was the "Memorandum on the Current Conditions in Germany, especially the *Judenfrage*," a joint effort by Kapler and others, most notably *Oberkonsistorialrat* Hans Wahl, the official responsible for ecumenical issues in the Federal Church Office.[79] This neatly structured nine-page memorandum encompassed all the factual arguments that Church leaders had used on earlier occasions when discussing the *Judenfrage*. It is therefore representative of the mindset and patterns of the Church leadership's argumentation.[80] It was sent not only to foreign Church leaders (such as Albert Beaven in response to his inquiry of 26 March) but also to pastors of German congregations abroad and German diplomatic missions.[81] Completed on 7 June 1933, that is, just within Kapler's tenure of office, it was the most widely disseminated of all the statements and comments on the "Jewish Question" by the

---

77. Boyens, *Kirchenkampf*, on 23 May 1933.   78. Ibid.
79. Ibid., 54; Wright, *Parteien*, 195–196. Ernst Christian Helmreich, in his carefully researched *The German Churches under Hitler. Background, Struggle, and Epilogue* (Detroit: Wayne State Press, 1979), 491, n. 62, maintained that Hans Wahl drew up the memorandum, though it is likely that Hermann Kapler and other DEKA members also contributed to it.
80. The collation of points summarizes the Church leadership's pattern of argumentation as an ideal-type, focusing on the key constructs of the Church's position. Wright argued that "the Federal Church Office did not want this memorandum to be considered as an official statement by the Church, but merely use it to explain the silence of the Protestant Church." Wright, *Parteien*, 195–196.
81. The State Secretary in the Reich Chancellery, Hans Heinrich Lammers, who also received a copy, characterized it as "quite interesting." He mentions that fifty copies had been sent to the Foreign Office. See 4 July 1933 at BA Berlin, R 43 II, no. 161, fol. 92; 15 June 1933 at NEKA Kiel, Bestand 32.01, no. 2268, fol. 3.

Church leadership, and is thus to be found in Church as well as in State archives.[82]

The memorandum begins with revealing comments on "the German revolution of 1933" that made possible "a reassessment of German *Kulturgüter* (cultural endowments)"—a reassessment that would be "more fundamental, the deeper the intellectual roots of the revolution reach." The new regime was seen as a redemption from the wretched Weimar governments, which constituted a mixture of "liberal and Marxist" ideas that "left their mark on the conditions of post-war Germany" and did not prove to be "fruitful for the life of the people."[83] From the outset, foreign readers of this document thus gain the impression that the German Protestant Church vastly preferred the National Socialist regime to the Weimar State. In the spring of 1933 this was indeed the case. An even more detailed positive appraisal of the new regime followed on the next pages: through its vast intellectual and organizational effort the new government was said to have reestablished "order and discipline," leading to a return of "industry and thrift, social peace, and the cultivation of the national heritage." The new leaders, it was argued, stood for peace: Hitler's speech on 23 March, as well as his disarmament speech on 17 May, gave ample testimony to that. It was also "noted with regret, that influential foreign newspapers deemed it appropriate to withhold from their readers the sentences [in Hitler's speech of 17 May] concerning professions of peace." With regard to the character of the political revolution, "the overall judgment that it happened in a disciplined way will always remain historically valid," despite the occurrence of "isolated acts of violence – also against Jews, but not solely or primarily against them." The contrast to the revolution of 1918 could therefore not be

---

82. BA Berlin, R 43 II, no. 161, fols. 82–86v.; NEKA Kiel, Bestand 32.01, no. 2268, following fol. 7. After Kapler left office, Friedrich Seetzen sent the memorandum to the Reich Chancellery. Since Seetzen's letter contained formulations that Wahl had himself used word for word in the Church Executive Committee meeting of 26 April, it may be assumed that Wahl co-operated in writing the letter. See BA Berlin, R 43 II, no. 161, fols. 80–81.
83. Ibid., fol. 82.

greater, particularly since the new rulers emphatically stood up for "Christianity and Church."[84]

Next, the authors turned to the "Jewish Question:" In truth, they wrote, one ought to be surprised that it attracted "such enormous interest" abroad, while "the severe injustices and breaches of the law in recent years" committed against German minorities abroad "had been accepted more or less in silence" by the world. Here we encounter again the theme of the implicit identification of two very different kinds of injustice that are not causally connected. Yet again, transgressions against Germans in the wake of World War I are meant to excuse the current antisemitic outrages. In particular the reasons provided for antisemitic attacks and legislative measures disclose the Church leaders' way of thinking: after the war, given the impact of the 1918 revolution and the Versailles Treaty, the *"Judenfrage"* attained "the critical culmination point characteristic of the present situation," in particular the fact that "vast sections of the people [interpreted]...the attitude of some Jewish circles during the war, and particularly in its immediate aftermath, as ambiguous or even hostile toward our own people's struggle for life."[85] Thanks to their good relationship with Marxist parties, Jews had gained "a disproportionately large number of public offices and other positions," and German governments had opened up the eastern borders for Jewish immigration after 1918, whereby "countless Eastern Jews of culturally inferior standing could settle in Germany...." This statement was buttressed by statistical documentation regarding Jewish over-representation in certain professions. The examples are taken from Berlin, Frankfurt, and Breslau—the three cities with the highest proportion of Jewish inhabitants.[86] What had further agitated the people was "the realization...that the Jewish intellect, especially in literature, theatre, and film, corroded the life of the

---

84. Ibid., fols. 82, 82v., 83.
85. Ibid., fol. 83. On figures regarding the Jewish contribution to World War I, see Chapter 14 below.
86. Ibid., fol. 83v. See the statement of the Vice President of the Frankfurt *Oberlandesgericht*. The respective percentages are: Berlin (3.8%), Frankfurt (4.7%), and Breslau (3.2%) (Thamer, *Verführung*, 258), though percentages of Jewish lawyers and doctors are much higher.

family and *Volkstum*, and finally, all those human bonds without which the preservation of the life of the nation and the State are not possible."[87] For a long time the Churches had observed "with deep regret...how the spirit of decomposition of all traditional foundations of German communal life was nourished by a widely disseminated negative Jewish body of literature." The positive contribution of "distinguished Jews to German culture" must also not be overrated.[88] The "strong monopolization (*Besetzung*) of the academic professions by Jews" in no way signified "their intellectual superiority" in these fields, but stemmed from the fact that "with Jews certain talents are prevalent," combined with the "demonstrably ruthless use of their connections and their support of each other." Reading passages such as these, the reader might well assume that the memorandum was written by someone close to the NSDAP. The simple fact of the matter is that the consensus of a general "cultural" antisemitism was very broad, its spectrum reaching from the national-liberal and Catholic to the conservative and into the National Socialist milieux.

All of these factors combined had brought "even thoughtful people to the realization that something had to be done to ward off the danger threatening...our Volkstum." The "severity that made itself felt in this resistance"—a more explicit word of excuse or explanation for the unbridled brutality of the antisemitic attacks is not to be found—had its source "in the foreign [policy] situation of our Fatherland," notably "the humiliating conditions in which Germany has been kept by the Versailles Treaty until today," as well as in "the war guilt question, the reparations, and the unfulfilled disarmament obligations [on the part of the Allies]."[89] All of that the German people had "endured with at times inconceivable patience," until the "dreadful emotional pressure" had

---

87. Ibid., fol. 84. This was a recurring theme of conservative Church leaders, as we have seen in the case of Dibelius and others.
88. Ibid. The complete sentence reads: "This is not to deny the positive contribution of distinguished Jews to German culture, though one must caution not to overrate it."
89. Ibid., fol. 84.

erupted—here the implication is "in antisemitic aggression," even though that was never stated explicitly. Another surprising turn of the argument follows: in that aggression, the authors warn, one should beware "not to see only the negative," but one must recognize that "antisemitism is only the reverse side of a deep inner consciousness of German uniqueness and of the determination to form and organize the German State and German destiny in accordance with its true character."[90] The memorandum sums up all the judgments and biases the Protestant Church leadership shared with a large part of the *Bildungsbürgertum*. Even from the mouth of a politician, one would hardly receive a more heartfelt endorsement of National Socialism and clear vindication of antisemitism as an essential precondition for national self-realization.

After a detailed justification of the boycott that was purportedly "started by Jewish circles abroad," and that had revived "the memory of the atrocity propaganda against Germany during the World War, which was built on lies," the antisemitic legislation of April 1933 was discussed and vindicated.[91] In this context it was emphasized that a "struggle against the Jewish religion or the free expression of the Jewish cult" was not part of the legislation. In stark opposition to everything that had been said before, the memorandum emphasized in conclusion that "the German Protestant Churches, which know themselves to be bound to God's word, sharply condemn any act of violence and vilification against members of another race."[92] Given Church leaders' deliberations and failure to act on spiritual platitudes, this appears as merely formulaic and written with little regard for taking deliberate action, despite the surprising resolution that the Church would look after "the suffering Judeo-Christians as its own members by practicing brotherly love."[93]

90. Ibid., fol. 84v. 91. Ibid., fols. 84v.–85v.
92. Ibid., fol. 85v. 93. Ibid., fol. 86.

12

THE GERMAN CATHOLIC CHURCH BETWEEN DOCTRINE AND SELF-PRESERVATION

The German Catholic Church, though not as large or influential as its Protestant counterpart, was deeply rooted in society: it served as a moral authority for its members, its bishops' pastoral instructions were heeded by German Catholics, and it had made its voice heard in the political arena of the Weimar Republic. In 1933, the Catholic Church counted 21.172 million members (in a population of 65.2 million) and about 20,000 priests by the end of the 1920s; it also commanded a multitude of vibrant organizations, including the People's League for German Catholics with more than 500,000 members, the Catholic Youth of Germany (1.5 million members) with its numerous suborganizations, Catholic workers' and civil servants' organizations, and a Catholic League of German Women.[1] Gradually growing since the 1870s, a well-organized and tightly-knit Catholic milieu had come into being as a defensive reaction against a State that was seen as hostile during the *Kulturkampf* (1871–87) between Bismarck and the Catholic Church. This "cultural battle" greatly increased cohesion and solidarity among German Catholics. In 1931, Karl Bachem, the historian of the nine-volume history of the Catholic Center Party, could proudly maintain that Germany possessed a developed system of Catholic organizations that was unique

---

1. Heinz Hürten, *Deutsche Katholiken 1918–1945* (Paderborn: Schöningh, 1992), 559; Guenter Lewy, *The Catholic Church and Nazi Germany*, first pub. 1964 (Boston: Da Capo, 2000), 4–5; Hürten, *Deutsche Katholiken*, 565, provides a more detailed membership breakdown.

Before the Holocaust: Antisemitic Violence and the Reaction of German Elites and Institutions during the Nazi Takeover.
Hermann Beck, Oxford University Press. © Hermann Beck 2022. DOI: 10.1093/oso/9780192865076.003.0013

throughout the world.[2] In ways comparable to the socialist milieu that surrounded and supported German Social Democracy, Catholic Church organizations offered sustenance and support to German Catholics throughout their entire personal and political lives.[3]

Before 30 January 1933

In 1933, the German Catholic Church was subdivided into twenty-five dioceses, each presided over by a bishop or archbishop. The episcopate of German bishops was organized in two main conferences, the Freising Conference of Bavarian Bishops, including the Church Province of Munich and Freising (the Archbishop of Munich and Freising, the Bishops of Augsburg, Passau, and Regensburg) and the Church Province of Bamberg (the Archbishop of Bamberg, the Bishops of Eichstätt, Speyer, and Würzburg), as well as the more encompassing Fulda Conference of Bishops.[4] They had met separately from 1873 to May 1933 and began to meet regularly in Fulda only between 1933 and 1938, though the heads of both—Cardinal Archbishop Michael von Faulhaber presiding over the Freising Conference and Cardinal Archbishop Adolf Bertram presiding over its Fulda counterpart—usually consulted each other before making important decisions or sending a delegate to the other's conference.[5] The Fulda Conference included the bishops of the Upper Rhenish Church Province (the Archbishop of Freiburg, the Bishops of Mainz and Rottenburg in Württemberg), the Church Province of Breslau

---

2. Lewy, *Catholic Church*, 5.
3. Historians of the Catholic Church can rely on the meticulously edited volumes containing pertinent archival documents on the Church and its relationship to the Nazi state. As Klaus Scholder pointed out, relevant holdings of Catholic archives had been published in a series of volumes "issued by the Catholic Academy in Bavaria which can scarcely have been equaled in contemporary history for comprehensiveness, wealth of data, and editorial quality;" Scholder, *Kirchen und Drittes Reich*, vii–ix. This chapter draws on these published sources.
4. Lewy, *Catholic Church*, 3–5; 342–344.
5. Lewy, *Catholic Church*, 4–15; *Akten Deutscher Bischöfe über die Lage der Kirche 1933–1945*, vol. I, 1933–1934, ed. Bernhard Stasiewski (Mainz: Grünewald, 1968), IXL–XLII.

(the Archbishop of Breslau, the Bishops of Ermland and Berlin, and the Prelate Nullius—that is, not subject to a diocesan bishop—of Schneide-mühl), the Church Province of Cologne (the Archbishop of Cologne, the Bishops of Trier, Limburg, Aachen, Münster and Osnabrück), the Church Province of Paderborn (the Archbishop of Paderborn, the Bishops of Fulda and Hildesheim), and the Bishop of Meissen in Saxony, a so-called exempt diocese, meaning it was not under the authority of an archbishop but directly subject to the Holy See in Rome.[6]

The relationship between the Catholic Church and the Nazi movement had never been easy, though National Socialism drew open episcopal criticism only after its breakthrough at the polls in 1930. In the fall of 1930, throughout 1931, and then again in August 1932, members of the Catholic episcopate repeatedly distanced themselves from the Nazi movement on ideological grounds. At the end of December 1930, the Archbishop of Breslau, Cardinal Adolf Bertram, head of the Fulda Conference, criticized National Socialism in a sharply worded statement that was widely publicized in the *Amtsblätter* (official gazettes) of the Catholic Church,[7] affirming that "often in times of bitterest misery and collapse of public mores, alluring seducers commandeer the soul of the people," and he castigated "exaggerated nationalism, glorification of race," and demanded "to cast away the treacherous illusion of a national religious community...based on race."[8] Still, the episcopate had not worked out a common policy on this issue, as became clear earlier that fall. Supported by his bishop, the Vicar General of the diocese of Mainz publicly argued that Catholics could not be permitted to become members of the NSDAP and that Nazi Party members could not be admitted to the sacraments; Cardinal Faulhaber in a 6 December memorandum to Bavarian bishops, in contrast, held that it was untenable to deny Nazi Party members the

---

6. Ibid., IXL–XLII; Lewy, *Catholic Church*, 342–344.
7. *Akten deutscher Bischöfe 1933–1934*, 800–806; the exchange of preceding notes and memoranda by Bertram and Faulhaber, 787–799.
8. 31 December 1931, "Kundgebung Bertrams," *Akten deutscher Bischöfe*, 800–806; quotations at 800, 801, 803.

sacraments without examining each individual case; Bishop Christian Schreiber of Berlin tried to steer a more permissible course by indicating in November 1930 that Catholics were not forbidden to become Party members.[9]

On 10 February 1931, the eight Bavarian bishops warned in a severely worded pastoral instruction for the clergy that the cultural program of National Socialism contained false teachings, since it sought to replace Christian faith with a new secular *Weltanschauung*. Bishops were to continue to issue warnings against the movement "as long as and insofar as it propagates cultural teachings that are incompatible with Catholic doctrine;" for Catholic clergy it was "strictly forbidden to participate in the National Socialist movement in any form."[10] On 5 March 1931, the six bishops of the Cologne Church Province also publicly warned "with deep earnestness against National Socialism," highlighting again its "cultural teachings." In stark contrast to the National Socialist goals of creating a unified Reich Church, they argued that "we Catholics do not know a national Church structure," even though at the same time they welcomed the fact that "in our poor, humiliated Fatherland that is held in servitude and torn apart by antagonism of all sorts, a feeling of togetherness of the German people amongst themselves is revived."[11] On 10 March 1931, the bishops of the Paderborn Church Province made it clear in their long and detailed public statement that "for Catholic Christians membership in the NSDAP is impermissible," since National Socialism behaved in a hostile way toward the Catholic Church, with "the swastika as a battle cry against the cross of Christ," stressing the international and universal character of Catholicism that was wholly incompatible with National Socialist ideology.[12] On 19 March, the bishops of the Upper Rhenish Church

---

9. On Faulhaber see *Akten deutscher Bischöfe*, 789; on Schreiber, see Lewy, *Catholic Church*, 8–9. The *Generalvikar* is the deputy of a bishop, responsible for the administration of a diocese.
10. 10 February 1931, "Pastorale Anweisung des bayerischen Episkopates," *Akten deutscher Bischöfe*, 806–809, esp. 807; Lewy, *Catholic Church*, 9, gives the date as 12 February.
11. 5 March 1931, "Kundgebung der Bischöfe der Kölner Kirchenprovinz," *Akten deutscher Bischöfe*, 814–818, esp. 816.
12. 10 March 1931, "Kundgebung der Bischöfe der Paderborner Kirchenprovinz," *Akten deutscher Bischöfe*, 818–824, esp. 824, 823, 821.

Province warned against the dangers of National Socialism in a statement that in parts resembled a kind of cultural criticism decrying the excessive denunciations of public personalities, and the divisions, discord, violence, and revolutionary unrest of the present age, using the tried and tested phrase of "as long as it propagates teachings that are incompatible with Catholic doctrine." The Fulda Bishops' Conference, held on 3–5 August 1931, decided on more general guidelines for the clergy, contenting itself with a condemnation of extreme nationalism, alongside socialism and communism, and not even mentioning Nazism by name.[13] In mid-August 1932, however, the Fulda bishops released a strongly worded communiqué that prohibited Nazi Party membership in all of its dioceses, not only because the Party's official program contained false teachings and hostility to the faith shown by its leading figures, but also because the Catholic clergy was convinced that "if the Party were to achieve its hotly sought-after monopoly of power in Germany, this would result in dire prospects for Church interests."[14]

These repeated and often sharply worded public declarations against National Socialism on the part of the German episcopate, which were often published in Catholic *Amtsblätter*, suffered from several severe shortcomings that may have limited their efficacy. First, the various pronouncements issued by the different Church provinces and bishops' conferences made it obvious that German Catholicism did not speak with one united voice, since the diverse statements showed marked differences in nuance and were not equally pointed in their condemnation of National Socialism, so that German Catholics received noticeably dissimilar messages. Secondly, in an age of virulent nationalism, when every institution was eager to emphasize its patriotism, the Catholic Church was no exception. Thus, while condemning Nazism as incompatible with the teachings of the Church, these warnings were

13. 19 March 1931, "Kundgebung der Bischöfe der Oberrheinischen Kirchenprovinz," *Akten deutscher Bischöfe*, 824–828, quotation 827; 3–5 August 1931, "Richtlinien der Fuldaer Bischofskonferenz," *Akten deutscher Bischöfe*, 828–832.
14. 17 August 1932, "Protokoll der Fuldaer Bischofskonferenz," *Akten deutscher Bischöfe*, 843–844.

accompanied by professions of national solidarity and devotion to the Fatherland—they decried the "burning shame of our Fatherland bleeding from a thousand wounds," and emphasized that "we love *Volk* and Fatherland and value German characteristics," even though professions of patriotism were often attended by warnings against excessive nationalism.[15] All declarations deliberately shied away from politics, instead confining their warnings to the ideological aspects of National Socialism and its orientation toward Catholicism. In the pastoral instructions of the Bavarian episcopate, this is explicitly stated: "It is far from our minds to deal with the political aims of National Socialism; we are merely concerned with its position towards Catholic Christianity."[16]

This political abstemiousness, for which Catholic bishops have been rightly criticized, may in part be due to their generational experience.[17] As was the case with the dignitaries of the Protestant *Landeskirchen*, the political opinions of German bishops had been formed during life in the German Empire, so that many remained monarchist in outlook and distrusted liberalism and democracy. In January 1933, a good many members of the German episcopate were in their seventies, including the Archbishop of Bamberg (born 1861), Archbishop of Breslau (1859), Bishop of Fulda (1858), Bishop of Münster (1862), Bishop of Passau (1855), and Bishop of Speyer (1862); that is, they were born well before the foundation of the Empire, while most others were in their sixties, born between 1865 and 1872.[18] Given their age, the formative generational experience of the German episcopate included living through Bismarck's *Kulturkampf* against the Catholic Church. In 1871, the Reichstag and *Bundesrat* (Federal Council) decided on tightening Article 130 of the penal code, the so-called "*Kanzelparagraph*" ("pulpit clause") that threatened with

---

15. The first quotation is from the Paderborn Church Province, the second from that of the Upper Rhine. *Akten deutscher Bischöfe*, 819, 828.
16. *Akten deutscher Bischöfe*, 807.   17. Lewy, *Catholic Church*, 8–9.
18. These include the Bishops of Aachen (born 1865), Augsburg (1869), Berlin (1872), Hildesheim (1871), Mainz (1871), Rottenburg (1870), Trier (1866) Würzburg (1871); and the Archbishops of Cologne (1871), Munich and Freising (1869), and Paderborn (1865). This point is also made in Lewy, *The Catholic Church*, 12. For information on German bishops (1930–4), see *Akten deutscher Bischöfe*, XL–XLII.

punishment every member of the Catholic clergy who discussed matters of State in the course of his clerical duties.[19] Avoiding politics had thus been inculcated from early on: having experienced the *Kulturkampf*, Catholic bishops may also have been wary of maneuvering the Catholic Church into the role of a pariah once again.

Despite these qualifications, it is worth emphasizing that the German episcopate was far more critical of National Socialism than the leaders of Protestant *Landeskirchen*. Warnings against National Socialism as laid down in pastoral instructions and public proclamations were detailed and unsparing, especially, as mentioned above, those of the Bavarian bishops and the Cologne, Paderborn, and Upper Rhenish Church Provinces in 1931.[20] Before 1933, any attempt by Nazi leaders to enlist the Catholic Church as an ally against communism was doomed to failure, while the electorate of the Catholic Center Party, unlike that of parts of the mostly Protestant DNVP, remained largely immune to the temptations of National Socialism.[21] Even though there was some ideological overlap, such as the *Reichsideologie* that harked back to the idea of a universal empire with its concept of a greater Germany including Austria—widespread also among Catholic academics and the Catholic youth movement—Nazism failed to make substantial inroads into the Catholic milieu before Hitler came to power.[22]

---

19. Wilfried Loth, *Das Kaiserreich. Obrigkeitsstaat und politische Mobilisierung* (Munich: DTV, 1996), 50–59, esp. p. 54.
20. There were other institutions besides the Catholic Church that excluded National Socialists: in June 1930 Prussian civil servants were prohibited from joining the NSDAP, while the *Reichswehr* dismissed party members from its associated organizations as early as July 1929, and army members were not allowed to attend meetings at which Nazis appeared in uniform or swastika flags were flown.
21. Ludwig Volk, *Der Bayerische Episkopat und der Nationalsozialismus 1930–1934*, 2nd ed. (Mainz: Grünewald, 1966), 59–61. The electorate of the Catholic parties, the Center and the Bavarian People's Party, remained relatively stable throughout the Republic, their combined number of deputies oscillating between 78 (elections of May 1928) and 97 (July 1932). Eberhard Kolb, *Die Weimarer Republik*, 7th ed. (Munich: Oldenbourg, 2009), 316–317.
22. Klaus Breuning, *Die Vision des Reiches. Deutscher Katholizismus zwischen Demokratie und Diktatur, 1929–1934* (Munich: Hueber, 1969), 225–238; 326–340; Joachim Maier, "Die Katholische Kirche und die Machtergreifung," in Wolfgang Michalka, ed., *Die nationalsozialistische Machtergreifung* (Paderborn, Schöningh, 1984), 152–167.

After 30 January 1933

In the campaign for the 5 March 1933 elections, the German episcopate, Catholic organizations, and the Catholic Center Party maintained their policy of strict opposition to National Socialism. In an electoral appeal from 17 February 1933, leading to the prohibition of about twenty newspapers that reprinted it, Catholic organizations inveighed against the new government's lack of respect for constitutional rights, the replacement of due process by "arbitrariness and favoritism," and incitement of hatred against political opponents. They made it clear that they would combat this "Bolshevism in a nationalist key," while on 20 February the Fulda Conference of Bishops called on Catholic voters to cast their ballots for "deputies whose character...provides testimony of their defense of peace,...confessional schools, Christian religion, and the Catholic Church."[23] In accordance with its slogan, "Hitler is the figurehead—Hugenberg and Papen the proprietors of the firm," the electoral strategy of the Center Party was initially directed mainly against the German Nationals. From the beginning the party was hampered by the government's decree of 4 February ("Protection of the German People") that curbed the freedom of the press and could quickly lead to the banning of newspapers. By mid-February, the campaign for the March elections was decidedly no longer democratic: SA attacks on Center Party press organs, meetings, and prominent speakers—some of whom, such as Adam Stegerwald, were physically attacked—multiplied, and two days before the elections, the government prohibited the radio transmission of Brüning's speech in the Berlin Sportpalast.[24]

Despite these adverse conditions, the Center Party largely maintained its former strength: its numbers of deputies slightly rose from seventy to seventy-four, though, due to increased voter participation, its relative share of the electorate declined from 11.9 percent (in November 1932) to

23. "Wahlaufruf katholischer Organisationen," *Akten deutscher Bischöfe*, 3–5; "Kundgebung der Fuldaer Bischofskonferenz," *Akten deutscher Bischöfe*, 6–7; quotations 4 and 6.
24. Morsey, "Zentrumspartei," 345–353.

11.2 percent.[25] Yet after the elections the party was seized by a kind of paralysis that was characteristic for all democratic forces that opposed National Socialism in March 1933.[26] This was due to several reasons: as a political factor the Center had become negligible since the NSDAP–DNVP coalition enjoyed a clear 51.9 percent majority—in fact, without Communist representatives in the Reichstag, the Nazi Party alone had ten more deputies than all other parties combined. The NSDAP was also buttressed by the rapid and virtually unopposed takeover between 5 and 10 March of those German states not yet in Nazi hands; the defeatism and resignation of its powerful former opponents, such as the republican *Reichsbanner*; and, most importantly, a decisive swing in the public mood in favor of the new government that hastened a mass exodus of members of democratic parties and made it seem as if the future inexorably belonged to Hitler's followers. The gnawing feeling of insignificance that contributed to the Center's support of the Enabling Act (thus providing Hitler with the two-thirds majority needed for the bill to pass), was intensified by local indicators of the party's powerlessness. In Cologne, for example, one of Germany's traditional strongholds of Catholicism, the NSDAP furloughed Konrad Adenauer, Lord Mayor of long standing, on 13 March, and a few days later, some of Cologne's prominent landmarks were renamed in an attempt to denigrate the Republic and pay tribute to the spirit of the new Germany.[27]

Bishops also began to waver and betray signs of insecurity. In a letter to Hindenburg of 10 March, Cardinal Bertram, who had already turned to the President for help before the elections, now showed grave concern as to "whether the movement that had attained power will respect...the position of the Church in public life;" he expressly sought Hindenburg's

---

25. Kolb, *Weimarer Republik*, 7th ed., 316–317.
26. See also Introduction, above; Morsey, "Zentrumspartei," 354.
27. This included, for example, the renaming of the "Platz der Republik" to "Adolf-Hitler Platz" and "Erzberger Platz" to "Königin-Luise Platz." See Morsey, "Zentrumspartei," 356. In 1933, 75.3% of Cologne's population were Catholic. With 756,605 inhabitants, it was the largest Catholic city in Germany in 1933, slightly ahead of Munich (735,388 inhabitants); see Thamer, *Verführung*, 258. Center Party politician Konrad Adenauer, the future Chancellor of West Germany (1949–63), was Lord Mayor of Cologne from 1920 to 1933.

"protection for the Church and its life and works."[28] Freiburg Archbishop Conrad Gröber's message to the papal envoy Eugenio Pacelli on 18 March, when the power relationship had further changed in favor of the NSDAP, bears witness to the increasingly fragile position in which the Church found itself during the second half of March. A concerned Gröber argues that "we must avoid everything that looks like a provocation of the new rulers and might influence them against the Church and the clergy," and uneasily deplores that "even in my own diocese a larger number of Catholic congregations [*Gemeinden*] defect to this Party in droves."[29] Gröber viewed the standing of the German Catholic Church as precarious, for in contrast to the situation in Italy, in Germany "Protestantism will use every political opportunity to express its hate and its will to destroy against the Catholic Church." It was also alarming that "Catholic organizations, which formerly loyally adhered to the Center Party, now timidly draw back or sign up with the National Socialists," though this was hardly surprising, "given the repressive methods National Socialism habitually employs."[30]

On 19 March, two days before the historic "Day of Potsdam," a milestone on the new regime's road to winning over the old conservative elites, Cardinal Bertram, while seemingly still refusing to amend his attitude towards National Socialism, reminded his fellow bishops that "previous warnings [against National Socialism] by bishops are valid only insofar as the doubts and reservations communicated to the clergy continue to exist." Once they fell by the wayside, "they will cease being valid."[31] Beneath the surface such a sea change in the position of the Church was in the offing. On 9 March, Cardinal Faulhaber went on his ad

---

28. 10 March 1933, "Bertram an Hindenburg," *Akten deutscher Bischöfe*, 7–8.
29. 18 March 1933, "Gröber an Pacelli," *Akten deutscher Bischöfe*, 9–10, esp. 10. Gröber and Pacelli, the future Pope Pius XII, had been collaborating on the Concordat between the Vatican and the German state of Baden, concluded on 12 October 1932 and ratified on 11 March 1933.
30. Ibid., 10; Volk, *Bayerischer Episkopat*, 50–62; Ernst Deuerlein, *Der deutsche Katholizismus 1933* (Osnabrück: Fromm, 1963).
31. 19 March 1933, "Bertram an die Mitglieder der Fuldaer Bichofskonferenz," *Akten deutscher Bischöfe*, 11–12, esp. 12.

limina visit to Rome to report on the state of his diocese.[32] During the course of this visit several articles appeared in press organs close to the Vatican that heralded a political volte-face toward National Socialism, indicating that the Vatican was anxious to establish friendly relations between German Catholics and the new regime.[33] Hitler's declaration before the Reichstag in the early afternoon on 23 March, designed to signify reconciliation with political Catholicism, was a further step toward making any reservations on the part of the Church leadership seemingly irrelevant. In this Reichstag speech, which preceded the vote on the Enabling Act, Hitler emphasized that "the National government sees in the two Christian confessions the most important factors for the preservation of the character of our nation."[34] This was followed by the Center Party's approval of the Enabling Act in the evening hours of 23 March.[35] Ultimately responsible for the timing of the rather precipitate turnaround of German bishops' attitude toward National Socialism was the publication of Hitler's "grievance" on 22 March that Catholic bishops, "in a series of declarations, acted on by the Catholic clergy," had denunciated "leaders and members of the NSDAP as apostates of the Church, who must not get the benefit of the sacraments." The official act of State called the "Day of Potsdam" on 21 March had been preceded by festive Protestant and Catholic Church services, but since these disparaging

32. The ad limina visits, which obligated all bishops to travel to Rome once every five years, also required German bishops to report personally and directly to the Pope on the state of their dioceses.
33. Lewy, *Catholic Church*, 31, 38; *Akten deutscher Bischöfe*, 11, n. 1.
34. *Akten deutscher Bischöfe*, 15, n. 1.
35. The dramatic events are well captured in Morsey, "Zentrumspartei," 353–367. The once influential thesis that there was a causal connection between Center Party deputies voting for the Enabling Act and Catholic bishops rescinding their warnings on 28 March, on the one hand, and the conclusion of the *Reichskonkordat* (the so called "*Junktimthese*"), on the other, has few advocates today. There is no evidence for such a connection in contemporary sources. In late March a Concordat between the Reich and the Vatican had not been expected. Center Party politician Prelate Joseph Föhr, who had negotiated the Concordat with the state of Baden, noted just before the vote, "other Concordats secured; Reich Concordat not intended." See Hürten, *Deutsche Katholiken*, 187; Matthias Strickler, "Kollaboration oder weltanschauliche Distanz? Katholische Kirche und NS-Staat," in Karl-Joseph Hummel and Michael Kißner, eds., *Die Katholiken und das Dritte Reich*, 2nd ed. (Paderborn: Schöningh, 2010), 83–99, esp. 84–85, Michael Kißener, *Das Dritte Reich* (Darmstadt: WBG, 2005), 67–70.

statements about National Socialists had not been revoked, "[Hitler] had regrettably not been in a position to participate in the Potsdam Catholic service."[36]

This line of wounded respectability made it seem as if the Catholic episcopate had unjustly excluded loyal Catholics from practicing their religion. Due to Hitler's public complaint, Catholic bishops felt under pressure to seek accommodation with the regime, given the favor the Protestant Church seemed to enjoy. Catholic Church leaders saw themselves as locked into a kind of awkward competition with the Protestant churches to curry favor with the new regime—feelings that were entirely mutual. In the larger scheme of things, Catholic organizations had to find a place in the new order, especially in view of the hazardous situation of Catholic civil servants close to the Center Party, some of whom were threatened with dismissal unless a *modus vivendi* could be found. The episcopate also did not want to see the patriotism of German Catholics called into question and have them excluded from participation in the much discussed "rebuilding" of the new Reich. This had happened once before during the *Kulturkampf* and should not happen again, especially since influential Catholic newspapers already called for support of the new Reich and Catholic participation in it; numerous Catholic organizations were also eager to be involved in the new Germany.[37] In light of the political turnaround of the Center Party in supporting the new government's emergency powers, there was now indeed little reason to hold back. On 28 March, in a rather precipitate announcement that left no time for careful consultation with the different dioceses, Cardinal Bertram of Breslau rescinded former warnings and reservations. The final text is more sharply worded than Bertram's initial conciliatory

36. *Akten deutscher Bischöfe*, 14–15, n. 3.
37. Such as the *Augsburger Postzeitung*: "We want to be inside the new German community, for we love Germany. And it is unworthy, especially for the Catholic attitude of mind, to persist in negative opposition when the hour calls for work and positive goals" (Lewy, *Catholic Church*, 31). The origins of the *Postzeitung* go back to 1686; it was banned in 1935. The Catholic Teachers' Association enthusiastically endorsed the new government on 30 March; Gruber, *Katholische Kirche*, 42–43.

version; it carries the short preamble that, *"Without annulling the censure of certain religious-moral errors,* the Episcopate believes it has reason to be confident that the former general injunctions and warnings are no longer necessary." Hitler's "public and solemn declaration" to respect the integrity of the Churches before the Reichstag on 23 March is cited as the reason for the cancellation of warnings.[38] Up to this point, the fate of Jews had not been a topic in the intra-episcopal correspondence. In the wake of the dramatic events in March 1933, the German bishops had been too pre-occupied with their own fate and that of the Church to care very much about what was happening outside the confines of the Catholic milieu.

The Church, the April Boycott, and Intervention on Behalf of Jews

A few days later, this issue could no longer be avoided. Oscar Wasser-mann, a director of the Deutsche Bank in Berlin, himself of Jewish descent and actively involved in Zionist causes, had approached Cardinal Bertram as *primus inter pares* among Germany's archbishops to request that he intercede with the government to stop the boycott.[39] Bertram, who was clearly not eager to perform this task, told Wassermann that it was beyond his competence to speak on behalf of the German bishops and that he was not in a position to judge whether the reasons given for the boycott were justified or if an intervention had any chance of success. All he could offer Wassermann was to ask "the archbishops of the Church provinces if such a step was opportune."[40] In his circular to his

---

38. For the text see Gruber, *Katholische Kirche,* 39–40; *Akten deutscher Bischöfe,* 30–32.
39. Oscar Wassermann was the speaker of the Deutsche Bank's Management Board; in May 1933 he was forced to resign his position. Wassermann had been recommended to Bertram by Berlin's St. Hedwig Cathedral's *Domkapitular* (Canon) Monsignor Bernhard Lichtenberg (1875–1943), who openly opposed the Nazi regime. Lichtenberg died during his transport to the Dachau concentration camp in November 1943. On Wassermann, see Harold James, *The Deutsche Bank and the Nazi Economic War against the Jews* (Cambridge: Cambridge University Press, 2001), 16–17; 24–26.
40. *Akten deutscher Bischöfe,* 42, n. 3; repr. in Gruber, *Deutsche Katholiken,* 41–42, esp. 41.

peers Bertram began by laying out a series of reservations, making it clear that he himself was opposed to any intervention: at issue was, after all, "an economic struggle of a circle not close to us from the viewpoint of the Church." Moreover, such a step "can only be considered interference in matters that do not concern the Episcopate, which has good reason to confine itself to its own sphere of work." In all likelihood, he wrote, an intervention might not be successful anyway and might harm the Church, since it could not be kept confidential "and would certainly meet with the worst possible interpretation all over Germany." And finally, had not in the past "the largely Jewish-dominated press consistently observed silence when Catholics in different countries were persecuted?"[41] Faced with such manifest doubts regarding the advisability of an appeal to the government, the other archbishops, who were asked to respond via telegram with a short "grant wish" or "refrain from granting wish," mostly fell into line. Archbishop Cardinal Faulhaber telegraphed back, "Granting of wish [has] no chance of success. Would only aggravate situation. Action already receding," while Archbishop Gröber, who remained in the minority, wrote, "Grant wish out of consideration for those without guilt and converts." No further action ensued since the boycott ended on the evening of 1 April and the bishops remained silent.[42]

Throughout the Third Reich, Cardinal Bertram would try to avoid having to take a stand when asked for intervention on behalf of German Jews and was averse to taking any risk that might jeopardize the Catholic Church's position. His Munich confrère Cardinal Faulhaber, by contrast, in open defiance of the regime's official religious policy, defended in a series of sermons (in December 1933 and January 1934) the importance of Old Testament religious values to Christianity, and in March 1939 directed a fervently worded appeal to the new Pope Pius XII to assist "Christian non-Aryans" to emigrate to Brazil by requesting from Brazilian President Getúlio Vargas an expeditious endorsement of 3,000 visas

41. Akten deutscher Bischöfe, 42–43, n. 3; Gruber, Deutsche Katholiken, 41–42.
42. Volk, Bayerischer Episkopat, 77.

for German immigrants.[43] In mid-November 1941, when it had become clear that the war in the East could not be won (at least, not in 1941), the dictatorship had tightened its reins and deportations were under way, Faulhaber requested that Bertram support him in a petition of German archbishops asking for better treatment for baptized Catholics of Jewish descent in the round-ups and transports that had recently begun in Munich and other cities. As Faulhaber wrote to Bertram, these transports were carried out "in the darkness of night" and "in brutal form and under inhuman conditions," whereby "scenes occur which, in the chronicle of our age, will eventually be equated with the haulages of African slave traders," and which were accompanied "by suicides."[44] Even these graphic descriptions failed to move Bertram, who argued that little could be accomplished by such a step since, as with everything connected with "non-Aryans," this issue was part of "the implementation of a fundamental principle of an ideology," the episcopal offices did not possess "conclusive materials for putting together such a petition" and it was more important for the episcopate "to concentrate on other matters, more consequential and far-reaching for the Church."[45] In 1933 and in later years, Cardinal Adolf Bertram thus often eschewed involving his Church in helping Jews or even baptized Catholics of Jewish decent, since this might entangle the institution in difficulties with the Nazi regime.

In the spring of 1933, Faulhaber, too, was still anxious to toe the line with the new regime. In a letter of 30 March to the American Cardinal George W. Mundelein, he adopted the narrative of the German government regarding the April boycott by arguing, "The untrue reports about

---

43. Michael von Faulhaber, *Judentum, Christentum, Germanentum*, 7–26; partly repr. in Gruber, *Katholische Kirche*, 143–147; 31 March 1939, "Faulhaber an Papst Pius XII," *Akten Kardinal Michael von Faulhabers*, vol. II: 1935–1945, ed. Ludwig Volk (Mainz: Grünewald, 1978), 630–632; repr. in Gruber, *Katholische Kirche*, 396–398.

44. 13 November 1941, "Faulhaber an Bertram," *Akten Faulhabers*, vol. II, 824–825; partly repr. in Gruber, *Katholische Kirche*, 462–463. Faulhaber makes the point that "to speak up for non-Aryans in general" would not "meet with the understanding" of executive organs, but that the German episcopate had the obligation to stand up for the "children of the Catholic Church."

45. 17 November 1941, "Bertram an Faulhaber," *Akten Faulhabers*, vol. II, 844–845, Gruber, *Katholische Kirche*, 465–466.

bloodstained terror in Germany, which have appeared in American and foreign newspapers...have induced the German government to take countermeasures and conduct a boycott against Jewish shops in all severity."[46] Here Faulhaber's line of argumentation even denied the fact that attacks had taken place. "Foreign correspondents have not considered the difficult situation they created for Jews in Germany," he continued, and then went on to ask Mundelein "to muster all your influence to compel foreign newspapers, which reported about acts of terror, to make a declaration indicating they are convinced that their former allegations are groundless."[47] This was a thoroughly naïve attempt to influence the American Cardinal, but not unlike similar endeavors made by members of the Protestant Church hierarchy. In a letter to Eugenio Pacelli of 10 April Faulhaber bluntly explained the reasons why the Catholic Church should avoid taking a public stand: "At present we Catholic bishops are confronted with the question of why the Catholic Church does not speak out on behalf of the Jews, as she so often did before in her history. This is currently not possible, since a struggle against Jews would quickly turn into a struggle against Catholics and because Jews can help themselves, as the rapid termination of the boycott has shown."[48] Already on 31 March he had written in a similar vein to Bavarian bishops that "the current harassment of Jews might quickly change into harassment of Jesuits."[49]

Among the questions and protestations of Catholic clergy in early April 1933 a few are noteworthy. On 5 April 1933 Alois Wurm, a Catholic priest and editor of a monthly magazine, wrote to Faulhaber and directed the Cardinal's attention to the fact that "in this age of extreme incitement

---

46. 30 March 1933, "Faulhaber and Mundelein," *Akten Kardinal Michael von Faulhabers*, vol. I: *1917–1945*, ed. Ludwig Volk (Mainz: Grünewald, 1975), 682.
47. *Akten Faulhabers*, vol. I, 683.
48. Quoted in Volk, *Bayerischer Episkopat*, 78.
49. Ibid. And this despite the fact that during the Weimar Republic Faulhaber had become a "fairly committed critic of antisemitism." See Philipp Nielsen, *Between Heimat and Hatred. Jews and the Right in Germany, 1871–1935* (New York: Oxford University Press, 2019), 229; Derek Hastings, *Catholicism and the Roots of Nazism: Religious Identity and National Socialism* (New York: Oxford University Press, 2019), 104, 142.

to hatred against Jewish citizens who are certainly up to 99 percent innocent, not one single Catholic paper, as far as I can see, has had the courage to promulgate the basic Catholic catechism teaching that one must not hate and prosecute any man – least of all because of his race. To many this appears as a grave Catholic error."[50] Wurm points out that since the *Frankfurter Zeitung* dared to oppose the boycott, "a Catholic paper would hardly have been attacked for asserting Catholic teachings at a time when they are infringed upon," and laments that "the Catholic population was left without Catholic guidance through its press in this time of greatest confusion" as result of which "the authority of the bishops has greatly suffered."[51] In his slightly condescending response Faulhaber tells Wurm that he should have "addressed himself to a different recipient." Besides, Faulhaber contends, "for the higher authorities of the Church far more pressing contemporary issues exist [than the persecution of Jews]; since schools, the continued existence of Catholic associations, [and] sterilizations are more important for Christianity in our country, especially since one can assume and have partly experienced that Jews can help themselves, so that we have no cause to give the government reason to turn persecution of Jews into persecution of Jesuits. From various sides I receive questions as to why the Church does nothing about the persecution of Jews. I am displeased about this, for when Catholics or bishops are oppressed no one asks what one could do to stop this harassment."[52] Undaunted by Faulhaber's dismissive rebuttal, Wurm insists that he had addressed the correct recipient, "for who but our God-given Church leaders can provide guidance, including to the press, in such difficult, confused times," and he maintains that a press reception "clearly defining the position of the Church" would be effective. In an unflattering comparison with Faulhaber, Wurm mentions

---

50. 5 April, "Wurm an Faulhaber," *Akten Faulhabers*, vol. I, 701.
51. Ibid., 701. Wurm ends by confronting Faulhaber with another unwelcome truth, namely that "it is quite a different and more difficult question as to how to get through to the millions of Catholics who support National Socialism" (ibid., 702).
52. 8 April 1933, "Faulhaber an Wurm," *Akten Faulhabers*, vol. I, 705.

that Bischof von Ketteler (one of the great figures of the German Catholic Church in the nineteenth century) "in the present situation would not have renounced the creation of a united front of the Episcopate to help the confused people and serve the cause."[53]

Faulhaber's stock-in-trade arguments are in this instance entirely misplaced, since in the spring of 1933 the unrelenting harassment of the Jewish minority was so obviously unique and without parallel to the discrimination of others. In his rejoinder to an obstreperous underling Faulhaber was obviously carried away by the conviction that, since the entire microcosm of Catholic organizations was under attack in April 1933, from Catholic teachers' unions to Catholic journeymen's associations and youth organizations, everything had to be done not to give the government a pretext to attack the Church on yet another front. It was this attitude of complete appeasement and fear of undermining personal and institutional interests that lay in part behind the silence of Germany's once powerful institutions in the face of antisemitic violence.

Among the very few Catholic voices publicly protesting against the boycott and anti-Jewish violence was the Franconian Catholic priest, Alois Eckert, who wrote a courageous newspaper article, published on 4 April, in which he accused the government of "implementing a new code of law" divorced from Christian ethics:

> We do not consider the solution to the *Judenfrage* as it is attempted today correct and just in light of our Christian conscience, neither in its methods nor its moral attitude. The solution to the *Judenfrage* cannot be sought and found from the standpoint of race. No man may lose rights and be discriminated against on account of his race.... Here manifest injustice is occurring in Germany. And in the long run, wrongs always fall back more heavily on those who perpetrate than on those who suffer them.[54]

---

53. 9 April 1933, "Wurm an Faulhaber," *Akten Faulhabers*, vol. I, 706–707. Wilhelm Emmanuel von Ketteler (1811–77), Bishop of Mainz, pioneer of political Catholicism and champion of Catholic social policies.
54. Published in the *Rhein-Mainische Volkszeitung* on 4 April 1933, reprinted in Gruber, *Katholische Kirche*, 47–49, esp. 48–49. The *Volkszeitung* began publication in 1923. It was close to the Catholic Left. After most of its editors were arrested in 1933, it lost subscribers and ceased publication in 1935.

The most vociferous protest came from Franziskus Stratmann OP to Faulhaber.[55] Stratmann argued that "the minds of the right-thinking are churned up by the National Socialist rule of terror . . . and the authority of bishops was shaken in the eyes of countless Catholics and non-Catholics by their quasi endorsement of the National Socialist movement," a reference to the 28 March declaration of the episcopate. What was happening was "a barbaric, never experienced mental and material dispossession carried out against tens of thousands of innocent people, who are without defense and rights, and no authoritative voice is raised in public against this abuse."[56] Stratmann charges that "especially the persecution of Jews tramples underfoot every sense of justice" and complains that "while bishops spoke out against the dispossession of princes [in the 1926 referendum], . . . they remain silent to this far worse expropriation." From what Stratmann writes, it is clear that antisemitic violence was widely known:

> What is called atrocity propaganda from abroad refers 80% to real atrocities. Every acquaintance with whom I discuss it can testify to specific details. I myself, here in the St. Norbert hospital where I am Chaplain, have seen the naked body of a Jewish merchant, which showed the cruelest traces of abuse. The gentleman, who is completely a-political, and had been a *Frontkämpfer* for four years and was badly wounded [in World War I], has been beaten for hours with canes and whips on the day of the boycott, together with other Jews, for no other reason than because he is Jewish. Numerous similar cases are being related by credible witnesses. A Jewish academic told me that he knew of several murders in his circle of acquaintances. A patient here in the hospital told me that he personally had not heard about murders, but of cases of death following maltreatment, as well as of suicides. Most valuable and highly intelligent individuals are mentally crushed underfoot by berserk people who are morally and intellectually beneath them. . . . But no one effectively protests against this indescribable

---

55. 10 April 1933, "Stratmann an Faulhaber," *Akten Faulhabers*, vol. I, 709–711; repr. in Gruber, *Katholische Kirche*, 55–58. The Dominican Franziskus Stratmann OP (1883–1971) (OP stands for "Ordinis Praedicatorum") was a *Studentenseelsorger* in Berlin and, until the dissolution of the organization, active in the *Friedensbund Deutscher Katholiken*.
56. Gruber, *Katholische Kirche*, 56.

German and Christian shame. Even priests feel their antisemitic instincts satisfied by this sinful hounding.[57]

On 24 April, Joseph Kumpfmüller, Bishop of Augsburg since 1930, who had two weeks previously informed Faulhaber of the "continued taking into protective custody of decent Catholics,"[58] wrote about the predicament of "patriotic Jews and their descendants who converted to Christianity" and the dismay among his congregation that "the Episcopate has not taken a more decisive stand on this."[59] Yet, in the spring of 1933, in the face of all the outrages, Faulhaber and the Catholic episcopate chose to remain silent.

There were several reasons why German bishops chose not to take a more active role and refrained from speaking out against anti-Jewish violence and boycott measures. As Faulhaber wrote to Alois Wurm in early April, in the eyes of the Church leadership "far more pressing contemporary issues exist," by which he meant protecting the integrity of the Church and its organizations against further Nazi encroachments.[60] Since mid-March bishops had been confronted with a wave of arrests of Catholic civil servants, as well as officials close to the Catholic Center and Bavarian People's Party. As the Regensburg Bishop Michael Buchberger impressed on Faulhaber on 27 March,

> Many of our best Catholics have been deprived of their positions in the face of tumult and mayhem, many languish like convicts in prisons, others have been chased out of their posts like criminals, and still nothing has happened to contain violent intrusions or make amends for injustices. We must not now abandon our loyal Catholic people and their leaders.[61]

---

57. Ibid., 57.
58. 10 April 1933, "Kumpfmüller an Faulhaber," *Akten Faulhabers*, vol. I, 709.
59. 24 April 1933, "Kumpfmüller an Faulhaber," *Akten Faulhabers*, vol. I, 716.
60. 8 April 1933, "Faulhaber an Wurm," *Akten Faulhabers*, vol. I, 705.
61. 27 March 1933, "Buchberger and Faulhaber," *Akten Faulhabers*, vol. I, 27. Written the day before Bertram rescinded previous injunctions against National Socialism on 28 March, this was also meant as a warning not to be too hasty in making concessions to the regime.

In the spring of 1933, a time of rapidly growing enthusiasm and hopes for the new regime, coupled with all-pervasive Nazi terror against real or perceived enemies and the ruthless *Gleichschaltung* of organizations that had rejected or stood aloof from National Socialism in the past, the higher Church leadership was anxious not to add to possible reprisals against Catholics by drawing attention to itself in standing up for the persecuted Jewish minority. On the other hand, the Church was prepared to take a very active stand whenever Catholic interests were concerned, as they did in the case of the civil service legislation.[62]

Secondly, and this already became manifest in Bertram's 31 March circular to the German archbishops, there was a lack of interest in (as Bertram disparagingly put it) "an economic struggle of a circle not close to us," so that active help "can only be considered interference in matters that do not concern the Episcopate."[63] This emotional distance was based partly on a tradition of latent Catholic resentments against Jews, reaching back into the nineteenth century, that stood in the way of solidarity with the victims of Nazi violence.[64] Then there was Faulhaber's (at least professed) conviction that German Jews "can help themselves," as he had written to Wurm, and his belief that anti-Jewish atrocities had partly been invented, as he indicated in his 30 March letter to Cardinal Munde- lein in Chicago, in which he spoke of "untrue reports about bloodstained terror in Germany."[65] Finally, as becomes apparent from the correspond- ence among bishops, there was the palpable fear that, by not removing its warnings against National Socialism and by involving itself in further opposition to the regime, formerly devout Catholics who were clearly attracted to the regime in ever growing numbers would be forced to choose between their loyalty to the Church and active participation in

---

62. See Chapter 10 above (also in *Akten deutscher Bischöfe*, 51, 59, 60). In this context the Church interceded solely for "exceptionally competent Catholic civil servants," not on behalf of Jews.
63. *Akten deutscher Bischöfe*, I, 42, n. 3 (also quoted above); Volk, *Bayerischer Episcopat*, 77.
64. See Olaf Blaschke, *Katholizismus und Antisemitismus im Deutschen Kaiserreich* (Göttingen: Vandenhoeck & Ruprecht, 1999).
65. *Akten Faulhabers*, vol. I, 705 and 682.

the new Germany. Given the atmosphere in the spring of 1933, they may well have been tempted to opt for the latter.[66]

Heinz Hürten has argued that from Bertram's perspective "the competency of the Church in helping to maintain the order of society was limited" (meaning that it was not the place of the Church to involve itself in politics and speak on behalf of persecuted minorities) and, in support of his argument, he cites an August 1945 memorandum by Archbishop Cardinal Joseph Frings of Cologne, in which Frings maintained that "the Church is not an organization to control the State in the sense that she is obligated to protest publicly through its priests or bishops against any kind of injustice."[67] This is not a convincing contention, given that in the spring of 1933 Jews in Germany were attacked with a hitherto unknown ferociousness, first by organizations of the stronger party in the coalition government and then (with the April boycott and legislation) directly by ministries and organs of State, far exceeding a simple injustice. In direct contradiction to this line of reasoning, the Church had formerly involved itself actively in politics during Weimar's last years by speaking out against communism and, after September 1930, against National Socialism. It is therefore hardly persuasive to argue that the Church could not be expected to take a public stance on behalf of victims of persecution, especially since a few Catholic bishops, such as Clemens August von Galen of Münster and Konrad von Preysing, first of Eichstätt and then of Berlin, would very actively oppose the regime (though in Galen's case, not in support of Jews) in the far more perilous context of the radicalized Nazi regime during the Second World War.[68]

---

66. From their correspondence it is clear that German bishops were aware that many Catholics were all too eager to join in with the spirit of the new Germany and anxious to avoid another *Kulturkampf* situation and their concomitant ostracization from the mainstream of society.
67. Hürten, *Deutsche Katholiken*, 196.
68. In the spring of 1933 Galen still agreed with basic tenets of the new regime and welcomed its struggle against "Liberalism, Marxism, Godlessness, and public immorality." See Michael Grüttner, *Das Dritte Reich 1933–1939* (Stuttgart: Klett-Cotta, 2014), 439; and Beth Griech-Polelle, *Bishop von Galen. German Catholicism and National Socialism* (New Haven: Yale University Press, 2002); on Preysing, see Kevin Spicer, *Resisting the Third Reich. The Catholic Clergy in Hitler's Berlin* (DeKalb: Northern Illinois Press, 2004).

Thirteen years after these events, on 26 February 1946, Konrad Adenauer, Lord Mayor of Cologne until mid-March 1933 and Chancellor of West Germany from 1949 to 1963, and himself a devout Catholic, wrote to the Bonn theologian Bernhard Custodis that,

> in my opinion the German people and the bishops and clergy bear their fair share of the blame for the events in the concentration camps.... The Jewish pogroms of 1933 and 1938 happened in full public view.... I believe that if all the bishops had publicly protested from their pulpits on a given day, much could have been avoided. This did not happen and there is no excuse for it.[69]

Quite obviously Adenauer was not aware of his own wishful thinking: the basis for such a remonstration had been entirely absent in 1933, for the major impediment to any kind of protest against the persecution of Germany's Jews was the very mentality and outlook of German bishops themselves.

69. Adenauer, *Briefe*, 172–173.

13

REACTIONS OF THE GERMAN ADMINISTRATIVE AND JUDICIAL BUREAUCRACY

The way in which authorities dealt with violent attacks, in particular with respect to "*Ostjuden*," can best be demonstrated by the case of the highly industrialized state of Saxony. With 346 inhabitants per square kilometer, it was the most densely populated state in the Reich (excepting city-states),[1] and it incorporated several large cities with a high proportion of Jews from the East, including Leipzig, Dresden, and Chemnitz.[2] In this predominantly Protestant state, the NSDAP was stronger than in the Reich overall; the same was true for Communists and Social Democrats: in the 5 March 1933 elections the NSDAP received 43.9 percent of the national vote (45.0 percent in Saxony); the SPD 18.3 percent (26.2 percent in Saxony); and the KPD 12.3 percent (16.5 percent in Saxony). More than 90 percent of Saxony's population were Protestant (1925).[3] Numbers of reported attacks on East European Jews were high. A 24 April 1933 listing of arrests and cases of bodily injury, sent by the Saxon Ministry for Foreign Affairs to the Interior Ministry with the request to review the information, records "fifty known arrests of Polish citizens – predominantly

---

1. *Statistisches Jahrbuch* (1933), 5. The Reich average was 140.6 inhabitants per square kilometer. Saxony had an area of 14,986 sq. km and, with 5,196,000 inhabitants (1933), was thus smaller than Baden, which had half as many inhabitants.
2. In 1933 Leipzig was the fifth largest (713,470 inhabitants), Dresden the seventh largest (642,143), and Chemnitz the seventeenth largest (350,734) German city in the Reich. See Thamer, *Verführung*, 258. On the "*Ostjuden*" in Saxony, see SHStA Dresden, Bestand 10736, no. 11708, "Einwanderung und Ausweisung von Ostjuden," fol. 126.
3. *Statistisches Jahrbuch* (1933), 540–41, 18.

Before the Holocaust: Antisemitic Violence and the Reaction of German Elites and Institutions during the Nazi Takeover. Hermann Beck, Oxford University Press. © Hermann Beck 2022. DOI: 10.1093/oso/9780192865076.003.0014

those of the Jewish race" and "twenty-five arrests of Czech citizens." Of the fifty cases of "bodily injury of Polish citizens . . . police inquiries still have not led to the identification of perpetrators in any single case." The report conceded that "according to the information that reached us it cannot be denied that some cases involved considerable mistreatment."[4] The Saxon Foreign Ministry asserted that it had "up to this point refrained from providing answers to queries from the Polish Consul in all cases, since any official reference to these matters – excepting denials – merely furnished foreign Consuls with further material to hinder the rejection of atrocity propaganda."[5] Thus, the bureaucracy dealt with antisemitic attacks ultimately on the basis of *raison d' état*.

As numbers of attacks rose, the Saxon Foreign Ministry enacted guidelines "for the response to complaints levied by foreign Consulates regarding the mistreatment of their citizens."[6] These should be characterized by "uniform interpretations." Police authorities were told never to respond directly to complaints, but to first convey the results of police investigations to the Interior Ministry, which would then forward the outcome of its inquiry to the Foreign Ministry.[7] For complaints issued by the Polish Diplomatic Mission in Berlin, the complicated route through administrative channels did not end here: Saxony's Foreign Ministry was to forward its reports to the Reich Interior Ministry. In general, inquiries were to be "handled in a dilatory fashion," – that is, delaying tactics were to be applied to the whole process.[8]

A review of the complaints lodged by the Polish Consulate in Leipzig indicates that these dealt with different cases than those that the Polish

---

4. 24 Apr. 1933 at SHStA Dresden, Bestand 10717, no. 4846,"Verhaftungen."
5. Ibid.
6. 12 May 1933 at SHStA Dresden, Bestand 10717, no. 4846, "Entwurf an Innenministerium."
7. Ibid.
8. 30 Aug. 1933 at SHStA Dresden, Bestand 10717, no. 4846, "Reichsminister des Innern an Landesregierungen." The Reich Interior Ministry also demanded to be "informed of all cases in which foreigners are taken into protective custody, so that the necessary material is immediately at hand to respond to diplomatic protests."

Diplomatic Mission in Berlin had listed as having taking place in Saxony.[9] The Polish Consulate in Leipzig and the Polish Embassy in Berlin apparently had not compared their rolls of complaints. This would have been difficult, given the large number of attacks. Poland's Consulate in Leipzig, for example, sent a list of complaints to Saxony's Foreign Ministry in Dresden, in which the Polish Consul complained that his earlier "interventions from the 10th, 11th, 13th, 17th, 18th, 20th, and 23rd of the month [March] regarding excesses against Polish citizens of the Jewish faith" remained without response. On 28 March the Consulate presented a list of further complaints that cited another twenty-five cases.[10] Even though it is impossible to cite definitive numbers in light of sketchy records and missing archival files, it can safely be assumed that in the Free State of Saxony alone the number of assaults on Polish Jews amounted to several hundred.[11]

In dealing with the brutal attacks on "*Ostjuden*," Saxon officials found themselves caught between the Scylla of expected national solidarity with the perpetrators and the Charybdis of their own sense of justice, for they knew all too well that reports about the SA's brutal maltreatment of victims were true. In the conflict between nationalist sensibilities and the rule of law, *raison d'état* prevailed. The authorities distorted the truth to protect the reputation of the Reich. For some officials it may have been an easy choice on account of their own prejudices. The *post factum* recording of the progression of events in assault cases by the police makes it clear that the brutality of the attacks was minimized and that victims were intimidated and put under pressure not to press their cases too strongly. As a result, victims often downplayed what had happened to them.

9. See the aforementioned petitions of the Polish Envoy to the German Foreign Ministry of 11 March, 23 March, 27 March, and 5 April 1933 at BA Berlin, R43 II, no. 1195, fols. 113–120; 164–174; 199–204; and R43 II, no. 603, fols. 15–29.
10. 28 March 1933 at SHStA Dresden, Bestand 10717, no. 4846.
11. In the Hauptstaatsarchiv Dresden a total of eleven *Aktenbestände* (nos. 4847–4857) are missing from series 10717, which deals with "Complaints of foreign diplomatic missions concerning attacks on their Jewish citizens." In other words, countless complaints that had been registered in 1933 have disappeared.

Officials Minimize Attacks

It became apparent from a 5 April 1933 report of the Chemnitz police presidium to the Saxony Interior Ministry that officials minimized attacks.[12] The merchant Littmann Grebler had been forced by the SA to scrape political graffiti off of the sides of buildings on 25 March. His statement reads as follows: "I have not been beaten. My wife, mentioned here, was in no way bothered. I have not reported the incident to the Consulate and also do not know who has."[13] The commercial assistant Markus Reich, born in 1898 in Galicia, was abducted on 8 March by Dresden SA members together with his brother Simon and other Polish Jews. While Simon Reich stated that he had been beaten by SA men, Markus Reich declared that "he had been treated very correctly and politely and thought highly of the SA men, who [even] in this excitable time had not said one impolite word to him."[14] It is obvious that Markus Reich wanted to protect himself with this soothing statement from retaliation by Nazi stormtroopers. The hairdresser Alex Kamelhar, born in 1914, who had also been forced by the SA to rub communist political slogans off buildings, and whose hair, like that of others, was cut off, could not appear in person owing to "illness." Apparently, he had been beaten up by the SA and lay in hospital. His mother made the following statement: "An SA man used very small scissors to cut off a portion of the hair."[15]

Victims had been savagely abused and now felt compelled to downplay the offense for fear of the SA. Efforts to minimize attacks are consistently apparent. The merchant Jakob Salomon Pfeffer, born in 1880 in Poland, admitted to being repeatedly hit "by several SA men" and had to be treated by a doctor, yet apologized for the Polish

12. 5 Apr. 1933 at SHStA Dresden, Bestand 10717, no. 4846, "Polizeipräsidium Chemnitz an Ministerium des Innern."
13. 5 Apr. 1933, ibid.
14. 30 May 1933 at SHStA Dresden, Bestand 10717, no. 4846, "Sächsisches Innenministerium an Ministerium der auswärtigen Angelegenheiten."
15. 5 Apr. 1933, ibid.

Consulate's complaint: "I did not turn to the Consulate and also cannot state on whose part this action was taken."[16] The police report mentioned that Pfeffer and his daughter, who was arrested with him, "are accused of high treason," that is, of being involved in politically subversive activities. This was clearly a trumped-up allegation, used to explain Pfeffer's injuries. The Polish Jews who had been attacked and subsequently arrested consisted of small shopkeepers, office workers, the owner of a bakery, and a hairdresser, rendering the assertion that "with respect to these people, the…Chemnitz NSDAP has established that Jews support leftist political parties and finance their election campaigns" absurd. The report ends with the usual observation: "Despite detailed investigations, the persons who assaulted Jews have not been apprehended."[17] Such allegations merely served as a standing excuse and justification for the brutal attacks of the perpetrators. The all-pervasive fear that so obviously dictated the statements of the victims to the police was justified, since attackers were clearly not held accountable for their actions and might well strike again.

On 13 April, Hans Pfundtner, Undersecretary of State in the Reich Interior Ministry, sent a further list with about fifteen "attacks against foreigners" to the Reich Commissar for the state of Saxony, Manfred von Killinger, regarding arrests and severe maltreatment in Saxon cities. He concluded with a comment typical for the mindset of the bureaucracy: "I respectfully request that these complaints be verified and the results of the investigation shared with me. At the same time, I request that it be examined to what extent undesirable, especially Jewish, foreigners can be deported."[18] For the authorities, the victims of attacks were evidently considered responsible for their own plight. Deportation thus seemed the best solution, also to avoid provoking the SA unnecessarily by their very presence. The reports of Saxony's Interior Ministry, which "interpreted" police accounts of the incidents before transmitting them to the Saxon

16. Ibid.   17. Ibid.
18. 13 Apr. 1933 at SHStA Dresden, Bestand 10717, no. 4846, "Reichsministerium des Innern an Killinger."

Foreign Ministry, consistently explain attacks in such a way as to provide excuses for the perpetrators. Flimsy reasons are cited that supposedly justify attacks or explain them away as practically "within rights." Specific charges against victims are fabricated and the construed incriminating evidence is put forward to excuse attacks, exonerate attackers, and provide justification for their actions as a form of self-defense against communists, subversives, and other dubious elements.[19] Incriminating material against victims was also fabricated to enable officials to take the moral high ground when confronted by the complaints of Polish diplomats. Toward that end, the Interior Ministry often directly adopted the SA version of events.

Fabricated Charges against Victims

To give but a few examples from archival documents: in response to a complaint by the Polish Consulate in Leipzig about an attack on a synagogue in Dresden, the Saxon Interior Ministry stated in its report: "The Dresden police presidium declared that on the day in question it was suspected that in the synagogue in the Sporergasse 2 a political meeting was to be held."[20] Against the opposition of the police, the SA had then "brought the Jews to the *Volkshaus* [by then an SA meeting place]," but "interrogations failed to produce incriminating materials."[21] The pretext that the raid was staged as a response to a (supposedly Communist Party) meeting was evidently contrived by the SA to give their action a veneer of legality. In a 9 May report, the arrest of Josef and Chane Weiner was explained thus: "[T]he husband Weiner had been charged with fomenting agitation among his Jewish co-religionists and communists against the regime." It soon became evident that "sufficient proof thereof could not

19. 28 Apr., 9 May, 23 May, 27 May, 30 May, 22 June, 19 July, and 22 July 1933 at SHStA Dresden, Bestand 10717, no. 4846, "Sächsisches Ministerium des Innern an Ministerium der auswärtigen Angelegenheiten." In all cases presented here, Polish Jews were assaulted, mistreated, and also often robbed.
20. 28 Apr. 1933, ibid.   21. 28 Apr. 1933, ibid.

be furnished."[22] The arrest of Sabina Haspel, born in 1907 in Galicia, was based on the supposition that "in a letter that became known, [she] spread rumors of alleged violent acts against Jews."[23] During the Nazi takeover, spreading this particular rumor was not an unusual "crime."

Officials in the Interior Ministry were frequently confronted with antisemitic attacks and were well aware that Sabina Haspel was innocent and had been arrested solely because she was foreign-born and Jewish. In the same vein, Juda Tager, who was mentioned earlier, was accused of disseminating "atrocity propaganda" and "according to a credible witness... [of having] spread the following seditious statement:... 'In Chemnitz SA-men had cut off the beard of an old Jew. In the Dresden Brüdergasse they had threatened and extorted 200 Reichsmarks from a sick Jew.'"[24] It says much about the lack of political independence of Interior Ministry officials that they considered this a criminal act, even though they knew perfectly well that the "seditious statements" were true. Despite the Reich Interior Ministry's frequent warnings to "diligently and promptly investigate [attacks] against foreign citizens that were allegedly committed by members of the SA and SS," the procedure among Saxon officials continued unaltered: assaults were minimized and victims were incriminated with fabricated crimes.[25] This didn't always work, as became clear in the case against Heinrich Leßmann, who was taken into "protective custody" because he "was about to flee to Poland... [to] disseminate atrocity propaganda about the treatment of Jews in Germany," and who (allegedly) had also made disparaging remarks about Reichskanzler Hitler.[26] Of the eight witnesses supporting the accusations, seven withdrew their testimony after being summoned by the police. A witness by the name of Kiesauer claimed that Leßmann had

22. 9 May 1933, ibid.   23. 13 May 1933, ibid.

24. 13 May 1933, ibid. In its report, Saxony's Foreign Ministry adopted the Interior Ministry's version almost verbatim.

25. 22 May 1933, ibid. This could indicate that Saxon officials were closer than officials in the capital to local SA members who committed the attacks, though it is more likely that, in demanding diligent investigations, the Reich Interior Ministry officials merely wanted to uphold a facade to satisfy foreign consulates and embassies.

26. 27 May 1933, ibid.

said that "the Germans are pigs, just as is Hitler's party." Leßmann denied this charge, and when Kiesauer was interrogated again on 12 May, he conceded that he had been "mistaken." Leßmann was released the next day after the fabricated case against him collapsed.[27]

In cases where no plausible charges could be construed, other pretexts were put forward to provide reasons for arrests and shroud them in legality: "The police had to put Milewsky in protective custody since the public mood against Jewish traders, especially against Milewsky himself, was so hostile that acts of violence against him were to be feared."[28] Where beatings had been exceptionally brutal, authorities asserted that the case happened "at a time of greatest national excitement,"[29] or, as the Saxon Interior Ministry commented on 22 June, "In reviewing the cases before us, it must be taken into account that all of them took place during the first weeks after the national revolution. Insofar as ill-treatment occurred, this is regrettable; yet with major political upheavals, such as happened in the wake of the national revolution, this cannot be avoided completely even when authorities are fully alert."[30]

Another method to excuse perpetrators was to discredit the "moral character" of the victim: "Löwenkron, Max, has been taken into protective custody on 11 April, released again on 9 May 1933 and consigned to the Dresden-Friedrichstadt hospital.... Löwenkron is a man suffering from a serious venereal disease."[31] This suggests that Max Löwenkron was hospitalized not because of injuries inflicted by the SA, but because of a venereal disease which, in turn, was meant to indicate a questionable lifestyle. As far as the authorities were concerned, cases occasionally took care of themselves: "Steinitz, Anna, has poisoned herself with gas on 7 April 1933 in Chemnitz for unknown reasons. Therefore, she could not have been taken into custody on 24 April 1933."[32]

---

27. 27 May 1933, ibid.   28. 30 May 1933, ibid.   29. 30 May 1933, ibid.
30. 22 June 1933, ibid. Officials also knew that due to the amnesties crimes would be forgiven in any case.
31. 19 July 1933, ibid.
32. 19 July 1933, ibid. On suicides of German Jews in 1933, see Goeschel, "Suicides," 22–45, esp. 23–24.

In those rare instances when officials in subordinate administrative branches acted in ignorance of instructions that prescribed standardized responses and replied directly to complaints by the Polish Consulate in Leipzig, the same pattern of argumentation is prevalent. The district administration office (*Landratsamt*) in Zwickau, for example, responded to the Polish Consulate in the case of the painter Moses Scheiner (who had been taken into "protective custody") that Scheiner had been arrested because he was "under the well-founded suspicion of supporting communist subversion." Authorities also claimed to be worried that Scheiner was in personal danger during the national revolution, "because he was very unpopular in wide circles of Plauen's population due to existing suspicion of treasonous and subversive objectives and his affiliation with the Judentum."[33]

In August 1933, when the wave of antisemitic violence had passed its zenith and officials in both Saxony and the Reich had been confronted with many hundreds of cases, a directive of Reich Interior Minister Frick regarding the "treatment of Polish Jews" summed up the issue from the perspective of the bureaucracy: "Let me note that from the standpoint of my portfolio, I consider it necessary that Germany be freed as soon as possible from those eastern Jewish types who do not belong to the Reich and have shown themselves unworthy of German hospitality by dint of their personal conduct and business practices."[34] Even contemporary Prussian or Saxon officials (though bound by the strictures of their mindset) may have thought that this was an odd kind of "hospitality" that expressed itself in robbery, attacks, and assaults designed to humiliate the guests. The intra-bureaucratic correspondence as a whole leaves no doubt that the authorities tried to place blame for the attacks squarely on the shoulders of the victims. In the end, those Prussian and Saxon

33. 15 July 1933 at SHStA Dresden. Bestand 10717, no. 4846, "Kreishauptmannschaft Zwickau an polnisches Konsulat Leipzig." Plauen had 113,860 inhabitants in 1933; *Statistisches Jahrbuch* (1933), 7.
34. 24 Aug. 1933 at SHStA Dresden, Bestand 10717, no. 4846, "Reichsminister des Innern an preußischen Minister des Innern und sächsisches Ministerium der auswärtigen Angelegenheiten."

officials who so shrewdly manipulated the truth may have come to believe their own lies.

A memorandum of the German Foreign Office to the Interior Ministry of 22 June also throws light on the attitude of Polish authorities toward their Jewish subjects:[35] the Polish government wished, "after the recent welcome relaxation of tensions in German-Polish relations...to avoid new aggravations in mutual relations due to incidents with Polish Jews."[36] The Polish side had emphasized that conflicts regarding the "Jewish Question" in the spring "had to do with ill-treatment or other excesses that took place in the wake of revolutionary turbulences," whereas now the "destruction of the livelihood of Polish Jews in Germany" was at risk. At stake was the treatment of those Polish Jews "who travel from marketplace to marketplace to sell their merchandise," and the "expulsion of Polish Jews from Germany."[37] According to the German Foreign Office, the Polish government was concerned mainly that Polish Jews could maintain their already meager existence in Germany and that they would not be expelled on account of minor misdemeanors relating to passports or the failure to renew residence permits in time. In other words: Poland's main concern was for as many Polish Jews as possible to remain in Germany, while Germany wanted to expel the largest possible number of Polish Jews.[38] According to the German Foreign Office, Polish authorities therefore were not primarily interested in protecting their Jewish nationals from attacks by the SA. Their priority was that Polish Jews could remain in

---

35. 22 June 1933 at SHStA Dresden, Bestand 10717, no. 4846, "Auswärtiges Amt, abschriftlich dem Reichsministerium des Innern."
36. Ibid.
37. Ibid. In the summer of 1933, the German side emphasized that with regard to the expulsion of Eastern Jews (which had been speeded up since March), "interstate relations with Poland" should be considered. 24 August 1933 at SHSta Dresden, Bestand 10717, no. 4846.
38. Already on 17 February 1933 an edict of the Prussian Interior Ministry to the police was issued whereby the standing order not to expel "Ostjuden" was rescinded. On 15 March a decree of the Reich Interior Ministry followed, mandating that further immigration of "Ostjuden" be avoided. Eastern Jews should no longer be granted citizenship and those without valid residence permits deported. See Walk, ed., Das Sonderrecht, 3–4. On antisemitism in Poland, see William W. Hagen, "Before the 'Final Solution:' Toward a Comparative Analysis of Political Anti-Semitism in Interwar Germany and Poland," Journal of Modern History 68 (1996), 351–381.

Germany for economic reasons. Beginning in the summer of 1933, both sides seemed interested in a further relaxation of tensions, and the Polish side put forward instrumental reasons for ending transgressions against Polish Jews in Germany: attacks "triggered strong repercussions with the Jewish population in Poland, so that it would become ever more difficult for the Polish government to work toward consolidating an easing of tensions."[39]

Humanitarian considerations never entered into the German authorities' field of vision, as illustrated by the case of Salomon Kopf. The Polish Jews Kopf, Engel, and Lewin, as well as the Austrian citizen Leo Grummer, were beaten up and badly mistreated in the Hainewalde camp in Saxony and then expelled to Czechoslovakia during the night of 31 March/1 April. The case had bureaucratic repercussions through the end of 1933 because one of the abused victims, Salomon Kopf, died of his severe injuries ten days later in a hospital in the town of Warnsdorf in the German-speaking Sudetenland and was buried in Teplitz on 15 April.[40] Since Kopf left behind his father, mother, and two daughters, whom he had cared for while alive, the family presented the Saxon authorities with a compensation payment bill of 186,000 Reichsmarks—a significant sum at the time—of which 180,000 Reichsmarks were meant "for the death of the son and caregiver."[41]

In bureaucratic communications about Salomon Kopf, Saxon officials were preoccupied mostly with protecting "the Saxon state treasury against liability" and making sure that the case "could not be exploited

39. 22 June 1933, "Auswärtiges Amt, abschriftlich dem Reichsministerium des Innern," ibid.
40. SHStA Dresden, Bestand 10717, no. 4858, fols. 207–216; and 26 August, 9 September, and 29 September 1933 at SHStA Dresden, Bestand 10717, no. 4846.
41. 19 August 1933 at SHStA Dresden, Bestand 10717, no. 4846, "Reichsminister des Innern an Sächsisches Ministerium der auswärtigen Angelegenheiten." Salomon Kopf was a salesman, born in Kalisch, a city in central Poland (Kalisz), in 1904. Kopf, badly beaten again during his forced expulsion and left at the border with a broken skull, was found by the Czech border patrol on 1 April 1933 and transported to a hospital in Warnsdorf (occasionally also spelled Varnsdorf), a Czech town on the border with Saxony, where he died on 10 April 1933. See also Gesellschaft für Christlich-Jüdische Zusammenarbeit Dresden, e.V., ed., *Buch der Erinnerung. Juden in Dresden: Deportiert, Ermordet, Verschollen 1933–1945* (Dresden: Universitätsverlag & Richter, 2006).

abroad to the disadvantage of the German Reich and the National Socialist movement."[42] Consenting to compensation payments might be viewed as an admission of guilt, which was also to be avoided. The Saxon authorities had before them Kopf's death certificate, as well as detailed records specifying the severity of the injuries to his face and skull, wounds to which he succumbed after a painful ten-day struggle for his life.[43] These records testify to the savagery with which Kopf's murder by installments had been carried out. In intra-bureaucratic correspondence no mention is made of the brutality with which Kopf's murderers proceeded, no doubt because it would have made the SA and the Nazi government appear in a bad light. Even though an official investigation was carried out, the assembled materials about Kopf's case disappeared shortly after they had been sent to the SA for further comment.[44] It was events like these that documented the unambiguously corrupt and criminal character of the regime, even at this very early stage.

SA Colonel (*Standartenführer*) Unterstab in Löbau (Saxony), who had been responsible for the documents, freely admitted that "he regretfully had to acknowledge that the documents could no longer be located" and that he did not know "if the documents had been intentionally suppressed or simply got lost."[45] This transparent maneuver of destroying incriminating evidence was not punished by the authorities. Surviving investigation reports are replete with the usual euphemisms and false statements—such as, for example, that in the course of the expulsion, Kopf had "fallen in the treacherous terrain at night and thereby sustained his injuries." And even in this murder case the victims are slandered in an

---

42. 21 November 1933 at SHStA Dresden, Bestand 10717, no. 4858, "Sächsisches Ministerium des Innern an Ministerium der auswärtigen Angelegenheiten." In terms of criminal law, the case involved *"schwere Körperverletzung mit Todesfolge"* ("severe bodily injury resulting in death").

43. 19 August 1933 at SHStA Dresden, Bestand 10717, no. 4846, "Reichsminister des Innern an sächsisches Ministerium der auswärtigen Angelegenheiten."

44. 26 August 1933 at SHStA Dresden Bestand 10717, no. 4846, "Ministerium des Innern an Ministerium der auswärtigen Angelegenheiten." Despite the disappearance, Kopf's case was briefly referred to at the time in a report from the Jewish Telegraphic Agency and is documented in written accounts and databases. See n. 41 above.

45. Ibid.

attempt to exonerate the perpetrators. In this vein, all the victims are smeared as "traveling Jews of the worst kind," and Kopf is accused of "having had an illegitimate child in Germany for whom he refused to pay child support."[46] This is merely another example of the well-known pattern by which the SA tried to vindicate the criminal acts of its members by fabricating incriminating evidence and unsubstantiated accusations meant to discredit the victims. While SA Major (*Sturmbann-führer*) Hans Müller, the commandant of the Hainewalde camp where Kopf had been tortured, was put on mandatory leave, the Saxon authorities' zeal in following through the criminal prosecution quickly waned.[47] After all, German Reich and state authorities shared similar orientations on this and pursued the same strategy: minimize the crimes and protect the perpetrators. In intra-bureaucratic correspondence the victims appear to have caused the crimes, simply by virtue of their very presence.

Antisemitic Attacks and the Reaction of the Judicial Bureaucracy

In cases regarding attacks on German Jews, the documentary evidence in the files of the Prussian Ministry of Justice allows us a glimpse of reactions in the judicial branch of the bureaucracy to violence against German Jews. In the Prussian province of Hesse, raids and assaults in the spring of 1933 were often coupled with extortion. A typical case was that of SA First Lieutenant (*Sturmführer*) Friedrich Best, who, with a posse of his men, raided the premises of Jewish livestock dealers, mistreated them, and extorted small sums of money (the modesty of the sums was dictated by the general poverty of the rural population). Allegedly, the victims had aroused the ire of the rural population by virtue of purportedly dubious (though unspecified) machinations. On 15 May 1933 Best and his group

46. 30 April 1933 at SHStA Dresden, Bestand 10717, no. 4846, "Schutzhaftlager Hainewalde."
47. 18 December 1933 at SHStA Dresden, Bestand 10717, no. 4846, "Sächsisches Ministerium der auswärtigen Angelegenheiten an Reichsministerium des Innern."

invaded the home of the livestock dealer Max Oppenheimer, beat him with truncheons, and extorted 90 Reichsmarks (since the badly roughed-up Oppenheimer's blood had soiled Best's coat); on 20 May Best attacked the livestock dealer Adolf Frankenberg with another group and extorted a slightly larger sum, out of which Frankenberg had allegedly swindled Best's friends. According to the report by the Marburg prosecutor *Oberstaatsanwalt* Heintzmann, both Oppenheimer and Frankenberg declared themselves to be "not interested in the punishment of the perpetrators," and Oppenheimer's wife withdrew the charges she had made with the police for fear of reprisals.[48] Regarding the reaction of the authorities, it is conspicuous that the public prosecutor in charge of the investigation saw himself in the role of defending counsel. The injuries of the victims were dismissed as "numerous, but merely external and not very serious" in the case of Frankenberg; and "considerable, but merely external wounds" in the case of Oppenheimer. In his report transmitted via the state attorney general in Kassel to the Prussian Ministry of Justice in Berlin, the Marburg prosecutor adopted a defense counsel's version of events by slandering the victims: Oppenheimer had "made himself very unpopular with the population because of disparaging remarks against the NSDAP;" he was said "to have threatened SA men with beatings" (an unlikely charge), and was generally considered to be a "parasite of the people" (*Volksschädling*).[49] Adolf Frankenberg was "so much hated in the population on account of his deceitful dealings...that people wanted to hang him," so that Best had to take him into protective custody.[50] Frankenberg's alleged fraudulent dealings with Best's acquaintances, which had been used as a transparent pretext for Best's extortions, are accepted as fact in the prosecutor's report. It therefore comes as no surprise that in both cases the prosecutor's office requested the termination of legal proceedings,

48. 3 August 1933 at GStAPK Dahlem, Rep. 84a, no. 54804, fol. 3; 4 August 1933 at GStAPK Dahlem, Rep. 84a, no. 54805, fol. 4. As to the "moral" assessment of the case, the public prosecutor commented in Max Oppenheimer's case: "Although the attacks committed are severe, it is especially the financial extortion that we strongly object to." (no. 54804, fol. 3).
49. 3 August 1933 at GStAPK Dahlem, Rep. 84a, no. 54804, fol. 4.
50. 4 August 1933 at GStAPK Dahlem, Rep. 84a, no. 54805, fol. 5.

especially since the offenses were carried out "in connection with the National Socialist revolution for the enforcement of National Socialist State policies."[51] In both cases this request was granted a few days later.[52]

The tendentious report of the public prosecutor, which cast aspersions on the victims by labelling them "people's parasites," swindlers, and opponents of the national government (thereby creating extenuating circumstances for the perpetrators), was bound to lead to this result. Already months after Hitler's accession to the chancellorship, the administration of justice was thus unable to act with any degree of objectivity. A combination of political pressure and the expectations of those in power, which judicial officials anxiously strove to fulfill, played a decisive role in this. While reports detail the mistreatments inflicted on victims, the general tenor of these reports turns victims into villains, exculpates the attackers, and makes the violent assaults appear as a kind of self-defense against an existing gangrene in the body politic. In the present case, the Marburg public prosecutor does his best to indicate in his report that he is on the side of the perpetrators, that is, the National Socialist State, even though his professionalism forces him to recount the facts, while at the same time minimizing the severity of the attack and finding excuses for the criminals to indicate that he is fully behind the new government.

In the first phase of the National-Socialist revolutionary takeover, much remained undecided and held in abeyance, so that judicial officials, who were also concerned about their careers, felt under great pressure to live up to what the zeitgeist seemed to demand of them. Their reports were thus ideologically colored, which endowed every anti-Jewish crime with a certain "moral" justification. Perpetrators knew quite well that they could count on this. As a consequence, they not only felt free to behave

51. Ibid.
52. 14 August 1933 at GStAPK Dahlem, Rep. 84a, no. 54804; 16 August at GStAPK Dahlem, Rep. 84a, no. 54805. This so-called "Issuing of pardons on the occasion of the completion of the National Socialist revolution" was based on an ordinance by Göring of 22 July 1933 in connection with a general instruction of the Justice Ministry of 25 July 1933.

in a brazen and impertinent fashion but often saw themselves as agents restoring "moral justice." In the mindset of the average Nazi stormtrooper, Jews had a lot to answer for: according to National Socialist propaganda, they had financially bled Germany for decades. The "stab in the back"—defeat and the sudden inglorious end to the war—the punitive Versailles Treaty, a threatening Communist Party, the denigration of national symbols and shrines, and the weakening of the national fiber were all laid at their door.[53] They were also considered an alien body that had built its wealth on the misery of the people and whose members were far better off than members of the SA. In the mental climate prevailing in the spring of 1933, SA men would have felt "morally" justified in their deeds, even while serving jail time.[54] The bias of the judicial system in conjunction with the amnesty for "crimes committed during the National Socialist Revolution" ensured that there would be no punishment for their crimes. In instances of robbery and pillage, perpetrators could also make themselves believe that they were only seeking compensation for the damages that, according to Nazi propaganda, Jews had inflicted on the German people, while physical attacks could be construed as retribution for other crimes Jews had allegedly perpetrated. In Nazi eyes, after 5 March 1933 the time had come to seek revenge and demand punishment for all the alleged wrongs suffered.

A typical example of this "righteous retribution" is the assault on Rudolf Boldes, a furniture dealer in Recklinghausen, a city in the Prussian Rhine province, by SS member Emil Somplatzki. Somplatzki's brother-in-law, the miner Friedrich Jewski, had ordered bedroom furnishings from Boldes before the Nazis came to power but then cancelled the order. Boldes thereupon sued him and Jewski had to pay the furniture

---

53. These factors and others were often cited by perpetrators as pretexts for their attacks.
54. Richard Evans mentions that for National Socialists Jews were scapegoats for a wide variety of issues; they were blamed for everything that Nazis hated: "Communism and finance capitalism, social democracy and liberalism, pacifism and international understanding, openness to compromise and tolerance, homosexuality and the emancipation of women, critical journalism, satire and cabaret, sexual emancipation and personal freedom, atonal music and abstract art, experimental literature and concrete poetry." Evans, *Drittes Reich*, vol. I: *Aufstieg*, 555.

dealer more than 300 Reichsmarks in compensation. On 30 March 1933, when the political situation had undergone a complete transformation, Somplatzki appeared in Boldes's shop with a second SS man and menacingly demanded 350 Reichsmarks from Boldes.[55] When Boldes refused to pay, he was "hit in the face about 10 times and kicked in the shins," and then threatened with execution at gunpoint. Boldes's mother-in-law, who happened to be in the shop during the raid, was also mistreated.[56] The Recklinghausen lower court thereupon charged Somplatzki with coercion and bodily harm and mandated that he pay a fine to the victims as punishment. When Somplatzki protested against the payments imposed on him—50 Reichsmarks to Boldes and 30 Reichsmarks to Boldes's mother-in-law—judicial proceedings ensued. Somplatzki's defense counsel moved to dismiss proceedings, since there had been no witnesses except for the injured parties, and Boldes was not to be trusted, for he had "a bad reputation," used "various tricks" in his rental-purchase business, "proceeded ruthlessly against buyers" when they "did not meet their obligations," and "also had previous convictions for fraud."[57] Somplatzki's defense counsel not only failed to provide proof for these serious allegations but went further, adding to his unsubstantiated accusations that "Boldes has the reputation of a man who, regardless of the misery of his compatriots, brutally uses any legal means at his disposal to get his money." Since Boldes had merely demanded what was his due, Somplatzki's lawyer basically implied that it was immoral to use legal means to safeguard one's rights. In contrast to Boldes, the defense counsel continued, the SS man Somplatzki was someone "who is completely committed to the national movement."[58]

Instructive again is the reaction of the judicial authorities—in this instance, that of the Bochum prosecutor *Oberstaatsanwalt* Dresler, who

---

55. GStAPK Dahlem, Rep. 84a, no. 54913, "Wegen Nötigung und Körperverletzung des jüdischen Möbelhändlers Rudolf Boldes," fols. 11–17; 43–46.
56. 27 October 1933 at GStAPK Dahlem, Rep. 84a, no. 54913.
57. 17 October 1933, ibid.
58. 17 October 1933, ibid. "One even gets the idea that, in this case, [Somplatzki] acted without having been aware that he contravenes the law."

provided a final summing up of the case. Dresler minutely listed the details of Somplatzki's offense, even mentioning that Somplatzki took away Boldes's wallet and tried to rip his watch from its chain. This seems to indicate that the prosecution was convinced of Somplatzki's guilt. Yet, in the final summary of his report, the prosecutor fully adopted the (unverified) incriminating charges advanced by the defense counsel against Boldes, who, he charged, worked "with methods characteristic of those businessmen" (a clear reference to the fact that Boldes was Jewish) and callously proceeded against those "who cannot meet their obligations." Somplatzki's anger was therefore only too understandable, since his brother-in-law had "a wife and seven children." In this line of reasoning, prejudice assumed the force of legal facts. The public prosecutor then moved to dismiss proceedings since the offense had been committed in the context of the National Socialist revolution. His motion was granted.[59]

Other offenses, even raids involving entire gangs of perpetrators, were treated along the same lines. On the evening of the nationwide boycott of 1 April 1933, for example, a group of about twenty SA and SS men raided two country inns in the Fritzlar-Homberg region in northern Hesse.[60] The first victim was the innkeeper Loeb, from whom a sum of money was extorted and who then, after handing over the money, was beaten with truncheons by a group of ten to twelve men. The motive of the attack was ostensibly revenge, since the popular local teacher Knoche had allegedly lost his position at Loeb's instigation. Shortly thereafter, the same group raided the inn of Levi Gutheim and subjected him and his family to the same ordeal of extortion and beating. Gutheim was reproached with "having torn down a swastika pennant." In both raids,

---

59. 27 October, 7 November, and 10 November 1933 at GStAPK Dahlem, Rep. 84a, no. 54913.
60. GStAPK Dahlem, Rep. 84a, no. 54813, "Untersuchung wegen Überfalls auf jüdische Gastwirtschaften. Ermittlungsverfahren gegen den Lehrer Knoche und Genossen." Fritzlar an der Eder, a town in the administrative district of Kassel, had 4,600 inhabitants in 1933; Homberg, a town in the same district, had 4,000 inhabitants; *Neuer Brockhaus*, 4 vols., Leipzig, 1938.

the gang of SA and SS men left the scene of the crime only after "having appropriated the existing supplies of cigars, cigarettes, and liquor."[61]

The acting district governor (Regierungspräsident) in Kassel remarked on the case that "perpetrators should be prosecuted, especially with regard to property thefts."[62] The serious injuries of the victims—Gutheim's son had severe concussion as well as wounds on his arms and legs—had been stressed in the district administrator's (Landrat) report to the Regierungspräsident, but they played no role in bringing criminal charges against the offenders.[63] The report of the Kassel prosecutor Ludwig, following the usual pattern, advocated dismissing the case. Since nothing was known to the detriment of the victims, Ludwig confined himself to speculating that "in the final analysis the central motivation for the actions of the offenders has to be sought in the embitterment . . . about the behavior of the Jewish population."[64] The main offender, the teacher Knoche, who had close ties to the NSDAP, was defended by the Landrat: "I have known the teacher Knoche for years; he is full of spirit, but otherwise nothing is known against him. As I confidentially heard, he is slated to become a member of the County Board."[65] In fact, the raids against Jewish inns were the beginning of a brilliant career for Knoche. By 1936, the former village school teacher had become County Supervisor for Schools (Kreisschulrat).[66]

As it can safely be assumed that the estimated number of unrecorded attacks against foreign Jews in the German Reich was high, we may infer from the many hundreds of reported cases in the spring of 1933 alone that possibly as many as a thousand attacks on "Ostjuden" and other foreign

61. 25 August 1933 at GStAPK Dahlem, Rep. 84a, no. 54813, fol. 7v.
62. 5 April 1933 at GStAPK Dahlem, Rep. 84a, no. 54813. He also emphasized that the local police of the district in question (Dorfpolizisten) should not interrogate the perpetrators.
63. 2 April 1933 at GStAPK Dahlem, Rep. 84a, no. 54813, fol. 44. Those who took part in the raid were mentioned by name in the Landrat's report, wherein it was established that it was their SA regiment that had granted the authorization for the trip to Fritzlar-Homberg.
64. 25 August 1933 at GStAPK Dahlem, Rep. 84a/=, no. 54813, fol. 8.
65. 2 April 1933, ibid., fol. 45.
66. 4 March 1936, ibid. His name resurfaces in the files in 1936 because renewed proceedings were opened against Knoche that year and the Kassel prosecutor's office requested the old files from 1933.

Jews took place. Just weeks after Hitler became Chancellor, Eastern Jews especially were without protection or rights and were exposed to the wanton brutality of the SA, since the police, for the most part, failed to intervene. The fact that there was a pogrom-like climate only weeks into Hitler's chancellorship points not only to the effectiveness of antisemitic indoctrination among Nazi formations but also to significant antisemitic orientations in some parts of German society.

Authorities of the *Reich* and the German states knew quite well what was going on, but did everything to minimize crimes and shield the perpetrators, thereby becoming willing accomplices of the attackers.[67] The bureaucratic correspondence makes it appear as if victims triggered attacks against them by virtue of their very presence in Germany. This was also the case with the reaction of the judicial bureaucracy in instances of attacks against German Jews, to the point that readers of the intra-bureaucratic exchanges are left with the impression that the bureaucracy invented reasons to minimize and excuse the crimes committed by the SA. Quite often, judicial officials' own prejudices provided extenuating circumstances. By getting away with attacks that occasionally included murder, and seeing that the perpetrators got off scot-free, Nazi formations quickly understood that the bureaucracy was willing to cover up their criminal acts. To the SA this was a sign of encouragement and a signal to keep on going, for they would suffer no consequences. This attitude of the bureaucracy toward the multitude of brutal antisemitic attacks in the spring of 1933 makes it painfully obvious that, in the event of future outrages committed against Germany's Jewish community, no help could be expected from administrative or judicial officials— those same people who prided themselves on being the standard-bearers of Germany's *Rechtsstaat*, with its emphasis on both law and justice.

---

67. This complicity is astonishing, given the fact that, during the last months of Weimar, judges, public prosecutors, and the conservative *Preußischer Richterverein* (Prussian Association of Judges) were the repeated targets of Nazi attacks that made it obvious that, once in power, the NSDAP would not respect the independence of the judiciary. See Fattmann, *Bildungsbürger* 223.

14

REACTIONS OF HITLER'S CONSERVATIVE COALITION PARTNER

Hitler's coalition partner, the German National People's Party (DNVP or German Nationals) was the only political party in a position to react to the antisemitic violence that set in after the 5 March 1933 elections. The KPD had been banned after the Reichstag Fire Decree, the Social Democrats had to fend off increasing persecution themselves, and even the Catholic Center Party and the once influential liberal parties, now reduced to splinter parties with a total of seven deputies between them, were primarily concerned with their own political survival in March 1933.[1] Even so, the German Nationals were unlikely defenders of the rights of German Jews since their leaders and members were themselves antisemitic, although their own brand of antisemitism traditionally differed in tone, if not ultimately in outcome after 30 January 1933, from that of their coalition partner. As George Mosse has emphasized, the anti-Jewish orientations of conservatives were partly rooted in a long-standing cultural heritage dating back to the nineteenth century, when they were widely disseminated among the conservative middle-class milieu through a series of popular novels, in particular Gustav Freytag's

---

1. Larry E. Jones, *German Liberalism and the Dissolution of the Weimar Party System 1918-1933* (Chapel Hill and London: University of North Carolina Press, 1988); Matthias and Morsey, "Die Deutsche Staatspartei," in Matthias and Morsey, *Das Ende der Parteien* (Düsseldorf: Droste, 1960), 31–97; Hans Booms, "Die Deutsche Volkspartei," in Matthias and Morsey, *Ende der Parteien*, 523–539; Ludwig Richter, *Die Deutsche Volkspartei 1918–1933* (Düsseldorf: Droste, 2002).

Before the Holocaust: Antisemitic Violence and the Reaction of German Elites and Institutions during the Nazi Takeover.
Hermann Beck, Oxford University Press. © Hermann Beck 2022. DOI: 10.1093/oso/9780192865076.003.0015

Soll und Haben (1855) and Wilhelm Raabe's *Der Hungerpastor* (1864).[2] Their main Jewish protagonists, Veitel Itzig in Freytag's bestselling novel and Moses Freudenstein in Raabe's *Hungerpastor*, were depicted as stereotypical caricatures of allegedly typical Jewish characteristics to the point that the term "Itzig" was used as a derogatory synonym for Jew or Jewish.[3] These characters attained considerable notoriety in German educated society and shaped the indelibly negative image of the supposedly devilishly cunning Jew. Occasional positive images of Jewish characters, such as Bernhard Ehrenthal in Freytag's *Soll und Haben*, pale by comparison.[4]

The DNVP and the "Jewish Question" during the Weimar Republic

There was no consensus among DNVP leaders and rank-and-file members regarding the "Jewish Question" and thus no unified or consistent opinion about how the party should position itself on the issue. The multitude of viewpoints within the DNVP reflected the party's disparate roots, since upon its foundation it provided a home for former members of the conservative parties of the Empire, the German-Conservative and Free Conservative parties, and Christian Socials and members of *völkisch*

---

2. Mosse, "Deutsche Rechte," in Werner E. Mosse, ed., *Entscheidungsjahr 1932*, 183–246, esp. 184, 212.
3. As, for example in "Schieber-Itzig" (i.e., "racketeering Jew"); see Stephan Malinowski, *Vom König zum Führer. Deutscher Adel und Nationalsozialismus* (Frankfurt: Fischer, 2016), 484, 497; Ernest K. Bramsted, *Aristocracy and the Middle Classes in Germany. Social Types in German Literature 1830–1900*, rev. ed. (Chicago: University of Chicago Press, 1964). 132–150.
4. See Chapter 10, above, on Otto Dibelius. While some literary scholars have claimed that neither Freytag nor Raabe had antisemitic motivations, readers of these novels will find it difficult to absolve the two authors from anti-Jewish prejudices, since the fiendish cunning of both Itzig and Freudenstein are carefully developed throughout the novels and dwelled upon in such detail by their authors that it is well-nigh impossible to acquit them of intent. See Bernt Ture von zur Mühlen, *Gustav Freytag: Biographie* (Göttingen: Wallstein, 2016); Jörg Thunecke, "Es sind nicht alle frei, die ihrer Ketten spotten," in Sigrid Thielking, ed., *Raabe-Rapporte. Literaturwissenschaftliche und literatur-didaktische Zugänge zum Werk Wilhelm Raabes* (Wiesbaden: Universitätsverlag, 2002), 57–67; Ruth Klüger, "Die Säkularisierung des Judenhasses am Beispiel von Wilhelm Raabes 'Der Hungerpastor,'" in Klaus-Michael Bogdal, Klaus Holz, and Matthias N. Lorenz, eds., *Literarischer Antisemitismus nach Auschwitz* (Stuttgart: Metzler, 2007), 103–110.

groups, as well as some National Liberals.[5] Throughout the Weimar Republic, the DNVP's position on antisemitism depended on the party's changing orientation toward the Republic itself, the ups and downs of the economy, and various tactical electoral strategies. A marked discrepancy in attitude existed between the party's national leadership, which by and large tended to eschew antisemitic themes, and its regional (*Land*) associations, which enjoyed considerable autonomy from the party center and were more likely to exhibit antisemitic orientations.[6] This was the case particularly at the beginning of the Republic, since the initial DNVP leadership was comprised of moderate conservatives, such as the first party chairman, Oskar Hergt, but this changed soon after 30 January 1933, when party leaders were anxious not to appear lenient regarding the "Jewish question." Unlike most other parties, the DNVP also had no elaborate party program other than a few guiding principles, such as the 1919 *Wahlaufrufe* (electoral proclamations) or the 1920 *Grundsätze* (Basic Principles).[7]

Antisemitic statements and actions played a role from early on. During the campaign for the election of the National Assembly in Weimar on 19 January 1919, DNVP propaganda ranted against the German Democratic Party (DDP), labeling it a "*Judenpartei*" and condemning its "Jewish press." Given the decentralized structure of the party organization, the national leadership could not control what was happening at the regional level, where discrimination was not limited to slander against other parties.[8] In 1920 Anna von Gierke (1874–1943), DNVP deputy in the National Assembly in 1919 and daughter of the prominent legal scholar Otto von Gierke

5. Larry E. Jones, *The German Right, 1918–1930: Political Parties, Organized Interests, and Patriotic Associations in the Struggle against Weimar Democracy* (Cambridge: Cambridge University Press, 2020), 17–32.
6. Jones, *German Right*, 11–14; 32–38; 151–156; Werner Liebe, *Die Deutschnationale Volkspartei, 1918–1924* (Düsseldorf: Droste, 1956); Christian F. Trippe, *Konservative Verfassungspolitik 1918–1923. Die DNVP als Opposition in Reich und Ländern* (Düsseldorf: Droste, 1995). In 1919, the DNVP had thirty-five *Land* associations; between 1924 and 1928, the number rose to about forty-five. Party membership fluctuated between 300,000 and 400,000 in 1919, then rose to 950,000 in 1923, before declining to just under 700,000 in 1928. Beck, *Fateful Alliance*, 19.
7. Dirk Lau, *Wahlkämpfe in der Weimarer Republik. Propaganda und Programme der politischen Parteien bei den Wahlen zum Deutschen Reichstag von 1924 bis 1930*, 3rd ed. (Baden-Baden: Tectum, 2018), 64.
8. Jan Striesow, *Die Deutschnationale Volkspartei und die Völkisch-Radikalen, 1918–1922*, vol. I. (Frankfurt: Haag, 1981), 44–62; Jones, *German Right*, 35–38.

(whose wife was Jewish), saw her nomination for a Reichstag seat thwarted by antisemitic obstructionism within her own party.[9] The DNVP's 1920 *Grundsätze*, the closest the DNVP ever came to a formal program, contained the unambiguous passage: "We emphatically oppose the increasingly calamitous predominant power of Jewry since the revolution in government and public life. We need to put an end to the influx of foreign elements over our borders."[10] In contrast, the party's more moderate leadership under Oskar Hergt, together with Karl Helfferich and Otto Hoetzsch, rejected three motions in November 1921 that would have barred Jews from joining the party and then adopted a resolution that prevented *Land* associations from amending their statutes to exclude Jews from party membership.[11]

The year 1922 saw a showdown between the DNVP leadership and the figureheads of the party's antisemitic wing, Wilhelm Henning, Reinhold Wulle, and Albrecht von Graefe, after Henning wrote a venomous article that included an implicit threat regarding Walter Rathenau and his dealings with the Soviets at the Rapallo Conference.[12] When Rathenau was murdered shortly after the publication of the article, the *völkisch* wing became a liability to the DNVP. Rathenau's death had triggered a wave of support for the Republic as well as indignant outrage against the murderers and all who could be considered intellectual sponsors of the deed, so that party leaders felt compelled to disassociate themselves from

---

9. Trippe, *Verfassungspolitik*, 68; Larry E. Jones; "Conservative Antisemitism in the Weimar Republic. A Case Study of the German National People's Party," in Larry E. Jones, *The German Right in the Weimar Republic. Studies in the History of German Conservatism, Nationalism, and Antisemitism* (New York and Oxford: Berghahn, 2014), 79–107, esp. 82, 90; Jones, *German Right*, 107–8; Beck, *Fateful Alliance*, 37.

10. Wilhelm Mommsen, ed., *Deutsche Parteiprogramme*, vol. 1 (Munich: Olzog, 1960), 533–543, esp. 538; Liebe, *Deutschnationale Volkspartei*, 115.

11. Though, as Jones writes, it remained unclear "how this would pertain to the two or three district organizations that had already adopted the so-called Jewish paragraph," Jones, *German Right*, 153–4; Stefan Breuer, *Die Völkischen in Deutschland*, 2nd ed. (Darmstadt: WBG, 2010), 185.

12. "The Real Face of the Rapallo Treaty," *Konservative Monatsschrift*, 79 (June 1922), 521–526. "German honor is not something for international Jewish trade to haggle over … German honor will be expiated. But you, Herr Rathenau … will be held to account by the German nation;" quoted in Liebe, *Deutschnationale Volkspartei*, 159.

radical antisemitic members to avoid having the DNVP as a whole accused of sanctioning political murder.[13] At the Görlitz party conference in October 1922, the leaders of the *völkisch* wing left the party when the DNVP leadership refused to accept its existence as an organized party subgroup, and founded the German *Völkisch* Freedom Party in December 1922.[14] DNVP leaders were initially concerned that an exodus to the German *Völkisch* Freedom Party might weaken the electoral base of the DNVP, but the drain remained limited, since not a single DNVP *Land* association joined those who left. These tensions simply reflected the division over the *völkisch* issue that had always existed within the DNVP. On the one hand, leaders were concerned that if the *völkisch* wing became prominent, "the entire world of business, especially heavy industry, the wholesale trade, and the big banks" would turn away from the party, and the DNVP's employee wing (*Reichsarbeiterausschuss*) feared that an exclusion of all Jews would lead to "the immediate resignation of several renowned party leaders, entire groups of industrialists, and certain groups of organized Christian workers."[15] There was also a general reluctance to emphasize antisemitic themes too strongly for fear of alienating potential coalition partners and voters in the areas that bordered Poland.[16] On the other hand, the German Nationals did not want to lose *völkisch* support completely, given its potential to form a mass base of support, and thus agreed to the establishment of a *Völkisch* Reich Committee of the German National People's Party (*Völkischer*

13. Hagen Schulze, *Weimar. Deutschland 1917–1933* (Berlin: Siedler, 1982), 242–245; Maik Ohnezeit, *Zwischen "schärfster Opposition" und dem "Willen zur Macht." Die Deutschnationale Volkspartei (DNVP) in der Weimarer Republik 1918–1928* (Düsseldorf: Droste, 2011), 134–58; Jones, *German Right*, 151–57; Jones "Conservative Antisemitism," 83–84; Lewis Hertzmann, *DNVP: Right-Wing Opposition in the Weimar Republic, 1918–1924* (Lincoln: University of Nebraska Press, 1963); Beck, *Fateful Alliance*, 36–38.
14. Rainer Hering, *Konstruierte Nation. Der Alldeutsche Verband 1890 bis 1939* (Hamburg: Christians, 2003), 474–475; Barry Jackisch, *The Pan-German League and Radical Nationalist Politics in Interwar Germany, 1918–1939* (London and New York: Routledge, 2012), 54–62; Jones, *German Right*, 157–161.
15. Quotations in Breuer, *Die Völkischen*, 186, and Amrei Stupperich, *Volksgemeinschaft oder Arbeitersolidarität. Studien zur Arbeitnehmerpolitik in der deutschnationalen Volkspartei, 1918–1933* (Göttingen: Muster-Schmidt, 1982), 91.
16. Breuer, *Die Völkischen*, 183.

Reichsausschuss der Deutschnationalen Volkspartei) in February 1923, thereby stemming any future losses to the German *Völkisch* Freedom Party and also providing the Pan-German League with a platform within the DNVP from which they could pursue their objectives.[17] In addition, antisemitic tendencies inherited from the Christian Social movement during the Empire and former liberals who had been active in the Fatherland Party in 1917–18 continued to play an important role in the DNVP in the person of the Reichstag deputy Gottfried Traub.[18]

The campaign for the elections of 4 May 1924, as a result of which the DNVP temporarily became the strongest party in the Reichstag, saw the high point of *völkisch* influence and antisemitic agitation. The demands to "eliminate the subversive Jewish influence in politics" was a constant refrain of German National electioneering throughout the spring of 1924: DNVP posters emphasized that to be German National meant being *völkisch* and that the party wanted to be "free of Jewry, [which is] allied with Marxism," while the DNVP's main opponent, the SPD, was reproached with protecting Jews.[19] In the fall of 1924 party leaders hoped for DNVP participation in government, given the DNVP's strong showing in the May elections; consequently, antisemitic issues did not play a major role in the campaign for the elections of 7 December 1924, which were portrayed as a decisive battle between the Right and Left. But anti-Jewish themes did not disappear altogether. DNVP propaganda contended that the SPD politicians Otto Braun and Carl Severing were responsible for the allegedly unrestrained influx of *"Ostjuden"* into Prussia, the SPD was accused of having its party coffers filled by "Jewish racketeers," and tradesmen and artisans were warned that "whoever does not

17. Hering, *Konstruierte Nation*, 470–479; Jackisch, *Pan-German League*, 95–100; Jones, *German Right, 1918–1930*, 160–161; Jones, "Conservative Antisemitism," 85.
18. Mosse, "Deutsche Rechte," 226–235; Berding, *Moderner Antisemitismus*, 213–214; Jones, *German Right*, 27–28, 77, and Wolfgang Benz, ed., *Handbuch des Antisemitismus. Judenfeindschaft in Geschichte und Gegenwart*, vol. 2: *Personen* (Berlin: De Gruyter Saur, 2009), 837–838.
19. Lau, *Wahlkämpfe*, 372, 373, 375, 376; Jones, "Conservative Antisemitism," 85; Jones, *German Right*, 216–220.

vote" is "Juda's slave, France's coolie, calls Bolshevism into the country, [and] sacrifices his children."[20]

The years between 1925 and 1928 were dominated by Kuno Graf von Westarp, who led the DNVP's parliamentary faction from 1925 to 1929 and was party chairman from March 1926 to October 1928. Though by no means free of antisemitic prejudice, Westarp had made it clear in 1919 that the religious and civic equality of Jews must not be infringed upon, and he later voted against the introduction of so-called "Aryan paragraphs" in the DNVP and in the *Deutsche Adelsgenossenschaft*, the largest association of German aristocrats.[21] He was also prepared to recognize national-minded deeds and actions of German Jews and emphasized as understood that "every serious politician loathes violence perpetrated against Jews."[22] It obviously mattered to Westarp that, philosophically, he could reconcile his own and the party's antisemitic prejudices with the modern democratic state based on the rule of law, and that politically these prejudices should not impede the maneuverability of the DNVP in the electoral arena.[23] While emphasizing that antisemitic propaganda had its usefulness, Westarp did not regard antisemitism from a purely instrumental angle. As his biographer emphasizes, the "Jewish question" was more to him than a means to gain votes; he regarded Jews as an "alien *Volkstum*" and he deplored what he considered the harmful influence of Jewish leaders on German workers.[24]

20. Lau, *Wahlkämpfe*, 434, 435. Heinrich-August Winkler, *Mittelstand, Demokratie und Nationalsozialismus. Die politische Entwicklung von Handwerk und Kleinhandel in der Weimarer Republik* (Cologne: Kiepenheuer, 1972), 132; Winkler argues that "the agitation of the DNVP during the 1924 elections evinced unmistakably fascist traits and, in many ways, anticipated... the style of national socialist campaigns in the 1930s" (248).
21. See also G. H. Kleine, "Adelsgenossenschaft und Nationalsozialismus," *VJHZ*, 26:1 (1978), 100–143.
22. Stephan Malinowski, "Kuno Graf Westarp – ein *missing link* im preußischen Adel," in Larry E. Jones and Wolfram Pyta, eds., *"Ich bin der letzte Preuße." Der politische Lebensweg des konservativen Politkers Kuno Graf Westarp* (Cologne, Weimar, and Vienna: Böhlau, 2006), 9–32, esp. 19–20; Karl J. Mayer, "Kuno Graf Westarp als Kritiker des Nationalsozialismus," in Jones and Pyta, *Letzte Preuße*, 189–216, esp. 201. Quotation in James Retallack, "Zwei Vertreter des preußischen Konservatismus im Spiegel ihres Briefwechsels: Die Heydebrand - Westarp Korrespondenz," in Jones and Pyta, *Letzte Preuße*, 33–60, esp. 56; see also Ohnezeit, *Zwischen*, 124–126.
23. Breuer, *Die Völkischen*, 184.
24. Daniela Gasteiger, *Kuno von Westarp, 1864–1945: Parlamentarismus, Monarchismus, und Herrschaftsutopien in deutschen Konservatismus* (Berlin and Boston: De Gruyter, 2018), 191–93.

He adamantly opposed the immigration of "*Ostjuden*," whom he blamed for the increase in public expressions of antisemitism after 1918, and he supported reducing Jewish influence in economic, political, and cultural affairs.[25] In all of these orientations, Westarp's antisemitism was typical of moderate conservatives and, as we have seen, was also widespread among Protestant Church leaders.

Already before the May 1928 elections, confrontation between the pan-German wing around Alfred Hugenberg, who rejected participation in coalition governments and other forms of active collaboration within the Republic, and the more pragmatic wing around Westarp had become more acrimonious.[26] Following the electoral setback of May 1928, in which the DNVP lost almost two million votes and fell from 20.5 to 14.2 percent of the popular vote (103 to 73 mandates), Hugenberg's more uncompromisingly anti-Republican course began to prevail, and on 20 October 1928 Hugenberg was elected chairman by a wafer-thin majority, a victory due largely to the personnel policy of the Pan-German League.[27] Ironically, Alfred Hugenberg, who was after all the man who led his party into a coalition with Hitler on 30 January 1933, was among the least antisemitic of all leading German Nationals. As George Mosse emphasized, in Hugenberg's speeches no mention is made of the "Jewish problem," and the long-time DNVP Reichstag deputy (1920–33) and economic expert Reinhold Quaatz, whose mother was Jewish and who was related to Ludwig Holländer, the director of the *Centralverein*, remained one of Hugenberg's closest collaborators until March 1933.[28]

25. Retallack, "Zwei Vertreter," 55, 57; Mayer, "Kuno Graf Westarp," 201.
26. Lau, *Wahlkämpfe*, 488; Jones, *German Right*, 372–387.
27. Pan-Germans, who favored Hugenberg, had come to dominate many *Land* associations. See the detailed accounts in Jackisch, *Pan-German League*, 146–158, and Björn Hofmeister, "Between Monarchy and Dictatorship: Radical Nationalism and Social Mobilization of the Pan-German League, 1914–1939" (Diss., Georgetown University, Washington, 2012), 269–298, esp. 293 (where Hofmeister provides a breakdown of which *Land* associations had supported Westarp and which Hugenberg).
28. Mosse, "Deutsche Rechte," 231–232; John A. Leopold, *Alfred Hugenberg: The Radical Nationalist Campaign against the Weimar Republic* (New Haven and London: Yale University Press, 1977), 22; Jones, "Conservative Antisemitism," 91; Hermann Weiß and Paul Hoser, eds., *Die Deutschnationalen und die Zerstörung der Weimarer Republic. Aus dem Tagebuch von Reinhold Quaatz 1928–1933* (Munich: Oldenbourg, 1989), 7–18.

Apart from Anna von Gierke and the industrialist Richard Friedländer, who had (unsuccessfully) been nominated for the National Assembly in Silesia, Quaatz was the only prominent person of Jewish ancestry in the DNVP.[29] At the same time, however, Hugenberg was on a similarly friendly footing with Paul Bang, his Undersecretary of State in the Ministry of Economics after 30 January, a rabid antisemite who, under the pen name Wilhelm Meister, had published the notorious and widely read pamphlet *The Jew's Debt Register: A German Statement of Account*.[30]

During the campaigns for the 14 September 1930 and 31 July 1932 elections, anti-Jewish themes played no role in the electoral strategy of the DNVP, nor were they mentioned at the Harzburg Front meeting of DNVP, NSDAP, and other organizations of the national Right.[31] In the summer of 1930 the party's electoral efforts focused wholly on Hugenberg, with slogans such as "One Man – One Movement – One Program" or "The German people want a leader, the leader is here: Hugenberg."[32] Here emerge the beginnings of what would become a powerful trend after 30 January 1933: the imitation of National Socialist styles, techniques, and propaganda methods that became especially pronounced after the elections of 5 March 1933.[33] German National criticism of the NSDAP during Weimar's last elections in 1932 focused on social and economic issues, while antisemitism was never a direct matter of debate or confrontation between the two parties. After Nazi attacks on *Stahlhelm* leader Theodor Duesterberg during the July 1932 election campaigns on account of his Jewish grandfather, the DNVP felt called upon to defend its antisemitic pedigree by publishing anti-Jewish articles by Paul Bang and

29. Peter Pulzer, *Jews and the German State. The Political History of a Minority* (Oxford: Blackwell, 1992), 237.
30. Friedländer, "Politische Veränderungen," 27–66, esp. 65. Wilhelm Meister's *Judas Schuldbuch: Eine deutsche Abrechnung*, published in 1919, was very successful commercially and went through several editions, with more than 30,000 copies printed. Uwe Lohalm, *Völkischer Radikalismus. Die Geschichte des Deutschvölkischen Schutz- und Trutz-Bundes. 1919–1923* (Hamburg: Leibnitz, 1970), 180.
31. Mosse, "Deutsche Rechte," 232, argues that due to Hugenberg's influence "not a word was said about Jews at the Harzburg meeting." See also Jones, *Hitler versus Hindenburg*, 106–129.
32. Lau, *Wahlkämpfe*, 554; Jones, *German Right*, 566–570; 578–585.
33. Beck, *Fateful Alliance*, 246–250.

praising Paul de Lagarde and Houston Stuart Chamberlain in its official party organs.[34] Throughout the Republic, though less during its final phase, the DNVP clearly spoke of the need to address a "Jewish problem." Yet there existed significant differences between the antisemitism of the DNVP and that of the National Socialists.

Antisemitism, both ideologically and practically in terms of day-to-day politics, played a less significant role for the German Nationals than it did for the National Socialists. For the most part, DNVP leaders and members alike renounced violence and terror against Jews. Even at the height of antisemitic fervor during the campaign for the May 1924 elections, the DNVP clearly delineated their own brand of antisemitism from that of the *völkisch* parties on the extreme right. As Larry Jones emphasizes, German Nationals remained critical of the hostility the National Socialist Freedom Party (the electoral alliance of the German *Völkisch* Freedom Party and what remained of the NSDAP after the failed 1923 coup) displayed towards religion, the monarchy, and the capitalist system, and they looked askance at what they perceived as the plebeian quality that characterized *völkisch* agitation against Jews.[35] The majority of the party's members and leaders, who exhibited more moderate antisemitic orientations, at least recognized "national actions" of Germany's Jews, such as active participation in World War I; this was not the case in Hitler's party. Traditional conservative antisemitism had begun as anti-modernism in the 1840s and 1850s and the pronounced hostility against the *homo novus*, who upset the traditional hierarchical order.[36] In the 1870s, conservative resistance to the influx of Eastern Jews from the Russian Empire became pronounced. This attitude continued to characterize the conservative

---

34. Mosse, "Deutsche Rechte," 228–229; Jones, "Conservative Antisemitism," 94–95. Duesterberg had run for the DNVP in the March 1932 presidential elections.

35. Jones, *German Right*, 219–220.

36. As, for example, when the Prussian conservative (and later Prussian Foreign Minister) Joseph Maria von Radowitz wrote in the 1840s: "Formerly a Jew could never become truly powerful, however much money and mortgage bonds he might have possessed." Quoted in Hermann Beck, *The Origins of the Authoritarian Welfare State in Prussia: Conservatives, Bureaucracy, and the Social Question, 1815–1870* (Ann Arbor: University of Michigan Press, 1995), 74.

position until 1933: across the board, German Nationals were critical of *"Ostjuden"* and opposed to the immigration of Jews from the East, continually stressing differences between *"Ostjuden"* and established German Jews who had been in the country for generations, and whom they wanted to see treated differently. National Socialists were far less likely to recognize any distinction.[37] The German National attitude towards *"Ostjuden"* was similar to that of the majority of Protestant Church leaders.

Prussian conservatives from Ewald von Kleist-Schmenzin to Kuno Graf von Westarp claimed that Christian theology formed the moral basis of the State.[38] While this did not prevent a pronounced antisemitic outlook, it tended to moderate more extreme antisemitic resentments, which then did not come to the fore with the same level of brutality as was the case with ardent National Socialists.[39] Belief in the rule of law (as in Westarp's case), the rootedness in Protestant Christianity that was strong in some Prussian conservatives, and, above all, conviction about the necessity of social order and rules of behavior, which the State was meant to uphold, could act as a moderating factor and brake on their own marked antisemitism. Yet, as will be shown below, in 1933 these moderating elements were not sufficient to compel conservatives to protest against Nazi crimes. And, though only in a minority, the DNVP did include racial antisemites of the most radical kind, such as Hugenberg's Undersecretary of State in the Ministry of Economics, Paul Bang, and other cases discussed below.

37. Hans Mommsen, "Konservatismus und Faschismus. Zur Einschätzung der NSDAP durch die deutsche politische Rechte vor der nationalsozialistischen Machteroberung," in Helga Grebing and Klaus Kinner, eds., *Arbeiterbewegung und Faschismus. Faschismus-Interpretationen in der europäischen Arbeiterbewegung* (Essen: Klartext, 1990), 29–38, esp. 31–32.
38. See Mayer, "Kuno Graf Westarp," 202; Bodo Scheurig, *Ewald von Kleist-Schmenzin. Ein Konservativer gegen Hitler* (Berlin: Propyläen, 1994); Jeremy Noakes, "German Conservatives and the Third Reich: An Ambiguous Relationship," in Martin Blinkhorn, ed., *Fascists and Conservatives. The Radical Right and the Establishment in Twentieth-century Europe* (London: Unwin Hyman: 1990), 71–97, esp. 75–79.
39. See Gellately, *Hitler's True Believers*, 13–65; 239–264.

The Wehrmacht general Gotthard Heinrici (1886–1971), son of a conservative Prussian parson and church administrator, is in many ways representative of conservative antisemitism. Heinrici left an extensive literary bequest, consisting of diary notes and letters, in which he frankly communicates his political views on the Nazi regime.[40] In the Republic's last phase, Heinrici was a moderate conservative who initially supported Hindenburg against both Hitler and Hugenberg's more radical-conservative candidate Theodor Duesterberg in the March 1932 presidential elections, but he then developed considerable enthusiasm for the Nazi regime.[41] In a letter to his parents on 12 February 1933 Henrici wrote about his confidence that "things will continue improving" and his hope that "we will now finally escape from this Marxist-Jewish mess." He rationalizes and downplays reports of violent antisemitic attacks, arguing that "occasional transgressions pale . . . in comparison to this great overall success." On 1 April, Heinrici recorded that he found the anti-Jewish boycott of that day to be "a very infelicitous measure, which will lead to countless injustices and insults," but, as his 9 April letter indicated, it was also important to "keep in view the great things and amazing feats that have been accomplished and will be accomplished in the future." Heinrici would maintain this basic attitude until the outbreak of the war: in his letter of 7 July 1934 he endorsed Hitler's elimination of parts of the SA leadership in the stillborn Röhm Putsch a week earlier and only regretted that it had not taken place sooner. He minimized the Nuremberg Laws in September 1935 and, as a practicing Lutheran, lamented the hostility of the regime toward the Churches. He strongly rejected the Reich-wide pogrom during the so-called "Kristallnacht" on 9/10 November 1938, but he offered no active protest. Taken as a whole, consent and support for the regime predominated in Henrici's thinking.

For National Socialists, in contrast to the prevarication of the DNVP and most of its members, antisemitism and the "Jewish Question" played

---

40. Parts of the diary (also for the 1930s) have been published by Hürter, *Vernichtungskrieg*.
41. The following quotations are taken from Hürter, *Vernichtungskrieg*, 165–187.

a central, often *the* central, role within the party—it was important for the "inner integration" of its members, and for Hitler, it was the key to solving all political and economic problems. In addition to open terror against Jews, rejected by most, though not all, German Nationals, there were other main differences between conservatives and Nazis. The first pertained to language and behavior and can best be illustrated by virtue of the very specific vocabulary Hitler used to shape the narrative in addressing the "Jewish Question." Eberhard Jäckel collected a series of relevant phrases from the first volume of Hitler's *Mein Kampf* that make this clear:

> The Jew is the maggot in the rotting body, pestilence, worse than the black death of the past, a germ carrier of the worst kind, the eternal spirit of discord of humanity, the parasite that worms its way into humanity, the spider that slowly sucks the blood out of the pores of the people, a bloody infighting horde of rats, the blood sucker in the body of other peoples, the typical parasite, a freeloader that continues to widely multiply like a harmful bacillus, the eternal leech, the parasite of peoples, the vampire of national communities.[42]

This radical language became reflected in the propaganda and behavior of those who subscribed to National Socialism. In his book about the discourse of the Third Reich, Victor Klemperer, who had been forced to wear the yellow star since 19 September 1941, describes his experience as a publicly recognizable Jew and how language translated itself into behavior: "A car stopped after passing by me on an empty street and an unknown person stuck his head out of the window: 'Are you still alive, you damn swine? One should just run over you...'" As Klemperer later stood with his face against the wall in Dresden's Gestapo headquarters,

---

42. Eberhard Jäckel, *Hitlers Weltanschauung. Entwurf einer Herrschaft*, 3rd ed. (Stuttgart: DVA, 1986), 69. See also Gellately, *Hitler's True Believers*, 15–16; 21–22; 45–55; Thomas Pegelow, *The Language of Genocide. Linguistic Violence and the Struggle of Germans of Jewish Ancestry* (Cambridge: Cambridge University Press, 2009); and Thomas Nipperdey and Reinhard Rürup, "Antisemitismus – Entstehung, Funktion und Geschichte eines Begriffs," in Thomas Nipperdey, *Gesellschaft, Kultur, Theorie. Gesammelte Aufsätze zur neueren Geschichte* (Göttingen: Vandenhoeck & Ruprecht, 1976), 113–132.

passersby hurled gratuitous insults at him: "Just hang yourself, you Jewish dog, what are you waiting for?"[43]

Another main difference concerns methods, and the cold determination, dissimulation, and underhanded tactics that Nazis were prepared to employ in their anti-Jewish policies. These are best encapsulated in a speech given by Goebbels in 1935 after the passing of the Nuremberg Laws:

If I were to express in my propaganda: the Jews have *absolutely* nothing more to lose! – well then, you shouldn't wonder if they fight...If you don't offer them any chance, no – one always has to leave things open. Take for example what the Führer did in such a masterful way in his speech yesterday: "We hope that with these Jewish laws the possibility now exists to bring about a tolerable relationship between the German and Jewish peoples and..." (laughter of those present). I call that *skillful*! That is *masterful*! If one had followed this up by saying: So, these are the *current* Jewish laws; but don't think that this is all, next month – and here there is *absolutely nothing* more that can be changed – next month the new ones will come and so on until you will again sit dirt poor in the ghetto – yes, in that case you shouldn't wonder if Jews mobilized the entire world against us. But if, on the other hand, you appear to give them a chance, even a *slim* opportunity to stay afloat, then the Jews will say: "Ha, if people abroad start agitating [against Germany] again, it'll only get worse, so folks, be quiet, *maybe* it'll still be alright!" (laughter and applause from those present)...And above all: the Jews aren't going anywhere...and their property is also still here. It's just as well that they are here. It is quite possible that in coming difficult confrontations they will serve as a very useful bargaining chip (applause of those present). We have to get out of our heads once and for all this asinine bourgeois phrase: "Viel Feind, viel Ehr" [the more enemies you have, the more laurels]. No, we have to choose our enemies. Especially when we know that the aim is their annihilation.[44]

43. Victor Klemperer, *LTI. Notizbuch eines Philologen*, 23rd ed. (Stuttgart: Reclam, 2007), 225, 231. Inspiration for such insults could be found on *Stürmer* bulletin boards, proclaiming: "Whoever does not know the Jew, does not know the devil" (ibid., 236).
44. Helmut Heiber, ed., *Goebbels-Reden*, vol. 1, 1932–1939 (Düsseldorf: Droste, 1971), 248–250; repr. in Helmut Berding, *Moderner Antisemitismus in Deutschland. Quellen zur Geschichte und Politik* (Stuttgart: Klett, 1988), 63–64. (All emphasis in the original.)

The German National approach was not so cynical, and there was no unanimity among its members. If left to their own devices, many of even the party's more radical members would have stopped at a legislative "solution," though, as will be seen below, during the April boycott they willingly adopted Nazi methods, and throughout the spring of 1933 were prepared to do almost anything to avoid being considered "*judenfreundlich.*"

The DNVP and National-minded German Jews in March 1933

Nationally oriented Jewish Germans were the most likely to turn to the DNVP for help. This group included those close to conservative parties, and also national-minded voters of liberal parties and the Center, as well as the overwhelming majority of those who had served in World War I.[45] Most of them shared basic ways of thinking, modes of behavior, and values with politically like-minded non-Jewish Germans. Psychologically, they were possibly the hardest hit by attacks and boycotts, since many of them identified with Germany and had sacrificed much for their country. At the end of March 1933, the conservative *Deutsche Allgemeine Zeitung* published an open letter dated 21 March with the title, "Declaration of a Jewish Frontline Soldier," in which the dilemma of nationally oriented Jewish Germans was graphically laid out:

> I was a soldier for almost four and a half years, always served only on the front line, fought in Flanders and France, and lost my only brother on the western front. When I now hear and read that Jews as a whole are characterized as un-German, I find that to be bitterly unjust. Then I tear

45. On the political orientation of Jewish Germans, see Jacob Toury, *Die politischen Orientierungen der Juden in Deutschland. Von Jena bis Weimar* (Tübingen: Mohr Siebeck, 1966). Jakob Wassermann's observations about himself and the German language are instructive in this context; Jakob Wassermann, *Mein Weg als Deutscher und Jude*, 2nd ed., (Munich: DTV, 1999), 48.

open my military ID and run my eyes over the long list of battles and skirmishes in which I took part and see the commendations "Very Good" and "Excellent." The unadorned Iron Cross lies alongside. Must I, in the homeland of my parents and forefathers, who fought and suffered for this homeland as the others did, have to live from now on as a social outcast? Must I be separated from the world of my friends because I am of Jewish ancestry?[46]

This open letter reflected the situation of tens of thousands. Gerhard Lissa, for example, a Jewish businessman from Berlin-Zehlendorf, reported on a meeting of former frontline soldiers, organized by the Reich Association of Jewish Frontline Soldiers, the SA, and the veterans' organizations *Stahlhelm* and the *Kyffhäuserbund*.[47] At this meeting "many disgraceful things took place. Jews wounded in the war, some of them now blind, were reviled and insulted by young rascals who never even heard the sound of a bullet whistle past them."[48] Given the fact that "savings accumulated through hard work and invested in war bonds have melted away, that already my uncles volunteered to serve in the war of 1870, and that my family and I have spiritually long converted to the German culture," Lissa was overcome by "an unending fury over the injustice" with which "every Jew is thrown into the same pot with fraudsters, scoundrels, and traitors to the Fatherland."[49] As he explains, all of the sacrifices made by the sons, fathers, and brothers killed in the Great War, and the painstakingly accumulated savings forfeited in the inflation of 1923, had now lost all meaning and value. And there was no help in sight. Lissa was just as suspicious and disdainful of foreign

46. BA Berlin, R 8005, no. 19, "DNVP: Politischer Schriftwechsel 1933," fol. 56. The *Deutsche Allgemeine Zeitung* (until 1918, "*Norddeutsche Allgemeine Zeitung*") was one of the most internationally respected daily newspapers in the Reich. The *DAZ* had advocated Hitler's participation in a governmental coalition since the summer of 1932. See Norbert Frei and Johannes Schmitz, *Journalismus im Dritten Reich*, 3rd ed. (Munich: Beck, 1999), 59–63.
47. BA Berlin, R 8005, no. 19, "Lissa to Lindner," Letter of 27 March 1933, fol. 57. In 1921, the *Deutscher Kriegerbund* (founded in 1872) merged with the *Kyffhäuserbund* (founded in 1898) to form the *Deutscher Reichskriegerbund Kyffhäuser* with 3 million members in 1930. On conservative German Jews and the First World War, see Nielsen, *Between Heimat and Hatred*, 73–113.
48. BA Berlin, R 8005, no. 19, "Lissa to Lindner," Letter of 27 March 1933, fol. 57.
49. Ibid., fol. 57.

protests against the anti-Jewish measures as other national-oriented Germans: "The voices from abroad are crude nonsense and a blasted nuisance. Here we are dealing with the same people who spread slander- and atrocity-propaganda against us during the war."[50] His psychological predicament was compounded by the threat of economic ruin, since "lately the payment of bills is refused with the explanation that one no longer needs to pay a Jew given that a new administration of justice will soon take effect in Germany."[51]

In the eyes of the new regime, military service, sacrifices made in the name of Germany, and an impeccable national-minded family back- ground meant nothing when the person concerned was Jewish. This becomes apparent from a multitude of cases in the DNVP files. Though most DNVP members and leaders were not as stridently antisemitic as their Nazi coalition partner and unwilling to go to the same lengths to reduce Jewish influence, in the spring of 1933 they felt under pressure to reject even nationally oriented Jews from membership in the party. The DNVP local association (*Kreisverein*) in Frankfurt am Main, for example, requested a membership decision concerning a Dr. A. Vogel, who had been warmly recommended by the association leader for acceptance. The characterization of Dr. Vogel is significant: "He was a Jew, two years ago he was baptized as a Protestant. According to the testimony of his minister, has always been absolutely non-Jewish and oriented toward the political Right. Vogel lost his wealth in the Inflation and is respected everywhere as a poor, upstanding and decent person."[52] In the short and terse reply received from Berlin, the "admission of Herr Dr. Vogel" was advised against: "The provision in our statutes that prohibits the accept- ance of Jews is most definitely not based on religion." No reference was made to Vogel's political orientation or personal qualities.[53] In the climate of the Nazi takeover, personal character, political orientation,

50. Ibid., fol. 58.
51. 31 March 1933, BA Berlin, R 8005, no. 19, "DNVP, Politischer Schriftwechsel 1933," fols. 52–54.
52. 18 April 1933 at BA Berlin, R 8005, no. 48, "Kirchen- und Religionsangelegenheiten," fol. 47.
53. 5 May 1933 at BA Berlin, R 8005, no. 48, fol. 46.

and religious affiliation were meaningless as the DNVP tacitly accepted the Nazis' "racial" characterization of "Jewishness."

In a similar case, the jurist Dr. Erich Gisbert received only a curt formal response when he appealed for help in a matter that concerned his very material existence. Gisbert, a former DNVP member and signatory to the referendum against the Young Plan, related through his mother to Prussian generals, and baptized and confirmed as a Protestant, had been forced to resign from his position at the Berlin Industry and Trade Chamber by the Association of National Socialist German Jurists.[54] In order to try to prove his credentials, he requested attestation from the DNVP's head office acknowledging his membership in the party and his participation in the referendum against the Young Plan.[55] In response he was only bluntly referred to his former DNVP *Land* Association, whereby words of regret or empathy were noticeably avoided.[56]

In certain ways typical for the witch-hunting climate of the spring of 1933 was the behavior of the DNVP in the case of the Bonn judicial counselor (*Justizrat*) Wassermeyer, the head of the DNVP Mittelrhein *Land* Association. Wassermeyer was concerned that his son Dr. Hans Wassermeyer, who worked in Altona near Hamburg, might get into difficulties with National Socialists and therefore asked the Altona DNVP chairman to watch over him.[57] Wassermeyer emphasized that his son had always voted for the DNVP, had taken part as a frontline soldier in World War I, and later joined the fight against communists as a student in Marburg in the summer of 1920.[58] When shortly after this request the son, Dr. Hans Wassermeyer, presented himself to the DNVP Altona local association to apply for admission to the party, the head of the association experienced an unpleasant surprise, as he related in his letter to the DNVP Headquarters: "When he appeared before us, we were

---

54. 3 April 1933 at BA Berlin, R 8005, no. 48, fols. 56–58.

55. Ibid., 54, 55. Philipp Nielsen argues that there might have been considerable support among German Jews for the DNVP, had the party not been antisemitic; Nielsen, *Between Heimat and Hatred*, 222–228.

56. 3 April 1933 at BA Berlin, R 8005, no. 48, fol. 53.

57. 14 March 1933 at BA Berlin, R 8005, no. 48, fol. 36.   58. Ibid., 36.

astonished that we had to deal with a Jew; subsequent inquiries established that his wife also comes from a well-known Hamburg Jewish
family."[59] Filled with uneasy foreboding, the Altona DNVP chairman
now requested information from Berlin about the elder Wassermeyer,
"especially if he is a Jew and as such the head of a [DNVP] party
organization."[60] As it quickly transpired, the concern of the DNVP's
Altona chairman was precipitate, for two days later the DNVP Mittelrhein
Land Association reported that Dr. Hans Wassermeyer was "not Jewish"
and that the Wassermeyer family was "a well-established Christian family
from Bonn." Dr. Hans Wassermeyer's mother, in like measure, was from
an old Christian family, so that "assumptions concerning the Jewish
ancestry of Dr. Hans Wassermeyer are absolutely incorrect."[61] In the
spring of 1933, every German—even those in nationalist circles who
held leading positions in the DNVP—lived under a cloud of suspicion.

Protests by Members of the DNVP and Active Help

Those German Nationals who had maintained friendly relations with
Jewish Germans occasionally perceived the violent attacks and blanket
discrimination as extremely unjust. Voices of protest were most apparent
in Frankfurt am Main, where many Jewish Germans had achieved prestige and prosperity and lived for generations in harmony with their
surroundings.[62] Even though the percentage of the Jewish population
had been declining in the city since the end of the Empire, in 1933 4.7
percent of the 555,857 inhabitants were Jewish, meaning that Frankfurt
had the highest percentage of Jews of all large German cities, more than
Berlin (3.8 percent) and Breslau (3.2 percent).[63]

59. 29 March 1933 at BA Berlin, R 8005, no. 48, fol. 35.   60. Ibid.
61. 31 March 1933 at BA Berlin, R 8005, no. 48, fol. 34.
62. On Frankfurt's Jews, see also Leo Löwenthal, *Mitmachen wollte ich nie. Ein autobiographisches Gespräch mit Helmut Dubiel* (Frankfurt: Suhrkamp, 1980), 13–63.
63. Thamer, *Verführung*, 258. In Frankfurt 7% of the population were Jewish in 1905. Thomas Nipperdey, *Deutsche Geschichte 1866–1918*, 399.

The long-time Frankfurt DNVP member Adele Kappus was one voice of protest: she wrote an open letter about the boycott of Jewish shops to Hugenberg,[64] complaining that it was "imprudent and unworthy of Germany to suddenly treat as pariahs Jewish people who have lived here for centuries, feel themselves to be German, and for centuries have provided valuable services to the Fatherland and their Christian compatriots."[65] In Frankfurt, Kappus wrote, "the Christian and Jewish economies [are] so intertwined with each other that one cannot harm one part of the economy without also badly hitting the other."[66] On the impact of the boycott she observed that "the arrow turns back on the archer."[67] She herself had been an employee at a large Jewish antiquarian bookstore whose owner "served four years on the front" and who, in all her time working for him, had treated her "justly and with goodwill."[68] Now the business stood on the brink of ruin and she and her colleagues had been told that they had to be let go. Kappus ended her letter to Hugenberg on a warning note: "If things continue like this, then many who welcomed the national revolution with their whole hearts will resentfully draw away from it. Do not fool yourself when it comes to the mood of the masses – it is not far removed from embittered anger."[69] In April 1933, however, there was little trace of public embitterment, and the Nazi regime was becoming so firmly ensconced in power that it would have been a far cry from disgruntlement to open revolt. Aside from the admission that "the measures were extraordinarily severe, therefore calling forth justified ill-feeling,"[70] the response sent to Kappus in Hugenberg's name emphasized that the DNVP was not responsible for the boycott, but "rather the NSDAP and not least those citizens who, instead of voting for the *Kampffront Schwarz-Weiß-Rot*, followed the swastika banner in masses, not to mention the [national liberal] German People's Party, which in Frankfurt especially enjoyed marked Jewish approval." The reply not only

---

64. 12 April 1933 at BA Berlin, R 8005, no. 48, fols. 63–64.
65. Ibid., 64.   66. Ibid., fol. 64.   67. Ibid., fol. 63.
68. Ibid., fols. 63, 64.   69. Ibid., fol. 64.   70. Ibid., fol. 64.

lacked any words of empathy but ended by holding the victims responsible: "If one considers this last fact, then your former employers and those that followed them are partly to be blamed for the current development."[71]

The most sweeping and emphatically articulated accusation against Nazi terror also came from Frankfurt, directly out of the head office of the local DNVP association and written by the DNVP member and Vice President of the Frankfurt *Oberlandesgericht*, Dr. Heinrich Heldmann.[72] According to Heldmann, the city of Frankfurt was "pressurized by the NSDAP leadership, creating an atmosphere worse than that during the 1918 revolution. Fear and trepidation hover over the whole of public and family life."[73] On 30 March, Roland Freisler (who had become *Minister-ialdirektor* in the Prussian Ministry of Justice in March 1933 and later achieved dubious fame as the president of the *Volksgerichtshof*), "gave a violent inflammatory speech against Jews, transmitted by loudspeaker, as a result of which a pogrom might break out any day now."[74] Heldmann especially emphasized the deeply rooted national orientation of Frankfurt's Jews:

> The majority of local Jews have lived in Frankfurt and surrounding areas for centuries. Among them are personages on whom practically all public charity and largesse depends. A great many Jews have served in the field or lost sons in the war. Frankfurt's great cultural institutions could never have

71. Ibid., fol. 60.
72. 3 April 1933 at BA Berlin, R 8005, no. 19, "DNVP: Politischer Schriftwechsel 1933:" "Dr. Heldmann an Dr. Hergt," fols. 63–64. Arnim und Renate Schmid, *Frankfurt in stürmischer Zeit 1930–1933* (Stuttgart: Theiss, 1987), 177–180, esp. 178. The *Oberlandesgerichte* evolved from the highest territorial courts of the Holy Roman Empire. In 1879, there were twenty-eight *Oberlandesgerichte* in the second Empire; the number rose to thirty-six by 1942. Moritz von Köckeritz, *Die deutschen Oberlandesgerichts-Präsidenten im Nationalsozialismus, 1933–1945* (Frankfurt: Lang, 2011); Arthur von Gruenewaldt, *Die Richterschaft des Oberlandesgerichts Frankfurt am Main in der Zeit des Nationalsozialismus* (Tübingen: Mohr Siebeck, 2015), 155–158.
73. 3 April 1933 at BA Berlin, R 8005, no. 19, "DNVP: Politischer Schriftwechsel 1933:" "Dr. Heldmann an Dr. Hergt," fol. 63.
74. Ibid. A "*Ministerialdirektor*" is the second-highest ministry official after the undersecretary. Roland Freisler (1893–1945) began his career as an attorney in Kassel and then became an NSDAP deputy in the parliament of the Prussian province of Hesse-Nassau, thus explaining his proximity to Frankfurt.

been established without Jewish charitable contributions. The spirit that predominates in these old Jewish families must in part be seen as genuinely conservative."[75]

Heldmann regretted that he had not been able to prevent discrimination and terror from finding their way into even the *Oberlandesgericht*. The court's Jewish judges, who included "the most capable and industrious members of the courts of law," were put on compulsory leave, and "the terror against Jewish lawyers" was so terrible that they were "downright driven to commit suicide." Among the lawyers, "whose impeccable character and flawless management have been known to me for many years," there is "bitter despair, since only few of them still have even a modest fortune, their savings having been lost in the Inflation and Great Depression."[76]

Heldmann also complained about the "horrible terror in public life"[77] and the fact that the SA could commit with impunity offenses that were "not only tolerated but even encouraged by the police."[78] Thirty-five Jewish merchants, for example, had been led with raised hands "through the busiest streets of the city," and "children of Jewish families, who are no longer connected with Judaism but have been raised as Christians, are chased from the schools."[79] It was obvious that these occurrences were detrimental to the standing of the DNVP and that it was high time to take action: "There is so much despair throughout our entire citizenry that it is incompatible with the reputation and dignity of the DNVP not to act and to offer relief."[80] As the Vice President of Frankfurt's highest court, Heldmann was painfully aware that judges dare not risk "to come out against the terror, since they no longer trusted that the administration of justice was still independent."[81] While a majority of judges still hoped that the German National members of the Cabinet might, "at least in the short term," succeed in salvaging the constitutionally established

---

75. Ibid., fol. 63.   76. Ibid., fol. 63v.   77. Ibid., fol. 63v.
78. Ibid., fols. 63, 63v.   79. Ibid., fol. 64.   80. Ibid., fol. 64.
81. Ibid.

foundations of the *Rechtsstaat*, "in view of the complete silence on the part of these Cabinet members, trust in their influence is shrinking with each passing day."[82] Even though the words of this German National jurist make clear his outrage about Nazi violence, anger about the crimes perpetrated against Frankfurt's Jews, embarrassment over the powerlessness and passivity of his own party, and dismay over the erosion of the rule of law, he realizes that worse is yet to come: "Even our *Frankfurter Post* would not dare publish a very moderate article of mine entitled, 'Return to the Law,' because the publisher has reason to fear that the SA will smash its printing press. I myself have been advised by friends not to put my name to this article, for otherwise I might be taken into protective custody."[83] This letter from the senior judge and Vice President of the Frankfurt *Oberlandesgericht* indicates that attacks were widely known; indeed, that one would consciously have to look the other way not to be aware of them. It also shows that as early as March 1933 even members of the elite were no longer secure and could find themselves threatened with "protective custody," for whose standing would seem to be more secure than that of a senior German National judge? Even where the will and readiness to help existed, the opportunity to intervene without endangering one's own position might already in some cases have been very limited by late March 1933. If the German National Vice President of an *Oberlandesgericht* saw himself unable to help, others may have felt even more powerless.

Archival files contain few cases of active help. In most instances, this was not only because intervention on behalf of the victims might endanger one's own life or that of one's family, but because there was no will or readiness to help. DNVP leader Alfred Hugenberg had created the aura of an extremely busy minister (with several portfolios) around himself, whose vital work for his ministries was essential for the health of the German economy.[84] Since Hugenberg even neglected his party

---

82. Ibid.   83. Ibid., fols. 63v., 64.

84. Leopold, *Alfred Hugenberg*, 22. "Hugenberg considered antisemitism a tool which could be exploited and discarded; he himself measured a man by his loyalty to the nation rather than by the purity of his racial pedigree."

responsibilities to the point that his deputy, Friedrich von Winterfeld, to all intents and purposes took over his work as head of the party, he could believably claim to have no time for other "problems," especially since the almost 68-year-old was plagued by health problems. That Hugenberg, who was grandiloquently stylized by the party press as the German National "leader," would not actively address the discrimination, humiliation, and violent attacks suffered by national-minded Jewish Germans at Nazi hands becomes apparent from the pretext to which his colleagues resorted when pressed for help: his busy schedule and poor health prevented him from being available to meet and pay attention to affairs other than those pertaining to his four ministries.[85] It was Papen's Vice Chancellor's Office that gradually rose to the level of the "Reich Complaint Center."[86] Especially since Göring had replaced Papen as *Reichskommissar* for Prussia (Göring had become Prussian Minister-President on 11 April 1933), Papen was available for other matters. One case in which Papen actively intervened was that of the historian Ludwig Dehio, archivist at the Prussian State Archive in Berlin-Dahlem, whom he helped to retain his position. A flawless national pedigree and a prominent name also played their part. Dehio, son of the famous art historian Georg Dehio,[87] was a victim of the 7 April Law on the Restoration of the Civil Service. Dehio also had the good fortune to have well-connected friends who used their influence on his behalf, such as Edgar Wedepohl, member of the *Deutscher Herrenclub*[88] and close to Papen. In a long letter to Papen, Wedepohl, having first met Dehio as an infantry officer during the war,

85. Weiß and Hoser, eds., *Die Deutschnationalen*, 231–244. In Cabinet discussions Hugenberg equally showed an interest only in economic matters. *Akten der Reichskanzlei*, part I, vol. I, 95–102; 159–166; 197–203; 238–255; 265–281; 292–295; 311–328.
86. BA Berlin, R 53, *Akten des Stellvertreters der Reichskanzlei: Kanzlei von Papen*. On the term *Reichsbeschwerdestelle* (Reich Complaint Center), see Norbert Frei, *Der Führerstaat. Nationalsozialistische Herrschaft 1933 bis 1945*, 6th ed. (Munich, DTV, 2001), 26.
87. Georg Dehio (1850–1932) was the editor of the *Handbuch der deutschen Kunstdenkmäler*, published between 1905 and 1912, as well as the author of the *Geschichte der deutschen Kunst* (1919–25).
88. The German Gentlemen's club was a social club for the country's aristocratic and bourgeois elites.

praised Dehio's national-minded views.[89] Wedepohl further related that, already as a child, Dehio had been cordially received in the home of Paul de Lagarde (the famous orientalist and figurehead of conservative anti-semitic cultural pessimism, who was held in high honor in the Third Reich), while Dehio's father had received the "highest honors of the German Reich."[90] In Dehio's case, the ring of his name and the national significance of his father's achievements appear to have moved Papen to take action. At Wedepohl's suggestion, Papen immediately turned to Hindenburg's Undersecretary of State Otto Meissner with the request that he plead Dehio's case to Hindenburg.[91] Meissner responded in the most obliging manner, assuring Papen that Dehio's case had been for-warded, with Hindenburg's special recommendation for a "benevolent examination," to the Prussian Minister of Culture. In his communication to Prussia's Culture Minister, Meissner emphasized that in 1930 Hinden-burg had awarded Dehio's father the *Adlerschild*, one of the Reich's highest honors for service to the Fatherland for "the national importance of his achievements." Papen's office lost no time in informing Wedepohl of Meissner's intervention; the tone of the communication made it clear that a positive result was to be expected.[92]

The Boycott and *Völkisch* Antisemitism

On the whole, German Nationals and other conservatives did not view their role in these early months of 1933 as censors of Nazi attacks or helpless observers filled with rage. A section of the DNVP did disapprove of the lawlessness of the antisemitic discrimination and the brutality of

---

89. BA Berlin, R 53, no. 86, "Anfragen wegen politischer Verhaftungen," fols. 76–80.
90. Ibid., fols. 77, 78. On Paul de Lagarde (1827–91), until 1834 Paul Bötticher, see Stern, *Politics of Cultural Despair, passim.*
91. 19 June 1933, BA Lichterfelde, R 53, no. 86, fol. 82.
92. Ibid., fols. 83, 85. On Ludwig Dehio as a historian, see Volker Berghahn, "Ludwig Dehio," in Hans-Ulrich Wehler, *Deutsche Historiker*, vol. IV (Göttingen: Vandenhoeck & Ruprecht, 1972), 97–116; Theodor Schieder, "Ludwig Dehio zum Gedächtnis," *Historische Zeitschrift*, 201 (1965), 1–12.

the attacks, though the reasons varied: some party members, such as Adele Kappus, were personally affected by the boycott, others thought that a distinction should be made between established German Jews and "*Ostjuden*" when it came to discriminatory measures, and still others complained about the erosion of the rule of law and clearly realized that with it a part of the German identity was in danger of being obliterated. Taken as a whole, however, the DNVP's dominant reaction to National Socialist outrages was the re-emergence of prejudices and resentments as part of the traditional antisemitic consensus within the party, whose members had always seen in German Jews the unwelcome element of modernism and the undermining of customs and the traditional way of life. Added to these traditional anti-Jewish motivations, already evident in nineteenth-century German conservatives, were two further elements specific to the period of the Nazi takeover of power: when it came to supporting the new nationalist and antisemitic orientation, DNVP members did not want to be "surpassed" by National Socialists and be seen as lukewarm; and secondly, in the atmosphere of spring 1933, some DNVP members no longer felt compelled to conceal their own often extreme *völkisch* attitudes. The DNVP's disparate roots were reflected in the levels of intensity of party members' manifest antisemitism that now came to light: from the moderate liberal-conservative influence of the Free Conservatives, who were often politically closer to the National Liberals than to the German Conservative Party, all the way to the extreme antisemitic elements of *völkisch* groups and Christian Socials. Even though a part of the *völkisch* racist wing had been forced out of the party in 1922, *völkisch* attitudes and ways of thinking had continued to live on in the DNVP.[93]

While the NSDAP bore the main responsibility for organizing the 1 April 1933 boycott, a large part of the German National Party organization was also involved in the event. A series of documents confirm that the order to participate actively in the boycott was issued by the party

93. Lohalm, *Völkischer Radikalismus*, 216–221, 325, 425.

head office. On 1 April 1933, for example, the DNVP Grenzmark Posen-West Prussia *Land* Association reported to Berlin: "Telephoned instructions to immediately put the *Kampfring* in service for the propaganda campaign, 'Germans buy only German goods' have been put into effect without delay." The response was encouraging: "We had the signs carried through all the streets of the city many times over and have also achieved a good propagandistic effect, especially since we were the first to appear on the scene."[94] Already on 28 March a circular had been sent to twenty-five DNVP *Land* Associations north of the Main river: "Organize immediately processions with signs reading, 'Germans buy only German goods' and 'Germans buy only from Germans.'"[95] The instructions from the DNVP head office to the party *Land* Associations were passed on to the local organizations, which in turn sent their reports back to Berlin that orders had been executed.[96] The DNVP's Gotha party organization reported that they would not arrange for signs to be carried through the streets: "The Nazis have already been doing that for days, and if we appeared on the scene now, it would only look as if we were imitating them, and it will make no impression at all." Instead, the Gotha group would put up signs "in our display and newspaper cases."[97] As far as the DNVP party organization was concerned, it seemed that from the national head office in Berlin down to the local organizations, the entire party took pains to actively participate in the April boycott to the best of its ability, and if a local organization failed to take part the reasons had nothing to do with moral scruples, humanitarian motives, or adherence to the rule of law.

Some DNVP members did speak out against the harshness and injustices of the boycott, but the reactions were predictably measured, even when national-minded Jews were concerned. One DNVP member from

94. 1 April 1933 at BA Berlin, R 8005, no. 48, fol. 104.
95. BA Berlin, R 8005 , fol. 106. The telegram made the rounds, among other places, to the DNVP *Land* Associations in Niederrhein, Westphalen-Ost, Arnsberg, Mittelrhein, Düsseldorf-Ost, Hanover-Süd, Braunschweig, Merseburg, Magdeburg, Dresden, and Leipzig.
96. Ibid., fol. 107.   97. 30 March 1933, ibid., fol. 108.

Hattingen/Ruhr complained that a resident Jewish dentist, "a through and through strictly national-oriented man," who "because of that had to endure a lot of nastiness from the Left," now had to give up his entire practice, while a Jewish factory owner, "a benefactor the likes of which Hattingen and its surroundings has not seen a second time," was now ostracized like everyone else.[98] The answer from Berlin was telling: the "so-called Jewish action" might not appeal to everyone, but one should take into consideration that "we find ourselves in a revolution and some things that in normal times would not be tolerated are now unavoidable."[99] What is more, "the question of one's attitude toward Jews is one of principle that cannot depend on whether or not the individual Jew is a decent human being or not."[100] The DNVP head office made its position absolutely clear: "Religious considerations play no role whatsoever in our attitude toward Jews; we disapprove of them out of political considerations."[101]

During the Republic the issue of religion versus race had been left open (in fact, it was not a matter of dispute, since religion was clearly deemed the decisive factor). Now in the atmosphere of the Nazi takeover, when everything seemed to flow in the one unstoppable direction of the Nazi Party, the DNVP leadership was anxious to follow what was considered the "politically correct" policy. The initial concept from the days of the Empire was that Jews should not have too strong a position in a Christian society; the religious criterion was thus decisive. In the late winter and spring of 1933, the DNVP leadership followed unequivocally in the footsteps of the NSDAP and committed itself to the national revolution, surrendering the rights of the individual, including those of religious freedom and legal protection, to the NSDAP's vision of a racial "national community." For the DNVP, German Jews lost their rights as individuals

---

98. 1 April 1933, ibid., fols. 68–69.   99. 20 April 1933, ibid., fol. 67.
100. Ibid., fol. 67.
101. Ibid., fol. 67. The DNVP head office stated, in conclusion, that the boycott was now over, "and any further measures will be based on a legal foundation."

in the spring of 1933 and became subordinated to its political strategy of keeping pace with its NSDAP coalition partner.

There were also strongly *völkisch*-oriented German Nationals for whom antisemitism was a central issue. How large the percentage of such *völkisch*-minded conservatives in the DNVP was at the end of the Republic cannot be established with certainty, though it is safe to assume that by 1932 many of them may have converted to Nazism. But there remained *völkisch*-leaning German Nationals who held prominent positions, such as the Württemberg physician Bubenhofer, senior medical consultant at the Freudenstadt district hospital in the Black Forest, member of the executive committee of the Württemberg chapter of the party, and, as he wrote about himself in a letter to Papen, "a man well-known for his nationalist convictions throughout the *Land* of Württemberg."[102] Bubenhofer's 11 April 1933 letter to Papen was accompanied by a treatise, in which he laid out his political ideas and asked Papen for his comments. The physician's observations offer revealing insights into the mental universe of the DNVP's *völkisch* wing.[103]

Bubenhofer positioned himself as an enemy of the left wing of the Nazi party. In a meeting of the Württemberg executive committee, he had already demanded in 1932 that the DNVP switch *en bloc* to the NSDAP to strengthen the non-socialist wing of the party as well as Hitler's position within it. The latter point was important to him, since Bubenhofer felt himself in harmony with Hitler's policies, and saw no notable difference "between his [Hitler's] views about solutions to social problems and those of the German Nationals."[104] A strong German National wing would have the effect of strengthening the "Christian-conservative" worldview within the NSDAP. Even today, Hitler was said to be helpless in the face of unauthorized SA actions.[105] On the other hand, Bubenhofer

102. 11 April 1933, BA Berlin, R 53, no. 80, "Akten der Vizekanzlei Papen," fol. 157v.
103. BA Berlin, R 53, no. 80, "Vizekanzlei Papen," fols. 157–162; see also Werner Braatz, "The counter-revolution of 1933 as viewed in two documents addressed to Vice-Chancellor Papen," *International Review of Social History*, 19 (1974), 115–127.
104. BA Berlin, R 53, no. 80, "Vizekanzlei Papen," fol. 158v.
105. Ibid., fol. 159.

was enthusiastic about the "magnificent crackdown since 5 March," an obvious reference to the suppression of the opposition and the swift establishment of the dictatorship. He emphasizes that he wholeheartedly agrees with most of the NSDAP's positions,[106] though he professes dismay that "the revolution" had been proceeding in "too bloodless a fashion," and that socialists and their intellectual leaders, "alien races, the Jews," had gotten off too lightly.[107] Bubenhofer's verdict that the revolution had not been radical enough underlines the chillingly uncompromising nature of his antisemitism, so that it comes as no surprise that he wants the "alien-race elements" completely annihilated: "These leaders must be killed and in abundance at that. We will again come back to the soul of the German worker only once this poison has been eliminated."[108]

To Bubenhofer the "boycott against Jewry" appears "to have been a very inadequate measure," as he does not believe that "a revolution without consciously applied terror really penetrates."[109] Germans were in any case too good-natured for that kind of horror, whereas in Russia the scale of terror had petrified the entire world:

> And who, at the end of the day, were the fathers of the Russian revolution? Jews. I do not want to say that we should imitate these Jewish methods, but through tough measures against the Jews in Germany and their dominance in various fields, we must fill their blood relations throughout the world with such a holy dread that they will be silenced. We have to use German Jews as hostages against Jewish financial power. This is the idiom they understand.[110]

Here the antisemitism and political radicalism of the *völkisch* German National Bubenhofer is no different from that of even the most extreme

---

106. Ibid., fol. 159.   107. Ibid., fols. 159v., 160.

108. Ibid., fol. 160. On this standard accusation of the Right ever since 1918 that Jewish leaders had steered the labor movement into increasingly radical waters, see also Chapter 2 above, and Friedländer, "Politische Veränderung," 27–67.

109. BA Berlin, R 53, no. 80, fol. 160.

110. Ibid., fol. 160. Bubenhofer's proximity to Nazism also become clear from his remarks on eugenics, wherein he speaks of making the population more "Nordic" ("*Aufnordung*," 160), of "compulsory sterilization of all racially-inferior people" (fol. 160v.), and the need for "gradual de-urbanization," since "large cities mean the death of a people" (fol. 160v.).

National Socialists. The main difference between Bubenhofer's radical *völkisch* conservatism and National Socialism lay paradoxically in the fact that Bubenhofer rejected any form of public health care and welfare policies, as he indicated when arguing: "It was not despite, but rather because of social welfare legislation that we lost the war." National Socialists took pride in Germany's social legislation; they also would hardly have spoken of the "pointless and immoral right to an equal, direct, secret vote."[111]

Lacking Determination and Fearing to Decide

While Bubenhofer was not an exceptional case, German Nationals in the mold of Bubenhofer were also not typical. Bubenhofer's ilk were mostly to be found in the *Bildungsbürgertum* or in parts of the Protestant aristocracy.[112] In the months during the Nazi takeover, the German Nationals made desperate efforts not to be seen as "Jew friendly" ("*judenfreundlich*"), for fear of falling out of favor with their domineering coalition partner and so as not to appear out of sync with the prevailing anti-Jewish mood of the spring of 1933. To National Socialists, on the other hand, it seemed that German Nationals had evinced too little enthusiasm for the boycott and generally remained on the sidelines when it came to Nazi anti-Jewish measures. German National apprehensions were reflected in the concerned tone in which the *Altenburger Landes-Zeitung* turned to the DNVP head office with an inquiry about how to handle the following accusation: "In the course of discussions with a National Socialist about antisemitism, one of our readers was reproached on account of German Nationals protecting Jews; 40–50% of the editors in Hugenberg's

---

111. Ibid., fols. 160v., 161. In the Third Reich voting was virtually compulsory, though secrecy was a sham; see the interesting piece by Hedwig Richter and Ralph Jessen, "Elections, Plebiscites, and Festivals," in Gellately, *Oxford Illustrated History of the Third Reich*, 85–117.
112. Malinowski, *Vom König zum Führer*, 482–488; Stephan Malinowski, "Vom blauen zum reinen Blut. Antisemitische Adelskritik und adliger Antisemitismus 1871–1944," *Jahrbuch für Antisemitismusforschung*, 12 (2003), 147–168; Jones, *The German Right 1918–1930*, 304–311.

publishing house [Scherlverlag] are said to be Jewish."[113] The DNVP's main office hastily affirmed that of about 100 editors at the publishing house, "most recently only four would meet this description. Numbers may have been reduced still further in the meantime, though a total elimination can be attained only gradually."[114] The head office clearly took pains to dispel any suspicion that Hugenberg employed a significant number of Jewish editors in his publishing house.

German Nationals were conscious of a predicament when reviewing membership applications of Jews. This becomes starkly evident from the convoluted and twisting tactics they employed when rejecting Jews and half-Jews for DNVP membership between February and the late spring of 1933. Still, almost every case was handled on an individual basis. The *Land* and local party committees, which were more in tune with local conditions and often impressed by the nationalist merits and good character of the applicant (whereby only those Jewish Germans who felt close to conservative causes would apply for membership anyway), were, as a rule, more open to accept applications from Jewish Germans than the DNVP head office in Berlin. The Berlin party headquarters desperately tried to fend off the calamitous reputation of being favorably predisposed towards Jews and was thus consistent in maintaining its disapproving attitude.[115] In the deliberations about each individual application, there was no unified policy approach that guided the outcome. The later a case came forward, the greater the chance of refusal. What was still subject to a long debate in the first months of 1933 was likely to be dismissed without much ado in April or May. This rapid increase in anti-Jewish sentiment on the part of the DNVP leadership reflects the speed of Hitler's successful establishment of the dictatorship and the party's acknowledgement of that fact. The party leadership obviously felt it had to join the

---

113. 11 April 1933 at BA Berlin, R 8005, no. 48, fol. 52.
114. 3 May 1933 at BA Berlin, R 8005, no. 48, fol. 51.
115. In November 1932, Nazis had repeatedly tried to insinuate that Jewish organizations endorsed the DNVP, thereby trying to discredit the party in the eyes of its voters; Nielsen, *Between Heimat and Hatred*, 227–228.

fray or suffer the potentially debilitating political consequences. But there were exceptions even to this rule of thumb. At the beginning of 1933, any case that appeared ambiguous was still disputed at length and produced an extensive correspondence, in which contradictory opinions clashed.

One case in particular, that of the practicing physician Dr. Behrend from Pomerania, illustrates how deeply antisemitism was rooted in the DNVP and how much the party membership was torn over this issue. In February and March 1933, the Behrend case divided the entire Pomerania *Land* Association, the DNVP's largest and most influential regional organization since the founding of the party.[116] In mid-February 1933 a prominent member of the DNVP's Kolberg local group wrote a letter requesting mediation from the *Land* Association in the provincial capital of Stettin in a matter regarding Dr. Behrend, who was described as "the son of a Jewish father and a Christian mother. The father converted to Christianity upon his marriage."[117] Dr. Behrend and his non-Jewish wife had joined the party at the request of Kolberg's local DNVP leader. "Behrend did his duty in the war and occupied a position of considerable prominence in Kolberg, ... frequented the best social circles," and "up to now has never stood out" politically. Despite "his only inherent flaw" consisting in the fact that "he is the son of a Jewish father and so a half Jew," a whole series of DNVP members expressed grave misgivings concerning Behrend's membership in the DNVP.[118] Other DNVP members, in contrast, recommended that Behrend retain his membership and even threatened to leave the party if he were forced out. In this difficult situation, the local group hoped for help from the *Land* Association.[119]

116. Traditionally, the DNVP had been most successful in Pomerania. In the elections for the provincial Diet, the party received 48.5% of the vote in 1925, 40.8% in 1929, and 18.4% in 1933. Jürgen Falter, Thomas Lindenberger, and Siegfried Schumann, eds., *Wahlen und Abstimmungen in der Weimarer Republik. Materialien zum Wahlverhalten, 1919–1933* (Munich: Beck, 1986), 104.

117. 14 February 1933 at BA Berlin, R 8005, no. 48, "DNVP, Kirchen- und Religionsangelegen-heiten," fol. 147.

118. Ibid., fol. 147v.   119. Ibid., fol. 147.

Behrend's opponents also turned to the *Land* Association. One of Behrend's colleagues, Chief Medical Officer Dr. Haenisch, argued that Behrend's continuing membership would only cause the party harm, because "it would leave us wide open to Nazi attacks."[120]

Just as Behrend's supporters had done, Haenisch threatened to leave the party if Behrend were to remain a member. He also made it plain that he was not alone in his opinion—other German Nationals, he argued, also "take a harsh view of those who belong to Judaism from the racial-*völkisch* standpoint and refuse to work closely with people who are so strongly Jewish by dint of their blood."[121] The retired Captain von Hertzberg, a cousin of the Pomeranian DNVP chairman Georg von Zitzewitz[122] and prominent Kolberg DNVP member, who was also a strong opponent of Behrend's continuing membership, complained in his letter to the *Land* Association that half-Jews, "who cannot be accepted by the Nazis," now seek admission to the DNVP only "because they need a back-up plan."[123] Hertzberg warned that the DNVP stood in danger of losing its best members if indiscriminate admission into the party was not curtailed. Then "inferior scum" would gain the upper hand in the party. Therefore, the party must not "burden itself with Jews and Jewish riff-raff;" rather, it must "be *völkisch* and free of Jews or it won't exist at all."[124] If Behrend should remain a member, Hertzberg threatened, as others had before him, to leave the party. Once again, in its quest to mimic its more successful coalition partner, the DNVP appeared to jettison the worth of individual achievement and emphasize racial criteria.

Shortly before the 5 March elections, the DNVP Pomeranian *Land* Association, to whom all these communications were sent, found itself in an awkward predicament. It did not want to hazard a decision since

---

120. 21 February 1933 at BA Berlin, R 8005, no. 48, fols. 146–146v.
121. Ibid., fol. 146v.
122. Georg von Zitzewitz, born in 1892, member of the Prussian Landtag 1932–1933, DNVP Reichstag deputy in 1924 and 1933.
123. 21 February 1933 at BA Berlin, R 8005, no. 48, "DNVP, Kirchen- und Religionsangelegenheiten," fol. 142.
124. Ibid.

some party members would be antagonized regardless of the outcome. The matter was thus referred to Berlin with the recommendation that "the affair is not to be considered in haste." Instead, dilatory tactics were to be pursued: "We have advised the Kolberg local association to appeal to party mediation, in order to drag this matter out."[125] Now the decision lay in the hands of Berlin, where it would not be taken lightly. Major Hans Nagel, the manager of the party's day-to-day affairs, with whom the ultimate decision lay, drafted a carefully worded response to Stettin, which he diligently revised before sending the final letter to the Stettin *Land* Association on 23 March.[126] In his letter Nagel urgently recommended "to refrain from an appeal to party arbitration," because if "this produces a general decision, the party will be damaged in any case."[127] Nagel clearly articulated the party's dilemma: "Doubts may exist about whether the provision of the statutes according to which Jews may not become members refer to religion or race." If in the sensitive issue of accepting half-Jews as members, "a fundamental decision is made to the effect…that half-Jews can be admitted, this would greatly damage us among *völkisch*-oriented circles and cost us a great many members."[128] In addition, it would provide "National Socialists with unmatched propaganda materials against us," so that it would be best "to make a decision in each individual case."[129]

By mid-May, the DNVP had lost most of its local strongholds to the more dynamic Nazi Party, whose predominance had increased steadily after the 5 March elections. Symbolic of the party's increasing alignment

---

125. 2 March 1933 at BA Berlin, R 8005, no. 48, fol. 141.
126. BA Berlin, R 8005, no. 48, fol. 140–140v. In his draft, Nagel emphasized that in case of an overall decision against the acceptance of half-Jews, "a great many very valuable members might be lost to us." He omitted this sentence from the final version, since it might well be construed as "pro-Jewish." Thus, even in intra-party correspondence, fear of appearing favorably disposed toward what now had become the "national enemy" was pervasive.
127. 23 March 1933 at BA Berlin, R 8005, no. 48, fol. 136.
128. Ibid., vol. 136.
129. Ibid., fols. 136–136v. After the dissolution of the DNVP, Hans Nagel (1882–1964) became a member of the *Wehrwirtschaftsamt* within the German army. A general (*Generalmajor*) during World War II, he held important positions in the economic administration of the "Eastern Operations Area" after Germany's invasion of the Soviet Union in June 1941.

with the Nazis and adoption of their methods, the DNVP renamed itself the "German National Front" at the beginning of May. After that party leaders took pains to avoid any political move that might be construed as a provocation to its coalition partner. In May 1933, the Frankfurt am Main local association, for example, warmly recommended "the admission of a gentleman who is Jewish." The applicant was "*Generaldirektor* Professor Dr. Salomon, [who] according to the information of one of our prominent members, [was] baptized forty years ago [and who] enjoys a distinguished reputation here in Frankfurt;" he was a man on whom one could "rely absolutely."[130] Despite this glowing recommendation, the Berlin head office immediately issued a negative answer.[131]

The changing decision-making process of the DNVP central office in Berlin and the concomitant uncertainty that affected both membership applicants and the local offices to which they applied were connected with the political developments in the spring, such as the waning strength of the German Nationals and the concomitant growth of Nazi power, and with the absence of binding guidelines. Efforts in that direction lacked resoluteness. On 27 March 1933, for example, Major Hans Nagel wrote to the Berlin *Land* Association:

> The DNVP statutes include the passage that Jews may not be accepted into the party. There are no details in the statutes as to a specific definition of who is a Jew. However, in the committees responsible for accepting new members the opinion has gained ground that persons who have been born Jewish and then became Christian cannot be accepted into the party.[132]

---

130. 2 May 1933 at BA Berlin, R 8005, no. 48, , "DNVP, Kirchen- und Religionsangelegenheiten," fol. 29.

131. 10 May 1933 at ibid., fol. 28.

132. 27 March 1933 at BA Berlin, R 8005, no. 48, fol. 125. This is not strictly true: throughout the Republic a general prohibition against Jews becoming party members remained a bone of contention within the party. It was never introduced, though individual *Land* associations, such as Pomerania, pushed through such a ban for their own particular area. Walter, *Antisemitische Kriminalität*, 44–46.

In mid-May, only six weeks later, much more decisive language was used. The answer to a letter from a Jewish party member who had been expelled from his local branch was unmistakable:

> According to the party statutes, Jews cannot be accepted into the German National Front. For the characterization as a Jew, it is not religion, but ethnic origin that is decisive. For this reason, if you as a member of the Jewish race have been accepted into our party, that can only have happened because we had no knowledge of this fact. Therefore, we cannot consider the expulsion from your local group as incorrect.[133]

Given the party's inbred antisemitism, the multitude of opinions within it, and the vacillation of the DNVP regarding the "Jewish Question," there was never a chance that Hitler's coalition partner could or even would wish to mitigate Nazi racial policies. Nevertheless, there were many who overrated the DNVP's potential positive influence in this regard, such as the prominent Weimar journalist and former editor of the liberal *Vossische Zeitung*, Georg Bernhard, who, overoptimistically as it happens, wrote in 1933 that "in the long run German Nationals are bound to constitute an obstacle to the implementation of Nazism's racial idiocies."[134]

---

133.   14 May 1933 at BA Berlin, R 8005, no. 48, fol. 25.
134.   Georg Bernhard, *Die deutsche Tragödie. Der Selbstmord einer Republik* (Prague: Orchis, 1933), 25.

EPILOGUE

How Could it Happen?

Contemporaries who lived through the events of the late winter and spring of 1933 have repeatedly emphasized

> a complete change in popular mood between the Reichstag election of 5 March and the summer of 1933. It is something that cannot be documented, but anyone who was there remembers it well.... Despite all the lawlessness of that period, despite the concentration camps and arbitrary arrests, despite the first unmistakable signs of official antisemitism, there was a growing sense that great times lay ahead.[1]

This popular mood and political atmosphere, characteristic for the spring of 1933, forms the context in which the events examined here unfolded. Its distinguishing trait was a mixture of enthusiasm and fear: genuine and passionate agreement with the goals professed by the new regime, on the one hand, and fear of the terror it spread, on the other.

In hindsight, the initial allure the new government exerted on patriotic Germans of all classes has often been underrated. First there was the certainty that the nation had been rescued from the mortal danger of communism, then the hope for unity—a domestic solidarity reminiscent of the frequently conjured-up "spirit of August 1914" that would replace the party strife and bitter social and political conflict of Weimar's final

---

1. Sebastian Haffner, *The Ailing Empire. Germany from Bismarck to Hitler* (New York: Fromm, 1989), 184 and 186. According to Haffner, who lived in Berlin as a lawyer-in-training at the time, this change in public feeling "created the real power base for the future Führer state" (185).

Before the Holocaust: Antisemitic Violence and the Reaction of German Elites and Institutions during the Nazi Takeover.
Hermann Beck, Oxford University Press. © Hermann Beck 2022. DOI: 10.1093/oso/9780192865076.003.0016

years. Otto Dibelius, the Protestant *Generalsuperintendent* of the Kurmark, epitomized this mood of national rebirth when he proclaimed in his 4 April radio address to an American audience: "Today the German Reich is as united and firmly joined together as never before in our history."[2] This newly found unity was a source of pride that revitalized the national-minded part of the population, which at the time constituted a large majority. The strength and seeming determination of the government to stand up to hostile neighbors and former World War I antagonists, so conspicuously absent in the governments of the Weimar Republic, added to its popularity. While virtually no one wanted war,[3] it was generally hoped that the ruthless implacability Hitler showed toward his domestic opponents would also be applied in foreign affairs, especially in view of the widespread feeling that Germany had been wronged at Versailles and throughout the 1920s. The extreme national pride the regime evinced from its inception, even if at times bordering on the ridiculous, was seen as an asset, while the brutality with which domestic political opponents were dealt was tempered by the fact that these were mostly communists and socialists, the instinctive foe of law-abiding and patriotic Germans.[4] To many, the determination Hitler had shown in cracking down on the domestic opposition made them respect the new regime, for it indicated that Germany once again had a strong national government. Heinrich Rendtorff, the Protestant Bishop of Mecklenburg, summarized this sentiment when he spoke with relief about Germany finally having an *"Obrigkeit"* again—a determined government, for which

2. 4 April 1933 at EZA Berlin, Bestand 51, E2e8,1, "Die nach Amerika gerichtete Rundfunkrede des Herrn General-superintendenten Dibelius vom 4. April 1933," fol. 4.
3. See Marlis Steinert, "Hitlers Krieg und die Deutschen," in Gerhard Schulz, ed., *Die Große Krise der dreißiger Jahre. Vom Niedergang der Weltwirtschaft zum Zweiten Weltkrieg* (Göttingen: Vandenhoeck & Ruprecht, 1985), 137–153.
4. In his *The Nazi Seizure of Power*, which meticulously traces the rise of the Nazi party in the northern German town of Northeim, William S. Allen argues that "The victory of Nazism can be explained to a large extent by the desire on the part of Northeim's middle class to suppress the lower class and especially its political representatives, the Social Democratic party. Nazism was the first effective instrument for this....In many ways the actions and beliefs of Northeimers during the last years of the Weimar era were the same as if World War I had never ended. It was in this sort of atmosphere that the SPD might seem treasonable and the Nazis reasonable" (296, 297).

citizens had reason to be grateful and whose occasional revolutionary "excesses should be overlooked."[5]

In the same vein, the majority of the population, from the aristocracy down to the petty bourgeoisie, was in accord with the new regime's policy of deliberately placing itself into an unbroken line of continuity with the conservative traditions of the Prussian past, as encapsulated in the "Day of Potsdam." Even prominent members of the 20 July 1944 conspiracy to assassinate Hitler, such as Hellmuth Stieff, Henning von Tresckow, and Claus Graf von Stauffenberg, had high hopes and considerable enthusiasm for Hitler's government in 1933, while Ludwig Beck, the intended Head of State in a post-Hitlerite Germany, wrote in a letter of 17 March 1933 that the political transformation of 30 January 1933 had been "the first great ray of light since 1918."[6] Among younger German historians, the "national revolution" was interpreted as a seminal event that re-established continuity with the Prussian German past, after overcoming the inglorious episode of the Republic of Weimar and alien Western influence, thus making possible Germany's political and spiritual rebirth. The Nazi takeover was also likened to other "German revolutions," in particular to the Reformation, the uprising against Napoleon in 1813, and the period of unification between 1864 and 1871. For Rudolf Stadelmann, the "revolution of 1933" was an upheaval of European, if not universal, significance, since it established values that widely transcended German borders, while Wilhelm Mommsen argued that the age of liberalism and the bourgeoisie had now come to an end. Common to all interpretations was the underlying hope that the "national awakening" of 1933 consolidated the continuation of vaunted German traditions, while at the same time ushering in an era of promising new beginnings.[7]

5. In the decisive 26 April meeting on the "Judenfrage," see EZA Berlin, Bestand 1, no. 3210, fol. 275, for the original version of the meeting minutes; EZA Berlin, Bestand 1, no. 2411, fol. 16 for the edited version.
6. See Joachim Fest, *Staatsstreich. Der lange Weg zum 20. Juli* (Berlin: Siedler, 1994); Becker and Becker, eds., *Hitlers Machtergreifung*, 146.
7. Bernd Faulenbach, "Tendenzen der Geschichtswissenschaft im Dritten Reich," in Renate Knigge-Tesche, ed., *Berater der braunen Macht. Wissenschaft und Wissenschaftler im NS-Staat* (Frankfurt: Anabas, 1999), 26–52 esp. 31–33.

The emphasis on social equality, and the propaganda regarding the elimination of the socially privileged position of the upper bourgeoise (also intended as an indirect attack on the DNVP and its followers), struck a receptive chord with many in the economically difficult times of 1933 and was apt to render the regime more popular with those less fortunate. Some Center Party and liberal deputies, who had voted for the Enabling Act in March 1933, claimed after the war that their constituents had urged them to vote in the affirmative, thereby signaling that a more dictatorial form of government and the elimination of the multi-party system enjoyed considerable popularity.[8] After bleak years of depression, Weimar democracy, which to many stood for inflation, mismanagement, and humiliation by former wartime enemies, additionally came to denote mass unemployment, rising crime, and a deepening hopelessness.[9] As Part III of this book has shown, the conservative elites in the Churches and elsewhere vehemently rejected what they considered the shallow mass culture of the Weimar Republic, which to them represented licentiousness and a weakening of the national fiber. The present, by contrast, shone all the brighter.

This enlivening sentiment of a leap into a happier future was paradoxically coupled with the fear of falling victim to the pervasive violence of the SA and other Nazi organizations, which spared no one who fell afoul of the new masters regardless of social station or proven nationalist pedigree. Even prominent conservative politicians were in danger of literally being thrown down a flight of stairs, and knowledge of the torture cellars and other "extra-legal spaces," inaccessible to the law, was widespread.[10] In addition to fear of the SA, there was the by no means groundless dread of being held up to public ridicule and seeing

---

8. Dirk Schumann also emphasizes the increasing acceptance of a "legal dictatorship" on the part of the bourgeoisie, who welcomed that the country was run by one "strong and unambiguous will." See Schumann, "Gewalt als Methode," 135–155, esp. 148.
9. In describing the public mood in the spring of 1933, Haffner writes, "It was – and there is no other way of putting it – a widespread feeling of deliverance, of liberation from democracy" (Ailing Empire, 185).
10. Hermann Beck, "Konflikte zwischen Deutschnationalen und Nationalsozialisten während der Machtergreifungszeit," Historische Zeitschrift, 292 (2011), 645–690, esp. 664.

one's name all over the local paper, read aloud in a large assembly (for being photographed while entering a Jewish-owned store), or even of becoming the victim of a "pillory march," as quite a few German Jews and others who helped them did. Nazi violence was particularly insidious, since it had come to be viewed as a legitimate counterweight against communist violence, thereby meeting with increasing acceptance by the German *Bürgertum*.[11] In conjunction with the growing popularity of the regime in whose name the perpetrators acted and the inability (and frequent unwillingness) of the police to protect the victims, no defense against the violence seemed possible, regardless of how egregiously it manifested itself.

Looking back on the late winter and spring of 1933, the speed and character of events are difficult to fathom: exactly five weeks to the day after Hitler had become Chancellor (Monday, 30 January—Monday, 6 March), Germany was inundated by a wave of anti-Jewish violence, with thousands of attacks against *"Ostjuden"* living in Germany and hundreds against German Jews, including pillory marches, assaults with robbery, grievous bodily harm, abductions, extortions, and murder. At the same time the nascent dictatorship quickly repudiated any respect for the private life of individuals, freely intruding into other people's affairs in the name of the new Germany. The resurrection of medieval punishments, such as the pillory marches, was probably more instinctive than calculated. Very much in the same spirit of tearing down barriers between public and private spheres of life was the *Heimtücke-Verordnung* that punished the spreading of rumors, even if they originated in strictly private conversations. A confidential tête-à-tête could thus have fateful consequences when informers were taken at their word. This "Perfidy Decree" stifled personal communication, especially about political issues, and often left people with the feeling of having confided too much.

Boycott actions were also a form of antisemitic crime, especially since (contrary to the accepted view of 1 April 1933) the day of the boycott was

---

11. A point also made by Schumann, "Gewalt als Methode," 135–155, esp. 145.

replete with violent attacks and abductions of Jewish victims, so that one might argue with some justification that the boycott constituted a nationwide pogrom. In Berlin, Hesse, and the Prussian Rhine province, Eastern Jews were subjected to brutal abuse, in Regensburg Jewish businessmen were taken into "protective custody," in the Saxon cities of Plauen, Chemnitz and Zittau, Jews were tortured and killed, and from Breslau Walter Tausk reported in his diary that the boycott had "turned into a frenzy of bloodlust all over Silesia, into open pillage, acts of violence and revenge."[12] In short, it was a far cry from the largely peaceful boycott as depicted in diplomatic reports from British and American diplomats, and it gives the lie to Nazi claims (and Protestant Church leader Otto Dibelius's radio address to American listeners) that the boycott had passed without violence.[13]

Violence also played an important role in the April 1933 legislation, which constituted a first decisive step toward the exclusion of German Jews from the civil service, judiciary, and medical profession, while significantly limiting their access to higher education. The trail for standardized discriminatory national legislation was blazed by innumerable actions of local violence as well as regional administrative measures directed against Jews. In fact, one central objective behind national legislation was to put a lid on local actions and violence that threatened to interrupt due administrative process. Notably in the case of the legal profession, violent disturbances and "unauthorized actions" against Jewish lawyers and judges were widespread. While historians are well aware of the 1938 Reich-wide pogrom (*Kristallnacht*), the plethora of violent attacks in the spring of 1933 remains largely unknown in historical literature or at best unrecognized in its true dimensions. Contemporaries, on the other hand, were fully aware of the antisemitic attacks of March and April 1933, as evidenced by Konrad Adenauer's 1946 letter to a fellow Catholic, in which he averred that "[t]he Jewish pogroms of 1933 and 1938

---

12. Tausk, *Breslauer Tagebuch*, 57.
13. See also Asher, *Was Hitler a Riddle?*, 23–24. The one incident that was widely reported was the murder of Friedrich Schumm in Kiel (discussed in Chapters 6 and 10).

happened in full public view."[14] This includes the leadership groups of those institutions still in a position to act—the Protestant and Catholic Churches, the administrative and judicial bureaucracy, and the conservative German National People's Party (the leaders of the SPD, Center, and liberal parties were under Nazi attack and threatened by persecution). How did they react to what was to all intents and purposes a monstrous violation of the values their institutions professed to uphold?

In the spring of 1933, the most influential of these was arguably the German Protestant Church, which represented almost two-thirds of all Germans with its over 40 million members. During the Weimar Republic, especially its latter years, the Church had frequently been involved in politics. In December 1931, for example, Interior Minister Wilhelm Groener turned to Hermann Kapler, the head of the *Kirchenausschuss*, the Church's highest executive committee, requesting that the Protestant Church aid the State in preventing violence.[15] The Protestant Church saw itself as the conscience of the nation whose task it was to enjoin "moral" behavior (and correct ethically deviant conduct) and see to fair play in society. We have seen that while several dignitaries of the Protestant Church wanted to protest at the end of March, by the time of the decisive 26 April meeting the number of the courageous few had shrunk to but one, Wilhelm von Pechmann. His impassioned plea for action was heard, but still fell on deaf years. The overwhelming majority, led by Kapler, justified their inactivity and compliant submissiveness towards the regime with a series of rationalizations, including deprecation of foreign protests, fear of alienating an increasingly powerful regime, obvious satisfaction about the fact that "foreign infiltration" had finally been stopped, agreement with the government's "justified" use of "protective measures," and wholehearted, even passionate, endorsement of National Socialist policies.[16] The dignitaries of the Protestant Church

---

14. Adenauer, *Briefe*, 172–173.   15. Scholder, *Churches*, 178.
16. Since the analysis here focuses on the reaction of the Protestant Church as an institution and not on the scholarly tracts and lectures of its members (unless they were discussed by the Church leadership), I have not included a discussion of Dietrich Bonhoeffer's April 1933

went with the flow, terrified to find themselves in a minority opinion and, as shown by the crucial 26 April meeting, even afraid to mention arguments in favor of national-minded German Jews (such as, for example, their steadfast service for their country). The conduct of the Protestant Church leadership was to a certain extent similar to elite behavior in other nationalist frenzies in the twentieth century, albeit with infinitely more catastrophic results in the end.[17] Yet in 1933 it was certainly not merely fear of the new regime but a combination of strong prejudice against Jews and genuine admiration for the accomplishments of the "national revolution" that held German Church leaders back from voicing remonstrations and disapproval. Those German Protestant voices that reached an international audience in the spring of 1933 underlined pride in the new regime and emphasized that Hitler's government had rekindled "a sense of honor in the nation."

Letter exchanges between high-ranking Church leaders about the antisemitic terror spread by the new regime show that conservative Protestant dignitaries blamed what they considered the pernicious "Jewish influence in German cultural life" for the moral lassitude and profligacy (and indirectly also the political weakness) of the Weimar Republic. Throughout the Republic, prominent Protestant theologians had held, and some publicly expressed, antisemitic views. Recent research has revealed that Martin Niemöller (who rose to national prominence with the *Pfarrernotbund* only in the second half of 1933 and is thus not part of this study), for example, was imbued with radical nationalist and *völkisch* notions in the 1920s.[18] Deep-seated and seemingly indelible

---

lecture "Die Kirche vor der Judenfrage." Here Bonhoeffer argued that the Church should inquire whether the State had legitimate reasons for its actions, dispense "diakonische Hilfe" to its victims and, if required, act politically, that is, by directly opposing State action, though this latter course first needed to be decided by a *Konzil*.

17. Similarities exist to August 1914 and to McCarthyism, when few dared to voice arguments in favor of the national enemy (in 1914) or communist sympathizers (in the late 1940s and early 1950s).
18. Benjamin Ziemann, "Martin Niemöller als völkisch-nationaler Studentenpolitiker in Münster 1919–1923," VJHZ, 67 (2019), 209–234. This had already been pointed out in the 1970s

notions about the negative influence of Jewish predominance in public life, and a "provocative lack of consideration and respect" (as Wilhelm von Pechmann once put it), were so widespread that they even extended to those who, like Pechmann himself, continued advocating protest against antisemitic violence and legislation. Pervasive cultural-religious antisemitism further numbed any wish to protest.[19] Throughout discussions among Church leaders in March and April, the pro-Nazi "German Christians" played no role. It was traditional Church leaders, whose average age was well over 60 and who had been educated and molded by the values of their class during the German Empire, who chose inactivity. Luther's "Zwei-Reiche-Lehre," separating the religious realm of Christ from the secular realm of politics, cannot serve as an excuse for the Protestant Church's silent collusion, since Church leaders had been actively involved in politics during the Weimar Republic and clearly taken sides (in fact, had been asked to do so by the *Reichsinnenminister*).

Yet it is striking that the Church was not even prepared to take up the cause of its own members—Jews who had been baptized—even though internal memoranda continually emphasized that "Judeo-Christians" needed and deserved protection and, in a manner of speaking, even paid for it in the form of Church taxes (*Kirchensteuer*). The exculpating argument that the Protestant Church would not have survived open resistance but rather been forced into a *Gleichschaltung* with regime organizations and goals, like other institutions from trade unions to artisan guilds and sports clubs, misses the point. Open resistance would not have

by Klaus Theweleit in his *Männerphantasien*, though it was not buttressed by the same amount of documentation.

---

19. The *Honoratiorenantisemitismus* (antisemitism of notabilities) of Protestant Church leaders was interspersed with a certain snobbism and elitism, comparable to the antisemitism of the Protestant upper classes in the United States in the 1920s, who wanted to keep American Jews out of university humanities faculties and social clubs. Dinnerstein, *Antisemitism*, 78–104; Peter Novick, *That Noble Dream. The "Objectivity Question" and the Historical Profession* (Cambridge: Cambridge University Press, 1988), 172–174. On one German Jewish emigrant's perception of American antisemitism, see Leo Löwenthal, *Mitmachen wollte ich nie. Ein autobiographisches Gespräch mit Helmut Dubiel* (Frankfurt: Suhrkamp, 1980).

been necessary; even a limited form of protest regarding an issue that had direct bearing on the Ten Commandments and went to the heart of religious belief (*Nächstenliebe*) and the Church's mission to be the moral conscience of the nation may have compelled Church dignitaries to voice their disapproval of anti-Jewish violence and offer solace to those German Jews who turned to the Church for help. But the guardians of morality and tradition failed in their self-proclaimed mission. What undoubtedly contributed to the silence and inactivity of Church leaders was the broad consensus with the basic domestic and foreign policy goals of the new regime, even though a majority of Church dignitaries, such as Kapler, had voted for Hindenburg, not Hitler, in the 1932 presidential elections. Yet, even if they found the violent aspects of Nazi antisemitism repugnant, they were prepared to take the rough with the smooth and overlook antisemitic violence and the April boycott, since they were in basic harmony with the tenets of the new government, especially since the DNVP, the party for which many of them had voted during the Weimar Republic, formed part of it.

Catholic bishops, who were equally aware of the extent of the violence, were also concerned about the potential fallout that criticism of the regime might bring in its wake. Until the end of March, they managed to evade the issue of antisemitic violence. Archbishop Adolf Bertram's circular to German archbishops at the very end of March, inquiring whether the Church should intervene to stop the boycott, set the confines of how the German episcopate would approach the issue in the spring of 1933. In a distancing bureaucratic tone Bertram made it clear that he was opposed to any intervention: the boycott was concerned with the "economic struggle" of an "interest group" not close to the Church, German bishops had better concentrate on their own affairs, intervention would certainly not meet with success and only bring Catholics into disrepute, and in the past the "largely Jewish-owned press" had remained silent on the persecution of Catholics in different countries. This would essentially be the line followed by Catholic bishops in 1933. In his communications with American cardinals, the Munich Archbishop

Michael von Faulhaber adopted the narrative of the government regarding the April boycott (just as Otto Dibelius had done in the Protestant Church), and assured them that "reports about bloodstained terror in Germany" were essentially untrue. In his correspondence with Catholics who had urged that the Catholic Church speak out publicly, he emphasized that Catholic protest would turn the fight against Jews into a fight against Catholics and repeatedly stressed that Jews could help themselves: Catholic schools, the salvaging of Catholic associations from being affected by Gleichschaltung and losing their independence, and the protection of Catholic civil servants were more pressing concerns. Thus, while a few courageous individual voices vehemently urged that the Catholic Church speak out, the episcopate remained silent about anti-Jewish attacks and boycotts.[20] On the whole the Catholic Church, much like its Protestant counterpart, was not shy when it came to raising its voice in the political arena, as German bishops demonstrated when they condemned communism, complained about the shallowness of public morals during the Weimar Republic, disparaged the cultural teachings of National Socialism in 1931 and 1932, and pleaded with the regime on behalf of Catholic civil servants in April 1933. During the war, Catholic bishops, such as Clemens August von Galen, would again raise their voices—just not on behalf of the persecuted Jewish minority.

Administrative and judicial officials assiduously "worked towards" what they assumed the new regime expected from them.[21] The administrative and judicial bureaucracy was the institution most responsible for

20. There was far greater continuity in leadership of the German Catholic Church than in the Protestant Church in the late spring and summer of 1933. Following Hermann Kapler's retirement in early June, the government-appointed commissar for the Prussian Protestant Church, August Jäger, furloughed most of the Generalsuperintendenten and (temporarily) replaced them with representatives of the German Christians. Most of them were later reinstated. See Kurt Meier, Kreuz und Hakenkreuz. Die evangelische Kirche im Dritten Reich, 2nd ed. (Munich: DTV, 2008), 32–59.

21. This was reminiscent of what Ian Kershaw described in his chapter "Working towards the Führer" in the first part of his biography of Hitler, Hitler. Hubris 1889–1936, 527–591: an attempt by many to work in the spirit of what they thought the regime wanted without having received express orders.

the implementation of any antisemitic policy.[22] It could act as a retarding or accelerating force, hold back or speed up governmental policies. In the late winter and spring of 1933 German administrative officials were even closer to the impact of antisemitic violence, since they were directly involved in the handling of complaints from foreign embassies and consulates about attacks on their Jewish citizens, while members of the upper echelon of the judicial branch, in particular public prosecutors, dealt with antisemitic crimes. In "interpreting" the course of assaults and occasionally recording what had happened from the mouths of the frightened victims, police officials and others could exercise a great deal of latitude. It is obvious that most officials involved, from those who recorded the crimes to higher-ranking civil servants who prepared reports for the Interior Ministry, did their best to minimize the extent of the attacks. To provide legitimate reasons for attacks and as a way to justify them, victims were often labelled communists or communist sympathizers, who had allegedly made seditious statements supporting communist subversion. This tactic was used even in cases of affluent middle-class Jews, on whom it was manifestly absurd to cast such aspersions. But then, administrative officials stood firmly behind the new government. Commenting on the "Day of Potsdam," the journal of the Reich Association of Higher Administrative Officials commented: "The National Uprising has been welcomed by all higher officials, but by none so warmly and with such an open heart as by administrative officials."[23]

In the judicial branch, public prosecutors aided and abetted crimes in cases ranging from theft to murder. Given the political and psychological climate during the spring of 1933 and the amnesties of 21 March and 25 July, they knew full well that offenders would inevitably be released in any case. In their reports and summings-up, they worked toward that end by exculpating perpetrators with specious excuses. To prejudice the

22. Horst Matzerath, "Bürokratie und Judenverfolgung," in Ursula Büttner, ed., *Die Deutschen und die Judenverfolgung im Dritten Reich* (Hamburg: Christians, 1992), 105–129.
23. See Fattman, *Bildungsbürger*, 225, n. 222.

outcome, a branding label was put on victims from the beginning: the file of the murder victim Max Kassel from Wiesbaden, for example, a reasonably well-off and completely apolitical dairy merchant, was headed "communist from Wiesbaden," though in Kassel's case the assigned political affiliation was farcical, with not a shred of evidence to support it. The all-too-willing complicity of the judiciary in the spring of 1933 cannot be explained solely with reference to opportunism, though concern about one's career undoubtedly did play a role. The other obvious reason, accounting for the often creative besmirching of victims, was the deep-seated antisemitic prejudice with which members of the judiciary were suffused.

And the leadership of Hitler's embattled coalition partner, the DNVP, desperately tried not to appear "*judenfreundlich*." Some Germans, including German Jews, assumed in 1933 that the DNVP would resist "the implementation of Nazism's racial idiocies," as the prominent Weimar journalist Georg Bernhard asserted, that the antisemitism in Hitler's program would be tempered by bourgeois sensibilities, and that prominent German Jews would suffer no harm.[24] The DNVP and conservatives in general would fulfill none of the expectations or hopes placed in them. Already during the Weimar Republic, the DNVP had excluded German Jews from some of its *Land* organizations and, even though the party's antisemitism abated somewhat after 1924, its leadership group was permeated by an antisemitism comparable to the views held by Protestant Church leaders, that is, a religious and cultural anti-Judaism mixed with a political antisemitism that automatically associated Jews with left-wing politics, advocated the removal of "*Ostjuden*" from Germany, and favored restrictions on and a general resistance to Jewish influence. Extreme radical *völkisch* currents, comparable to the "redemptive antisemitism" Saul Friedländer has connected with die-hard Nazis, were rare in the DNVP, but by no means non-existent. During the period of the Nazi

---

24. Georg Bernhard quoted in Beck, *Fateful Alliance*, 176; see also Ebermayer, *Denn heute gehört uns Deutschland*, 23–24.

takeover, the DNVP endorsed its regional associations' participation in the April boycott, while at the same time trying not to close the door completely to national-minded Jews and those who had been baptized.[25] A few of its members protested against Nazi violence, but none of its leaders joined in. Here, too, we observe the phenomenon of an anxious *"Zuarbeiten"* toward the actions and decisions DNVP leaders felt their overpowering coalition partner expected of them. Their indecisiveness and teetering opportunism were a sorry spectacle for a party that shared power during a period when political institutions were being radically transformed.

What thus astonishes is not just the shrinking back from any form of open (or even veiled) protest, but the anxious anticipation of the wishes of the new regime's dominant coalition partner that we observe in both the bureaucracy and the DNVP. What can explain this phenomenon? Three interconnected and mutually overlapping reasons account for it: the growing popularity of a regime that propagated antisemitism and made it socially and politically acceptable; fear of Nazi terror and repressive measures; and, most importantly, antisemitic prejudice on the part of the German elite. For many national-minded conservative Germans, these prejudices encompassed a cluster of perceptions that came to the fore in the wake of World War I, including the purported link between Jews and communism, accusations of their having triggered the post-World War I revolution—thereby "stabbing the German army in the back" and consequently holding Jews responsible for military defeat and the humiliation of Versailles.[26] Adding to the political prejudices was the

25. According to Philipp Nielsen, even at the end of the Weimar Republic there remained a sizeable contingent of conservative Jews who may well have been close to the DNVP if the party had moderated its antisemitic stance. See Nielsen, *Between Heimat and Hatred*, 224–226.

26. The *Ostdeutsche Rundschau* summarized the feelings of many German nationalists and antisemites in June 1919: "The Jews have obstructed our military winning run and defrauded us of the fruits of our victories. The Jews have laid an axe to the thrones and smashed the monarchical constitution to pieces. The Jews have destroyed our middle classes, spread profiteering like the plague, stirred up the cities against the countryside, and the workers against the State and Fatherland. The Jews have brought us the revolution, and if now after the lost war we also lose the peace, then the Jew [Juda] has amassed his fair share of guilt." Quoted in Friedländer, "Politische Veränderungen," 53.

cultural-religious antisemitism of conservative Church dignitaries, such as Otto Dibelius, who openly acknowledged that his family, as those of "most families of higher officials in the old Germany," was antisemitic to the point where "you avoided personal dealings with [Jews]," not because of "a hostile attitude, but still in a way that sensed the foreignness in their manner."[27] This attitude, embraced by conservative Church dignitaries and DNVP leaders, acted as a break on any willingness to help or protest, even in cases where Nazi actions were considered repugnant and despicable. It was the perceived "foreignness" in manner to which Dibelius alluded that made the Heidelberg bookstore owner Wilhelmine Wolff denounce her long-time customer Heinz Stern, because she disliked his "mocking superior tone" and "the impudent taunting way in which he comports himself."[28] These remarks highlight one of the conundrums Jews in Germany encountered in 1933: if they remained true to their cultural and religious heritage, as did many "*Ostjuden*," they were vilified, attacked, and treated with contempt. Yet, even if they were completely assimilated, had become fully "German" and converted to Christianity, they were still perceived, at best, as somehow "foreign," and, at worst, as scheming pretenders to the *Volksgemeinschaft*.

Admittedly, by the second half of March open resistance on the part of individuals would have required extraordinary personal courage; following one's conscience became a matter of character, since every individual's personal and material existence was at stake. Under the conditions of the emerging dictatorship there were few alternatives to becoming culpable, as Joachim Scholtyseck has convincingly argued.[29] The surprising factor in all of this, given Germany's much-vaunted *Rechtsstaat* tradition and emphasis on upright behavior on the part of its public servants, is the extent of eager complicity by higher officials who often falsely

27. Gerlach, *Als die Zeugen schwiegen*, 42. Dibelius no doubt felt free to honestly reminisce about the past because he had protected (and presumably saved) two Jewish families during the war.
28. 22 July 1933 at LABW Karlsruhe, Bestand 507, no. 11669a, fols. 29–30 (see Chapter 6 above).
29. Joachim Scholtyseck, "Die deutschen Eliten im Jahr 1933: War Widerstand möglich?" in Wirsching, ed., *Das Jahr 1933*, 110–131.

depicted the Jewish victims of SA violence as communists, child molesters, or seducers and rapists of "German women" as a way to justify SA violence and provide an alibi for the attackers, who could thus be presented as righteous avengers instead of the thugs they were. However unlikely these invented charges and moral slurs cast upon the victims, officials understood that they would get away with them, for they appreciated that their own preconceived and previously privately held notions about "Ostjuden" and German Jews were shared not only by their superiors but also by the bulk of the German conservative elite. As shown by the examples of Dibelius and others, the leaders of the institutions discussed in this book had long held antisemitic beliefs, even if, for the most part, they had rarely been aired. The zeitgeist of spring 1933 gave these orientations public legitimacy.[30] Previous checks and balances, such as Rechtsstaat conventions that emphasized the rights of citizens, Christian morals, and a national patriotism that did not distinguish between Jewish and non-Jewish Germans had fallen by the wayside in March and April 1933. Now people's personal prejudices—cultural, political, and racial antisemitism—could be freely expressed in public. They had become central to the Nazi vision of Germany's transformation into an "Aryan" Volksgemeinschaft and were thus to some extent even expected. In the conditions of spring 1933, with the NSDAP in power and antisemitism an officially encouraged ideology that legitimated "politically correct" antisemitic behavior, higher officials, Church leaders, and other members of conservative leadership groups could thus give free rein to their prejudices. With antisemitism now a public ideology fueled by formerly private prejudices, it was easier to ignore or find excuses for

30. Shulamit Volkov has argued that in the German Empire antisemitism had become a "cultural code," denoting hatred against "Bildung, Freiheit und Menschlichkeit," as Theodor Mommsen once put it. Antisemitism was associated with radical anti-modernism, the rejection of liberalism and socialism, and the espousal of nationalism and a preindustrial value system; opposition to antisemitism signified support of social and political emancipation and a progressive attitude toward Jews and society in general. By the spring of 1933, the former had become the sole socially acceptable outlook. Shulamit Volkov, "Antisemitismus als kultureller Code," in Volkov, Jüdisches Leben und Antisemitismus im 19. und 20. Jahrhundert (Munich: Beck, 1990), 13–36, esp. 20 and 35.

the many acts of violence perpetrated against Jews in Germany. In his autobiography centering on the year 1933, Sebastian Haffner wrote about the month of March: "People began to join in – at first mostly from fear. After they had participated, they no longer wanted to do so just from fear. That would have been mean and contemptible. So, the necessary ideology was also supplied. That was the spiritual basis of the victory of the National Socialist revolution."[31] With regard to anti-Jewish sentiments, this "ideology" had become firmly embedded in conservative leadership groups well before the "national revolution."

Already in the spring of 1933, the Nazi regime succeeded in "making the personal the political"—erasing the boundaries between private life and the public sphere. Decisively for the fate of Jews in Germany, this included deep-seated personal antisemitism that could now be freely vented in public. Given their leadership role in the few institutions that might have halted the sweeping tide of often violent anti-Jewish sentiment that pervaded Germany in the late winter and spring of 1933—the Protestant and Catholic Churches, the administrative and judicial bureaucracy, and Hitler's coalition partner, the German National People's Party—conservative German elites bear a heavy responsibility not only for failing to protest but for making antisemitism socially acceptable and increasingly publicly *de rigueur* in the emerging Nazi state. The progressive radicalization of antisemitic legislative measures and violence in the second half of the 1930s would hardly have been possible if the institutions and elites discussed in this book had taken a stand in the spring of 1933.[32] Their behavior made it clear to those in power that Germany's respected and "respectable people"—its traditional religious, political, and administrative elites—would decline to interfere with the regime's antisemitic violence and legislation when opposition was still feasible. In

31. Sebastian Haffner, *Defying Hitler. A Memoir*, trans. Oliver Pretzel (New York: Picador, 2003), 129. The German original (*Geschichte eines Deutschen*, 126) uses "Gesinnung" for ideology. This could also be translated as "basic convictions" or "way of thinking."
32. The inbuilt mechanism of this radicalization is outlined in Goebbels's 1935 speech at Nuremberg; see Chapter 14, n. 44.

the late 1930s and during the war, when anti-Jewish atrocities reached hitherto unimaginable proportions in the increasingly repressive Nazi dictatorship, even if these elites had had a change of heart, for opposition and any significant mobilization of support for the victims of terror it was now far too late.

Bibliography

Archival Sources

Archiv der sozialen Demokratie, Bonn
Emigr. Sopade, Mappe 2, 1933 (Film 1); Mappe 6, (Film 2); Mappe 58 (Film 8); Mappe 105 (Film 17) Allgemeine Korrespondenz, 1933–1945; Mappe 113 (Film 18)
Nachlaß Carl Severing
Nachlaß Dr. Paul Hertz, Film 17
Nachlaß Wilhelm Keil

Bayerisches Hauptstaatsarchiv, München
Bayerisches Staatsministerium des Innern: Minn, Nr. 73708: Anti-Judendemonstration in Gunzenhausen und Umgebung
Presseausschnitts-Sammlung, Sammlung Rehse: PrASlg.: nos. 199, 3915, 3918, 3929, 3939
V. Hauptabteilung, Sammlung Varia, no. 231: "The Persecution of the Jews in Germany"

Bundesarchiv Berlin-Lichterfelde
NS 5-VI, Deutsche Arbeitsfront, no. 17187, Presseausschnitts-Sammlung
NS 5-VI, Deutsche Arbeitsfront, no. 17196, Presseberichte zur Judenfrage
NS 5 VI, Deutsche Arbeitsfront, no. 17208, Geschichte, Volks- und Rassenkunde, Judenfrage
NS 5-VI, Deutsche Arbeitsfront, no. 17209, Judenfrage, Allgemeines, Antisemitismus
NS 22, Reichsorganisationsleiter der NSDAP, no.568, Presseausschnitts-Sammlung, vol. II, 1933–1942
R 43 I, Reichskanzlei, no. 2655, DNVP
R 43 II, Reichskanzlei, no. 161, Evangelische Kirche, vol. III, März 1933–Januar 1934
R 43 II, Reichskanzlei, no. 480, Judenfrage, vol. V, 1933–34
R 43 II, Reichskanzlei, no. 594, Jüdische Angelegenheiten im Allgemeinen, vol. II, 1933–34
R 43 II, Reichskanzlei, no. 600, Judentum: Stellung und Behandlung der Juden im national- sozialistischen Deutschland, vol. I, Februar–September 1933
R 43 II, Reichskanzlei, no. 602, Judentum: Stellung und Behandlung der Juden im national- sozialistischen Deutschland, vol. II, 1933–1935

R 43 II, Reichskanzlei, no. 603, Judentum: Stellung und Behandlung der Juden im national- sozialistischen Deutschland, vol. III, 1933

R 43 II, Reichskanzlei, no. 603a, Proteste Einzelfälle

R 43 II, Reichskanzlei, no. 1195, NSDAP

R 43 II, Reichskanzlei, no. 1273, Militärisches Wehrgesetz, vol. II, Juli 1933–Oktober 1935

R 43 II, Reichskanzlei, no. 1374, Akten betreffend Württemberg, Kirche, Judenfrage, vol. II

R 43 II, Reichskanzlei, no. 1399, Judenverfolgung in Deutschland, vol. IV

R 43 II, Reichskanzlei, no. 1480, Judenverfolgung

R 72, Stahlhelm, no. 1476, 1477, Antisemitismus, Diskriminierung der Juden, März 1925–April 1935

R 8005, DNVP, no. 48, Kirchen- und Religionsangelegenheiten, September 1931–Juni 1933

R 8034 II, Pressearchiv Reichslandbund, no. 9251, Nationalsozialistisches Parteileben, 5. März–20 August 1933

Bundesarchiv Koblenz

Z 38, Oberster Gerichtshof für die Britische Zone, no. 213, Verbrechen gegen die Menschlichkeit, Öffentliche Anprangerung in Goslar

Z 38, no. 216, Strafsache gegen Karl Saucke wegen Freiheitsberaubung und Misshandlung von Angehörigen linksgerichteter Parteien und Juden in Seesen

Z38, no. 239, Tötung eines jüdischen Hauptschriftleiters des sozialdemokratischen Volksblattes in Detmold

Z 38, no. 389, Öffentliche Anprangerung zweier Juden

Z 38, no. 391, Anprangerung eines jüdischen Geschäftsmanns, Pinneberg 1933

Z 38, no. 401, Strafsache gegen Hubert König wegen Verbrechen gegen die Menschlichkeit

ZSg (Zeitgeschichtliche Sammlung): 103, no. 214, Kirchenkampf 1933–1945

ZSg. 103, no. 795, NSDAP und Bürgertum

ZSg. 103, no. 3101, Boycott gegen jüdische Geschäfte

Bundesarchiv-Militärarchiv Freiburg

Allgemeines Wehrmachtsamt, RW 6, no. 73a

Allgemeines Wehrmachtsamt, RW6, no. 73b

N5, no. 27, Stülpnagel, 75 Jahre meines Lebens

Zeitschriften:

Deutsche Wehr (Z 66), 1933

Militär-Wochenblatt, 1933

Evangelisches Zentralarchiv, Berlin

Bestand 1, Kirchenkanzlei der deutschen Evangelischen Kirche, no. 1339, Kirchenpolitische Vorgänge, Generalia: Juni 1933–Februar 1934

Bestand 1, Kirchenkanzlei der deutschen Evangelischen Kirche, no. 2411, Kirchenkanzlei

Bestand 1, Kirchenkanzlei der deutschen Evangelischen Kirche, no. 2867, Kirche und politisches Leben, März 1933–Ende 1933

Bestand 1, Kirchenkanzlei der deutschen Evangelischen Kirche, no. 3069, Judenmission, Februar–Dezember 1933

Bestand 1, Kirchenkanzlei der deutschen Evangelischen Kirche, no. 3176, Rundschreiben

Bestand 1, Kirchenkanzlei der deutschen Evangelischen Kirche, no. 3210, Sitzungen des DEKA, Februar 1933–Juni 1935

Bestand 5, Kirchliches Außenamt, no. 802, Behandlung der Judenfrage

Bestand 7, Evangelischer Oberkirchenrat, no. 949, Deutsche Christen, März–Oktober 1933

Bestand 7, Evangelischer Oberkirchenrat, no. 997, Neugestaltung der Verfassung der Evangelischen Kirche der Altpreußischen Union

Bestand 7, Evangelischer Oberkirchenrat, no.1087, Besprechungen des EOKR

Bestand 7, Evangelischer Oberkirchenrat, no. 3688, Akten betreffend das Judentum und die antisemitische Bewegung, Mai 1931-Juni 1941

Bestand 50, Geschichte des Kirchenkampfes, no. 949, Kirche und Judentum, 1933–1942

Bestand 51, E2e8,1, Politische Weltbundkorrespondenz

Zeitschriften
Allgemeine Evangelisch-Lutherische Kirchenzeitung
Das Evangelische Deutschland
Deutsches Pfarrerblatt
Die Reformation 1933 (Deutsche Evangelische Kirchenzeitung für die Gemeinde)
Glaube und Volk, 1933
Junge Kirche, Mitteilungsblatt der Jungreformatorischen Bewegung
Monatsblatt der Vereinigung der Evangelisch-Lutherischen innerhalb der preußischen Landeskirche
Protestantenblatt, Wochenschrift für den deutschen Protestantismus
Zwischen den Zeiten (ed. Georg Merz)

Geheimes Staatsarchiv preußischer Kulturbesitz, Dahlem

I. HA., Preußisches Justizministerium, Rep. 84a, no. 53389, Ermittlungsverfahren gegen Unbekannt wegen Ermordung des jüdischen Zahnarztes Dr. Alfred Meyer, Kommunist in Wuppertal-Barmen

I. HA, Rep. 76, Ministerium der Geistlichen, Unterrichts, etc. Angelegenheiten, no. 21675, Nationalsozialismus und Katholische Kirche vom April 1931 bis Dezember 1933

I. HA, Rep. 77, Titel 4043, Preußisches Innenministerium, Politische Polizei, no. 123, Politische Ausschreitungen und Zusammenstöße, vol. IV, 1933

I. HA, Rep. 77, Titel 4043, Preußisches Innenministerium, Politische Polizei, no. 127, Politische Ausschreitungen und Zusammenstöße

I. HA., Rep. 77, Titel 4043, Preußisches Innenministerium, Politische Polizei, no. 259, Antisemitische Ausschreitungen

I. HA, Rep. 77, Titel 4043, Preußisches Innenministerium, Politische Polizei, no. 278, Deutschnationale Volkspartei, 1925–1933

I. HA, Rep. 77, Titel 4043, Preußisches Innenministerium, Politische Polizei, no. 295, Beziehungen der NSDAP zu anderen Organisationen und Verbänden

I. HA, Rep. 90, Annex B, Der Preußische Ministerpräsident, no. 146, Bescheinigung des jüdischen Gemeindevorstehers dass keine Übergriffe der NSDAP vorgekommen sind

I. HA, Rep. 90, Annex P, Preußisches Staatsministerium, no. 71, Heft 1, Ausschreitungen, März 1933

I. HA, Rep. 90, Annex P, Preußisches Staatsministerium, no. 71, Heft 2, Ausschreitungen, März 1933

I. HA, Rep. 90, Annex P, Preußisches Staatsministerium, no. 5813, Überwachung von Juden und Emigranten

I. HA, Rep. 120BB, XVI, 1, Ministerium für Handel und Gewerbe, no. 1, Nichtzulassung jüdischer Markthändler

Rep. 84a, no. 54771, Untersuchung gegen SA-Mann Wilhelm Abesser in Berlin wegen Amtsanmaßung gegenüber jüdischen Geschäftsleuten

Rep. 84a, no. 54782, Untersuchung gegen SA Mitglieder in Bad Freienwalde

Rep. 84a, no. 54804 and 54805, Ermittlungsverfahren gegen den Landwirt und SS-Sturmführer Friedrich Best und Genossen wegen Freiheitsberaubung, Körperverletzung, und Erpressung

Rep. 84a, no. 54813, Untersuchung wegen Überfalls auf jüdische Gastwirtschaften; Ermittlungsverfahren gegen den Lehrer Otto Knoche u. Genossen

Rep. 84a, no. 54815, Wegen Ermordung des jüdischen Milchhändlers Max Kassel

Rep. 84a, no. 54847, Wegen Verschleppung und Misshandlung des jüdischen Kaufmanns Ignaz Merker in Köln 1933

Rep. 84a, no. 54897, Wegen Ermordung des jüdischen Rechtsanwalts Schumm aus Neidenburg

Rep. 84a, Nr. 54913, Wegen Nötigung und Körperverletzung des jüdischen Möbelhändlers Rudolf Boldes, Kopiert insgesamt 16 Blatt; handschriftliche Notizen 1 Seite

Hauptstaatsarchiv Stuttgart
Nachlaß Eugen Bolz, NL Bolz, no. 36, Vorgänge während der Machtergreifung in Stuttgart

Hessisches Hauptstaatsarchiv Wiesbaden
Abt. 423, no. 1069, Landratsamt Wetzlar, Sonderakten betreffend Gesetze und Verordnungen zum Schutze von Volk und Staat: Inschutzhaftnahme von Juden, März bis Anfang April 1933

Abt. 461, no. 7331, Prozessakten des Sondergerichts Frankfurt: Strafsache gegen Wilhelm Dietz

Abt. 462, no. 73556, Prozessakten des Sondergerichts Frankfurt: Verbreitung von Greuelmärchen

Abt. 468, no. 424, Staatsanwaltschaft beim Landgericht Wiesbaden. Ermittlungsakte im Mordfall Max Kassel am 22. April 1933

Abt. 469/33, no. 4345, Überfall auf den Wiesbadener Rechtsanwalt und Notar, Dr. Emil Höchster

Abt. 483, no. 4156a, Anti-jüdische Ausschreitungen in Gladenbach, Hessen, März bis August 1933

Abt. 518, no. 76, David Abramowicz

Abt. 518, no. 896, Baruch Steinlauf, geb. am 11.7.1880

Abt. 518, no. 2980, Paul Aron

Abt. 518, no. 3112, August und Amalie Bender, Eltern von Karl Bender, geb. am 30.12. 1908

Abt. 518, no. 3299, Arnold Aron

Abt. 518, no. 3542, Norbert Weil, geb. am 25.1.1904

Abt. 518, no. 4634, Max Goldschmidt, geb. 18.3.1906

Abt. 518, no. 4636, Max Goldschmidt, geb. 11.3.1894

Abt. 518, no. 5165, Ludwig Wolfgang Schwarzschild, geb. am 23. Dezember 1900

Abt. 518, no. 5578, Jakob Stein, geb. am 6.7.1896

Abt. 518, no. 33295, Joseph Aron, geb. 13.5.1914

Abt. 518, no. 48634, Entschädigungsakte Salomon Rosenstrauch

Abt. 520/BW, no. 2085, Spruchkammerakte zu Ernst Franzreb

Abt. 40914, no. 789, Gefangenenakte des Strafgefängnisses Frankfurt-Preungesheim, Sondergericht Kassel

Institut für Zeitgeschichte München

Ed 1: Aufzeichnungen des Generals der Infanterie Curt Liebmann, 41–90

Ed 303, vol. I, Entrechtung der Juden in Baden

Ed 414/155, Herbert Frank, Zeitungsausschnitte zum Boycott

Ed 714/1, Sammlung DNVP in Bayern, Rundschreiben, Februar und Juni 1933

Ed 714/3, DNVP und NSDAP. Was uns einigt und was uns trennt, Zeitungsausschnitte

Fa 282, vol. I, Aktenstücke zur Judenverfolgung

GK 08.11, vol. I, Misshandlung eines jüdischen Viehhändlers mit Todesfolge in Köln

Zeitzeugenschrifttum: ZS 10 Karl Bodenschatz

Zeitzeugenschrifttum: ZS 13 Freiherr Friedrich von Bötticher

Zeitzeugenschrifttum: ZS 17 Schipp von Branitz

Zeitzeugenschrifttum: ZS 63 Paul Hauser

Zeitzeugenschrifttum: ZS 72 Karl Hollidt

Zeitzeugenschrifttum: ZS 91-1 Georg von Kuechler

Zeitzeugenschrifttum: ZS 105 Horst von Mellenthin

Zeitzeugenschrifttum: ZS 171 Generalmajor Hans Friedrichs

Zeitzeugenschrifttum: ZS 173-1 General a. D. Kurt Haseloff
Zeitzeugenschrifttum: ZS 182 Maximilian von Weichs
Zeitzeugenschrifttum: ZS 198 Kurt Zeitzler
Zeitzeugenschrifttum: ZS 208-1 Günther Blumentritt
Zeitzeugenschrifttum: ZS 215 Emil Buhl
Zeitzeugenschrifttum: ZS 246 Hellmuth Heye
Zeitzeugenschrifttum: ZS 279 Eugen Ott, General
Zeitzeugenschrifttum: ZS 282-1 Werner Pfafferott
Zeitzeugenschrifttum: ZS 328-1 Generalmajor H. Reinhardt
Zeitzeugenschrifttum: ZS 332 Josef Sellmayr
Zeitzeugenschrifttum: ZS 335 Freiherr von Ledebar
Zeitzeugenschrifttum: ZS 340-1 Generalleutnant von Zanthier
Zeitzeugenschrifttum: ZS 344-1 Werner Reichel
Zeitzeugenschrifttum: ZS 354 Franz von Papen
Zeitzeugenschrifttum: ZS 654-1 Ida Oberfohren
Zeitzeugenschrifttum: ZS 1606-1 Ludwig Foerder (Übergriffe in Breslau)
Zeitzeugenschrifttum: ZS 2501 Heinrich Bosse

Landesarchiv Baden-Württemberg (formerly Generallandesarchiv Karlsruhe)
Bestand 233, Badisches Staatsministerium, no. 27737, Archivalien über die Juden
Bestand 235, Badisches Kultusministerium, no. 12748, Politische Betätigung der evangelischen Geistlichen, 1877–1940
Bestand 235, Badisches Kultusministerium, no. 12809, Verhältnis der Kirchen zur NSDAP, 1933–1942
Bestand 465c, Document Center, Mannheim: NSDAP, Verbände und Polizei in Mannheim
Bestand 507, Sondergericht Mannheim, no. 11752, Verfahren gegen Minna Bloch, geb. 29.01.1888

Landesarchiv Berlin
F-Rep. 240, no. 291B, Wille und Werk des Nationalsozialismus
F-Rep. 240; no. 336B, Das neue Deutschland und das Judentum

Tageszeitungen

Berliner Illustrierte Nachtausgabe
Der Tag
Kreuzzeitung

Landesarchiv Schleswig-Holstein, Schleswig
Politische Polizeiabteilung des preußischen Oberpräsidiums, Abt. 301, nos. 4507–4508, Schutz der Republik

Staatsanwaltschaft Kiel, Abt. 352.3, no. 879, Rantzau, Otto, Graf zu, geb. 14.07.1888, ehemaliger Polizeipräsident in Kiel

Staatsanwaltschaft Kiel, Abt. 352.3, no. 885, Ermordung des Rechtsanwalts Spiegel 1933 in Kiel

Staatsanwaltschaft Kiel, Abt. 352.3, no.1697, Köhler, Walter, geb. 14.02.1900, aus Bordesholm; Verbrechen gegen die Menschlichkeit

Staatsanwaltschaft Kiel, Abt. 352.3, no. 2689, Zerstörung des Hauses des jüdischen Arztes Dr. Steilberger im Mai 1933

Staatsanwaltschaft Kiel, Abt. 352.3, nos. 4498–4499, Verbrechen gegen die Menschlichkeit: Ermordung des jüdischen Rechtsanwalts und SPD-Kommunalpolitikers Wilhelm Spiegel am 12.03.1933 in Kiel

Staatsanwaltschaft Kiel, Abt. 352.3, nos. 4500–4501, Ermordung des jüdischen Rechtsanwalts Friedrich Schumm am 1.04.1933 im Polizeigefängnis Kiel

Staatsanwaltschaft Lübeck, Abt. 352.4, no. 540, Verdacht eines Verbrechens gegen die Menschlichkeit: Beteiligung an der Verlegung des Redakteurs Dr. Fritz Solmitz in das KZ Fuhlsbüttel.

Staatsanwaltschaft Flensburg, Abt. 354, no. 801, Verbrechen gegen die Menschlichkeit: Beteiligung an einem sogenannten Prangermarsch in Flensburg

Staatsanwaltschaft Flensburg, Abt. 354, no. 2940, Beteiligung am Prangermarsch

Landeshauptarchiv Schwerin
Bestand 4.12-211, Mecklenburg-Strelitzsches Staatsministerium, no. 576, Veranstaltungen politischer Verbände

Bestand 4.12-211, Mecklenburg-Strelitzsches Staatsministerium, no. 577, NSDAP Tätigkeit in Mecklenburg-Strelitz

Bestand 5.12-1/1, Mecklenburg-Schwerinsches Staatsministerium, no. 515, Akten betreffend den Oberkirchenrat

Bestand 5.12-1/1, Mecklenburg-Schwerinsches Staatsministerium, no. 516, Landessynode und die Verfassung der Evangelisch-Lutherischen Kirche

Bestand 5.12-1/1, Mecklenburg-Schwerinsches Staatsministerium, no. 517, Die Neuregelung der landeskirchlichen Verhältnisse in Mecklenburg ab dem 22. April 1933

Bestand 5.12-3/1, Mecklenburg-Schwerinsches Ministerium des Innern, no. 1147, Staatsangehörigkeitsangelegenheiten

Bestand 5.12-3/1, Mecklenburg-Schwerinsches Ministerium des Innern, no. 11148a–11148b, Widerruf von Einbürgerungen aus politischen Gründen

Bestand 5.12-7/11, Mecklenburg-Schwerinsches Ministerium für Unterricht und Kultus, no. 9012

Bestand 10.72-3/1, Jüdische Gemeinden, Mecklenburg-Schwerin, no. 147, Tagebuch des Juden Meinungen aus Hagenow

Landeskirchenarchiv Dresden
Bestand 5, LBR 138, Sammlung Judenfrage

Bestand 36, no. 113, Arierfrage, 1933–1945

Niedersächsisches Landesarchiv—Hauptstaatsarchiv Hannover
Hann. 150, Provinziallandtag, no. 464, Wahlen und Sitzungen 1933
Hann. 310 II A, no. 41, 1932–1933, Austritte aus der SPD vom März 1933

Nordelbisches Kirchenarchiv (Landeskirchliches Archiv der Evangelisch-Lutherischen Kirche Norddeutschlands in Kiel)
Bestand 32.01, no. 2268, Judenverfolgungen

Sächsisches Hauptstaatsarchiv Dresden
Außenministerium, Bestand 10717, no. 1723, Judentum, 1933–1935
Außenministerium, Bestand 10717, no. 2167, Judenfrage
Außenministerium, Bestand 10717, no. 4846, Beschwerden ausländischer Vertretungsbehörden wegen Übergriffen an ihren jüdischen Staatsbürgern
Außenministerium, Bestand 10717, no. 4858, Beschwerden ausländischer Vertretungsbehörden wegen Übergriffen an ihren jüdischen Staatsbürgern
Außenministerium, Bestand 10717, no. 8335, Widerruf von Einbürgerungen; Aberkennung der deutschen Staatsangehörigkeit, 1933–1935
Außenministerium, Bestand 10717, no. 8357, Fremdblütige Ausländer, Dresden
Außenministerium, Bestand 10717, no. 9202, Deutsche Evangelische Kirche, 1933–1935
Innenministerium, Bestand 10736, no. 11708, Einwanderung und Ausweisung von Ostjuden
Innenministerium, Bestand 10736, no. 22517, Kirchen-Angelegenheiten: Denunziation von Pfarrern

Staatsarchiv Hamburg
Bestand 131-4, 1933: A 35/34, Boykottmaßnahmen gegen Juden wegen der Veröffentlichung in ausländischen Zeitungen 1933
Bestand 132-1, Reichs- und auswärtige Angelegenheiten, no. 828, Boykottbewegung im Ausland als Gegenbewegung zu antisemitischen Bewegungen in Deutschland
Bestand 241-1 I, no. 1010, Antisemitismus
Bestand 361-2 V, no. 154e, vol. I, Verteilung von Flugblättern und Werbematerial der kommunistischen und nationalsozialistischen Parteien
Bestand 363-3, no. A 155, Senatsakten, Deutsche Evangelische Kirche 1933

Staatsarchiv München
Polizeidirektion München, Nos. 6758, 6761–6764, 6766–6771

Landesarchiv Nordrhein-Westfalen (formerly Hauptstaatsarchiv Düsseldorf)
Staatsanwaltschaft Bonn, Gerichte Rep. 268, no. 3, Antisemitische Straftaten, vol. I
Staatsanwaltschaft Düsseldorf, Gerichte Rep. 372, nos. 121–122; 123–131, Wegen Mordes an dem jüdischen Zahnarzt, Dr. Alfred Meyer am 16.5. in Düsseldorf

Staatsanwaltschaft Düsseldorf, Gerichte Rep. 372, nos. 461–467, Ermordung des jüdischen Zahnarztes Meyer, Dr. Alfred in der "Stabswache" im Schloss Jägerhof in Düsseldorf am 16.5. 1933

Staatsanwaltschaft Kleve, Gerichte Rep. 224, no. 147, Max Frochel wegen Misshandlung von Kommunisten, Juden und Gefängnisinsassen 1933

Staatsanwaltschaft Köln, Gerichte Rep. 231, no. 120, Misshandlung jüdischer Händler 1933 im Schlachthof Köln

Staatsanwaltschaft Köln, Gerichte Rep. 231, no. 309, Verfolgung (Schutzhaftbefehl) der Halbjuden Gebrüder Karl und Johann Heinrich 1933 in Gummersbach

Staatsanwaltschaft Köln, Gerichte Rep. 231, nos. 1429–1430, Körperverletzung mit Todesfolge an dem jüdischen Viehhändler Max Moses

Staatsanwaltschaft Krefeld, Gerichte Rep. 0008, no. 9, Polizeimeister Fritz Graaf in Krefeld wegen Verbrechens gegen die Menschlichkeit (Misshandlung von Juden)

Staatsanwaltschaft Mönchengladbach, Gerichte Rep. 10, no. 201, Ausschreitungen gegen Juden

Memoirs, Document Collections, Diaries, and other Printed Primary Sources

Adenauer, Konrad. *Briefe 1945–1947*, ed. Hans-Peter Mensing (Berlin: Siedler, 1983).

Akten der Reichskanzlei. Die Regierung Hitler. Part I, vols. 1 and 2, 1933/34, ed. Karl-Heinz Minuth (Boppard: Boldt, 1983).

Akten deutscher Bischöfe über die Lage der Kirche 1933–1945. Vol. I: 1933–1934, ed. Bernhard Stasiewski (Mainz: Matthias-Grünewald-Verlag, 1968).

Akten Kardinal Michael von Faulhabers. Vol. I: 1917–1934, ed. Ludwig Volk (Mainz: Grünewald, 1975).

Akten Kardinal Michael von Faulhabers. Vol. II: 1935–1945, ed. Ludwig Volk (Mainz: Grünewald, 1978).

Akten zur Deutschen Auswärtigen Politik, 1918–1945, Series C, 1933–1937. Vol. I, parts 1 and 2. *Das Dritte Reich: Die ersten Jahre, 30. Januar bis 14. Oktober 1933* (Göttingen: Vandenhoeck & Ruprecht, 1971).

Bajohr, Frank, Beate Meyer, and Joachim Szodrzynski. *Bedrohung, Hoffnung, Skepsis. Vier Tagebücher des Jahres 1933* (Göttingen: Wallstein, 2013).

Bajohr, Frank, and Christoph Strupp, eds. *Fremde Blicke auf das "Dritte Reich." Berichte ausländische Diplomaten über Herrschaft und Gesellschaft in Deutschland 1933–1945* (Göttingen: Wallstein, 2011).

Baum, Hannelore, and Gertraud Grünzinger, eds. *Personenlexikon zum deutschen Protestantismus 1919–1949* (Göttingen: Vandenhoeck & Ruprecht, 2006).

Becker, Josef, and Ruth Becker, eds. *Hitlers Machtergreifung. Dokumente vom Machtantritt Hitlers 30. Januar 1933 bis zur Besiegelung des Einparteienstaates 14. Juli 1933*, 2nd ed. (Munich: DTV, 1992).

Bedürftig, Friedemann. *Taschenlexikon Drittes Reich* (Munich: Piper, 1997).

Benz, Wolfgang, Hermann Graml, and Hermann Weiß, eds. *Enzyklopädie des Nationalsozialismus* (Munich: DTV, 1997).

Berding, Helmut. *Moderner Antisemitismus in Deutschland. Quellen zur Geschichte und Politik* (Stuttgart: Klett, 1988).

Bernhard, Georg. *Die deutsche Tragödie. Der Selbstmord einer Republik* (Prague: Orbis, 1933).

Boberach, Heinz, Carsten Nicolaisen, and Ruth Papst, eds. *Handbuch der deutschen evangelischen Kirchen 1918–1949: Organe-Ämter-Verbände-Personen*, vol. 1 (Göttingen: Vandenhoeck & Ruprecht, 2010).

Bonhoeffer, Dietrich. "Die Kirche vor der Judenfrage," in Bonhoeffer, *Gesammelte Schriften*, vol. II: *Kirchenkampf und Finkenwalde*, ed. Eberhard Bethke (Munich: Kaiser, 1959), 44–53.

Braunbuch über Reichstagsbrand und Hitler-Terror (Basel: Universum-Bücherei, 1933). Repr.: World Committee for the Victims of German Fascism. *Braunbuch über Reichstagsbrand und Hitler-Terror. Das Originalbuch von 1933* (Frankfurt: Röderberg, 1973).

Brecht, Bertold. *Furcht und Elend des dritten Reiches* (Frankfurt: Suhrkamp, 1970).

Brügel, Johann Wilhelm, and Norbert Frei, eds. "Berliner Tagebuch 1932–1934: Aufzeichnungen des tschechoslowakischen Diplomaten Camill Hoffmann," *Vierteljahrshefte für Zeitgeschichte*, 36, no. 1 (1988): 131–183.

Brüning, Heinrich. *Memoiren 1918–1934* (Stuttgart: DVA, 1970).

Cohn, Willy. *Kein Recht-Nirgends. Breslauer Tagebücher* (Cologne: Böhlau, 2008).

Comité des Délégations Juives, ed. *Das Schwarzbuch. Tatsachen und Dokumente. Die Lage der Juden in Deutschland 1933* (Paris: Edition du Rond-Point, 1934).

Das Evangelische Deutschland. Kirchliche Rundschau für das Gesamtgebiet des Deutschen Evangelischen Kirchenbundes (1933). *Das evangelische Berlin* (Berlin-Steglitz: Evangelische Preßverb. für Deutschland, 1924–1945).

Dehn, Günther. *Die alte Zeit, die vorigen Jahre. Lebenserinnerungen* (Munich: Kaiser, 1962).

Delmer, Sefton. *Trail Sinister. An Autobiography* (London: Secker & Warburg, 1961).

Der Neue Brockhaus. Vols. I-IV (Leipzig: Brockhaus, 1938).

"Der Soldat und die nationale Revolution," *Militär-Wochenblatt*, 118, no. 18 (August 1933): 209–211.

Deutsches Historisches Museum Berlin, *Die Letzten Tage der Menschheit. Bilder des ersten Weltkrieges* (Berlin: DHM, 1994).

Dibelius, Otto. *Ein Christ ist immer im Dienst. Erlebnisse und Erfahrungen in einer Zeiten-wende* (Stuttgart: Kreuz, 1963).

Documents Diplomatiques Français 1932–1939. Series I: 1932–1935. Vol. II: *15 November 1932 to 17 March 1933*, ed. Commission de publication des documents relatifs aux origines de la guerre 1939–1945 (Paris: Imprimerie Nationale, 1964).

Documents Diplomatiques Français 1932–1939. Series I: 1932–1935. Vol. III: *17 March 1933 to 15 July 1933*, ed. Commission de publication des documents relatifs aux origines de la guerre 1939–1945 (Paris: Imprimerie Nationale, 1967).

Documents on British Foreign Policy 1919–1939. Series 2: 1929–1939. Vol. IV: *Disarmament Conference: Herr Hitler's accession to office 1932–1933*, ed. E.L. Woodward, Rohan Butler, J. P. T. Bury, Douglas Dakin, M. E. Lambert, and W. N. Medlicott (London: HMSO, 1950).

Documents on British Foreign Policy 1919–1939. Series 2. Vol. V: *European affairs, March-October, war debts 1933*, ed. E. L. Woodward, Rohan Butler, J. P. T. Bury, Douglas Dakin, M. E. Lambert, and W. N. Medlicott (London: HMSO, 1956).

Documents on German Foreign Policy, 1918–1945. Series C: *1933–1937. The Third Reich, First Phase.* Vol. I: *30 January to 14 October 1933,* ed. Paul R. Sweet, et al. (London: HMSO, and Washington, D.C.: Government Printing Office, 1957).

Dodd, Martha. *My Years in Germany* (London: Gollancz, 1939).

Dodd Jr., William E., and Martha Dodd, eds. *Ambassador Dodd's Diary, 1933–1938* (New York: Gollancz, 1941).

Dokumente über die Verfolgung der jüdischen Bürger in Baden-Württemberg durch das nationalsozialistische Regime 1933–1945, vols I and II, ed. Paul Sauer (Stuttgart: Kohlhammer, 1966).

Dokumente zur Kirchenpolitik des Dritten Reiches. Vol. I: *Das Jahr 1933. Im Auftrag der Evangelischen Arbeitsgemeinschaft für kirchliche Zeitgeschichte,* ed. Georg Kretschmar and Carsten Nicolaisen (Munich: Kaiser, 1971).

Domarus, Max, ed. *Hitler. Reden und Proklamationen, 1932–1945.* Vol. 1, *Triumph,* part 1 (Wiesbaden: Löwit, 1973).

Ebbinghaus, Julius. "Hermann Cohen," in *Encyclopedia of Philosophy,* vol. 2 (New York: Macmillan, 1972): 125–128.

Ebermayer, Erich. *Denn heute gehört uns Deutschland . . . Persönliches und politisches Tagebuch. Von der Machtergreifung bis zum 31. Dezember 1935* (Hamburg and Vienna: Zsolnay, 1959).

Eschenburg, Theodor. *Letzten Endes meine ich doch. Erinnerungen, 1933–1999* (Berlin: Siedler, 2000).

Fallada, Hans. *In meinem fremden Land. Gefängnistagebuch 1944* (Berlin: Aufbau, 2009).

Faulhaber, Michael von. "Die religiösen Werte des Alten Testamentes und ihre Erfüllung im Christentum," in Kardinal Faulhaber, *Judentum, Christentum, Germanentum: Adventspredigten, gehalten in St. Michael zu München 1933* (Munich: Huber, 1933), 5–26.

Foreign Relations of the United States. Diplomatic Papers 1933. Vol. II: *The British Commonwealth, Europe, Near East, and Africa,* ed. Rogers P. Churchill, Matilda F. Axton, Newton O. Sappington, Morrison B. Giffen, and Francis C. Prescott (Washington: U.S. Government Printing Office, 1949).

François-Ponçet, André. *The Fateful Years. Memoirs of a French Ambassador in Berlin 1931–1938* (New York: Harcourt Brace, 1949).

Friedrichs, Axel, ed. *Dokumente der Deutschen Politik.* Vol. 1: *Die nationalsozialistische Revolution, 1933* (Berlin: Hochschule für Politik, 1939).

Gay, Peter. *My German Question* (New Haven: Yale University Press, 1997).

Gesellschaft für Christlich-Jüdische Zusammenarbeit Dresden, e.V., ed. *Buch der Erinnerung. Juden in Dresden: Deportiert, Ermordet, Verschollen 1933–1945* (Dresden: Universitätsverlag & Richter, 2006).

Göring, Hermann. *Reden und Aufsätze,* ed. Erich Gritzbach (Munich: Zentralverlag der NSDAP, F. Eher Nachfolger, 1938).

Göring, Hermann. *Reden und Aufsätze,* 8th ed., ed. Erich Gritzbach (Munich: Zentralverlag der NSDAP, F. Eher Nachfolger, 1943).

Gruber, Hubert. *Katholische Kirche und Nationalsozialismus 1930–1945. Ein Bericht in Quellen* (Paderborn: Schöningh, 2006).

Gruner, Wolf, ed. *Die Verfolgung und Ermordung der europäischen Juden durch das nationalsozialistische Deutschland 1933–1945.* Vol. 1, *Deutsches Reich 1933–1937* (Munich: Oldenbourg, 2008).

Haffner, Sebastian. *Defying Hitler. A Memoir*, trans. Oliver Pretzel (New York: Picador, 2003). German original: *Geschichte eines Deutschen, Die Erinnerungen 1914–1933* (Munich: DTV, 2002).

Handbuch der Evangelischen Presse (Leipzig: Wallmann, 1929).

Heiber, Helmut, ed. *Goebbels-Reden*. Vol. 1, *1932–1939* (Düsseldorf: Droste, 1971).

Heiber, Helmut, and Beatrice Heiber, eds. *Die Rückseite des Hakenkreuzes. Absonderliches aus den Akten des Dritten Reiches*, 2nd ed. (Munich: DTV, 1994).

Hermle, Siegfried, and Jörg Thierfelder, eds. *Herausgefordert. Dokumente zur Geschichte der Evangelischen Kirche in der Zeit des Nationalsozialismus* (Stuttgart: Calwer, 2008).

Hoffman, Martin, Hans Friedrich Lenz, Paul Gerhard Schäfer, and Johannes Stoll, eds. *Dokumentation zum Kirchenkampf in Hessen und Nassau*. Vol. I, *Jahrbuch der Hessischen kirchengeschichtlichen Vereinigung*, no. 25 (Darmstadt: Verlag der Hessischen kirchengeschichtlichen Vereinigung, 1974).

Kalshoven, Hedda. *Between Two Homelands. Letters Across the Borders of Nazi Germany*, trans. and with a preface by Peter Fritzsche (Urbana: University of Illinois Press, 2014).

Kantzenbach, Friedrich Wilhelm, ed. *Widerstand und Solidarität der Christen in Deutschland 1933–1945. Eine Dokumentation zum Kirchenkampf aus den Papieren des D. Wilhelm Freiherrn von Pechmann* (Neustadt/Aisch: Landessynode der Evangelisch-Lutherischen Kirche in Bayern, 2000).

Kirchliches Jahrbuch für die Evangelischen Landeskirchen Deutschlands, 1932, ed. Hermann Sasse (Gütersloh: Bertelsmann, 1932).

Klemperer, Viktor. *Ich will Zeugnis ablegen bis zum letzten*. Vol. I: *1933–1941* (Berlin: Aufbau, 1995).

Klemperer, Victor. *LTI. Notizbuch eines Philologen*, 23rd ed. (Stuttgart: Reclam, 2007).

Klepper, Jochen. *Unter dem Schatten Deiner Flügel: Aus den Tagebüchern der Jahre 1932–1942* (Stuttgart: DVA, 1956).

Klöss, Erhard, ed. *Reden des Führers. Politik und Propaganda Adolf Hitlers 1922–1945* (Munich: DTV, 1967).

Klotz, Leopold, ed. *Die Kirche und das Dritte Reich. Fragen und Forderungen deutscher Theologen*, vol. I (Gotha: Klotz, 1932).

Kraus, Wolfgang, ed. *Auf dem Weg zu einem Neuanfang. Dokumentation zur Erklärung der Evangelisch-Lutherischen Kirche in Bayern zum Thema Christen und Juden* (Munich: Evangelischer Presseverband, 1999).

Kretschmar, Georg, and Carsten Nicolaisen, eds. *Dokumente zur Kirchenpolitik des Dritten Reiches*. Vol. I: *Das Jahr 1933* (Munich: Kaiser, 1971).

Kretschmar, Georg, and Carsten Nicolaisen, eds. *Dokumente zur Kirchenpolitik des Dritten Reiches*. Vol. II: *Von Beginn des Jahres 1934 bis zur Errichtung des Reichsministeriums für die kirchlichen Angelegenheiten am 16. Juli 1935* (Munich: Kaiser, 1975).

Kübel, Johannes. *Erinnerungen: Mensch und Christ, Theologe, Pfarrer und Kirchenmann*, ed. Martha Frommer (Villingen-Schwenningen: Selbstverlag, 1973).

Kulka, Otto Dov, and Eberhard Jäckel, eds. *Die Juden in den geheimen NS-Stimmungsberichten 1933-1945* (Düsseldorf: Droste, 2004). Book and CD-ROM.

Künneth, Walter. *Was haben wir als evangelische Christen zum Rufe des Nationalsozialismus zu sagen?* (Dresden: Landesverein für innere Mission, 1931).

Laible, Wilhelm. "'Deutschkirche' und 'Deutsche Christen,'" *Allgemeine Evangelisch-Lutherische Kirchenzeitung*, 66, no. 34 (25 Aug. 1933): 786–788.

Landau, Edwin. "Mein Leben vor und nach Hitler," in *Jüdisches Leben in Deutschland, Selbstzeugnisse zur Sozialgeschichte, 1918–1945*, vol. III, ed. Monika Richarz (Stuttgart: DVA, 1982), 99–108.

Loerke, Oskar. *Tagebücher 1903–1939*, 2nd ed., ed. Hermann Kasack (Heidelberg and Darmstadt: Lambert Schneider, 1956).

Löwenthal, Leo. *Mitmachen wollte ich nie* (Frankfurt: Suhrkamp, 1981).

Mann, Thomas. *Tagebücher, 1918–1921*, ed. Peter de Mendelssohn (Frankfurt: Fischer, 1979).

Mann, Thomas. *Tagebücher 1933–1934*, ed. Peter de Mendelssohn (Frankfurt: Fischer, 1979).

March, Ottokar Stauf von der, ed. *Die Juden im Urteil der Zeiten. Eine Sammlung jüdischer und nichtjüdischer Urteile* (Munich: Boepple, 1921).

Marum, Ludwig. *Briefe aus dem Konzentrationslager Kislau*, ed. Elisabeth Marum-Lanau and Jörg Schadt (Karlsruhe: Müller, 1984).

Marx, Jakob. *Das deutsche Judentum und seine jüdischen Gegner* (Berlin: Philo, 1925).

Meissner, Otto. *Staatssekretär unter Ebert-Hindenburg-Hitler. Der Schicksalsweg des Deutschen Volkes 1918–1945* (Hamburg: Hoffmann & Campe, 1950).

Meyers Großes Konversations-Lexikon, 6th ed., vols. 1–20. (Leipzig: Bibliographisches Institut, 1902–8).

Michaelis, Herbert, and Ernst Schraepler, eds. *Ursachen und Folgen. Vom deutschen Zusammenbruch 1918 bis zur staatlichen Neuordnung Deutschlands in der Gegenwart. Eine Urkunden- und Dokumentensammlung zur Zeitgeschichte*, Vol. IX (Berlin: Wendler, 1958–80).

Müller-Jabusch, Maximilian. *Handbuch des öffentlichen Lebens*, 5th ed. (Leipzig: Koehler, 1929).

Münch, Ingo von., ed. *Gesetze des NS-Staates*, 3rd. ed. (Paderborn: UTB, 1994).

Nathorff, Hertha. *Das Tagebuch der Hertha Nathorff: Berlin–New York. Aufzeichnungen 1933–1945* (Frankfurt: Fischer, 1988).

Noske, Gustav. *Erlebtes aus Aufstieg und Niedergang einer Demokratie* (Offenbach: Drott, 1947).

Oppeln-Bronikowski, Friedrich von., *Gerechtigkeit! Zur Lösung der Judenfrage* (Berlin: Huch, 1932).

Preußische Statistik, vol. 299 (Berlin: Statistisches Amt, 1930).

Radbruch, Gustav. *Der innere Weg: Aufriss meines Lebens* (Göttingen: Vandenhoeck & Ruprecht, 1961).

Reich-Ranicki, Marcel, ed. *Meine Schulzeit im Dritten Reich. Erinnerungen deutscher Schriftsteller*, 7th ed. (Munich: DTV, 1998).

Reich-Ranicki, Marcel. *Mein Leben* (Stuttgart: DVA, 1999).

Rougemont, Denis de. *Journal aus Deutschland 1935–1936* (Berlin: Aufbau, 2001).

Rückleben, Hermann, and Hermann Erbacher, eds. *Die Evangelische Landeskirche in Baden im "Dritten Reich." Quellen zu ihrer Geschichte*. Vol. I: *1931–1933* (Karlsruhe: Evangelischer Presseverband, 1991).

Sauer, Paul, ed. *Dokumente über die Verfolgung der jüdischen Bürger in Baden-Württemberg durch das nationalsozialistische Regime 1933–1935*, part 2 (Stuttgart: Kohlhammer, 1966).

Schäfer, Gerhard. *Die Evangelische Landeskirche in Württemberg und der Nationalsozialismus. Eine Dokumentation zum Kirchenkampf.* Vol. I: *Um das politische Engagement der Kirche 1932–1933,* and Vol. II: *Um eine Deutsche Reichskirche 1933* (Stuttgart: Calwer, 1971).

Schmidt, Kurt Dietrich, ed. *Die Bekenntnisse und grundsätzlichen Äußerungen zur Kirchenfrage.* Vol. I: *Des Jahres 1933* (Göttingen: Vandenhoeck & Ruprecht, 1934).

Schmidt, Paul. *Statist auf diplomatischer Bühne 1923–1945. Erlebnisse des Chefdolmetschers im Auswärtigen Amt mit den Staatsmännern Europas* (Bonn: Athenäum, 1950).

Schoeps, Hans-Joachim. *Die letzten dreißig Jahre. Rückblicke* (Stuttgart: Klett, 1956).

Schütt, Ernst Christian. *Chronik 1933. Tag für Tag in Wort und Bild,* 2nd ed. (Dortmund: Chronik 1993).

Schwarz, Angela. *Die Reise ins Dritte Reich. Britische Augenzeugen im nationalsozialistischen Deutschland, 1933–1939* (Göttingen and Zurich: Vandenhoeck & Ruprecht, 1993).

Severing, Carl. *Mein Lebensweg* (Cologne: Greven, 1950).

Sobański, Antoni Graf. *Nachrichten aus Berlin 1933–1936,* trans. from the Polish by Barbara Kulinska-Krautmann (Berlin: Parthas, 2007).

Stasiewski, Bernhard. *Akten deutschen Bischöfe über die Lage der Kirche 1933–1945,* vol. I, *1933–1934* (Mainz: Grünewald, 1968).

Statistisches Jahrbuch für das Deutsche Reich, 49 (Berlin: Hobbing, 1933).

Statistisches Jahrbuch für das Deutsche Reich, 52 (Berlin: Hobbing, Statistisches 1933).

Steuwer, Janosch. *"Ein Drittes Reich, wie ich es auffasse." Politik, Gesellschaft und privates Leben in Tagebüchern 1933–1939* (Göttingen: Wallstein, 2017).

Stroop, Paul, ed. *Geheimberichte aus dem Dritten Reich 1933–1935. Der Journalist H.J. Noordewier als politischer Beobachter* (Berlin: Argon, 1990).

Tausk, Walter. *Breslauer Tagebuch,* ed. Ryszard Kincel (Berlin: Siedler, 1988).

Tschirschky, Fritz Günther von. *Erinnerungen eines Hochverräters* (Stuttgart: DVA, 1972).

Volk, Ludwig, ed. *Akten Kardinal Michael von Faulhabers 1917–1945.* Vol. I: *1917–1934* (Mainz: Grünewald, 1975).

Walk, Joseph, ed. *Das Sonderrecht für die Juden im NS-Staat: eine Sammlung der gesetzlichen Maßnahmen und Richtlinien—Inhalt und Bedeutung,* 2nd ed. (Heidelberg: Müller, 1996).

Wassermann, Jakob. *Mein Weg als Deutscher und Jude,* 2nd ed. (Munich: DTV, 1999).

Weiß, Hermann, ed. *Biographisches Lexikon zum dritten Reich* (Frankfurt: Fischer, 2002).

Weiß, Hermann, and Paul Hoser, eds. *Die Deutschnationalen und die Zerstörung der Weimarer Republik. Aus dem Tagebuch von Reinhold Quaatz 1928–1933* (Munich: Oldenbourg, 1989).

Wistrich, Robert S. *Who's Who in Nazi Germany* (London: Routledge, 1995).

Zweig, Stefan. *Die Welt von gestern. Erinnerungen eines Europäers* (Frankfurt: Fischer, 2010).

Secondary Literature

Adam, Uwe Dietrich. *Judenpolitik im Dritten Reich* (Düsseldorf: Droste, 1972).

Adler-Rudel, Scholem. *Ostjuden in Deutschland 1880–1940* (Tübingen: Mohr Siebeck, 1959).

Ahlheim, Hannah. *"Deutsche, kauft nicht bei Juden!" Antisemitismus und politischer Boycott in Deutschland 1924 bis 1935,* 2nd ed. (Göttingen: Wallstein, 2011).

Albers, Jens. "Nationalsozialismus und Modernisierung," *Kölner Zeitschrift für Soziologie und Sozialpsychologie*, 41 (1989): 345–365.

Allen, William S. *The Nazi Seizure of Power. The Experience of a Single German Town, 1922–1945*, rev. ed. (New York: Franklin Watts, 1984).

Althusser, Louis. *Ideologie und ideologische Staatsapparate* (Hamburg: VSA, 1977).

Angermund, Ralph. *Deutsche Richterschaft 1919–1945. Krisenerfahrung, Illusion, politische Rechtsprechung* (Frankfurt: Fischer, 1990).

Angress, Werner T. "Juden im politischen Leben der Revolutionszeit," in *Deutsches Judentum in Krieg und Revolution 1916–1923*, ed. Werner E. Mosse (Tübingen: Mohr Siebeck, 1971), 127–315.

Angress, Werner T. "Prussia's Army and the Jewish Reserve Officer Controversy before World War I," in *Imperial Germany*, ed. James Sheehan (New York: Franklin Watts, 1976), 93–128.

Ascher, Abraham. *Was Hitler a Riddle? Western Democracies and National Socialism* (Stanford: Stanford University Press, 2012).

Aschheim, Steven E. *Brothers and Strangers. The East European Jew in German and German Jewish Consciousness, 1800–1923* (Madison: University of Wisconsin Press, 1982).

Bader-Weiß, Grete, and Karl-Siegfried Bader. *Der Pranger. Ein Strafwerkzeug und Rechtswahrzeichen des Mittelalters* (Freiburg: Waibel, 1935).

Baier, Helmut. *Die Deutschen Christen Bayerns im Rahmen des bayerischen Kirchenkampfes* (Nuremberg: Selbstverlag des Vereins für bayerische Kirchengeschichte, 1968).

Bajohr, Frank. *"Arisierung" in Hamburg. Die Verdrängung der jüdischen Unternehmer 1933–1945*. Hamburger Beiträge zur Sozial- und Zeitgeschichte, 35, 2nd ed. (Hamburg: Christians, 1998). English trans.: *"Aryanisation" in Hamburg. The Economic Exclusion of Jews and the Confiscation of their Property in Nazi Germany* (New York and Oxford: Berghahn, 2002).

Bajohr, Frank. *"Unser Hotel ist judenfrei." Bäder-Antisemitismus im 19. und 20. Jahrhundert* (Frankfurt: Fischer, 2003).

Bajohr, Frank, and Dieter Pohl. *Der Holocaust als offenes Geheimnis. Die Deutschen, die NS-Führung und die Alliierten* (Munich: Beck, 2006).

Bajohr, Frank, and Christoph Strupp, eds. *Fremde Blicke auf das "Dritte Reich." Berichte ausländischer Diplomaten über Herrschaft und Gesellschaft in Deutschland 1933–1945*, 2nd ed. (Göttingen: Wallstein, 2012).

Bankier, David. *The Germans and the Final Solution. Public Opinion Under Nazism* (Oxford: Blackwell, 1992).

Bankier, David. "German Social Democrats and the Jewish Question," in *Probing the Depths of German Anti-Semitism, German Society and the Persecution of the Jews, 1933–1941*, ed. David Bankier (New York: Berghahn, 2000), 511–532.

Bankier, David, ed. *Probing the Depths of German Antisemitism. German Society and the Persecution of the Jews, 1933–1941* (New York: Berghahn, 2000).

Baranowski, Shelley. "The 1933 German Protestant Church Elections: Machtpolitik or Accommodation," *Church History*, 49 (1980): 298–315.

Barkai, Avraham. "Der wirtschaftliche Existenzkampf der Juden im Dritten Reich, 1933–1938," in *Die Juden im nationalsozialistischen Deutschland/The Jews in Nazi Germany, 1933–1943*, ed. Arnold Pauker (Tübingen: Mohr Siebeck, 1986), 153–166.

Barkai, Avraham. *Vom Boycott zur "Entjudung." Der wirtschftliche Existenzkampf der Juden im Dritten Reich 1933–1943* (Frankfurt: Fischer, 1988).

Barkai, Avraham. *"Wehr Dich!" Der Centralverein deutscher Staatsbürger jüdischen Glaubens 1893–1938* (Munich: Beck, 2002).

Bärsch, Claus-Ekkehard. *Die politische Religion des Nationalsozialismus: Die religiösen Dimensionen der NS-Ideologie in den Schriften von Dietrich Eckart, Joseph Goebbels, Alfred Rosenberg und Adolf Hitler*, 2nd ed. (Munich: Fink, 2002).

Barth, Boris. *Dolchstosslegenden und politische Desintegration. Das Trauma der deutschen Niederlage im ersten Weltkrieg 1914–1933* (Düsseldorf: Droste, 2003).

Bartov, Omer. *The Eastern Front, 1941–1945. German Troops and the Barbarization of Warfare* (London: Macmillan, 1985).

Bartov, Omer. *Hitler's Army. Soldiers, Nazis, and War in the Third Reich* (Oxford: Oxford University Press, 1991).

Bartov, Omer. *Murder in Our Midst. The Holocaust, Industrial Killing, and Representation* (New York: Oxford University Press, 1996).

Bauer, Gisa. *Kulturprotestantismus und frühe bürgerliche Frauenbewegung in Deutschland: Agnes von Zahn-Harnack, 1884–1950* (Leipzig: Evangelische Verlagsanstalt, 2006).

Beck, Hermann. *The Origins of the Authoritarian Welfare State in Prussia: Conservatives, Bureaucracy, and the Social Question, 1815–1879* (Ann Arbor: University of Michigan Press, 1995).

Beck, Hermann. "Between the Dictates of Conscience and Political Expediency: Hitler's Conservative Alliance Partner and Antisemitism during the Nazi Seizure of Power," *Journal of Contemporary History*, 41 (2006): 611–640.

Beck, Hermann. *The Fateful Alliance: German Conservatives and Nazis in 1933. The Machtergreifung in a New Light* (New York and Oxford: Berghahn, 2010).

Beck, Hermann. "Konflikte zwischen Deutschnationalen und Nationalsozialisten während der Machtergreifungszeit," *Historische Zeitschrift*, 292 (2011): 645–681.

Beck, Hermann. "The Antibourgeois Character of National Socialism," *Journal of Modern History*, 88, no. 3 (September 2016): 572–609.

Beck, Hermann. "The Nazi Seizure of Power," in *The Oxford Illustrated History of the Third Reich*, ed. Robert Gellately (Oxford: Oxford University Press, 2018), 51–84.

Beck, Hermann. "Violence Against 'Ostjuden' in the Spring of 1933 and the Reaction of German Authorities," in *From Weimar to Hitler. Studies in the Dissolution of the Weimar Republic and the Establishment of the Third Reich, 1932–1934*, ed. Hermann Beck and Larry E. Jones (New York: Berghahn, 2019), 163–193.

Beck, Hermann, and Larry E. Jones, eds. *From Weimar to Hitler. Studies in the Dissolution of the Weimar Republic and the Establishment of the Third Reich, 1932–1934* (New York: Berghahn, 2019).

Behrens, Beate. *Mit Hitler zur Macht. Aufstieg des Nationalsozialismus in Mecklenburg und Lübeck 1922–1933* (Rostock: Neuer Hochschul-Schriften-Verlag, 1998).

Bennathan, Esra. "Die demographische und wirtschaftliche Struktur der Juden," in *Entscheidungsjahr 1932. Zur Judenfrage in der Endphase der Weimarer Republik*, ed. Werner A. Mosse (Mohr: Tübingen, 1966), 87–131.

Benz, Wigbert. *Hans-Joachim Riecke, NS-Staatssekretär: Vom Hungerplaner vor, zum "Welternährer" nach 1945* (Berlin: Wissenschaftlicher Verlag, 2014).

Benz, Wolfgang, ed. *Antisemitismus in Deutschland. Zur Aktualität eines Vorurteils* (Munich: DTV, 1995).

Benz, Wolfgang, ed. *Handbuch des Antisemitismus. Judenfeindschaft in Geschichte und Gegenwart*, vol. 2: *Personen (A-K; L-Z)* (Berlin: De Gruyter Saur, 2009).

Berding, Helmut. *Moderner Antisemitismus in Deutschland* (Frankfurt: Suhrkamp, 1988).

Bergen, Doris L. *Twisted Cross. The German Christian Movement in the Third Reich* (Chapel Hill: University of North Carolina Press, 1996).

Berghahn, Volker. "Ludwig Dehio," in *Deutsche Historiker*, vol. IV, ed. Hans-Ulrich Wehler (Göttingen: Vandenhoeck & Ruprecht, 1972), 97–116.

Bergmann, Werner. *Geschichte des Antisemitismus*, 2nd ed. (Beck: Munich, 2004).

Bergmann, Werner, and Ulrich Sieg, eds. *Antisemitische Geschichtsbilder* (Essen: Klartext, 2009).

Bernhard, Georg. *Die deutsche Tragödie. Der Selbstmord einer Republik* (Prague: Orbis, 1933).

Bessel, Richard. "The Potempa Murder," *Central European History*, 10 (1977): 241–54.

Bessel, Richard. *Political Violence and the Rise of Nazism. The Storm Troopers in Eastern Germany 1926–1934* (New Haven and London: Yale University Press, 1984).

Bessel, Richard. "The Nazi Capture of Power," *Journal of Contemporary History*, 39 (2004): 169–188.

Beyrau, Dietrich. "Antisemitismus und Judentum in Polen, 1918–1939," *Geschichte und Gesellschaft*, 8 (1982): 205–233.

Bigler, Robert M. *The Politics of German Protestantism. The Rise of the Protestant Church Elite in Prussia, 1815–1848* (Berkeley: University of California Press, 1972).

Bily, Lothar. "Max Maurenbrecher," in *Biographisch-Bibliographisches Kirchenlexikon*, vol. V (Herzberg: Bautz, 1993): 1051–1055.

Blanke, Richard. "The German Minority in Interwar Poland and German Foreign Policy – Some Reconsiderations," *Journal of Contemporary History*, 25, no. 1 (1990): 87–102.

Blanke, Richard. *Orphans of Versailles: The Germans in Western Poland, 1918–1939* (Lexington: University of Kentucky Press, 2014).

Blaschke, Olaf. *Katholizismus und Antisemitismus im Deutschen Kaiserreich* (Göttingen: Vandenhoeck & Ruprecht, 1999).

Blasius, Dirk. "Zwischen Rechtsvertrauen und Rechtszerstörung: Deutsche Juden 1933–1935," in *Zerbrochene Geschichte: Leben und Selbstverständnis der Juden in Deutschland*, ed. Dirk Blasius and Dan Diner (Frankfurt: Fischer, 1991), 121–137.

Bleuel, Hans Peter, and Ernst Klinnert. *Deutsche Studenten auf dem Weg ins Dritte Reich* (Gütersloh: Mohn, 1967).

Bloch, Charles. *Die SA und die Krise des NS-Regimes 1934* (Frankfurt: Suhrkamp, 1970).

Boberach, Heinz. "Quellen für die Einstellung der deutschen Bevölkerung zur Judenverfolgung. Analyse und Kritik," in *Die Deutschen und die Judenverfolgung im Dritten Reich*. Hamburger Beiträge zur Sozial- und Zeitgeschichte 29, ed. Ursula Büttner (Hamburg: Christians, 1992), 31–50.

Boblenz, Frank, and Bernhard Post. *Die Machtübernahme in Thüringen 1932/33* (Erfurt: Landeszentrale für politische Bildung Thüringen, 2013).

Bodo, Béla. "The Role of Anti-Semitism in the Expulsion of non-Aryan Students, 1933–1945," *Yad Vashem Studies*, 30 (2002): 189–227.

Booms, Hans. "Die Deutsche Volkspartei," in *Das Ende der Parteien 1933*, ed. Erich Matthias and Rudolf Morsey (Düsseldorf: Droste, 1960), 523–539.

Borgstedt, Angela. *Entnazifizierung in Karlsruhe 1946–1951* (Konstanz: UVK, 2001).

Boyens, Armin. *Kirchenkampf und Ökumene 1933–1939* (Munich: Kaiser, 1969).

Braatz, Werner. "The Counter-Revolution of 1933 as Viewed in Two Documents Addressed to Vice-Chancellor Papen," *International Review of Social History*, 19, no. 1 (April 1974): 115–127.

Bracher, Karl Dietrich. *Die nationalsozialistische Machtergreifung. Stufen der Machtergreifung* (Ullstein: Berlin, 1974).

Bracher, Karl Dietrich. *Die deutsche Diktatur. Entstehung, Struktur, Folgen des Nationalsozialismus*, 7th ed. (Berlin: Ullstein, 1997). English trans.: *The German Dictatorship. The Origins, Structure, and Effects of National Socialism* (New York: Holt, Rinehart & Winston, 1970).

Bracher, Karl Dietrich, Wolfgang Sauer, and Gerhard Schulz. *Die nationalsozialistische Machtergreifung. Studien zur Errichtung des totalitären Herrschaftssystems in Deutschland 1933–34*, 2nd ed. (Cologne and Opladen: Westdeutscher Verlag, 1962).

Brakelmann, Günter. *Evangelische Kirche und Judenverfolgung. Drei Einblicke*. Schriften der Hans Ehrenberg Gesellschaft 7. (Waltrop: Spenner, 2001).

Bramsted, Ernest K. *Aristocracy and the Middle Classes in Germany. Social Types in German literature 1830–1900*, rev. ed. (Chicago: University of Chicago Press, 1964).

Braubach, Max. "Hitler's Machtergreifung: Die Berichte des französischen Botschafters Francois-Poncet über die Vorgänge in Deutschland von Juli 1932 bis Juli 1933," in *Festschrift für Leo Brandt*, ed. Josef Miexner and Gerhard Kegel (Cologne: VS Verlag für Sozialwissenschaften, 1968), 443–464.

Brechenmacher, Thomas. "Die Kirche und die Juden," in *Die Katholiken und das Dritte Reich. Kontroversen und Debatten*, 2nd ed., ed. Karl-Joseph Hummel and Michael Kißener (Paderborn: Schöningh, 2010), 125–144.

Brechtken, Magnus. *Madagaskar für die Juden: Antisemitische Idee und politische Praxis, 1885–1945* (Munich: Oldenbourg, 1997).

Bredel, Willi. *Die Prüfung. Roman aus einem Konzentrationslager* (Berlin: Aufbau, 1968).

Bremm, Klaus-Jürgen. *Propaganda im 1. Weltkrieg* (Darmstadt: Theiss, 2013).

Breuer, Stefan. *Die radikale Rechte in Deutschland 1871–1945. Eine politische Ideengeschichte* (Ditzingen: Reclam, 2010).

Breuer, Stefan. *Die Völkischen in Deutschland*, 2nd ed. (Darmstadt: WBG, 2010).

Breuning, Klaus. *Die Vision des Reiches. Deutscher Katholizismus zwischen Demokratie und Diktatur, 1929–1934* (Munich: Hueber, 1969).

Broszat, Martin. "Aussen- und innenpolitische Aspekte der preußisch-deutschen Minderheitenpolitik in der Ära Stresemann," in *Politische Ideologien und Nationalstaatliche Ordnung*, ed. Kurt Kluxen and Theodor Schieder (Munich: Oldenbourg, 1968), 393–445.

Broszat, Martin. *Der Staat Hitlers*. 7th ed. (Munich: Deutsche Taschenbuch Verlag), 1978. English trans.: *The Hitler State. The Foundation and Development of the Internal Structure of the Third Reich* (London and New York: Longman, 1981).

Broszat, Martin. "Siegerjustiz oder strafrechtliche 'Selbstreinigung'. Aspekte der Vergangenheitsbewältigung der deutschen Justiz während der Besatzungszeit," *Vierteljahrshefte für Zeitgeschichte*, 29 (1981): 477–544.

Broszat, Martin. "Nationalsozialistische Konzentrationslager 1933–1945," in *Anatomie des SS-Staates*, 6th ed., ed. Hans Buchheim, Martin Broszat, and Hans-Adolf Jacobsen (Munich: DTV, 1994), 323–449.

Broszat, Martin, Elke Fröhlich, and Falk Wiesemann. *Bayern in der NS Zeit*. Vol. 1: *Soziale Lage und politisches Verhalten der Bevölkerung im Spiegel vertraulicher Berichte* (Munich and Vienna: Oldenbourg, 1977).

Buchheim, Hans, ed. *Anatomie des SS-Staates*, 4th ed. Vol. 1: *Die SS—das Herrschaftsinstrument Befehl und Gehorsam. Gutachten des Instituts für Zeitgeschichte*. (Munich: DTV, 1984).

Buchheim, Hans, Martin Broszat, and Hans-Adolf Jacobsen, eds. *Anatomie des SS-Staates*, 6th ed. Gutachten des Instituts für Zeitgeschichte (Munich: DTV, 1994).

Buchheim, Hans, Martin Broszat, Hans-Adolf Jacobsen, and Helmut Krausnick, eds. *Anatomie des SS-Staates*, 5th ed. Vol. 2: *Konzentrationslager, Kommissarbefehl, Judenverfolgung* (Munich: DTV, 1989).

Burleigh, Michael. *The Third Reich. A New History* (New York: Hill & Wang, 2000).

Buss, Hansjörg. *"Entjudete" Kirche. Die Lübecker Landeskirche zwischen christlichem Antijudaismus und völkischem Antisemitismus, 1918–1950* (Paderborn: Schöningh, 2011).

Buss, Hansjörg, Annette Göhres, Stephan Linck, and Joachim Liß-Walther, eds. *"Eine Chronik gemischter Gefühle." Bilanz der Wanderausstellung "Kirche, Christen, Juden in Nordelbien 1933–1945"* (Bremen: Edition Temmen, 2005).

Büttner, Ursula. "Die deutsche Gesellschaft und die Judenverfolgung – ein Forschungsproblem," in *Die Deutschen und die Judenverfolgung im Dritten Reich*, ed. Ursula Büttner. Hamburger Beiträge zur Sozial- und Zeitgeschichte, 29 (Hamburg: Christians, 1992), 7–29.

Büttner, Ursula, and Martin Greschat. *Die Verlassenen Kinder der Kirche. Der Umgang mit Christen jüdischer Herkunft im "Dritten Reich."* (Göttingen: Vandenhoeck & Ruprecht, 1998).

Campbell, Bruce. B. "Autobiographies of Violence: The SA in its Own Words," *Central European History*, 46 (2013): 217–237.

Campbell, Bruce B. "The SA in the Gleichschaltung: The Context of Pressure and Violence," in *From Weimar to Hitler. Studies in the Dissolution of the Weimar Republic and the Establishment of the Third Reich, 1932–1934*, ed. Hermann Beck and Larry E. Jones (New York: Berghahn, 2019), 194–221.

Caplan, Jane. *Government without Administration. State and Civil Service in Weimar and Nazi Germany* (Oxford: Oxford University Press, 1988).

Carsten, Francis L. *The Reichswehr and Politics 1918–1933* (Oxford: Oxford University Press, 1966).

Carstens, Uwe. *Ferdinand Tönnies. Friese und Weltbürger. Eine Biographie*, 2nd ed. (Bredstedt: Nordfriisk Instituut, 2013).

Chamberlain, Houston Stewart. *Die Grundlagen des 19. Jahrhunderts*. Ungekürzte Volksausgabe, 17th ed. (Munich: Bruckmann, 1933).

Chickering, Roger. "The Reichsbanner and the Weimar Republic, 1924–1926," *Journal of Modern History*, 40, no. 4 (December 1968): 524–34.

Childers, Thomas. *The Third Reich. A History of Nazi Germany* (New York: Simon & Schuster, 2018).

Clark, Christopher M. *The Politics of Conversion. Missionary Protestantism and the Jews in Prussia 1728–1941* (Oxford: Clarendon Press, 1995).

Cohen, Hermann. "Der polnische Jude," *Der Jude*, 1 (1916/17): 149–156.

Confino, Alon. "Why Did the Nazis Burn the Hebrew Bible? Nazi Germany, Representations of the Past, and the Holocaust," *Journal of Modern History*, 84, no. 2 (June 2012): 369–400.

Confino, Alon. *A World Without Jews. The Nazi Imagination from Persecution to Genocide* (New Haven and London: Yale University Press, 2014).

Conway, John L. "Between Pacifism and Patriotism. A Protestant Dilemma: The Case of Friedrich Sigmund-Schultze," in *Germans against Nazism. Nonconformity, Opposition and Resistance in the Third Reich. Essays in Honor of Peter Hoffmann*, rev. ed., ed. Francis R. Nikosia and Lawrence D. Stokes (Oxford and New York: Berghahn, 2015), 87–114.

Conze, Eckart, Norbert Frei, Peter Hayes, and Moshe Zimmermann. *Das Amt und die Vergangenheit. Deutsche Diplomaten im Dritten Reich und in der Bundesrepublik* (Munich: Pantheon, 2012).

Corni, Gustavo. "Alfred Hugenberg as Minister of Agriculture: Interlude or Continuity?" *German History*, 7 (1989): 204–225.

Crim, Brian E. *Antisemitism in the German Military Community and the Jewish Response, 1916–1938* (Lanham, MD: Lexington, 2014).

Crouthammel, Jason, Michael Geheran, Tim Grady, and Julia Barbara Köhne, eds. *Beyond Inclusion and Exclusion. Jewish Experiences of the First World War in Central Europe* (New York and Oxford: Berghahn, 2019).

Dahm, Karl Wilhelm. *Pfarrer und Politik. Soziale Positionen und politische Mentalität des deutschen evangelischen Pfarrerstandes zwischen 1918 und 1933* (Cologne: Westdeutscher Verlag, 1965).

Dahrendorf, Ralf. *"Homo Sociologicus." Ein Versuch zur Geschichte, Bedeutung und Kritik der Kategorie der sozialen Rolle*, 14th ed. (Wiesbaden: Westdeutscher Verlag, 1974).

Dahrendorf, Ralf. *Gesellschaft und Demokratie in Deutschland*, 5th ed. (Munich: DTV, 1977).

Davis, Belinda J. *Home Fires Burning: Food, Politics, and Everyday Life in World War I Berlin* (Chapel Hill: University of North Carolina Press, 2000).

Deuerlein, Ernst. *Der deutsche Katholizismus 1933* (Osnabrück: Fromm, 1963).

Dibelius, Otto. *Das Jahrhundert der Kirche*, 2nd ed. (Berlin: Furche, 1928).

Dibelius, Otto. *Ein Christ ist immer im Dienst*, 2nd ed. (Stuttgart: Kreuz, 1963).

Diels, Rudolf. *Luzifer ante Portas. Zwischen Severing und Heydrich* (Stuttgart: DVA, 1950).

Diewald-Kerkmann, Gisela. *Politische Denunziation im NS-Regime oder die kleine Macht der Volksgenossen* (Bonn: Dietz, 1995).

Dinnerstein, Leonard. *Antisemitism in America* (New York and Oxford: Oxford University Press, 1994).

Dippel, John V. H. *Bound upon a Wheel of Fire. Why so many German Jews made the Tragic Decision to Remain in Nazi Germany* (New York: Basic Books, 1996).

Dörner, Bernward. *"Heimtücke": Das Gesetz als Waffe. Kontrolle, Abschreckung und Verfolgung in Deutschland 1933–1945* (Paderborn: Schöningh, 1998).

Dreyfus, Jean-Marc, ed. *Geheime Depeschen aus Berlin. Der französische Botschafter François-Poncet und der Nationalsozialismus* (Darmstadt: WBG, 2018).

Drobisch, Klaus, and Günther Wieland. *Das System der NS-Konzentrationslager 1933–1939* (Berlin: Akademie, 1993).

Dülffer, Jost. *Deutsche Geschichte 1933–945. Führerglaube und Vernichtungskrieg* (Stuttgart: Kohlhammer, 1992). English trans.: *Nazi Germany. Faith and Annihilation 1933–1945* (London: Arnold, 1996).

Dülmen, Richard van. *Kultur und Alltag in der Frühen Neuzeit. Dorf und Stadt*, 2nd ed. (Munich: Beck, 1999).

Dunker, Ulrich. *Der Reichsbund jüdischer Frontsoldaten. Geschichte eines Abwehrvereins* (Düsseldorf: Droste, 1977).

Echternkamp, Jörg. *Nach dem Krieg. Alltagsnot, Neuorientierung und die Last der Vergangenheit 1945–1949* (Zurich: Pendo, 2003).

Erb, Dirk, ed. *Gleichgeschaltet. Der Nazi-Terror gegen Gewerkschaften und Berufsverbände 1930–1933. Eine Dokumentation* (Göttingen: Steidl, 2001).

Erdmann, Karl-Dietrich. "Professoren unter Hitler. Dargestellt am Beispiel der Universität Kiel." *Frankfurter Allgemeine Zeitung*, 137 (16 June 1965): 15.

Ericksen, Robert P. *Theologians under Hitler: Gerhard Kittel, Paul Althaus, Emmanuel Hirsch* (New Haven: Yale University Press, 1985). German trans.: *Theologen unter Hitler. Das Bündnis zwischen evangelischer Dogmatik und Nationalsozialismus* (Munich: Hanser, 1986).

Esser, Ingo. *"Volk, Staat, Gott!" Die deutsche Minderheit in Polen und ihr Schulwesen 1918–1939* (Wiesbaden: Harrassowitz, 2010).

Evans, Richard J. *The Coming of the Third Reich* (New York: Penguin, 2004). German trans.: *Das Dritte Reich*. Vol I: *Aufstieg* (Munich: DTV, 2005).

Evans, Richard J. *The Third Reich in Power 1933–1939* (New York: Penguin, 2005). German trans.: *Das Dritte Reich*. Vol. II: *Diktatur* (Munich: DTV, 2010).

Eyck, Erich. *Geschichte der Weimarer Republik*, vol. I (Zurich: Rentsch, 1956).

Falter, Jürgen, Thomas Lindenberger, and Siegfried Schumann, eds. *Wahlen und Abstimmungen in der Weimarer Republik. Materialien zum Wahlverhalten, 1919–1933* (Munich: Beck, 1986).

Fattmann, Rainer. *Bildungsbürger in der Defensive. Die akademische Beamtenschaft und der "Reichsbund der höheren Beamten" in der Weimarer Republik* (Göttingen: Vandenhoeck & Ruprecht, 2001).

Faulenbach, Bernd. "Tendenzen der Geschichtswissenschaft im 'Dritten Reich,'" in *Berater der braunen Macht. Wissenschaft und Wissenschaftler im NS-Staat*, ed. Renate Knigge-Tesche (Frankfurt: Anabas, 1999), 26–52.

Faust, Anselm. *Der nationalsozialistische Studentenbund*, vol. II (Düsseldorf: Schwann, 1973).

Faust, Anselm. "Professoren für die NSDAP. Zum politischen Verhalten der Hochschullehrer 1932/33," in *Erziehung und Schulung im Dritten Reich*, vol. II, ed. Manfred Heinemann (Stuttgart: Klett, 1980), 31–49.

Feldman, Gerald D. *The Great Disorder. Politics, Economics, and Society in the German Inflation, 1914–1924* (Oxford: Oxford University Press, 1993).

Fest, Joachim. *Staatsstreich. Der lange Weg zum 20. Juli* (Berlin: Siedler, 1994).

Feuchtwanger, Lion. *The Oppermanns*, 2nd ed. (New York: Carroll & Graf, 2001).

Fischer, Conan. *Stormtroopers. A Social, Economic and Ideological Analysis 1929–1935.* (London: George Allen & Unwin, 1983).

Fischer, Lars. *The Socialist Response to Antisemitism in Imperial Germany* (Cambridge: Cambridge University Press, 2007).

Flemming, Jens. "Konservatismus als 'nationalrevolutionäre Bewegung'. Konservative Kritik an der Deutschnationalen Volkpartei 1918–1933," in *Deutscher Konservatismus im 19. Und 20. Jahrhundert. Festschrift für Fritz Fischer*, ed. Dirk Stegmann, Bernd-Jürgen Wendt, and Peter-Christian Witt (Bonn: Neue Gesellschaft, 1983), 295–331.

Förster, Jürgen. "Das Verhältnis von Wehrmacht und Nationalsozialismus im Entscheidungsjahr 1933." *German Studies Review*, 18 (1995): 471–480.

Fraenkel, Ernst. *Der Doppelstaat* (Hamburg: Europäische Verlagsanstalt, 1974).

Frank, Walter. *Hofprediger Adolf Stoecker und die christliche Bewegung*, 2nd ed. (Hamburg: Hanseatische Verlagsanstalt, 1935).

Franz, Eckhart G. *Juden als Darmstädter Bürger* (Darmstadt: Roether, 1984).

Frei, Norbert. *Vergangenheitspolitik. Die Anfänge der Bundesrepublik und die NS-Vergangenheit* (Munich: DTV, 1996).

Frei, Norbert. *Der Führerstaat. Nationalsozialistische Herrschaft 1933 bis 1945*, 6th ed. (Munich: DTV, 2001). English trans.: *National Socialist Rule in Germany. The Führer State 1933–1945* (Oxford: Blackwell, 1993).

Frei, Norbert, ed. *Hitlers Eliten nach 1945*, 2nd ed. (Munich: DTV, 2004).

Frei, Norbert, and Johannes Schmitz. *Journalismus im Dritten Reich*, 3rd. ed. (Munich: Beck, 1999).

Friedländer, Saul. "Die politischen Veränderungen der Kriegszeit und ihre Auswirkungen auf die Judenfrage," in *Deutsches Judentum in Krieg und Revolution 1916–1923*, ed. Werner E. Mosse (Tübingen: Mohr Siebeck, 1971), 27–66.

Friedländer, Saul. "The Demise of the German Mandarins. The German University and the Jews, 1933-1939," in *Von der Aufgabe der Freiheit. Politische Verantwortung und bürgerliche Gesellschaft im 19. und 20. Jahrhundert. Festschrift für Hans Mommsen*, ed. Christian Jansen, Lutz Niethammer, and Bernd Weisbrod (Berlin: Akademie, 1995), 69–82.

Friedländer, Saul. *Nazi Germany and the Jews*. Vol. I: *The Years of Persecution, 1933–1939* (New York: HarperCollins, 1997). German trans.: *Das dritte Reich und die Juden*. Vol. I: *Die Jahre der Verfolgung, 1933–1939* (Munich: Beck, 1998).

Friedrichs, Axel, ed. *Die nationalsozialistische Revolution 1933* (Berlin: Junker & Dünnhaupt, 1935).

Fritsche, Christiane. *Ausgeplündert, zurückerstattet und entschädigt. Arisierung und Wiedergutmachung in Mannheim*, 2nd ed. (Ubstadt-Weiher: Regionalkultur, 2013).

Fritsche, Christiane. "*Du sollst nicht begehren deines Nächsten Haus*": die "*Arisierung*" von *Grundstücken in Mannheim durch Institutionen der Evangelischen Kirche* (Ubstadt-Weiher: Regionalkultur, 2014).

Fritsche, Christiane, and Johannes Paulmann, eds. "*Arisierung*" und "*Wiedergutmachung*" *in deutschen Städten* (Cologne: Böhlau, 2014).

Fritz, Hartmut. *Otto Dibelius. Ein Kirchenmann in der Zeit zwischen Monarchie und Diktatur* (Göttingen: Vandenhoeck & Ruprecht, 1998).

Fritzsche, Peter. *Germans into Nazis* (Cambridge, MA: Harvard University Press, 1998).

Fritzsche, Peter. *Life and Death in the Third Reich* (Cambridge, MA: Harvard University Press, 2008).

Fritzsche, Peter. *The Turbulent World of Franz Göll* (Cambridge, MA: Harvard University Press, 2011).

Fritzsche, Peter. *Hitler's First Hundred Days* (New York: Basic Books, 2020).

Gailus, Manfred, ed. *Pöbelexzesse und Volkstumulte in Berlin: Zur Sozialgeschichte der Straße 1830–1980* (Berlin: Europäische Perspektiven, 1984).

Gailus, Manfred. *Protestantismus und Nationalsozialismus. Studien zur nationalsozialistischen Durchdringung des Protestantischen Sozialmilieus in Berlin* (Cologne: Böhlau, 2001).

Gailus, Manfred. "Kirchenbücher, Arier-Nachweise und kirchliche Beihilfen zur Judenverfolgung. Eine Einführung," in *Kirchliche Amtshilfe*, ed. Manfred Gailus (Göttingen: Vandenhoeck & Ruprecht, 2008), 7–27.

Gailus, Manfred, *Die Kirche und die Judenverfolgung im "Dritten Reich,"* ed. Kirchliche Amtshilfe. (Göttingen: Vandenhoeck & Ruprecht, 2008).

Gall, Lothar, Gerald Feldman, Harold James, Carl-Ludwig Holtfrerich, and Hans E. Büschgen, eds. *Die Deutsche Bank, 1870–1995* (Munich: Beck, 1995).

Gasteiger, Daniela. *Kuno von Westarp, 1864–1945. Parlamentarismus, Monarchismus und Herrschaftsutopien im deutschen Konservatismus* (Berlin: De Gruyter, 2018).

Gay, Peter. *My German Question. Growing Up in Nazi Berlin* (New Haven and London: Yale University Press, 1998).

Geheran, Michael. *Comrades Betrayed. Jewish World War I Veterans under Hitler* (Ithaca: Cornell University Press, 2020).

Gellately, Robert. *The Gestapo and German Society. Enforcing Racial Policy 1933–1945* (Oxford: Clarendon Press, 1990).

Gellately, Robert. "Denunciations in Twentieth-Century Germany: Aspects of Self-Policing in the Third Reich and the German Democratic Republic," in *Denunciatory Practices. Denunciation in Modern European History, 1789–1989*, ed. Sheila Fitzpatrick and Robert Gellately (Chicago: University of Chicago Press, 1997), 185–221.

Gellately, Robert. "Crime, Identity and Power: Stories of Police Imposters in Nazi Germany," *Crime, Histoire & Sociétés*, 4, no. 2 (2000): 5–18.

Gellately, Robert. *Backing Hitler. Consent and Coercion in Nazi Germany* (Oxford and New York: Oxford University Press, 2001).

Gellately, Robert. *Hitler's True Believers: How Ordinary People Became Nazis* (Oxford: Oxford University Press, 2020).

Gellately, Robert, and Nathan Stoltzfus. *Social Outsiders in Nazi Germany* (Princeton: Princeton University Press, 2001).

Genschel, Helmut. *Die Verdrängung der Juden aus der Wirtschaft im Dritten Reich* (Göttingen: Musterschmidt, 1966).

Gerlach, Wolfgang. *Als die Zeugen schwiegen: Bekennende Kirche und die Juden* (Berlin: Institut Kirche und Judentum, 1987).

Gerst, Thomas. "Vor 80 Jahren: Ausschluss jüdischer Ärzte aus der Kassenpraxis," *Deutsches Ärzteblatt*, 110, no. 16 (19 April 2013): 770–772.

Geyer, Michael. "Etudes in Political History: Reichswehr, NSDAP, and the Seizure of Power," in *The Nazi Machtergreifung*, ed. Peter Stachura (London: Allen & Unwin, 1983), 101–123.

Gies, Horst. *Geschichtsunterricht unter der Diktatur Hitlers* (Cologne: Böhlau, 1992).

Giles, Geoffrey J. *Students and National Socialism in Germany* (Princeton: Princeton University Press, 1985).

Giles, Geoffrey J. "Die Fahne hoch, die Reihen dicht geschlossen: Die Studenten als Verfechter der völkischen Universität?" in *Die Freiburger Universität in der Zeit des Nationalsozialismus*, ed. E. John, B. Martin, M. Mück, and H. Ott (Freiburg and Würzburg: Ploetz, 1991), 43–56.

Goeschel, Christian. "Suicides of German Jews in the Third Reich," *German History*, 25 (2007): 22–45.

Goeschel, Christian. *Suicide in Nazi Germany* (Oxford: Oxford University Press, 2009).

Goeschel, Christian, and Nikolaus Wachsmann, eds. *The Nazi Concentration Camps, 1933–1939: A Documentary History* (Lincoln and London: University of Nebraska Press, 2012).

Goldmann, Felix. "Deutschland und die Ostjudenfrage," *Zeitschrift des Centralvereins deutscher Staatsbürger jüdischen Glaubens*. 21 (November/December 1915): 195–213.

Göppinger, Horst. *Juristen jüdischer Abstammung im "Dritten Reich." Entrechtung und Verfolgung*, 2nd ed. (Munich: Beck, 1990).

Gordon, Sarah Ann. *Hitler, the Germans and the Jewish Question* (Princeton, NJ: Princeton University Press, 1984).

Görtemaker, Manfred, and Christoph Safferling. *Die Akte Rosenburg. Das Bundesministerium der Justiz und die NS-Zeit* (Munich: Beck, 2016).

Gosewinkel, Dieter. *Einbürgern und Ausschließen. Die Nationalisierung der Staatsangehörigkeit vom Deutschen Bund bis zur Bundesrepublik Deutschland*. Vol. 150: *Kritische Studien zur Geschichtswissenschaft* (Göttingen: Vandenhoeck & Ruprecht, 2001).

Grady, Tim. *The German-Jewish Soldiers of the First World War in History and Memory* (Liverpool: Liverpool University Press, 2011).

Grady, Tim. *A Deadly Legacy. German Jews and the Great War* (New Haven and London: Yale University Press, 2017).

Greschat, Martin. "Die Haltung der deutschen evangelischen Kirchen zur Verfolgung der Juden im Dritten Reich," in *Die Deutschen und die Judenverfolgung im Dritten Reich. Hamburger Beiträge zur Sozial- und Zeitgeschichte*, 29, ed. Ursula Büttner (Hamburg: Christians, 1992), 273–292.

Griech-Polelle, Beth A. *Bishop von Galen: German Catholicism and National Socialism* (New Haven: Yale University Press, 2002).

Griffin, Roger, ed. *Fascism* (Oxford: Oxford University Press, 1995).

Gruber, Hubert. *Katholische Kirche und Nationalsozialismus 1930–1945* (Paderborn: Schöningh, 2006).

Gruchmann, Lothar. "'Blutschutzgesetz' und Justiz. Entstehung und Anwendung des Nürnberger Gesetzes vom 15. September 1935," *Vierteljahrshefte für Zeitgeschichte*, 31 (1983), 418–442.

Gruchmann, Lothar. *Justiz im Dritten Reich 1933–1940. Anpassung und Unterwerfung in der Ära Gürtner*, 3rd ed. (Munich: Oldenbourg, 2001).

Gruenewald, Max. "The Beginning of the 'Reichsvertretung,'" *Leo Baeck Institute Year Book*, 1, no. 1 (1956): 57–67.

Gruner, Wolf, ed. *Die Verfolgung und Ermordung der europäischen Juden durch das nationalsozialistische Deutschland 1933–1945*, Vol. I: *Deutsches Reich, 1933–1937* (Munich: Oldenbourg, 2008).

Grüttner, Michael. *Studenten im Dritten Reich* (Paderborn: Schöningh, 1995).

Grüttner, Michael. *Das Dritte Reich 1933–1939* (Stuttgart: Klett-Cotta, 2014).

Gutman, Yisrael. "Poles and Jews between the Wars: Historic Overview," in *Hostages of Modernization. Studies on Modern Antisemitism, 1870–1933/39.* Vol. 3/2: *Austria-Hungary-Poland-Russia,* ed. Herbert A. Strauss (Berlin and New York: De Gruyter, 1993).

Haffner, Sebastian. *The Ailing Empire. Germany from Bismarck to Hitler* (New York: Fromm, 1989).

Haffner, Sebastian. *Germany: Jekyll and Hyde* (Berlin: Verlag 1900, 1996).

Hagen, William W. "Before the 'Final Solution': Toward a Comparative Analysis of Political Anti-Semitism in Interwar Germany and Poland," *Journal of Modern History,* 68 (1996): 351–381.

Hagen, William W. "Murder in the East: German-Jewish Liberal Reactions to Anti-Jewish Violence in Poland and Other East European Lands, 1918–1920," *Central European History,* 34, no. 1 (2001): 1–30.

Hambrock, Matthias. *Die Etablierung der Außenseiter. Der Verband nationaldeutscher Juden 1921–1935* (Cologne: Böhlau, 2003).

Hammer, Karl. *Deutsche Kriegstheologie 1870–1918* (Munich: DTV, 1974).

Harvey, David Allen. "Lost Children or Enemy Aliens? Classifying the Population of Alsace after the First World War," *Journal of Contemporary History,* 34, no. 4 (1999): 537–554.

Hastings, Derek. *Catholicism and the Roots of Nazism. Religious Identity and National Socialism* (New York: Oxford University Press, 2010).

Haynes, Stephen R. "Who needs Enemies? Jews and Judaism in Anti-Nazi Religious Discourse," *Church History,* 71 (2002): 341–367.

Hecht, Cornelia. *Deutsche Juden und Antisemitismus in der Weimarer Republik* (Bonn: Dietz, 2003).

Heidner, Georg. *Der politische Charakter der Deutschen* (Berlin: Hammer, 1919).

Heilbronner, Oded. "From Antisemitic Peripheries to Antisemitic Centres: The Place of Antisemitism in Modern German History," *Journal of Contemporary History,* 35 (2000): 559–576.

Heilbronner, Oded. "The Role of Nazi Antisemitism in the Nazi Party's Activity and Propaganda: A Regional Historiographical Study," *Leo Baeck Institute Yearbook,* 35 (2000): 397–439.

Heinemann, Ulrich. *Die verdrängte Niederlage. Politische Öffentlichkeit und Kriegsschuldfrage in der Weimarer Republik* (Göttingen: Vandenhoeck & Ruprecht, 1983).

Heinrichs, Wolfgang E. *Das Judenbild im Protestantismus des Deutschen Kaiserreichs. Ein Beitrag zur Mentalitätsgeschichte des deutschen Bürgertums in der Krise der Moderne,* 2nd ed. (Giessen: Brunnen, 2004).

Helmreich, Ernst Christian. *The German Churches under Hitler. Background, Struggle, and Epilogue* (Detroit: Wayne State Press, 1979).

Henke, Klaus-Dietmar, ed. *Totalitarismus. Sechs Vorträge über Gehalt und Reichweite eines klassischen Konzepts der Diktaturforschung* (Dresden: Hannah-Arendt-Institut für Totalitarismus Forschung, 1999).

Herbert, Ulrich. *Best: Biographische Studien über Radikalismus, Weltanschauung und Vernunft 1903–1989* (Bonn: J. H. W. Dietz, 2001).

Herbst, Ludolf. *Das nationalsozialistische Deutschland, 1933–1945. Die Entfesselung der Gewalt: Rassismus und Krieg* (Frankfurt: Suhrkamp, 1996).

Herf, Jeffrey. "'Der Krieg und die Juden.' Nationalsozialistische Propaganda im Zweiten Weltkrieg," in *Das Deutsche Reich und der zweite Weltkrieg*, vol. 9, part II, ed. Jörg Echternkamp. (Munich: DVA, 2005), 159–202.

Herf, Jeffrey. *The Jewish Enemy: Nazi Propaganda during World War II and the Holocaust* (Cambridge: Harvard University Press, 2006).

Hering, Rainer. *Die Bischöfe Simon Schöffel, Franz Tügel*. Hamburgische Lebensbilder in Darstellungen und Selbstzeugnissen, 10 (Hamburg: Verein für Hamburgische Geschichte, 1995).

Hering, Rainer. "Auf dem Weg in die Moderne? Die Hamburgische Landeskirche in der Weimarer Republik," *Zeitschrift des Vereins für Hamburgische Geschichte*, 82 (1996), 127–166.

Hering, Rainer. *Konstruierte Nation. Der Alldeutsche Verband 1890 bis 1939* (Hamburg: Christians, 2003).

Hering, Rainer, ed. *Die "Reichskristallnacht" in Schleswig-Holstein. Der Novemberpogrom im historischen Kontext* (Hamburg: Hamburg University Press, 2016).

Hering, Rainer. "From Collegiality to the Führerprinzip: The 1933 Introduction of the Episcopacy in the Hamburg Landeskirche," in *From Weimar to Hitler. Studies in the Dissolution of the Weimar Republic and the Establishment of the Third Reich, 1932–1934*, ed. Hermann Beck and Larry E. Jones (New York: Berghahn, 2019), 281–309.

Hermle, Siegfried. "Die Auseinandersetzung mit der nationalsozialistischen Judenverfolgung in der Evangelischen Kirche nach 1945," in *Die Deutschen und die Judenverfolgung im Dritten Reich. Hamburger Beiträge zur Sozial- und Zeitgeschichte*, 29, ed. Ursula Büttner. (Hamburg: Christians, 1992), 321–337.

Herrmann, Wilhelm. *Ethik*, 5th ed. (Tübingen: Mohr, 1913).

Hertzmann, Lewis. *DNVP: Right-Wing Opposition in the Weimar Republic, 1918–1924* (Lincoln: University of Nebraska Press, 1963).

Heschel, Susannah. *The Aryan Jesus: Christian Theologians and the Bible in Nazi Germany* (Princeton: Princeton University Press, 2008).

Hett, Benjamin Carter. *The Death of Democracy: Hitler's Rise to Power and the Downfall of the Weimar Republic* (New York: Henry Holt & Co., 2018).

Hilberg, Raul. *The Destruction of the European Jews*, 3rd ed., vol. 1 (New Haven: Yale University Press, 2003).

Hildebrand, Klaus. *Das Dritte Reich*, 3rd ed. (Munich: Oldenbourg, 1987). English trans.: *The Third Reich* (Winchester, MA: Allen & Unwin, 1984).

Hintze, Otto. "Der Beamtenstand," in *Otto Hintze, Soziologie und Geschichte, Gesammelte Abhandlungen*, 3rd ed., vol. 2, ed. Gerhard Oestreich (Göttingen: Vandenhoeck & Ruprecht, 1982), 66–126.

Hintze, Otto. *Soziologie und Geschichte, Gesammelte Abhandlungen*, 3rd ed., vol. 2, ed. Gerhard Oestreich (Göttingen: Vandenhoeck & Ruprecht, 1982).

Hockerts, Hans Günter. "Wiedergutmachung in Deutschland. Eine historische Bilanz 1945–2000," *Vierteljahrshefte für Zeitgeschichte*, 49, no. 2 (2001): 167–214.

Hockerts, Hans Günter, and Christiane Kuller, eds. *Nach der Verfolgung. Wiedergutmachung nationalsozialistischen Unrechts in Deutschland* (Göttingen: Wallstein, 2003).

Hoffmann, Christhard, Werner Bergmann, and Helmut W. Smith, eds. *Exclusionary Violence: Antisemitic Riots in Modern German History* (Ann Arbor: University of Michigan Press, 2002).

Hofmeister, Björn. "Between Monarchy and Dictatorship: Radical Nationalism and Social Mobilization of the Pan-German League, 1914–1939." Ph.D. Dissertation, Georgetown University (Washington, D.C., 2012).

Höhne, Heinz. *"Gebt mir vier Jahre Zeit." Hitler und die Anfänge des Dritten Reiches* (Frankfurt: Ullstein, 1996).

Holborn, Hajo, ed. *Republic to Reich: The Making of the Nazi Revolution. Ten Essays* (New York: Pantheon Books, 1972).

Höner, Sabine. *Der nationalsozialistische Zugriff auf Preußen. Preußischer Staat- und nationalsozialistische Machteroberungsstrategie 1928–1934* (Bochum: Brockmeyer, 1984).

Hördler, Stefan, ed. *Der SA-Terror als Herrschaftssicherung. "Kopinecker Blutwoche" und Öffentliche Gewalt im frühen Nationalsozialismus* (Berlin: Metropol, 2013).

Horkheimer, Max. "Die Juden und Europa," *Zeitschrift für Sozialforschung*, 8 (1939): 115–137.

Horne, John, and Alan Kramer. *German Atrocities 1914. A History of Denial* (New Haven and London: Yale University Press, 2001).

Hübner, Christoph. *Die Rechtskatholiken, die Zentrumspartei und die katholische Kirche in Deutschland bis zum Reichskonkordat von 1933. Ein Beitrag zur Geschichte des Scheiterns der Weimarer Republik* (Münster: LIT, 2014).

Huerkamp, Claudia. "Jüdische Akademikerinnen in Deutschland 1900–1938," *Geschichte und Gesellschaft*, 19 (1993): 311–331.

Hürten, Heinz. *Deutsche Katholiken 1918–1945* (Paderborn: Schöningh, 1992).

Hürter, Johannes, ed. *Notizen aus dem Vernichtungskrieg. Die Ostfront 1941/42 in den Aufzeichnungen des Generals Heinrici* (Darmstadt: WBG, 2016).

Jäckel, Eberhard. *Hitlers Weltanschauung. Entwurf einer Herrschaft*, 3rd ed. (Stuttgart: DVA, 1986).

Jackisch, Barry. *The Pan-German League and Radical Nationalist Politics in Interwar Germany, 1918–1939* (London and New York: Routledge, 2012).

Jacobsen, Ludwig August. *So hat es angefangen. Ein Bericht aus den Tagen der "nationalen Erhebung" in Köln* (Cologne: Volksblatt, 1987).

Jakob, Volker. "Wilhelm Spiegel: Jude-Anwalt-Sozialist. Das erste Mordopfer der antisemitischen Gewalt," in *Menora und Hakenkreuz. Zur Geschichte der Juden in und aus Schleswig-Holstein, Lübeck und Altona 1918–1998*, ed. Gerhard Paul and Miriam Gillis-Carlebach (Neumünster: Wachholtz, 1998), 205–213.

James, Harold. *The German Slump. Politics and Economics, 1924–1936* (Oxford: Oxford University Press, 1986).

James, Harold. "Die Deutsche Bank und die Diktatur 1933–1945," in *Die Deutsche Bank 1870–1995*, ed. Lothar Gall, Gerald Feldman, Harold James, Carl-Ludwig Holtfrerich, and Hans E. Büschgen (Munich: Beck, 1995), 315–408.

James, Harold. *The Deutsche Bank and the Nazi Economic War against the Jews* (Cambridge: Cambridge University Press, 2001).

Jansen, Christian. *Professoren und Politik* (Göttingen: Vandenhoek & Ruprecht, 1992).

Jansen, Christian, Lutz Niethammer, and Bernd Weisbrod, eds. *Von der Aufgabe der Freiheit. Politische Verantwortung und bürgerliche Gesellschaft im 19. und 20. Jahrhundert. Festschrift für Hans Mommsen* (Berlin: Oldenbourg, 1995).

Jarausch, Konrad. "The Crisis of German Professions 1918–1933," *Journal of Contemporary History*, 20 (1985): 379–398.

Jarausch, Konrad. *The Unfree Professions: German Lawyers, Teachers, and Engineers, 1900–1950* (Oxford: Oxford University Press, 1990).

Jarke, Jochen. *Kirche zwischen Monarchie und Republik. Der preußische Protestantismus nach dem Zusammenbruch von 1918* (Hamburg: Christians, 1976).

Jasper, Gotthard. *Die gescheiterte Zähmung. Wege zur Machtergreifung Hitlers 1930–1934* (Frankfurt: Suhrkamp, 1986).

Jochmann, Werner. "Die Ausbreitung des Antisemitismus," in *Deutsches Judentum in Krieg und Revolution 1916–1923*, ed. Werner E. Mosse (Tübingen: Mohr Siebeck, 1971), 409–510.

Jochmann, Werner. *Gesellschaftskrise und Judenfeindschaft in Deutschland 1870–1945*, 2nd ed. (Hamburg: Christians, 1991).

Jochmann, Werner. "Struktur und Funktion des deutschen Antisemitismus," in *Juden im Wilhelminischen Deutschland*, ed. Werner E. Mosse (Tübingen: Mohr Siebeck, 1998), 389–477.

Jones, Larry E. *German Liberalism and the Dissolution of the Weimar Party System, 1918–1933* (Chapel Hill and London: University of North Carolina Press, 1988).

Jones, Larry E. "Why Hitler Came to Power: In Defense of a New History of Politics," in *Geschichtswissenschaft vor 2000. Perspektiven der Historiographiegeschichte, Geschichtstheorie, Sozial- und Kulturgeschichte. Festschrift für Georg G. Iggers*, ed. Konrad H. Jarausch, Jörn Rüsen, and Hans Schleier (Hagen: Rottmann, 1991), 256–276.

Jones, Larry E. "Nazis, Conservatives, and the Establishment of the Third Reich, 1932–34," *Tel Aviver Jahrbuch für deutsche Geschichte*, 23 (1994): 41–64.

Jones, Larry E. "Franz von Papen, Catholic Conservatives, and the Establishment of the Third Reich, 1933-1934," *Journal of Modern History*, 83 (2011): 272–318.

Jones, Larry E. "Conservative Antisemitism in the Weimar Republic. A Case Study of the German National People's Party," in Larry E. Jones, *The German Right in the Weimar Republic. Studies in the History of German Conservatism, Nationalism, and Antisemitism* (New York and Oxford: Berghahn, 2014), 79–107.

Jones, Larry E. *Hitler versus Hindenburg. The 1932 Presidential Elections and the End of the Weimar Republic* (Cambridge: Cambridge University Press, 2016).

Jones, Larry E. *The German Right, 1918–1930: Political Parties, Organized Interests, and Patriotic Associations in the Struggle against Weimar Democracy* (Cambridge: Cambridge University Press, 2020).

Jones, Larry E., and Kevin Spicer. "In Search of Allies: Catholic Conservatives, the Alliance of Catholic Germans, and the Nazi Regime, 1933/34," in *From Weimar to Hitler. Studies in the Dissolution of the Weimar Republic and the Establishment of the Third Reich, 1932–1934*, ed. Hermann Beck and Larry E. Jones (New York: Berghahn, 2019), 339–365.

Junker, Detlef. *Die Deutsche Zentrumspartei und Hitler 1932/33: Ein Beitrag zu Problematik des politischen Katholizismus in Deutschland* (Stuttgart: Klett, 1969).

Jürgens, Christian. *Fritz Solmitz: Kommunalpolitiker, Journalist, Widerstandskämpfer und NS-Verfolgter aus Lübeck* (Lübeck: Schmidt-Römhild, 1996).

Kalshoven, Hedda, ed. *Between Two Homelands. Letters Across the Borders of Nazi Germany* (Urbana: University of Illinois Press, 2014).

Kammer, Hilde, and Elizabeth Bartsch, eds. *Nationalsozialismus. Begriffe aus der Zeit der Gewaltherrschaft 1933–1945* (Hamburg: Rowohlt, 1992).

Kasten, Bernd. "Deutschnationale Führungsschichten und der Aufstieg der NSDAP in Mecklenburg-Schwerin 1930–1933," *Mecklenburgische Jahrbücher*, 115 (2000): 233–257.

Kater, Michael H. *Studentenschaft und Rechtsradikalismus in Deutschland 1918–1933* (Hamburg: Hoffmann & Campe, 1975).

Kater, Michael H. "Hitler's Early Doctors: Nazi Physicians in Predepression Germany," *Journal of Modern History*, 59 (1987): 25–52.

Kater, Michael H. "Medizin und Mediziner im Dritten Reich," *Historische Zeitschrift*, 244, no. 2 (April 1987): 299–352.

Kater, Michael H. *Doctors under Hitler* (Chapel Hill: University of North Carolina Press), 1990.

Katzenbach, Friedrich Wilhelm. *Widerstand und Solidarität der Christen in Deutschland 1933–1945. Eine Dokumentation zum Kirchenkampf aus den Papieren des D. Wilhelm Freiherr von Pechmann*, repr. (Neustadt/Aisch: Landessynode der Evangelischen Kirche, 2000).

Kauders, Anthony. *German Politics and the Jews. Düsseldorf and Nürnberg, 1910–1933.* (Oxford: Clarendon Press, 1996).

Kershaw, Ian. *Hitler. 1889–1936: Hubris* (New York: Norton, 1999).

Kershaw, Ian. *Popular Opinion and Political Dissent in the Third Reich: Bavaria 1933–1945*, 2nd ed. (New York: Oxford University Press, 2002).

Kershaw, Ian. "Reactions to the Persecution of the Jews," in Ian Kershaw, *Hitler, the Germans, and the Final Solution* (New Haven and London: Yale University Press, 2008), 151–196.

Kershaw, Ian. "The 'Everyday' and the 'Exceptional': The Shaping of Popular Opinion, 1933- 1939," in *Hitler, the Germans, and the Final Solution*, ed. Ian Kershaw (New Haven and London: Yale University Press, 2008), 119–138.

Kim, Sun-Ryol. *Die Vorgeschichte der Trennung von Staat und Kirche in der Weimarer Verfassung von 1919. Eine Untersuchung über das Verhältnis von Staat und Kirche in Preußen seit der Reichsgründung von 1871* (Hamburg and London: LIT, 1996).

Kimmel, Günther. "Das Konzentrationslager Dachau. Eine Studie zu den nationalsozialistischen Gewaltverbrechen," in *Bayern in der NS-Zeit*. Vol. II: *Herrschaft und Gesellschaft im Konflikt*, ed. Martin Broszat and Elke Fröhlich (Munich and Vienna: Oldenbourg, 1979), 363–364.

Kisch, Egon Erwin. "Der Erste Schub," in Egon Erwin Kisch, *Nichts ist erregender als die Wahrheit*. Vol. II (Frankfurt: Büchergilde Gutenberg, 1981), 67–70.

Kißener, Michael. *Das Dritte Reich* (Darmstadt: WBG, 2005).

Kißener, Michael, ed. *Der Weg in den Nationalsozialismus 1933/34* (Darmstadt: WBG, 2009).

Kittel, Manfred. "'Steigbügelhalter' Hitlers oder 'stille Republikaner'? Die Deutschnationalen in neuer politikgeschichtlicher und kulturalistischer Perspektive," in *Geschichte der Politik. Alte und Neue Wege*, ed. Hans-Christof Kraus and Thomas Nicklas (Munich: Oldenbourg, 2007), 201–235.

Kleine, George H. "Adelsgenossenschaft und Nationalsozialismus," *Vierteljahrshefte für Zeitgeschichte*, 26 (1978): 100–143.

Klier, John D. *Imperial Russia's Jewish Question, 1855–1881* (Cambridge: Cambridge University Press, 1995).

Klüger, Ruth. "Die Säkularisierung des Judenhasses am Beispiel von Wilhelm Raabes 'Der Hungerpastor'," in *Literarischer Antisemitismus nach Auschwitz*, ed. Klaus-Michael Bogdal, Klaus Holz, and Matthias N. Lorenz (Stuttgart: Metzler, 2007), 103–110.

Kluke, Paul. "Der Fall Potempa," *Vierteljahrshefte für Zeitgeschichte*. 5 (1957): 279–297.

Knütter, Hans-Helmuth. "Die Linksparteien," in *Entscheidungsjahr 1932. Zur Judenfrage in der Endphase der Weimarer Republik*, ed. Werner E. Mosse (Tübingen: Mohr, 1966), 323–348.

Köckeritz, Moritz von. *Die deutschen Oberlandesgerichts-Präsidenten im Nationalsozialismus, 1933–1945* (Frankfurt: Lang, 2011).

Koehl, Robert. "Feudal Aspects of National Socialism," in *Nazism and the Third Reich*, ed. Henry Ashby Turner (New York: Quadrangle, 1972), 151–174.

Kolb, Eberhard. *Die Weimarer Republik*, 7th ed. (Munich: Oldenbourg, 2009).

Königseder, Angelika. *Recht und nationalsozialistische Herrschaft. Berliner Anwälte 1933–1945* (Bonn: Deutscher Anwaltsverlag, 2001).

Koonz, Claudia. *The Nazi Conscience* (Cambridge, MA: Harvard University Press, 2003).

Kopitzsch, Wolfgang. "Der 'Altonaer Blutsonntag'," in *Arbeiter in Hamburg. Unterschichten, Arbeiter, und Arbeiterbewegung seit dem ausgehenden 18. Jahrhundert*, ed. Arno Herzig, Dieter Langewiesche, and Arnold Sywottek (Hamburg: Erziehung & Wissenschaft, 1983), 509–516.

Kraus, Hans-Christof. "Altkonservatismus und moderne politische Rechte. Zum Problem der Kontinuität rechter politischer Strömungen in Deutschland," in *Weltbürgerkrieg der Ideologien. Antworten an Ernst Nolte. Festschrift zum 70. Geburtstag*, ed. Thomas Nipperdey, Anselm Doering-Manteuffel, and Hans-Ulrich Thamer (Berlin: Propyläen, 1993), 99–121.

Kraus, Hans-Joachim. "Die evangelische Kirche," in *Entscheidungsjahr 1932. Zur Judenfrage in der Endphase der Weimarer Republik*, 2nd ed., ed. Werner E. Mosse (Tübingen: Mohr Siebeck, 1966), 249–270.

Krausnick, Helmut. "Judenverfolgung," in *Anatomie des SS-Staates*, 5th ed,, vol. II, ed. Hans Buchheim, Martin Broszat, Hans-Adolf Jacobsen, and Helmut Krausnick (Munich: DTV, 1989), 257–260.

Kreutzmüller, Christoph. *Ausverkauf. Die Vernichtung der jüdischen Gewerbetätigkeit in Berlin 1930–1945*, 2nd ed. (Berlin: Metropol, 2013). English trans.: *Final Sale in Berlin. The Destruction of Jewish Commercial Activity 1930–1945* (New York: Berghahn, 2015).

Kreutzmüller, Christoph, and Eckart Schörle. *Stadtluft macht frei? Jüdische Gewerbetreibende in Erfurt 1919–1939* (Berlin: Hentrich, 2013).

Kruppa, Bernd. *Rechtsradikalismus in Berlin, 1918–1928* (Berlin: Overall, 1988).

Kulka, Otto D. "Major Trends and Tendencies in German Historiography on National Socialism and the 'Jewish Question' (1924–1984)," *Leo Baeck Institute Yearbook*, 30, no.1 (1985): 215–242.

Küllmer, Björn. *Die Inszenierung der Protestantischen Volksgemeinschaft. Lutherbilder im Lutherjahr 1933* (Berlin: Logos, 2012).

Kümmel, Werner F. "Die Ausschaltung rassisch und politisch mißliebiger Ärzte," in *Ärzte im Nationalsozialismus*, ed. Fridolf Kudlien (Cologne: Kiepenheuer, 1985), 56–81.

Kurlander, Eric. *Living with Hitler. Liberal Democrats in the Third Reich* (New Haven: Yale University Press, 2009).

Kwiet, Konrad. "Zur historiographischen Behandlung der Judenverfolgung im Dritten Reich," *Militärgeschichtliche Mitteilungen*, 1 (1980): 149–192.

Lahme, Tilmann. *Die Manns. Geschichte einer Familie* (Frankfurt: Fischer, 2015).

Lahusen, Benjamin. "Die Selbstermächtigung des Rechts: Breslau 1933. Zum 'Stillstand der Rechtspflege' in der Juristischen Zeitgeschichte," *Studies in Contemporary History*, 2 (2019): 258–277.

Lamberti, Marjorie. "German Schoolteachers, National Socialism, and the Politics of Culture at the End of the Weimar Republic," *Central European History*, 34, no. 1 (2001): 53–82.

Large, David Clay. "Out with the Ostjuden": The Scheunenviertel Riots in Berlin, November 1923," in *Exclusionary violence: antisemitic riots in modern German history*, ed. Christhard Hoffmann, Werner Bergman, and Helmut Walser Smith (Ann Arbor: University of Michigan Press, 2002), 123–140.

Larson, Erik. *In the Garden of Beasts: Love, Terror, and an American Family in Hitler's Berlin* (New York: Broadway, 2012).

Laswell, Harold. *Propaganda Technique in the World War* (Cambridge, MA: Harvard University Press, 1927).

Lau, Dirk. *Wahlkämpfe in der Weimarer Republik. Propaganda und Programme der politischen Parteien bei den Wahlen zum Deutschen Reichstag von 1924 bis 1930*, 3rd ed. (Baden-Baden: Tectum, 2018).

Ledford, Kenneth. "German Lawyers and the State in the Weimar Republic," *Law and History Review*, 13 (1995): 317–349.

Ledford, Kenneth. *From General Estate to Special Interest. German Lawyers 1978–1933* (Cambridge: Cambridge University Press, 1996).

Leibfried, Stephan and Florian Tennstedt. *Berufsverbote und Sozialpolitik 1933. Die Auswirkungen der nationalsozialistischen Machtergreifung auf die Krankenkassenverwaltung und die Kassenärzte*, 2nd ed. (Bremen: Universität Bremen, 1980).

Leibfried, Stephan, and Florian Tennstedt. "Health Insurance Policy and Berufsverbote in the Nazi Takeover," in *Political Values and Health Care. The German Experience*, ed. Donald W. Light (Cambridge, MA: MIT Press, 1986), 127–184.

Leicht, Johannes. *Heinrich Claß 1868–1953. Die politische Biographie eines Alldeutschen* (Paderborn: Schöningh, 2012).

Leopold, John A. *Alfred Hugenberg: The Radical Nationalist Campaign against the Weimar Republic* (New Haven and London: Yale University Press, 1977).

Lessing, Otto Edward, ed. *Minorities and Boundaries* (Dordrecht: Springer, 1931).

Levitt, Cyril. "The Prosecution of Antisemites by the Courts in the Weimar Republic: Was Justice Served?" *Leo Baeck Yearbook*, 36 (1991): 151–167.

Lewy, Guenter. *The Catholic Church and Nazi Germany* (Boston: Da Capo, 2000, first pub. 1964).

Liebe, Werner. *Die Deutschnationale Volkspartei, 1918–1924* (Düsseldorf: Droste, 1956).

Lill, Rudolf. "Die Deutschen Katholiken und die Juden in der Zeit von 1850 bis zur Machtübernahme Hitlers," in *Kirche und Synagoge: Handbuch zur Geschichte von Christen und Juden*, ed. Karl-Heinrich Rengstorf and Siegfried von Kortzfleisch (Stuttgart: Klett: 1970), 370–420.

Linck, Stefan. "'Vor zersetzendem jüdischen Einfluß bewahren.' Antisemitismus in der schleswig-holsteinischen Landeskirche," in *Als Jesus "arisch" wurde. Kirche, Christen, Juden in Nordelbien 1933–1945*, 2nd ed., ed. Annette Göhres, Stephan Linck, and Joachim Liß-Walther (Bremen: Edition Temmen, 2003), 132–146.

Lindemann, Albert S. *Anti-Semitism before the Holocaust* (London: Routledge, 2000).

Lipstadt, Deborah E. *Beyond Belief. The American Press and the Coming of the Holocaust 1933–1945* (London: Free Press, 1986).

Lohalm, Uwe. *Völkischer Radikalismus. Die Geschichte des Deutschvölkischen Schutz- und Trutz-Bundes 1919–1923* (Hamburg: Leibnitz, 1970).

Longerich, Peter. *Die braunen Bataillone. Geschichte der SA* (Munich: Beck, 1989).

Longerich, Peter. *Politik der Vernichtung. Eine Gesamtdarstellung de nationalsozialistischen Judenverfolgung* (Munich: Piper, 1998).

Longerich, Peter. *"Davon haben wir nichts gewusst!" Die Deutschen und die Judenverfolgung 1933–1945* (Munich: Pantheon, 2007).

Loth, Wilfried. *Das Kaiserreich. Obrigkeitsstaat und politische Mobilisierung* (Munich: DTV, 1996).

Loth, Wilfried, and Bernd-A. Rusineck, eds. *Verwandlungspolitik—NS-Eliten in der westdeutschen Nachkriegsgesellschaft* (Frankfurt and New York: Campus, 1998).

Löwe, Heinz-Dietrich. "Anti-Semitism at the Close of the Tsarist Era," in *Hostages of Modernization. Current Research on Antisemitism*. Vol. 3/2: *Austria-Hungary-Poland-Russia*, ed. Herbert A. Strauss (Berlin and New York: De Gruyter, 1993), 1188–1207.

Löwenthal, Leo. *Mitmachen wollte ich nie. Ein autobiographisches Gespräch mit Helmut Dubiel* (Frankfurt: Suhrkamp, 1980).

Lübbe, Hermann. *Politische Philosophie in Deutschland* (Munich: DTV, 1974).

Lubrich, Oliver, ed. *Travels in the Reich, 1933–1945: Foreign Authors Report from Germany* (Chicago: University of Chicago Press, 2010).

Lukaschek, Hans. "The Germans in Upper Polish Silesia," in *Minorities and Boundaries*, ed. Otto Eduard Lessing (The Hague: Nijhoff, 1931), 96–108.

McElligot, Anthony. "Street Politics in Hamburg 1932–1933," *History Workshop*, 16 (1983): 83–90.

McElligott, Anthony. *Contested City. Municipal Politics and the Rise of Nazism in Altona, 1917–1937* (Ann Arbor: University of Michigan Press, 1998).

Maier, Joachim. "Die Katholische Kirche und die Machtergreifung," in *Die nationalsozialistische Machtergreifung*, ed. Wolfgang Michalka (Paderborn: Schöningh, 1984), 152–167.

Malinowski, Stephan. "Vom blauen zum reinen Blut. Antisemitische Adelskritik und adliger Antisemitismus 1871–1944," *Jahrbuch für Antisemitismusforschung*, 12 (2003): 147–168.

Malinowski, Stephan. "Kuno Graf Westarp – ein missing link im preußischen Adel," in *"Ich bin der letzte Preuße." Der politische Lebensweg des konservativen Politkers Kuno Graf*

Westarp, ed. Larry E. Jones and Wolfram Pyta (Cologne, Weimar, and Vienna: Böhlau, 2006), 9–32.

Malinowski, Stephan. *Vom König zum Führer. Deutscher Adel und Nationalsozialismus* (Frankfurt: Fischer, 2016).

Mallmann, Klaus-Michael, and Gerhard Paul. "Allwissend, allmächtig, allgegenwärtig? Gestapo, Gesellschaft und Widerstand," *Zeitschrift für Geschichtswissenschaft*, 41 (1993): 984–999.

Maser, Peter, and Adelheid Weiser. *Juden in Oberschlesien*. Part I: *Historischer Überblick: Jüdische Gemeinden* (Berlin: Mann, 1992).

Matthias, Erich. "Die Sozialdemokratische Partei Deutschlands," in *Das Ende der Parteien 1933*, ed. Erich Matthias and Rudolf Morsey (Düsseldorf: Droste, 1960), 101–278.

Matthias, Erich, and Rudolf Morsey. "Die deutsche Staatspartei," in *Das Ende der Parteien 1933*, ed. Erich Matthias and Rudolf Morsey (Düsseldorf: Droste, 1960), 31–97.

Matzerath, Horst. "Bürokratie und Judenverfolgung", in *Die Deutschen und die Judenverfolgung im Dritten Reich*. Hamburger Beiträge zur Sozial- und Zeitgeschichte, 29, ed. Ursula Büttner (Hamburg: Christians, 1992), 105–129.

Mauersberger, Volker. *Hitler in Weimar. Der Fall einer deutschen Kulturstadt* (Berlin: Rowohlt, 1999).

Maurenbrecher, Max. *Der Heiland der Deutschen* (Göttingen: Vandenhoeck & Ruprecht, 1933).

Maurer, Trude. "Ausländische Juden in Deutschland, 1933–1939," in *Die Juden im nationalsozialistischen Deutschland/The Jews in Nazi Germany, 1933–1943*, ed. Arnold Pauker (Tübingen: Mohr Siebeck, 1986), 189–210.

Maurer, Trude. *Ostjuden in Deutschland 1918–1933* (Hamburg: Christians, 1986).

Mayer, Irene. "Berlin-Tiergarten," in *Der Ort des Terrors. Geschichte der nationalsozialistischen Konzentrationslagers*, vol. 2, ed. Wolfgang Benz and Barbara Distel (Munich: Beck, 2005), 64.

Mayer, Karl J. "Kuno Graf Westarp als Kritiker des Nationalsozialismus," in *"Ich bin der letzte Preuße." Der politische Lebensweg des konservativen Politkers Kuno Graf Westarp*, ed. Larry E. Jones and Wolfram Pyta (Cologne, Weimar, and Vienna: Böhlau, 2006), 189–216.

Mehnert, Gottfried. *Evangelische Kirche und Politik. Die politischen Strömungen im deutschen Protestantismus von der Julikrise 1917 bis zum Herbst 1919* (Düsseldorf: Droste, 1959).

Meier, Kurt. *Die deutschen Christen. Das Bild einer Bewegung im Kirchenkampf des Dritten Reiches* (Halle: Niemeyer, 1965).

Meier, Kurt. *Kirche und Judentum. Die Haltung der evangelischen Kirche zur Judenpolitik des Dritten Reiches* (Halle: Niemeyer, 1968).

Meier, Kurt. *Kreuz und Hakenkreuz. Die evangelische Kirche im Dritten Reich*, 2nd ed. (Munich: DTV, 2008).

Menke, Martin. "Misunderstood Civic Duty: The German Center Party and the Enabling Act," *Journal of Church and State*, 51 (2009): 236–264.

Messerschmitt, Manfred. *Die Wehrmacht im NS-Staat. Zeit der Indoktrination* (Hamburg: Decker, 1969).

Meyer, Markus. "Ein schwieriger Patient. Ein Bremer Rechtsanwalt und der 'Juden-boykott' im April 1933," *Arbeiterbewegung und Sozialgeschichte. Zeitschrift für die Regionalgeschichte Bremens im 19. und 20. Jahrhundert*, 11 (2003): 16–29.

Michalka, Wolfgang. *Die nationalsozialistische Machtergreifung* (Paderborn: Schöningh, 1984).

Michalka, Wolfgang, and Martin Vogt, eds. *Judenemanzipation und Antisemitismus in Deutschland im 19. und 20. Jahrhundert* (Eggingen: Edition Isele, 2003).

Mitchell, Allan. *Revolution in Bavaria 1918–1919. The Eisner Regime and the Soviet Republic* (Princeton: Princeton University Press, 1965).

Mommsen, Hans. *Beamtentum im Dritten Reich* (Stuttgart: DVA, 1966).

Mommsen, Hans. "Konservatismus und Faschismus. Zur Einschätzung der NSDAP durch die deutsche politische Rechte vor der nationalsozialistischen Machterober-ung," in *Arbeiterbewegung und Faschismus. Faschismus-Interpretationen in der europäischen Arbeiterbewegung*, ed. Helga Grebing and Klaus Kinner (Essen: Klartext, 1990), 29–38.

Mommsen, Hans. "State and Bureaucracy in the Brüning Era," in *From Weimar to Auschwitz*, ed. Hans Mommsen (Princeton: Princeton University Press, 1991), 79–118.

Mommsen, Hans. *Aufstieg und Untergang der Republik von Weimar 1918–1933* (Berlin: Ullstein, 1998).

Mommsen, Hans. "Die nationalsozialistische Machteroberung: Revolution oder Gegenrevolution?" in *Europäische Socialgeschichte. Festschrift für Wolfgang Schieder*, ed. Christof Dipper, Lutz Klinkhammer, and Alexander Nützenadel (Berlin: Duncker & Humblot, 2000), 41–56.

Mommsen, Hans. *Das NS-Regime und die Auslöschung des Judentums in Europa* (Göttingen: Wallstein, 2014).

Mommsen, Wilhelm, ed. *Deutsche Parteiprogramme*, vol. 1 (Munich: Isar Verlag Olzog, 1960).

Morgenthaler, Sybille. "Countering the pre-1933 Nazi Boycott against Jews," *Leo Baeck Institute Yearbook*, 36 (1991): 127–149.

Morsey, Rudolf. "Die Deutsche Zentrumspartci," in *Das Ende der Parteien 1933*, ed. Erich Matthias and Rudolf Morsey (Düsseldorf: Droste, 1960), 281–453.

Morsey, Rudolf. *Der Untergang des politischen Katholizismus: Die Zentrumspartei zwischen christlichem Selbstverständnis und 'Nationaler Erhebung' 1932/33* (Stuttgart and Zurich: Belser, 1977).

Morsey, Rudolf. *Das Ermächtigungsgesetz* (Düsseldorf: Droste, 1992).

Mosse, George L. "Die deutsche Rechte und die Juden," in *Entscheidungsjahr 1932. Zur Judenfrage in der Endphase der Weimarer Republik*, 2nd ed., ed. Werner E. Mosse (Tübingen: Mohr Siebeck, 1966), 183–246.

Mosse, George L. "Das deutsch-jüdische Bildungsbürgertum," in *Bildungsbürgertum im 19. Jahrhundert*. Vol. II: *Bildungsgüter und Bildungswissen*, ed. Reinhart Koselleck (Stuttgart: Klett, 1990), 168–180.

Mosse, George L. *Confronting History. A Memoir* (Madison: University of Wisconsin Press, 2000).

Mosse, Werner E. "Der Niedergang der Weimarer Republik und die Juden," in *Entscheidungsjahr 1932. Zur Judenfrage in der Endphase der Weimarer Republik*, 2nd ed., ed. Werner E. Mosse (Tübingen: Mohr Siebeck, 1966), 3–49.

Mosse, Werner E., ed. *Entscheidungsjahr 1932. Zur Judenfrage in der Endphase der Weimarer Republik* (Tübingen: Mohr Siebeck, 1966).

Mosse, Werner E., ed. *Deutsches Judentum in Krieg und Revolution 1916–1923*. Schriftenreihe Wissenschaftlicher Abhandlungen des Leo Baeck, 25 (Tübingen: Mohr Siebeck, 1971).

Mosse, Werner E., ed. *Juden im Wilhelminischen Deutschland* (Tübingen: Mohr Siebeck, 1998, first pub. 1976).

Mosse, Werner E. "German Jews: Citizens of the Republic," in *Juden im nationalsozialistischen Deutschland*, ed. Arnold Paucker (Tübingen: Mohr Siebeck, 1986), 45–55.

Mosse, Werner E. "Die Juden in Wirtschaft und Gesellschaft," in *Juden im Wilhelminischen Deutschland*, ed. Werner E. Mosse (Tübingen: Mohr Siebeck, 1998), 57–113.

Mühlen, Bernt Ture von zur. *Gustav Freytag: Biographie* (Göttingen: Wallstein, 2016).

Müller, Christine-Ruth. "Die Judenfrage im Bereich der APU 1933–1945," in *Die Geschichte der Evangelischen Kirche der Union*, vol. III, ed. Gerhard Besier and Eckhart Lessing (Leipzig: Evangelische Verlagsanstalt, 1999), 509–548.

Müller, Hans Peter. "Die Bürgerpartei/Deutschnationale Volkspartei (DNVP) in Württemberg 1918–1933. Konservative Politik und die Zerstörung der Weimarer Republik," *Zeitschrift für Württembergische Landesgeschichte*, 61 (2002): 374–433.

Müller, Ingo. *Hitler's Justice. The Courts of the Third Reich* (Cambridge, MA: Harvard University Press, 1991).

Müller, Klaus-Jürgen. *Das Heer und Hitler. Armee und nationalsozialistisches Regime 1933–1940* (Stuttgart: DVA, 1969).

Müller, Klaus-Jürgen. "Die Reichswehr und die Machtergreifung," in *Die Nationalsozialistische Machtergreifung*, ed. Wolfgang Michalka (Paderborn: Schöningh, 1984), 137–151.

Müller, Klaus-Jürgen. *Armee und Drittes Reich 1933–1939*, 2nd ed. (Paderborn: Schöningh, 1987).

Mulligan, William. "The Reichswehr and the Weimar Republic," in *Weimar Germany*, ed. Anthony McElligott (Oxford: Oxford University Press, 2009), 78–101.

Münch, Ingo von. *Die deutsche Staatsangehörigkeit. Vergangenheit—Gegenwart—Zukunft* (Berlin: De Gruyter, 2007).

Münch, Paul. *Lebensformen in der Frühen Neuzeit* (Frankfurt and Berlin: Ullstein, 1996).

Naser, Gerhard, ed. *Lebenswege Creglinger Juden. Das Pogrom von 1933. Der schwierige Umgang mit der Vergangenheit*, 3rd ed (Bergatreute: Eppe, 2002).

Naumann, Max. *Vom nationaldeutschen Juden* (Berlin: Goldschmidt, 1920).

Neiss, Marion. "Diffamierung mit Tradition – Friedhofschändungen," in *Antisemitismus in Deutschland. Zur Aktualität eines Vorurteils*, ed. Wolfgang Benz (Munich: DTV, 1995), 140–155.

Neitzel, Sönke. *Deutsche Krieger. Vom Kaiserreich zur Berliner Republik—eine Militärgeschichte* (Berlin: Ullstein, 2020).

Neliba, Günter. *Wilhelm Frick. Der Loyalist des Unrechtsstaates. Eine politische Biographie* (Paderborn: Schöningh, 1992).

Nellessen, Bernd. "Die schweigende Kirche. Katholiken und Judenverfolgung," in *Die Deutschen und die Judenverfolgung im Dritten Reich*. Hamburger Beiträge zur Sozial- und Zeitgeschichte, 29, ed. Ursula Büttner (Hamburg: Christians, 1992), 259–271.

Neugebauer, Wolfgang, ed. *Handbuch der preußischen Geschichte*, vol. 3 (Berlin and New York: De Gruyter, 2001).

Neumann, Margarete. *Von Potsdam bis Moskau* (Stuttgart: DVA, 1958).

Nielsen, Philipp. *Between Heimat and Hatred: Jews and the Right in Germany 1871–1935* (New York: Oxford University Press, 2019).

Niethammer, Lutz. *Die Mitläuferfabrik. Die Entnazifizierung am Beispiel Bayerns* (Berlin: Dietz, 1982).

Niewyk, Donald L. *Socialist, Anti-Semite, and Jew. German Social Democracy Confronts the Problem of Anti-Semitism, 1918–1933* (Baton Rouge: Louisiana State University Press, 1971).

Niewyk, Donald L. "The Economic and Cultural Role of Jews in the Weimar Republic," *Leo Baeck Institute Yearbook*, 16 (1971): 163–173.

Niewyk, Donald. "Jews and the Courts in Weimar Germany," *Jewish Social Studies*, 37 (1975): 99–113.

Niewyk, Donald L. *The Jews in Weimar Germany* (Baton Rouge: Louisiana State University Press, 1980).

Niewyk, Donald L. "Solving the 'Jewish Problem': Continuity and Change in German Antisemitism, 1871–1945," *Leo Baeck Institute Yearbook*, 35 (1990): 335–370.

Nikosia, Francis R., and Lawrence D. Stokes. *Germans against Nazism. Nonconformity, Opposition and Resistance in the Third Reich. Essays in Honor of Peter Hoffmann*, rev. ed. (Oxford and New York: Berghahn, 2015).

Nipperdey, Thomas. "Die deutsche Studentenschaft in den ersten Jahren der Weimarer Republik," in *Gesellschaft, Kultur, Theorie: Gesammelte Aufsätze zur neueren Geschichte*. Kritische Studien zur Geschichtswissenschaft, 18, ed. Thomas Nipperdey (Göttingen: Vandenhoeck & Ruprecht, 1976), 390–416.

Nipperdey, Thomas. *Deutsche Geschichte 1800–1866. Bürgerwelt und starker Staat* (Munich: Beck, 1983).

Nipperdey, Thomas. *Deutsche Geschichte 1866–1918*. Vol. I: *Arbeitswelt und Bürgergeist* (Munich: Beck, 1990).

Nipperdey, Thomas, and Reinhard Rürup. "Antisemitismus – Entstehung, Funktion, und Geschichte eines Begriffs," in *Gesellschaft, Kultur, Theorie. Gesammelte Aufsätze zur neuern Geschichte*. Kritische Studien zur Geschichtswissenschaft, 18, ed. Thomas Nipperde (Göttingen: Vandenhoeck & Ruprecht, 1976), 113–132.

Noakes, Jeremy. *The Nazi Party in Lower Saxony 1921–1933* (Oxford: Oxford University Press, 1971).

Noakes, Jeremy. "German Conservatives and the Third Reich: An Ambiguous Relationship," in *Fascists and Conservatives. The Radical Right and the Establishment in Twentieth-century Europe*, ed. Martin Blinkhorn (London: Unwin Hyman: 1990), 71–97.

Nolte, Ernst. "Konservatismus und Nationalsozialismus," *Zeitschrift für Politik*, 11 (1954): 5–20.

Nolte, Ernst. "Europäische Revolutionen des 20. Jahrhunderts. Die nationalsozialistische Machtergreifung im historischen Zusammenhang," in *Die Nationalsozialistische Machtergreifung*, ed. Wolfgang Michalka (Paderborn: Schöningh, 1984), 395–410.

Nolzen, Arnim. "The Nazi Party and its Violence against the Jews, 1933–1939: Violence as a Historiographical Concept," *Yad Vashem Studies*, 31 (2003): 245–285.

Norden, Günther van. *Kirche in der Krise. Die Stellung der evangelischen Kirche zum nationalsozialistischen Staat im Jahre 1933* (Düsseldorf: Presseverband der Evangelischen Kirche, 1963).

Norden, Günther van. *Der deutsche Protestantismus im Jahr der nationalsozialistischen Machtergreifung* (Gütersloh: Mohn, 1979).

Novick, Peter. *That Noble Dream. The "Objectivity Question" and the American Historical Profession* (Cambridge: Cambridge University Press, 1988).

Novick, Peter. *The Holocaust in American Life* (Boston and New York: Houghton Mifflin, 1999).

Nowak, Kurt. *Evangelische Kirche und Weimarer Republik. Zum politischen Weg des deutschen Protestantismus zwischen 1918 und 1932* (Göttingen: Vandenhoeck & Ruprecht, 1981).

Nowak, Kurt. "Die evangelischen Kirchenführer und das Präsidialsystem: Konfessionelle Politik im Spannungsfeld von autoritärem Staatsgeist und kirchenbehördlicher Pragmatik (1930–1932)," in *Die deutsche Staatskrise 1930–1933*. Schriften des Historischen Kollegs, 26, ed. Heinrich-August Winkler (Munich: Oldenbourg, 1992), 19–38.

Nowak, Kurt, and Gérard Raulet, eds., *Protestantismus und Antisemitismus in der Weimarer Republik* (Frankfurt: Campus, 1994).

Ohnezeit, Maik. *Zwischen "schärfster Opposition" und dem "Willen zur Macht." Die Deutschnationale Volkspartei (DNVP) in der Weimarer Republik 1918–1928* (Düsseldorf: Droste, 2011).

Olenhusen, Albrecht Götz von. "Die 'nichtarischen' Studenten an den deutschen Hochschulen: Zur nationalsozialistischen Rassenpolitik 1933–1945," *Vierteljahrshefte für Zeitgeschichte*, 14, no. 2 (April 1966): 175–206.

Ostrowski, Siegfried. "Vom Schicksal Jüdischer Ärzte im Dritten Reich. Ein Augenzeugenbericht aus den Jahren 1933–1939," *Bulletin des Leo-Baeck Instituts*, 6, no. 24 (1963): 313–351.

Paschen, Joachim. *Hamburg zwischen Hindenburg und Hitler. Die nationalsozialistische Machteroberung in einer roten Festung* (Bremen: Edition Temmen, 2013).

Patch, William L. Jr. "Nationalism, Socialism and Organized Labor's Response to the Dissolution of the Weimar Republic," in *From Weimar to Hitler. Studies on the Dissolution of Weimar Democracy and the Establishment of the Third Reich, 1932–34*, ed. Hermann Beck and Larry E. Jones (Oxford and New York: Berghahn Books, 2019), 248–280.

Pätzold, Kurt. *Faschismus, Rassenwahn, Judenverfolgung. Eine Studie zur politischen Strategie und Taktik des faschistischen deutschen Imperialismus* (Berlin/GDR: Verlag der Wissenschaften, 1975).

Paucker, Arnold. "Der jüdische Abwehrkampf," in *Entscheidungsjahr 1932. Zur Judenfrage in der Endphase der Weimarer Republik*, 2nd ed., ed. Werner E. Mosse (Tübingen: Mohr Siebeck, 1966), 405–499.

Paucker, Arnold, ed. *Die Juden im nationalsozialistischen Deutschland* (Tübingen: Mohr 1986).

Paul, Gerhard. *Aufstand der Bilder. Die NS-Propaganda vor 1933* (Bonn: J. H. W. Dietz, 1990).

Paul, Gerhard, and Miriam Gillis-Carlebach, eds. *Menora und Hakenkreuz. Zur Geschichte der Juden in und aus Schleswig-Holstein, Lübeck und Altona, 1918–1998* (Neumünster: Wachholtz, 1998).

Payne, Stanley G. *Fascism. Comparison and Definition* (Madison: University of Wisconsin Press, 1980).

Payne, Stanley G. *A History of Fascism, 1914–1945* (Madison: University of Wisconsin Press, 1995).

Pegelow, Thomas. "'German Jews', 'National Jews', 'Jewish Volk', or 'Racial Jews'? The Constitution and Contestation of 'Jewishness' in Newspapers of Nazi Germany, 1933–1938," *Central European History*, 35, no. 2 (2002): 195–221.

Pegelow, Thomas. *The Language of Nazi Genocide. Linguistic Violence and the Struggle of Germans of Jewish Ancestry* (Cambridge: Cambridge University Press, 2009).

Petter, Wolfgang. "Wehrmacht und Judenverfolgung," in *Die Deutschen und die Judenverfolgung im Dritten Reich*. Hamburger Beiträge zur Sozial- und Zeitgeschichte, 29, ed. Ursula Büttner (Hamburg: Christians, 1992), 161–178.

Petzina, Dietmar, Werner Abelshauser, and Anselm Faust. *Sozialgeschichtliches Arbeitsbuch, 1914–1945* (Munich: Beck, 1978).

Pine, Lisa. *Nazi Family Policy, 1933–1945* (Oxford: Oxford University Press, 1997).

Pohl, Monika. *Ludwig Marum. Gegner des Nationalsozialismus. Das Verfolgungsschicksal eines Sozialdemokraten jüdischer Herkunft* (Karlsruhe: Info, 2013).

Pommerin, Reiner. "Die Ausweisung von 'Ostjuden' aus Bayern 1923. Ein Beitrag zum Krisenjahr der Weimarer Republik," *Vierteljahrshefte für Zeitgeschichte*, 34 (1986): 311–340.

Ponsonby, Arthur. *Falsehood in Wartime. Containing an Assortment of Lies Circulated throughout the Nations during the Great War* (London: Allen & Unwin, 1928).

Popper, K. R. *The Open Society and its Enemies*. Vol. 2: *Hegel and Marx* (London and Henley: Routledge & Kegan Paul, 1966).

Proctor, Robert N. *Racial Hygiene: Medicine under the Nazis* (Cambridge, MA: Harvard University Press, 1988).

Prolingheuer, Hans. *Kleine politische Kirchengeschichte. Fünfzig Jahre Evangelischer Kirchenkampf von 1919 bis 1969* (Cologne: Pahl-Rugenstein, 1984).

Pulzer, Peter. *The Rise of Political Anti-Semitism in Germany and Austria*, rev. ed. (Cambridge, MA: Harvard University Press, 1988).

Pulzer, Peter. *Jews and the German State. The Political History of a Minority* (Oxford: Blackwell, 1992).

Pulzer, Peter. "Die jüdische Beteiligung an der Politik," in *Juden im Wilhelminischen Deutschland 1890–1914; ein Sammelband*. 2nd ed., ed. Werner E. Mosse (Tübingen: Mohr Siebeck, 1998), 143–239.

Rahden, Till van. *Juden und andere Breslauer. Die Beziehungen zwischen Juden, Protestanten und Katholiken in einer deutschen Großstadt von 1860 bis 1925* (Göttingen: Vandenhoeck & Ruprecht, 2000).

Raschke, Rainer, and Verein Stiftung Scheunenviertel, eds. *Spuren eines verlorenen Berlin. Das Scheunenviertel* (Berlin: Haude & Spener, 1994).

Read, James Morgan. *Atrocity Propaganda 1914–1919* (New Haven: Yale University Press, 1941).

Reichardt, Sven. *Faschistische Kampfbünde. Gewalt und Gemeinschaft im italienischen Squadrismus und in der deutschen SA* (Cologne, Weimar, and Vienna: Böhlau, 2002).

Reiche, Eric G. "From 'Spontaneous' to Legal Terror: SA Police and the Judiciary in Nürnberg, 1933–34," *European Studies Review*, 9 (1979): 237–264.

Reiche, Eric G. *The Development of the SA in Nürnberg, 1922–1934* (Cambridge: Cambridge University Press, 1986).

Reichmann, Eva. "Diskussionen über die Judenfrage 1930–1932," in *Entscheidungsjahr 1932. Zur Judenfrage in der Endphase der Weimarer Republik*, 2nd ed., ed. Werner E. Mosse (Tübingen: Mohr Siebeck, 1966), 503–531.

Reichmann, Eva."Der Bewußtseinswandel der deutschen Juden," in *Deutsches Judentum in Krieg und Revolution 1916–1923*, ed. Werner E. Mosse (Tübingen: Mohr Siebeck, 1971), 511–612.

Retallack, James. "Zwei Vertreter des preußischen Konservatismus im Spiegel ihres Briefwechsels: Die Heydebrand – Westarp Korrespondenz," in *"Ich bin der letzte Preuße." Der politische Lebensweg des konservativen Politkers Kuno Graf Westarp*, ed. Larry E. Jones and Wolfram Pyta (Cologne, Weimar, and Vienna: Böhlau, 2006), 33–60.

Rheins, Carl J. "The Verband nationaldeutscher Juden 1921–1922," *Leo Baeck Institute Yearbook*, 25, no. 1 (1980): 243–268.

Ribbe, Wolfgang, ed. *Geschichte Berlins*. Vol. 2: *Von der Märzrevolution bis zur Gegenwart* (Munich: Beck, 1987).

Richarz, Monika, ed. *Jüdisches Leben in Deutschland. Selbstzeugnisse zur Sozialgeschichte, 1918–1945*, vol. III (Stuttgart: DVA, 1982).

Richter, Hedwig, and Ralph Jessen. "Elections, Plebiscites, and Festivals," in *The Oxford Illustrated History of the Third Reich*, ed. Robert Gellately (Oxford: Oxford University Press, 2018), 85–117.

Richter, Ludwig. *Die Deutsche Volkspartei 1918–1933* (Düsseldorf: Droste, 2002).

Rogger, Hans. "Reforming Jews – Reforming Russians," in *Hostages of Modernization. Current Research on Antisemitism*. Vol. 3/2: *Austria-Hungary-Poland-Russia*, ed. Herbert A. Strauss (Berlin and New York: De Gruyter, 1993), 1208–1229.

Rohe, Karl. *Das Reichsbanner Schwarz-Rot-Gold* (Düsseldorf: Droste, 1966).

Röhm, Eberhard, and Jörg Thierfelder. "Die evangelische Kirche und die Machtergreifung," in *Die nationalsozialistische Machtergreifung*, ed. Wolfgang Michalka (Paderborn: Schöningh, 1984), 168–181.

Röhm, Eberhard, and Jörg Thierfelder. *Juden, Christen, Deutsche*. Vol 1: *1933–1935*, 2nd ed. (Stuttgart: Calwer, 2004).

Roos, Daniel. *Julius Streicher und "Der Stürmer"* (Paderborn: Schöningh, 2014).

Rosenthal, Jacob. *"Die Ehre des jüdischen Soldaten." Die Judenzählung im Ersten Weltkrieg und ihre Folgen* (Frankfurt and New York: Campus, 2007).

Rother, Rainer, ed. *Die letzten Tage der Menschheit. Bilder des ersten Weltkrieges* (Berlin: Deutsches Historisches Museum, 1994).

Rürup, Reinhard. "Das Ende der Emanzipation: Die antijüdische Politik in Deutschland von der 'Machtergreifung' bis zum Zweiten Weltkrieg," in *Die Juden im nationalsozialistischen Deutschland/The Jews in Nazi Germany, 1933–1943*, ed. Arnold Pauker (Tübingen: Mohr Siebeck, 1986), 97–114.

Rürup, Reinhard. "Emanzipation und Krise – Zur Geschichte der 'Judenfrage' in Deutschland vor 1890," in *Juden im Wilhelminischen Deutschland 1890–1914; ein Sammelband*, 2nd ed., ed. Werner E. Mosse (Tübingen: Mohr Siebeck, 1998), 1–56.

Rüthers, Bernd. *Die unbegrenzte Auslegung. Zum Wandel der Privatrechtsordnung im Nationalsozialismus*, 7th ed. (Tübingen: Mohr Siebeck, 2012).

Ryback, Timothy W. *Hitler's First Victims. The Quest for Justice* (New York: Knopf, 2014).

Sanders, Michael, and Philip Taylor. *British Propaganda during the First World War, 1914–1918* (London: Palgrave Macmillan, 1982).

Schäfer, Kirstin, and Werner von Blomberg. *Hitlers erster Feldmarschall. Eine Biographie* (Paderborn: Schönigh, 2006).

Scheurig, Bodo. *Ewald von Kleist-Schmenzin. Ein Konservativer gegen Hitler* (Berlin: Propyläen, 1994).

Schieder, Theodor. "Ludwig Dehio zum Gedächtnis," *Historische Zeitschrift*, 201 (1965): 1–12.

Schild, Wolfgang. *Folter, Pranger, Scheiterhaufen. Rechtssprechung im Mittelalter* (Munich: Bassermann, 2010).

Schleunes, Karl. *The Twisted Road to Auschwitz. Nazi Policy toward German Jews* (Urbana: University of Illinois Press, 1970).

Schmid, Arnim, and Renate Schmid. *Frankfurt in stürmischer Zeit 1930–1933* (Stuttgart: Konrad Theiss, 1987).

Schnabel, Franz. *Deutsche Geschichte im 19. Jahrhundert*, 4th ed., vol. I (Freiburg: Herder, 1948).

Schnabel, Thomas, ed. *Die Machtergreifung in Südwestdeutschland. Das Ende der Weimarer Republik in Baden und Württemburg 1928–1933* (Stuttgart: Kohlhammer, 1986).

Schneider, Michael. "The Development of State Work Creation Policy in Germany, 1930–1933," in *Unemployment and the Great Depression in Weimar Germany*, ed. Peter Stachura (London: Macmillan, 1986), 163–186.

Schneider, Michael. *Unterm Hakenkreuz. Arbeiter und Arbeiterbewegung 1933 bis 1939* (Berlin: Aufbau, 1999).

Schoeps, Hans-Joachim. *Die letzten dreißig Jahre. Rückblicke* (Stuttgart: Klett, 1956).

Scholder, Klaus. "Die Krise der dreißiger Jahre als Fragen an Christentum und Kirche," in *Die Große Krise der dreißiger Jahre. Vom Niedergang der Weltwirtschaft zum Zweiten Weltkrieg*, ed. Gerhard Schulz (Göttingen: Vandenhoeck & Ruprecht, 1985), 101–119.

Scholder, Klaus. *Die Kirchen und das Dritte Reich. Vorgeschichte und Zeit der Illusionen* (Frankfurt: Propyläen, 1977). English trans.: *The Churches and the Third Reich*. Vol. I: *Preliminary History and the Time of Illusions, 1918–1934* (Philadelphia: Fortress Press, 1988, first pub. 1977).

Scholder, Klaus. *Die Kirchen zwischen Republik und Gewaltherrschaft; gesammelte Aufsätze*, ed. Karl Otmar von Aretin and Gerhard Besier (Berlin: Siedler, 1988).

Scholder, Klaus. *Die Kirchen und das Dritte Reich. Vorgeschichte und Zeit der Illusionen* (Berlin: Ullstein, 2000).

Scholtyseck, Joachim. "Die deutschen Eliten im Jahr 1933: War Widerstand möglich?" in *Das Jahr 1933: Die nationalsozialistische Machteroberung und die deutsche Gesellschaft*. Dachauer Symposien zur Zeitgeschichte, 9, ed. Andreas Wirsching (Göttingen: Wallstein, 2009), 110–131.

Scholz, Robert. "Ein unruhiges Jahrzehnt: Lebensmittelunruhen, Massenstreiks und Arbeitslosenkrawalle in Berlin 1914–1923," in *Pöbelexzesse und Volkstumulte in Berlin: Zur Sozialgeschichte der Straße 1830–1980*, ed. Manfred Gailus (Berlin: Europäische Perspektiven, 1984), 79–123.

Schönhoven, Klaus. *Die deutschen Gewerkschaften* (Frankfurt: Suhrkamp, 1987).

Schönhoven, Klaus, and Hans-Jochen Vogel, eds. *Frühe Warnungen vor dem Nationalsozialismus* (Bonn: Dietz, 1998).

Schramm, Michael. *Das Deutschlandbild in der britischen Presse 1912–1919* (Munich: De Gruyter, 2007).

Schramm, Percy Ernst. *Neun Generationen. Dreihundert Jahre deutsche Kulturgeschichte im Licht der Schicksale einer Hamburger Bürgerfamilie (1648–1948)*, vol. I (Göttingen: Vandenhoeck & Ruprecht, 1963).

Schröder, Joachim. "Der erste Weltkrieg und der 'jüdische Bolschewismus,'" in *Nationalsozialismus und Erster Weltkrieg*, ed. Gerd Krumeich (Essen: Klartext, 2010), 77–96.

Schüler, Hermann. *Auf der Flucht erschossen. Felix Fechenbach 1894–1933* (Cologne: Kiepenheuer & Witsch, 1981).

Schüler-Springorum, Stefanie. *Die jüdische Minderheit in Königsberg/Preußen, 1871–1945* (Göttingen: Vandenhoeck & Ruprecht, 1996).

Schulze, Hagen. *Weimar. Deutschland 1917–1933* (Berlin: Siedler, 1982).

Schumann, Dirk. "Gewalt als Methode der nationalsozialistischen Machteroberung," in *Das Jahr 1933. Die nationalsozialistische Machteroberung und die deutsche Gesellschaft*, ed. Andreas Wirsching (Göttingen: Wallstein, 2009), 135–156.

Schumann, Dirk. *Politische Gewalt in der Weimarer Republik 1918–1933. Kampf um die Straße und Furcht vor dem Bürgerkrieg* (Essen: Klartext, 2001). English trans.: *Political Violence in the Weimar Republic 1918–1933. Fight for the Streets and Fear of Civil War* (New York: Berghahn, 2009).

Schurr, Stefan. "Die 'Judenaktion' in Creglingen am 25. März 1933. Eine Quellendokumentation," in *Lebenswege Creglinger Juden. Das Pogrom von 1933. Der schwierige Umgang mit der Vergangenheit*, 3rd ed., ed. Gerhard Naser (Bergatreute: Eppe, 2002), 59–82.

Schwabe, Klaus. *Weltmacht und Weltordnung. Amerikanische Außenpolitik von 1898 bis zur Gegenwart* (Paderborn: Schöningh, 2006).

Seghers, Anna. *Das Siebte Kreuz* (Berlin: Aufbau, 1996; first pub. 1942).

Seton-Watson, Hugh. "Two Contending Policies Toward Jews: Russia and Hungary," in *Hostages of Modernization. Studies on Modern Anti-Semitism 1870–1933/1939*. Vol. 3/2: *Austria-Hungary-Poland-Russia*, ed. Herbert A. Strauss (Berlin and New York: De Gruyter, 1993), 948–960.

Seul, Stephanie. "Herr Hitler's Nazis Hear an Echo of World Opinion: British and American Press Responses to Nazi Anti-Semitism, September 1930- April 1933," *Politics, Religion, and Ideology*, 14 (September 2013): 412–430.

Siemens, Daniel. *Stormtroopers. A New History of Hitler's Brownshirts* (New Haven: Yale University Press, 2017).

Silverman, Dan P. "Nazification of the German Bureaucracy Reconsidered: A Case Study," *Journal of Modern History*, 60 (1988): 496–539.

Silverman, Dan P. "Fantasy and Reality in Nazi Work-Creation Programs, 1933–1936," *Journal of Modern History*, 65 (1993): 113–151.

Smelser, Ronald, and Enrico Syring, eds. *Die SS. Elite unter dem Totenkopf. 30 Lebensläufe* (Paderborn: Schöningh, 2000).

Smid, Marikje. *Deutscher Protestantismus und Judentum 1932/33* (Munich: Kaiser, 1990).

Sommer, Wolfgang. *Wilhelm Freiherr von Pechmann. Ein konservativer Lutheraner* (Göttingen: Vandenhoeck & Ruprecht, 2010).

Spicer, Kevin. *Resisting the Third Reich. The Catholic Clergy in Hitler's Berlin* (De Kalb: Northern Illinois Press, 2004).

Steigmann-Gall, Richard. *The Holy Reich. Nazi Conceptions of Christianity 1919–1945* (Cambridge: Cambridge University Press, 2003).

Steinert, Marlis. "Hitler's Krieg und die Deutschen," in *Die Große Krise der dreißiger Jahre. Vom Niedergang der Weltwirtschaft zum Zweiten Weltkrieg,* ed. Gerhard Schulz (Göttingen: Vandenhoeck & Ruprecht, 1985), 137–153.

Stern, Frank. "Evangelische Kirche zwischen Antisemitismus und Philosemitismus." *Geschichte und Gesellschaft,* 18 (1992): 22–50.

Stern, Fritz. *The Politics of Cultural Despair: A Study in the Rise of Germanic Ideology.* (Berkeley, Los Angeles, and London: University of California Press, 1974).

Stern, Fritz. *Gold and Iron. Bismarck, Bleichröder, and the Building of the German Empire* (New York: Vintage, 1979).

Stern, Fritz. "National Socialism as Temptation," in Fritz Stern, *Dreams and Delusions. The Drama of German History* (New York: Vintage, 1979), 147–191.

Stern, Fritz. *Dreams and Delusions. The Drama of German History* (New York: Vintage, 1989).

Stern, Fritz. "Germany 1933: Fifty Years Later," in Fritz Stern, *Dreams and Delusions. The Drama of German History* (New York: Vintage, 1989), 119–146.

Stern, Fritz. "Das Feine Schweigen und seine Folgen," in Fritz Stern, *Das Feine Schweigen. Historische Essays* (Munich: Beck, 1999), 158–173.

Stern, Fritz. *Five Germanies I Have Known* (New York: Farrar, Straus, & Giroux, 2007).

Stoll, Gerhard E. *Die evangelische Zeitschriftenpresse im Jahre 1933* (Witten: Luther-Verlag, 1963).

Stolleis, Michael. "Gemeinschaft und Volksgemeinschaft. Zur juristischen Terminologie im Nationalsozialismus," *Vierteljahrshefte für Zeitgeschichte,* 20 (1972): 16–38.

Strauss, Herbert A. ed. *Hostages of Modernization, Studies on Modern Anti-Semitism 1870–1933/1939.* Vol. 3/2: *Austria-Hungary-Poland-Russia* (Berlin and New York: De Gruyter, 1993).

Strenge, Irene. *Machtübernahme 1933 – Alles auf legalem Weg* (Berlin: Duncker & Humblot, 2002).

Strickler, Matthias. "Kollaboration oder weltanschauliche Distanz? Katholische Kirche und NS-Staat," in *Die Katholiken und das Dritte Reich,* 2nd ed., ed. Karl-Joseph Hummel and Michael Kißner (Paderborn: Schöningh, 2010), 83–99.

Striesow, Jan. *Die Deutschnationale Volkpartei und die Völkisch-Radikalen, 1918–1922,* 2 vols. (Frankfurt: Haag, 1981).

Stupperich, Amrei. *Volksgemeinschaft oder Arbeitersolidarität. Studien zur Arbeitnehmerpolitik in der Deutschnationalen Volkspartei, 1918–1933* (Göttingen: Muster-Schmidt, 1982).

Stupperich, Robert. *Otto Dibelius. Ein evangelischer Bischof im Umbruch der Zeiten* (Göttingen: Vandenhoeck & Ruprecht, 1989).

Süle, Tibor. *Preußische Bürokratietradition* (Göttingen: Vandenhoeck & Ruprecht, 1988).

Thadden, Rudolf von. "Die Geschichte der Kirchen und Konfessionen," in *Handbuch der preußischen Geschichte*, vol. III, ed. Wolfgang Neugebauer (Berlin and New York: De Gruyter, 2001).

Thamer, Hans-Ulrich. *Verführung und Gewalt. Deutschland 1933–1945* (Berlin: Siedler, 1986).

Thieme, Karl. "Deutsche Katholiken," in *Entscheidungsjahr 1932. Zur Judenfrage in der Endphase der Weimarer Republik*, 2nd ed., ed. Werner E. Mosse (Tübingen: Mohr Siebeck, 1966), 271–289.

Thunecke, Jörg. "Es sind nicht alle frei, die ihrer Ketten spotten," in *Raabe-Rapporte. Literaturwissenschaftliche und literatur-didaktische Zugänge zum Werk Wilhelm Raabes*, ed. Sigrid Thielking (Wiesbaden: Deutscher Universitätsverlag, 2002), 57–67.

Tinnemann, Ethel Mary. "Attitudes of the German Catholic Hierarchy toward the Nazi Regime: A Study in German Psycho-Political Culture," *The Western Political Quarterly*, 22 (1969): 333–349.

Tomaszewski, Jerzy. "Położenie Żydów w Niemczech na Wiosnę 1933 r. w Reportach Poselstwa RP oraz Konsulatu Generalnego RP w Berlinie" ("The Situation of the Jews in Germany in Spring 1933 as Reflected in Reports of the Polish Republic Legation and Consulate General in Berlin"). *Biuletyn Żydowskiego Instytutu Historycznego*, Nos. 3–4 (1986): 131–142.

Tomaszewski, Jerzy. "Polish Diplomats and the Fate of Polish Jews in Nazi Germany," *Acta Poloniae Historica*, 61 (1990): 183–204.

Toury, Jacob. *Die politischen Orientierungen der Juden in Deutschland. Von Jena bis Weimar* (Tübingen: Mohr Siebeck, 1966).

Treue, Wilhelm. "Zur Frage der wirtschaftlichen Motive im deutschen Antisemitismus," in *Deutsches Judentum in Krieg und Revolution 1916–1923*, ed. Werner E. Mosse. (Tübingen: Mohr Siebeck, 1971), 387–408.

Trippe, Christian F. *Konservative Verfassungpolitik 1918–1923. Die DNVP als Opposition in Reich und Ländern* (Düsseldorf: Droste, 1995).

Tuchman, Barbara. *The Proud Tower. A Portrait of the World Before the War, 1890–1914.* (New York: Bantham, 1969).

Turner, Henry A., ed. *Nazism and the Third Reich* (New York: Quadrangle, 1972).

Turner, Henry A. *Hitler's Thirty Days to Power: January 1933* (New York: Addison-Wesley, 1996).

Tyrell, Albrecht. *Führer befiel . . . Selbstzeugnisse aus der "Kampfzeit" der NSDAP* (Düsseldorf: Droste, 1969).

Uhlig, Heinrich. *Die Warenhäuser im Dritten Reich* (Cologne: Westdeutscher Verlag, 1956).

Ulbrich, Bernd G. *Nationalsozialismus und Antisemitismus in Anhalt. Skizzen aus den Jahren 1932 bis 1942* (Dessau: Edition RK, 2005).

Vogt, Stefan. *Nationaler Sozialismus und soziale Demokratie. Die sozialdemokratische Junge Rechte 1918–1945* (Bonn: Dietz, 2006).

Vogt, Stefan. "Nationalist Socialism against National Socialism? Perceptions of Nazism and Anti-Nazi Strategies in the Circle of the Neue Blätter für den Sozialismus, 1930–1934," in *From Weimar to Hitler. Studies in the Dissolution of the Weimar Republic and the Establishment of the Third Reich, 1932–1934*, ed. Hermann Beck and Larry E. Jones (New York: Berghahn, 2019), 222–247.

Volk, Ludwig. *Der bayerische Episkopat und der Nationalsozialismus 1930–1934*, 2nd. ed. (Mainz: Grünewald, 1966).

Volk, Ludwig. *Katholische Kirche und Nationalsozialismus. Ausgewählte Aufsätze* (Mainz: Grünewald, 1987).

Volkmann, Peer Oliver. *Heinrich Brüning (1885–1970). Nationalist ohne Heimat. Eine Teilbibliographie* (Düsseldorf: Droste, 2007).

Volkov, Shulamit. "Antisemitismus als kultureller Code," in *Jüdisches Leben und Antisemitismus im 19. und 20. Jahrhundert*, ed. Shulamit Volkov (Munich: Beck, 1990), 13–36.

Volkov, Shulamit. "Die Dynamik der Dissimilation: Deutsche Juden und die ostjüdischen Einwanderer," in *Jüdisches Leben und Antisemitismus im 19. und 20. Jahrhundert*, ed. Shulamit Volkov (Munich: Beck, 1990), 166–180.

Wachsmann, Nikolaus. *KL: A History of the Nazi Concentration Camps* (New York: Farrar, Straus, & Giroux, 2015).

Walter, Dirk. *Antisemitische Kriminalität und Gewalt. Judenfeindschaft in der Weimarer Republik* (Bonn: Dietz, 1999).

Wassermann, Henry, and Eckhart G. Franz. "'Kauft nicht beim Juden.' Der politische Antisemitismus des späten 19. Jahrhunderts," in *Juden als Darmstädter Bürger*, ed. Eckhart G. Franz (Darmstadt: Roether, 1984), 123–136.

Weber, Reinhold. *Bürgerpartei und Bauernbund in Württemberg. Konservative Parteien im Kaiserreich und in Weimar (1895–1933)* (Düsseldorf: Droste, 2004).

Weber, Thomas. *Becoming Hitler. The Making of a Nazi* (Oxford: Oxford University Press, 2017).

Wehler, Hans-Ulrich. *Deutsche Gesellschaftsgeschichte*, vols. IV and V (Munich: Beck, 2008).

Wein, Martin. *Willy Brandt, Das Werden eines Staatsmannes* (Berlin: Aufbau, 2003).

Weiß, Hermann, and Paul Hoser, eds. *Die Deutschnationalen und die Zerstörung der Weimarer Republik. Aus dem Tagebuch von Reinhold Quaatz 1928–1933* (Munich: Oldenbourg, 1989).

Weiss, Yfaat. "'Ostjuden' in Deutschland als Freiwild. Die nationalsozialistische Außenpolitik zwischen Ideologie und Wirklichkeit," *Tel Aviver Jahrbuch für deutsche Geschichte*, 23 (1994): 215–232.

Wenth, Frederick K. "American Protestant Journals and the Nazi Religious Assault." *Church History*, 23 (1954): 321–338.

Wertheimer, Jack. *Unwelcome Strangers: East European Jews in Imperial Germany* (New York: Oxford University Press, 1987).

Wette, Wolfram. *Die Wehrmacht. Feindbilder, Vernichtungskrieg, Legenden* (Frankfurt/Main: Fischer, 2002).

Whalen, R. W. *Bitter Wounds: German Victims of the Great War, 1914–1939* (Ithaca: Cornell Press, 1984).

Wiener, Philip B. "Die Parteien der Mitte," in *Entscheidungsjahr 1932. Zur Judenfrage in der Endphase der Weimarer Republik*, 2nd ed., ed. Werner E. Mosse (Tübingen: Mohr Siebeck, 1966), 289–321.

Wildt, Michael. "Violence against Jews in Germany, 1933–1939," in *Probing the Depths of German Antisemitism. German Society and the Persecution of the Jews, 1933–1941,* ed. David Bankier (New York: Berghahn, 2000).

Wildt, Michael. *Generation des Unbedingten. Das Führungskorps des Reichssicherheitshauptamtes* (Hamburg: Hamburger Edition, 2003).

Wildt, Michael. *Volksgemeinschaft als Selbstermächtigung. Gewalt gegen Juden in der Deutschen Provinz 1919 bis 1939* (Hamburg: Hamburger Edition, 2007).

Wildt, Michael. *Hitler's Volksgemeinschaft and the Dynamics of Racial Exclusion* (New York: Berghahn, 2012).

Wildt, Michael. "Volksgemeinschaft: A Modern Perspective on National Socialist Society," in *Visions of Community in Nazi Germany: Social Engineering and Private Lives,* ed. Martina Steber and Bernhard Gotto (Oxford: Oxford University Press, 2014).

Wilhelmi, Heinrich. *Die Hamburger Kirche in der nationalsozialistischen Zeit 1933–1945. Arbeiten zur Geschichte des Kirchenkampfes,* vol. 5 (Göttingen: Vandenhoeck & Ruprecht, 1968).

Williams, Jenny. *Mehr Leben als eins. Hans Fallada. Biografie* (Berlin: Aufbau, 2011).

Winkler, Heinrich August. *Mittelstand, Demokratie und Nationalsozialismus. Die politische Entwicklung von Handwerk und Kleinhandel in der Weimarer Republik* (Cologne: Kiepenheuer, 1972).

Winkler, Heinrich August. *Der Weg in die Katastrophe. Arbeiter und Arbeiterbewegung in der Weimarer Republic 1930–1933,* 2nd ed. (Bonn: Dietz, 1990).

Winkler, Heinrich August. *Weimar 1918–1933,* 4th ed. (Munich: Beck, 2005).

Wirsching, Andreas. *Vom Weltkrieg zum Bürgerkrieg? Politischer Extremismus in Deutschland und Frankreich, 1918–1933/39. Berlin und Paris im Vergleich* (Munich: Oldenbourg, 1999).

Wirsching, Andreas, ed. *Das Jahr 1933: Die nationalsozialistische Machteroberung und die deutsche Gesellschaft.* Dachauer Symposien zur Zeitgeschichte, 9. (Göttingen: Wallstein, 2009).

Wolf, Hubert. *Papst und Teufel. Die Archive des Vatikan und das Dritte Reich* (Munich: Beck, 2012).

Wright, Jonathan R. C. *"Über den Parteien." Die politische Haltung der evangelischen Kirchenführer 1918–1933* (Göttingen: Vandenhoeck & Ruprecht, 1977).

Wünschmann, Kim. *Before Auschwitz: Jewish Prisoners in the Prewar Concentration Camps* (Cambridge, MA: Harvard University Press, 2015).

Zechlin, Egmont. *Die deutsche Politik und die Juden im Ersten Weltkrieg* (Göttingen: Vandenhoeck & Ruprecht, 1969).

Ziemann, Benjamin. "Martin Niemöller als völkisch-nationaler Studentenpolitiker in Münster 1919 bis 1923," *Vierteljahrshefte für Zeitgeschichte,* 67, no. 2 (2019): 209–234.

Zilkenat, Rainer. "Der Pogrom am 5. und 6. November 1923," in *Spuren eines verlorenen Berlin. Das Scheunenviertel,* ed. Thomas Raschke and Verein Stiftung Scheunenviertel (Berlin: Haude & Spener, 1994).

Zimmerman, Moshe. *Die Deutschen Juden 1914–1945.* (Munich: Oldenbourg, 1997).

Zmarzlik, Hans-Günter. "Der Antisemitismus im Zeiten Reich," *Geschichte in Wissenschaft und Unterricht,* 14 (1963): 272–286.

Zmarzlik, Hans-Günter. "Der Sozialdarwinismus in Deutschland als geschichtliches Problem," *Vierteljahrshefte für Zeitgeschichte,* 11 (1963): 246–273.

ACKNOWLEDGEMENTS

My first debt of gratitude goes to the many archivists without whose invaluable assistance the archival research for this work would not have been possible. I am especially grateful to the following achivists and archives: Dr. Christoph Bachmann, Staatsarchiv München; Dr. Bernhard Grau, Bayerisches Hauptstaatsarchiv München; Dr. Klaus A. Lankheit, Institut für Zeitgeschichte, München; Marco Birn, Landesarchiv Baden-Württemberg, Hauptstaatsarchiv Stuttgart; Dr. Martin Stingl and Andreas Neuburger, Landesarchiv Baden-Württemberg, Generallandes-archiv Karlsruhe; Dr. Volker Eichler, Hessisches Landesarchiv, Haupt-staatsarchiv Wiesbaden; Reinhold Bauer, Alois Fischer, and Annegret Neupert, Bundesarchiv Koblenz; Carina Notzke and Jana Brabant, Bundesarchiv-Militärarchiv Freiburg; Regina Hönerlage, Dr. Brachtendorf, and Dr. Astrid Küntzel, Landesarchiv Nordrhein-Westfalen; Dr. Jörg Ludwig, Hauptstaatsarchiv Dresden; Kristin Schubert, Landeskirchen-archiv Dresden; Matthias Meissner, Simone Langner, and Torsten Zarwel, Bundesarchiv Berlin-Lichterfelde; Dr. Ulrich Kober, Geheimes Staatsarchiv Preußischer Kulturbesitz, Berlin-Dahlem; Wolfgang Krogel, Dr. Karin Köhler, and Dr. Peter Beier, Evangelisches Zentralarchiv Berlin; Dr. Ilse Fischer, Archiv der sozialen Demokratie der Friedrich-Ebert Stiftung, Bonn; Denia Kalinowsky and Dr. Claudia Kauertz, Niedersäch-sisches Landesarchiv, Hauptstaatsarchiv Hannover; Dr. Matthias Manke and Christine Buchta, Landeshauptarchiv Schwerin; Dr. Bernd Ulbrich, Moses Mendelssohn Gesellschaft Dessau; Kristin Kalisch, Staatsarchiv Hamburg; Dr. Stephan Linck and Angelika Mittelsteiner, Archiv der Nordkirche, Kiel; Prof. Dr. Dr. Rainer Hering and Dr. Elke Imberger, Landesarchiv Schleswig-Holstein in Schleswig; and Dr. Frank Boblenz, Landesarchiv Thüringen in Weimar.

The College of Arts & Sciences at the University of Miami and its Dean, Leonidas Bachas, provided perhaps the most precious gift of all—free time to pursue my research and writing in the form of two sabbaticals, a Cooper Research Leave, and a fellowship from the UM Center for the Humanities. For this consistent support and encouragement, I remain grateful. I also wish to thank Al Nahmad for his generous research support.

From among my colleagues at the University of Miami who helped me the most while this book was in the making, occasionally more than they knew themselves, my special thanks go to Daniel Pals, Haim Shaked, and Donald Spivey. History colleagues who generously facilitated and furthered work on this book in various ways from collaboration on panels, invitations to give talks, or extensive correspondence include Joseph Bendersky, Robert Gellately, Rainer Hering, and Larry E. Jones.

This book owes more than words can express to my wife, who diligently and repeatedly read every word of the manuscript, made valuable suggestions as to its contents, critiqued every chapter, and fine-tuned its wording and style by compelling me to be more detailed and specific, as well as economical in wording. Her unflagging attention to detail was also crucial in the copy-editing process and her help with the translation of opaque German passages was invaluable. Because of her efforts this is a better and more readable book. It goes without saying that all remaining errors are my own.

INDEX

For the benefit of digital users, indexed terms that span two pages (e.g., 52–53) may, on occasion, appear on only one of those pages.

Aachen 100n.111
Abraham, Martes 70–1
Abramowicz, David 224–5
Adam, Uwe Dietrich 40–1, 271n.119
Adenauer, Konrad 47–8, 300–1, 384–5, 385n.27, 399, 462–3
ADGB (see also trade unions) 10–11, 305–8, 306n.104
Adler, Adolf. 147–8
Adler, Felix 147–8
Agriculture 267–71
    farmers' associations 269–70
Ahlheim, Hannah 39–40
Allen, William S. 11n.23, 168–9, 458n.4
Alsfeld 132
Altenstadt 157–8
Althaus, Paul 285, 292–3
Althusser, Louis 257n.73
Altona (see also Preußenschlag, SA) 287n.35, 437–8
    Altonaer Blutsonntag 286–7
Alzenau 145, 145n.73
American League for the Defense of Jewish Rights 312–13
amnesties (see also decrees) 145–6, 176–7, 182n.23, 407n.30, 414n.52
    for crimes, early 1933 23–4, 175n.1, 468–9
    for crimes, July 1933 4, 23–4, 67–8, 108–10, 118n.69, 131n.29, 175–6, 178, 208, 208n.119, 414–15, 468–9
Andersen, Friedrich 293–4

Angress, Werner 42–3
antisemitism (see also "Aryan clause;" attacks, antisemitic; boycotts; citizenship; crimes; legislation, Nuremberg Laws; "Ostjuden;" Perfidy Decree; pillory marches; violence; Weimar Republic) 51n.19, 73, 181–2, 189–90, 217, 234–5, 253–4, 254n.64, 319, 331, 338, 346–7, 375–6, 411–12, 418–21, 421n.4, 428–34, 442n.84, 449–50, 457, 464–5, 471–4, 472n.30
    in agricultural and artisanal trades 267–71
    among doctors 249–50, 249n.47, 250n.48
    cultural 285, 341–2, 361–2, 374–6, 442–4, 470–1
    economic discrimination 57–62, 211–12, 241–3, 260, 409–10
    motivations for 57, 66, 73–5, 76n.9
    and name changes 87–92, 88n.53, 92n.74
    political 79n.24
    psychological impact of 136–7
    racial 76n.9, 219–20, 238, 240–1, 291–2, 351–2, 394, 430, 436–7, 449n.110, 452–3, 471–3
    social ostracization 236, 434–5, 446–7
    spa and seaside resort bans 265–7
    and tradesmen 267–71
    "redemptive," 76n.9, 469–70
Apen 270–1

Apolda 58–9

Appel, Marta 223–4

Arnim, Detlev von 284n.27

Aron, Joseph 141, 141n.59

Aron, Paul 224–5

"Aryan clause" (*see also* antisemitism,
Hindenburg, Jews, legislation) 16–18,
240–5, 240n.8, 247–8, 250–1, 250n.51,
255–7, 259–62, 261n.83, 265, 271,
366n.68

and economic discrimination 25

and prohibitions against entering
towns 25

Aschaffenburg 145

Aschheim, Steven 101–2

Association of National German Jews
99–101

Association of Private Health
Insurance Companies of
Germany (*Verband Privater
Krankenversicherungsunternehmungen
Deutschlands*) 250–1

Asthalter, Wilhelm 63–4, 190–3,
191n.56

"atrocity propaganda" (*Greuelpropaganda*),
(*See also* First World War) 28, 60–1,
61n.58, 67–70, 94–5, 111, 166–7, 170–1,
175–6, 213–19, 216n.20, 219n.28, 221–2,
224–5, 229–31, 313–21, 314n.10, 315n.13,
316n.14, 319n.22, 342–3, 369–70, 395–6,
400–1, 406–7, 435–6

attacks, antisemitic (*see also* crimes, Jews,
murders, Perfidy Decree, pillory
marches; SA; SS; violence) 53–63, 73,
99n.105, 108–10, 114–15, 123–50, 214–15,
218n.24, 237, 245–6, 257–9, 311, 313,
346–7, 350–1, 356–7, 367–70, 374–5,
395–6, 400–3, 405, 412, 461–3, 471–3

on "Jew-friendly" Germans 152–3,
160–2, 214–15, 217–19

pograms and pogram-like 24, 47–8, 52,
71–2, 82–5, 105–6, 124–5, 171n.64,
178–80, 228, 243–6, 311–12, 431, 461–3

attacks, political (*see also* crimes, camps,
Communist Party; Social Democratic
Party) 198–204, 214–15

Augsburg 100n. 111, 276n.4, 396

Austria/Austrians 57–8, 67–8, 88–90,
95–7, 95n.92, 114–15, 142, 277, 410

Axelrod, Towia 73–5, 74n.4, 78–9

Bachem, Karl 377–8

Bad Nauheim 251–2

Baden 8–9, 49–50, 90–1, 139n.54, 198–9,
242–3, 251–2, 268–9, 305–8, 329–30,
357–9

Landeskirche in 317, 356n.33, 357–9, 364–5,
368n.74, 386n.29, 387n.35

Baeck, Leo 47–8, 98–9, 237, 238n.4,
239–40, 261–2

Baerwald, Rabbi Leo 105–6

Bajohr, Frank 39–40

Bamberg 378–9, 382–3

Bang, Paul 427–30, 428n.30

Bankier, David 136n.49, 259–60

Barkai, Avraham 39–40, 42–3, 231n.67

Barteld, John Adam Heinrich 127–9,
127n.14

Bartels, Adolf 293–4

Barth, Karl 300–1, 301n.84

Bauer, Gustav 75

Bautzen 57–9

Bavaria 8–9, 38–9, 49–50, 73–5, 80–1,
8on.29, 86–90, 139n.54, 172, 232–3,
242–3, 244n.23, 245–8, 250, 305–8,
306n.102, 378n.3, 379–82, 391–2

deportation policy in 79n.24, 80–1

"racial cleansing" in 309–10

Soviet Republic of (*See also* revolution,
1918) 73–5, 74n.4, 78–9, 94–5, 99–101,
342–3

Bavarian People's Party 383n.21, 396

Beaven, Albert W. 318n.20, 319–20, 372–3

Beck, Ludwig 459–60

Becker, Hans 144–5

Behrens, Walter 191–2, 201–2

Behringersdorf 265–6

Belgium 60–1, 142–3, 313–15, 316n.15, 318–19

Bender, Amalie 141n.61

Bender, August 141n.61

Bender, Karl 141, 141n.61

Bendix, Hans 326–7, 326n.53

Bennathan, Esra 78n.19, 231n.67

Bendix, Hans 326–7, 326n.53

Benoist-Méchin, Jacques 75n.6

Berding, Helmut 40–1

Bereisch, Jakob 63–4

Berger, Alfred 84

Berlin 2, 48–50, 50n.12, 53, 55–6, 62–3, 65–9, 77–8, 80–4, 95–7, 98n.102, 104–7, 111–16, 132, 151–2, 177, 188n.46, 208, 208n.119, 222–6, 230n.63, 242–3, 246–7, 251–2, 262n.89, 288n.41, 296–9, 299n.76, 348–9, 369–70, 374–5, 379–80, 384, 398, 401–2, 435–8, 457n.1, 461–2

    Charlottenburg 112–13

    Dahlem 130–1, 178–80, 442–4

    Kreuzberg 160–1

    Kurfürstendammkravalle, 1931 124–5, 285–6

    Lichterfelde 130–1

    police in 65–7, 103–5, 112–16, 126–7, 161–2

    SA in 126–7, 139–40, 245–6

    Scheunenviertel 53–5, 77–8, 82n.36, 83–5, 95–7, 124–5, 222n.39

    Schöneberg 140, 263–4

Bernhard, Georg 456, 469–70

Bertram, Cardinal Archbishop Adolf 29–31, 323–4, 378–80, 382–3, 385–6, 388–91, 389n.39, 391n.44, 396n.61, 397–8, 466–7

Bertram, Ernst 75

Bessel, Richard 33–4

Best, Friedrich 412–14

Beuel 126–7

Beuthen 52n.25, 56, 82–3, 232–3, 287

Biedenkopf 147–8, 148n.83

Birkenstock, Hermann 206–7, 209

Bismarck, Otto von 278–9, 377–8, 382–3

Blankenburg 197–8

Bleichröder, Gerson 98n.102

Bloch, Minna 171–2

Bochum 264n.93, 416–17

Böhme, Ernst 197n.79

Boldes, Rudolf 415–16

Bonhoeffer, Dietrich 346n.1, 348–9, 463n.16

Bonn 14–16, 126–7

Bornkamm, Heinrich 292–3

Bötticher, Paul. *See* Lagarde, Paul de

bourgeoisie 73, 75, 77–8, 132, 271–2, 308, 443n.88, 459–60, 460n.8, 469–70

boycott, 1 April 1933 (*see also* attacks, antisemitic; Jews, German; violence; SA; SS) 1–2, 24, 47–8, 59, 66, 69–70, 159–61, 190–1, 213–14, 216–19, 232–3, 243–4, 250, 258–9, 271, 319, 327–32, 342–4, 352–3, 398, 417–18, 461–2

    connection to antisemitic attacks 149–50

    financial ruin as a result of 327–8

    lack of support for/opposition to 25, 213–14, 223–4, 228–9, 259–60, 271–2

    motivations for 212, 217–20, 231–2

    psychological impact of 228, 434

    and violence 69–70, 224–8, 243–4

boycotts (*see also* boycott, 1 April 1933; violence) 39–40, 211, 213–14, 231, 237, 264–5, 327, 461–2

    against Nazi Germany 103–4, 213–15, 258–9, 312–14, 313n.5, 343–4

    "from below" 213–14

    and denunciation of violators 235

    pressures to join in 232–5

    tradition in Germany 211

    and violence 212–13

Bracher, Karl Dietrich 10n.20, 36–7

Brandenburg 90–1, 132, 232–3, 251–2, 304–5, 334, 340–1

Braun, Otto 7–8, 425–6

Braunschweig 197–8, 197n.79, 204n.104, 263–4, 279, 279n.9, 288n.41, 299n.77, 446n.95

Brecht, Bertolt 174

Brecht, Hermann 329–30

Bredel, Willi 200–1

Bremen 8–9, 139n.54, 228–9, 305–8

Breslau (see also SA) 29–30, 56–7, 142–3, 147, 151–2, 222–4, 223n.43, 226–7, 229–31, 245–7, 374n.86, 378–9, 382–3, 438

Broszat, Martin 36–8, 240–1

Bruchsal 171–2, 181n.19, 230n.63

Brüning, Heinrich 239–40, 384

Bubenhofer, Dr. med. 448–51, 449n.110

Buchberger, Michael 396, 396n.61

Buchheim, Meier 172, 178–80

Bülow-Schwante, Vicco Karl Alexander von 55–6, 56n.37, 95–7, 96n.93

bureaucracy/civil service (see also antisemitism; crimes; judicial system; legislation; public prosecutors) 24–5, 31, 234, 239, 256–7, 388–9, 396–7, 397n.62, 470–4

administrative branch of 16–18, 403, 405, 418–19, 462–3, 467–8

composition of 239n.5, 241n.12

judicial branch of 16–18, 31–2, 136–7, 412, 419, 462–3, 467–8

response to antisemitic attacks 176, 209–10, 403, 405, 419

Buren, Michael van 68–9

Burgbernheim 156

Bürgertum/Bildungsbürgertum 340, 375–6, 450–1, 460–1

Burghart, Georg 294–5, 317, 335n.77, 346–50, 346n.1

Burleigh, Michael 37–8

Cadman, Samuel Parkes 317

camps, concentration, detention, internment (see also SA) 35–6, 78–9, 81, 82n.35, 84–5, 93–4, 141, 194–5, 195n.71, 203–4, 270–1, 305–8, 337–8, 399, 457

Auschwitz 146n.78

Dachau 13–14, 34–5, 195–6, 305–8, 337–8, 389n.39

Fuhlsbüttel 199–201, 201n.95, 203–4

Hainewald 410–12

Kislau 181n.19, 198–9, 203–4

Osthofen 157n.21

Cannstadt 71

Catholics/Catholicism 230n.63, 299, 310n.112, 324, 374–5, 377–82, 384–90, 385n.27, 392–4, 393n.51, 396–8, 398n.66, 462–3, 466–7

networks of organizations 377–8, 388–9, 388n.37, 392–4, 395n.55, 466–7

Catholic Church (see also Bertram; Center Party, Faulhaber, Hitler) 29–30, 221n.37, 257n.73, 299–301, 300n.80, 337–8, 355–6, 377–99

and antisemitism 29–31, 323–4, 379–80, 389–90, 394, 466–7

on antisemitic attacks and discrimination 324, 466–7

and 1 April 1933 boycott 29–30, 389, 466–7

and April 1933 legislation 29–31, 466–7

clergy of 310n.112, 380–3, 385–8, 392–4, 399

concordats of 386n.29, 387n.35

episcopate of (see also Catholic Church leaders) 29–31, 378–84, 388–9, 392–8, 466–7

Fulda Bishops Conference 323–4, 378–81, 384

and Jewish converts 323–4, 390–1, 391n.44, 396

and Jewish Germans 30–1, 388–9

on the "Jewish Question," 394

and the Kanzelparagraph 397–8

Kulturkampf against 30n.43, 377–8, 382–3, 388–9, 398n.66

on leftist ideologies 380–1, 384, 398, 398n.68
and National Socialism 29–30, 309–10, 379–88, 395, 396n.61, 398
on nationalism 379–84
and the NSDAP/Nazi regime 30–1, 310n.112, 378n.3, 379–80, 383n.20, 385–8, 390–4, 396–8, 398n.68, 466–7
organizations of (*see also* Catholics/Catholicism) 29–30, 385–6, 396
and the Protestant Church 309–10, 385–6, 388–9
structure of 378–9
and Weimar Republic 398, 466–7
Catholic Church leaders 322–6, 337–8, 381–90, 387nn.32,35, 392–8, 398n.66, 399, 462–3, 466–7, 467n.20
Center Party (*see also* Catholic Church; Enabling Act) 7–8, 10–12, 129n.22, 240–1, 276, 294–5, 300–1, 305–8, 323–6, 377–8, 383–9, 383n.21, 385n.27, 387n.35, 396, 420–1, 434, 459–60, 462–3
Central Organization of German Consumer Cooperatives 212–13
Centralverein deutscher Staatsbürger jüdischen Glaubens (*Centralverein*) 98–101, 105–6, 124–5, 211, 215–17, 216n.19, 217n.21, 226, 231–2, 231n.68, 427–8
Chamberlain, Austin 311–12
Chamberlain, Houston Stewart 293–4, 428–9
Chemnitz (*see also* SA) 51–6, 99–101, 226, 245–6, 263–4, 264n.93, 400–1, 403–4, 406–7, 461–2
Churches (*see also* Catholic Church; Protestant Church) 459–60, 471–4
foreign 111–12, 309–11, 319–20, 319n.25, 347–53, 364–5, 371–2, 371n.76
citizenship and residency (*see also* antisemitism; law) 19, 49–50, 78–9, 97–8
difficulties of obtaining 62–3, 86–91

exclusion from 409n.38
laws relating to 86–7, 87n.52, 93–4, 97–8
civil service (*see* bureaucracy)
coalition government, NSDAP–DNVP (*see also* German National People's Party; laws; legislation; National Socialism; National Socialist German Workers' Party/Nazi regime; Reich, Third, government) 1–2, 9–10, 91–8, 95n.92, 109n.25, 130, 213–14, 216–19, 224–5, 227, 231–2, 242–3, 247–8, 257–8, 297–8, 384–5, 420–1, 427–8, 435n.46, 441–2, 443n.85, 456–9, 469–71, 473–4
overestimation of DNVP influence in 300–1
Cohen, Hermann 101–2, 102n.119
Cohen, Siegfried 112–13
Cohn, Willy 142–3
Cologne 56, 64, 126–7, 144, 144n.68, 149–50, 150n.92, 187–9, 188n.46, 212–13, 242–3, 245–6, 250–2, 300–1, 323–4, 378–81, 383–5, 385n.27, 398–9
communism/communists (*see also* attacks, political; Communist Party of Germany) 204–5, 217–19, 342–3, 351–2, 457–9, 464n.17
alleged ties of Jews to 23–4, 29, 73–5, 79n.24, 95–7, 176, 181–4, 325–6, 341–2, 348–9, 374–5, 403–6, 408, 425–6, 431, 449, 467–8, 470–1, 470n.26
and antisemitic violence 57, 118–19, 204–6, 467–8, 471–3
perceived threat of 9–10, 169–70, 212–13, 258n.75, 298–300, 325–6, 344–5, 414–15
Communist Party of Germany (KPD) 9–11, 13–14, 52, 71–2, 173, 182–6, 240–1, 285–6, 299, 360n.49, 384–5, 400–1, 414–15, 420–1
outlawing of 8–9
violence against members of 185–6, 203–4, 305–8, 331–2

Compensation Law, postwar (*see also* attacks; crimes; murders) 130–1, 206–7
  claims filed under 4, 4n.9, 70–1, 130–1, 131n.25, 138–41, 140n.58, 146n.78, 147, 185–6, 186n.38, 224–5, 225n.52
Confino, Alon 35–6
conservatives (*see also* "Day of Potsdam;" German National People's Party; Protestant Church leaders) 32–3, 221–2, 292–3, 300–1, 308, 318, 325–6, 331–3, 348–9, 361–2, 364–5, 374–5, 375n.87, 386–8, 419n.67, 420–2, 426–7, 429–32, 429n.36, 434, 435n.47, 442–5, 451–2, 459–61, 464–5, 469–73, 470n.25
Convention on the Protection of Minorities, 1922 (*see also* Upper Silesia) 56, 56n.39, 254–5
Cottbus 81, 262n.89
courts (*see also* judicial system; Perfidy Decree; police; public prosecutors; SA; Great Britain) 168–9, 198–9, 205–6, 209–10
  German postwar denazification (*Spruchkammern*) 183n.26, 185–6, 186n.38
  Oberlandesgerichte 440–2, 440n.72
Cramer, Wilhelm 228–9
Creglingen 178–80
crimes, antisemitic (*see also* amnesties; Compensation Law; murders; public prosecutors; violence) 2, 16–18, 441–2, 461–2, 467–8
  abductions, deportations and expulsions 65–70, 78–81, 84–5, 88–94, 99–101, 115–16, 143–5, 206–7, 390–1, 403–5, 409–12, 409nn.37–8
  absence of full documentation of 209–10
  documentary evidence for 130–8
  extortion 412–14, 413n.48, 417–18
  grievous bodily harm and murder (*See* murder)

post-WWII reopening of cases 2, 4–5, 22–4, 130–1, 137n.52, 160–1, 161n.33, 164–5, 170–1, 175–7, 178n.10, 180, 183–5, 183n.26, 191–201, 194, 195nn.67–69, 200n.89, 201n.95, 203n.100
Custodis, Bernhard 399
Czechoslovakia 60–1, 68–9, 114–15, 142–3, 367–70, 410, 410n.41

Dahrendorf, Ralf 275–6, 283–4
Danzig 155n.12
Darmstadt 141
Darré, Walter 353n.23
Daum, Adam 184–5
"Day of Potsdam" 308–9, 310n.112, 333–4, 337–8, 342–3, 386–8, 459–60, 467–8
decrees (*see also* amnesties; laws; Perfidy Decree; Reichstag fire)
  For the protection of the German People (4 February 1933) 7, 195n.71, 297–8, 384
  For the Protection of the People and the State (28 February 1933) 7–8, 195n.71, 420–1
Deggendorf 57
Dehio, Georg 442–4, 443n.87
Dehio, Ludwig 442–4
Dehn, Gunther 295–6
Delmenhorst 234
Dessau 58–9
Detmold 195–6, 196n.74
Deutsch, Albert 115
Deutsch-Krone 229–31
Dibelius, Otto 28, 190–1, 191n.56, 280–2, 281n.13, 288, 304–9, 305n.98, 334–8, 346–9, 361–2, 375n.87, 457–9, 461–2, 466–7, 470–3, 471n.27
Dickinson, Lord Willoughby 346–7, 346n.1
Diels, Rudolf 226
Dietrich, Hermann 11–12
Dietz, Wilhelm 173–4

Diplomatic Missions, foreign (*see also* Great Britain; The Netherlands; Poland, Switzerland; United States) 31, 51–2, 70–1, 113n.42, 130, 142–3, 176, 257–8, 401, 401n.8, 402n.11, 406n.25, 467–8

Ditzen, Rudolf (pen name Hans Fallada) 196–7, 196nn.75–6, 209–10

Dodd, Ambassador William 161–2

Doehring, Canon Bruno 284n.27, 292–3

Dolgesheim 178–80

Dominicus, Alexander 81n.33, 82n.35

Dörner, Bernward 167n.53

Dortmund 71, 212–13, 223–4, 270, 270n.117

Dresden 3–4, 49–50, 50n.12, 56, 67–70, 88–90, 99–101, 110–11, 148–9, 214–15, 226, 245–6, 263–4, 400–2, 405–7
police/Gestapo headquarters in 432–3

Dresler, *Oberstaatsanwalt* 416–17

Duesterberg, Theodor 294–5, 361–2, 428–9, 429n.34, 431

Duisburg- Hamborn 51–2, 56, 61–4, 66, 224–5, 262n.89, 264n.93

Dülffer, Jost 37–8

Durst, Chaim Baruch 53–5

Düsseldorf 11–12, 56, 62–3, 126–7, 143, 206–10, 207n.118, 212–13, 226, 331

Ebert, Friedrich 76n.9

Eckert, Alois 292n.52, 394

Ehrlich, Mojzeszoni 224–5

Eisner, Kurt 73–5

Elend, Leo 226

Elbing 132, 212

elections
1919, January 14, 422–3
1924, May 425–6, 429–30
1924, December 425–6, 426n.20
1928, May 427–8
1930, September 428–9
1932, March presidential 429n.34, 431, 465–6

1932, July 14–16, 294–5, 428–9

1933, 5 March 5–10, 28, 31–2, 47–8, 52, 123, 129, 197–8, 205–6, 212–14, 243n.22, 257–8, 301–5, 337–8, 360n.49, 384, 400–1, 420–1, 428–9, 448–9, 454–5, 457

Eltz-Rübenach, Paul von 221–2, 221n.37

Empire, German 14, 51–2, 73–5, 86, 229–31, 241n.14, 275–6, 382–3, 421–5, 447–8, 464–5, 472n.30

Enabling Act (*Ermächtigungsgesetz*) (*see also* Center Party) 11–12, 14, 242n.17, 305–10, 388–9, 459–60

Erfurt 58–9, 125–8, 268–9

Erlich, Cyla 53–5

Erlich, Mojzes 53–5

Erzberger, Matthias 110n.28

Eschenburg, Theodor 9–10

Essen 52, 56, 212–13, 219–20

Esslingen 71

Evans, Richard 37–8

expulsions 138–50

Fallada, Hans (*see* Ditzen, Rudolf)

Faulhaber, Michael von 30–1, 299–301, 300n.80, 378–80, 386–8, 390–8, 391n.44, 392n.49, 393n.51, 396n.61, 466–7

Fauszlegier, Lajbus 66–7

Fechenbach, Felix 5nn.11–12, 195–7, 195–6nn.72–4

Feith, Rudolf Ernst 173

Feuchtwanger, Lion 115, 178–80

First World War (*see also* "atrocity propaganda;" Jews, German) 49–50, 60–1, 61n.58, 73–5, 76n.9, 79n.24, 97n.98, 99–102, 175–6, 181–2, 212, 215–19, 216n.20, 303–4, 308–9, 314–15, 330–1, 357–9, 376, 395–6, 414–15, 435–6, 435n.47, 457–9, 458n.4, 470–1, 470n.26

Fischbeck, Otto 99–101

Fischl, Dr. Hermann 90–1, 90n. 67

Fischl, Markus 90–1 90
Flensburg 160–1
Föhr, Joseph 387n.35
Fraenkel, Ernst 59
France 2, 56n.39, 60–1, 86, 98n.102, 142–3,
    146, 146n.78, 175–6, 178–82, 186n.38,
    214–15, 229–31, 313–15, 357–9
Franconia 11–12, 34–5, 156–8, 220n.30,
    265–6, 266n.98, 394
Frank, Hans 244n.23, 245–8, 253
Fränkel, Dr. Fritz 139–41, 139n.56
Franken, Max 112–13
Frankenberg (town) 172
Frankenberg, Adolf 412–14
Frankfurt am Main 64, 127–8, 159–60,
    160n.27, 173–4, 182–3, 224–5, 321–2,
    322n.40, 367–9, 374n.86, 440n.74,
    441–2
  DNVP in 436–7, 440–1, 454–5
  Jewish life in 438–41, 438n.63
  SA in 147–8, 245–6, 441–2
Franzreb, Ernst 183–6, 183n.26
Frei, Norbert 37–8
Freiburg 58–9, 378–9
Freienwalde 157–8
Freikorps 110n.28, 204–5
Freising 378–9
Freisler, Roland 207–8, 207n.118, 245–8,
    440, 440n.74
Freudenberg, Walter 329n.62
Freytag, Gustav 77–8, 420–1, 421n.4
Frick, Wilhelm 53–5, 86, 88–93, 103–4,
    103n.1, 160–1, 219–20, 242n.17, 258–9,
    353–4, 408–9
Friedberg 181–2
Friedländer, Richard 427–8
Friedländer, Saul 40–3, 49–50, 75n.6,
    76n.10, 240–1, 242n.17, 249–50,
    469–70
Friedmann, Anatole 115–16
Frings, Archbishop Cardinal Josef 398
Frisch, Hermann 87–90, 88n.53, 92n.74
Fritsch, Werner von 16–18, 17n.38

Fritzlar-Homberg 417–18, 417n.60, 418n.63
Fritzsche, Peter 35–6
Froebel, Max 148–9
Fuchs, Ernst 268–9
Fuchs, Julian 104–5
Fürstenwalde 196–7

Galen, Clemens August von 398, 398n.68,
    466–7
Gandersheim 197–8
Ganz, Gustav 53–5
Gedern 132–7
Gellately, Robert 40–1
Gelsenkirchen 53–6, 262–3
Gennrich, Paul 294–5
Genschel, Helmut 39–40
Gercke, Dr. Achim 219–20
Gerlach, Wolfgang 339n.89
German Bar Association (Deutscher
    Anwaltsverein, DAV) 244–5, 247n.34
  banning of Jewish members in 246–8
German Christians' Faith Movement
    (Glaubensbewegung Deutsche Christen;
    German Christians) (See also
    Protestant Church) 291–4,
    292nn.52–3, 344n.105, 354–5, 359–62,
    359n.46, 367–9, 464–5, 467n.20
German Democratic Party (DDP) (see also
    Staatspartei) 14, 20, 81, 81nn.32–33,
    99–101, 129n.22, 284n.26, 422–3
German Medical Association 252
German National Front (see German
    National People's Party, DNVP)
German Nationals (see German National
    People's Party)
German National People's Party (DNVP)
    (see also coalition government,
    NSDAP-DNVP; conservatives; Hitler
    Cabinet; Hugenberg; Jews, German;
    Protestant Church) 14–16, 101n.113,
    109n.25, 130, 160n.27, 246–7, 259–60,
    302n.86, 384, 441–50, 447n.101, 462–3,
    469–71

and antisemitic violence 420–1, 426–7,
  429–31, 438, 442–5
and antisemitism 14–16, 73, 75, 220–1,
  420–1, 426–8, 430, 436–7, 437n.55,
  442n.84, 444, 450, 469–70,
  470n.25
appeals/complaints by Jews to 1–2, 5–7,
  32–3, 130–1, 438
"Aryan clauses" within 423n.11, 426–7
and boycotts 33, 220–1, 431, 434,
  439–40, 444, 450–1, 469–70
divisions within party 421–5, 434
Görlitz party conference, 1922 423–5
and the "Jewish Question," 32–3, 421,
  434, 456
Kampfring 13–14, 445–6
Kampfstaffeln 305–8
Land associations in 33, 220–1, 421–3,
  422n.6, 423n.11, 427n.27, 436–8, 440,
  445–6, 446n.95, 448–50, 469–70
membership of Jewish Germans in
  32–3, 423n.11, 436–8, 450, 469–70
and national-minded Jewish
  Germans 426–7, 429–30, 434,
  437n.55, 446–7, 469–70
and National Socialism 383
and the NSDAP/Nazi regime 1–2, 33,
  426n.20, 428–32, 434, 436–7, 444–5,
  447–56, 449n.110, 451n.115, 459–60
and "*Ostjuden*," 78–9, 79n.26, 425–7,
  429–30, 444–5, 469–70
overestimation of influence of 26–7,
  456, 469–70
and the Pan German League 423–5,
  427–8, 427n.27
roots of 421–5, 444–5
SA attacks against 33
in the Weimar Republic 32–3, 421,
  447–8, 455n.132, 469–70, 470n.25
völkisch element within 33, 421–6, 438,
  444, 453, 469–70
and *völkisch* political parties 423–5,
  429–30

German People's Party (DVP) 284n.26,
  295n.66, 439–40
Gernstein, Israel 53–5
Gestapo (*see also* police) 168n55, 339–40,
  432–3
Gierke, Anna von 422–3, 427–8
Gierke, Otto von 422–3
Gisevius, Johannes 325–6, 325n.50
Gladenbach 147–8, 148n.83
Gleichschaltung ("co-ordination"
  policy) 397, 465–7
  of German *Länder* 8–11, 359–60,
    360n.49, 384–5
  of *Landeskirchen* 353–6, 353n.23,
    354nn.26–27, 355–6nn.29–32, 359–60,
    360nn.50–51, 465–6
Gleiwitz 56, 245–6, 263–4
Glogau 219–20
Goebbels, Joseph 11–12, 128n.17, 173,
  219n.28, 433, 473n.32
Goethe, Johann Wolfgang von 280–2,
  282n.16
Goldmann, Felix 98–9
Goldschmidt, Max (Limburg) 147, 147n.81
Goldschmidt, Max (Melsungen) 147–8,
  148n.82
Göring, Hermann 3–4, 7–8, 13–14, 33–4,
  103–4, 103n.1, 161–2, 173, 219–20,
  414n.52, 442–4
Görlitz 245–6
Goslar 164–5
Graef, Albrecht von 423–5
Granzow, Walter 353–4, 353n.23
Great Britain 60–1, 113–14, 175–6, 186n.38,
  214–15, 246–7, 311–15, 461–2
  military government, postwar
    Germany 2, 5–7, 193–4, 202–3
  Supreme Court of British Zone, postwar
    WWII 130–1, 164–5, 166n.52
Grebler, Littmann 403
Greece/Greeks 69–70, 113–14
Gröber, Archbishop Conrad 324, 385–6,
  386n.29, 389–90

Groener, Wilhelm 285–6, 463–4
Groß-Strelitz 61–2
Grummer, Leo 410
Grünebaum, Hermann 64
Grzesinski, Albert 7–8
Guggenheim, Willy 112–13
Gürtner, Franz 247–8, 248n.41, 253
Güstrow 90–1 90
Gutheim, Levi 417–18
Gyssling, Walter 105–6, 105n.7

Haas, Johann 182–3
Haber, Mendel Zelig 71
Haffner, Sebastian 71–2, 222–3, 264–5, 457,
    457n.1, 460n.9, 471–3
Halle 58–9, 295–6
Hamborn 61–2, 159–60
Hamburg 8–9, 48n.5, 87–90, 103–4,
    139n.54, 188n.46, 214–15, 217–19,
    262n.89, 305–8, 306n.102, 313–14,
    314n.8, 329–30, 437–8
    German Israelite community in 216–17,
        217n.22
    Protestant Church in 368n.74
Hanover 100n.111, 113, 127–8, 232–3, 278–9,
    279n.8, 288n.41, 299n.77, 354–5,
    359–60, 446n.95
Hansen, Dr. Hans 160–1
Harnack, Adolf von 128n.15, 301–3
Hartmannbund 252
Haspel, Sabina 405–7
Häusler, Fischel 63
Hecht, Cornelia 38–9, 84
Heidelberg 90–1, 169–70, 173, 295–6
Heilberg, Alfred 187, 187n.40
Heilberg, Liselotte 187
Heilbronn 178–80
Heimtücke-Verordnung (see Perfidy Decree)
Heine, Wolfgang 86–7
Heines, Edmund 57, 147, 147n.80, 227,
    227n.56
Heinrici, Gotthard 341–2, 431
Heldmann, Dr. Heinrich 440–1

Helfferich, Karl 422–3
Helmreich, Ernst Christian 372n.79
Henning, Wilhelm 423–5
Henriod, Henri-Louis 29, 317, 347–50,
    348n.6, 349nn.8–9, 352–3
Herbst, Ludolf 37–8
Hergt, Oskar 246–7, 422–3
Herne 219–20, 264n.93
Herrmann, Wilhelm 280–4
Herszberg, Simon Leib 61–2
Hesse 123, 132, 140–1, 224–5, 233–4, 247–8,
    269–71, 412–14, 440n.74, 461–2
Hesse-Darmstadt 8–9, 139n.54, 305–8,
    306n.102
Hesse, Hermann Albert 354–5, 359–60,
    360n.51
Heydner, Georg
"Hilfspolizisten" (auxiliary police) (see police)
Hildebrand, Klaus 10n 20, 37–8
Hindenburg (town) 56, 61–2, 65, 132
Hindenburg, President Paul von (see also
    decrees; legislation) 18n.40, 76n.9,
    95n.88, 166–7, 294–5, 311–12, 323–4,
    353–4, 354n.27, 361–2, 385–6, 431,
    442–4, 465–6
    and "Aryan Clause" exceptions 94–5,
        95n.87, 241–2, 241n.14, 242n.15, 250–1,
        253, 256
    and "Ostjuden" 94–7
    and Hitler 94–5
    and the Perfidy Decree 21–2
Hirsch, Emanuel 292–3
Hitler, Adolf (see also Catholic Church;
    coalition government, NSDAP/
    DNVP; National Socialism; NSDAP;
    Hitler Cabinet; Protestant Church;
    Reich, Third) 11–12, 26–7, 86, 97–8,
    97n.98, 107–8, 108n.21, 111–12, 125–6,
    128n.17, 156–62, 168–9, 171–3, 183–4,
    196–7, 201–2, 219–22, 227, 227n.56,
    238, 238n.4, 240–1, 242n.17, 247–50,
    258–9, 258n.76, 261–2, 285, 287–8,
    292–3, 300–1, 301n.84, 308–10,

310n.112, 335–9, 338n.87, 342–3, 345–7, 351–4, 354n.27, 355n.30, 356n.32, 361–2, 373–4, 384–5, 385n.27, 406–7, 427–8, 431–3, 448–9, 451–2, 457–60, 465–6

accession to the chancellorship 31–2, 111–12, 118–19, 300–1, 414, 418–19

adulation of in popular culture 11–12

and antisemitism 431–3

and the "Aryan clause" 94–5, 323–4

appeals to stop grassroots violence 132, 136–7, 136n.49, 147, 212–14, 213n.10, 216–17, 257–9, 258n.75

and boycotts 217–19

and Churches 290n.48, 297–8, 309–10, 335–8, 352, 359–60, 360n.51, 370, 386–9, 431

foreign policy speech, 17 May 1933 347n.2, 373–4

Hitlerterror (*see also* terror) 34–5, 217–19, 313

Königsberg speech 298–9, 298n.75, 305n.98

Potsdam Garrison Church speech 308

Putsch of 1923 147n.80

Hitler Cabinet (*see also* coalition government, NSDAP/DNVP; Third Reich) 92–3, 214–15, 221–2, 242n.17, 244–5, 247–50, 247n.37, 253–4, 258n.76, 261–3, 300–1, 441–2, 443n.85

Höchster, Dr. Emil 146, 146n.78

Höchster, Johanna 146, 146n.78

Hoetzsch, Otto 422–3

Hoffmann, Adolf 279n.9

Holländer, Ludwig 427–8

Homberg 147

Horhausen 234–5

Horkheimer, Max 71–2

Horn, Karl Albert 367–9, 368n.74

horror propaganda (*see* atrocity propaganda)

Hosemann, Johannes 354–5

Hugenberg, Alfred (*see also* German National People's Party) 7–8,

100n. 112, 109n.25, 300–1, 384, 427–31, 427n.27, 428n.31, 439–40

Scherl-Verlag of 450–1

Hundt, Ernst 335n.77, 364–5, 365n.65, 369–70

Hürten, Heinz 398

Hürter, Johannes 341–2

inflation 32–3, 77–8, 78n.19, 80–1, 84, 125–6, 246–7, 435–6, 440, 459–60

Ingolstadt 82n.35

Insterburg 262n.89

Issler, Josef 53–5

Italy/Italians 103–4, 112–13, 113n.42, 385–6

Jäckel, Eberhard 431–2

Jäger, August 467n.20

Jahnke, Fritz 194n.67

Jewish Workers' Welfare Bureau 81n.33, 84, 268–9

Jews (*see also* antisemitism; attacks; communism; crimes; Jews, German; Jews, professional; "*Ostjuden;*" violence) 34–5, 78n.19, 84

American 19–20, 104–12

economic ruin of 231–2

émigrés 229–31

demographics of 49–50, 90n.62, 108n.23, 223n.43, 230n.63, 322n.40, 374n.86, 438, 438n.63

East European other than Polish 48–51, 114–18, 400–1

refugees 97n.97, 111–12, 142–3, 350

Russian 48–9, 48n.4, 75, 79n.24, 98n.102

West European 112–14

Jews, German (*see also* laws; legislation; professionals) 24–5, 51–2, 59, 63, 70–1, 94–5, 130–1, 166–7, 171–2, 223–4, 229–31, 229n.62, 236, 257–9, 346, 356, 371, 429–30, 450, 460–1, 466–7, 470n.25, 471–3

attitudes toward "*Ostjuden*" 19, 48–9, 73, 95–102

Jews, German (*cont.*)
 biases against 29, 67–8, 95–8, 118–19,
  204–5, 253–4, 325–6, 330, 332–3, 341–2,
  346–50, 367–71, 374–5, 449, 464–7,
  470n.26
 characterization as "foreigners" and
  "alien" 236, 241–2, 254–5, 330–1,
  364–5, 370–1, 414–15, 422–3, 426–7,
  448–9, 463–4, 470–1
 Christian converts (*see also* Catholic
  Church; Protestant Church) 326
 and erosion of rights (see also
  Rechtsstaat) 116–19, 447–8
 national-minded 16–18, 33, 99–102,
  204–5, 208, 434
 service in First World War 16–18,
  17n.37, 32–3, 60–1, 67–8, 76–7, 77n.12,
  139–40, 159–60, 171–2, 181–2, 201–2,
  204–5, 209–10, 223–4, 229–31, 241–2,
  246–7, 246n.33, 251–2, 255–6, 327–8,
  332–3, 346–7, 374–5, 395–6, 434,
  440–1
 social ostracization of 229–31, 235, 237,
  259–60
 suicides of 178n.8, 227, 246–7, 390–1,
  395–6, 407, 407n.32, 440
Jews, Polish (*see also* attacks; "*Ostjuden*;"
  Poland) 18–19, 50–1, 53–66, 70–2, 75,
  86–8, 98–9, 107, 143
Jews, professional (*see also* boycott, 1 April
  1933; legislation) 24–5, 214–15, 217–19,
  221–2, 242–3, 245–8, 271–2, 374n.86,
  441–2, 462–3
Jewski, Friedrich 415–16
Jézéquel, Jules 347–8, 347n.2,
  348nn.6–7
Jochmann, Werner 42–3
Jonas, Max 147–8
Jones, Larry E. 423n.11, 429–30
judicial system (*see also* bureaucracy/civil
  service; public prosecutors) 31–2,
  148–50, 419n.67, 435–6

betrayal of legal principles 23–4,
  176–8, 414
expulsion of Jews from 245–8
lack of independence of 441–2
mentality of officials in 176–7, 414–15,
  468–9
"moral" justification of antisemitic
  crimes in 414–17
postwar composition of 4–5

Kahr, Gustav von 78–81, 80n.29
Kalb, Isaak Moses 7–8, 62–3
Kamelhar, Alex 403
Kant, Immanuel 283n.23
Kanthak, Kurt 202–3
Kapler, Albrecht 295n.66
Kapler, Hermann 28, 279–80, 285–6,
  294–6, 295n.66, 317, 317n.16, 319–23,
  319n.25, 325–8, 335–7, 335n.77, 346–50,
  347n.2,5, 348–50, 352–73, 355n.29,
  356n.32, 360n.51, 361n.52, 365n.66,
  371n.76, 373n.82, 463–6, 467n.20
Kapp Putsch 78–9, 82–3, 82n.35, 201–2
Kappus, Adele 439–40, 444–5
Kardorff, Siegfried von 12
Karlsruhe 58–9, 99–101, 198–9, 268–9
Karow, Emil 288n.41, 294–5
Kassel (town) 152–3, 163, 180n.18, 269–70,
  412–14, 418, 418n.66, 440n.74
Kassel, Max 5nn.11–12, 181–6, 182n.23,
  183n.26, 468–9
Kattowitz 56n.39, 82–3
Keller, Adolf 347–8, 348n.6
Kerrl, Hanns 244n.23, 245–8, 248n.41, 253
Kershaw, Ian 37–8, 467n.21
Ketteler, Wilhelm Emmanuel von 392–4,
  394n.53
Kiel 137–8, 190–1, 192n.60, 201–4,
  203n.100, 224–5, 343–4, 462n.13
Killinger, Manfred von 105–6, 110n.28,
  404–5
Kisch, Egon Erwin 114–15, 114n.49

Klagges, Dietrich 197–8, 197n.79
Klauber, Jean 104–5
Klein, Fritz 178–80
Kleist-Schmenzin, Ewald von 292–3, 430
Klemperer, Victor 148–9, 148n.84, 160n.32, 229–31, 432–3
Kleve 148–9
Koch, Erich 226, 226n.55
Koch, Karl 284n.27
Koch, Wilhelm 284n.27
Koch-Weser, Erich 128n.15
Köhler, Walter 193–4, 194n.69
König, Hubert 149–50, 150n.92
Königsberg 132, 224–5, 263–4, 285
Königshütte 56n.39
Konstanz 58–9, 157–8
Kopf, Salomon 410–12, 410n.41, 411n.44
Kortheuer, August 294–5
Krankenkassen (see Statutory Health Insurance Funds)
Krausnick, Helmut 40–1
Kreutzmüller, Christoph 39–40
Krieger, Alma, 163–4
Kristallnacht 430
Krüger, Gustav 322–3
Kruppa, Bernd 84
Kube, Wilhelm 291–2, 292n.52, 304–5, 344n.105, 361–2
Kübel, Johannes 321–2, 322n.40, 365–9
Kühlewein, Prelate Julius 329–30, 368n.74
Kumpfmüller, Joseph 396
Künneth, Walter 296–7, 296n.70
Kwami, Robert 289–91
Kyffhäuser/Kriegerbund 435n.47

Laas, Salomon 62–3
Laband 52n.25
Lagarde, Paul de 293–4, 294n.60, 428–9, 442–4
Lammers, Hans Heinrich 91–2, 91n.72, 92–3, 103–4, 238n.4, 258–9, 313n.5, 319–20, 361–2, 372n.81

Landau, Edwin 229–31
Landauer, Gustav 74n.4
Länder (German states) (see also Gleichschaltung; legislation; Protestant Church) 3–4, 31, 78–9, 86–90, 87n.52, 92–3, 108–10, 127–9, 138–9, 216–17, 237–8, 240–6, 241n.12, 243n.22, 247n.37, 254–5, 261, 263–4
interior ministers of 8–9, 31, 93–4, 130, 176
NSDAP takeover of 139n.54, 337–8, 384–5
Landfried, Staatssekretär 64n.71, 132n.30
Landgraf, Georg 204n.104
Landshut 58–9
Langen 132
Large, David Clay 82n.36, 84–5
law (see also antisemitism; decrees; legislation; Nuremberg Laws; public prosecutors; Rechtsstaat) 7, 24–5, 145, 258–61, 333–4, 402, 430, 441–2, 444–5
against the Establishment of Political Parties, July 1933 160–1
Constitutio Criminalis Carolina 154–5, 154n.10
on the Coordination of the Länder with the Reich 243n.22
Criminal Code Amendments, 1933 93–4
"Kanzelparagraph," 382–3
on the Reduction of Unemployment (Reinhardt Program) 262–3
on the Revocation of Naturalizations and Rescinding of German Citizenship, July 1933 90–3, 91n.70, 93n.78
"retroactive legality" 260–1, 271, 271n.119
"spontaneous" local ordinances and decrees 59, 258–9
League of Nations 146, 215–16, 264n.93
Lebenbaum, Hans 329–30
Leder, Berthold 147–8
Leffler, Siegfried 292–3

legislation, antisemitic 1–2, 24–5, 29, 47–8, 237, 256, 265, 271, 305–8, 322–6, 329–30, 348–9, 356–9, 366–7, 398, 462–3, 473–4
  as attempt to deter violence 237–8, 242–3
  Decree on Physicians and the Statutory Health Insurance System (22 April 1933) 249, 249n.47, 251n52
  Law on Admission to Legal Practice (7 April 1933) 244–8, 244n.23, 246–7nn.33–34, 247n.37, 248n.41, 253, 326n.53
  Law Against the Overcrowding of German Schools and Universities (25 April 1933) 94, 253
  Law on the Appointment of Reich Governors (Reichsstatthaltergesetz)
  Law on the Reconstruction of the Reich, 1934
  Law on the Restoration of a Professional Civil Service (7 April 1933) (see also "Aryan clause;" Hindenberg, "Aryan clause" exceptions) 239–44, 240n.10, 241–2nn.14–15, 242n.17, 361–2, 397, 442–4
Lehmann, Hans 199–200
Leibowitz, Wolf 53–5
Leipart, Theodor 305–8
Leipzig 19–20, 49–56, 58–9, 66–70, 99–101, 107–11, 108n.23, 176, 400–2, 405–6, 408
Leitner, Hermann 115–16
Leitner, Selma 115–16
Lerch, Johannes 182–5, 183n.26
Leßmann, Heinrich 406–7
Leutheuser, Julius 292–3
Levien, Max 78–9
Leviné-Nissen, Eugen 73–5, 74n.4, 78–9
leftist political parties/opposition (see also Communist Party of Germany; Social Democratic Party of Germany) 13–14, 84–5, 160–1, 169–70, 197–8, 279n.9, 341–2, 403–4
liberal political parties (see also German Democratic Party) 11–12, 420–1, 434, 459–60, 462–3
Lichtenberg, Monsignor Bernhard 389n.39
Lieberg, Walter 163
Liegnitz 219–20, 264n.93
Limburg an der Lahn 147, 147n.81
Lippe 195–6
Lissa, Gerhard 435–6
Lloyd George, David 315–16
Löbau 411–12
Lohse, Hinrich 203n.100
Longerich, Peter 40–1, 217–19, 231n.68, 259–60
Löwenfeld, Philipp 80–1
Löwenkron, Max 407
Lübeck 8–9, 139n.54, 199–200, 305–8
Ludwig, Emil 91–2
Ludwigshafen 219–20
Luther, Martin 464–5
Luxemburg, Rosa 73–5

Machtergreifung (Nazi seizure of power) 1–2, 5–7, 11–14, 31–4, 64, 160–1, 175–7, 180, 198, 228, 256–8, 279–80, 313–14, 414–15, 436–7, 444–5, 447–8, 450–1, 459–60, 469–70
  absence of resistance to; defeatism 10–11
  DNVP complicity towards 32–3
  semi-legal nature of 10–12, 10n.20, 40n.66
Magdeburg 232–3
Mainz 100n.111, 184–5, 378–80
Mann, Thomas 75, 259–60, 272n.121, 283n.20
Mannheim 65, 163–4, 170–1, 219–20, 230n.63, 234–5
Marahrens, August 354–5, 359–60, 360n.51
Marburg an der Lahn 157–8, 163n.43, 412–14, 437–8

Marienburg 132

Martin, Ernst 284n.26

Marum, Ludwig 181n.19, 198–9, 203–4

Marx, Jakob 99–101, 100n.110

Maurenbrecher, Max 293–4,
    294nn.59–60

Maurer, Trude 38–9, 80–1, 84, 85n.44

Mecklenburg-Schwerin 86–90, 90n.62,
    263–4, 353–5, 353n.23, 457–9
  Nazi attempt to co-opt *Landeskirchen* in
    (see also *Gleichschaltung*) 353–6,
    353n.23, 359–60, 366–7

Meissen 262–3, 378–9

Meissner, Otto 354n.27, 442–4

Meister, Wilhelm (*see* Bang, Paul)

Melsungen 147

Menn, Wilhelm 331, 338–9

Merker, Ignaz 143–5, 144n.68

Meusel, Admiral Ernst 111

Meyer, Dr. Alfred 5n.11, 204–10, 205n.107,
    207n.118, 208n.119, 209n.121

Michael, Ernst 147–8

Michael, Julius 147–8

Michaelis, Walter 365–7, 366n.68, 370

Miller, David 52n.25

Molo, Walter von 128n.15

Mommsen, Hans 109n.25

Mommsen, Theodor 472n.30

Mommsen, Wilhelm 459–60

Mond, Joseph 66

Moses, Max 187–90, 187n.41

Mosse, George L. 42–3, 420–1, 427–8,
    428n.31

Mosse, Werner E. 42–3

Mühsam, Erich 74n.4

Mülheim (Ruhr) 219–20

Müller, Hans 411–12

Müller, Ludwig 111, 111n.34, 353–4, 354n.27,
    355n.30, 356n.32, 360n.51

Müller-Otfried, Paula 284n.27

Mumm, Reinhard 284n.27

Mundelin, Cardinal George W. 391–2,
    397–8

Munich (*see also* Bavaria) 30–1, 38–9,
    49–50, 50n.12, 53–5, 74n.4, 82–3,
    88–90, 99–101, 104–6, 173–4, 178–80,
    182–4, 223–4, 250, 332–3, 378–9,
    385n.27, 390–1
  Israelite Religious Community in 105–6
  revolution in (*see also* revolution,
    1918–1919) 78–9, 332–3
  SA headquarters in 105–6

murders (*see also* antisemitism; crimes;
    Compensation Law; police; public
    prosecutors; SA; SS; violence) 2–4,
    47–8, 70–2, 175, 208–10, 235, 395–6,
    410–12, 410n.41, 411–12, 461–2, 468–9
  numerical estimates of 5–7, 175–8
  "shot while trying to escape" 22–3,
    180, 194
  spontaneous 22–3, 180–1

Murr, Wilhelm 288–9, 289n.42

Nagel, Hans 453–5, 454nn.126,129

Nambiar, Narayanan 113–14, 114n.47

Nathorff, Hertha 112n.39, 225n.52

national revolution (*see also* amnesties;
    National Socialism; National Socialist
    revolution; zeitgeist) 20–1, 107–8,
    130, 173–4, 190–1, 212–13, 217–19,
    323–4, 332–5, 342–3, 346–7, 349–50,
    361–2, 373–4, 407–8, 439–40, 446–9,
    459–60, 463–4, 467–8, 471–3
  official end of 108–10, 160–1

National Socialism (*see also* coalition
    government, NSDAP-DNVP; national
    revolution; National Socialist German
    Workers' Party; National Socialist
    revolution; Perfidy Decree;
    propaganda; zeitgeist) 16–18, 50–1,
    155–7, 183–4, 228, 249n.47, 277–8,
    295–6, 308, 344n.105, 345, 351–2,
    366–7, 369n.75, 380–1, 384–6, 393n.51,
    397, 410–17
  anti-bourgeois, anti-elitist orientation
    of 158–9

National Socialism (*cont.*)
politicization of private life in 20–2, 117–18, 155–6, 158–9, 163–4, 167–9, 461, 473–4
and decline in foreign tourism 111–12, 161–2, 162n.41, 170–1
National Socialist German Workers' Party (NSDAP)/Nazi regime (*see also* antisemitism; attacks; boycott, 1 April 1933; boycotts; coalition government; German National People's Party; national revolution; National Socialist revolution; press; propaganda; SA; SS; zeitgeist) 7–12, 20–1, 24–5, 31–2, 52, 63, 66–9, 66n.75, 75–6, 86, 107–12, 108n.21, 116–17, 127–30, 132, 138–9, 142–3, 145–6, 148n.83, 150n.92, 155–9, 156n.15, 168–70, 173, 178–94, 183n.26, 192n.59, 196–7, 196n.76, 199–203, 203nn.100–102, 208, 211–14, 219–25, 220n.32, 221n.37, 228–35, 231n.68, 237, 239–40, 243–4, 247–8, 249n.47, 252–5, 257–9, 263–9, 271n.119, 277–8, 285–6, 289–92, 290n.46, 292n.52, 294–301, 297n.72, 303–8, 318n.21, 331–2, 343–5, 344n.105, 345n.107, 351–4, 360n.49, 361–2, 364–9, 369n.75, 374–5, 380–1, 384–8, 393n.51, 400–1, 403–4, 406–7, 410–21, 419n.67, 428–34, 436–40, 445–6, 449–50, 457–63, 458n.4, 469–74
attacks against DNVP 13–14
attacks against the political Left 169–70
and dissolution of political parties 14–16
organizations of 219–24, 247–8, 252, 267–8, 289n.42, 303n.93, 437, 460–1
seizure/takeover of power (see *Machtergreifung*)
takeover of *Länder*, March 1933 (see also *Gleichschaltung; Länder*) 8–10

and violence 12, 71–2, 84–5, 126–7, 149–50, 288–9, 305–8, 348–9, 397–8, 441–4, 460–1
National Socialist revolution/German revolution (*see also* amnesties) 2–4, 24, 130, 131n.29, 156–7, 175–6, 178, 203n.99, 208n.119, 252, 351–2, 412–17, 414n.52, 471–3
Nazi seizure of power (see *Machtergreifung*)
Naumann, Max 99–102, 100n.112
Necheles-Magnus, Henriette 223–4
Neidenburg 190–1
Neimann, Jakob 53–5
Netherlands, The 97n.97, 112–13, 142–3, 313–14, 352–3
Neurath, Freiherr Konstantin von 53–5, 103–4, 103n.1, 112–13, 221–2, 258–9
Neustettin 269–70
Nielsen, Philipp 437n.55, 470n.25
Niemöller, Martin 464–5
Niewyk, Donald L. 101–2
Noakes, Jeremy 288n.41
Noelle, Hermann 209
Nolzen, Armin 34–5
Norden, Günther van 332n.66
Norderney 266–7, 267n.103
Northeim 168–9, 458n.4
Novick, Peter 111–12
Nuremberg 58–9, 161–2, 247–8, 265–6
Nuremberg Laws 109n.25, 153n.5, 163–4, 431, 433

Oberhausen 152, 219–20
Oels 226
Öhringhausen 159–60
Oldenburg 234, 289n.44
Kwami controversy in 289–91
Oling, Robert Rubin 116–17, 116n.59
Oppeln-Bronikowski, Friedrich von 101n.113
Oppenheimer, Max 412–14, 413n.48
Oppenheimer, Richard 327–8
Optionsgebiet (*see* Poland; Upper Silesia)

Ormianer, Chaim 64
Ormianer, Milan 64
Ossietzky, Carl von 300–1
"*Ostjuden*" (*see also* antisemitism; Bavaria;
    crimes; Jews; Prussia; violence)
    47–102, 176, 253–4, 348–9, 374–5,
    425–6, 429–30, 470–3
    prejudices against 73–8, 77n.16
    stigmatization of 78–85
    violence against 47–72, 212–13, 213n.10,
    226, 400–3, 405, 418–19, 461

Pacelli, Eugenio 385–6, 386n.29, 390–2
Paderborn 234, 378–9
Papen, Franz von (*see also* German National
    People's Party; Prussia) 217–19,
    299–301, 384, 399, 448
    government of 287
    and overthrow of Prussia
    government 7–8, 286–7
    and the "Reich Complaint
    Office" 218n.24, 442–4
Pätzold, Kurt 40–1, 228
Paucker, Arnold 42–3
Pechmann, Wilhelm von 303, 303n.91,
    305–8, 320–2, 321nn.30,33, 322n.40,
    332–3, 356n.32, 359–69, 360n.50,
    362n.56, 363n.59, 364n.62, 461, 463–5
Perfidy Decree/Perfidy Law (*see also*
    antisemitism; National Socialism;
    NSDAP; propaganda) 20–2, 21n.42,
    130–1, 166, 178–80
    special courts (*Sondergerichte*) related
    to 130–1, 168–71
Perpessa, Charilaos 69–70
Pfeffer, Jakob Salomon 403–4
Pfeiffer, Hans 209n.121
Pfeiffer, Hermann 144–5
Pforzheim 232–3
Pfundtner, Hans 108–10, 109n.25, 256,
    404–5
Pietczuch, Konrad 287–8

pillory marches (*Prangermärsche*) (*see also*
    antisemitism; attacks; crimes;
    police) 2, 5–7, 18–21, 25, 40–1, 47–8,
    51–3, 62–5, 147, 151, 173–4, 197n.79,
    198–9, 460–1
    contemporary knowledge of 159
    historical roots of 153–6
Pinneberg 165–6
Pirna 57–8
Plauen 56, 226, 408, 461–2
Poland (see also *Ostjuden*; Jews, Polish;
    Reich; Upper Silesia) 54n.28, 87–8,
    214–15, 313–14, 400–1, 403–4, 409–10,
    410n.41, 423–5
    on attacks on Jewish Poles 48–9, 61–4,
    70–1, 103–5, 144–5, 224–5, 400–2,
    402nn.9,11, 405–6, 408
    Diplomatic Missions of 53–6, 58–9, 65,
    67–8, 143, 403
    German minority in 18–19, 59–61, 357–9,
    366–70, 367n.70, 374–5
    territorial dispute with Germany 56,
    56n.39, 82–3
police (*see also* "protective custody;" public
    prosecutors; SA; SS) 13–14, 57–9, 63–4,
    67–70, 83–4, 92–4, 105–6, 108–10,
    113–14, 117–18, 126–7, 137–8, 144–6, 152–3,
    161–2, 168–70, 181–3, 185–7, 190–4,
    192n.59, 194nn.67,69, 199–200, 206–10,
    207n.118, 208–10, 212–13, 262–3, 266–7,
    324, 343–4, 401–7, 409n.37,
    412–14, 418n.62, 467–8
    auxiliary ("*Hilfspolizisten*") 7–8, 51–2,
    55–6, 62–3, 65–6, 68–9, 115–16, 132,
    138–9, 147, 201–2
    failure to intervene in antisemitic
    attacks 33–4, 51–2, 66, 71, 107–10,
    112–13, 124, 148–9, 400–1, 460–1
    failure to record antisemitic crimes 1–4,
    51–2, 66–7, 70–1, 115–16,
    145, 175–6
    refusal to intervene against SA 441–2

Pomerania 33–4, 212–13, 219–20, 452–4, 452n.116, 455n.132

Ponsonby, Arthur 61n. 58, 315–16, 316n.14

Pope Pius XII (*see* Pacelli, Eugenio)

Poppe, Hugo 328

Popper, Karl 156n.15

"positive Christianity" 290–1, 290n.48, 296–7, 297n.72

Potempa (*See also* murders) 287, 345, 345n.107

Potsdam (*see also* "Day of Potsdam")
Garrison Church in 308–9, 338–9, 338n.87

press (*see also* "atrocity propaganda") 7
Catholic 324, 379–80, 386–9, 388n.37, 392–4, 394n.54
foreign 5–7, 28, 60–1, 60n.57, 103–4, 111–12, 112n.38, 123–4, 124n.3, 130, 139n.56, 169–70, 176–7, 214–15, 216n.20, 217–19, 223–5, 246–7, 311, 313, 316–17, 352–3, 373–4, 391–2, 411n.44
German, non-Nazi 60–1, 67–8, 70–2, 75–6, 78–9, 81–2, 84–5, 99–102, 123, 127–9, 151–2, 157–8, 163–7, 163n.43, 169–70, 173, 187–8, 212–13, 215–19, 223–5, 231–3, 263–4, 270, 288, 303, 313, 318–19, 319n.22, 333, 337–8, 353–4, 384, 389–90, 392–4, 434–6, 435n.46, 441–4, 450–1, 470n.26
Nazi 67–8, 118n.68, 128n.17, 234–5, 245–8, 264n.93, 267–8, 298–9, 298n.75, 304–5, 317–19
Protestant 290–1, 291n.50

Pressel, Wilhelm 288–9, 289n.42

Preysing, Konrad von 398

prisons (*see also* Compensation Law; police; public prosecutors)
sentences 21–2, 137–8, 147–50, 150n.92, 167–8, 170–4, 183–4, 193–4, 195n.71, 199–200, 201n.95, 209
treatment of Jews in 148–50

propaganda (*see also* antisemitism; "atrocity propaganda;" Goebbels, Joseph; NSDAP/DNVP coalition government; Perfidy Decree) 180
NSDAP 11–12, 75–7, 95–7, 118–19, 204–5, 213–14, 259–60, 414–15, 418–19, 432–3, 433n.43, 459–60

"protective custody" (*see also* police; camps; SA; SS) 114–18, 152–3, 195–6, 195n.71, 205–7, 226, 396, 401n.8, 406–8

Protestant Church (*see also* Catholic Church; Hitler; Protestant Church leaders; Protestantism/Protestants; Prussia) 16–18, 291–2, 301n.85, 386–8
Altona Confession 286–7
and antisemitism 283–4, 290–1, 291n.49, 293–4, 325–6, 347n.5, 348–51, 356, 366–7, 371
appeals for help from 320–1, 326, 465–6
and boycotts 319, 347–8, 348n.6, 376, 465–6
and the Catholic Church 335–6
confessions within 278–80, 354–5, 355n.29
and Christian converts 321–2, 322n.40, 323n.41, 341, 356–9, 357n.36, 363–5, 367–9, 371, 465–6
as "conscience of the nation" 16–18, 28, 280, 304–5, 309–10, 321–2, 329n.62
on creation of unified national Church (see also *Gleichschaltung*) 278, 291–4, 294n.60, 303n.93, 320–1, 335–7, 352, 359–60, 465–6
and the DNVP 14–16, 284, 465–6
Executive Committee (*Deutscher Evangelischer Kirchenausschuss*, DEKA) of 279–80, 280n.12, 301–4, 302n.89, 303n.91, 317, 320–1, 355–9, 361–3, 362n.56, 363n.59, 365–6, 368n.74, 371–2, 372n.79, 373n.82. 463–4

and foreign Church leaders 28–9,
277–8, 277n.6, 314, 319–20, 347–9,
351–2, 364–5, 372–3
and the German Christian
movement 291–2, 336–7
and the "Jewish Question" 329–30,
346–7, 351–4, 356, 371, 459n.5
Landeskirchen (Land churches) of 26–7,
276, 278–80, 285–6, 291–5, 301–3,
305–8, 320–3, 328, 353–5, 355n.29,
359–60, 363–4, 363n.59, 382–3
and National Socialism 25–7, 277–8,
283n.23, 286–92, 295–7, 334–6
and the NSDAP/NSDAP regime 16–18,
25–6, 295–6, 335, 361–2, 370
and NSDAP/DNVP coalition
government 26–7
political divisions within 27, 291
reaction to foreign protests 314,
355–6
relationship to State and Nation 25–6,
275–7, 283–4, 290–1, 301–3, 333–5,
370–2, 371n.76, 463–4, 463n.16
and the Sahm Ausschuss 294–5, 295n.64
structure of 276, 276n.4, 278–80,
289n.45
and the Weimar Republic 25–6, 276–8,
280–2, 284–91, 284nn.26–7, 301–3,
335–6, 463–5
and First World War 275–6
Protestant Church leaders (see also
Dibelius, Otto; Kapler, Hermann;
Prussia)
26–7, 111, 277, 284–91, 294–5, 301–4,
308, 316–23, 325–30, 332–4, 338–9,
347–51, 353–5, 359–62, 364–70, 372–6,
375n.87, 391–2, 426–7, 429–30, 457–9,
462–6, 467n.20
on antisemitic April 1933
legislation 271–2
and antisemitism 28–9, 209–10, 259–60,
275n.1, 285, 296–7, 303–4, 465–6,
465n.19
and "atrocity propaganda" 28, 60–1,
314n.10, 316–17, 319–21, 357–9,
369–70, 376
attempts to downplay antisemitic
attacks 28
and the coalition government 28
and foreign protests 314
and German Jews 27, 356, 371
on the "Jewish Question" 28–9, 356
mindset of 27, 325–6, 346–7, 357–9,
369–76, 372n.80, 375n.87
and National Socialism 28–9, 277–8,
320–1
and the NSDAP 16–18, 288–91, 288n.41,
289n. 42, 371, 373–6
and the Weimar Republic 27, 277,
367–9, 373–4, 464–6
Protestant German Youth group 318
Protestantism/Protestants 230n.63, 280–4,
283n.20, 292–3, 299, 308, 348–9,
351–5, 355n.29, 359–60, 400–1, 430,
450–1
Prussia (see also Göring, Hermann) 7,
7n.17, 11–12, 33–4, 58–9, 77–8, 78n.19,
78n.21, 81–2, 81n.33, 86, 87n.52, 88–90,
99–101, 104–5, 123, 128, 128n.15, 132,
159–60, 192–3, 195n.71, 201–2,
208n.119, 212–13, 220n.32, 223–4, 226,
229n.62, 231n.68, 247–8, 262–3,
279n.9, 308, 341–2, 357–9, 425–6, 430,
442–6, 453n.122, 459–62
civil servants in 136–7, 383n.21
Culture Ministry of 361–2, 442–4
deportations of Jews from 80–2,
80n.27, 82n.35
Interior Ministry of 87n.52, 90, 124–5,
202–3, 226, 246n.33, 266–7,
409n.38
Internment Decree in 19, 81, 81nn.32–33
Justice Ministry of 130–1, 176–7, 182–3,
192–3, 207n.118, 208n.119, 244n.23,
245–8, 326n.53, 412–14, 440
police in 3–4, 7–8, 226–7

Prussia (*see also* Göring, Hermann) (*cont.*)
  Preußenschlag 7–8, 437n.54
  Protestant Church in 276, 276n.4,
    278–9, 278n.7, 284–5, 294–5, 334–6,
    364–5
  "racial cleansing" in 309–10
public prosecutors (*see also* bureaucracy/
    civil service; crimes; judicial system;
    police, SA; SS) 4, 70–1, 148–9,
    148n.83, 150n.92, 171–2, 176–7, 182–3,
    187–90, 193–4, 207–8, 245–7, 416–17,
    419n.67, 467–8
  acquittals of SA perpetrators 131n.29,
    176–7
  and antisemitism 245–6
  and blaming victims for crimes 31–2,
    183–4, 412–14, 467–8
  lack of objectivity of 31–2, 176, 178,
    182–5, 412–14
  leniency toward antisemitic violence
    23–4, 31–2, 108–10, 113n.42,
    192–3, 209–10, 412–14, 413n.48, 418
  and "moral justification" of antisemitic
    crimes 414–17
Pulzer, Peter 42–3
Pump, Heinrich 165–6

Quaatz, Reinhold 427–8

Raabe, Wilhelm 77–8, 420–1,
    421n.4
Rabiner, Frieda, alias Friedjung 74n.4
Radowitz, Joseph Maria von 429n.36
Rameil, Josef 148–9
Rand, Jahnka 61–2
Rantzau, Count von 191–3, 192n.59
Rathenau, Walter 285, 423–5, 423n.12
Rathenow 267–8
Rechtsstaat (*see also* law; legislation)
    196n.76, 249–50, 419, 426–7, 441–2,
    471–3
Recklinghausen 262–3, 415–16
Regensburg 226, 461–2

Reich Association of Jewish Frontline
    Soldiers 83–4, 130–1, 215–16, 217n.21,
    226, 229–31, 435–6
Reich Association for Jewish Settlement 267–8
Reich, Marcus 403
Reich Ranicki, Marcel 94
Reich Representation of Jews in Germany
    (*Reichsvertretung der Juden in
    Deutschland*) 237–40, 238n.4, 261–2,
    261n.84, 264n.93
Reich, Simon 403
Reich, Third (*see also* coalition government,
    NSDAP-DNVP; law; NSDAP;
    National Socialism; zeitgeist) 93,
    103–4, 109n.25, 156n.15, 175–6, 202–3,
    335, 343–4, 371–2, 371n.76, 387n.35,
    388–90, 400–2, 408–12, 409n.37,
    442–4, 450n.111, 457–9
  Constitution in 266–7
  lawlessness in 203–4
  relations with Poland (*see also* Poland;
    Upper Silesia) 103–4, 409–10
  totalitarian nature of 174, 240–1
Reich, Third, government in (*see also* Hitler
    Cabinet; coalition government,
    NSDAP-DNVP; law; legislation;
    NSDAP; National Socialism)
  Chancellery (*see also* Hitler Cabinet)
    130–1, 238n.4, 258–9, 372–3nn.81–82
  Culture Ministry of 289–90
  Diplomatic Missions of 88–90, 139–40,
    139n.56, 313n.5, 372–3
  Economics Ministry of 212–13, 221–2,
    427–8
  Finance Ministry of 261, 261n.83,
    262n.87
  Foreign Ministry/Foreign Office of
    53–6, 59, 95–7, 103–4, 106n.12, 108–10,
    113n.42, 117–18, 139n.56, 258–9, 314n.8,
    371–2, 371n.76, 372n.81, 401, 402n.9,
    409–10
  Interior Ministry of 91–2, 94, 107–8,
    109n.25, 130, 176, 219–20, 240–1,

253–4, 256, 258–9, 266, 400–1, 401n.8, 404–10, 406nn.24–25, 467–8

Justice Ministry of 244n.23, 247n.37, 253, 414n.52

Labor Ministry of 250–2

Propaganda Ministry of 263n.91, 371–2, 371n.76

Reichswehr Ministry of 256

Transportation Ministry of 214–15, 221–2

Reichardt, Wilhelm 360n.51

Reichsbanner Black-Red-Gold 10–11, 13–14, 129, 129n.22, 140–1, 304–5

  reaction to Nazi takeover 305–8, 384–5

  rank and file of 11n.23

Reichenbach 57–8

Reichmann, Eva 42–3

Reichskonkordat (*see under* Catholic Church)

Reichstag fire (*see also* decrees) 8–10, 34–5, 105–6, 169–70, 173–4, 214–15, 299, 305–8, 338–9

Reichswehr (*see also under* Third Reich; Wehrmacht) 16–18, 16n.36, 17n.37, 383n.21

Reinhardt, Fritz 262–3, 262n.87

Remmele, Adam 198–9

Rendsburg 191–2

Rendtorff, Franz 366–7, 367n.70

Rendtorff, Heinrich 294–5, 322–3, 323n.41, 353–4, 359–60, 366–7, 371, 457–9

Rennertehausen 233–4

revolution, 1918–1919 (*see also* Bavaria; Munich) 304–5, 342–3, 373–5, 440, 470n.26

Rheinbischofsheim 171–2

Riecke, Hans-Joachim 196n.74

Röhm, Ernst 183–4, 201–2

Röhm Putsch 431

Romania 116–18

Rosenbaum, Berta 57–8

Rosenfeld, Arnold 178–80

Rosenstrauch, Salomon 70–1

Rostock 73–5, 212–13

Röver, Carl 289n.44, 290–1

Rüffer, Paul 13–14

Ruhmann, Dr. Kuno 168–9

Ruhr 49–51, 219–20

Ruhrort 159–60

Rumbold, Sir Horace 113–14

Rupprecht, Luise 57

Rürup, Reinhard 42–3

Russia 48–9, 48n.4, 90n.67, 97–8, 101n.116, 229–31, 299, 429–30

  revolution in, 1917 75, 342–3, 449

  revolutionaries in Germany 73–9

Rust, Bernhard 298–9, 299n.77

Ryback, Timothy 34–5

SA (*Sturmabteilung*) (*see also* antisemitism; attacks, antisemitic; camps; murders; protective custody; police; public prosecutors; violence) 3–5, 7–8, 12–14, 18–24, 31, 33, 35–6, 47–8, 52, 55–7, 60, 64, 66–71, 66n.75, 103–5, 107–8, 108n.21, 138–48, 151–2, 159–65, 173, 176, 194, 201, 212–14, 219–27, 257–9, 258n.75, 267–8, 285–8, 298–9, 305–8, 337–8, 384, 411–12, 414–15, 418n.63, 431, 433n.43, 435–6, 441–2, 448–9, 460–1, 471–3

  motivations for violence in 19–20, 23–4, 31–2, 48–9, 52, 71–2, 104–5, 107, 115–19, 136–9, 414–15, 418

  no fear of law in 22–4, 31, 55–6, 73, 106–10, 118–19, 145, 180, 203–4, 209–10, 227, 411–12, 414–15, 471–3

  occupation of law courts by 212–13, 245–6, 309–10

  torture cellars of 13–14, 47–8, 123, 138–9, 305–8, 460–1

  violence of 3–4, 33–4, 36–7, 47–8, 55–6, 105–8, 112–19, 126–7, 132, 136–7, 178–94, 179n.15, 227, 309–10, 402–7, 406n. 25, 409–14, 413n.48, 417–19, 460–1, 471–3

Saarbrücken 146
Sabatzky, Kurt 226, 226n.55
Safier, Chaim Juda 66–7
Sahm Ausschuss (Sahm Committee) 294–5,
    295n.64
Sahm, Heinrich 295n.64
Saper, Herszlik 65
Sasse, Hermann 296–7, 296n.70
Sauer, Karl 198–9
Sauer, Wolfgang 36–7
Sauke, Standartenführer 197–8, 198n.80
Saxony 8–9, 49–51, 51n.19, 57, 86–90,
    108–10, 139n.54, 212–15, 226, 279n.9,
    298–9, 305–8, 306n.102, 365n.66,
    378–9, 400–3, 405
  Economics Ministry of 57–8
  Foreign Ministry of 111n.33, 400–2,
    404–5, 406n.24
  Interior Ministry of 50–1, 58–60, 67–9,
    110–11, 116–18, 404–7
  police in 57–8, 110n.31
  SA in 108–11, 110n.31
Schaumburg-Lippe 8–9, 305–8
Scheck, Gedalli 65–6
Scheck, Isaak Leib 65–6
Schegel, Aron 62–3
Scheiner, Moses 408
Schenker, Uszer Haim 53–5
Schiff, August 147–8
Schiff, Max 147–8
Schiller, Friedrich 280–2, 282n.16
Schimmel, David 63–4
Schivelbein 233–4
Schlegelberger, Franz 247n.37
Schleicher, Kurt 18n.40
Schleswig-Holstein 5–7, 160–1, 212–13
Schleunes, Karl 40–1, 40n.66, 87n.49
Schleusingen 157–8
Schneekloth, Wilhelm 202–3, 203n.102
Schoeps, Hans-Joachim 100n.112
Schöffel, Bishop Simon 329–30
Scholder, Klaus 37–8, 280–2, 293n.56,
    360n.51, 361n.52, 378n.3

Scholtyseck, Joachim 471–3
Scholz, Robert 84–5
Schreiber, August Wilhelm 350–1, 350n.11
Schreiber, Christian 379–80
Schröder, Walter 199–201
Schulz, Gerhard 36–7, 241n.12
Schumacher, Kurt 7–8, 300–1
Schumann, Dirk 38–9, 460n.8
Schumm, Friedrich 5n.11, 190–1, 191n.56,
    192nn.58–9, 193n.62, 194n.69, 201–2,
    224–5, 343–4, 462n.13
Schupp, Johann Bathasar 327n.54
Schupp, Dr. Johannes 326–7, 327n.54
Schussler, Max 106–7
Schwarzschild, Ludwig 142, 142n.63
Schwerin 212–13, 322–3, 353–4
Schwerin von Krosigk, Lutz Graf 221–2
Seeckt, Hans von 16–18, 17n.38
Seesen 197–8
Seetzen, Friedrich 365n.66, 373n.82
Seghers, Anna 23–4
Seile, Abraham Pinkus 66–7
Seligenstadt 141n.61
Selz, Otto 178–80
Severing, Carl 81nn.32–33, 82, 82n.35,
    425–6
Siegel, Dr. Michael 105–6
Siegmund-Schultze, Friedrich 346n.1,
    350–1, 351nn.13–14
Siekmann, Adolf 165–6
Silesia (see also Upper Silesia) 33–4, 52n.25,
    57, 132, 219–20, 226–7, 234–5, 461–2
Simons, Walter 346n.1
Social Democratic Party of Germany
    (SPD)/socialists 7–8, 10–11, 14–16, 20,
    52, 71–2, 81–4, 95–7, 129n.22, 141,
    164–5, 170–1, 181n.19, 209–10, 240–1,
    294–6, 294n.59, 300–1, 304–8,
    307n.105, 347n.2, 377–8, 400–1, 425–6,
    448–9, 457–9, 458n.4, 462–3
  attacks against 13–14, 160–1, 197–204,
    204n.104, 209–10, 305–8, 420–1
Söffge, Wilhelm 164–5

Solmitz, Fritz 5n.11, 198–201, 200n.89, 201n.95

Solmitz, Karolina 199–201, 201n.95, 203–4

Solmssen, Georg 264–5

Somplatzki, Emil 415–17, 416n.58

Soviet Union (*see also* Russia) 93–4, 97–8, 423–5, 454n.129

Speyer 262–3, 382–3

Spiegel, Wilhelm 5n.11, 201–4, 203nn.99–103

Spira, Abraham 115–16

SS (*Schutzstaffel*) (*see also* attacks, antisemitic; crimes; public prosecutors; violence) 3–5, 7–8, 18–19, 48–9, 52, 55–6, 108n.21, 118–19, 137–9, 141–2, 149–53, 158n.22, 159–63, 165–6, 180–2, 184–5, 185n.31, 187, 190–4, 191n.56, 192n.60, 194n.69, 201, 212–31, 233–4, 257–8, 258n.75, 406–7, 415–18

Staatspartei (*see also* German Democratic Party, DDP) 127–8

Stadelmann, Rudolf 459–60

Stahlhelm 3–4, 7–8, 10–11, 117–18, 304–8, 434–6

Stange, Erich 318, 318n.21

Stargard 81, 82n.35, 157–8

Statutory Health Insurance Funds (*Krankenkassen*) (*see also* legislation) 47–8, 249
expulsion of Jewish doctors from 250–3, 251n.52, 253n.59

Stauffenberg, Claus Graf von 459–60

Stegerwald, Adam 384

Stein, Jakob 142, 142n.64

Steinitz, Anna 407

Steinlauf, Baruch 141–2, 142n.62

Stern, Fritz 228, 369n.75

Stern, Heinz 169–71, 173–4, 470–1

Stern, Hermann 178–80

Stern, Moritz 147–8

Stettin 219–20, 452–3

Stieff, Helmut 5n.11

Stieldorf, Peter 187–90, 187n.40

Stoeker, Adolf 275n.1

Stolp 269–70

Stoltenhoff, Ernst 331, 335–7

Strathmann, Hermann 284n.27

Stratmann, Franziskus 395, 395n.55

Straubing 178–80, 232–3

Strauss, Albert 147–8

Streicher, Julius 161–2, 162n.40, 219–20, 220n.30

Stresemann, Gustav 19–20, 215–16, 295n.66

students (*see also* legislation, April 1933) 24–5, 226, 250, 253–4
Association of German Students (VDSt) 339–40

Stülpnagel, Joachim von 17n.38

Stuttgart 88–90, 100n.111, 112–13, 288–9

Suhl 157–8

Switzerland 2, 112–13, 139–40, 142–3, 347–8, 350–2

Syne, Moszek Aron 53–5

Tager, Juda 67–8, 406–7

Tanne, Abraham 53–5

Tausk, Walter 222–4, 226–7, 229–31, 461–2

terror (*see also* boycott, 1 April 1933; *Hitlerterror*; NSDAP; Perfidy Decree; SA; SS; violence) 12–14, 108–10, 168–9, 205n.107, 217–19, 258–9, 305–8, 337–8, 391–2, 395, 397–8, 431–2, 440–2, 449, 457, 464–5, 473–4

Thamer, Hans-Ulrich 37–8

Theisen, Matthias 204n.104

Theweleit, Klaus 464n.18

Thuringia 93–4, 125–6, 242–3, 247–8, 268–9, 279n.9, 342–3

Tietz department store 226

Tilemann, Heinrich 290–1

Tillich, Paul 295–6, 295n.68

Tilling, Magdalena von 284n.27

Titius, Arthur 364–5, 364n.62, 365n.64, 370–1
Toller, Ernst 74n.4
Tönnes, Ferdinand 98n.103, 202–3
torture (*see also* SA; terror) 199–201, 200n.89, 305–8, 460–2
trade unions (*see also* ADGB) 13–14, 197–8, 305–8, 465–6
Traub, Gottfried 423–5
Trebnitz 128–9, 129n.18
Tresckow, Henning von 459–60
Treue, Wilhelm 42–3, 77–8, 78n.21
Trier 144–5
Tübingen 288–9

Uhlig, Heinrich 39–40
Union of White Collar Employees (*Gewerkschaftsbund der Angestellten*) 221–2
United States 2, 60–1, 110–12, 175–6, 186n.38, 214–15, 217–19, 277–8, 277n.6, 312–13, 342–4, 357–9, 457–9, 461–2, 465n.19
    Diplomatic Mission of 106–10, 106n.12, 112n.39, 177
Untermyer, Samuel 312–13, 312n.3
Upper Silesia (*see also* Poland; Convention; Third Reich) 82–3
    German-Polish relations in 254–5
    Optionsgebiet in 56, 56n.39
    plebiscite in (1921) 56, 82–3, 83n.38, 277
Urbig, Franz 264–5

Versailles Treaty 56n.39, 75–6, 76n.9, 81, 175–6, 277, 277n.6, 303–4, 316–17, 374–6, 414–15, 457–9, 470–1
violence (*see also* antisemitism, attacks; boycott, 1 April 1933; boycotts; crimes; SA; SS) 20, 36–7, 53–62, 78–9, 84–5, 112–13, 123–4, 176–7, 177n.7, 183–4, 199–204, 217, 242–3, 250, 253–4, 257–60, 264–5, 271–2, 285–7, 305–8, 332, 357–9, 373–4, 376, 394–6, 408–9, 412–14, 460–2, 473–4

against Jewish livestock dealers 148
antisemitic, documentary evidence for 130
antisemitic, in jails 148
antisemitic in Weimar Republic 124
and forcible expulsions 138
grassroots 147, 271
motivations for 47–9, 62, 71–2, 136–8, 147, 150n.92, 176–7, 180, 196n.76, 197–202, 264–5, 332, 414–15, 415n.54, 418, 461–2
völkisch orientations (*see also* German National People's Party; NSDAP) 75, 85n.44, 91–3, 152, 155–6, 158–9, 211, 292–4, 293n.56, 340–1, 429–30, 444, 453–4, 464–5
Volkov, Shulamit 472n.30
Volksgemeinschaft 71–2, 88–90, 156n.15, 235, 326–7, 364–5, 447–8, 470–3

Wadler, Arnold 74n.4
Wagner, Gerhard 252–3
Wagner, Karl 193–4
Wagner, Robert 198–9
Wahl, Hans 372–3, 372n.79, 373n.82
Waldenburg 157–8
Walter, Dirk 37–8, 79n.26, 84–5, 85n.44
Wandsbeck 223–4, 224n.45
Wanne-Eickel 51–2, 56
Wassermeyer, Dr. Hans 437–8
Wassermann, Jakob 434n.45
Wassermann, Oscar 389–90, 389n.39
Wassermeyer, *Justizrat* 437–8
Wedepohl, Edgar 442–4
Weenen 162–3
Wehrmacht (*see also* Reichswehr) 16n.36, 431, 454n.129
Weiden 232–3
Weil, Norbert 141, 141n.60
Weimar (town) 125–6
Weimar Republic 1–2, 14–16, 50–2, 102n.118, 113–14, 118–19, 138–9, 158–9, 196n.76, 213–14, 216n.20, 229n.62, 231–2, 249n.47, 304–5, 333–4, 338–9,

383n.21, 384–5, 385n.27, 392n.49, 419n.67, 457–60, 458n.4
antisemitism in 14, 20, 78–9, 91–2, 211, 392n.49
antisemitic violence in 71, 73, 124
Constitution of 16n.35
popular culture in 101–2, 196n.76, 344–5, 361–2
Weiner, Chane 405–6
Weiner, Josef 405–6
Weiss, Emanuel 224–5
Weißenburg 232–3
Weissmann, Hersz 53–5
Wellner, Erwin 66–7
Wenings 157n.21
Wertheim department store 226
Wesel 234
Wesseling 187–8
Westarp, Kuno Graf von 426–8, 427n.27, 427n.27, 430
Westerland 267n.104
Wienecke, Friedrich 292n.52
Wienstein, Richard 238n.4
Wiesbaden 53–6, 70–1, 141, 146, 181–6, 468–9
Wiese, Paul 195–6
Wildt, Michael 34–5, 71–2
Wilhelm, Crown Prince 299n.76
Williams, Michael 5–7, 176–8
Wilm, Werner 292–3
Wilson, Woodrow 277
Winkler, Heinrich August 37–8, 74n.3, 426n.20
Winterfeld, Friedrich von 442–4
Wismar 87–90, 90n.67
Wittemann, Valentin 173
Witten 219–20
Wolff, Katharina 173–4
Wolff, Nathaniel S. 106–7
Wolff, Wilhelmine 169–70, 470–1
Wolzogen, Hans von 293–4
World Alliance for International Friendship Through the Churches

(see also Henriod, Henri-Louis) 29, 277–8, 317, 346, 352–3, 368n.74
German National Council of 346–7, 346n.1, 350–2
Worms 56, 64–5, 178–80
Wright, Jonathan 372n.80
Wulle, Reinhold 75, 423–5
Wünschmann, Kim 35–6
Wuppertal 195–207, 206n.111, 212–13
Wurm, Alois 288–9, 392–4, 393n.51, 396–8
Wurm, Theophil 301–4, 302n.86, 320–1, 365–9
Wurth, Klaus 317, 330–1, 330n.64, 364–5, 367–9, 368n.74, 370–1
Württemberg 8–9, 86–90, 93–4, 139n.54, 288–9, 294–5, 303n.93, 305–8, 306n.102, 378–9, 448–9
Protestant Church in 299, 302n.86, 324, 367–9
Würzburg 100n.111, 212–13, 234–5, 265–6

Young Men's Christian World Alliance 318

Zahn-Harnack, Adolf von 301–3
Zahn-Harnack, Agnes von 301–3, 302n.89
Zechlin, Egmont 98–9
zeitgeist, 1933 11–14, 23–4, 27–8, 31–3, 117–19, 146, 174, 183–4, 209–10, 212–13, 221–2, 229–33, 243–4, 249n.47, 305–8, 363, 367–9, 384–5, 392–4, 397–8, 414–15, 414n.52, 418–19, 437–40, 444–5, 450–1, 457–9, 460n.9, 468–9, 471–3
Zerbes, Ludwig 199–200
Zilkenat, Rainer 84
Zimmermann, Moshe 99n.105
Zittau 226, 232–3, 461–2
Zitzewitz, Georg von 453, 453n.122
Zöllner, Wilhelm 176, 359–60
Zuckerman, Philip 107–11
Zweig, Stefan 95n.92
Zwickau 60, 408